1001
Kitchen Favorites

Culinary Arts Institute

A DIVISION OF DELAIR PUBLISHING COMPANY INC.

Cover Photo:
Sweet and Sour Chicken, page 341
Chicken and Shrimp Egg Roll, page 324

ISBN: 0-8326-0625-1

Contents

Note: A black circle: ● is used throughout this book to alert you to the fact that an additional recipe is involved in the one you are working on. The reference will be found in bold type and in its exact wording in the index.

Appetizers

1 *Appetizer Puffs*

These tiny cream puffs may be filled as you wish to make dainty and appealing hors d'oeuvres.

1 cup beer
½ cup butter or margarine
½ teaspoon salt
1 cup all-purpose flour
4 eggs

1. Heat beer, butter, and salt to boiling in a saucepan.
2. Add flour all at once. Beat vigorously with a wooden spoon until mixture leaves sides of pan and forms a smooth ball.
3. Add eggs, one at a time, beating until smooth.
4. Drop mixture by rounded teaspoonfuls onto a greased cookie sheet, 1 inch apart.
5. Bake at 450°F 10 minutes. Turn oven control to 350°F and bake 5 to 10 minutes more, or until lightly browned and puffed.
6. Cool. Split and fill with desired filling.

About 40 puffs

2 *Pickled Shrimp*

With small to medium shrimp, serve this appetizer on cocktail rye rounds. Larger shrimp may be served on fancy picks.

1 can or bottle (12 ounces) beer
¼ cup oil
1 tablespoon lemon juice
1 teaspoon sugar
1 teaspoon salt
½ teaspoon each dill seed, dry mustard, and celery salt
¼ teaspoon tarragon
⅛ teaspoon ground red pepper
2 bay leaves, halved
2 medium onions, chopped
1 package (10 ounces) small to medium frozen cooked shrimp, thawed

1. Place all ingredients except shrimp in a saucepan. Simmer 10 to 15 minutes, or until onions are just tender.
2. Add shrimp; remove from heat. Turn into a small casserole. Cover and refrigerate at least 1 day.
3. Remove bay leaves; drain off marinade. Let guests spoon shrimp and onions onto **cocktail rye rounds.**

About 25 appetizers

Note: With larger shrimp to be served on fancy picks, use only one onion and slice it. Remove onion before serving. Recipe may also be made with uncooked shrimp. Add them 4 to 5 minutes before end of cooking time; cover and simmer until shrimp turn pink. Continue as in above recipe.

3 Shrimp Dunk

This is the famous shrimp boiled in beer served as an appetizer. Instead of cocktail sauce or melted butter, try cold beer for dunking.

1 can or bottle (12 ounces) beer
   plus ½
   cup water
1 small onion, sliced
   Top and leaves of 1 stalk celery
1 tablespoon salt
3 or 4 peppercorns
1 bay leaf
1 garlic clove
1 pound very large shelled
   shrimp, uncooked

1. Combine ingredients except shrimp in a large saucepan. Cover; heat to boiling. Boil 10 minutes.
2. Add shrimp. Cover and boil 5 minutes, or just until shrimp turn pink. Remove from heat; chill in cooking liquid.
3. Serve cold with dunking bowls of cold beer. Serve as hors d'oeuvres or as a summertime main entrée.

25 to 30 shrimp

4 Shrimp Spread

Serve this spread at a cocktail party—on fancy crackers or inside tiny beer-flavored cream puffs.

½ cup butter or margarine,
   softened
2 green onions with some tops
2 parsley sprigs
¼ teaspoon salt
⅛ teaspoon garlic powder
   Dash pepper
1 package (12 ounces) frozen
   cooked shrimp, thawed
½ cup beer
1 tablespoon capers (optional)
   Fancy crackers or tiny cream
   puffs

1. Using a food processor or blender, process butter, onions, parsley, and seasonings until vegetables are minced and mixture is smooth. (With blender, prepare in 2 or 3 batches.)
2. Add shrimp, beer, and capers. Process to a smooth paste.
3. Serve at room temperature on crackers or in tiny cream puffs. Use a rounded teaspoon for each. One half recipe of Shrimp Spread fills one recipe Appetizer Puffs ●

2 ¾ cups spread for about 7 dozen crackers or tiny cream puffs

5 Marinated Mushrooms

Serve hot or cold as light hors d'oeuvres before a dinner party, or as part of an array of cocktail party nibbling foods.

1 pound small fresh mushrooms
⅔ cup vegetable oil
½ cup beer
¼ cup minced green onion with
   tops
2 tablespoons lemon juice
1 tablespoon chopped parsley
1 large garlic clove, minced
½ teaspoon salt
   Dash pepper

1. Wash mushrooms, remove stems, and pat dry. Reserve stems for later use.
2. Combine remaining ingredients in a shallow glass or ceramic dish. Add mushrooms. Cover and let stand at room temperature about 3 hours, stirring occasionally.
3. Place mushrooms, cup side up, on a broiler pan. Spoon some marinade over each. Broil 3 inches from heat about 2 minutes, or until lightly browned. Serve warm with picks.

40 to 50 mushrooms

Note: Marinated Mushrooms may also be served cold. Marinate in refrigerator. Do not broil. Turn into a serving bowl with marinade; serve with picks. Canned button mushrooms may also be used when serving this dish cold.

6 Tangy Cheese Dip

4 ounces Muenster cheese or other semisoft cheese, finely shredded (1 cup)
3 ounces blue cheese, crumbled
1 package (3 ounces) cream cheese, softened
⅛ teaspoon garlic powder
¾ cup beer (about)

1. After shredding, let Muenster cheese stand at room temperature at least 1 hour.
2. Using an electric blender or food processor, blend cheeses and garlic. Gradually add enough beer to make a mixture of dipping consistency.
3. Serve at room temperature with crackers for dipping.

About 2 cups

7 German Beer Cheese (Bierkäse)

Serve as a spread for hors d'oeuvres at a party or before dinner. It's especially good on rye rounds with glasses of cold beer to drink.

½ pound Cheddar cheese
½ pound Swiss cheese
2 teaspoons Worcestershire sauce
1 teaspoon dry mustard
1 small garlic clove, mashed
½ cup beer (about)

1. Shred cheeses finely. Or put through a meat grinder, using finest blade.
2. Add Worcestershire sauce, dry mustard, garlic, and enough beer to make a mixture of spreading consistency.
3. Turn into a 3-cup rounded bowl or mold; pack firmly. Chill. Unmold and serve at room temperature with **small rye rounds** or **crackers.**

3 cups

8 Cocktail Party Sausages

• 1½ cups Mustard Sauce or Savory Barbecue Sauce
4 dozen (about) cocktail frankfurters, vienna sausages, cocktail smoked sausage links, or chunks of frankfurters

1. Prepare desired sauce and heat with your choice of sausage.
2. Turn into a chafing dish. Serve warm with decorative picks.

About 4 dozen

9 Chili Nuts

These zippy nuts are nice to nibble on while drinking a glass of cold beer.

1 package (12 ounces) shelled raw peanuts
2 tablespoons peanut or vegetable oil
2 teaspoons chili powder
1 teaspoon salt

1. Combine ingredients in a large baking pan; spread thinly.
2. Bake at 325°F 25 minutes. Cool on waxed paper.

2 cups

10 Hot Crab Spread

1 package (8 ounces) cream cheese,
   softened
1 tablespoon milk
2 teaspoons Worcestershire sauce
1 can (7½ ounces) Alaska King crab,
   drained and flaked, or 1 package
   (6 ounces) frozen crab meat,
   thawed, drained, and flaked
2 tablespoons chopped green onion
2 tablespoons toasted slivered
   almonds

1. Combine cream cheese, milk, Worcestershire sauce, crab, and green onion. Place in small individual casseroles. Sprinkle with almonds.
2. Bake, uncovered, at 350°F 15 minutes. Serve with **assorted crackers.**

2 cups

11 Crab Meat Newburg Appetizer

2 tablespoons butter or margarine
2 tablespoons flour
½ teaspoon salt
2 cups milk
2 cups (8 ounces) shredded Cheddar
   cheese
2 cans (7½ ounces each) Alaska King
   crab, drained and flaked
3 hard-cooked eggs, grated
½ cup finely chopped onion
   Dash ground red pepper
1 tablespoon snipped parsley

1. Melt butter in a saucepan. Add flour and salt. Gradually add milk, stirring until thickened and smooth.
2. Add cheese, stirring until blended. Blend in remaining ingredients, except parsley. Put into a 1½-quart casserole.
3. Bake, covered, at 325°F 15 minutes, or until heated through. Sprinkle with parsley. Serve with **Melba toast** or **toast-points.**

25 servings

12 Crab Meat Quiche

1 unbaked 9-inch pie shell
2 eggs
1 cup half-and-half
½ teaspoon salt
   Dash ground red pepper
¾ cup (3 ounces) shredded Swiss
   cheese
¾ cup (3 ounces) shredded Gruyère
   cheese
1 tablespoon flour
1 can (7½ ounces) Alaska King crab,
   drained and flaked

1. Prick bottom and sides of pie shell. Bake at 450°F 10 minutes, or until delicately browned.
2. Beat together eggs, half-and-half, salt, and red pepper.
3. Combine cheeses, flour, and crab; sprinkle evenly in pie shell. Pour in egg mixture.
4. Bake, uncovered, at 325°F 45 minutes, or until tip of knife inserted 1 inch from center comes out clean. Let stand a few minutes. Cut into wedges to serve.

16 appetizers

13 *Barbecue Fondue*

2 cans (15¼ ounces each) barbecue
  sauce and beef for Sloppy Joes
1 teaspoon instant minced onion
1 teaspoon oregano
1½ cups (6 ounces) shredded Cheddar
  cheese

1. Combine all ingredients in a 1-quart casserole.
2. Bake, covered, at 350°F 30 minutes, or until heated through, stirring occasionally. Serve with **French bread cubes** on wooden picks.

3½ cups

14 *Mexican Chili-Bean Dip*

1 pound ground beef
½ cup finely chopped onion
½ cup ketchup
1 tablespoon chili powder
1 teaspoon salt
⅛ teaspoon garlic powder
  Dash ground red pepper
1 can (15½ ounces) red kidney beans
  (with liquid), mashed
1 cup (4 ounces) shredded Monterey
  Jack cheese

1. Brown ground beef and onion in a skillet; drain off excess fat.
2. Add remaining ingredients, except cheese. Put into a 1-quart casserole.
3. Bake, covered, at 350°F 30 minutes, or until heated through. Sprinkle with cheese. Serve with **corn chips.**

8 servings

15 *Hot Artichoke-Cheese Squares*

¼ cup finely chopped onion
1 garlic clove, minced
1 tablespoon shortening
4 eggs, well beaten
1 can (14 ounces) artichoke hearts,
  drained and chopped
¼ cup dry bread crumbs
2 cups (8 ounces) shredded Cheddar
  or Swiss cheese
2 tablespoons snipped parsley
  Few drops Tabasco

1. Sauté onion and garlic in shortening in a skillet.
2. Combine all ingredients. Pour into an 11x7-inch baking dish.
3. Bake, uncovered, at 325°F 30 minutes, or until filling is set. Let stand a few minutes. Cut into squares to serve.

24 appetizers

16 *Sausage and Applesauce Appetizers*

1 package (12 ounces) smoked link
    sausage, cut in 1-inch pieces
1 jar (15 ounces) applesauce
1 tablespoon caraway seed
1½ teaspoons instant minced onion

1. Broil sausage pieces until evenly browned.
2. Combine with applesauce, caraway seed, and onion. Put into a 1-quart casserole.
3. Bake, covered, at 250°F 2 hours. Serve with wooden picks.

About 32 appetizers

17 *Baked Carrot Spread*

1 cup grated carrot
1 cup mayonnaise
1 cup (4 ounces) grated Romano
    cheese
½ teaspoon garlic salt
½ teaspoon lemon pepper seasoning

1. Combine all ingredients in a 1-quart casserole.
2. Bake, uncovered, at 350°F 25 minutes, or until heated through. Serve with **assorted crackers.**

3 cups

18 *Baked Mushrooms*

1½ pounds fresh mushroom caps*
1 cup butter or margarine, melted
2 teaspoons finely chopped onion
1 garlic clove, minced
½ teaspoon rosemary
¾ teaspoon Worcestershire sauce

1. Place mushroom caps in a 1½-quart casserole.
2. Combine remaining ingredients. Pour over mushrooms.
3. Bake, covered, at 325°F 30 minutes, or until tender.

12 servings

* The mushroom stems can be sautéed and added to **hot, cooked green beans.**

19 *Onion Appetizers*

4 medium onions, finely chopped
3 tablespoons butter or margarine
½ cup dairy sour cream
1 tablespoon flour
½ teaspoon salt
    Dash pepper
1 teaspoon caraway seed
3 eggs, beaten
4 bacon slices, cooked and crumbled
1 unbaked 9-inch pie shell

1. Sauté onion in butter in a skillet.
2. Blend sour cream, flour, salt, pepper, and caraway seed. Beat in eggs. Stir in bacon and onion. Pour into pie shell.
3. Bake, uncovered, at 325°F 35 to 40 minutes, or until filling is set. Let stand a few minutes. Cut into wedges to serve.

16 appetizers

20 Wine-Cheese Canapés

½ cup whipped unsalted butter
4 teaspoons Roquefort cheese
4 toasted bread rounds
2 packages (3 ounces each) cream cheese
2 tablespoons sauterne
Parsley, minced
Pimento-stuffed olive slices
Paprika
Clear Glaze (see recipe)

1. Whip together butter and Roquefort cheese. Spread onto toasted bread rounds.
2. Whip cream cheese with sauterne.
3. Pipe a swirl of the mixture onto each canapé. Roll edges in minced parsley. Top with pimento-stuffed olive slice; sprinkle with paprika.
4. Glaze and chill.

Clear Glaze: Soften **1 envelope unflavored gelatin** in ⅔ **cup cold water** in a bowl. Pour **1 cup boiling water** over softened gelatin and stir until gelatin is dissolved. Chill until slightly thickened. To glaze canapés: Place canapés on wire racks over a large shallow pan. Working quickly, spoon about 2 teaspoons of slightly thickened gelatin over each canapé. (Have ready a bowl of ice and water and a bowl of hot water. The gelatin may have to be set over one or the other during glazing to maintain the proper consistency.) The gelatin should cling slightly to canapés when spooned over them. Any drips may be scooped up and reused.

21

About 24 canapés

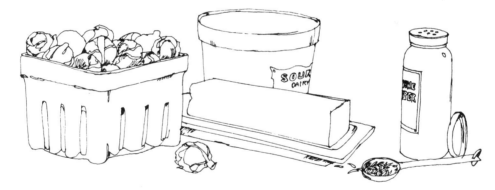

22 Liver Pâté

This is not baked, but made with gelatin and chilled. Calories can be cut by serving with vegetables rather than the usual crackers.

1½ cups chopped onion
1 cup chopped celery
1½ cups Chicken Stock
1 cup dry white wine
1 teaspoon paprika
⅛ teaspoon ground allspice or cloves
¼ teaspoon garlic powder
4 drops Tabasco
1¼ teaspoons salt
1½ pounds chicken livers, membranes removed
2 envelopes unflavored gelatin
½ cup cold water
Assorted vegetable relishes

1. Simmer onion and celery in stock and wine in an uncovered saucepan until liquid is reduced to 2 cups (about 15 minutes). Stir in paprika, allspice, garlic powder, Tabasco, and salt; simmer 2 minutes. Stir in livers; simmer covered until livers are tender (about 15 minutes). Drain; discard liquid.
2. Sprinkle gelatin over cold water; let stand 3 minutes. Set over low heat, stirring occasionally, until gelatin is dissolved (about 5 minutes).
3. Purée half the livers and vegetables along with half the gelatin mixture in a food processor or blender. Repeat with remaining ingredients; combine the two mixtures.
4. Pour mixture into a lightly oiled 1½-quart mold or bowl or ten 6-ounce custard cups. Chill until set (about 4 hours).
5. Serve from mold, or unmold onto platter and accompany with assorted vegetables.

10 to 12 servings

23 Puff Shrimp with Orange Ginger Sauce

Orange Ginger Sauce (see recipe)
Fat for deep frying heated to 375°F
2 pounds medium raw shrimp (20 to 25 per pound)
3 egg yolks
½ cup white wine
¾ cup all-purpose flour
1 teaspoon salt
¼ teaspoon pepper
3 egg whites

Orange Ginger Sauce:
1 cup orange marmalade
2 tablespoons soy sauce
¼ cup sherry
1 piece whole ginger root
1 clove garlic, minced

1. Prepare and cool Orange Ginger Sauce.
2. Fill a deep saucepan or automatic deep fryer one-half to two-thirds full with fat for deep frying; heat slowly to 375°F.
3. Shell and devein raw shrimp and set aside.
4. Beat together in a bowl egg yolks, wine, flour, salt, and pepper until smooth.
5. Beat egg whites until stiff, not dry, peaks are formed. Fold egg whites into egg yolk mixture.
6. Dry shrimp thoroughly and dip into batter, coating well.
7. Deep-fry one layer deep in heated fat 2 to 3 minutes on each side, or until golden brown. Remove from fat with a slotted spoon. Drain on absorbent paper. Be sure temperature of fat is 375°F before frying each layer. Serve shrimp hot accompanied with the Orange Ginger Sauce for dipping.
8. For Orange Ginger Sauce, combine in a saucepan marmalade, soy sauce, sherry, ginger root, and minced garlic. Stir over low heat until mixture bubbles. Remove from heat. Cool. Remove ginger before serving.

40 to 50 appetizers

24 Oysters Rockefeller

2 tablespoons butter or margarine
2 tablespoons flour
½ teaspoon salt
⅛ teaspoon pepper
1 cup milk (use light cream for richer sauce)
1 egg, well beaten
2 dozen oysters in shells
2 tablespoons sherry
2 tablespoons butter or margarine
1 tablespoon finely chopped onion
1 pound fresh spinach, cooked, drained, and finely chopped
1 tablespoon minced parsley
½ teaspoon Worcestershire sauce
6 drops Tabasco
¼ teaspoon salt
Few grains ground nutmeg
¼ cup shredded Parmesan cheese

1. For sauce, heat 2 tablespoons butter in a saucepan. Blend in flour, salt, and pepper; heat and stir until bubbly.
2. Gradually add the milk, stirring until smooth. Bring to boiling; cook and stir 1 to 2 minutes longer.
3. Stir the egg into white sauce; set aside.
4. Pour **coarse salt** into a 15×10×1-inch jelly roll pan to a ¼-inch depth. Open oysters and arrange the oysters, in the shells, on the salt; sprinkle ¼ teaspoon sherry over each.
5. Heat 2 tablespoons butter in a heavy skillet. Add the onion and cook until partially tender. Add the chopped spinach, 2 tablespoons of the white sauce, parsley, Worcestershire sauce, and Tabasco to the skillet along with salt and nutmeg; mix thoroughly. Heat 2 to 3 minutes.
6. Spoon spinach mixture over all of the oysters; spoon remaining white sauce over spinach. Sprinkle each oyster with cheese.
7. Bake at 375°F 15 to 20 minutes, or until tops are lightly browned.

4 to 6 servings

25 Avocado Sandwiches on Sour Dough

2 avocados, thinly sliced and salted
¼ cup butter (½ stick), softened
½ teaspoon oregano leaves
¼ teaspoon each chervil, parsley flakes, and grated lemon peel
Dash onion powder
8 slices sour dough or Italian bread, diagonally cut

1. Prepare avocado slices.
2. Cream butter with seasonings. Spread thinly over bread.
3. Top with avocado slices. Serve with white wine.

8 servings

26 Wine-Pickled Mushrooms

1 pound fresh mushrooms, sliced lengthwise
1 cup water
⅔ cup white vinegar
½ cup sugar
1 teaspoon salt
½ teaspoon monosodium glutamate
½ teaspoon celery salt
4 sprigs parsley
2 small stalks celery
1 tablespoon mixed pickling spices
1 bay leaf
6 whole cloves
12 peppercorns
½ teaspoon whole allspice
1 cup dry white wine

1. Prepare mushrooms and set aside in a bowl.
2. Mix remaining ingredients, except wine, in a saucepan; bring rapidly to boiling, reduce heat and simmer 10 minutes.
3. Strain the mixture over mushrooms and stir in the wine.
4. Cover and refrigerate several days before serving.

1 quart pickled mushrooms

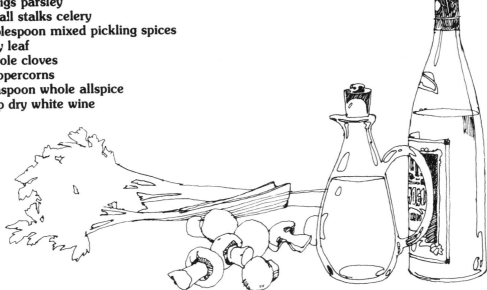

27 Cocktail Meatballs with Mushroom Curry Sauce

Meatballs:
1 pound ground beef
½ cup fine soft bread crumbs
¼ cup milk
¼ cup sherry
1 egg, slightly beaten
2 tablespoons grated onion
¼ teaspoon ground ginger
1 teaspoon salt
¼ teaspoon pepper
2 tablespoons bacon drippings or other fat
Mushroom Curry Sauce:
1 can (about 10 ounces) condensed cream of mushroom soup
¼ cup sherry
1 teaspoon curry powder

1. For meatballs, mix beef, bread crumbs, milk, wine, egg, onion, ginger, salt, and pepper; shape mixture into little balls, using about one level teaspoon for each.
2. Heat bacon drippings in a large heavy skillet; add a single layer of meatballs and cook, slowly, for about 10 minutes, or until meat is done, shaking pan gently from time to time to cook and brown evenly.
3. When all meat is cooked, spear each with a pick and arrange in hot serving dish.
4. For sauce, combine soup, wine, and curry powder. Heat through and serve piping hot with meatballs.

About 60 meatballs

28 Hot Crab Meat Canapés

2 cups (about 8 ounces) fresh lump crab meat (bony tissue removed)
1 tablespoon chopped pimento
3 tablespoons butter or margarine
1 tablespoon finely chopped green pepper
1 teaspoon finely chopped onion
3 tablespoons flour
½ teaspoon salt
¼ teaspoon dry mustard
Few grains white pepper
Few grains cayenne pepper
½ teaspoon Worcestershire sauce
¾ cup milk
1 egg yolk, slightly beaten
2 tablespoons sherry
5 slices white bread
Butter
5 teaspoons grated Parmesan cheese
2½ teaspoons melted butter or margarine
Paprika

1. Set out crab meat and pimento.
2. Heat 3 tablespoons butter in a heavy 2-quart saucepan; add green pepper and onion. Cook over low heat 2 to 3 minutes, or until partially tender. Blend in flour, salt, dry mustard, white pepper, cayenne pepper, and Worcestershire sauce. Heat until mixture bubbles. Add the milk gradually, stirring constantly. Bring mixture rapidly to boiling, stirring constantly; cook 1 to 2 minutes longer. Vigorously stir about 3 tablespoons hot mixture into egg yolk. Immediately blend into mixture in saucepan and cook, stirring constantly, about 5 minutes. Add crab meat and pimento to saucepan and mix gently until thoroughly blended. Cook over low heat, stirring gently, 2 to 3 minutes or until crab meat is thoroughly heated. Remove from heat and stir in sherry. Cool.
3. For canapés, trim crust from bread and toast until golden brown. Lightly spread toast with butter. Cover toast with crab meat mixture. Top each slice with 1 teaspoon grated cheese and ½ teaspoon of melted butter. Sprinkle with paprika.
4. Cut each toast slice diagonally into 4 triangles and place on a baking sheet.
5. Bake at 425°F 8 to 10 minutes.
6. Place canapés on broiler rack and place rack under broiler with tops of canapés 2 to 3 inches from heat. Broil 1 to 2 minutes.
7. Serve piping hot with **lemon wedges.** If desired, garnish with sprigs of parsley.

20 canapés

29 Fabulous Cheese Mousse

¼ cup cold water
1 envelope unflavored gelatin
3¾ ounces (three 1¼-ounce packages) Roquefort cheese
2⅔ ounces (two 1⅓-ounce packages) Camembert cheese
1 egg yolk, slightly beaten
1 tablespoon sherry
1 teaspoon Worcestershire sauce
½ cup chilled whipping cream
1 egg white
Pimento-stuffed olive slices

1. Lightly oil a fancy 1-pint mold with salad or cooking oil (not olive oil); set aside to drain. Chill a small bowl and rotary beater.
2. Pour the cold water into a small cup or custard cup. Sprinkle the gelatin evenly over the water. Let stand about 5 minutes to soften. Dissolve completely by placing cup over very hot water.
3. Force the Roquefort and Camembert cheeses through a fine sieve. Blend in the egg yolk, sherry, and Worcestershire sauce. Stir the dissolved gelatin and add to the cheese mixture, blending thoroughly.
4. Using the chilled bowl and beater, beat whipping cream until it is of medium consistency (piles softly).
5. Using clean beater, beat egg white until rounded peaks are formed. Fold whipped cream and egg white into the cheese mixture. Turn into the mold. Chill until firm.
6. Unmold onto chilled plate and garnish with olive slices. Serve with **crackers.**

One 1-pint mold

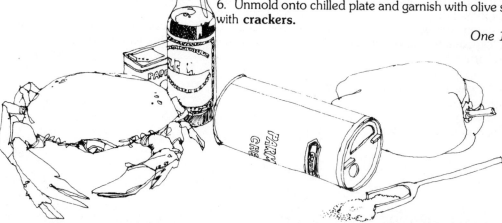

Salads

30 Sauerkraut Slaw

2 cups (16-ounce can) sauerkraut, drained and snipped with scissors
1 onion, chopped (about ½ cup)
1 green pepper, sliced (about ¾ cup)
1 unpared red apple, diced (about 1 cup)
⅓ to ½ cup sugar
1 can (16 ounces) sliced tomatoes or tomato wedges, drained
Seasoned pepper

1. Combine sauerkraut, onion, green pepper, apple, and sugar in a serving bowl; toss until well mixed. Cover and refrigerate.
2. Before serving, overlap tomato slices around edge of bowl. Sprinkle slices with seasoned pepper.

8 to 12 servings

31 Stuffed Eggplant Salad

2 large eggplants
4 medium tomatoes, peeled and diced
⅓ cup thinly sliced green onion
⅓ cup olive or salad oil
½ cup fresh lemon juice
¼ cup chopped parsley
1 tablespoon sugar
2½ teaspoons salt
2 teaspoons oregano
¼ teaspoon ground black pepper

1. Wash and dry eggplants; place on a cookie sheet. Bake in a 375°F oven 35 to 45 minutes, or until tender when pierced with a fork. Cool.
2. Cut a thin lengthwise slice from the side of each eggplant; carefully spoon out pulp. Chill shells.
3. Dice pulp and put into a bowl. Add tomatoes, green onion, oil, lemon juice, parsley, sugar, salt, oregano, and pepper; toss to mix. Chill.
4. Before serving, drain off excess liquid from salad mixture. Spoon salad into shells.

6 servings

32 Bacon-Bean Salad

⅔ cup cider vinegar
¾ cup sugar
1 teaspoon salt
1 can (16 ounces) cut green beans
1 can (16 ounces) cut wax beans
1 can (16 ounces) kidney beans, thoroughly rinsed and drained
1 medium onion, quartered and finely sliced
1 medium green pepper, chopped
½ teaspoon freshly ground black pepper
⅓ cup salad oil
1 pound bacon, cut in 1-inch squares
Lettuce (optional)

1. Blend vinegar, sugar, and salt in a small saucepan. Heat until the sugar is dissolved and set aside.
2. Drain all beans and toss with onion, green pepper, vinegar mixture, and ground pepper. Pour oil over all and toss to coat evenly. Store in a covered container in refrigerator.
3. When ready to serve, fry bacon until crisp; drain on absorbent paper. Toss the bacon with bean mixture. If desired, serve the salad on crisp lettuce.

About 12 servings

Note: If desired, omit bacon.

33 Mixed Vegetable Salad

1 cup diced cooked potatoes
1½ cups cooked sliced carrots
1½ cups cooked whole or cut green beans (fresh, frozen, or canned)
1½ cups cooked green peas (fresh, frozen, or canned)
1 cup sliced or diced cooked beets
Bottled Italian-style salad dressing
Lettuce
1 cup sliced celery
1 small onion, chopped
2 hard-cooked eggs, chopped
¾ cup small pimento-stuffed olives
¾ cup mayonnaise
¼ cup chili sauce
1 teaspoon lemon juice

1. Put potatoes, carrots, beans, peas, and beets into separate bowls. Pour salad dressing over each vegetable; chill thoroughly.
2. To serve, drain vegetables and arrange in a lettuce-lined salad bowl along with celery, onion, eggs, and olives.
3. Blend mayonnaise, chili sauce, and lemon juice. Pass with the salad.

About 8 servings

34 Beef Salad Acapulco

3 cups cooked beef strips
¾ cup salad oil
½ cup red wine vinegar
1½ teaspoons salt
¼ teaspoon ground pepper
⅛ teaspoon cayenne pepper
1 tablespoon chili powder
Salad greens
Avocado slices, brushed with marinade
Onion and green pepper rings
Tomato wedges
Ripe olives

1. Put beef strips into a shallow dish. Combine oil, vinegar, salt, pepper, cayenne pepper, and chili powder in a bottle; cover and shake vigorously. Pour over beef strips. Cover; marinate several hours or overnight.
2. Remove beef from marinade and arrange on crisp greens on chilled salad plates. Garnish with avocado slices, onion rings, green pepper rings, tomato wedges, and ripe olives. Serve the marinade as the dressing.

4 to 6 servings

35 *Greek-Style Lamb-and-Olive Salad*

Greek-Style Salad Dressing:
- ½ cup olive or salad oil
- 1 cup red wine vinegar
- 3 to 4 tablespoons honey
- 1½ teaspoons salt
- ⅛ teaspoon dry mustard
- 2 teaspoons crushed dried mint leaves
- ¼ teaspoon crushed oregano
- ¼ teaspoon crushed thyme
- ¼ teaspoon anise seed

Salad:
- 1½ pounds roast lamb, trimmed of fat and cut in strips
  Curly endive
- 1 large cucumber, pared and sliced
- 4 medium tomatoes, sliced and quartered
- 1 cup pitted ripe olives

1. For dressing, mix oil, vinegar, honey, salt, dry mustard, mint, oregano, thyme, and anise.
2. Pour the dressing over cooked lamb in a bowl, cover, and marinate in refrigerator at least 1 hour, or until thoroughly chilled.
3. To serve, arrange curly endive in a large salad bowl. Toss cucumber, tomatoes, and olives with some of the dressing and turn into salad bowl. Spoon meat over vegetables and pour more dressing over all.

6 servings

36 *Molded Spinach Cottage Cheese on Platter*

- 1 package (10 ounces) frozen chopped spinach
- 2 envelopes unflavored gelatin
- ¾ cup water
- 2 chicken bouillon cubes
- 2 tablespoons lemon juice
- 1½ cups creamed cottage cheese
- ½ cup dairy sour cream
- ½ cup sliced celery
- ⅓ cup chopped green pepper
- 2 tablespoons minced green onion

1. Cook and drain spinach, reserving liquid. Add enough water to liquid to make ½ cup. Set spinach and liquid aside.
2. Soften gelatin in ¾ cup water in a saucepan; add bouillon cubes. Set over low heat; stirring occasionally, until gelatin and bouillon cubes are dissolved. Remove from heat; stir in spinach liquid and lemon juice. Set aside.
3. Beat cottage cheese until fairly smooth with mixer or in electric blender. Blend with sour cream and then gelatin mixture. Stir in spinach, celery, green pepper, and onion. Turn into a 5-cup mold. Chill until firm.
4. Unmold onto a chilled large platter. If desired, arrange slices of summer sausage around the mold.

6 to 8 servings

37 *Chicken-Fruit Salad*

- Creamy Cooked Salad Dressing (page 82)
- 3 cups cubed cooked chicken
  Bottled French dressing
- ½ cup diced celery
- 1 cup small seedless grapes
- ½ cup drained crushed pineapple; reserve syrup for dressing
- 1 orange, sectioned and sections cut in halves
- ½ cup toasted salted almonds, coarsely chopped
- 1 tablespoon minced crystallized ginger

1. Prepare Creamy Cooked Salad Dressing; refrigerate.
2. Toss chicken in a bowl with enough French dressing to coat thoroughly; cover and set in refrigerator to marinate about 3 hours, mixing occasionally.
3. Lightly toss together chicken, celery, grapes, pineapple, orange, almonds, and ginger. Pour desired amount of the dressing over chicken mixture and toss gently. Cover and chill thoroughly.
4. To serve, line a salad bowl with chilled crisp greens. Fill bowl with chicken salad.

About 8 servings

38 *Tossed Supper Salad*

Dressing:
- 1 cup salad oil
- ½ cup cider vinegar
- 1 teaspoon salt
- 1 teaspoon sugar
- ½ teaspoon onion salt
- ¼ teaspoon crushed tarragon
- ¼ teaspoon paprika
- ¼ teaspoon dry mustard
- ¼ teaspoon celery salt
- ⅛ teaspoon garlic salt
- ⅛ teaspoon ground black pepper

Salad:
- 2 cans (6½ or 7 ounces each) tuna
- ½ head lettuce
- 1 cup spinach leaves, washed
- 1 cup diced celery
- ¾ cup chopped green pepper
- ½ cup cooked green peas
- 4 sweet pickles, chopped
- 4 radishes, thinly sliced
- 2 hard-cooked eggs, sliced
- 2 tablespoons chopped pimento
- 2 tomatoes, rinsed and cut in eighths
- 1 teaspoon salt
- Tomato wedges
- Ripe olives

1. For dressing, put oil and vinegar into a jar; mix salt, sugar, and seasonings; add to jar, cover, and shake well. Refrigerate until needed. Shake before using.
2. For salad, drain tuna well and separate into small chunks; put into a bowl. Toss tuna with ½ cup prepared dressing; cover and refrigerate 1 to 2 hours.
3. Tear lettuce and spinach into pieces and put into a large bowl. Add celery, green pepper, peas, pickles, radishes, eggs, and pimento; add the tuna with its dressing and tomatoes. Sprinkle with salt. Toss lightly until ingredients are mixed and lightly coated with dressing; add more dressing, if desired.
4. Garnish with tomato wedges and ripe olives.

8 to 10 servings

Note: Two cups of diced cooked chicken, turkey, veal, or pork may be substituted for tuna.

39 *Hearty Bean Salad*

- 1 can (15 ounces) kidney beans, drained
- 2 hard-cooked eggs, diced
- ¼ cup chopped onion
- ½ cup diced celery
- ⅓ cup drained sweet pickle relish
- ½ cup shredded sharp Cheddar cheese
- ½ cup dairy sour cream
- Lettuce

1. Mix kidney beans, eggs, onion, celery, relish, and cheese in a large bowl. Add sour cream and toss together lightly; chill.
2. Serve the salad on lettuce.

4 to 6 servings

40 *Cinnamon Waldorf Molds*

- ⅓ cup red cinnamon candies
- 3 cups water
- 2 packages (3 ounces each) cherry-flavored gelatin
- 1 tablespoon lemon juice

1. Heat cinnamon candies and water to boiling in a saucepan. Remove from heat and add gelatin and lemon juice; stir until gelatin and candies are dissolved.
2. Chill until slightly thickened.
3. Mix in celery, apples, marshmallows, and walnuts. Spoon

      2 cups chopped celery
      2 cups chopped unpared red apples
      1 cup miniature marshmallows
      ½ cup chopped walnuts
        Lettuce

into 6 to 8 individual fancy molds or turn into a 1½-quart mold. Chill until firm.
4. Unmold onto lettuce.

6 to 8 servings

41 *Chef's Fruit Salad*

Cinnamon-Buttered Raisins:
      1 tablespoon butter or margarine, melted
      ½ cup dark raisins
      ½ cup golden raisins
      ½ teaspoon ground cinnamon

Salad:
        Salad greens
      1 quart shredded salad greens
      6 cups mixed fruit
        Creamy Lemon Celery-Seed Dressing or Celery-Seed Salad Dressing
      1½ cups Swiss cheese strips
      1½ cups cooked ham or turkey strips

1. For Cinnamon-Buttered Raisins, melt butter in a skillet. Mix in raisins and cinnamon. Set over low heat 5 minutes, stirring frequently. Cool.
2. Line a salad bowl with salad greens. Add shredded greens.
3. Arrange fruit in bowl. Spoon some of the desired dressing over all. Top with cheese and ham strips alternated with Cinnamon-Buttered Raisins. Serve with remaining dressing.

About 6 servings

Creamy Lemon Celery-Seed Dressing: Blend thoroughly 1½ cups mayonnaise, ¼ cup unsweetened pineapple juice, 1 teaspoon grated lemon peel, 1 tablespoon lemon juice, ½ teaspoon celery seed, and few drops Tabasco. Cover and refrigerate at least 1 hour to blend flavors.   42

About 1½ cups dressing

Celery-Seed Salad Dressing: Combine in a small bowl ¼ cup sugar, ⅓ cup light corn syrup, ¼ cup cider vinegar, 1½ to 2 teaspoons celery seed, 1 teaspoon dry mustard, 1 teaspoon salt, few grains white pepper, and 1 teaspoon grated onion. Beat with a rotary beater until mixture is thoroughly blended. Add 1 cup salad oil very gradually, beating constantly. Continue beating until mixture thickens. Cover and chill thoroughly. Shake before serving.   43

2 cups dressing

44 *Salade à la Crème (Green Salad with Cream Dressing)*

      1 quart mixed greens (such as iceberg, Boston, or Bibb lettuce, romaine, escarole, or chicory)
      ½ cup dairy sour cream
      2 tablespoons chopped parsley
      2 tablespoons dry white wine (such as chenin blanc)
      ½ teaspoon salt
      ⅛ teaspoon freshly ground pepper

1. Using only perfect leaves, wash, dry, tear into pieces, and chill greens before combining with dressing. Cold, dry leaves ensure a crisp salad.
2. Combine sour cream, parsley, wine, salt, and pepper.
3. At serving time, transfer greens to a large bowl, add dressing, and toss well.

About 6 servings

45 *Garden-Green Salad Mold*

1 package (3 ounces) lime-flavored
   gelatin
¼ teaspoon salt
1 cup boiling water
1 cup cold water
1 ripe medium avocado
1 tablespoon lemon juice
2 cups finely shredded cabbage
½ cup thinly sliced radishes
½ cup thinly sliced green onions with
   tops
  Crisp greens

1. Put gelatin and salt into a bowl; add boiling water and stir until completely dissolved. Blend in cold water. Chill until slightly thickened.
2. Mash avocado and stir in lemon juice; blend thoroughly with gelatin. Mix in cabbage, radishes, and green onions.
3. Turn into a 1-quart mold or individual molds and chill until firm. Unmold onto chilled serving plate and garnish with salad greens.

About 8 servings

46 *Stewed Tomato Aspic*

1 envelope unflavored gelatin
½ cup cold water
1 can (16 ounces) stewed tomatoes
1 tablespoon sugar
¼ teaspoon salt
1 tablespoon cider vinegar
1½ teaspoons prepared horseradish
1½ teaspoons grated onion
¼ teaspoon Worcestershire sauce
2 hard-cooked eggs, cut in quarters
  Salad greens

1. Sprinkle gelatin over water to soften.
2. Turn tomatoes into a saucepan and break up any large pieces with a spoon. Stir in sugar, salt, vinegar, horseradish, onion, and Worcestershire sauce and heat to boiling. Add softened gelatin and stir until dissolved.
3. Chill gelatin until slightly thickened.
4. Arrange egg quarters around bottom of a 3- or 4-cup mold. Spoon slightly thickened gelatin mixture into mold. Chill until firm.
5. Unmold and garnish with crisp greens.

4 to 6 servings

47 *Rice Salad with Assorted Sausages*

⅓ cup white wine vinegar
1 teaspoon lemon juice
¼ teaspoon French mustard
1 teaspoon salt
¼ teaspoon ground black pepper
⅓ cup salad oil
3 cups cooked enriched white rice,
   cooled
3 cups finely shredded red cabbage
½ cup raisins
½ cup walnut pieces
  Greens
  Link sausage (such as bratwurst,
   smoky links, and frankfurters),
   cooked

1. Put vinegar into a bottle. Add lemon juice, mustard, salt, and pepper. Cover and shake. Add oil and shake well.
2. Combine rice, cabbage, raisins, and walnuts in a bowl; chill.
3. When ready to serve, shake dressing well and pour over salad; toss until well mixed.
4. Arrange greens on luncheon plates, spoon salad on greens, and accompany with assorted sausages.

6 to 8 servings

48 Shimmering Strawberry Mold

2 packages (3 ounces each)
  strawberry-flavored gelatin
1½ cups boiling water
2 bottles (7 ounces each) lemon-lime
  carbonated beverage
1 pint fresh ripe strawberries,
  rinsed and hulled
⅓ cup sugar
  Salad greens
  Whole strawberries (optional)

1. Turn gelatin into a bowl, add boiling water, and stir until completely dissolved. Mix in carbonated beverage. Stir frequently over ice and water until slightly thicker than consistency of thick unbeaten egg white.
2. Meanwhile, cut berries lengthwise into halves, if large; sprinkle with sugar and set aside.
3. Stir the berries into the slightly thickened gelatin. Spoon into a 2-quart fancy tubed mold (or 10 individual molds). Chill until firm.
4. Unmold onto a chilled serving plate; garnish with crisp salad greens and, if desired, strawberries.

About 10 servings

Note: If desired, nut-coated cream cheese balls may be added to the salad. Soften 1 package (8 ounces) cream cheese; shape into ½-inch balls and roll in finely chopped walnuts (about ¾ cup). Arrange 5 or 6 balls in bottom of 2-quart mold; spoon enough of the slightly thickened gelatin-strawberry mixture into mold to cover cheese balls. Continue layering with remaining balls and gelatin mixture. Chill until firm.

49 Wilted Cabbage

4 cups shredded cabbage
6 slices bacon
½ cup cider vinegar
¼ cup water
3 tablespoons sugar
½ teaspoon salt
¼ teaspoon dry mustard

1. Turn cabbage into a bowl.
2. Cook bacon until crisp in a skillet; drain, reserving ¼ cup drippings. Crumble bacon onto cabbage; set aside.
3. Put reserved drippings into skillet. Add vinegar, water, sugar, salt, and dry mustard. Heat to boiling, stirring to blend.
4. Pour dressing over cabbage and bacon; toss lightly to mix.

6 to 8 servings

50 Ham Mousse Piquant

2 packages (3 ounces each)
  lemon-flavored gelatin
¼ teaspoon salt
2 cups boiling water
1 cup cold water
¼ cup cider vinegar
2 teaspoons grated onion
¼ cup water
⅔ cup chopped sweet pickle
¼ cup diced pimento
⅔ cup mayonnaise or salad dressing
1 teaspoon Worcestershire sauce
1 cup chilled whipping cream,
  whipped
4 cups firmly packed coarsely ground
  cooked ham
1 cup sliced celery
  Watercress

1. Turn gelatin and salt into a bowl. Add boiling water and stir until gelatin is dissolved. Stir in cold water, vinegar, and onion.
2. Remove 2 cups of the mixture and stir in ¼ cup water; chill until mixture thickens slightly.
3. Mix pickle and pimento into the slightly thickened gelatin. Turn into a ring mold (11 to 12 cups). Chill until just set but not firm.
4. Meanwhile, chill remaining gelatin over ice and water, stirring frequently, until slightly thickened, then whip with rotary beater until fluffy.
5. Blend mayonnaise and Worcestershire sauce; fold into whipped cream. Combine whipped cream mixture, ham, celery, and whipped gelatin. Turn into mold over pickle layer. Chill until firm.
6. Unmold onto a chilled serving plate. Fill center of mold with watercress.

About 12 servings

51 *Frosty Fruit Salad*

1 cup chopped soft dried prunes
1 cup orange pieces (1 to 2 oranges)
1 can (13¼ ounces) pineapple tidbits,
    drained; reserve ¼ cup syrup
½ cup sliced maraschino cherries,
    well drained on absorbent paper
1 envelope unflavored gelatin
⅓ cup cold water
2 cups creamed cottage cheese
1 cup dairy sour cream
1 cup whipping cream, whipped
¾ cup sugar
¾ teaspoon salt
1 large ripe banana, sliced
½ cup chopped salted almonds

1. Prepare fruits and set aside.
2. Soften gelatin in cold water in a small saucepan. Set over low heat and stir until gelatin is dissolved.
3. Sieve cottage cheese into a bowl. Blend in reserved pineapple syrup, sour cream, whipped cream, sugar, and salt; stir in the dissolved gelatin. Add the reserved fruits, banana, and almonds; mix well. Turn into refrigerator trays and freeze.
4. Allow salad to soften slightly at room temperature before serving. To serve, cut into wedges.

About 12 servings

52 *Vegetable Medley Salad Dressing Deluxe*

1 cup salad oil
3 tablespoons cider vinegar
2 tablespoons prepared horseradish
1 tablespoon sugar
1 teaspoon dry mustard
1 teaspoon paprika
½ teaspoon seasoned salt
¾ teaspoon salt
⅛ teaspoon ground black pepper
    Few grains cayenne pepper
1 medium ripe tomato, peeled and
    cut in pieces
1 small onion, peeled and cut in
    pieces
½ small cucumber, pared and cut in
    pieces
⅓ small ripe avocado, peeled and cut
    in pieces
1 large clove garlic, peeled

1. Put oil, vinegar, horseradish, sugar, seasonings, vegetables, avocado, and garlic into an electric blender container and blend thoroughly. Chill.
2. Serve on a tossed vegetable salad.

About 3½ cups dressing

53 *Jiffy French Dressing*

1 tablespoon sugar
1 teaspoon paprika
1 teaspoon dry mustard
1 teaspoon salt
⅛ teaspoon ground black pepper
1 cup salad oil
¼ cup vinegar or lemon juice

1. Blend sugar, paprika, dry mustard, salt, and pepper; put into a jar. Add oil and vinegar. Cover jar tightly and shake vigorously to blend. Store in refrigerator.
2. Before serving, shake dressing thoroughly.

1¼ cups dressing

54 *Gourmet French Dressing*

¾ cup olive oil
¼ cup vinegar (tarragon or cider)
¼ teaspoon Worcestershire sauce
1 clove garlic, cut in halves
1 teaspoon sugar
½ teaspoon salt
¼ teaspoon paprika
¼ teaspoon dry mustard
⅛ teaspoon ground black pepper
⅛ teaspoon ground thyme

1. Combine oil, vinegar, Worcestershire sauce, garlic, sugar, salt, paprika, dry mustard, pepper, and thyme in a jar; cover and shake well. Chill in refrigerator.
2. Before serving, remove garlic and beat or shake dressing thoroughly.

About 1 cup dressing

Roquefort French Dressing: Follow recipe for Gourmet French Dressing. Blend **3 ounces (about ¾ cup) Roquefort cheese,** crumbled, and **2 teaspoons water** until smooth. Add dressing slowly to cheese, blending well.

55

56 *No-Oil Salad Dressing*

½ cup water
½ cup white wine vinegar
1 tablespoon cold water
2 teaspoons cornstarch
1 tablespoon sugar
1 tablespoon chopped parsley
1 teaspoon salt
½ teaspoon basil
¼ teaspoon paprika
¼ teaspoon dry mustard
⅛ teaspoon ground white pepper

1. Heat ½ cup water and vinegar to boiling. Blend 1 tablespoon cold water and cornstarch; pour into vinegar mixture, stirring constantly.
2. Cook and stir until slightly thickened. Stir in sugar, parsley, salt, basil, paprika, dry mustard, and pepper. Chill thoroughly.
3. Serve on tossed salad greens.

About 1 cup dressing

57 *Cooked Salad Dressing*

¼ cup sugar
1 tablespoon flour
½ teaspoon dry mustard
½ teaspoon salt
⅛ teaspoon ground pepper
1 cup water
¼ cup cider vinegar
4 egg yolks, fork beaten
2 tablespoons butter or margarine

1. Blend sugar, flour, dry mustard, salt, and pepper in a heavy saucepan. Add water gradually, stirring constantly. Bring rapidly to boiling; cook and stir mixture 2 minutes. Stir in vinegar.
2. Stir about 3 tablespoons of the hot mixture into the beaten egg yolks. Immediately blend into mixture in saucepan. Cook and stir until slightly thickened.
3. Remove from heat and blend in butter. Cool; chill. Store in a covered jar in refrigerator.

About 1½ cups dressing

58 *Creamy Cooked Salad Dressing*

2 tablespoons sugar
⅛ teaspoon salt
2 tablespoons cider vinegar
2 tablespoons pineapple syrup
3 egg yolks, slightly beaten
1 tablespoon butter or margarine
1 cup chilled whipping cream, whipped

1. Mix sugar and salt in a heavy saucepan. Stir in vinegar and pineapple syrup. Bring to boiling, stirring constantly.
2. Stir about 2 tablespoons of the hot mixture into egg yolks until blended. Immediately blend into mixture in saucepan. Cook and stir until slightly thickened.
3. Remove from heat; blend in butter. Cool and chill.
4. Blend chilled mixture into whipped cream. Cover and refrigerate until ready to use.

About 2 cups dressing

59 Refreshing Salad Mold

A nice accompaniment to a savory meat dish, especially on warm days.

1 can or bottle (12 ounces) beer
2½ cups ginger ale
2 envelopes unflavored gelatin
2 medium grapefruit, peeled and sectioned

1. Sprinkle gelatin over beer in a saucepan; let stand to soften. Stir over low heat until gelatin is dissolved. Add ginger ale.
2. Chill until partially thickened. Fold in grapefruit sections.
3. Turn into a lightly oiled 5-cup mold. Chill until set. Unmold onto a platter before serving.

8 servings

60 Golden Glow Salad

1 package (6 ounces) lemon-flavored gelatin
2 cups boiling water
1 can (20 ounces) crushed pineapple
1 cup dry white wine, such as chablis
2 cups grated carrots
Crisp salad greens

1. Dissolve gelatin in boiling water.
2. Drain pineapple, reserving 1 cup syrup.
3. Add pineapple syrup and wine to gelatin mixture. Chill until partially set.
4. Fold in carrots and pineapple. Fill 12 individual molds or one 1½-quart mold.
5. Chill until firm and unmold on greens.

12 servings

61 Gourmet Potato Salad

5 cups cubed cooked potatoes
½ teaspoon salt
⅛ teaspoon ground black pepper
4 hard-cooked eggs, chopped
1 cup chopped celery
⅔ cup sliced green onions with tops
¼ cup chopped green pepper
1 cup large curd cottage cheese
¼ teaspoon dry mustard
½ teaspoon salt
Few grains black pepper
⅔ cup (6-ounce can) undiluted evaporated milk
½ cup crumbled blue cheese
2 tablespoons cider vinegar
Lettuce

1. Put potatoes into a large bowl and sprinkle with salt and pepper. Add eggs, celery, onions, and green pepper; toss lightly.
2. Put cottage cheese, dry mustard, salt, pepper, evaporated milk, blue cheese, and vinegar into an electric blender container. Blend thoroughly.
3. Pour dressing over mixture in bowl and toss lightly and thoroughly. Chill before serving to blend flavors.
4. Spoon chilled salad into a bowl lined with lettuce. Garnish as desired.

About 8 servings

62 *Piquant Perfection Salad*

1½ cups boiling water
1 package (6 ounces)
    lemon-flavored gelatin
1 can (8 ounces) crushed
    pineapple in juice
    Water
1 can or bottle (12 ounces) beer
3 medium carrots, shredded
    (about 1½ cups)
½ small head cabbage, finely
    shredded (about 3 cups)

1. Pour boiling water over gelatin; stir until dissolved.
2. Drain pineapple, thoroughly pressing out and reserving juice. Add enough water to juice to measure ¾ cup.
3. Add juice and beer to gelatin. Chill until partially thickened.
4. Stir in carrots, cabbage, and pineapple. Turn into a shallow pan or oiled 6½-cup ring mold or any 1½-quart mold. Chill until set.
5. Dip mold briefly in hot water; invert on a serving platter.
6. Serve with a dressing of **1 cup mayonnaise** blended with **2 tablespoons beer.**

12 half-cup servings

63 *Beermato Aspic*

A refreshing complement to many meat, poultry, and fish dishes.

1 can (18 ounces) tomato juice
    (2¼ cups)
1 can or bottle (12 ounces) beer
⅓ cup chopped onion
⅓ cup chopped celery leaves
    (optional)
2½ tablespoons sugar
1 tablespoon lemon juice
½ teaspoon salt
1 bay leaf
2 envelopes unflavored gelatin
¼ cup cold water

1. Combine tomato juice (reserve ¼ cup), beer, onion, celery leaves, sugar, lemon juice, salt, and bay leaf in a saucepan. Simmer, uncovered, 10 minutes.
2. Meanwhile, sprinkle gelatin over cold water and reserved tomato juice in a large bowl; let stand to soften.
3. Strain hot tomato juice mixture into bowl; stir until gelatin is completely dissolved.
4. Pour into a lightly oiled 1-quart mold. Chill until firm. Unmold onto crisp **salad greens.**

8 servings

Note: For individual aspics, turn mixture into 8 oiled ½-cup molds. Chill until firm.

64 *Beer-Curried Fruit*

An unusual accompaniment for baked ham, pork, poultry, or lamb. A nice winter brunch dish, too. It's pretty on a buffet table.

½ cup packed brown sugar
1 tablespoon cornstarch
2 to 3 teaspoons curry powder
¾ cup beer
¼ cup butter or margarine
1 tablespoon grated orange peel
1 can (30 ounces) cling peach
    slices, drained
1 can (29 ounces) pear halves or
    slices, drained
2 cans (11 ounces each) mandarin
    oranges, drained
2 bananas, thinly sliced

1. In a large saucepan, combine sugar, cornstarch, and curry powder. Stir in beer. Cook, stirring constantly, until thickened and clear.
2. Add butter and orange peel; stir until melted.
3. Add peaches, pears, and mandarin oranges. (If using pear halves, cut into slices.) Cover and simmer about 10 minutes. Stir in bananas.
4. Turn into a serving dish, chafing dish, or warming dish. Sprinkle with **flaked coconut.**

7 cups

65 Gourmet Salad Dressing

3 ounces Roquefort cheese,
   crumbled (about ¾ cup)
1 package (3 ounces) cream
   cheese, softened
1 cup dairy sour cream
⅓ cup sherry
1 tablespoon grated onion
½ teaspoon salt
¼ teaspoon paprika
1 or 2 drops Tabasco

1. Put Roquefort cheese into a bowl. Blend in cream cheese until smooth.
2. Add sour cream, sherry, onion, salt, paprika, and Tabasco; blend until creamy. Store dressing, covered, in refrigerator.

About 2 cups dressing

66 Enchanting Fruit Dressing

A fitting partner for fruit.

½ cup water
½ cup honey
8 mint leaves
⅛ teaspoon whole cardamom
   seed (contents of 3
   cardamom pods), crushed
¼ teaspoon salt
½ cup sherry, madeira, or port
1 tablespoon lemon juice

1. Put water, honey, mint leaves (bruise the mint with the back of a spoon), and cardamom seed into a small saucepan with a tight-fitting cover. Set over low heat and stir until mixed. Cover saucepan and bring rapidly to boiling. Boil gently 5 minutes. Remove from heat and stir in salt. Set aside to cool.
2. When mixture is cool, strain it and blend in sherry and lemon juice.

About 1 ⅓ cups dressing

67 Chicken Mousse Amandine

½ cup dry white wine, such as
   sauterne
2 envelopes unflavored gelatin
3 egg yolks
1 cup milk
1 cup chicken broth

1. Place a small bowl and a rotary beater in refrigerator to chill.
2. Pour wine into a small cup and sprinkle gelatin evenly over wine; set aside.
3. Beat egg yolks slightly in top of a double boiler; add milk gradually, stirring constantly.
4. Stir in the chicken broth gradually. Cook over simmering

½ cup (about 3 ounces) almonds, finely chopped
3 cups ground cooked chicken
¼ cup mayonnaise
2 tablespoons minced parsley
2 tablespoons chopped green olives
1 teaspoon lemon juice
1 teaspoon onion juice
½ teaspoon salt
½ teaspoon celery salt
Few grains paprika
Few grains cayenne pepper
½ cup chilled heavy cream
Sprigs of parsley

water, stirring constantly and rapidly until mixture coats a metal spoon.

5. Remove from heat. Stir softened gelatin and immediately stir it into the hot mixture until gelatin is completely dissolved. Cool; chill in refrigerator or over ice and water until gelatin mixture begins to gel (becomes slightly thicker). If mixture is placed over ice and water, stir frequently; if placed in refrigerator, stir occasionally.

6. Blend almonds and chicken into chilled custard mixture along with mayonnaise, parsley, olives, lemon juice, onion juice, and a mixture of salt, celery salt, paprika, and cayenne pepper.

7. Using the chilled bowl and beater, beat cream until of medium consistency (piles softly).

8. Fold whipped cream into chicken mixture. Turn into a 1½-quart fancy mold. Chill in refrigerator until firm.

9. Unmold onto chilled serving plate and, if desired, garnish with sprigs of parsley.

8 servings

68 *Dubonnet Chicken Salad Mold*

2 envelopes unflavored gelatin
1 cup cranberry juice cocktail
1 cup red Dubonnet
1 cup red currant syrup
1 envelope unflavored gelatin
¾ cup cold water
1 tablespoon soy sauce
1 cup mayonnaise
1½ cups finely diced cooked chicken
½ cup finely chopped celery
¼ cup toasted blanched almonds, finely chopped
½ cup whipping cream, whipped
Leaf lettuce
Cucumber slices, scored
Pitted ripe olives

1. Soften 2 envelopes gelatin in cranberry juice in a saucepan; set over low heat and stir until gelatin is dissolved. Remove from heat and stir in Dubonnet and currant syrup.

2. Pour into a 2-quart fancy tube mold. Chill until set but not firm.

3. Meanwhile, soften 1 envelope gelatin in cold water in a saucepan. Set over low heat and stir until gelatin is dissolved.

4. Remove from heat and stir in soy sauce and mayonnaise until thoroughly blended. Chill until mixture becomes slightly thicker. Mix in chicken, celery, and almonds. Fold in whipped cream until blended.

5. Spoon mixture into mold over first layer. Chill 8 hours or overnight.

6. Unmold onto a chilled serving plate. Garnish with lettuce, cucumber, and olives.

About 10 servings

69 *Peach Wine Mold*

1 can (29 ounces) sliced peaches
1 package (6 ounces) lemon-flavored gelatin
1½ cups boiling water
1 cup white wine
⅓ cup sliced celery
⅓ cup slivered blanched almonds
Curly endive

1. Drain peaches thoroughly, reserving 1¼ cups syrup. Reserve and refrigerate about 8 peach slices for garnish. Cut remaining peaches into pieces; set aside.

2. Pour gelatin into a bowl, add boiling water, and stir until gelatin is dissolved. Stir in reserved syrup and wine. Chill until partially set.

3. Mix peaches, celery, and almonds into gelatin. Turn into a 1½-quart fancy mold. Chill until firm.

4. Unmold salad onto a serving plate. Garnish with curly endive and reserved peach slices.

About 8 servings

70 Tangy Cabbage Mold

A cool, tart taste that is nice with a hearty main dish. If you wish, serve with mayonnaise.

1 envelope unflavored gelatin	1. Soften gelatin in cold water in a saucepan. Stir over low heat until dissolved.
¼ cup cold water	
¼ cup sugar	2. Add sugar, lemon juice, and salt; stir until dissolved. Add beer. Chill until partially thickened.
2 tablespoons lemon juice	
½ teaspoon salt	3. Stir in cabbage and green pepper.
1 can or bottle (12 ounces) beer	4. Turn into a 3½-cup mold, a shallow 1½-quart oblong casserole (8x6 inches), or 6 individual molds.
1½ cups shredded cabbage (about ¼ of a 2-pound head)	
½ green pepper, shredded	

6 servings

71 Hot Potato Salad

Bacon and beer flavor the slightly sweet sauce on these German-style potatoes. Serve with hot dogs, bratwurst, or Polish sausage. Beer is the perfect beverage.

6 medium boiling potatoes (2 pounds)	1. Place unpeeled potatoes in a large saucepan; add water to cover. Heat to boiling. Boil, uncovered, for 20 minutes, or until tender. Peel and cube; turn into a serving dish.
10 slices bacon (½ pound)	2. Meanwhile, cook bacon until crisp; leave drippings in skillet. Crumble bacon over potatoes.
½ cup chopped onion	
½ cup beer	3. Add onion to skillet. Sauté until tender. Add beer, sugar, salt, and celery seed. Heat to boiling, stirring occasionally. Pour over potatoes; toss lightly.
1 to 1½ tablespoons sugar	
1 to 1½ teaspoons salt	
1 teaspoon celery seed	

6 servings

72 Shrimp Salad with Coral Dressing

2 cups cooked, peeled, and deveined shrimp	1. Toss shrimp, rice, celery, cucumbers, and chives together.
1½ cups cooked rice	2. Blend ingredients for dressing. Pour over shrimp mixture and toss thoroughly. Chill.
½ cup sliced celery	
½ cup chopped unpeeled cucumbers	3. Serve on salad greens. Top with a little horseradish, if desired, and garnish with lemon wedges.
¼ cup chopped chives	
⅓ cup mayonnaise	4. Accompany with champagne.
¼ cup dairy sour cream	
1 tablespoon chili sauce	
¼ teaspoon onion salt	
⅛ teaspoon pepper	
1½ teaspoons tarragon vinegar	
Salad greens	
Horseradish (optional)	
Lemon wedges	

6 servings

73 *Salde Siciliano*

1 whole clove garlic
4 anchovy fillets
  Juice of 1 lemon
6 tablespoons dry red wine, such as burgundy
¾ cup olive oil
  Oregano leaves (¼ ounce or 2½ tablespoons)
  Peppercorns, crushed (⅛ ounce or ¾ teaspoon)
2 cloves garlic, minced
1 pimento, diced
3 tomatoes, diced
1 cup cooked green beans
1 cup diced hearts of artichoke
1 cup diced hearts of palm
1 head romaine lettuce, torn in pieces
1 head iceberg lettuce, torn in chunks
2 slices bread, toasted and cut in cubes
¼ pound Gorgonzola cheese, crumbled

1. Rub a large wooden salad bowl with the whole clove of garlic. Add anchovy fillets. Rub bowl again with the garlic and anchovies; mash together forming a paste. Blend in, stirring vigorously, the lemon juice, burgundy, olive oil, oregano, and pepper. (If necessary, correct seasonings to taste.)
2. Blend in minced garlic, diced pimento, and tomatoes. Add green beans, hearts of artichoke and palm, romaine, and iceberg lettuce. Toss lightly.
3. Add croutons and cheese. Again, toss lightly. Serve immediately on chilled salad plates.

4 to 8 servings

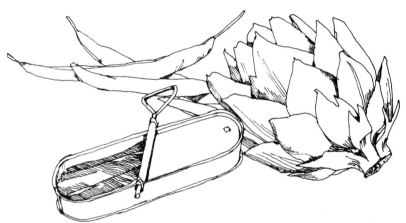

74 *White Wine Aspic*

1½ tablespoons unflavored gelatin
2 tablespoons sugar
¼ teaspoon salt
⅔ cup cold water
1¼ cups apple juice
1 cup dry white wine, such as chablis
1 tablespoon sweet pickle syrup
1 tablespoon lemon juice
½ cup dairy sour cream

1. Blend gelatin, sugar, and salt in a saucepan; add water. Place over low heat, stirring constantly, until gelatin and sugar are thoroughly dissolved.
2. Stir in apple juice, white wine, pickle syrup, and lemon juice. Chill until slightly thickened. Immediately blend with sour cream.
3. Pour into a fancy 1-quart ring mold and chill until firm. Unmold onto a serving plate and surround with fresh fruits, such as peach or pear halves or wedges, bunches of Tokay or green grapes, sweet red cherries, orange segments, or other colorful fruits in season.

About 6 servings

Note: If desired, fold 1½ cups shredded vegetables such as carrots, cabbage, cucumber, and green pepper into sour cream-gelatin mixture and turn into an 8×8×2-inch pan. Chill until firm, cut into squares, and serve in crisp lettuce cups.

Soups

75 Chicken Soup Tortellini

2 quarts water
1 broiler-fryer chicken (about 2½ pounds)
1 onion, sliced
2 teaspoons fresh minced parsley or 1 teaspoon dried parsley
1½ teaspoons salt
1 teaspoon rosemary or chervil
⅛ teaspoon pepper
1 cup sliced celery with leaves
1 cup sliced fresh mushrooms
½ cup dry white wine
32 tortellini (see recipe)

1. Place water, chicken, onion, parsley, salt, rosemary, and pepper in a large saucepan. Bring to boiling; simmer covered 1 hour, or until chicken is tender.
2. Remove chicken; cool. Discard chicken skin. Remove meat from bones and chop fine. Reserve for tortellini filling.
3. Bring stock to boiling; stir in remaining ingredients. Simmer 15 minutes, or until tortellini are done. (If using frozen tortellini, simmer about 30 minutes.)

8 to 10 servings

76 Tortellini

Dough:
2 eggs
2 egg whites
2 tablespoons olive or vegetable oil
2 teaspoons salt
3 cups all-purpose flour

Filling:
2½ cups finely chopped chicken
¼ cup grated Parmesan cheese
2 egg yolks

1. Prepare dough by combining eggs, egg whites, oil, and salt in a bowl. Gradually add flour, mixing well until mixture forms a soft dough. Turn onto a floured surface and knead in remaining flour to form a very stiff dough.
2. Wrap dough in waxed paper; let rest 10 minutes.
3. Combine chicken, cheese, and egg yolks in a bowl. Set aside.
4. Divide dough in quarters. Roll each quarter into a large circle as thin as possible. Cut into about 32 (2-inch) rounds.
5. For each tortellini, place about 1 teaspoon chicken mixture in center of round. Moisten edges with water. Fold in half; seal edges. Shape into rings by stretching the tips of half circle slightly and wrapping the ring around your index finger. Gently press tips together (tortellini may be frozen at this point).
6. Cook as directed in recipe for Chicken Soup Tortellini.

About 128 tortellini

77 French Onion Soup *(Soupe à l'Oignon)*

The originator of this famous French soup was King Louis XV, who returned late one night to his hunting lodge and found only onions, butter, and champagne on hand. So hungry and weary was he that he simply mixed them together. Voilà—French Onion Soup! A toasted cheese crouton is traditionally part of the recipe, so there's no need to serve additional bread.

5 medium onions, sliced (4 cups)
3 tablespoons butter or margarine
1½ quarts beef broth
½ teaspoon salt
⅛ teaspoon pepper
Cheese Croutons

1. Sauté onions in melted butter in a large saucepan. Cook slowly, stirring until golden (about 10 minutes).
2. Blend in beef broth, salt, and pepper. Bring to boiling, cover, and simmer 15 minutes.
3. Pour soup into warm soup bowls or crocks. Float a cheese crouton in each bowl of soup.

6 servings

78 Cheese Croutons

6 slices French bread, toasted
2 tablespoons butter or margarine
¼ cup (1 ounce) grated Gruyère or Swiss cheese

1. Spread one side of each bread slice with butter. If necessary, cut bread to fit size of bowl. Sprinkle cheese over buttered toast.
2. Place under broiler until cheese melts.

79 Hungarian Goulash Soup

The Hungarians use grated potato for a thickening in this soup, with wonderful results.

1½ pounds beef for stew, cut into ½-inch cubes
1 tablespoon shortening or vegetable oil
1 large onion, chopped
1 quart water
¾ cup grated potato (about 1 large)
1 tablespoon paprika
1 tablespoon tomato sauce or ketchup
1 teaspoon salt
½ teaspoon caraway seed (optional)
¼ teaspoon crushed thyme
Pinch red pepper
1 cup chopped pared raw potato (about 1 large)
1 cup uncooked egg noodles

1. Brown meat in shortening in a large saucepan. Add onion; cook until tender.
2. Add water, grated potato, and seasonings. Bring to boiling; cover. Simmer 1½ hours, or until beef is tender.
3. Stir in potatoes and noodles. Cook until tender, 10 to 20 minutes.

4 to 6 servings

Hungarian Goulash Soup with Spaetzle: Follow recipe for Hungarian Goulash Soup, omitting chopped potato and noodles. Serve with **hot buttered spaetzle.**

80

81 Spaetzle

2 cups all-purpose flour
1 teaspoon salt
1 egg
¼ to ½ cup water

1. Combine flour and salt; stir in egg. Gradually add water until batter is stiff, but smooth. Place on wet cutting board; flatten.
2. With a wet knife, scrape small pieces of dough off and drop into boiling salted water. Cook only one layer of spaetzle at a time, boiling gently 5 to 8 minutes, or until done. Remove with perforated spoon.

Note: Spaetzle may be served in pea, lentil, or tomato soup or as a side dish, either tossed with hot melted butter or sautéed in butter. For variety, sprinkle with toasted bread crumbs or grated Parmesan cheese.

82 *Mulligatawny Soup*

Mulligatawny soup is from India, and as you might expect, the distinctive flavor is curry. Curry recipes do not always call for curry powder. The authentic ones call for a combination of spices, such as turmeric, cumin, coriander, dill, and cardamom. This version of mulligatawny calls for both curry powder and several other seasonings.

1 cup diced uncooked chicken (see Note)
¼ cup chopped onion
¼ cup chopped celery
¼ cup diced carrot
2 tart apples, pared and sliced
¼ cup fat or margarine
¼ cup flour
1 teaspoon curry powder
1½ quarts chicken broth
1 tomato, peeled and chopped, or 1 cup drained canned tomatoes, chopped
½ green pepper, minced
1 teaspoon minced parsley
1 teaspoon salt
1 teaspoon sugar
⅛ teaspoon pepper
⅛ teaspoon mace
2 whole cloves
1 cup cooked rice (optional)

1. Cook chicken, onion, celery, carrots, and apple in melted fat in a large saucepan until lightly browned.
2. Stir in flour and curry powder. Gradually add chicken broth, stirring constantly.
3. Stir in remaining ingredients. Cook, covered, over low heat until chicken is tender.
4. Remove and reserve chicken. Strain soup, discarding cloves.
5. Purée vegetables in an electric blender or force through a sieve or food mill. Return soup and vegetable purée to saucepan. Mix in chicken and heat to serving temperature.
6. If desired, mix in hot cooked rice.

8 servings

Note: If making your own chicken broth, substitute the cooked chicken meat for the uncooked chicken and add to soup for final heating.

83 *Tomato-Cheese Soup*

1 can (about 10 ounces) condensed tomato soup
1 soup can milk
1 cup (4 ounces) shredded Cheddar, American, or Colby cheese
¼ teaspoon finely crushed basil (optional)

1. Turn soup into a large saucepan; gradually blend in milk. Stir until hot and blended.
2. Mix in cheese and, if desired, basil.

3 servings

84 *Greek Egg-Lemon Soup*

Lemons are to Greece as oranges are to Florida—they just can't seem to get enough of them. And this soup is as common to them as chicken-noodle is to Americans.

6 cups rich veal or chicken broth (page 62) or 6 bouillon cubes in 6 cups water
⅓ cup uncooked rice
3 eggs
¼ cup lemon juice

1. Bring broth to boiling in a large saucepan. Add rice; cover and simmer until rice is tender, about 20 minutes.
2. Beat eggs until frothy in a bowl; add lemon juice. Beat in 2 cups of broth very slowly; stir the mixture into the remaining soup.
3. Heat to serving temperature, being very careful not to let it boil (boiling will curdle the egg).

4 to 6 servings

Basic White Bread, page 62

85 *Alphabet Soup*

½ pound ground beef
1 onion, chopped
5 cups water
1 can (16 ounces) tomatoes
3 potatoes, cubed
2 carrots, sliced
2 stalks celery, sliced
2 teaspoons salt
1 teaspoon Worcestershire sauce
1 beef bouillon cube
¼ teaspoon garlic powder
¼ teaspoon pepper
3 sprigs fresh parsley, minced, or 2
    tablespoons dried
1 cup uncooked alphabet macaroni

1. Brown meat in a large saucepan; drain off fat.
2. Add remaining ingredients, except macaroni. Bring to boiling; cover and simmer 1 hour.
3. Stir in macaroni; cook 20 minutes.

6 to 8 servings

86 *Homemade Chicken-Noodle Soup*

2 quarts water
1 broiler-fryer chicken (about 2½
    pounds), cut up
1 finely chopped onion
1 cup finely chopped celery
2 tablespoons minced fresh parsley
    or 1 teaspoon dried
2 teaspoons salt
1 teaspoon crushed rosemary or
    chervil
⅛ teaspoon pepper
2 cups uncooked homemade (see
    page 60) or packaged noodles

1. Place all ingredients except noodles in a kettle or Dutch oven. Bring to boiling; simmer 1 hour, or until chicken is tender.
2. Remove chicken; cool. Discard skin. Remove meat from bones and chop.
3. Return chicken to stock; bring to boiling. Stir in noodles. Simmer 20 to 30 minutes, or until noodles are done.

8 servings

87 *Homemade Noodles*

2 eggs
½ teaspoon salt
1 cup all-purpose flour

1. Beat eggs and salt in a mixing bowl. Gradually add flour, mixing well until mixture forms a soft dough. Turn onto a floured surface; knead in remaining flour to form a very stiff dough.
2. Cover; let rest 10 to 15 minutes.
3. Roll dough as thin as possible, turning dough over as you roll.
4. Roll dough up tightly, jelly-roll fashion. Cut off thin slices. Toss to separate. Spread out on baking sheets; toss periodically until thoroughly dry.

2 cups noodles

Lettuce Soup, page 49

88 *Hot Dog! It's Soup*

One way of improving your child's acceptance of food is to allow him or her to have a hand in its preparation. With this soup we are mixing two favorite children's foods—corn and hot dogs. You might ask your child to help you shred the cheese (under your supervision, of course) or slice the hot dogs (a table knife will do). Serve with buttered slices of homemade white bread. That's one of their favorites, too.

½ cup chopped onion
⅓ cup sliced celery
2 tablespoons margarine
1 cup water
2 cups (16-ounce can) cream-style corn
1 bay leaf
½ teaspoon basil
1½ cups milk
1 pound frankfurters, sliced
1 teaspoon salt
⅛ teaspoon pepper
½ cup shredded process American cheese
Minced parsley

1. Sauté onion and celery in margarine in a medium saucepan. Add water, corn, bay leaf, and basil. Cook 5 minutes.
2. Remove bay leaf. Add remaining ingredients except parsley. Cook over low heat until cheese melts.
3. Garnish with parsley.

6 to 8 servings

89 *Beef Stock*

Because during simmering the liquid is reduced, salt lightly initially and correct salt level before serving.

3 pounds lean beef (chuck or plate), cut in 1-inch pieces
1 soup bone, cracked
3 quarts cold water
1 tablespoon salt
2 large onions, peeled
2 whole cloves
5 carrots, cut in large pieces
3 stalks celery with leaves, sliced
4 sprigs parsley
1 bay leaf
1 teaspoon thyme
8 peppercorns

1. Put meat and soup bone into a large saucepan; add water and salt. Cover saucepan and simmer about 2 hours, removing foam as necessary.
2. Slice 1 onion; insert the cloves into second onion. Add onions, remaining vegetables, and seasonings to saucepan. Cover and bring to boiling. Reduce heat and simmer about 1½ hours.
3. Remove from heat; remove soup bone and strain stock through a fine sieve. Allow to cool. Chill. (The meat and vegetables strained from stock may be served as desired.)
4. Remove fat that rises to surface (reserve for use in other food preparation). Reheat and serve with slices of crisp toast.

About 2½ quarts stock

Brown Stock: Follow recipe for Beef Stock. Cut meat from soup bone and brown it along with beef pieces in ¼ **cup fat** in saucepan before cooking. Proceed as in Beef Stock.

90 *Baked Minestrone*

1½ pounds lean beef for stew, cut
 in 1-inch cubes
1 cup coarsely chopped onion
2 cloves garlic, crushed
1 teaspoon salt
¼ teaspoon pepper
2 tablespoons olive oil
3 cans (about 10 ounces each)
 condensed beef broth
2 soup cans water
1½ teaspoons herb seasoning
1 can (16 ounces) tomatoes
 (undrained)
1 can (15¼ ounces) kidney beans
 (undrained)
1 can (6 ounces) pitted ripe olives
 (undrained)
1½ cups thinly sliced carrots
1 cup small seashell macaroni
2 cups sliced zucchini
 Grated Parmesan cheese

1. Mix beef, onion, garlic, salt, and pepper in a large saucepan. Add olive oil and stir to coat meat evenly.
2. Bake at 400°F 30 minutes, or until meat is browned, stirring occasionally.
3. Turn oven control to 350°F. Add broth, water, and seasonings; stir. Cover; cook 1 hour, or until meat is tender.
4. Stir in tomatoes, kidney beans, olives, carrots, and macaroni. Put sliced zucchini on top. Cover; bake 30 to 40 minutes, or until carrots are tender.
5. Serve with grated cheese.

10 to 12 servings

91 *Brown Vegetable Stock*

Use assorted vegetables from your refrigerator, or purchase a package of soup vegetables from your produce counter.

2 pounds mixed vegetables
 (carrots, leeks, onions, celery,
 turnips, etc.)
¼ cup butter or margarine
2½ quarts water
½ teaspoon salt
½ teaspoon thyme
3 sprigs parsley
½ bay leaf
 Dash of pepper

1. Chop vegetables. Brown in butter.
2. Add water and seasonings. Cover.
3. Simmer 1½ hours or until vegetables are tender.
4. Strain and chill.

About 2 quarts stock

White Vegetable Stock: If a lighter, clearer stock is desired, omit butter and do not brown vegetables.

92

93 Red and White Bean Soup

There are many dried white beans on the market—great northern, navy, white, kidney, and lima are some. They may be used interchangeably and are all high in protein.

2 cups dried navy beans, soaked overnight
2 cups chopped onion
1 tablespoon salt
10 whole peppercorns
1 stalk celery with leaves, sliced
¼ cup minced parsley or 2 tablespoons dried parsley
½ teaspoon crushed thyme or basil
2 cups chopped potato
¼ cup butter or margarine
¼ cup flour
1 can (15 ounces) tomato sauce
1 can (14 ounces) brown beans in molasses sauce

1. Drain soaked beans, reserving liquid. Add enough water to bean liquid to measure 6 cups. Combine in a large saucepan soaked beans, bean liquid, onion, salt, peppercorns, celery, parsley, and thyme. Heat to boiling; simmer 45 minutes.
2. Stir in potato. Simmer 20 minutes or until tender.
3. In a separate saucepan, stir flour into melted butter; cook until bubbly. Gradually add tomato sauce; mix well.
4. Stir tomato mixture and brown beans into soup. Simmer 5 minutes.

8 servings

94 Chili Soup

½ pound ground beef
1 cup chopped onion
5 cups water
1 can (28 ounces) tomatoes
1 can (15 ounces) tomato sauce
1 clove garlic, crushed
1 tablespoon chili powder
1 teaspoon salt
1 teaspoon cumin
½ teaspoon oregano
1 cup uncooked macaroni
1 can (about 15 ounces) kidney or chili beans

1. Brown meat in a large saucepan; drain off fat. Stir in onion; cook 1 minute.
2. Add water, tomatoes, tomato sauce, garlic, chili powder, salt, cumin, and oregano. Simmer 30 minutes.
3. Add remaining ingredients; cook until macaroni is done (about 10 to 15 minutes).

8 to 10 servings

95 Farm-Style Leek Soup

2 large leeks (1 pound) with part of green tops, sliced
2 medium onions, sliced
1 large garlic clove, minced
¼ cup butter or margarine
4 cups chicken stock or bouillon
2 cups uncooked narrow or medium noodles (3 ounces)
1 can or bottle (12 ounces) beer
1½ cups shredded semisoft cheese (Muenster, brick, process, etc.)
Salt and pepper

1. Cook leek, onion, and garlic in butter for 15 minutes, using low heat and stirring often.
2. Add stock. Cover and simmer 30 minutes.
3. Add noodles. Cover and simmer 15 minutes, or until noodles are tender.
4. Add beer; heat to simmering. Gradually add cheese, cooking slowly and stirring until melted. Season to taste with salt and pepper.

6 servings, about 1½ cups each

96 *Bean and Prosciutto Soup*

2 cups (about ¾ pound) dried
    beans, soaked overnight
5 cups water
2 cups sliced celery
3 to 4 ounces sliced prosciutto, cut
    in thin strips
1 can (16 ounces) tomatoes
1 can (about 10 ounces) condensed
    beef broth
1 teaspoon salt
1 garlic clove, crushed
2 packages (9 ounces each) frozen
    Italian green beans
3 sprigs fresh parsley, minced
    (about 2 tablespoons)

1. Combine soaked dried beans, water, celery, prosciutto, tomatoes, beef broth, salt, and garlic in a 5-quart saucepot. Bring to boiling; simmer, covered, 30 minutes.
2. Mix in green beans and parsley; simmer 5 to 10 minutes.

10 to 12 servings

97 *Tomato-Lentil Soup*

2 cups chopped carrots
1 cup chopped onion
1 cup sliced celery
2 tablespoons margarine, melted
1 clove garlic, crushed
1¼ cups (½ pound) dried lentils
2 quarts water
1 tablespoon salt
1 can (6 ounces) tomato paste
¼ teaspoon crushed dill weed or
    tarragon

1. Sauté carrots, onion, and celery in margarine in a large saucepan until tender.
2. Add garlic, lentils, water, and salt. Simmer 2 hours, or until lentils are tender.
3. Add tomato paste and dill weed; stir.

6 to 8 servings

98 *Split Pea Soup with Ham Bone*

2 cups dried green split peas
1½ quarts water
1 ham bone (about 1½ pounds)
1 onion, sliced
1 cup sliced celery
1 cup grated carrot
2 teaspoons salt
1 teaspoon crushed basil
¼ cup butter or margarine
¼ cup flour
2 cups milk

1. In a large saucepan, combine peas, water, bone, onion, celery, carrot, salt, and basil. Bring to boiling; simmer 1½ to 2 hours.
2. Stir flour into melted butter in a separate saucepan; cook until bubbly. Gradually add milk, stirring constantly. Bring to boiling; cook 1 minute.
3. Stir white sauce into soup.

8 servings

99 *Lentil Soup*

1¼ cups (about ½ pound) lentils, soaked overnight
2 quarts beef broth
6 frankfurters, cut diagonally in ½-inch slices
2 onions, thinly sliced
2 carrots, sliced
2 stalks celery, sliced
3 sprigs chervil or parsley or 1 tablespoon dried chervil
2 teaspoons salt
¼ teaspoon pepper

Combine all ingredients in a large saucepan. Bring to boiling; simmer 35 minutes, or until lentils are tender.

100 *Chicken Succotash Soup with Parsley Dumplings*

1 broiler-fryer chicken (2 to 3 pounds), cut up
2 quarts water
2 teaspoons salt
½ teaspoon crushed rosemary
Pinch pepper
Parsley Dumplings
1 cup sliced carrots
¼ cup chopped onion
1 package (10 ounces) frozen corn
1 package (10 ounces) frozen lima beans

1. Combine chicken, water, salt, rosemary, and pepper in a large saucepan. Bring to boiling; simmer 45 minutes, covered, or until chicken is tender.
2. Remove chicken from broth; cool, skin, and cut into pieces.
3. Skim fat or chill to remove fat
4. Prepare Parsley Dumplings.
5. Add vegetables and chicken to stock. Bring to boiling. Drop dumplings by teaspoonfuls onto gently simmering soup. Cover; cook 10 minutes. Uncover; cook 5 to 10 minutes.
6. Serve each portion with one or two dumplings.

6 to 8 servings

101 *Parsley Dumplings*

2 cups all-purpose flour
2 teaspoons baking powder
1½ teaspoons salt
⅛ teaspoon pepper
3 tablespoons butter or margarine
1 egg
Milk
¼ cup minced parsley

1. Combine flour, baking powder, salt, and pepper in a bowl.
2. Cut in butter until mixture resembles coarse meal.
3. Break egg into measuring cup. Add enough milk to make 1 cup liquid. Beat well. Add to dry ingredients along with parsley and stir just until flour is moistened.
4. Proceed as directed.

102 *Lebanon Lentil Soup*

2 quarts beef broth
1 ham bone
1¼ cups (about ½ pound) lentils
2 stalks celery, sliced
2 carrots, sliced
1 onion, sliced
1 teaspoon salt
¼ teaspoon pepper
½ teaspoon crushed thyme or ¼ teaspoon dill weed

1. Combine all ingredients in a large saucepan. Bring to boiling. Cover; simmer 1 to 2 hours, or until lentils are tender.
2. Remove ham bone. Force soup mixture through a coarse sieve or food mill, or purée in an electric blender.
3. Heat, if necessary.

8 servings

Cream of Lentil Soup: Follow recipe for Lebanon Lentil Soup. After puréeing, stir in **1 cup half-and-half** or **whipping cream.** 103

104 *Italian White Bean Soup*

2 cups (about ½ pound) dried navy beans, soaked overnight
2 quarts water
2 cups chopped potato (about 1 large)
1 can (16 ounces) tomatoes (undrained)
¼ cup chopped onion
2 teaspoons salt
1 clove garlic, crushed
1 teaspoon crushed basil
1 cup (about 2 ounces) broken vermicelli or shell macaroni

1. Combine in a large saucepan beans, water, potato, tomatoes, onion, salt, garlic, and basil. Bring to boiling; simmer 1 hour, or until beans are tender.
2. Stir in vermicelli; cook 20 minutes.

8 to 10 servings

105 *Lancaster County Chicken-Corn Soup*

The "rivvels" served in this soup are a Pennsylvania Dutch dumpling made by rubbing bits of the dough mixture between the palms of your hands and dropping them into the soup.

1 stewing chicken (3 to 4 pounds), cut up
1 large onion, chopped
3 quarts water
2 teaspoons salt
¼ teaspoon pepper
4 cups corn (three 10-ounce packages frozen corn or two 16-ounce cans)
½ cup chopped celery with leaves
Rivvels

1. Place chicken, onion, water, salt, and pepper in a large saucepot. Bring to boiling; simmer 1 hour or until chicken is tender.
2. Remove chicken from stock, strip meat from bones, cut into bite-size pieces, and return to stock. Add corn and celery; simmer 30 minutes.
3. Drop rivvels into soup by rivveling; that is, rubbing dough between palms of your hands and dropping into soup. Cook in simmering soup 15 minutes, or until done.

10 servings

Rivvels: Combine 1 cup all-purpose flour, **½ teaspoon salt, 1 egg,** and enough **milk (about ¼ cup)** to make a crumbly semimoist mixture. 106

107 Chili-Chicken Soup

1 broiler-fryer chicken (about 3
  pounds), cut up
1½ quarts water
1 onion, studded with 2 or 3
  whole cloves
1 tablespoon salt
3 garlic cloves, crushed
1 bay leaf
1 can (about 15 ounces) red
  kidney beans
1 can (6 ounces) tomato paste
1 can (4 ounces) mild green
  chilies or 1 hot pepper,
  chopped
1 tablespoon chili powder
1 teaspoon crushed basil
Cooked rice

1. Combine chicken, water, onion, salt, garlic, and bay leaf in a large saucepan. Bring to boiling; simmer 45 minutes, or until chicken is tender.
2. Remove chicken and onion from stock; cool. Discard chicken skin; remove meat from bones and chop. Skim fat from stock. Remove cloves from onion; discard. Chop onion.
3. Stir chicken, onion, and remaining ingredients, except rice, into stock. Heat. Serve with rice.

6 to 8 servings

108 Burgundy Oxtail Soup

2 oxtails (about 3 pounds), cut up
¼ cup flour (about)
3 tablespoons bacon fat or
  shortening
2 quarts water
1 onion, chopped
¾ cup tomato juice
2 teaspoons salt
1 bay leaf
4 peppercorns
1 garlic clove, crushed
1 cup sliced celery with leaves
1 cup sliced carrot
¾ cup burgundy or other dry red
  wine
½ teaspoon crushed tarragon
1 cup sliced fresh mushrooms
¼ cup chopped fresh parsley

1. Coat oxtails with flour. Brown in hot fat in a large saucepan.
2. Add water, onion, tomato juice, salt, bay leaf, peppercorns, and garlic. Bring to boiling; simmer 2 to 3 hours.
3. Strain stock. Chill; remove fat. Return stock to saucepan.
4. Bring stock to boiling; add celery, carrot, burgundy, and tarragon. Simmer 30 minutes.
5. Stir in remaining ingredients. Cook 5 minutes.

8 servings

109 Belgian Beer Soup

Soups provide great ways to cook less-tender cuts of meat. Most of these meats are flavorful and relatively inexpensive, and best of all they become tender through long, slow simmering.

2 pounds beef chuck, cut in ½-inch
  cubes; reserve bone
7 cups water
1 cup beer
2 teaspoons salt
1 bay leaf

1. Trim fat from meat.
2. Brown meat and bone in a large saucepan without fat. Stir in water, beer, salt, bay leaf, pepper, allspice, and bouillon cubes. Heat to boiling; simmer 2 hours.
3. Stir in onion, potatoes, celery, and carrots; simmer 30 minutes.

½ teaspoon pepper
½ teaspoon allspice
2 beef bouillon cubes
½ cup chopped onion
4 cups chopped potatoes (about 6 medium potatoes)
2 cups sliced celery
2 cups sliced carrots
1 package (10 ounces) frozen Brussels sprouts

4. Stir in Brussels sprouts; simmer 15 minutes, or until sprouts are tender.

6 to 8 servings

110 *Sherried Chicken Chowder*

10 cups water
1 broiler-fryer chicken (about 2½ pounds)
1 carrot, coarsely chopped
1 stalk celery, coarsely chopped
1 onion, halved
4 whole cloves
2 teaspoons salt
1 teaspoon crushed tarragon
1 bay leaf
½ cup uncooked barley or rice
½ teaspoon curry powder
¼ cup dry sherry
1 cup half-and-half

1. Place water, chicken, carrot, celery, onion halves studded with cloves, salt, and tarragon in Dutch oven or saucepot. Bring to boiling; simmer 1 hour, or until chicken is tender.
2. Remove chicken; cool. Discard skin; remove meat from bones; chop.
3. Strain stock. Discard cloves and bay leaf. Reserve stock and vegetables. Skim fat from stock.
4. Purée vegetables and 1 cup stock in an electric blender.
5. Return stock to Dutch oven; bring to boiling. Stir in barley and puréed vegetables. Simmer 1 hour, or until barley is tender. Stir in chicken, curry, sherry, and half-and-half.

8 servings

111 *Meatball Soup*

1 pound ground beef
1 onion, chopped
1½ quarts water
1 can (16 ounces) tomatoes
3 potatoes, cubed
2 carrots, sliced
2 stalks celery, sliced
3 sprigs fresh parsley, minced, or 2 tablespoons dried
½ cup uncooked barley
2 teaspoons salt
½ teaspoon crushed thyme or basil
¼ teaspoon garlic powder
¼ teaspoon pepper
1 bay leaf
1 teaspoon Worcestershire sauce
1 beef bouillon cube

1. Shape beef into tiny meatballs. Brown meatballs and onion in a large saucepan, or place in a shallow pan and brown in a 400°F oven. Drain off excess fat.
2. Add remaining ingredients. Bring to boiling, simmer 1½ hours, or until vegetables are tender.

8 servings

112 *Vegetable Medley Soup*

8 slices bacon
½ cup chopped onion
½ cup sliced celery
5 cups water
1½ cups fresh corn or 1 package
    (about 10 ounces) frozen corn
½ cup sliced carrots
1 potato, pared and sliced
1 tablespoon salt
1 teaspoon sugar
¼ teaspoon pepper
¼ teaspoon crushed thyme or basil
1 cup fresh green beans, cut in
    1-inch pieces
4 cups chopped peeled tomatoes
    (4 to 5 tomatoes)

1. Cook bacon until crisp in a Dutch oven or kettle. Drain off all but 2 tablespoons fat.
2. Sauté onion and celery in bacon fat.
3. Stir in water, corn, carrots, potato, salt, sugar, pepper, and thyme. Bring to boiling; simmer covered 30 minutes.
4. Stir in green beans; simmer 10 minutes, or until beans are crisp-tender.
5. Stir in tomatoes; heat 5 minutes.

About 6 servings

113 *Vegetarian Chowder*

4 cups sliced zucchini
½ cup chopped onion
⅓ cup butter or margarine
⅓ cup flour
2 tablespoons minced parsley
1 teaspoon crushed basil
1 teaspoon salt
⅛ teaspoon pepper
3 cups water
1 chicken bouillon cube
1 package (10 ounces) frozen corn
    or 2 cups fresh corn
1 can (13½ ounces) evaporated
    milk
1 can (16 ounces) tomatoes, broken
    up, or 3 tomatoes, skinned
    and chopped
1 cup shredded Monterey Jack
    cheese (optional)

1. Sauté zucchini and onion in butter in a large saucepan. Stir in flour, parsley, basil, salt, and pepper.
2. Gradually add water, stirring constantly. Add remaining ingredients. Bring to boiling; simmer 10 to 15 minutes.
3. If desired, stir in Monterey Jack cheese.

6 to 8 servings

114 *Beef Barley Soup*

2 quarts water
1 soup bone with meat
½ cup chopped celery tops
1 tablespoon salt
½ teaspoon pepper
½ cup uncooked regular barley

1. Combine water, bone, celery tops, salt, and pepper in a Dutch oven. Bring to boiling; cover tightly and simmer 1 to 2 hours.
2. Remove bone from stock; cool. Remove meat from bone; chop. Return to stock.
3. Stir in barley; continue cooking 30 minutes.

3 cups coarsely chopped cabbage
1 cup sliced carrots
1 cup sliced celery
2 cups sliced parsnips
2 cups thinly sliced onion
1 can (12 ounces) tomato paste

4. Add remaining ingredients; simmer 30 minutes, or until vegetables are tender.

8 to 10 servings

115 Cheddar-Corn Chowder

2½ cups water
1½ cups chopped potatoes
1 cup sliced carrots
½ cup sliced celery
¼ cup chopped onion or scallions
1½ teaspoons salt
¼ teaspoon pepper
¼ cup butter or margarine
¼ cup flour
2 cups milk
2½ cups shredded sharp Cheddar
    cheese (10 ounces)
1 can (16 ounces) cream-style
    corn or 2 cups fresh corn

1. Combine water, potatoes, carrots, celery, onion, salt, and pepper in a large saucepan. Cover; bring to boiling. Simmer 10 minutes, or until vegetables are tender.
2. Melt butter in a saucepan. Stir in flour; cook until bubbly. Gradually add milk, stirring constantly. Bring to boiling; cook 1 minute. Add cheese; stir until melted.
3. Gradually add cheese sauce to soup, stirring constantly. Stir in corn.

6 servings

116 Vegetable-Beer Chowder

1 package (9 ounces) frozen green
    beans, thawed
1 package (10 ounces) frozen corn,
    thawed
¼ cup chopped onion
¼ cup butter or margarine
¼ cup flour
1 teaspoon salt
½ teaspoon dry mustard
2 cups milk
1 cup beer
2 cups shredded Cheddar cheese (8
    ounces)

1. Sauté vegetables in melted butter in a large saucepan.
2. Stir in flour, salt, and dry mustard; cook until bubbly, stirring constantly.
3. Gradually add milk and beer, stirring constantly. Bring to boiling; cook 1 minute.
4. Stir in cheese until melted.

4 to 6 servings

117 *New England Clam Chowder*

2 tablespoons butter or margarine
½ cup finely diced celery
¼ cup thinly sliced leek (white part only)
¼ cup minced onion
¼ cup minced green pepper
3 tablespoons flour
1¾ cups milk
1 cup whipping cream or half-and-half
½ cup finely diced potato
12 large hard-shelled clams (to prepare, see Note), or 2 cans (about 7 ounces each) minced clams, drained (reserve liquid)
½ teaspoon salt
⅛ teaspoon thyme
3 drops Tabasco
Pinch white pepper
½ teaspoon Worcestershire sauce
Finely chopped parsley

1. Melt butter over low heat in a heavy 3-quart saucepan. Add celery, leek, onion, and green pepper. Stirring occasionally, cook 6 to 8 minutes, or until partially tender.
2. Blend flour into the vegetable-butter mixture; heat until bubbly. Gradually add milk and cream, stirring constantly. Bring to boiling, stirring constantly; cook 1 to 2 minutes.
3. Stir in potato, reserved clam liquid, salt, thyme, Tabasco, and pepper. Bring to boiling and simmer 25 to 35 minutes, stirring frequently. Add minced clams and Worcestershire sauce.
4. Pour into soup tureen or individual soup bowls. Garnish with parsley.

4 to 6 servings

Note: To prepare clams and broth, rinse clams thoroughly under running cold water. Place clams in saucepan and add 3 cups water. Cook over medium heat until shells open completely. Drain the clams, reserving 2 cups of broth for chowder. Remove clams from shells. Cut off the hard outsides (combs) and chop clams into small, fine pieces. Decrease milk in chowder to 1 cup.

118 *Creamy Tuna-Broccoli Soup*

¼ cup butter or margarine
3 tablespoons minced onion
3 tablespoons flour
½ teaspoon salt
½ teaspoon celery salt
½ teaspoon ground sage
¼ teaspoon white pepper
Pinch cayenne pepper
1 quart milk
1 package (10 ounces) frozen chopped broccoli
1 can (6½ or 7 ounces) tuna, drained and flaked

1. Melt butter in a large, heavy saucepan over low heat. Add onion and cook until tender. Blend in flour, salt, celery salt, sage, and peppers. Heat until bubbly.
2. Gradually add milk, stirring constantly. Bring to boiling. Stir in broccoli. Cook over low heat, stirring occasionally, 10 to 12 minutes, or until broccoli is tender when pierced with a fork.
3. Mix in tuna and heat about 3 minutes.

About 6 servings

119 *Vegetable Oyster Soup*

4 cups chopped head lettuce
2 cups chopped spinach
1 cup chopped carrots
½ cup chopped onion
1½ cups chicken broth or 1 can
    (about 10 ounces) chicken
    broth
1 can (10 ounces) frozen oysters,
    thawed
2 tablespoons butter
2 tablespoons flour
1¼ teaspoons salt
2 cups milk
1 teaspoon grated lemon peel
1 tablespoon lemon juice
    Freshly ground pepper
    Lemon slices

1. Put lettuce, spinach, carrots, onion, ½ cup chicken broth, and oysters into a 3-quart saucepan. Cover and cook until carrots are just tender (about 5 minutes).
2. Turn half of cooked mixture into an electric blender container and blend a few seconds; repeat. Set vegetable mixture aside.
3. Melt butter in a saucepan. Stir in flour and salt. Gradually add milk and remaining 1 cup chicken broth, stirring until smooth. Bring to boiling, stirring occasionally, and cook until thickened. Add vegetable mixture, lemon peel and juice, and pepper; heat to desired serving temperature, stirring occasionally.
4. Serve garnished with lemon slices.

About 7 cups

120 *Cream of Broccoli Soup*

2 packages (10 ounces each)
    frozen chopped broccoli
1 cup water
½ cup sliced celery
1 small onion, sliced
2 tablespoons butter or margarine
2 tablespoons flour
1½ quarts chicken stock
2 egg yolks, beaten
½ cup half-and-half or milk
½ teaspoon salt
    Pinch pepper
    Paprika

1. Cook broccoli in water 3 to 5 minutes; reserve liquid.
2. Sauté celery and onion in butter; stir in flour. Gradually add stock and liquid from broccoli, stirring constantly, until thickened.
3. Add broccoli; put through a food mill or purée in an electric blender, if desired.
4. Stir egg yolks into half-and-half; gradually add to soup, being careful not to boil. Season with salt and pepper.
5. Garnish each serving with a sprinkle of paprika.

6 servings

121 *Chinese Cabbage Soup*

2 cups cooked chicken, cut into
    strips (about 1 chicken breast)
7 cups chicken broth
6 cups sliced Chinese cabbage
    (celery cabbage)
1 teaspoon soy sauce
1 teaspoon salt
¼ teaspoon pepper

Combine chicken and chicken broth; bring to boiling. Stir in remaining ingredients; cook only 3 to 4 minutes, or just until cabbage is crisp-tender. (Do not overcook.)

6 servings

Note: If desired, lettuce may be substituted for the Chinese cabbage. Reduce cooking time to 1 minute.

122 *Dill Cabbage Soup*

Cook the vegetables only until crisp-tender to keep the flavor and appearance attractive.

2 quarts beef stock
1 cup thinly sliced carrots
1 cup sliced celery
½ cup chopped onion
8 cups (about ½ head) thinly sliced cabbage
Salt and pepper to taste
3 tablespoons water
2 tablespoons flour
½ cup yogurt or dairy sour half-and-half
½ teaspoon minced dill or ¼ teaspoon dried dill weed
Minced parsley

1. Pour stock into a large saucepan. Add carrots, celery, and onion. Bring to boiling, reduce heat, and cook until vegetables are tender (about 10 minutes).
2. Add cabbage; continue cooking until crisp-tender (about 5 minutes). Season to taste with salt and pepper.
3. Stir water gradually into flour, stirring until smooth. Pour slowly into soup, stirring constantly. Bring to boiling; boil 1 minute.
4. Stir in yogurt and dill.
5. Garnish with parsley.

8 to 10 servings

123 *French Cauliflower Soup*

1 head cauliflower, cut in flowerets
5 cups chicken stock or 5 chicken bouillon cubes in 5 cups water
½ cup uncooked rice
¼ cup finely chopped celery
1 cup milk or half-and-half
¼ cup flour
Salt and pepper
Sliced green onion, snipped watercress, or snipped parsley

1. Put cauliflowerets, stock, rice, and celery into a large saucepan. Bring to boiling; simmer until cauliflower is crisp-tender and rice is cooked (about 10 minutes).
2. Gradually add milk to flour, blending until smooth; stir into soup. Bring to boiling, stirring constantly until thickened. Season to taste.
3. Sprinkle each serving with green onion, watercress, or parsley.

6 servings

Creamed French Cauliflower Soup: Follow recipe for French Cauliflower Soup; strain soup after Step 1. Purée vegetables and rice in an electric blender. Return vegetables and stock to saucepot. Continue with Step 2. Stir in **¼ cup white wine** and either **½ teaspoon basil** or **¼ teaspoon dill weed.** Garnish as suggested. **124**

125 *Cream of Turkey Soup*

½ cup butter
6 tablespoons flour
½ teaspoon salt
Pinch black pepper
2 cups half-and-half
3 cups turkey or chicken broth
¾ cup coarsely chopped cooked turkey

1. Heat butter in a saucepan. Blend in flour, salt, and pepper. Heat until bubbly.
2. Gradually add half-and-half and 1 cup of broth, stirring constantly. Bring to boiling; cook and stir 1 to 2 minutes.
3. Blend in remaining broth and turkey. Heat; do not boil. Garnish with grated carrot.

About 6 servings

126 *Frosty Cucumber Soup*

1 large cucumber, scored with a
    fork
¼ teaspoon salt
    Pinch white pepper
1½ cups yogurt
1¼ cups water
½ cup walnuts, ground in an
    electric blender
2 cloves garlic, minced
    Green food coloring (optional)

1. Halve cucumber lengthwise and cut crosswise into very thin slices. Rub inside of a large bowl with cut surface of ½ clove garlic. Combine cucumber, salt, and pepper in bowl. Cover; chill.
2. Pour combined yogurt and water over chilled cucumber; mix well. If desired, tint with 1 or 2 drops of food coloring. Chill.
3. Combine walnuts and garlic; set aside for topping.
4. Ladle soup into bowls. Place soup bowls over larger bowls of crushed ice. Serve with walnut topping.

4 servings

127 *Creamy Cheddar Cheese Soup*

2 tablespoons butter
2 tablespoons chopped onion
⅓ cup all-purpose flour
1¼ teaspoons dry mustard
¼ teaspoon garlic powder
¼ teaspoon paprika
2 teaspoons Worcestershire sauce
1½ quarts milk
3 tablespoons chicken seasoned
    stock base
1½ cups sliced celery
2½ cups (10 ounces) shredded
    Cheddar cheese

1. Melt butter in a 3-quart saucepan. Add onion and sauté until tender. Stir in flour, mustard, garlic powder, paprika, and Worcestershire sauce.
2. Remove from heat; gradually add milk, stirring constantly. Add chicken stock base and celery; mix well. Cook over low heat, stirring occasionally, until thickened. Add cheese and stir until cheese is melted and soup is desired serving temperature; do not boil.
3. Serve topped with **chopped green pepper, pimento strips, toasted slivered almonds,** or **cooked crumbled bacon.**

About 2 quarts

128 *Sweet Pea Soup*

1 small head lettuce, shredded
    (about 5 cups)
2 cups shelled fresh peas, or 1
    package (10 ounces) frozen
    green peas
1 cup water
½ cup chopped leek or green onion
2 tablespoons butter
2 teaspoons chervil
1 teaspoon sugar
½ teaspoon salt
¼ teaspoon black pepper
1 can (about 10 ounces) condensed
    beef broth
¾ cup water
2 cups half-and-half

1. Put lettuce, peas, 1 cup water, leek, butter, chervil, sugar, salt, and pepper into a large saucepan; stir and bring to boiling. Cover and cook until peas are tender.
2. Press mixture through a coarse sieve or food mill and return to saucepan. Stir in broth and ¾ cup water.
3. Just before serving, stir half-and-half into mixture and heat.

6 servings

129 Pumpkin Patch Soup

If zipped in the blender before cooking, this soup becomes light and fluffy. You'll be left with an extra cup of pumpkin, so use it in Pumpkin Spice Rolls

3 cups canned pumpkin or fresh
   cooked puréed pumpkin
2 cups milk, half-and-half, or 1
   can (13 ounces) evaporated
   milk
3 tablespoons maple syrup
1 teaspoon salt
½ teaspoon nutmeg
½ teaspoon cinnamon
¼ teaspoon cloves or allspice

Combine all ingredients in a large saucepan. Heat.

4 servings

130 Gazpacho

2 cans (6 ounces each) seasoned
   tomato juice
½ cucumber, coarsely sliced
1 tomato, quartered
¼ cup vinegar
¼ cup salad oil
1 tablespoon sugar
1 can or bottle (25.6 ounces)
   seasoned tomato juice
½ cucumber, chopped
1 tomato, chopped
1 small onion, chopped
   Minced parsley
   Chopped hard-cooked egg
   Chopped cucumber
   Croutons

1. Pour the 12 ounces tomato juice into an electric blender. Add sliced cucumber, tomato, vinegar, oil, and sugar; blend. Pour into a bowl and mix in remaining ingredients; chill.
2. Serve with bowls of parsley, hard-cooked egg, cucumber, and croutons.

4 servings

131 Tomato Cooler Gazpacho

2 cans (about 10 ounces each)
   condensed tomato soup
2 soup cans water
1 large clove garlic, crushed
1 tablespoon lemon juice
5 to 10 drops Tabasco
½ teaspoon crushed basil
½ cup chopped cucumber
½ cup chopped green pepper
2 tablespoons sliced green onion

1. Combine ingredients; chill several hours.
2. Serve in chilled sherbet glasses or bowls with garnishes suggested in Gazpacho.

6 servings

132 *Gazpacho Garden Soup*

3 large tomatoes, chopped
1 clove garlic, crushed
1 small cucumber, chopped
1 green pepper, chopped
½ cup sliced green onions
¼ cup chopped onion
¼ cup minced parsley
1 teaspoon crushed rosemary
¼ teaspoon crushed basil
½ teaspoon salt
¼ cup olive oil
¼ cup salad oil
2 tablespoons lemon juice
2 cups chicken broth or 3 chicken
    bouillon cubes dissolved in 2
    cups boiling water, then cooled

1. Combine all ingredients except chicken broth in a large bowl. Toss gently.
2. Stir in chicken broth; chill.
3. Serve in chilled bowls with garnishes suggested in Gazpacho.

6 servings

133 *Pioneer Potato Soup*

1 quart chicken stock
4 potatoes, chopped (about 4 cups)
2 cups sliced carrots
½ cup sliced celery
¼ cup chopped onion
1 teaspoon salt
½ teaspoon marjoram, dill weed, or
    cumin
⅛ teaspoon white pepper
1 cup milk or half-and-half
2 tablespoons flour
    Garnishes: paprika, sliced green
        onions, crisply cooked
        crumbled bacon, chopped
        pimento, snipped chives or
        parsley, or grated Parmesan
        cheese

1. Combine all ingredients except milk, flour, and garnishes in a large saucepan. Bring to boiling; simmer 30 minutes.
2. Gradually add milk to flour, stirring until smooth. Stir into soup.
3. Bring soup to boiling; boil 1 minute, stirring constantly.
4. Garnish as desired.

4 to 6 servings

Potato Soup with Sour Cream: Follow recipe for Pioneer Potato Soup. Before serving, stir in **½ cup dairy sour cream.** Heat; do not boil. 134

Puréed Potato Soup: Follow recipe for either Pioneer Potato or Potato Soup with Sour Cream, omitting the flour. Purée in an electric blender before serving. Reheat, if necessary. 135

136 *Lettuce Soup*

Lettuce need not be relegated only to the salad bowl. Chop it up, stir it into a rich broth, and eat it with some San Francisco Sourdough French Bread

2 tablespoons butter or margarine
2 tablespoons flour
1 can (about 10 ounces) condensed
    chicken broth
1 soup can water
½ small head lettuce, cored and
    coarsely chopped
¼ cup thinly sliced celery
1 tablespoon chopped watercress
    Salt and pepper

1. Melt butter in a saucepot; stir in flour and cook until bubbly.
2. Gradually stir in chicken broth and water; bring to boiling, stirring constantly. Cook 1 minute.
3. Stir in lettuce, celery, and watercress. Season with salt and pepper to taste. Cook until vegetables are crisp-tender, about 5 minutes.

About 3 servings

137 *Mixed Vegetables Soup*

3 cups beef broth or 3 beef
    bouillon cubes dissolved in 3
    cups boiling water
1 small potato, diced
2 carrots, diced
1 tomato, chopped
1 green onion, sliced
½ cup shredded cabbage or ½ cup
    sliced zucchini
½ teaspoon Beau Monde seasoning
    or seasoned salt
1 tablespoon minced parsley

1. Combine broth, potato, and carrot in a saucepan; bring to boiling. Simmer 30 minutes.
2. Add remaining ingredients; cook 5 minutes, or until cabbage is crisp-tender.

4 servings

138 *Celery-Crab Soup*

Quick, but elegant. Since it is so easy, you'll have time to make Popovers

2 cans (about 10 ounces each)
    condensed cream of celery
    soup
2 soup cans milk
1 cup flaked crab meat
1 teaspoon Worcestershire sauce
¼ teaspoon crushed tarragon
4 to 8 drops Tabasco
    Butter (optional)
    Paprika (optional)

1. Combine soup and milk in a saucepot. Stir in crab meat, Worcestershire sauce, tarragon, and Tabasco. Heat (do not boil); stir occasionally.
2. Garnish each serving with a pat of butter and a sprinkling of paprika, if desired.

6 servings

139 *Oyster Stew*

If you like oysters, you'll love this—it's hardly more than oysters and milk. Traditionally, this is served Christmas Eve with buttered toast.

¼ cup butter or margarine
1 pint fresh oysters, drained;
    reserve liquor
1½ cups milk
1 cup half-and-half
1 teaspoon salt
    Pinch black pepper or cayenne
    pepper
    Minced parsley

1. Melt butter in a saucepan. Add milk, half-and-half, and oyster liquor. Scald; do not boil.
2. Add oysters and seasonings. Heat; do not boil.
3. Garnish with parsley.

4 servings

140 *Lobster-Tomato Cream Soup*

When you use lobster, you are really going first class. Serve with a bread equally as classy—French Crescents

2 tablespoons minced onion
¼ cup butter
¼ cup flour
¼ teaspoon salt
Pinch black pepper
2 cups tomato juice
1 cup half-and-half
½ cup milk
1½ teaspoons Worcestershire sauce
4 drops Tabasco
1 can (about 6 ounces) lobster, drained and cut in pieces
3 tablespoons dry sherry
Whipped cream

1. Sauté onion in melted butter in a large saucepan. Stir in flour, salt, and pepper. Heat until mixture bubbles.
2. Gradually stir in tomato juice, half-and-half, milk, Worcestershire sauce, and Tabasco. Cook until sauce thickens, stirring constantly.
3. Add lobster, reserving a few pieces for garnish. Heat; do not boil. Stir in sherry.
4. Pour into a tureen or individual soup bowls. Garnish with reserved lobster meat and whipped cream.

6 servings

Crab-Tomato Cream Soup: Follow recipe for Lobster-Tomato Cream Soup, except substitute **1 cup** (about 4 ounces) **flaked fresh crab meat** for the lobster. 141

142 *Creamy Shrimp and Avocado Bisque*

Seafood and fruit join to make an elegant soup. Serve with bowknot-shaped Dinner Rolls

2 cans (about 10 ounces each) condensed cream of asparagus soup
2 cans (about 10 ounces each) condensed cream of potato soup
1 teaspoon curry powder
2 soup cans milk
2 soup cans half-and-half
2 cups cooked shrimp, cut in pieces (see Note)
1 avocado, peeled and chopped
2 tablespoons minced chives

1. Combine soups and curry in a large, heavy saucepan. Stir in milk and half-and-half. Set over low heat until thoroughly heated, stirring occasionally.
2. Mix in shrimp; heat thoroughly; do not boil.
3. Pour into soup tureen; gently stir in avocado. Sprinkle with chives. Serve at once.

10 servings

Note: When using fresh or fresh-frozen shrimp, shell and devein. To remove the vein, make a shallow cut lengthwise down back of each shrimp. Remove vein with point of knife.

Cool and Creamy Shrimp and Avocado Bisque: Follow recipe for Creamy Shrimp and Avocado Bisque; chill before serving. 143

144 *Consommé*

More than just a clear stock, consommé derives its special flavor from the vegetables used. Egg whites and shells clarify this traditional and elegant appetizer soup.

½ cup coarsely chopped celery leaves
½ cup chopped leek (green part only)
½ cup chopped carrots
¼ cup chopped parsley leaves and stems
2 tomatoes, chopped
3 egg whites
3 egg shells, crushed
2 quarts beef stock

1. Combine ingredients in a heavy 4- or 5-quart saucepot. Bring to boiling. Reduce heat; simmer 20 minutes, uncovered and undisturbed.
2. Pour soup into a sieve lined with a double thickness of dampened cheesecloth which has been placed over a large bowl. Serve hot.

6 servings

Double Consommé: Follow recipe for Consommé, adding **1 pound beef,** cut in pieces, with vegetables. Simmer 45 minutes. 145

Consommé with Vegetables: Follow recipe for Consommé. After straining, add **1 cup thinly sliced cooked vegetables.** Heat. 146

147 *Bouillabaisse*

Truly a bouillabaisse should be served after you've been fishing all day—so you can include your catch! But when you are buying, select 3 different fish plus seafood. Other possibilities besides those listed here are red snapper and whole clams.

⅔ cup chopped onion
2 leeks, chopped (white part only)
¼ cup olive oil
1 clove garlic, crushed
1 can (16 ounces) tomatoes
1 tablespoon minced parsley
½ bay leaf
½ teaspoon savory
½ teaspoon fennel
⅛ teaspoon saffron
1½ teaspoons salt
¼ teaspoon pepper
1 lobster (1½ to 2 pounds) cleaned and cut up, or 8 lobster tails
1½ pounds bass, boned and cut in 1-inch pieces
1 pound perch, boned and cut in 1-inch pieces
1 pound cod, boned and cut in 1-inch pieces
1 pound fresh shelled deveined shrimp
1 pound sea scallops (fresh or thawed frozen)
1 pint oysters
6 slices French bread, toasted

1. Sauté onion and leeks in olive oil in a large Dutch oven. Stir in garlic, tomatoes, parsley, bay leaf, savory, fennel, saffron, salt, pepper, lobster, and bass, and just enough water to cover (1 to 1½ quarts). Bring to boiling; simmer 10 minutes.
2. Add perch and cod; continue to simmer 10 minutes, or until fish are almost tender.
3. Add shrimp and scallops; cook 5 minutes longer.
4. Meanwhile, drain oysters, reserving liquor. Remove any shell particles. Simmer oysters in liquor in a saucepan 3 minutes, or until edges begin to curl. Add to fish mixture.
5. Line a deep serving dish with toasted bread. Cover with fish and pour sauce in which fish has been cooked over all. Serve at once.

About 8 servings

Note: If desired, substitute 1 cup sherry for 1 cup of the water in step 1.

148 *Vichyssoise (Chilled Leek and Potato Soup)*

Surprisingly enough, this is an American soup with a French name. Gourmets will insist that it be made with the white part of leeks. (The rest of us will settle for green onions.) Serve very cold.

4 to 6 leeks
2 tablespoons butter or margarine
4 potatoes, pared and sliced
1 quart chicken broth or 6 chicken bouillon cubes dissolved in 1 quart boiling water
1 cup half-and-half
1 cup chilled whipping cream
Snipped chives

1. Finely slice the white part and about an inch of the green part of each leek to measure about 1 cup.
2. Sauté leeks in butter in a heavy saucepan. Stir in potatoes and broth; bring to boiling. Simmer 40 minutes, or until potatoes are tender.
3. Sieve the cooked vegetables or blend until smooth in an electric blender. Mix in half-and-half; chill thoroughly.
4. Just before serving, stir in whipping cream. Garnish with chives.

8 servings

149 *Sour Cream Garlic Soup*

Garlic lovers—this one would be a nice beginning to a pork entrée.

8 cloves garlic, crushed or minced
⅓ cup butter or margarine
⅓ cup flour
¼ teaspoon crushed basil
⅛ teaspoon salt
⅛ teaspoon pepper
1½ quarts beef broth
 Dairy sour cream
 Chopped chives
 Sieved hard-cooked egg yolk

1. Carefully cook garlic in melted butter in a heavy saucepan until golden, stirring constantly. Stir in flour, basil, salt, and pepper; heat until bubbly. Gradually add broth, stirring constantly. Bring to boiling; cook 1 minute.
2. Serve hot or cold, topping each serving with a generous dollop of sour cream and a sprinkling of chives and egg yolk.

4 to 6 servings

150 *New Orleans Gumbo*

Gumbo, a Creole masterpiece, is traditionally made with filé, which is dried sassafras leaves. Because filé is not always available outside of Louisiana, okra is often substituted for it.

2 onions, chopped
½ cup butter or margarine
¼ cup flour
2 quarts chicken stock
1 can (28 ounces) tomatoes
½ pound okra, sliced
1 stalk celery, sliced
½ teaspoon thyme
1 bay leaf
½ teaspoon salt
 Pinch pepper
 Pinch cayenne pepper
6 hard-shell crabs
24 large peeled and deveined shrimp
24 oysters
2 cups cooked rice

1. Sauté onion in butter in a large saucepan. Mix in flour; cook until bubbly.
2. Gradually add chicken stock, tomatoes, okra, celery, and seasonings; add crabs. Simmer 1 hour.
3. Add shrimp and oysters; simmer 5 minutes.
4. Put ¼ cup rice into each soup bowl; ladle in hot gumbo.

8 servings

151 *Toasted Almond Soup*

This creamy soup is not only delicious but quick, because it is made in an electric blender.

1 cup water
1 cup salted roasted almonds
4 egg yolks
3 chicken bouillon cubes
1 small slice onion
½ teaspoon sugar
2 cups water
1 cup half-and-half

1. Put 1 cup water, almonds, egg yolks, bouillon cubes, onion, and sugar in an electric blender container. Blend until amonds are finely ground.
2. Pour into a saucepan; stir in 2 cups water. Cook over low heat about 5 minutes, or until mixture coats a spoon, stirring constantly (do not boil).
3. Stir in half-and-half and heat thoroughly without boiling. Garnish with **finely shredded orange peel.**

5 or 6 servings

152 *Crab Meat Bisque*

Bisques are cream soups usually containing shellfish, as here. Accompany any one of these bisques with crescent-shaped Dinner Rolls

½ cup chopped onion
⅓ cup chopped carrot
1 leek (white part only), minced
3 tablespoons butter or margarine
● 1 quart White Stock
1 teaspoon salt
⅛ teaspoon pepper
1 bay leaf
3 egg yolks, beaten
1 cup whipping cream
½ cup dry white wine
2 cups (8 ounces) flaked fresh crab
   meat
   Minced parsley

1. Sauté onion, carrot, and leek in melted butter in a large saucepan. Stir in white stock, salt, pepper, and bay leaf. Cover; simmer 10 minutes.
2. Push mixture through sieve or food mill or purée in an electric blender. Return to saucepan.
3. Stir about 3 tablespoons hot soup into egg yolks. Return mixture to soup, stirring constantly.
4. Stir in whipping cream, wine, and crab meat. Heat; do not boil.
5. Sprinkle parsley over each serving.

8 servings

Lobster Bisque: Follow recipe for Crab Meat Bisque, substituting **2 cans (about 6 ounces each) lobster meat,** drained, for the crab meat.

Shrimp Bisque: Follow recipe for Crab Meat Bisque, substituting **2½ cups chopped cooked shrimp** for crab meat.

153 *Crimson Soup*

4 cups puréed drained tomatoes
   (about 2 pounds ripe tomatoes)
1 tablespoon brown sugar
1 teaspoon salt
   Few grains freshly ground black
   pepper
½ teaspoon grated lemon peel
2 tablespoons lemon juice
½ teaspoon grated onion
1 cup finely chopped cantaloupe
½ cup finely chopped honeydew
   melon
¼ cup finely chopped cucumber

1. Combine tomato purée, brown sugar, salt, pepper, lemon peel and juice, and onion. Stir in remaining ingredients.
2. Chill several hours.
3. Serve in chilled bowls. If desired, garnish each serving with a lemon slice and a sprig of parsley or watercress. Accompany with a shaker of seasoned salt and a bowl of brown sugar.

6 servings

154 Swedish Fruit Soup

1 cup dried apricots
¾ cup dried apples
½ cup dried peaches
½ cup prunes
½ cup dark seedless raisins
2 quarts water
¼ cup sugar
3 tablespoons quick-cooking
    tapioca
1 piece stick cinnamon (3 inches)
1 teaspoon grated orange peel
1 cup red raspberry fruit syrup

1. Rinse dried fruits with cold water; remove pits from prunes. Place fruits in a large kettle with the water; cover and allow to soak 2 to 3 hours.
2. Add the sugar, tapioca, cinnamon, and orange peel to fruits; let stand 5 minutes. Bring to boiling and simmer covered 1 hour, or until fruit is tender.
3. Stir in syrup; cool, then chill thoroughly.
4. Serve with **whipped cream** and **slivered blanched almonds**.

12 to 16 servings

155 Breakfast Nog

¼ cup sugar
2 egg yolks
1 quart milk
¼ teaspoon salt
⅛ teaspoon nutmeg
1 teaspoon vanilla extract

1. Beat sugar into egg yolks in a large saucepan. Stir in milk, salt, and nutmeg. Cook over low heat, stirring constantly, until mixture coats a spoon.
2. Serve hot or cold in mugs.

4 servings

Banana Nog: Prepare Breakfast Nog. Chill. Stir in **1 or 2 sliced bananas.** If desired, sprinkle each serving with **grated chocolate** and **cinnamon.**   156

Fluffy Breakfast Nog: Prepare Breakfast Nog; chill. Beat **2 egg whites** until foamy. Gradually add **3 tablespoons sugar,** beating until soft peaks form. Fold into chilled custard. Top each serving with dollop of **whipped cream.**   157

158 Cherry Breakfast Soup

1 can (about 10 ounces) dark sweet
    cherries, drained; reserve liquid
4 whole cloves
1 stick cinnamon, broken in half
    Juice of ½ lemon (about 2
    tablespoons)
2 teaspoons cornstarch
1 can (16 ounces) sliced pears,
    drained; reserve juice
1 orange, peeled and sectioned

1. Combine cherry liquid, cloves, cinnamon, and lemon juice in a saucepan; bring to boiling. Simmer 5 minutes. Remove spices with slotted spoon.
2. Combine cornstarch and pear juice; gradually add to cherry mixture. Cook until thickened, stirring constantly.
3. Stir in remaining fruit. Serve hot or cold.

6 servings

159 *Apricot-Melon Soup*

2 cups chopped melon, cantaloupe, or honeydew
2 cups apricot nectar
2 tablespoons lemon juice
Dash salt
1 pint lemon sherbet

1. Combine melon, apricot nectar, lemon juice, and salt. Chill.
2. Serve in chilled bowls. Float a scoop of sherbet on each serving.

4 servings

160 *Green Pea Potage*

Water chestnuts are a unique soup ingredient, for no matter how long they sit in the soup, they never get soggy and lose their crunch.

¼ cup dairy sour cream
1 can (about 11 ounces) condensed green pea soup
1 soup can water
¼ cup sliced water chestnuts
1 tablespoon sliced green onion
1 tablespoon lemon juice
Toasted slivered almonds

1. Blend sour cream into soup in a bowl. Gradually add water, stirring until smooth. Mix in water chestnuts, green onion, and lemon juice. Chill 4 hours.
2. Garnish chilled soup with the almonds.

3 servings

161 *Tomato-Noodle Soup*

Tomatoes and noodles join to make this reminiscent of spaghetti!

2 cans (about 10 ounces each) condensed tomato soup
2 cans (about 10 ounces each) condensed cream of celery soup
1 can (6 ounces) tomato paste
¼ cup instant minced onion
1 can (1 ounce) dried instant mixed vegetables
1 teaspoon salt
¼ teaspoon pepper
1 teaspoon crushed basil
2 quarts water
8 ounces (about 4 cups) fine egg noodles
Milk

1. Combine soups and tomato paste in a large saucepan; mix in instant minced onion, instant vegetables, salt, pepper, and basil.
2. Gradually add water, stirring constantly. Bring to boiling, stirring occasionally.
3. Add noodles gradually so the mixture continues to boil. Cook, uncovered, until noodles are tender, about 10 minutes, stirring occasionally. Blend in milk to taste.

About 3½ quarts

162 *Creamy Shrimp Gumbo*

Shrimp makes it elegant, canned soups make it quick.

1 can (about 10 ounces) condensed
    cream of chicken soup
1 soup can milk
1 can (about 10 ounces) condensed
    chicken gumbo soup
½ cup chopped cooked shrimp
¼ teaspoon soy sauce
    Garlic powder to taste

1. Blend chicken soup and milk in a saucepan.
2. Stir in remaining ingredients. Heat (do not boil).

4 to 6 servings

163 *Chilled Dilled Chicken Soup*

2 cans (about 10 ounces each)
    condensed cream of chicken
    soup
2 soup cans milk
2 teaspoons chopped green onion
    with tops
½ cup chopped cucumber
2 teaspoons chopped fresh dill or
    ½ teaspoon dill weed

1. Mix soup and milk in a bowl; blend in the remaining ingredients.
2. Cover and refrigerate 3 to 4 hours to allow flavors to blend.
3. Serve soup thoroughly chilled, or heat and serve.

About 6 servings

164 *Cream of Everything Soup*

Mushroom, peas, tomato, rice are all blended to perfection.

1 can (about 10 ounces) condensed
    cream of mushroom soup
1 can (about 11 ounces) condensed
    green pea soup
1 can (about 10 ounces) condensed
    tomato-rice soup
3 soup cans water
½ teaspoon crushed dill weed
¼ teaspoon crushed tarragon
    Dairy sour cream

1. Combine all ingredients in a saucepan. Cover and simmer about 10 minutes.
2. Top individual bowls of soup with a dollop of dairy sour cream.

About 8 servings

165 Herbed Soup

Two herbs here you should get to know. Basil complements most tomato dishes, while fennel, a mild licorice flavor, enhances the taste of fish.

1 can (about 10 ounces) condensed
    chicken gumbo soup
1 can (about 10 ounces) condensed
    cream of celery soup
2 soup cans water
¼ teaspoon ground fennel
¼ teaspoon crushed basil
    Few grains ground ginger
    Avocado Sauce

1. Blend soups, water, herbs, and ginger in a saucepan. Simmer covered about 10 minutes.
2. Serve with Avocado Sauce.

6 servings

Avocado Sauce: Combine ½ **cup dairy sour cream** and ½ **cup mashed ripe avocado**; blend until smooth.

166

167 Canyon City Soup

Seasonings in this soup give it a southwestern flavor.

1 onion, sliced
2 tablespoons margarine
½ pound frankfurters, sliced
3½ cups (28 ounces) tomatoes
2 cups (about 15 ounces) kidney
    beans or chili beans, drained
½ to 1 teaspoon chili powder
½ teaspoon cumin powder
½ teaspoon garlic salt
    Salt and pepper

1. Sauté onion in margarine.
2. Add remaining ingredients; stir.
3. Simmer 10 minutes.

4 servings

168 Curried Potato-Apple Soup

1 can (about 10 ounces) condensed
    cream of potato soup
1 soup can milk
1 apple, quartered, pared, and
    cored
½ teaspoon curry powder

1. Combine all ingredients in electric blender container and blend until smooth.
2. Pour into a saucepan and heat thoroughly.
3. Garnish hot soup with **apple wedges.**

About 1 quart

169 *Zucchini Soup*

Zucchini grows so abundantly and quickly that it is a fun vegetable to watch in the garden.

2 cups diced zucchini
½ cup tomato juice
2 tablespoons chopped onion
⅛ teaspoon basil
1 package (8 ounces) cream cheese, cubed

1. Combine zucchini, tomato juice, onion, and basil; simmer 20 minutes.
2. Pour into an electric blender; add cream cheese and blend until smooth.
3. Serve hot, or chill to serve as cold soup or dip.

About 3 servings

170 *Vegetable-Sausage Soup*

1 can (about 10 ounces) condensed vegetable soup
1 soup can water
½ teaspoon prepared mustard
⅛ teaspoon pepper
1 cup cubed thuringer or cervelat sausage

1. Combine soup, water, mustard, and pepper in a saucepan. Set over moderate heat until mixture begins to simmer.
2. Add the sausage and simmer 10 minutes.

3 servings

171 *Caraway Bouillon*

1½ quarts boiling water
6 beef bouillon cubes
1 tablespoon crushed caraway seed

1. Add water to bouillon and caraway seed in a saucepan. Stir until cubes are dissolved. Cover; simmer 10 minutes.
2. Serve hot in mugs.

6 to 8 servings

172 *Vegetable Bouillon*

1 can (about 10 ounces) condensed beef broth
1 soup can water
1 can (6 ounces) cocktail vegetable juice
2 tablespoons finely chopped green pepper
3 radishes, finely chopped
½ teaspoon instant minced onion

1. Bring broth, water, and vegetable juice to boiling in a saucepan.
2. Add green pepper, radishes, and onion. Simmer, uncovered, 5 to 8 minutes.
3. Serve hot, garnished with sprigs of **parsley**.

4 servings

173 *California Cup*

Although the ingredients sound unusual, the combination is surprisingly good.

1 can (about 10 ounces) condensed
    tomato soup
½ soup can cranberry juice cocktail
½ soup can water
1 teaspoon lemon juice
    Dairy sour cream

1. Combine ingredients; chill until serving time.
2. Top each serving with dollop of sour cream.

3 servings

174 *Cabbage-Cheese Chowder*

The brisk autumn air and activities are sure to stimulate appetites.

1 can (about 10 ounces) condensed
    Cheddar cheese soup
1 soup can milk
½ teaspoon prepared mustard
4 slices (2 ounces) bologna, diced
3 cups thinly sliced cabbage

1. Combine soup, milk, and mustard in a medium saucepan. Stir in bologna and cabbage.
2. Cook over low heat until cabbage is crisp-tender, about 5 minutes.

4 servings

175 *Quick Mulligatawny*

Creamy curried chicken soup is a quick adaptation of a well-known Indian soup.

1 can (about 10 ounces) condensed
    cream of chicken soup
1 soup can milk
1 cup finely chopped cooked
    chicken
¼ cup packaged precooked rice
½ teaspoon curry powder
¼ teaspoon instant minced onion

1. Combine all ingredients in a medium saucepan.
2. Simmer 10 minutes.

4 servings

176 Egg Drop Soup

Oriental in origin, Egg Drop Soup is an appetizing first course.

¼ cup thinly sliced celery
2 tablespoons thinly sliced
    mushrooms
1 green onion, thinly sliced
3 cups chicken stock
½ teaspoon salt
    Few grains pepper
1 egg, well beaten

1. Combine vegetables and chicken stock in a saucepan. Stir in salt and pepper. Bring to boiling; simmer 5 minutes.
2. Reduce heat and drizzle egg slowly into stock while stirring. Stir until egg separates into shreds. Simmer 1 minute. Serve at once.

3 or 4 servings

177 Herbed Zucchini Soup

½ cup chopped onion
2 tablespoons bacon fat or
    margarine
4 medium zucchini, sliced (about 4
    cups)
1 can (about 10 ounces) condensed
    beef consommé or broth
2 cups water
1 teaspoon basil
½ teaspoon salt
¼ teaspoon garlic powder
⅛ teaspoon pepper
¼ cup minced parsley or 2
    tablespoons dried parsley
    Grated Parmesan cheese

1. Sauté onion in bacon fat in a large saucepan. Stir in remaining ingredients except Parmesan cheese. Heat to boiling; simmer until zucchini is tender, 3 to 5 minutes.
2. Sprinkle each serving with Parmesan cheese.

4 to 6 servings

Creamy Zucchini Soup without Cream: 178
Prepare Herbed Zucchini Soup. Purée in an electric blender. Reheat.

Breads

179 *Basic White Bread*

5½ to 6 cups flour
2 packages active dry yeast
2 tablespoons sugar
2 teaspoons salt
1 cup milk
1 cup water
2 tablespoons oil
Oil or butter

QUICK MIX METHOD
1. Combine 2 cups flour, yeast, sugar, and salt in a large mixing bowl.
2. Heat milk, water, and 2 tablespoons oil in a saucepan over low heat until very warm (120° to 130°F).
3. Add liquid to flour mixture; beat on high speed of electric mixer until smooth, about 3 minutes. Gradually stir in more flour to make a soft dough.
4. Turn onto lightly floured surface and knead until smooth and elastic (5 to 10 minutes).
5. Cover dough with bowl or pan; let rest 20 minutes.
6. For two loaves, divide dough in half and roll out two 14×7-inch rectangles; for one loaf roll out to 16×8-inch rectangle.
7. Roll up from narrow side, pressing dough into roll at each turn. Press ends to seal and fold under loaf.
8. Place in 2 greased 8×4×2-inch loaf pans or 1 greased 9×5×3-inch loaf pan; brush with oil.
9. Let rise in warm place until double in bulk (30 to 45 minutes).
10. Bake at 400°F 35 to 40 minutes.
11. Remove from pans immediately and brush with oil; cool on wire rack.

One 2-pound loaf
or two 1-pound loaves

CONVENTIONAL METHOD
1. Heat milk, sugar, oil, and salt; cool to lukewarm.
2. In a large bowl, sprinkle yeast in warm water (105° to 115°F); stir until dissolved.
3. Add lukewarm milk mixture and 2 cups flour; beat until smooth.
4. Beat in enough additional flour to make a stiff dough.
5. Turn out onto lightly floured surface; let rest 10 to 15 minutes. Knead until smooth and elastic (8 to 10 minutes).
6. Place in a greased bowl, turning to grease top. Cover; let rise in warm place until double in bulk (about 1 hour).
7. Punch down. Let rest 15 minutes.
8. Follow same shaping and baking instructions as Quick Mix Method.

You'll want to try these flavor variations to the Basic White Bread for something different. Shaping variations are also included.

Cheese Bread: Add **1 cup (4 ounces) shredded Cheddar cheese** before the last portion of the flour.   **181**

Onion Bread: Omit the salt and add **1 package (1⅜ ounces) dry onion soup mix** to the warm milk.   **182**

Mini Loaves: Divide dough into 10 equal pieces. Shape into loaves. Place in 10 greased 4½×2½×1½-inch loaf pans. Cover; let rise until double in bulk (about 20 minutes). Bake at 350°F 20 to 25 minutes.   **183**

Braided Egg Bread: Reduce milk to ½ cup. Add **2 eggs** with warm liquid to the flour mixture. Divide dough into 3 equal pieces. Form each into a rope, 15×12 inches. Braid. Tuck ends under. Place on a greased baking sheet or 9×5×3-inch loaf pan. Cover and let rise and bake the same as basic recipe.   **184**

French Bread: Omit the milk and oil and use **2 cups water.** Divide dough in half. Roll each half into 15×12-inch rectangle. Beginning at long side, roll up tightly. Seal seams. Taper the ends. With a sharp knife, make ¼-inch deep diagonal cuts along loaf tops. Cover. Let rise until less than double in bulk (about 20 minutes). Brush with water. Bake at 400°F 15 minutes, then reduce to 350°F and bake 15 to 20 minutes longer. For crisper crust, put pan of hot water in bottom of oven and 5 minutes before loaf is done, brush with glaze of **1 beaten egg white** and **1 tablespoon cold water.**   **185**

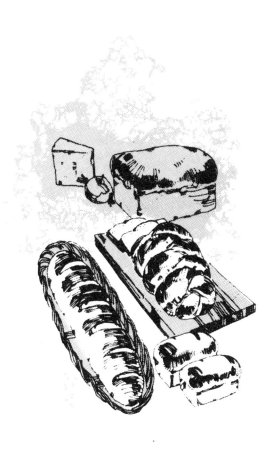

186 *Flavorful Herb Bread*

The delicious aroma of the herbs baking in this bread will draw everyone into the kitchen. Be prepared.

  ¾ **cup warm milk**
  2 **tablespoons melted bacon fat or butter**
  2 **tablespoons sugar**
1½ **teaspoons salt**
  1 **package active dry yeast**
  ¼ **cup warm water (105° to 115°F)**
  1 **egg**
  ¼ **cup chopped chives**
  2 **tablespoons minced parsley**
  1 **teaspoon crushed oregano**
  3 **to 3½ cups all-purpose flour**

1. Heat milk, bacon fat, sugar, and salt; cool to lukewarm.
2. Sprinkle yeast over warm water in a large mixing bowl; stir until dissolved.
3. Add the liquid, egg, chives, parsley, and oregano to yeast. Stir in 2 cups flour, beating until smooth. Add enough more flour to make a stiff dough.
4. Turn dough onto floured surface; knead until smooth and elastic (10 minutes).
5. Place in a greased bowl, turning to grease top of dough. Cover; let rise in a warm place until double in bulk (1 to 1½ hours).
6. Punch dough down. Shape into a round loaf. Place in a greased 9-inch pie pan. Cover; let rise until double in bulk (about 30 minutes).
7. Bake at 400°F 10 minutes; reduce to 375°F and bake 20 to 25 minutes longer, or until bread is well browned.

1 loaf

187 *100% Whole Wheat Bread*

Whole wheat flour gives a sweet, nutty flavor to this bread and is great for toasting. Remember the loaf will be low and compact because of the bran particles cutting through the gluten structure.

4¼ to 4¾ cups whole wheat flour
2 packages active dry yeast
1 tablespoon salt
¾ cup milk
¾ cup water
2 tablespoons oil
2 tablespoons honey
1 egg (at room temperature)
Oil

1. Combine 1¾ cups flour, yeast, and salt in a large mixing bowl.
2. Heat milk, water, oil, and honey over low heat until very warm (120° to 130°F).
3. Add the liquid and egg to flour mixture; beat until smooth, about 3 minutes on high speed of electric mixer.
4. Gradually stir in more flour to make a soft dough.
5. Turn onto a lightly floured surface and knead until smooth and elastic (5 to 8 minutes).
6. Cover dough with bowl or pan; let rest 20 minutes.
7. Roll out to 16×8-inch rectangle.
8. Roll up from narrow side, pressing dough into roll at each turn. Press ends to seal and fold under loaf.
9. Place in greased 9×5×3-inch loaf pan; brush with oil.
10. Let rise in a warm place (80° to 85°F) until double in bulk (30 to 45 minutes).
11. Bake at 375°F 35 to 40 minutes.
12. Remove from pans immediately and brush with oil or butter; cool on wire rack.

1 loaf

188 *Whole Wheat-Oatmeal Bread*

2¼ cups milk
¼ cup butter or margarine
1 tablespoon salt
¼ cup firmly packed brown sugar
2½ to 2¾ cups all-purpose flour
2 cups whole wheat flour
2 packages active dry yeast
2 cups uncooked oats
⅔ cup wheat germ

1. Heat milk, butter, salt, and sugar in a saucepan until lukewarm. Pour liquid into a large mixer bowl. Add 1 cup all-purpose flour and 1 cup whole wheat flour; beat 2 minutes at medium speed of electric mixer. Add remaining whole wheat flour and yeast; beat 2 minutes at medium speed. Stir in oats, wheat germ, and enough additional all-purpose flour to make a soft dough.
2. Turn dough onto a floured surface; knead until smooth and elastic (about 10 minutes). Round dough into a ball. Place in a greased bowl; lightly grease surface of dough. Cover; let rise in a warm place until nearly double in bulk (about 1 hour).
3. Punch dough down; shape into 2 large or 8 miniature loaves. Place in greased 8×4×2-inch or 4×3×2-inch loaf pans. Let rise in a warm place until nearly double in bulk.
4. Bake at 375°F 45 minutes for large loaves or 30 minutes for miniature loaves. Remove from pans immediately; cool on wire rack.

2 large loaves or 8 miniature loaves

189 Delicatessen Rye Bread

You'll notice when making rye breads that the dough is stickier and has a different consistency than whole wheat flour doughs.

2 to 2¾ cups all-purpose or
    unbleached flour
2 cups rye flour
2 teaspoons salt
2 packages active dry yeast
1 tablespoon caraway seed
1 cup milk
¾ cup water
2 tablespoons molasses
2 tablespoons oil

1. Combine 1¾ cups all-purpose flour, salt, yeast, and caraway seed in a large mixing bowl.
2. Heat milk, water, molasses, and oil in a saucepan over low heat until very warm (120° to 130°F).
3. Add liquid gradually to flour mixture, beating on high speed of electric mixer; scrape bowl occasionally. Add 1 cup rye flour, or enough to make a thick batter. Beat at high speed 2 minutes. Stir in remaining rye flour and enough all-purpose flour to make a soft dough.
4. Turn dough onto a floured surface; knead until smooth and elastic (about 5 minutes).
5. Cover with bowl or pan and let rest 20 minutes.
6. Divide in half. Shape into 2 round loaves; place on greased baking sheets. Cover; let rise until double in bulk (30 to 45 minutes).
7. Bake at 375°F 35 to 40 minutes, or until done.

2 loaves

190 Freezer Oatmeal Bread

This recipe lets you make your own convenience foods. Allow 4 hours after you pull the loaf out of the freezer before you enjoy hot homemade bread.

12 to 13 cups all-purpose flour
 4 packages active dry yeast
 2 tablespoons salt
 2 cups milk
 2 cups water
 ½ cup honey
 ¼ cup vegetable oil
 2 cups uncooked oats
 ½ cup wheat germ
    Oil

1. Combine 2 cups flour, yeast, and salt in a large mixing bowl.
2. Heat milk, water, honey, and oil in a saucepan until very warm (120° to 130°F).
3. Add the liquid gradually to flour mixture, beating 3 minutes on high speed of electric mixer until smooth. Stir in oats, wheat germ, and enough remaining flour to make a soft dough.
4. Turn dough onto a floured surface; knead until smooth and elastic (8 to 10 minutes).
5. Divide dough in quarters. Shape each quarter into a loaf, and either place in an 8×4×2-inch loaf pan or on a baking sheet. Freeze just until firm. Remove from pan. Wrap tightly in aluminum foil or freezer wrap. Dough will keep up to 2 weeks.
6. To bake, remove wrapping and place dough in a greased 8×4×2-inch loaf pan. Thaw in refrigerator overnight or at room temperature 2 hours. Brush with oil and let rise in a warm place until double in bulk (about 2 hours).
7. Bake at 400°F 30 to 35 minutes, or until done.

4 loaves

Freezer Whole Wheat Bread: Follow recipe for Freezer Oatmeal Bread, substituting **5 cups whole wheat flour** for 5 cups all-purpose flour.

191

Freezer White Bread: Follow recipe for Freezer Oatmeal Bread, omitting oats and wheat germ and increasing flour by about 1 cup.

192

193 *Family Wheat Bread*

This recipe is ideal for your family's everyday bread. It not only makes wonderful sandwiches and toast, but is high in protein due to the milk, eggs, and whole grains.

5 to 6 cups all-purpose or
    unbleached flour
2 packages active dry yeast
1 tablespoon salt
2 cups milk
½ cup water
¼ cup oil
3 tablespoons honey
3 eggs
2 cups whole wheat flour

1. Combine 2½ cups all-purpose flour, yeast, and salt in a large mixing bowl.
2. Heat milk, water, oil, and honey in a saucepan until very warm (120° to 130°F).
3. Add liquid to flour mixture and beat until smooth. Add eggs and continue beating about 3 minutes on high speed of electric mixer.
4. Stir in whole wheat flour and enough all-purpose flour to make a soft dough.
5. Turn dough onto a floured surface; allow to rest 10 minutes for easier handling. Knead until smooth and elastic (about 8 minutes). Let rest 20 minutes.
6. Divide dough in half. Roll each half into a 14×9-inch rectangle. Shape into loaves. Place in greased 9×5×3-inch loaf pans.
7. Cover with plastic wrap. Refrigerate 2 to 24 hours.
8. When ready to bake, remove from refrigerator. Let stand at room temperature 10 minutes.
9. Bake at 400°F 40 minutes, or until done.

2 loaves

Variations: Substitute 1 cup of any one of the following ingredients for 1 cup of the whole wheat flour: **uncooked oats, cornmeal, cracked wheat, soybean grits, millet, wheat germ, ground sunflower seeds, bran, crushed shredded wheat cereal,** or any flour of your choice.

194

195 *Refrigerator Rye Bread*

This lets you do all the mixing and clean up when you have the time and just shape and bake the loaf when you want to serve hot bread.

3 to 3½ cups unbleached or
    all-purpose flour
¼ cup firmly packed brown sugar
2 packages active dry yeast
1 tablespoon salt
1 tablespoon caraway seed or
    grated orange peel
2 cups hot water
¼ cup molasses
2 tablespoons softened butter or
    margarine
3 cups rye flour
Cornmeal

1. Combine 2 cups unbleached flour, brown sugar, yeast, salt, and caraway seed in a large mixing bowl.
2. Heat water, molasses, and butter until very warm (120° to 130°F).
3. Add liquid gradually to flour mixture and beat about 3 minutes on high speed of electric mixer. Stir in rye flour and enough unbleached flour to make a soft dough.
4. Turn dough onto a floured surface; knead until smooth and elastic (about 5 minutes). Let rest 20 minutes.
5. Divide dough in half. Shape into 2 long narrow loaves by rolling and stretching dough as for French Bread.
Place on a greased baking sheet sprinkled with cornmeal. Cover with plastic wrap or waxed paper; refrigerate 2 to 24 hours.
6. When ready to bake, remove plastic wrap carefully. Let rise in a warm place while oven is preheating, about 15 minutes. Brush loaves with water.
7. Bake at 400°F 40 minutes, or until done.

2 loaves

196 *Carrot Brown Bread*

The husky character of this bread makes it a good companion to soups and a tasty way to get vitamin A.

3 cups whole wheat flour
4 cups unbleached or all-purpose flour
2 packages active dry yeast
2 teaspoons salt
2 cups milk
½ cup water
¼ cup vegetable oil
2 tablespoons honey
2 tablespoons molasses
1 cup grated carrot

1. Mix flours.
2. Combine 2 cups flour mixture, yeast, and salt in a large mixing bowl.
3. Heat milk, water, oil, honey, and molasses in a saucepan until very warm (120° to 130°F).
4. Add liquid gradually to flour mixture, beating 3 minutes on high speed of electric mixer.
5. Stir in carrot and enough more flour to make a soft dough.
6. Turn dough onto a floured surface; allow to rest 10 minutes for easier handling. Knead until smooth and elastic (5 to 8 minutes).
7. Place dough in an oiled bowl; turn to oil top of dough. Cover; let rise in a warm place until double in bulk (about 1 hour).
8. Punch dough down; divide in half. Either shape into 2 round loaves and place on a greased baking sheet, or shape into 2 loaves and place in 2 greased 9×5×3-inch loaf pans. Cover; let rise until double in bulk (about 30 minutes).
9. Bake at 375°F 40 to 45 minutes, or until done.

2 loaves

197 *Mozzarella Egg Bread*

7 to 8 cups all-purpose flour
2 packages active dry yeast
1 tablespoon sugar
1 tablespoon salt
6 eggs (at room temperature)
1 cup plain yogurt
2 cups shredded mozzarella cheese (8 ounces)
½ cup hot tap water (120° to 130°F)

1. Combine 2 cups flour, yeast, sugar, and salt in a mixing bowl.
2. Stir eggs, yogurt, 1½ cups cheese, and water into flour mixture; beat until smooth, about 3 minutes on high speed of electric mixer.
3. Stir in enough more flour to make a soft dough.
4. Turn dough onto a floured surface; knead until smooth and elastic (5 to 8 minutes).
5. Place in an oiled bowl; turn to oil top of dough. Cover; let rise in a warm place until double in bulk (about 1 hour).
6. Punch dough down. Divide in half; shape into loaves, and place in 2 greased 9×5×3-inch loaf pans. Cover; let rise until double, about 30 minutes. Top loaves with remaining cheese.
7. Bake at 375°F 30 minutes, or until done.

2 loaves

198 *Hearty Potato Bread*

Potato adds wonderful flavor and moistness to bread. Now you have a chance to see why it has been an international favorite for years.

6½ to 7½ cups flour
2 packages active dry yeast
2 tablespoons sugar
1 tablespoon salt
2¼ cups hot potato water
1 cup warm unseasoned mashed potatoes
2 tablespoons oil

1. Combine flour, yeast, sugar, and salt in a large mixing bowl.
2. Add potato water (see Note), potatoes, and oil to flour mixture; beat about 3 minutes on high speed of electric mixer.
3. Stir in enough more flour to make a soft dough.
4. Turn dough onto a floured surface; knead until smooth and elastic (5 to 8 minutes).
5. Place in an oiled bowl; turn to oil top of dough. Cover; let rise in a warm place until double in bulk (about 1 hour).
6. Punch dough down. Divide in half; shape into loaves and place in 2 greased 9×5×3-inch loaf pans. Cover; let rise until double in bulk (about 45 minutes).
7. Bake at 375°F 40 to 45 minutes, or until done.

2 loaves

Note: To make potato water, cook 2 pared, cut-up potatoes until tender in about 3 cups water. Drain, reserving water. Mash potatoes and cool for bread.

199 *Colonial Bread*

2 cups whole wheat flour
2½ cups unbleached or all-purpose flour
¾ cup rye flour
½ cup yellow cornmeal
⅓ cup firmly packed brown sugar
2 packages active dry yeast
1 tablespoon salt
2½ cups hot tap water (120° to 130°F)
¼ cup vegetable oil
1 egg

1. Blend flours and cornmeal. Combine 2½ cups flour mixture, sugar, yeast, and salt in a large mixing bowl.
2. Stir water, oil, and egg into flour mixture; beat until smooth, about 3 minutes on high speed of electric mixer.
3. Gradually stir in enough more flour mixture to make a soft dough.
4. Turn dough onto a floured surface; knead until smooth and elastic (5 to 8 minutes).
5. Place in an oiled bowl; turn to oil top of dough. Cover; let rise in a warm place until double in bulk (about 1 hour).
6. Punch dough down. Divide in half; shape into loaves. Place in 2 greased 9×5×3-inch loaf pans. Cover; let rise until double in bulk (about 30 minutes).
7. Bake at 375°F 35 to 40 minutes, or until done.

2 loaves

200 Cornmeal French Bread

1 cup cooked cornmeal mush (see recipe)
2 packages active dry yeast
½ cup warm water
1 cup milk, scalded
1 tablespoon sugar
2½ teaspoons salt
4¾ to 5¼ cups all-purpose flour

1. Prepare cornmeal mush; cool slightly.
2. Dissolve yeast in warm water.
3. Pour scalded milk over sugar and salt in a large bowl. Add mush and mix well; cool to lukewarm. Beat in 1 cup flour. Mix in yeast and enough additional flour to make a soft dough.
4. Turn dough onto a lightly floured surface. Knead until smooth and satiny (about 10 minutes).
5. Put dough into a greased bowl; turn to grease top. Cover; let rise in a warm place until double in bulk (about 1 hour).
6. Punch dough down; cover and let rest 10 minutes. Form into a long thin roll on greased baking sheet. With a sharp knife, cut diagonal ¼-inch-deep slits about 2½ inches apart across the top. Brush top of loaf with salt water (**1 tablespoon salt** dissolved in **¼ cup water**). Cover; let rise until double in bulk (about 45 minutes).
7. Pour boiling water into a pie pan to a ½-inch depth; set on bottom rack of oven.
8. Bake at 400°F 15 minutes; turn temperature control to 350°F and bake 30 to 35 minutes longer. About 5 minutes before bread is finished baking, baste with salt water.

1 large loaf

Cornmeal Mush: Heat **3 cups water** to boiling in a saucepan. Mix **1 cup cornmeal, 1 teaspoon salt,** and **1 cup cold water.** Pour cornmeal mixture into boiling water, stirring constantly. Cook until thickened, stirring frequently. Cover; continue cooking over low heat 10 minutes.

201

4 cups

202 Here's-To-Your-Health Bread

Just about every ingredient in this bread is good for you. Whole grains and cottage cheese provide protein. Raisins and molasses contribute important minerals, especially iron. And besides all this, it tastes delicious.

4½ cups all-purpose or unbleached flour
3 cups whole wheat flour
1 cup uncooked oats
½ cup wheat germ
2 packages active dry yeast
2 teaspoons salt
2½ cups hot tap water (120° to 130°F)
1½ cups (12 ounces) creamed cottage cheese (at room temperature)
½ cup molasses or honey
2 tablespoons vegetable oil
1 cup raisins

1. Mix flours and oats.
2. Combine 3 cups flour mixture, wheat germ, yeast, and salt in a large mixing bowl.
3. Add water, cottage cheese, molasses, and oil to flour mixture; beat until smooth, about 3 minutes on high speed of electric mixer.
4. Stir in raisins and enough more flour to make a soft dough.
5. Turn dough onto a floured surface; let rest 10 minutes for easier handling. Knead until smooth and elastic (5 to 8 minutes).
6. Place in an oiled bowl; turn dough to oil top. Cover; let rise in a warm place until double in bulk (about 1 hour).
7. Punch dough down. Divide dough in thirds; shape into loaves and place in 3 greased 9×5×3-inch loaf pans. Cover; let rise until double in bulk (about 30 minutes).
8. Bake at 375°F 30 to 35 minutes, or until done.

3 loaves

203 *Cinnamon Swirl Loaves*

2 packages active dry yeast
½ cup warm water
2 cups milk, heated
⅓ cup honey
1 tablespoon salt
⅓ cup shortening
5 to 5½ cups all-purpose flour
2 cups uncooked oats
½ cup firmly packed brown sugar
2 tablespoons cinnamon

1. Dissolve yeast in warm water.
2. Pour hot milk over honey, salt, and shortening in a large bowl. Cool to lukewarm. Stir in 1 cup flour. Add softened yeast and oats. Stir in enough more flour to make a soft dough.
3. Turn dough onto a lightly floured surface; knead until smooth and satiny (about 10 minutes). Round dough into a ball and place in a greased bowl. Brush lightly with melted shortening. Cover; let rise in a warm place until double in bulk (about 1 hour).
4. Punch dough down; divide in half. Roll each half into a 14×7-inch rectangle. Brush with melted butter; sprinkle with brown sugar and cinnamon. Starting with short side, roll up as for jelly roll.
5. Place in 2 greased 8×4×2-inch loaf pans. Brush lightly with **melted shortening.** Cover; let rise until nearly double in bulk (about 45 minutes).
6. Bake at 375°F 45 to 50 minutes. Remove loaves from pans and brush with **melted butter.** Cool. Drizzle with a thin confectioners' sugar glaze, if desired.

2 loaves

204 *Triple Treat Bread*

If you don't have dry milk, you can replace 1 cup of the water with milk for the same tasty results.

4½ cups all-purpose or unbleached flour
2 cups whole wheat flour
1 cup rye flour
½ cup firmly packed brown sugar
½ cup instant nonfat dry milk
2 packages active dry yeast
1 tablespoon salt
2 cups hot tap water (120° to 130°F)
¼ cup vegetable oil

1. Mix flour.
2. Combine 2 cups flour mixture, sugar, dry milk, yeast, and salt in a large mixing bowl.
3. Stir water and oil into flour mixture; beat until smooth, about 3 minutes on high speed of electric mixer. Stir in enough remaining flour to make a soft dough.
4. Turn dough onto a floured surface; knead until smooth and elastic (5 to 8 minutes).
5. Place in an oiled bowl; turn to oil top of dough. Cover; let rise in a warm place until double (about 45 minutes).
6. Punch dough down. Divide in half; shape into loaves and place in 2 greased 9×5×3-inch loaf pans. Cover; let rise until double in bulk (about 30 minutes).
7. Bake at 375°F 35 to 40 minutes, or until done.

2 loaves

205 *Ground Nut Bread*

The electric blender or food processor is perfect for grinding the nuts and sunflower seeds for this bread.

3 cups all-purpose flour
1½ cups whole wheat flour
2 packages active dry yeast
2 teaspoons salt
1¾ cups hot tap water (120° to 130°F)
¼ cup honey

1. Mix flours.
2. Combine 1¾ cups flour mixture, yeast, and salt in a large mixing bowl.
3. Add water, honey, and oil to flour mixture; beat until smooth, about 3 minutes on high speed of electric mixer.
4. Stir in oats, nuts, sunflower seeds, cornmeal, and enough more flour to make a soft dough.

2 tablespoons vegetable oil
1 cup rolled oats
1 cup ground unsalted nuts
½ cup ground unsalted hulled
    sunflower seeds
½ cup cornmeal

5. Turn dough onto a floured board; knead until smooth and elastic (5 to 8 minutes).
6. Place in an oiled bowl; turn to oil top of dough. Cover; let rise in a warm place until double in bulk (about 1 hour).
7. Punch dough down. Divide in half, then each half in thirds. Form each piece into a rope 12 to 15 inches long. For each loaf, braid 3 pieces together. Tuck ends under; place in 2 greased 9×5×3-inch loaf pans or on greased baking sheets. Cover; let rise until double in bulk (about 1 hour).
8. Bake at 375°F 35 to 40 minutes, or until done.

2 loaves

206 *Harvest Bread*

1½ cups milk
⅓ cup margarine
2 tablespoons honey
2 tablespoons light molasses
2 teaspoons salt
2 large shredded wheat biscuits,
    crumbled
½ cup warm water (105° to 115°F)
2 packages active dry yeast
2 cups whole wheat flour
¼ cup wheat germ
2 to 3 cups all-purpose flour

1. Heat milk; stir in margarine, honey, molasses, salt, and shredded wheat biscuits. Cool to lukewarm.
2. Measure warm water into a large warm bowl. Sprinkle in yeast; stir until dissolved. Add lukewarm milk mixture and whole wheat flour; beat until smooth. Stir in wheat germ and enough all-purpose flour to make a stiff dough.
3. Turn dough onto a lightly floured surface; knead until smooth and elastic (8 to 10 minutes). Place in a greased bowl; turn to grease top. Cover; let rise in a warm place until double in bulk (about 1 hour).
4. Punch dough down; divide in half. Proceed, following directions below for desired shape.
5. Cover; let rise in a warm place until double in bulk (about 1 hour). If making sheaf, make diagonal snips with scissors along the bent portion of stalks above the twist. If desired, gently brush sheaf with beaten egg.
6. Bake on lowest rack position at 400°F about 20 minutes for sheaves and 25 to 30 minutes for loaves, or until done. Remove from baking sheets and cool on wire racks.

2 loaves

To Make Round Loaves: Shape each half of dough into a smooth round ball. Press each ball slightly to flatten into rounds 6 inches in diameter. Place on greased baking sheets.

To Make Wheat Sheaf: Divide one half of dough into 18 equal pieces. Roll 2 pieces into 12-inch ropes. Twist ropes together; set aside. Roll 8 pieces into 18-inch ropes and roll remaining 8 pieces into 15-inch ropes. Place one 18-inch rope lengthwise on center of a greased baking sheet, bending top third of rope off to the left at a 45-degree angle. Place a second 18-inch rope on sheet touching the first rope but bending top third off to the right. Repeat procedure using two more 18-inch ropes, placing them along outer edges of straight section and inside bent sections so that ropes are touching. Repeat, using two of the 15-inch ropes. Repeat, starting with the long ropes, placing them on top of the arranged long ropes and slightly spreading out ropes forming bottom of sheaf. Fill in by topping with the remaining 15-inch ropes, making shorter bends in two uppermost ropes. Cut twist in half. Arrange twists side by side around center of sheaf, tuck ends underneath. Repeat with remaining half of dough.

207 Mushroom Bread

¼ cup margarine
½ pound mushrooms, finely
    chopped
1 cup finely chopped onion
2 cups milk
3 tablespoons molasses
4 teaspoons salt
¼ teaspoon pepper
½ cup warm water (105° to 115°F)
2 packages active dry yeast
1 egg
1 cup wheat germ
8 to 9 cups all-purpose flour

1. Melt 2 tablespoons margarine in a large skillet over medium heat. Add mushrooms and onion; sauté until onion is tender and liquid has evaporated. Cool.
2. Heat milk; stir in molasses, salt, and pepper. Cool to lukewarm.
3. Measure warm water into a large warm bowl. Sprinkle in yeast; stir until dissolved. Add lukewarm milk mixture, egg, wheat germ, and 2 cups flour; beat until smooth. Stir in enough additional flour to make a stiff dough.
4. Turn dough onto a lightly floured surface; knead until smooth and elastic (8 to 10 minutes). Place in a greased bowl; turn to grease top. Cover; let rise in a warm place until double in bulk (about 1 hour).
5. Meanwhile, use four 30-ounce fruit cans to prepare Mushroom Pans (see below).
6. Punch dough down; turn onto lightly floured surface.

To Make Mushrooms: Divide dough onto 4 equal pieces. Shape each piece into a smooth round ball. Place in prepared Mushroom Pans. Let rise in a warm place until double in bulk (about 1 hour). With fingertips, gently press lower edge of mushroom cap down to meet foil-covered collar. Reshape cap if necessary. If desired, brush mushrooms with a mixture of 1 egg beaten with 1 tablespoon water. Bake on lowest rack position at 400°F about 40 minutes, or until done. Carefully remove from pans and cool on wire racks.

To Make Loaves: Divide dough in half. Roll each half to a 14×9-inch rectangle. Shape into loaves. Place in 2 greased 9×5×3-inch loaf pans. Cover; let rise in a warm place until double in bulk (about 1 hour). Bake at 400°F about 45 minutes, or until done. Remove from pans and cool on wire racks.

4 mushrooms
or 2 round loaves

Mushroom Pans: Cut 4 heavy cardboard squares 2 inches wider than can opening. Trace can opening in center of squares and cut out. Cover rings with foil. Place rings over cans so they fit tightly around opening. Grease cans and foil collars well.

208 Anadama Batter Bread

1 package active dry yeast
¼ cup warm water
1 cup cornmeal
2 teaspoons salt
½ teaspoon baking soda
⅓ cup dark molasses
3 tablespoons shortening
¾ cup boiling water

1. Dissolve yeast in warm water.
2. Combine cornmeal, salt, baking soda, molasses, and shortening in a large mixer bowl. Stir in boiling water; cool to lukewarm.
3. Add softened yeast, egg, and 1 cup flour to cornmeal mixture; beat 2 minutes on medium speed of electric mixer or 300 vigorous strokes with a wooden spoon. Stir in remaining flour.

1 egg
2¼ cups all-purpose flour
Melted butter

4. Spread batter in a well-greased 2-quart casserole. Cover; let rise in a warm place until nearly double in bulk (1 to 1½ hours).
5. Bake at 350°F about 40 minutes. Remove from casserole immediately. Brush top lightly with melted butter; cool.

1 loaf

209 *Aspen Batter Bread*

4 cups all-purpose flour
2 tablespoons sugar
1 package active dry yeast
1 teaspoon salt
¼ teaspoon ginger
1 can (13 ounces) evaporated milk
½ cup hot water
2 tablespoons vegetable oil

1. Combine 2 cups flour, sugar, yeast, salt, and ginger in a large mixing bowl.
2. Heat milk, water, and oil until very warm (120° to 130°F).
3. Stir in liquid with flour mixture; beat 2 minutes by hand or with electric mixer. Cover; let rise 15 minutes.
4. Beat in remaining flour by hand. Pour into 2 greased 1-pound coffee cans. Cover with greased plastic lids; let rise in a warm place until dough rises to top of cans (or until lids pop off), about 35 minutes. Remove lids.
5. Bake at 375°F 40 to 45 minutes, or until done. Place on wire racks to cool slightly before removing loaves from cans.

2 loaves

210 *Bran-New Batter Bread*

1 cup all-purpose flour
1 package active dry yeast
2 teaspoons salt
½ cup hot water
½ cup milk
½ cup vegetable oil
⅓ cup honey
2 eggs
1 cup whole bran cereal
½ cup wheat germ
1½ cups all-purpose flour

1. Combine 1 cup flour, yeast, and salt in large mixing bowl.
2. Heat water, milk, oil, and honey until very warm (120° to 130°F).
3. Add liquid and eggs to flour mixture and beat about 3 minutes at high speed of electric mixer.
4. Beat in bran cereal, wheat germ, and remaining flour by hand. Divide mixture into 2 well-greased 1-pound coffee cans. Cover with greased plastic lids and let rise in a warm place until dough rises almost to top of cans (about 35 minutes). Remove lids.
5. Bake at 375°F 35 minutes, or until done. Place on wire racks. Cool loaves slightly, then remove from cans and place on racks to cool.

2 loaves

211 *Dilly Cottage Batter Bread*

2½ cups all-purpose flour
1 package active dry yeast
1 tablespoon instant minced onion
1 teaspoon salt
½ teaspoon dill weed, thyme, or rosemary
1 cup creamed cottage cheese (at room temperature)
½ cup hot tap water (120° to 130°F)
1 egg (at room temperature)
1 tablespoon honey
1½ cups all-purpose flour

1. Combine 1 cup flour, yeast, onion, salt, and dill weed.
2. Add cottage cheese, water, egg, and honey to flour mixture; beat 3 minutes by hand or with electric mixer.
3. Beat in remaining flour. Cover; let rise in a warm place until double in bulk (about 1 hour).
4. Stir batter down; pour into a well-greased 1½-quart round casserole. Let rise in a warm place until light (30 to 40 minutes).
5. Bake at 375°F 50 to 55 minutes, or until done.

1 loaf

212 Basic Dinner Rolls

4 to 4¾ cups all-purpose flour
2 tablespoons sugar
2 packages active dry yeast
1 teaspoon salt
1 cup milk
½ cup water
¼ cup butter or margarine
1 egg (at room temperature)
Melted butter (optional)

1. Combine 1½ cups flour, sugar, yeast, and salt in a mixing bowl.
2. Heat milk, water, and butter until very warm (120° to 130°F).
3. Add liquid and egg to flour mixture; beat until smooth, about 3 minutes.
4. Stir in enough remaining flour to make a soft, sticky dough.
5. Turn dough onto a floured surface; continue to work in flour until dough can be kneaded. Knead until smooth and elastic, but still soft (about 5 minutes).
6. Cover dough with bowl or pan. Let rest 20 minutes.
7. Shape dough as desired. Cover and let rise until double in bulk (about 15 minutes).
8. Bake at 425°F about 12 minutes. Cool on wire racks. Brush with butter if desired.

2 to 2½ dozen rolls

Pan Rolls: Divide dough into 24 equal pieces by first dividing dough in half and then each half into 12 equal pieces. Roll into balls. Place in a greased 13×9×2-inch baking pan. Brush with melted butter, if desired. **213**

Cloverleaf Rolls: Pinch off bits of dough; roll into 1-inch balls. For each roll, place 3 balls in a greased muffin-pan well. **214**

Crescents: Divide dough in half. Roll each half into a 12-inch round about ¼ inch thick. Brush with **2 tablespoons melted butter.** Cut into 12 wedges. For each crescent, roll up wedge beginning at side opposite the point. Place point-side down on a greased baking sheet; curve ends. **215**

Snails: Roll dough into a rectangle ¼ inch thick. Cut off strips ½ inch wide and 5 inches long. Roll each piece of dough into a rope about 10 inches long. Wind into a flat coil, tucking ends under. Place on greased baking sheet. **216**

Figure Eights: Shape strips of dough ½ inch wide and 5 inches long into 10-inch ropes as in Snails (above). For each roll, pinch ends of rope together and twist once to form a figure 8. Place on greased baking sheets. **217**

Twists: Follow procedure for Figure Eights, giving each 8 an additional twist. **218**

Bowknots: Roll dough into a rectangle ¼ inch thick. Cut off strips ½ inch wide and 5 inches long. Roll each strip into a smooth rope 9 or 10 inches long. Gently tie into a single or double knot. Place on a greased baking sheet. **219**

Parker House Rolls: Roll dough ¼ inch thick. Brush with **3 or 4 tablespoons melted butter.** Cut with a 2½-inch round cutter. With a knife handle, make a crease across each circle slightly off center. Fold larger half over the smaller, pressing edges to seal. Place on a greased baking sheet or close together in a greased 13×9×2-inch baking pan. **220**

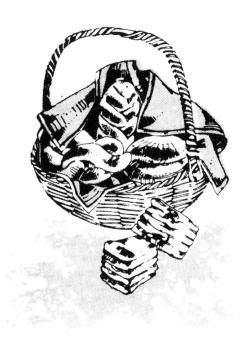

Braids: Form several ropes, ½ inch in diameter. Braid 3 ropes into a long strip; cut into 3-inch lengths. Pinch together at each end. Place on a greased baking sheet. **221**

Butterflies: Divide dough in half. Roll each half into a 24×6-inch rectangle about ¼ inch thick. Brush with **2 tablespoons melted butter.** Starting with long side, roll up dough as for jelly roll. Cut off 2-inch pieces. With handle of knife, press crosswise at center of each roll, forming a deep groove so spiral sides become visible. Place on a greased baking sheet. **222**

Fantans or Butterflake Rolls: Roll dough into a rectangle ¼ inch thick. Brush with **3 or 4 tablespoons melted butter.** Cut into 1-inch strips. Stack 6 or 7 strips; cut each into 1½-inch sections. Place on end in greased muffin-pan wells. **223**

224 *Crusty Hard Rolls*

If you like a crunchy roll, try this one. A shiny golden crust surrounds the snowy white and moist interior.

3½ **to 4½ cups all-purpose flour**
2 **packages active dry yeast**
1 **tablespoon sugar**
1½ **teaspoons salt**
1 **cup hot tap water (120° to 130°F)**
2 **tablespoons vegetable oil**
1 **egg white**
1 **egg yolk**
1 **tablespoon water**

1. Combine 1 cup flour, yeast, sugar, and salt in a large mixer bowl. Stir in water, oil, and egg white; beat until smooth, about 3 minutes on high speed of electric mixer. Gradually stir in more flour to make a soft dough.
2. Turn dough onto a floured surface; knead until smooth and elastic (3 to 5 minutes).
3. Cover with bowl or pan and let rest about 20 minutes.
4. Divide into 18 equal pieces. Form each into a smooth oval; place on a greased baking sheet. Slash tops lengthwise about ¼ inch deep. Let rise until double in bulk (about 15 minutes).
5. Brush with a mixture of egg yolk and 1 tablespoon water.
6. Bake at 400°F 15 to 20 minutes. For a crisper crust, place a shallow pan of hot water on lowest oven rack during baking.

1½ dozen rolls

Kaiser Rolls: Follow recipe for Crusty Hard Rolls, only flatten each of the 18 pieces of dough into 4- to 4-½-inch rounds. For each roll, lift one edge of the round and press it into center of circle. Then lift the corner of the fold and press it into the center. Continue clockwise around the circle until 5 or 6 folds have been made. Let rise and bake as directed above. **225**

226 French Crescents (Croissants)

Crescents are a lot of work but since they melt in your mouth they're worth every minute.

1 cup milk
1 tablespoon oil
1 tablespoon sugar
½ teaspoon salt
1 package compressed or active
    dry yeast
¼ cup warm water (105° to 115°F)
2¾ to 3 cups all-purpose flour
1 cup (½ pound) butter, softened
1 egg yolk
1 tablespoon milk

1. Heat 1 cup milk, oil, sugar, and salt in a saucepan; cool to lukewarm.
2. Dissolve yeast in warm water in a large bowl. Add milk mixture and 1 cup flour; beat until smooth. Stir in enough remaining flour to make a soft dough.
3. Turn dough onto a floured surface; continue to work in flour until dough can be kneaded. Knead until smooth and elastic (about 5 minutes).
4. Shape dough into a ball and place in an oiled bowl; turn to oil top of dough. Cover; let rise in a warm place until double in bulk (about 45 minutes).
5. Punch dough down. Roll out on floured surface to form a rectangle about ¼ inch thick.
6. Cut butter in slices (just soft enough to spread but not melted). Spread over center one-third section of rectangle. Fold each extending side over butter, pressing together the open edges to seal. Roll out again until rectangle is ⅜ inch thick. Turn dough occasionally, flouring surface lightly to prevent sticking. Fold in thirds again to make a squarish rectangle. Roll dough and fold again in the same manner. Wrap dough in waxed paper or foil; chill 30 minutes. If at any time dough oozes butter and becomes sticky while rolling, chill until butter is more firm.
7. Roll and fold again 2 more times exactly as directed before. Chill dough again another 30 minutes.
8. Roll dough into a rectangle about ⅛ inch thick. Cut into strips 6 inches wide. Cut triangles out of each strip to measure about 6×8×6 inches. Roll up each triangle of dough from a 6-inch edge, pinching tip to seal. Shape each roll into a crescent. Place, point down, 1½ inches apart on ungreased baking sheet.
9. Cover; let rise until double in bulk (30 to 45 minutes).
10. Brush each roll with mixture of egg yolk and 1 tablespoon milk.
11. Bake at 425°F 15 minutes, or until brown. Remove from baking sheet and cool on wire rack. Serve warm.

About 1½ dozen rolls

227 Pumpkin Spice Rolls

3½ to 4½ cups all-purpose flour
¼ cup firmly packed brown sugar
1 package active dry yeast
1 teaspoon salt
½ teaspoon cinnamon
¼ teaspoon nutmeg
⅛ teaspoon cloves
⅛ teaspoon ginger
1 cup milk
¼ cup water

1. Combine 1½ cups flour, brown sugar, yeast, salt, and spices in a large mixer bowl.
2. Heat milk, water, pumpkin, and oil in a saucepan until very warm (120° to 130°F).
3. Add liquid and egg to flour mixture and beat until smooth, about 3 minutes on high speed of electric mixer.
4. Stir in enough remaining flour to make a soft dough.
5. Turn dough onto floured board; continue to work in flour until dough is stiff enough to knead. Knead until smooth and elastic (about 5 minutes).

¾ cup canned pumpkin
¼ cup vegetable oil
1 egg
2 tablespoons melted butter

6. Cover with bowl or pan; let rest 20 minutes.
7. Shape into 2-inch balls; place each ball in a greased muffin-pan well. Brush with melted butter. Cover; let rise until double in bulk (about 20 minutes).
8. Bake at 375°F 20 minutes, or until done.

2 dozen rolls

228 Potato Pan Rolls

½ cup milk
1 tablespoon sugar
¾ teaspoon salt
2 tablespoons margarine
½ cup warm water (105° to 115°F)
1 package active dry yeast
1 egg
½ cup mashed potatoes (at room temperature)
3½ to 4½ cups all-purpose flour
Flour for dusting

1. Heat milk; stir in sugar, salt, and margarine. Cool to lukewarm.
2. Measure warm water into a large warm bowl. Sprinkle in yeast; stir until dissolved. Stir in lukewarm milk mixture, egg, mashed potatoes, and 2 cups flour. Beat until smooth. Stir in enough additional flour to make a soft dough.
3. Turn dough onto a lightly floured surface; knead until smooth and elastic (8 to 10 minutes). Place in a greased bowl; turn to grease top. Cover; let rise in a warm place until double in bulk (about 1 hour).
4. Punch dough down; turn out onto a lightly floured surface. Divide in half. Divide each half into 16 equal pieces; form into smooth balls. Place in 2 greased 9-inch round layer cake pans. Cover; let rise in a warm place until double in bulk (about 1 hour).
5. Dust rolls with flour.
6. Bake at 375°F about 25 minutes, or until done. Remove from pans and cool on wire racks.

32 rolls

229 Brown-and-Serve Rolls

9 to 10 cups all-purpose flour
½ cup sugar
2 packages active dry yeast
1 tablespoon salt
2 cups warm water
1 cup milk
½ cup butter or margarine

1. Stir together 3 cups flour, sugar, yeast, and salt in a large mixer bowl.
2. Heat water, milk, and butter until very warm (120° to 130°F).
3. Add liquid ingredients to flour mixture; beat until smooth, about 3 minutes on high speed of electric mixer.
4. Gradually stir in enough more flour to make a soft dough.
5. Turn out onto a floured surface; knead until smooth and elastic (5 to 8 minutes).
6. Shape dough into a ball, place in an oiled bowl, and turn to oil top of dough. Cover; let rise in a warm place until double in bulk (30 to 45 minutes).
7. Punch dough down. Divide in half. Shape each half into rolls (see page 26 for different shapes). Let rise in a warm place until double in bulk (30 to 45 minutes).
8. Bake at 375°F 20 to 25 minutes, or just until rolls begin to change color. Cool in pans 20 minutes. Finish cooling on wire racks. Wrap tightly in plastic bags and refrigerate up to 1 week, or freeze up to 2 months. Before serving, place rolls on ungreased baking sheet.
9. Bake at 400°F 10 to 12 minutes.

About 4 dozen rolls

230 Better Batter Rolls

These rolls resemble muffins in texture and shape, but the aroma as they bake is unmistakably and deliciously that of yeast. These go together quickly as they require no kneading.

3 cups all-purpose flour
1 package active dry yeast
1 teaspoon salt
1 cup hot water
¼ cup vegetable oil
¼ cup honey
1 egg

1. Combine 2 cups flour, yeast, and salt in a mixer bowl. Add water, oil, honey, and egg; beat until smooth, about 2 minutes on medium speed of electric mixer or 300 vigorous strokes by hand.
2. Beat in remaining flour by hand. Cover; let rise until double in bulk (about 30 minutes).
3. Fill greased muffin-pan wells half full. Let rise until double in bulk (about 30 minutes).
4. Bake at 400°F 10 to 12 minutes.

2 dozen rolls

231 English Muffins

3 to 3½ cups all-purpose flour
2 tablespoons sugar
1 package active dry yeast
1 teaspoon salt
¾ cup hot milk (120° to 130°F)
1 egg (at room temperature)
2 tablespoons vegetable oil
Cornmeal

1. Combine 1 cup flour, sugar, yeast, and salt in a mixer bowl.
2. Stir in milk, egg, and oil; beat until smooth, about 3 minutes on high speed of electric mixer.
3. Stir in enough remaining flour to make a soft dough.
4. Turn out onto floured board; knead until smooth and elastic (5 to 8 minutes).
5. Cover with bowl; let rest 20 minutes.
6. Roll out to ½-inch thickness. Cut into 3- or 4-inch rounds. Sprinkle with cornmeal. Cover; let rise until double in bulk (about 45 minutes).
7. Bake in a greased heavy skillet or on a griddle on top of the range over low heat 20 to 30 minutes, or until golden brown, turning once. Cool and store in an airtight container or plastic bag.
8. To serve, split with knife or fork. Toast. Serve hot.

About 1 dozen muffins

232 *Hurry-Up Dinner Rolls*

2½ to 3 cups all-purpose flour
2 tablespoons sugar
1 package active dry yeast
½ teaspoon salt
¾ cup hot tap water (120° to 130°F)
1 egg (at room temperature)
2 tablespoons vegetable oil
2 tablespoons melted butter or margarine

1. Combine 1 cup flour, sugar, yeast, and salt in a bowl. Stir in water, egg, and oil; beat until smooth. Cover; let rise in a warm place 15 minutes.
2. Stir in enough remaining flour to make a soft, sticky dough.
3. Turn dough onto a floured board; continue to work in flour until dough can be kneaded. Knead until smooth and elastic (about 3 minutes).
4. Divide dough into 16 pieces; shape into balls. Place in a greased 9-inch square pan. Brush tops with melted butter. Cover; let rise 20 minutes.
5. Bake at 425°F 8 to 10 minutes.

16 rolls

233 *Parmesan Bread Fingers*

2½ cups all-purpose biscuit mix
1 package active dry yeast
½ teaspoon salt
⅔ cup hot water
¼ cup butter or margarine, melted
¼ cup grated Parmesan cheese

1. Combine biscuit mix, yeast, and salt in a bowl.
2. Stir in water until mixture clings to itself.
3. Turn dough onto a floured surface. Knead 8 to 10 times.
4. Roll out into a 13×9-inch rectangle.
5. Brush half of butter in a 13×9×2-inch baking pan. Place dough in pan, pressing to fit. Cut crosswise into 16 strips, then lengthwise in half.
6. Brush with remaining butter and sprinkle with cheese. Cover; let rise 15 minutes.
7. Bake at 425°F 15 minutes. Turn off oven; allow sticks to remain in oven 15 minutes.

32 bread fingers

234 *Brooklyn Bagels*

4 to 5 cups all-purpose flour
1 package active dry yeast
2 teaspoons salt
1½ cups hot water (120° to 130°F)
2 tablespoons honey or sugar
1 egg white
1 teaspoon water

1. Combine 1 cup flour, yeast, and salt in a bowl.
2. Stir in hot water and honey; beat until smooth, about 3 minutes. Stir in enough remaining flour to make a soft dough.
3. Turn out onto a floured surface; continue to work in flour until dough is stiff enough to knead. Knead until smooth and elastic (about 5 minutes).
4. Cover with bowl. Let rest 15 minutes.
5. Divide into 12 equal parts. Shape each into a flattened ball. With thumb and forefinger poke a hole into center. Stretch and rotate until hole enlarges to about 1 or 2 inches. Cover; let rise about 20 minutes.
6. Boil water in a large shallow pan, about 2 inches deep. Reduce heat. Simmer a few bagels at a time about 7 minutes. Remove from pan; drain on a towel about 5 minutes. Place on a baking sheet; brush with mixture of egg white and water.
7. Bake at 375°F 30 minutes, or until done.
8. To serve, split and toast. Spread with **butter** and **jam** or **cream cheese**.

1 dozen bagels

235 *Basic Sweet Dough*

4 to 5 cups all-purpose flour
2 packages active dry yeast
1 teaspoon salt
¾ cup milk
½ cup water
½ cup melted butter
½ cup sugar
1 egg

1. Stir together 1¾ cups flour, yeast, and salt in a large mixer bowl.
2. Heat milk, water, butter, and sugar until very warm (120° to 130°F).
3. Add liquid ingredients to flour mixture; beat until smooth, about 2 minutes on electric mixer.
4. Add egg and ½ cup more flour and beat another 2 minutes.
5. Gradually add enough more flour to make a soft dough.
6. Turn out onto floured board; continue to work in flour until dough can be kneaded. Knead until smooth and elastic, but still soft (about 5 minutes).
7. Cover; let rest about 20 minutes.
8. Shape, let rise, and bake as directed in recipes that follow.

Cinnamon Rolls: Roll dough into a 13×9-inch rectangle. Spread with **2 tablespoons softened butter** or **margarine.** Sprinkle with mixture of **½ cup firmly packed brown** or **white sugar** and **2 teaspoons cinnamon.** Beginning with long side, roll dough up tightly jelly-roll fashion. Cut roll into 12 (1-inch) slices. Place slices in a greased 13×9×2-inch baking pan or greased muffin cups. Bake at 375°F 15 to 20 minutes.   236

1½ dozen

Glazed Raised Doughnuts: Follow recipe for Basic Sweet Dough. Roll out to about ½-inch thickness. Cut with doughnut cutter or make into shape of your choice, such as squares, twists, long johns, doughnut holes, or bismarcks. Let rise, uncovered, until light, 40 to 50 minutes. Fry in deep hot oil (375°F) 3 to 4 minutes, turning once. Drain on paper towels. Dip in a glaze of **1½ cups confectioners' sugar, 2 tablespoons warm water,** and **1 teaspoon vanilla extract.**   237

Apricot Crisscross Coffeecake: For one large coffeecake, roll dough into a 15×12-inch rectangle. For two small coffeecakes, divide dough in half. Roll each half into an 12×8-inch rectangle. Combine **½ cup apricot preserves, ½ cup raisins,** and **½ cup sliced almonds.** Spread half the filling lengthwise down the center of each rectangle. Make about 12 slashes, each 2 inches long, down the long sides of each coffeecake. Fold strips alternately over filling, herringbone fashion. Cover; let rise until double in bulk (50 to 60 minutes). Bake at 375°F 20 to 25 minutes for small coffeecakes and 35 to 40 minutes for large coffeecake.   238

239 *Refrigerator Sweet Dough*

5 to 6 cups all-purpose flour
2 packages active dry yeast
½ cup sugar
1½ teaspoons salt
1 cup milk
½ cup water
½ cup butter or margarine, softened
2 eggs

1. Stir 1¾ cups flour, yeast, sugar, and salt together in a large mixer bowl.
2. Heat milk, water, and butter to very warm (120° to 130°F).
3. Add liquid to dry ingredients and beat until smooth, about 2 minutes on electric mixer.
4. Add eggs and ½ cup flour and continue beating another 2 minutes.
5. Gradually stir in enough additional flour to make a soft dough.
6. Turn out onto floured board; continue to work in flour until dough can be kneaded. Knead until smooth and elastic, but still soft (5 to 8 minutes).
7. Cover with plastic wrap, then with a towel.
8. Let rest 20 minutes.
9. Divide in half and shape as desired.
10. Brush with **oil.** Cover with plastic wrap.
11. Refrigerate 2 to 24 hours. When ready to bake, remove from refrigerator and let stand 10 minutes.
12. Bake at 375°F 20 to 30 minutes.
13. Remove from pans and cool on rack.

2 coffeecakes

Cinnamon Slice Coffeecake: Follow shaping instructions as in Cinnamon Rolls ● , only omit 13×9×2-inch pan. Instead, place 6 slices, cut-side down, on bottom of a greased 10-inch tube pan. Place 6 more slices cut-side against outer side of pan. Cover first layer with remaining 6 rolls. Bake at 375°F 20 to 25 minutes.

240

Cinnamon Discs: Combine ¾ **cup firmly packed brown sugar, ¾ cup white sugar, ½ cup finely chopped pecans,** and **1 teaspoon cinnamon.** Divide dough in half. Roll each half into a 12-inch square. Melt ½ **cup butter.** Brush dough with 2 tablespoons of the butter. Sprinkle with ½ cup sugar mixture. Roll up jelly-roll fashion; pinch to seal edges. Cut into 1-inch slices. Place on greased baking sheets at least 3 inches apart. Cover with waxed paper. Flatten each to about 3 inches in diameter. Let rise 15 minutes. Flatten again. Brush with remaining butter; sprinkle with remaining sugar mixture. Cover with waxed paper; flatten again. Bake at 400°F 10 to 12 minutes.

241

2 dozen

Bubble Bread: Divide dough into 20 equal pieces; shape into balls. Combine ½ **cup sugar or firmly packed brown sugar, ½ cup finely chopped nuts,** and **1 teaspoon cinnamon.** Melt ½ **cup butter or margarine.** Roll balls in butter, then in sugar mixture. Arrange balls in a well-greased 10-inch tube pan. Cover; let rise until double in bulk (45 to 60 minutes). Bake at 350°F 30 to 35 minutes.

242

Orange Bubble Ring: Shape dough into 20 balls as for Bubble Bread. Roll each ball in **½ cup melted butter** and then a mixture of **½ cup sugar** and **1 tablespoon grated orange peel.** Arrange and bake as above. **243**

Apricot Bubble Bread: Shape dough into 20 balls as for Bubble Bread; roll balls in butter, then in sugar. Arrange 10 balls in bottom of a well-greased 10-inch tube pan. Top with **¼ cup apricot preserves.** Repeat layers. Cover; let rise until double in bulk (about 45 minutes). Bake as directed. **244**

245 *Sweet Maple Coffeecake*

3 to 3½ cups all-purpose flour
1 package active dry yeast
½ teaspoon salt
½ cup milk
¼ cup water
¼ cup butter or margarine
2 eggs
¼ cup honey or sugar
Maple Filling

1. Combine 1 cup flour, yeast, and salt in a mixer bowl.
2. Warm milk, water, and butter in a small saucepan.
3. Add liquid, eggs, and honey to flour mixture; beat until smooth, about 3 minutes on electric mixer.
4. Stir in enough remaining flour to make a soft, sticky dough.
5. Turn out onto floured board; continue to work in flour until dough can be kneaded. Knead until smooth and elastic, but still soft (about 5 minutes).
6. Cover with a bowl; let rest 30 minutes.
7. Divide dough in half; roll each half into a 15×12-inch rectangle. Spread with Maple Filling. Fold each rectangle in thirds, making a 15×4-inch strip. Cut in 10 equal pieces. Place strips of dough in greased 8×4×2-inch loaf pans, cut side down. Cover; let rise 30 minutes.
8. Bake at 350°F 35 to 40 minutes.

2 loaves

Maple Filling: Cream **½ cup firmly packed brown sugar** and **⅓ cup white sugar** with **¼ cup softened butter or margarine.** Stir in **¼ cup maple syrup, 2 tablespoons all-purpose flour, ½ teaspoon cinnamon,** and **½ cup chopped nuts.**

246 *Nutty Sweet Twists*

Now that you've mastered the basic yeast dough, you're ready for a new twist!

1 can (13 ounces) evaporated milk
or 1⅔ cups milk
1 tablespoon lemon juice or
vinegar
½ cup raisins
3 tablespoons sugar
2 tablespoons butter or margarine
3 to 3¼ cups all-purpose flour
1 package active dry yeast

1. Warm milk and lemon juice in a small saucepan. Add raisins, sugar, and 2 tablespoons butter.
2. Combine 2 cups flour, yeast, salt, and baking soda in a large mixer bowl. Stir in milk mixture and egg; beat until smooth.
3. Stir in enough remaining flour to make a soft, sticky dough.
4. Turn out onto a floured surface; continue to work in flour until dough can be kneaded. Knead until smooth and elastic,

1 teaspoon salt
½ teaspoon baking soda
1 egg
2 tablespoons butter or margarine, softened or melted
⅓ cup firmly packed brown sugar
⅓ cup finely chopped nuts
2 teaspoons cinnamon

but still soft (about 5 minutes). Let dough rest 5 minutes.
5. Roll dough into a 24×12-inch rectangle, about ⅛ inch thick. Spread or brush with 2 tablespoons butter. Sprinkle with a mixture of brown sugar, nuts, and cinnamon. Fold in half lengthwise, forming a 24×6-inch rectangle. Cut into 1-inch strips. For each roll, hold both ends of strip and twist. Place on greased baking sheet. (If shorter rolls are desired, cut twists in half.)
6. Bake at 375°F 10 to 15 minutes (see Note).

2 dozen long (6-inch) twists
or 4 dozen short (3-inch) twists

Note: For shinier twists, brush dough with mixture of **1 egg white** and **1 teaspoon water** just before baking.

Frosted Sweet Twists: Follow recipe for Nutty Sweet Twists and glaze baked rolls with a mixture of ½ cup confectioners' sugar and 1 tablespoon milk.   247

248 *Austrian Almond Braid*

5 to 5½ cups all-purpose flour
2 packages active dry yeast
1 cup milk
½ cup sugar
½ cup shortening or butter
¼ cup water
2 teaspoons salt
2 eggs (at room temperature)
½ cup golden raisins
½ cup candied mixed fruit, chopped
½ cup chopped blanched almonds
Almond Icing (see recipe)
Candied fruit and nuts for decoration (optional)

1. Combine 2 cups flour and yeast in a large mixer bowl.
2. Heat milk, sugar, shortening, water, and salt in a saucepan over low heat until very warm (120° to 130°F), stirring to blend. Add liquid to flour-yeast mixture and beat until smooth, about 3 minutes on medium speed of electric mixer. Blend in eggs. Add 1 cup flour and beat 1 minute. Stir in fruit and almonds; add more flour to make a soft dough.
3. Turn dough onto a lightly floured surface; knead until smooth and satiny (5 to 10 minutes). Cover dough and let rest 20 minutes. Divide dough in half.
4. For each braid, take two-thirds of one portion of dough and divide into thirds. Roll each piece with hands into a 15-inch strand. Braid strands on lightly greased baking sheet. Divide remaining third into thirds; form three 18-inch strands. Braid strands loosely; place on first braid, pressing in lightly. Tuck ends of top braid under ends of bottom braid. Brush with oil. Let rise in a warm place until double in bulk (about 45 minutes).
5. Bake at 350°F 25 to 30 minutes, or until golden brown. Remove from baking sheets to wire rack. While braids are still slightly warm, ice with almond icing. Decorate with candied fruit and nuts, if desired.

2 large loaves

Almond Icing: Put **1½ cups confectioners' sugar, 2 tablespoons milk,** and **1 teaspoon almond extract** into a small bowl; stir until smooth.

249 *Sally Lunn*

5 cups all-purpose flour
½ cup sugar
1 package active dry yeast
1 teaspoon salt
1½ cups milk
½ cup butter or margarine
3 eggs
¼ cup sugar
¼ teaspoon nutmeg

1. Combine 2 cups flour, ½ cup sugar, yeast, and salt in a mixer bowl.
2. Heat milk and butter in a small saucepan.
3. Add liquid with eggs to flour mixture; beat 2 minutes by hand or with electric mixer.
4. Stir in remaining flour by hand. Cover; let rise until double in bulk (about 1 hour).
5. Stir dough down. Pour into a greased and sugared 10-inch tube pan. Cover; let rise until double in bulk (about 30 minutes).
6. Combine ¼ cup sugar and nutmeg; sprinkle over dough.
7. Bake at 400°F 40 minutes. Cool in pan 5 minutes.
8. If desired, serve hot with strawberries and whipped cream.

One large loaf

250 *Russian Kulich*

5 cups all-purpose flour
2 packages active dry yeast
1 cup milk
½ cup sugar
¼ cup oil
2 teaspoons salt
2 eggs (at room temperature)
2 teaspoons grated lemon peel
½ cup chopped blanched almonds
¼ cup raisins
¼ cup chopped candied citron
¼ cup chopped candied orange peel
¼ cup chopped candied cherries
½ cup confectioners' sugar
1 tablespoon milk
  Candied fruit (optional)

1. Combine 1 cup flour and yeast in a large mixer bowl.
2. Heat 1 cup milk, sugar, oil, and salt in a saucepan over low heat until very warm (120° to 130°F), stirring to blend. Add liquid to flour-yeast mixture and beat until smooth, about 2 minutes on medium speed of electric mixer. Beat in eggs, lemon peel, almonds, raisins, and candied fruit. Add 1 cup flour and beat 1 minute on medium speed. Stir in more flour to make a soft dough.
3. Turn dough onto a lightly floured surface and knead until smooth and satiny (8 to 10 minutes). Shape into a ball and place in a lightly greased bowl; turn to grease surface. Cover; let rise in a warm place until double in bulk (about 1½ hours).
4. Punch dough down; divide into 2 or 3 equal portions and shape into balls. Let rest 10 minutes.
5. Grease generously two 46-ounce juice cans or three 1-pound coffee cans. Place dough in cans, filling about half full; brush with oil. Let rise until double in bulk (about 1 hour).
6. Bake at 350°F 30 to 35 minutes, or until golden brown. Immediately remove from cans and cool.
7. Blend confectioners' sugar and 1 tablespoon milk until smooth; ice top of loaves. Decorate with candied fruit, if desired.

2 large or 3 medium loaves

251 *Cottage Raisin Puffs*

Sweet enough for breakfast, but not too sweet for lunch or dinner. The cheeses add enough protein to make it a good match for one of our lighter soups.

3 to 3½ cups all-purpose flour
2 packages active dry yeast
1½ teaspoons salt
1 cup creamed cottage cheese
½ cup melted butter or margarine
½ cup hot water
¼ cup sugar or honey
1 egg
Raisin Cream Filling

1. Combine 1 cup flour, yeast, and salt in a mixer bowl.
2. Heat cottage cheese, butter, water, and sugar in a saucepan until very warm (120° to 130°F).
3. Add liquid and egg to flour mixture and beat until smooth, about 3 minutes.
4. Stir in enough remaining flour to make a soft dough.
5. Turn out onto floured board; continue to work in flour until dough can be kneaded. Knead until smooth and elastic, but still soft (about 5 minutes).
6. Place in an oiled bowl; turn to oil top of dough. Cover; let rise in warm place until double in bulk (about 1 hour).
7. Punch dough down. Roll into a rectangle 20×12 inches. Cut into 2-inch squares. Place about 1 teaspoon of Raisin Cream Filling in center of each square. Bring corners to center and press together. Place on greased baking sheets. Let rise 10 minutes.
8. Bake at 375°F 12 to 15 minutes, or until done.

2 dozen

Raisin Cream Filling: Stir **2 tablespoons milk** into **1 package (8 ounces) cream cheese, softened.** Blend in **½ cup raisins.**

Cottage Date Puffs: Prepare Cottage Raisin Puffs, substituting **chopped dates** for raisins and adding **¼ cup chopped nuts.**

252

253 *Kugelhupf*

3 to 4 cups all-purpose flour
2 packages active dry yeast
1 cup milk
1 cup raisins
½ cup water
½ cup sugar
½ cup butter
1 teaspoon salt
3 eggs (at room temperature)
2 teaspoons rum extract
Butter, softened
⅓ cup ground almonds
Sifted confectioners' sugar
Candied fruits and nuts
Corn syrup

1. Combine 2 cups flour and yeast in a large mixer bowl.
2. Heat milk, raisins, water, sugar, ½ cup butter, and salt in a saucepan over low heat until very warm (120° to 130°F), stirring to blend; add to flour-yeast mixture and beat until smooth, about 3 minutes on medium speed of electric mixer. Blend in eggs and rum extract; add ½ cup flour and continue to beat 2 minutes. Add enough flour to make a thick batter. Cover; let rise in a warm place until double in bulk and batter is bubbly (about 1 hour).
3. Stir batter down. Spoon into two 1½-quart or three 1-quart turk's-head or other fancy molds that have been buttered and dusted with ground almonds. Cover; let rise in a warm place until double in bulk (about 30 minutes).
4. Bake at 325°F 1 hour for 1½-quart loaves or 45 minutes for 1-quart loaves. If necessary to prevent excessive browning, cover during the last 10 minutes of baking. Unmold on wire racks. Dust with confectioners' sugar. Decorate with candied fruits and nuts that have been dipped in corn syrup.

2 large or 3 small loaves

Sourdough puts a little bit of history in your loaf pan. About 6,000 years ago the Egyptians accidentally discovered that when flour was exposed to water and the wild yeast in the air, it fermented and expanded. When the fermented dough was added to bread dough, the result was a lighter bread. The "starter" was passed down from generation to generation to produce the staff of life for thousands of years.

In this country, gold prospectors carried the starter with them everywhere they went, and soon they themselves became known as Sourdoughs.

Sourdough requires a little know-how in order to nurture it and see that it performs as expected. Read these helpful hints to guide you in making sourdough breads.

Hints: Use your starter often. Don't let it become tucked away in the back of the refrigerator where you'll forget about it. Sourdough that is allowed to sit unused for 2 or 3 months will spoil and have to be discarded.

If you have replenished the starter, make sure that you wait at least 8 hours before using it.

The old sourdoughs, the name given to prospectors who always carried the sourdough starter with them, referred to the process of replenishing the starter as "sweetening" it. When replenishing, use warm water (105° to 115°F) to provide the best environment for yeast growth. Just as packaged yeast is vulnerable to too high temperatures, so is the yeast in sourdough starters.

Store your starter in the refrigerator. You may want to keep as much as 2 cups on hand so you'll be ready either for quantity baking or for sharing with a friend.

254 *Sourdough Starter*

2 cups flour
1 package active dry yeast
1 tablespoon sugar
2 cups warm potato water (105° to 115°F)

1. Combine flour, yeast, and sugar in a nonmetal mixing bowl. Stir in potato water.
2. Cover; let stand in a warm place (80° to 85°F) for 48 hours.
3. Store in covered jar in refrigerator.

To use in recipe: Stir well before use. Pour out required amount called for in recipe and use as directed.

To replenish remaining starter: Mix in 1 cup each flour and warm water until smooth. Let stand in warm place a few hours until it bubbles again before covering and replacing in refrigerator.

Note: Use in recipe or remove 1 cup starter and replenish every week.

255 *Sourdough Sam's Skillet Loaves*

Sourdough and an iron skillet will carry you back to the early prospecting days. For authenticity and mighty good eating, serve it with honey and butter.

1 cup sourdough starter
2½ cups warm water
2 tablespoons honey or sugar
7 to 7½ cups all-purpose flour
¼ cup vegetable oil
1 tablespoon salt
1 teaspoon baking soda
6 tablespoons butter
4 tablespoons cornmeal

1. Combine starter, water, honey, and 5 cups flour in a large nonmetal mixing bowl. Cover with plastic wrap or a wet towel; let stand at room temperature 12 hours or overnight.
2. Stir in oil. Combine salt, soda, and 1 cup flour. Stir into dough; beat until smooth.
3. Stir in enough remaining flour to make a soft dough.
4. Turn dough onto a floured surface; continue to work in flour until dough is stiff enough to knead. Knead until smooth and elastic (about 5 minutes).
5. Divide dough in half. Roll each into a 10-inch round (see Note).
6. For each loaf, melt 3 tablespoons butter in a heavy 10-inch cast-iron skillet with heat-resistant handle. Sprinkle with 2 tablespoons cornmeal. Place dough in skillet. Turn over to coat top with butter and cornmeal. Let rise 15 minutes.
7. Bake at 400°F 25 to 30 minutes, or until done.
8. Serve hot with **butter** and **honey**.

2 loaves

Note: If you don't have 2 skillets, simply allow the second dough circle to rise while the first bakes—it will just have a lighter texture.

Sweet and Sourdough Granola Bread: 256
Prepare dough as in Sourdough Sam's Skillet Loaves. After dividing dough in half, roll out each half into a 16×6-inch rectangle. Brush each with **2 tablespoons melted butter** and sprinkle with half the Granola Cinnamon Filling. Beginning with narrow end of rectangle, roll up tightly as for jelly roll; seal edges. Place loaves in 2 greased 9×5×3-inch loaf pans. Cover; let rise until double in bulk (45 to 60 minutes). Bake at 350°F 40 to 45 minutes.

Granola Cinnamon Filling: Combine **1 cup granola, ½ cup firmly packed brown sugar, ½ cup chopped dates or raisins** (optional), and **1 teaspoon cinnamon**. 257

Sourdough Apple Kuchen: Prepare dough as in Sourdough Sam's Skillet Loaves. After dividing dough, roll out each half into a 10-inch round. Place dough in 2 greased 9- or 10-inch springform pans. Press dough about 1½ inches up sides of pan. Fill each kuchen with a mixture of **2 cups finely sliced pared apples, ½ cup firmly packed brown sugar, ¼ cup all-purpose flour,** and **1 teaspoon cinnamon**. Sprinkle with **¼ cup sliced almonds**. Dot with **2 tablespoons butter**. Let rise 30 minutes. Bake at 375°F 40 to 45 minutes, or until done. 258

259 Golden Sourdough Bread

1 package active dry yeast
1¼ cups warm water
¼ cup firmly packed brown sugar
2 teaspoons salt
⅓ cup butter or margarine
3½ to 4 cups all-purpose flour
• 1½ cups sourdough starter
3½ cups uncooked oats

1. Soften yeast in ¼ cup warm water. Pour remaining 1 cup water over sugar, salt, and butter in a large bowl. Stir in 2 cups of flour, sourdough starter, oats, and softened yeast. Stir in enough additional flour to make a stiff dough.
2. Knead dough on a floured surface until smooth and elastic (about 10 minutes). Round dough into a ball; place in a greased bowl. Lightly grease surface of dough. Cover; let rise in a warm place until nearly double in bulk (about 1 hour).
3. Punch dough down; shape into 2 round loaves. Place on greased cookie sheets. Let rise in a warm place until nearly double in bulk (about 40 minutes). Slash tops with sharp knife or kitchen shears.
4. Bake at 400°F 35 to 40 minutes. Cool on wire racks.

2 loaves

260 San Francisco Sourdough French Bread

• 1 cup sourdough starter
1½ cups warm water
2 tablespoons sugar
5 to 6 cups all-purpose flour
1 tablespoon salt
½ teaspoon baking soda

1. Combine starter, water, sugar, and 3 cups flour in a large nonmetal mixing bowl. Cover with plastic wrap or a towel; let stand at room temperature 12 hours or overnight.
2. Combine salt, soda, and 1 cup flour. Stir into dough; beat until smooth.
3. Stir in enough remaining flour to make a soft dough.
4. Turn dough onto a floured surface; continue to work in flour until dough is stiff enough to knead. Knead until smooth and elastic (5 to 8 minutes).
5. Shape dough into a long, narrow loaf by rolling and stretching dough as for French Bread (page 15). Place on a greased baking sheet. Cover; let rise in a warm place until double in bulk (1½ to 2 hours).
6. With a sharp knife, slash top ½ inch deep at 2-inch intervals. Brush loaf with **water.**
7. Bake at 375°F 30 to 35 minutes.

1 loaf

Note: For a browner and shinier crust, brush before baking with a mixture of **1 egg white** and ⅓ **cup water** instead of only water.

261 Quick Buttermilk Bread

1¾ cups all-purpose flour
2 teaspoons baking powder
¾ teaspoon baking soda
1 teaspoon salt
⅓ cup firmly packed brown sugar
1½ cups uncooked oats
1 cup buttermilk
½ cup vegetable oil
2 eggs, beaten
½ cup chopped pecans

1. Mix flour, baking powder, baking soda, and salt in a bowl. Stir in brown sugar and oats. Add remaining ingredients; stir only until dry ingredients are moistened.
2. Pour batter into a greased 9×5×3-inch loaf pan.
3. Bake at 350°F 50 to 55 minutes. Cool on wire rack about 10 minutes. Remove from pan; cool thoroughly.
4. Wrap and store. (Bread will slice better if stored a day before slicing.)

1 loaf

262 Cheddar Cornbread

1 cup yellow cornmeal
1 cup all-purpose flour
1 tablespoon baking powder
1 teaspoon salt
2 cups shredded Cheddar cheese (8 ounces)
1 cup milk
¼ cup melted butter or margarine or vegetable oil
1 egg
4 slices crisply cooked bacon, crumbled
1 green pepper, sliced (optional)

1. Combine cornmeal, flour, baking powder, salt, and 1 cup cheese in a mixing bowl.
2. Combine milk, butter, and egg in a separate bowl; beat well.
3. Add liquid ingredients to dry ingredients; stir just until flour is moistened. Pour into a greased 9-inch round layer cake pan. Sprinkle with remaining cheese and bacon. Top with green pepper rings, if desired.
4. Bake at 425°F 25 minutes, or until done.

About 8 servings

263 Pleasin' Pumpkin Bread

3½ cups all-purpose flour
3 cups sugar
2 cups cooked mashed pumpkin
1 cup vegetable oil
⅓ cup water
4 eggs
2 teaspoons baking soda
1½ teaspoons salt
2 teaspoons cinnamon
½ teaspoon nutmeg
¼ teaspoon cloves
¼ teaspoon ginger

1. Put flour, sugar, baking soda, salt, and spices into a large mixing bowl; mix well. Add pumpkin, oil, water, and eggs; beat until well blended.
2. Divide batter equally into 2 greased 9×5×3-inch loaf pans.
3. Bake at 350°F 70 minutes, or until done.
4. Cool before wrapping.

2 loaves

264 *Oklahoma Oatmeal Bread*

1 cup evaporated milk
2 tablespoons vegetable oil
1 tablespoon vinegar
1 cup uncooked oats
1 cup all-purpose flour
1 cup firmly packed brown sugar
1 teaspoon baking soda
½ teaspoon salt
1 cup raisins or chopped nuts

1. Beat milk, oil, and vinegar in a mixing bowl until smooth.
2. Add oats, flour, brown sugar, baking soda, and salt; mix until well blended.
3. Stir in raisins or nuts.
4. Turn into a greased 9×5×3-inch loaf pan or two 7×4×2-inch loaf pans.
5. Bake at 350°F 50 to 60 minutes, or until done.
6. Cool before wrapping.

1 large loaf or 2 small loaves

Light, flaky biscuits are a snap to make. They can be mixed minutes before the meal and served piping hot right from the oven.

The same biscuit dough can be either rolled or dropped onto a baking sheet, depending on your preference and time. Drop biscuits are dropped by spoonfuls onto a greased baking sheet just like a cookie. Then you pop them into the oven. To produce that wonderful flakiness and shape typical of the rolled biscuit, an additional step must be taken. The dough is gently kneaded about ½ minute, rolled or patted out, and cut with a biscuit cutter. Both kinds are baked in a hot (425°-450°F) oven 10 to 12 minutes.

A technique to remember to get straight, even sides is to push the biscuit cutter evenly, straight down, without twisting. If you like soft sides, place the biscuits close together in a shallow pan. For crusty sides, allow about an inch around each biscuit on the baking sheet.

To pull piping-hot, mouth-watering biscuits out of the oven just as everyone is sitting down to dinner or breakfast, you can cheat a little on the time schedule. Prepare the biscuits, put on a baking sheet, and cover with plastic wrap. Refrigerate up to one hour before you are ready to bake. Just allow a few extra minutes for them to bake.

265 *Biscuits*

2 cups all-purpose flour
1 tablespoon baking powder
1 teaspoon salt
⅓ cup butter or shortening
¾ cup milk

1. Combine flour, baking powder, and salt in a mixing bowl. Cut in butter with pastry blender or 2 knives until mixture resembles rice kernels.
2. Stir in milk with a fork just until mixture clings to itself.
3. Form dough into a ball and knead gently 8 to 10 times on lightly floured board. Gently roll dough ½ inch thick.
4. Cut with floured biscuit cutter or knife, using an even pressure to keep sides of biscuits straight.
5. Place on ungreased baking sheet, close together for soft-sided biscuits or 1 inch apart for crusty ones.
6. Bake at 450°F 10 to 15 minutes, or until golden brown.

About 1 dozen

Southern Buttermilk Biscuits: Follow recipe for Biscuits, substituting **buttermilk** for the milk and adding ¼

266

teaspoon baking soda to the dry ingredients and reducing baking powder to 2 teaspoons.

267

Drop Biscuits: Follow recipe for Biscuits, increasing milk to 1 cup. Omit rolling-out instructions. Simply drop from a spoon onto a lightly greased baking sheet.

268 *Scones*

1⅔ cups all-purpose flour
1 tablespoon sugar
1½ teaspoons baking powder
½ teaspoon baking soda
½ teaspoon salt
½ cup shortening
½ cup buttermilk

1. Combine flour, sugar, baking powder, baking soda, and salt in a mixing bowl. Cut in shortening with pastry blender or two knives until mixture resembles rice kernels.
2. Stir in buttermilk with a fork until mixture clings to itself.
3. Form dough into a ball and knead gently about 8 times on a floured surface. Divide dough in half; roll each into a round about ½ inch thick. Cut each round into 6 wedge-shaped pieces. Place on ungreased baking sheets.
4. Bake at 450°F 8 to 10 minutes. Serve warm.

1 dozen

269 *Savory Biscuit Bread*

1½ cups all-purpose flour
1 tablespoon baking powder
½ teaspoon salt
½ teaspoon paprika
½ teaspoon celery salt
¼ teaspoon pepper
¼ teaspoon poultry seasoning
¼ cup shortening
½ cup milk (about)

1. Combine flour, baking powder, and seasonings in a mixing bowl. Cut in shortening until mixture resembles rice kernels.
2. Stir in milk with a fork just until flour is moistened.
3. Pat into a greased 8-inch round layer cake pan.
4. Bake at 450°F 10 to 15 minutes, or until done.

6 servings

270 *Dakota Bran Muffins*

1 cup all-purpose flour
1 tablespoon baking powder
½ teaspoon salt
1½ cups ready-to-eat bran flakes
1 cup milk
1 egg
¼ cup vegetable oil
¼ cup honey or sugar

1. Combine dry ingredients in a mixing bowl.
2. Combine remaining ingredients in a separate bowl; beat well.
3. Add liquid ingredients to dry ingredients; stir just until flour is moistened. Spoon batter into 12 greased muffin-pan wells.
4. Bake at 400°F 20 to 25 minutes, or until golden brown.

1 dozen

271 *Buttermilk Coffeecake*

1 cup sugar
½ cup butter or margarine, softened
2 eggs
1 teaspoon vanilla extract
2 cups all-purpose flour
1 teaspoon baking powder
1 teaspoon baking soda
½ teaspoon salt
1 cup buttermilk
Topping:
　1 cup chopped nuts
　1 cup sugar
　⅓ cup firmly packed brown sugar
　1 teaspoon cinnamon
　½ cup butter or margarine

1. Cream sugar and butter; beat in eggs and vanilla extract until well blended.
2. Combine flour, baking powder, baking soda, and salt.
3. Add buttermilk and flour mixture alternately to sugar mixture, beating well after each addition.
4. For topping, combine nuts, sugar, brown sugar, and cinnamon. Cut in butter.
5. Sprinkle half of topping mixture in bottom of a greased and floured 13×9×2-inch baking pan. Pour in batter. Cover with remaining topping.
6. Bake at 350°F 25 to 30 minutes.
7. Serve warm.

1 coffeecake

272 *Rhubarb Bread*

1½ cups firmly packed brown sugar
⅔ cup vegetable oil
1 cup buttermilk
1 egg
1 teaspoon vanilla extract
2½ cups all-purpose flour
1 teaspoon salt
1 teaspoon baking soda
1½ cups finely chopped rhubarb
½ cup chopped nuts
2 tablespoons sugar

1. Beat brown sugar, oil, buttermilk, egg, and vanilla extract in a mixing bowl.
2. Mix flour, salt, and baking soda. Add to brown sugar mixture and stir until blended.
3. Stir in rhubarb and nuts.
4. Turn into 2 greased 8×4×2-inch loaf pans. Sprinkle 1 tablespoon sugar over each.
5. Bake at 325°F 1 hour, or until done.

2 loaves

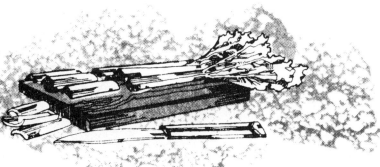

273 *Zucchini Bread*

2 cups sugar
1 cup vegetable oil
3 eggs
1 teaspoon vanilla extract
3 cups all-purpose flour
1 teaspoon salt
1 teaspoon baking soda
1 teaspoon cinnamon
2 cups shredded unpeeled zucchini
1 cup chopped nuts

1. Beat sugar, oil, eggs, and vanilla extract in a mixing bowl until fluffy.
2. Mix flour, salt, baking soda, and cinnamon. Add to egg mixture and stir until blended.
3. Stir in zucchini and nuts.
4. Turn into a greased 9×5×3-inch loaf pan.
5. Bake at 350°F 1 hour and 20 minutes, or until done.
6. Cool before wrapping.

1 loaf

274 *Waffles*

2 cups sifted all-purpose flour
1 tablespoon sugar
1 tablespoon baking powder
½ teaspoon salt
3 eggs, well beaten
2 cups milk
½ cup butter or margarine, melted

1. Mix flour, sugar, baking powder, and salt in a bowl.
2. Combine eggs, milk, and melted butter. Add liquid mixture to flour mixture; beat just until batter is blended.
3. Heat waffle baker. Pour enough batter into waffle baker to allow spreading to within 1 inch of edges. Lower cover and bake waffle; do not raise cover during baking. Lift cover and loosen waffle with a fork. Serve hot.

About 4 large waffles

Buttermilk Waffles: Follow recipe for Waffles; substitute **buttermilk** for milk. Decrease baking powder to 2 teaspoons and add **1 teaspoon baking soda**. **275**

Wheat Germ Pecan Waffles: Follow recipe for Waffles; decrease flour to 1½ cups. Stir **½ cup toasted wheat germ** into the flour mixture. Sprinkle **3 tablespoons coarsely chopped pecans** onto the batter before baking each waffle. **276**

Cheese Waffles: Follow recipe for Waffles. When batter is smooth, blend in **½ cup shredded cheese**. **277**

Chocolate Waffles: Follow recipe for Waffles. Generously sprinkle **semisweet chocolate pieces** over batter before closing waffle baker. **278**

Popovers, unlike the other quick breads, rely on steam as the leavening agent. (The others use baking powder or baking soda.) The steam is produced from the high amount of liquid present in popover batter. It is this steam that gives the popover its characteristic hollow interior. The crispy outside structure comes from eggs and gluten. If they turn out any other way, they just aren't popovers.

Failure of popovers to "pop" is probably due to one of two reasons. One is underbeating. The batter should be beaten vigorously to develop the gluten. The second reason may be the oven temperature. It must be hot enough to achieve a sudden rise to open up the inside of the popover.

279 *Popovers*

3 eggs
1 cup milk
2 tablespoons vegetable oil
½ teaspoon salt
1 cup sifted all-purpose flour

1. Beat eggs in a mixing bowl. Beat in milk, oil, and salt.
2. Beat in flour until mixture is smooth and well blended.
3. For best results, preheat iron popover pan after thoroughly coating pan wells with shortening or oil. Pour batter into 8 popover-pan wells or 8 greased heat-resistant custard cups.
4. Bake at 400°F 35 to 40 minutes, or until popovers are puffed and golden brown. Serve hot with butter.

8 popovers

Note: For a crispier popover, make slit in side of each baked popover to allow the steam to escape. Return popovers to oven for 10 minutes with the heat turned off.

280 *Sunshine Corn Muffins*

1½ cups all-purpose flour
1½ cups yellow cornmeal
  1 tablespoon baking powder
  ⅛ teaspoon salt
  1 cup milk
  ½ cup honey
  ½ cup vegetable oil
  2 eggs

1. Combine dry ingredients in a mixing bowl.
2. Combine remaining ingredients in a separate bowl; beat well.
3. Add liquid ingredients to dry ingredients; stir just until flour is moistened. Spoon into 24 greased muffin-pan wells.
4. Bake at 400°F 15 to 20 minutes, or until wooden pick inserted in muffin comes out clean.

2 dozen

281

Sunshine Cornbread: Follow recipe for Sunshine Corn Muffins, except pour mixture into a greased 9-inch square pan. Bake at 400°F 30 minutes, or until done.

6 servings

282 *Lemon Chiffon Muffins*

½ cup softened butter or margarine
½ cup sugar
  Grated peel of 1 lemon (about 1 tablespoon)
2 tablespoons milk
2 eggs, separated
3 tablespoons lemon juice (about 1 lemon)
1 cup all-purpose flour
1 teaspoon baking powder
¼ teaspoon salt
¼ cup chopped nuts
1 tablespoon sugar
1 teaspoon nutmeg

1. Cream butter, sugar, lemon peel, milk, and egg yolks in a mixing bowl until light and fluffy. Beat in lemon juice.
2. Combine flour, baking powder, and salt in a separate bowl. Add to batter and mix just until blended.
3. Beat egg whites until soft peaks form; fold into batter.
4. Spoon into 12 greased muffin-pan wells. Sprinkle with a mixture of nuts, sugar, and nutmeg.
5. Bake at 375°F 15 to 20 minutes, or until done.

1 dozen

283 *Maple Tree Muffins*

2 cups all-purpose flour
1 tablespoon baking powder
½ teaspoon salt
½ cup chopped nuts
⅔ cup milk
½ cup pure maple syrup or maple-blended syrup
1 egg
¼ cup vegetable oil

1. Combine flour, baking powder, salt, and nuts in a mixing bowl.
2. Combine remaining ingredients in a separate bowl; beat well.
3. Add liquid ingredients to dry ingredients; stir just until flour is moistened. Spoon into 12 greased muffin-pan wells.
4. Bake at 400°F 15 to 20 minutes, or until a wooden pick inserted in muffin comes out clean.

1 dozen

284 *Bran-Oatmeal Muffins*

¾ cup bran cereal
¾ cup milk
¼ cup butter or margarine
¼ cup molasses
1 egg
1 cup all-purpose flour

1. Combine bran cereal and milk to soften.
2. Beat butter and molasses together in a bowl. Add egg and mix well. Add bran-milk mixture.
3. Mix flour, sugar, baking powder, baking soda, and salt. Add dry ingredients to bran mixture; stir just until moistened. Stir in oats.

2 tablespoons sugar
1 teaspoon baking powder
½ teaspoon baking soda
½ teaspoon salt
1 cup uncooked oats

4. Spoon mixture into 12 greased medium-sized muffin-pan wells.
5. Bake at 400°F 15 to 18 minutes, or until golden brown.

1 dozen

Pancakes and waffles from a simple batter make possible a delicious array of combinations. Pancakes can be rolled, stuffed, or stacked with creamed meats or vegetables or sweet syrups for breakfast through dinner. You can add chopped nuts, raisins, coconut, fruits, and herbs to change the basic batter.

Two things to remember to make perfect pancakes or waffles. The batter should not be overmixed and the temperature of the griddle must be right. The dry ingredients are stirred with the liquid until just blended, and the batter should still be lumpy. You can make pancakes just how you like them, either thick or thin, by adding more or less liquid to the recipe.

The griddle is hot enough for baking when drops of cold water sprinkled on the surface dance in small beads.

285 *Pancakes*

1½ cups sifted all-purpose flour
1 tablespoon sugar
1½ teaspoons baking powder
¼ teaspoon salt
2 egg yolks, beaten
1⅓ cups milk
2 tablespoons butter or margarine, melted
2 egg whites

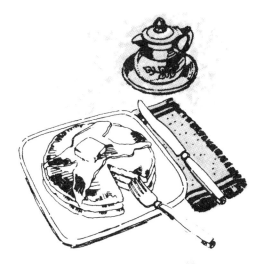

1. Start heating griddle or heavy skillet over low heat.
2. Mix flour, sugar, baking powder, and salt in a bowl.
3. Combine egg yolks, milk, and butter. Add liquid to flour mixture and beat until blended.
4. Beat egg whites until rounded peaks are formed. Spread beaten egg whites over batter and fold gently together.
5. Test griddle; it is hot enough for baking when drops of water sprinkled on surface dance in small beads. Lightly grease griddle, if so directed by manufacturer.
6. Pour batter onto griddle into pools about 4 inches in diameter, leaving at least 1 inch between cakes. Turn pancakes as they become puffy and full of bubbles. Turn only once.
7. Serve hot.

About 12 pancakes

Buttermilk Pancakes: Follow recipe for Pancakes; substitute ½ **teaspoon baking soda** for the baking powder and **buttermilk** for the milk. Do not separate eggs. Beat eggs with buttermilk and proceed as in step 3 above. 286

Cornmeal Pancakes: Follow recipe for Pancakes. Decrease flour to ¾ cup. Mix ¾ **cup yellow cornmeal** into dry ingredients. 287

Rye Pancakes: Follow recipe for Buttermilk Pancakes. Decrease flour to ¾ cup and mix in ¾ **cup rye flour.** Blend **3 tablespoons molasses** into buttermilk-egg mixture. 288

Blueberry Pancakes: Follow recipe for Pancakes; gently fold **2 cups rinsed and drained blueberries** into batter after folding in beaten egg whites. 289

Jiffy quick breads from convenience foods give you a head start on the road to home baking. Some of the following recipes use a biscuit mix which has the fat and leavening agents already preblended for you. Because most of them are mixed all in one bowl and then baked, you can enjoy hot, homemade breads in a twinkling.

290 Homemade Croutons

Day-old bread slices
Softened butter or margarine

1. Spread both sides of bread slices with butter.
2. Stack slices and cut into cubes.
3. Spread over baking sheet.
4. Bake at 275°F 25 to 35 minutes, stirring occasionally, until dry and lightly browned.

Parmesan Croutons: Follow recipe for Homemade Croutons, except sprinkle both sides of bread with **grated Parmesan cheese** before cubing and baking.

291

Crusty Croutons: Follow recipe for Homemade Croutons except use **French bread** slices instead of day-old bread slices and do not cube bread. Turn slices over once during baking.

292

293 Poppy Seed Cheese Bread

1 cup shredded Cheddar cheese (4 ounces)
1 cup all-purpose biscuit mix
⅓ cup milk
1 egg
¼ cup chopped onion
1 tablespoon poppy seed

1. Combine ½ cup cheese and biscuit mix in a mixing bowl.
2. Add milk; stir just until flour is moistened. Pat dough over bottom of a greased 8- or 9-inch pie plate.
3. Combine remaining cheese, egg, and onion. Spread over biscuit dough. Sprinkle with poppy seed.
4. Bake at 425°F 15 to 20 minutes.

About 6 servings

294 Sesame Seed Twists

2 cups biscuit mix
¼ cup chilled butter
3 tablespoons melted butter
2 tablespoons sesame seed
1 egg yolk
1 teaspoon milk

1. Prepare biscuit mix as directed on package for rolled biscuits. Roll out on a lightly floured surface into a 12-inch square.
2. Thinly slice 3 tablespoons of butter and place on half of dough; fold other half over it. With rolling pin, gently seal open edges. Repeat procedure, using remaining chilled butter. Fold other half over, forming a 6-inch square.
3. Roll dough into a 12-inch square. Divide in half. Set one half in refrigerator.
4. Brush surface with melted butter. Sprinkle with some of the sesame seed. Cut into twelve 6×1-inch strips. Twist each strip and place on an ungreased baking sheet. Brush with mixture of egg yolk and milk. Sprinkle with more sesame seed. Repeat with other half.
5. Bake at 425°F 10 minutes.

2 dozen twists

Roast Leg of Lamb with Spicy Wine Sauce, page 184
Peach Wine Mold, page 27

295 Quick Strips

1 loaf unsliced white bread
½ cup butter or margarine, melted
¼ teaspoon garlic salt
  Grated Parmesan cheese, sesame
    seed, or poppy seed

1. Cut four 1¼-inch slices from loaf of bread. Cut each slice into 1-inch strips.
2. Combine butter and garlic salt in a 13×9×2-inch baking pan.
3. Toss bread strips in butter; sprinkle with cheese.
4. Bake at 350°F 20 minutes.

About 20 strips

296 Garlic Bread

1 loaf French bread
½ cup butter or margarine, softened
¼ teaspoon garlic powder or garlic salt

1. Slice bread almost through to bottom crust at 1-inch intervals.
2. Thoroughly combine butter and garlic powder. Spread on both sides of each bread slice.
3. Place on baking sheet.
4. Bake at 350°F 15 to 20 minutes, or until hot and crispy.

About 1 dozen slices

297 La Verde Slices

1 loaf Italian bread, cut diagonally in 1-inch slices
½ cup softened butter or margarine
2 tablespoons finely chopped green pepper
2 tablespoons finely chopped onion

1. Broil bread slices until golden brown on each side.
2. Combine butter, green pepper, and onion. Spread on one side of each slice.
3. Broil until lightly browned.

About 1 dozen slices

298 Sugar Buns

1 cup firmly packed brown sugar
⅓ cup butter or margarine
1 tablespoon corn syrup
½ cup chopped pecans
2 cans refrigerated dough for butterflake dinner rolls

1. Combine brown sugar, butter, and corn syrup in a saucepan; bring to boiling, stirring occasionally.
2. Stir in pecans.
3. Divide mixture evenly among 12 muffin-pan wells.
4. Place 2 rolls in each cup.
5. Bake at 375°F 15 minutes. Remove from pans immediately.

1 dozen buns

299 Cranberry Swirl Rolls

1 package (about 14 ounces) hot roll mix
1 can (16 ounces) jellied cranberry sauce
¼ cup firmly packed brown sugar
1 teaspoon cinnamon

1. Prepare hot roll mix following package directions.
2. Roll half of dough at a time into a 12×8-inch rectangle. Spread each rectangle with cranberry sauce to within 1 inch of edge. Sprinkle with brown sugar and cinnamon. Starting with a 12-inch side, roll up jelly-roll fashion. Seal edges. Cut each into 1-inch slices and place cut-side down on greased baking sheets.
3. Bake at 375°F 10 minutes, or until done.

About 2 dozen rolls

Lamb Curry, page 177

300 Cinnamon Swirl Date Ring

3 cups all-purpose biscuit mix
¼ cup sugar
¼ cup butter or margarine
¾ cup milk
Cinnamon-Date Filling

1. Combine biscuit mix and sugar in a mixing bowl; cut in butter until mixture resembles rice kernels.
2. Gently stir in milk just until ingredients are moistened.
3. Drop half of dough by tablespoonfuls into a greased 6-cup ring mold. Sprinkle with Cinnamon-Date Filling. Top with remaining dough.
4. Bake at 350°F 25 to 30 minutes, or until a wooden pick inserted in cake comes out clean. Invert mold onto plate; leave over cake 5 minutes. Serve warm.

One coffeecake ring

Cinnamon-Date Filling: Combine ½ cup melted butter or margarine, ½ cup chopped dates, ¼ cup chopped nuts, and 1 teaspoon cinnamon.

Doughnuts are more than a sweet treat during coffee breaks; they help bring people together for enjoyable conversations and can even be the whole reason for the party.

Fry cakes, as they are sometimes called, can be rolled and cut into shapes, or dropped by spoonfuls into the hot fat. In both cases the temperature of the fat is very important. The fat should be heated slowly and be maintained at 375°F throughout the cooking. If the temperature is too low, the dough will soak up too much fat; if it is too hot, the outside will brown before the inside has completely cooked.

Pour in enough oil or fat to half fill a 3- to 4-quart saucepan. This leaves enough room for the bubbling action of the doughnuts cooking.

It is helpful to have a wire basket or slotted spoon to remove the doughnuts from the oil to absorbent paper to drain.

301 Lemon Doughnut Balls

2 cups all-purpose flour
¼ cup sugar
1 tablespoon baking powder
1 teaspoon salt
½ teaspoon baking soda
½ cup milk
¼ cup melted butter or margarine
2 tablespoons grated lemon peel
¼ cup lemon juice
1 egg
½ cup flaked coconut
Vegetable oil or shortening
   heated to 375°F
Confectioners' sugar

1. Combine flour, sugar, baking powder, salt, and baking soda in a mixing bowl.
2. Combine milk, butter, lemon peel and juice, egg, and coconut in a separate bowl; beat well.
3. Add liquid ingredients to dry ingredients. Stir just until flour is moistened.
4. Drop by teaspoonfuls into hot oil. Fry 3 minutes, or until golden brown. Drain on paper towels. Sprinkle with confectioners' sugar.

About 3 dozen

302 *Filled Berlin Doughnuts (Bismarcks)*

A hint of orange and rum extract flavors these puffy Bismarcks. Fill them with your favorite jelly.

1 package active dry yeast
¼ cup warm water
½ cup sugar
1 teaspoon salt
⅓ cup butter
1 tablespoon orange juice
2 teaspoons rum extract
1 cup milk, scalded
3½ to 4 cups all-purpose flour
2 eggs, well beaten
    Fat for deep frying heated to
      375°F
    Jam or jelly

1. Soften yeast in the warm water.
2. Put ½ cup sugar, the salt, butter, orange juice and rum extract into a large bowl. Pour scalded milk over ingredients in bowl. Stir until butter is melted. Cool to lukewarm.
3. Blend in 1 cup of the flour and beat until smooth. Stir in yeast. Add about half of the remaining flour and beat until smooth. Beat in the eggs. Then beat in enough of the remaining flour to make a soft dough.
4. Turn dough onto a lightly floured surface and let rest 5 to 10 minutes.
5. Knead until smooth and elastic. Form into a ball and put into a greased deep bowl; turn dough to bring greased surface to top. Cover; let rise in a warm place until double in bulk.
6. Punch down dough. Turn dough onto a lightly floured surface and roll ½ inch thick. Cut dough into rounds with a 3-inch cutter. Cover with waxed paper and let rise on rolling surface away from drafts and direct heat, until double in bulk (30 to 45 minutes).
7. About 20 minutes before deep frying, heat fat.
8. Fry doughnuts in heated fat. Put in only as many doughnuts at one time as will float uncrowded one layer deep in the fat. Fry 2 to 3 minutes, or until lightly browned; turn doughnuts with a fork or tongs when they rise to the surface and several times during cooking (do not pierce). Lift from fat; drain over fat for a few seconds before removing to absorbent paper. Cool.
9. Cut a slit through to the center in the side of each doughnut. Force about ½ teaspoon jam or jelly into center and press lightly to close slit. (A pastry bag and tube may be used to force jelly or jam into slit.) Shake 2 or 3 Bismarcks at one time in bag containing **sugar**.

About 2 dozen

303 *Crispy Breadsticks*

1 cup whole wheat flour
1 package active dry yeast
1 tablespoon sugar
1 teaspoon salt
⅔ cup hot water
2 tablespoons vegetable oil
1 to 1¼ cups all-purpose flour

1. Stir together whole wheat flour, yeast, sugar, and salt in a mixing bowl.
2. Blend in water and oil; beat until smooth.
3. Stir in enough flour to form a soft dough.
4. Turn onto a floured surface; continue to work in flour until dough is stiff enough to knead. Knead until smooth and elastic (about 5 minutes), working in as much flour as possible. (The more flour, the crispier the bread sticks.)
5. Cover with bowl; let rest about 30 minutes.
6. Divide dough in quarters. Divide each quarter into 8 equal pieces. For ease in shaping, allow dough to rest about 10 minutes. Roll each piece with palms of hands into 10-inch lengths.
7. Place on greased baking sheets about ½ inch apart. If desired, brush with a mixture of 1 egg white and 1 teaspoon water.
8. Bake at 325°F 20 minutes, or until golden brown and crispy.

32 bread sticks

304 *Peasant Black Bread*

3½ cups rye flour
½ cup unsweetened cocoa
¼ cup sugar
3 tablespoons caraway seed
2 packages active dry yeast
1 tablespoon instant coffee
    (powder or crystals)
2 teaspoons salt
2½ cups hot water (120°-130°F)
¼ cup vinegar
¼ cup dark molasses
¼ cup vegetable oil or melted
    butter
3½ to 4½ cups unbleached or
    all-purpose flour

1. Thoroughly mix rye flour, cocoa, sugar, caraway, yeast, coffee, and salt in a large mixing bowl.
2. Stir in water, vinegar, molasses, and oil; beat until smooth.
3. Stir in enough unbleached flour to make a soft dough.
4. Turn onto a floured surface. Knead until smooth and elastic (about 5 minutes).
5. Place in an oiled bowl; turn to oil top of dough. Cover; let rise in warm place until doubled (about 1 hour).
6. Punch dough down. Divide in half; shape each half into a ball and place in center of 2 greased 8-inch round cake pans. Cover; let rise until double in bulk (about 1 hour).
7. Bake at 350°F 40 to 45 minutes, or until done.

2 loaves

305 *Grandma Louise's Banana Loaf*

1 cup sugar
½ cup shortening
1 cup mashed fully ripe bananas
    (2 to 3 bananas)
1 egg
¼ cup buttermilk
1¾ cups all-purpose flour
1½ teaspoons baking powder
1 teaspoon baking soda
½ teaspoon salt

1. Combine sugar, shortening, bananas, egg, and buttermilk in a mixing bowl; beat well.
2. Blend remaining ingredients, add to banana mixture, and mix until blended (about 1 minute).
3. Turn into a greased 9×5×3-inch loaf pan.
4. Bake at 350°F 45 to 50 minutes, or until done.

1 loaf

306 *New England Blueberry Muffins*

In New England, they fill the muffin cups right up to the top with batter to produce these giant round-top muffins. If you like yours more petite, fill the muffin cups ⅔ full and reduce baking time by 5 minutes.

1 cup sugar
½ cup softened butter or margarine
2 eggs
½ cup milk
2 cups all-purpose flour
2 teaspoons baking powder
½ teaspoon salt
1 to 1½ cups fresh or frozen blueberries

1. Combine sugar, butter, eggs, and milk in a mixing bowl; beat well.
2. Blend flour, baking powder, and salt; add and mix until blended (about 1 minute). Fold in blueberries.
3. Spoon into 12 well-greased muffin cups, filling almost to the top of the cup.
4. Bake at 375°F 20 to 25 minutes.

12 large muffins

307 *Indian Flat Bread (Nan)*

From the northwest region of India comes Indian Flat Bread, baked at a high temperature in clay ovens. This is a richer, more sophisticated bread than the unleavened chapati eaten by most Indians. Both breads are literally the staff of life.

1 cup all-purpose flour
1 package active dry yeast
2 teaspoons salt
1 cup hot water (120°-130°F)
¼ cup buttermilk or yogurt
1 egg (at room temperature)
2 tablespoons vegetable oil
1 tablespoon honey or sugar
2 to 3 cups all-purpose flour
Melted butter (optional)
Cornmeal or sesame or poppy seeds (optional)

1. Combine 1 cup flour, yeast, and salt in a mixing bowl.
2. Stir in water, buttermilk, egg, oil, and honey; beat until smooth.
3. Stir in enough remaining flour to form a soft, sticky dough.
4. Turn onto a floured surface; continue to work in flour until dough is stiff enough to knead. Knead until smooth and elastic, but still soft (3 to 5 minutes).
5. Place in an oiled bowl; turning once to oil top of dough. Cover; let rise until double in bulk (about 45 minutes).
6. Punch dough down. Shape into 16 equal balls. Let rest 5 minutes. Roll out each ball to a ¼-inch-thick round. If desired, brush with melted butter and sprinkle with cornmeal, sesame, or poppy seeds. Set on baking sheets.
7. Bake at 450°F 5 to 8 minutes.

16 round loaves

308 *Pocket Bread*

2 cups all-purpose flour
2 packages active dry yeast
2 tablespoons sugar or honey
2 teaspoons salt
2½ cups hot water (120°-130°F)
¼ cup vegetable oil
5½ to 6 cups all-purpose flour

1. Combine 2 cups flour, yeast, sugar, and salt in a large mixing bowl.
2. Stir in water and oil; beat until smooth.
3. Stir in enough remaining flour to make a soft dough.
4. Turn onto a floured surface; continue to work in flour until stiff enough to knead. Knead until smooth and elastic (about 5 minutes).
5. Place in an oiled bowl; turn to oil top of dough. Cover; let rise in a warm place until double in bulk (about 45 minutes).
6. Punch dough down. Divide in half. Divide each half into 10 equal pieces. Roll each piece into a ball. Let dough rest 5 minutes. Roll balls into 3- or 4-inch rounds, ⅛ inch thick. Place on greased baking sheets. Cover; let rise 30 minutes (see Note).
7. Bake at 450°F 5 to 8 minutes, or until puffed and brown.

20 pocket breads

Note: Avoid pinching or creasing dough after rolling, or bread will not puff properly.

Pasta & Grains

309 *Lemony Meat Sauce with Spaghetti*

2 pounds ground beef
1½ cups finely chopped onion
1¼ cups chopped green pepper
2 cloves garlic, minced
¼ cup firmly packed brown sugar
1 teaspoon salt
¼ teaspoon ground black pepper
1 teaspoon thyme, crushed
½ teaspoon basil, crushed
2 cups water
2 cans (8 ounces each) tomato sauce
2 cans (6 ounces each) tomato paste
1 can (6 ounces) sliced broiled
   mushrooms (undrained)
1 tablespoon grated lemon peel
¼ cup lemon juice
1 pound enriched spaghetti
   Shredded Parmesan cheese

1. Put meat, onion, green pepper, and garlic into a heated large heavy saucepot or Dutch oven. Cook 10 to 15 minutes, cutting meat apart with fork or spoon.
2. Stir in brown sugar, salt, pepper, thyme, basil, water, tomato sauce, and tomato paste. Cover and simmer 2 to 3 hours, stirring occasionally. About 30 minutes before serving, mix in mushrooms with liquid and lemon peel and juice.
3. Meanwhile, cook spaghetti following package directions; drain.
4. Spoon sauce over hot spaghetti and sprinkle generously with cheese.

10 to 12 servings

310 *Polenta*

2 tablespoons olive oil
1 clove garlic, crushed
1 can (8 ounces) sliced mushrooms,
    drained, or 1 pound fresh
    mushrooms, sliced
1 can (16 ounces) tomatoes
    (undrained)
⅓ cup tomato paste
1 teaspoon salt
¼ teaspoon ground pepper
3 cups water
1½ teaspoons salt
1 cup enriched cornmeal
1 cup cold water
    Grated Parmesan or Romano
    cheese

1. Heat olive oil and garlic in a skillet. Add mushrooms and cook about 5 minutes, stirring occasionally. When lightly browned, stir in tomatoes with liquid, tomato paste, salt, and pepper. Simmer 15 to 20 minutes.
2. Meanwhile, bring 3 cups water and 1½ teaspoons salt to boiling in a saucepan. Mix cornmeal and 1 cup cold water; stir into boiling water. Continue boiling, stirring constantly to prevent sticking, until mixture is thick. Cover, reduce heat, and cook over low heat 10 minutes or longer.
3. Turn cooked cornmeal onto warm serving platter and top with the tomato-mushroom mixture. Sprinkle with grated cheese. Serve at once.

6 to 8 servings

311 *Fried Cornmeal Mush*

1 cup enriched yellow cornmeal
1 teaspoon salt
2¼ cups milk
1½ cups water
    Butter or margarine
    Syrup or honey

1. Combine cornmeal, salt, and 1 cup milk. Pour remaining milk and water into a saucepan and bring to boiling. Add cornmeal mixture gradually; cook and stir until thickened. Cover and cook over low heat 10 minutes. Pour into a buttered loaf pan, mold, or other container, and chill.
2. Turn out of pan and slice ½ inch thick. Cook on lightly buttered griddle or skillet until crisp and golden, turning once. Serve with butter and syrup or honey.

6 to 8 servings

312 *Bulgur, Pilaf Style*

½ cup butter or margarine
½ cup chopped onion
½ cup chopped green pepper
2 cups bulgur (cracked wheat)
4 cups boiling water
4 chicken bouillon cubes
1 teaspoon salt
¼ teaspoon ground black pepper
1 cup shredded carrot

1. Heat butter in a skillet with heat-resistant handle. Mix in onion and green pepper. Cook until onion is tender.
2. Stir in bulgur, cover, reduce heat, and cook 10 minutes over low heat; stir once or twice to prevent sticking.
3. Add boiling water and bouillon cubes; stir until cubes are dissolved; cover tightly.
4. Cook in a 350°F oven 30 minutes. Stir in salt, pepper, and carrot. Continue cooking 15 minutes, or until liquid is absorbed and bulgur is tender.

About 8 servings

313 *Baked Hominy Grits*

1 quart milk
½ cup butter or margarine, cut in
    pieces
1 cup enriched white hominy grits,
    quick or long-cooking
1 teaspoon salt

1. Heat milk to boiling. Add butter; then add hominy grits gradually, stirring constantly. Bring to boiling and boil 3 minutes, or until mixture becomes thick, stirring constantly. Remove from heat; add salt.
2. Beat mixture at high speed of an electric mixer 5 minutes, or until grits have a creamy appearance. Turn mixture into a greased 1½-quart casserole.
3. Bake at 350°F about 1 hour. Serve hot.

6 to 8 servings

314 *Spaghetti à la King Crab*

Parmesan Croutons
2 cans (7½ ounces each) Alaska king crab or 1 pound frozen Alaska king crab
2 tablespoons olive oil
½ cup butter or margarine
4 cloves garlic, minced
1 bunch green onions, sliced
2 medium tomatoes, peeled and diced
½ cup chopped parsley
2 tablespoons lemon juice
¼ teaspoon basil
¼ teaspoon thyme
½ teaspoon salt
1 pound enriched spaghetti

1. Prepare Parmesan Croutons; set aside.
2. Drain canned crab and slice. Or, defrost, drain, and slice frozen crab.
3. Heat olive oil, butter, and garlic in a saucepan. Add crab, green onions, tomatoes, parsley, lemon juice, basil, thyme, and salt. Heat gently 8 to 10 minutes.
4. Meanwhile, cook spaghetti following package directions; drain.
5. Toss spaghetti with king crab sauce. Top with Parmesan Croutons. Pass additional grated Parmesan cheese.

About 6 servings

Parmesan Croutons: Put **3 tablespoons butter** into a shallow baking pan. Set in a 350°F oven until butter is melted. Slice **French bread** into small cubes to make about 1 cup. Toss with melted butter. Return to oven until golden (about 6 minutes). Sprinkle with **2 tablespoons grated Parmesan cheese** and toss.

315 *White Clam Sauce for Linguine*

12 ounces enriched linguine
¼ cup olive oil
½ cup chopped onion
¼ cup snipped parsley
3 cloves garlic, minced
2 tablespoons flour
¼ to ½ teaspoon salt
Few grains pepper
3 cans (8 ounces each) minced clams, drained; reserve 1½ cups liquid

1. Cook linguine following package directions; drain and keep hot.
2. Meanwhile, heat oil in a large skillet. Add onion, parsley, and garlic; cook about 3 minutes, stirring occasionally.
3. Mix in flour, salt, and pepper; cook until bubbly. Add reserved clam liquid gradually, while blending thoroughly. Bring rapidly to boiling, stirring constantly, and boil 1 to 2 minutes. Mix in the minced clams and heat; do not boil.
4. Serve clam sauce on the hot linguine.

6 servings

316 *Fiesta Zucchini-Tomato Casserole*

1½ quarts water
2 packets dry onion soup mix
4 ounces enriched spaghetti, broken
⅓ cup butter or margarine
⅔ cup coarsely chopped onion
1 cup green pepper strips
2 or 3 zucchini (about ¾ pound), washed, ends trimmed, and zucchini cut in about ½-inch slices

1. Bring water to boiling in a saucepot. Add onion soup mix and spaghetti to the boiling water. Partially cover and boil gently about 10 minutes, or until spaghetti is tender. Drain and set spaghetti mixture aside; reserve liquid.*
2. Heat butter in a large heavy skillet. Add onion and green pepper and cook about 3 minutes, or until tender. Add zucchini; cover and cook 5 minutes. Stir in tomatoes, parsley, seasoned salt, and pepper. Cover and cook about 2 minutes, or just until heated.
3. Turn contents of skillet into a 2-quart casserole. Add

4 medium tomatoes, peeled and cut
   in wedges
¼ cup snipped parsley
1 teaspoon seasoned salt
⅛ teaspoon ground black pepper
⅔ cup shredded Swiss cheese

drained spaghetti and toss gently to mix. Sprinkle cheese over top. If necessary to reheat mixture, set in a 350°F oven until thoroughly heated before placing under broiler.

4. Set under broiler with top about 5 inches from heat until cheese is melted and lightly browned.

6 to 8 servings

*The strained soup may be stored for future use as broth or for cooking vegetables, preparing gravy or sauce, or as desired.

317 *Rice Pilaf Deluxe*

⅓ cup butter
1½ cups uncooked enriched white rice
⅓ cup chopped onion
1½ teaspoons salt
3 cans (13¾ ounces each) chicken
   broth
¾ cup golden raisins
3 tablespoons butter
¾ cup coarsely chopped pecans
½ teaspoon salt

1. Heat ⅓ cup butter in a heavy skillet. Add rice and onion and cook until lightly browned, stirring frequently.
2. Add 1½ teaspoons salt, chicken broth, and raisins; cover, bring to boiling, reduce heat, and simmer until rice is tender and liquid is absorbed (20 to 25 minutes).
3. Just before serving, heat 3 tablespoons butter in a small skillet. Add pecans and ½ teaspoon salt; heat 2 to 3 minutes, stirring occasionally.
4. Serve rice topped with salted pecans.

About 8 servings

318 *Spanish Rice au Gratin*

½ cup uncooked enriched white rice
1 cup water
½ teaspoon salt
1½ tablespoons butter or margarine
½ cup chopped onion
½ cup chopped celery
⅓ cup chopped green pepper
1 cup canned tomatoes, cut in
   pieces
½ teaspoon salt
½ teaspoon monosodium glutamate
1 teaspoon sugar
¾ teaspoon chili powder
¼ teaspoon Worcestershire sauce
1 cup (about 4 ounces) shredded
   Cheddar cheese

1. Combine rice, water, and ½ teaspoon salt in a saucepan. Bring to boiling, reduce heat, and simmer, covered, about 14 minutes.
2. Meanwhile, heat butter in a skillet. Mix in onion, celery, and green pepper. Cook until vegetables are tender. Mix in cooked rice, tomatoes, ½ teaspoon salt, monosodium glutamate, sugar, chili powder, and Worcestershire sauce. Simmer until thick.
3. Turn mixture into a greased baking dish. Top evenly with cheese.
4. Place under broiler 3 to 4 inches from heat until cheese is melted.

3 or 4 servings

319 *Cheese Risotta*

  1 **cup chopped onion**
  ¼ **cup butter or margarine**
  1 **cup uncooked white rice**
  1 **can (16 ounces) tomatoes**
      (undrained)
1½ **cups water**
  2 **chicken bouillon cubes**
  1 **can (3 ounces) mushroom slices,**
      drained
      Dash pepper
      Few grains saffron (optional)
  2 **cups (8 ounces) shredded sharp**
      Cheddar cheese

1. Sauté onion in butter in a skillet. Stir in rice; cook until lightly browned.
2. Add remaining ingredients, except cheese. Bring to a boil, stirring until bouillon cubes dissolve.
3. Place half the rice mixture in a 1½-quart casserole. Top with 1½ cups cheese. Evenly spoon remaining rice mixture over cheese.
4. Bake, covered, at 350°F 45 minutes, or until rice is tender. Remove cover; sprinkle with remaining ½ cup cheese. Bake an additional 5 minutes, or until cheese is melted.

6 servings

320 *Baked Rice*

  1 **cup uncooked white rice**
  1 **can (5 ounces) water chestnuts,**
      drained and sliced
  2 **cups boiling water**
  1 **package (1⅜ ounces) dry onion**
      soup mix
  2 **tablespoons chopped pimento**

1. Place rice in bottom of a 1½-quart baking dish. Toast at 350°F 10 minutes, stirring occasionally until lightly browned.
2. Stir in remaining ingredients.
3. Bake, covered, at 350°F 45 minutes, or until rice is tender.

6 servings

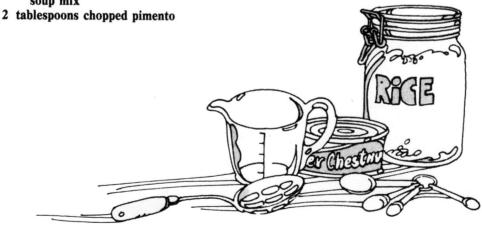

321 *Mushroom-Rice Casserole*

1 cup uncooked white rice
½ cup slivered almonds
1 small onion, chopped
1 can (4 ounces) sliced mushrooms, drained*
¼ cup butter or margarine
2 cups water
2 chicken bouillon cubes
2 tablespoons lemon juice
1 teaspoon soy sauce
Dash pepper
4 bacon slices, cooked and crumbled
2 tablespoons snipped parsley

1. Sauté rice, almonds, onion, and mushrooms in butter in a skillet. Stir in water, bouillon cubes, lemon juice, soy sauce, and pepper.
2. Heat to boiling. Cover and reduce heat to low. Cook until liquid is absorbed (about 20 minutes).
3. Stir in crumbled bacon and parsley. Put into a 1½-quart casserole.
4. Bake, covered, at 325°F 20 minutes, or until heated through.

6 servings

* The drained mushroom liquid can be used as part of the 2 cups water called for in the recipe.

322 *Italian Rice Casserole*

½ cup chopped onion
2 tablespoons oil
1 cup (4 ounces) shredded Cheddar cheese
1 cup sliced fresh mushrooms
¾ cup sliced pitted ripe olives
1 can (16 ounces) stewed tomatoes
1½ cups boiling water
1 package (6 ounces) long-grain and wild rice mix

1. Sauté onion in oil in a skillet. Combine with remaining ingredients. Put into a 2-quart baking dish.
2. Bake, covered, at 350°F 1 hour, or until rice is tender.

6 servings

323 *Rice Loaf*

2 cups cooked brown rice
½ cup finely chopped onion
½ cup finely chopped pecans
2 tablespoons snipped parsley
½ teaspoon salt
¼ teaspoon thyme
½ cup milk
1 egg, well beaten

1. Combine all ingredients. Put into a 1-quart casserole.
2. Bake, uncovered, at 350°F 35 to 40 minutes, or until set.

6 servings

324 Brunch Pilaf

1 package (6 ounces) long-grain and
    wild rice mix
½ pound pork sausage links, cut in
    1-inch pieces
½ pound fresh mushrooms, sliced
3 tablespoons butter or margarine
½ teaspoon salt
¼ teaspoon pepper
2 teaspoons instant minced onion
½ pound chicken livers, cut up

1. Prepare rice according to package directions.
2. Brown sausage in a skillet about 15 minutes. Drain and set aside.
3. Sauté mushrooms in 2 tablespoons butter. Toss with ¼ teaspoon salt, pepper, and minced onion; set aside.
4. Sauté chicken livers in remaining 1 tablespoon butter until lightly browned. Sprinkle with remaining ¼ teaspoon salt.
5. Combine all ingredients and put into a 1½-quart casserole.
6. Bake, covered, at 325°F 30 minutes, or until heated through.

6 to 8 servings

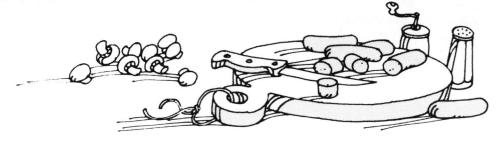

325 Mushroom Wild Rice

1 package (4 ounces) wild rice
1 medium green pepper, chopped
1 large onion, chopped
½ cup chopped celery
¼ cup butter or margarine
1 egg, beaten
1 can (10¾ ounces) condensed cream
    of mushroom soup
¼ cup sliced almonds
2 tablespoons snipped parsley

1. Prepare rice according to package directions.
2. Sauté green pepper, onion, and celery in butter in a skillet. Add to rice along with beaten egg. Put into a greased 1½-quart casserole.
3. Top with mushroom soup; mix slightly. Sprinkle with almonds.
4. Bake, covered, at 350°F 30 minutes, or until heated through. Sprinkle with parsley.

6 servings

326 Wild Rice Casserole

1 cup wild rice
2 tablespoons chopped onion
½ pound fresh mushrooms, sliced
½ cup butter or margarine
3 cups broth*
1 teaspoon salt
½ cup toasted slivered almonds

1. Sauté rice, onion, and mushrooms in butter in a skillet. Add broth and salt. Pour into a 1½-quart casserole.
2. Bake, covered, at 325°F 1 hour. Remove cover; top with almonds. Bake an additional 15 minutes, or until rice is tender. If desired, top with fresh tomato wedges.

6 servings

* Use beef broth when serving with meat and chicken broth when serving with poultry.

327 *Egg Noodle Supreme*

2 cups cooked noodles
¼ cup finely chopped green onion
1 garlic clove, minced
½ teaspoon tarragon
½ cup (2 ounces) shredded Colby cheese
½ cup milk
1 tablespoon butter or margarine, melted
½ cup dairy sour cream

1. Combine all ingredients, except sour cream. Put into a 1-quart casserole.
2. Bake, covered, at 350°F 25 minutes. Remove cover; stir in sour cream. Bake an additional 5 minutes, or until heated through.

4 servings

328 *Noodles au Gratin*

1 small onion, chopped
¼ cup butter or margarine
4 cups noodles, cooked and drained
½ cup dairy sour cream
6 slices (1 ounce each) American cheese, cut in pieces
½ teaspoon salt
½ cup milk
Paprika

1. Sauté onion in butter in a skillet. Combine with noodles, sour cream, cheese, and salt. Put into a 1½-quart casserole.
2. Pour milk over all. Sprinkle with paprika.
3. Bake, covered, at 350°F 40 minutes, or until golden brown.

6 to 8 servings

329 *Noodles Romanoff*

4 cups noodles, cooked and drained
1½ cups (12 ounces) cream-style cottage cheese
1 cup dairy sour cream
¼ cup finely chopped onion
1 teaspoon Worcestershire sauce
½ teaspoon salt
¼ teaspoon white pepper
½ cup (2 ounces) shredded Cheddar cheese
2 tablespoons snipped parsley

1. Combine all ingredients, except Cheddar cheese and parsley. Put into a 2-quart casserole. Sprinkle with cheese.
2. Bake, covered, at 325°F 40 minutes, or until heated through. Sprinkle with parsley.

6 servings

330 *Spaghetti Fromaggi*

¼ cup chopped onion
¼ cup chopped green pepper
¼ cup butter or margarine
¼ cup flour
1 teaspoon salt
¼ teaspoon pepper
3½ cups milk
1 cup (4 ounces) shredded Swiss cheese
1 cup (4 ounces) shredded Cheddar cheese
1 tablespoon Worcestershire sauce
1 tablespoon chopped pimento
1 package (16 ounces) spaghetti, cooked and drained
1 tablespoon snipped parsley

1. Sauté onion and green pepper in butter in a skillet. Stir in flour, salt, and pepper. Gradually add milk, stirring until thickened and smooth.
2. Stir in cheeses, Worcestershire sauce, pimento, and spaghetti. Put into a 3-quart casserole.
3. Bake, covered, at 350°F 45 minutes, or until heated through. Sprinkle with parsley.

8 servings

331 *Barley Italienne*

6 bacon slices, cut in 1-inch pieces
1½ cups quick-cooking barley
2¼ cups water
1 can (16 ounces) tomatoes (undrained)
1 can (8 ounces) tomato sauce
1 medium onion, sliced
1 garlic clove, minced
2 teaspoons salt
½ teaspoon oregano
¼ teaspoon pepper
8 ounces American cheese, sliced

1. Fry bacon in a skillet; drain off excess fat, reserving 2 tablespoons drippings.
2. Brown barley in bacon drippings in skillet. Add water and tomatoes. Bring to a boil; reduce heat. Cover and simmer 10 to 12 minutes, stirring occasionally.
3. Add bacon and remaining ingredients, except cheese. Cover and cook an additional 5 minutes.
4. Layer barley mixture and cheese alternately in a greased 2-quart casserole, ending with cheese on top.
5. Bake, covered, at 350°F 10 to 12 minutes, or until cheese is melted and mixture is heated through.

6 servings

332 *Barley-Mushroom Casserole*

½ cup finely chopped onion
½ pound fresh mushrooms, sliced
¼ cup butter or margarine
2 beef bouillon cubes
1 quart boiling water
1 teaspoon salt
1 cup barley

1. Sauté onion and mushrooms in butter in a skillet.
2. Dissolve bouillon cubes in boiling water. Mix with salt, barley, onion, and mushrooms. Pour into a 2-quart casserole.
3. Bake, uncovered, at 350°F 1 hour, stirring occasionally. Cover and bake an additional 30 minutes, or until barley is tender.

6 servings

Vegetables

333 *Flavor-Rich Baked Beans*

1½ quarts water
1 pound dried navy beans, rinsed
½ pound salt pork
½ cup chopped celery
½ cup chopped onion
1 teaspoon salt
¼ cup ketchup
¼ cup molasses
2 tablespoons brown sugar
1 teaspoon dry mustard
½ teaspoon ground black pepper
¼ teaspoon ground ginger

1. Grease 8 individual casseroles having tight-fitting covers. (A 2-quart casserole with lid may be used.)
2. Heat water to boiling in a large heavy saucepan. Add beans gradually to water so that boiling continues. Boil 2 minutes. Remove from heat and set aside 1 hour.
3. Remove rind from salt pork and cut into 1-inch chunks; set aside.
4. Add pork chunks to beans with celery, onion, and salt; mix well. Cover tightly and bring mixture to boiling over high heat. Reduce and simmer 45 minutes, stirring once or twice. Drain beans, reserving liquid.
5. Put an equal amount of beans and salt pork chunks into each casserole.
6. Mix one cup of bean liquid, ketchup, molasses, brown sugar, dry mustard, pepper, and ginger in a saucepan. Bring to boiling. Pour an equal amount of sauce over beans in each casserole. Cover casseroles.
7. Bake at 300°F about 2½ hours. If necessary, add more reserved bean liquid to beans during baking. Remove covers and bake ½ hour longer.

8 servings

334 *Lagered Sauerkraut with Apples*

Serve this German dish with sausage, roast pork, pork chops, or braised beef.

1 can (16 ounces) sauerkraut
1 medium apple
¾ cup beer
1 tablespoon sugar
1 tablespoon butter
½ teaspoon caraway seed
Dash pepper

1. Rinse sauerkraut in a large strainer; drain. Slice apple but do not peel.
2. Place all ingredients in a saucepan. Simmer, uncovered, for about 30 minutes, stirring occasionally, until most of liquid has evaporated and apples are tender.

4 servings

335 *Artichokes with Creamy Dill Sauce*

Cooked Artichokes
1 cup creamed cottage cheese
½ cup plain yogurt
1 tablespoon lemon juice
1 teaspoon instant minced onion
1 teaspoon sugar
½ teaspoon dill weed
½ teaspoon salt
Few grains pepper
2 parsley sprigs

1. Prepare desired number of artichokes.
2. Meanwhile, combine cottage cheese, yogurt, lemon juice, onion, sugar, dill weed, salt, pepper, and parsley in an electric blender container. Blend until smooth. Chill.
3. Serve artichokes with sauce for dipping.

About 1½ cups sauce

Cooked Artichokes: Wash **artichokes.** Cut off about 1 inch from tops and bases. Remove and discard lower outside leaves. If desired, snip off tips of remaining leaves. Stand artichokes upright in a deep saucepan large enough to hold them snugly. Add **boiling water** to a depth of 1 inch. Add **salt** (¼ teaspoon for each artichoke). Cover and boil gently 30 to 45 minutes, or until stems can easily be pierced with a fork. Drain artichokes; cut off stems.

336

337 *Stir-Fry Vegetables and Rice*

1 cup brown rice
¼ cup vegetable oil
1 medium onion, thinly sliced
1 cup thinly sliced carrot
1 clove garlic, crushed
1 green pepper, coarsely chopped
1 cup thinly sliced zucchini
1 cup thinly sliced mushrooms
2 cans (16 ounces each) bean sprouts, drained
¼ to ⅓ cup soy sauce

1. Cook rice following package directions; set aside.
2. Heat oil in a large skillet. Add onion, carrot, and garlic; cook and stir over medium high heat about 2 minutes.
3. Add green pepper, zucchini, and mushrooms; cook and stir 2 to 3 minutes.
4. Stir in cooked rice, bean sprouts, and soy sauce. Cook and stir 1 to 2 minutes, or until thoroughly heated.

6 to 8 servings

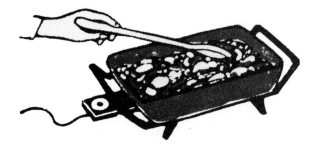

338 *Tangy Green Beans*

¾ pound fresh green beans, cut crosswise in pieces, or 1 package (9 ounces) frozen cut green beans
½ teaspoon salt
¼ cup butter or margarine
1 medium onion, quartered and thinly sliced
1 tablespoon wine vinegar
¼ teaspoon salt
⅛ teaspoon ground black pepper
¼ teaspoon dill weed
⅛ teaspoon crushed savory

1. Put beans and ½ teaspoon salt into a small amount of boiling water in a saucepan. Bring to boiling and cook, covered, until crisp-tender. Drain and set aside.
2. Heat 3 tablespoons butter in a skillet; add onion and cook 3 to 5 minutes. Mix in beans and cook about 4 minutes, or until thoroughly heated, stirring occasionally. Add remaining butter, wine vinegar, ¼ teaspoon salt, pepper, dill, and savory; toss over low heat until butter is melted.

About 4 servings

339 *Butter-Sauced Asparagus*

2 pounds fresh asparagus, washed,
    or 2 packages (10 ounces each)
    frozen asparagus spears, cooked
¼ cup butter
¼ cup chopped pecans
¼ cup finely chopped celery
1 tablespoon lemon juice

1. Put fresh asparagus into a small amount of boiling salted water in a skillet, bring to boiling, reduce heat, and cook 5 minutes, uncovered; cover and cook 10 minutes, or until just tender.
2. Meanwhile, heat butter in a small saucepan. Add pecans and celery and cook 5 minutes. Stir in lemon juice. Pour over asparagus and serve immediately.

About 6 servings

340 *Lima Beans New Orleans*

1 package (10 ounces) frozen lima
    beans
1 tablespoon vinegar
2 tablespoons olive oil
½ teaspoon salt
    Dash pepper
2 tablespoons chopped parsley
½ clove garlic, minced
1 teaspoon lemon juice

1. Cook lima beans following package directions; drain if necessary.
2. Add vinegar, olive oil, salt, pepper, parsley, and garlic to limas in saucepan. Heat thoroughly, then mix in lemon juice. Serve immediately.

4 servings

341 *Broccoli with Buttery Lemon Crunch*

1½ pounds broccoli, washed
¼ cup butter or margarine
½ cup coarse dry enriched bread
    crumbs
1 tablespoon grated lemon peel
3 tablespoons butter or margarine
1 small clove garlic, crushed in a
    garlic press or minced
½ teaspoon salt
    Few grains black pepper

1. Cook broccoli in a small amount of boiling salted water until just tender. (Cook uncovered 5 minutes, then cover and cook 10 to 15 minutes, or cook, covered, the full time and lift the lid 3 or 4 times during cooking.)
2. Meanwhile, heat ¼ cup butter in a large skillet; add bread crumbs and heat, stirring frequently, until well browned. Remove crumbs from butter with a slotted spoon and mix with the lemon peel.
3. Put 3 tablespoons butter, garlic, salt, and pepper into skillet; heat until butter is lightly browned. Add broccoli and turn gently until well coated with butter.
4. Arrange broccoli in a heated vegetable dish and pour remaining garlic butter over it. Top with the "lemoned" crumbs.

About 6 servings

342 *Brussels Sprouts in Herb Butter*

2 pounds fresh Brussels sprouts
⅓ cup butter
1 tablespoon grated onion
1 tablespoon lemon juice
¾ teaspoon salt
¼ teaspoon thyme
¼ teaspoon marjoram
¼ teaspoon savory

1. Cook Brussels sprouts in boiling salted water until just tender.
2. Put butter, onion, lemon juice, salt, thyme, marjoram, and savory into a saucepan. Set over low heat until butter is melted, stirring to blend.
3. When Brussels sprouts are tender, drain thoroughly and turn into a warm serving dish. Pour the seasoned butter mixture over the Brussels sprouts and toss gently to coat sprouts evenly and thoroughly.

About 8 servings

343 *Zesty Beets*

1 can or jar (16 ounces) small whole
  beets
2 tablespoons butter or margarine
2 tablespoons prepared horseradish
½ teaspoon prepared mustard
½ teaspoon seasoned salt

Heat beets in liquid; drain. Add butter, horseradish, prepared mustard, and seasoned salt; stir gently.

About 4 servings

344 *Cabbage Rolls Paprikash*

8 large cabbage leaves
2½ cups diced cooked chicken
2 tablespoons chopped onion
½ cup finely chopped celery
¼ pound chopped fresh mushrooms
1 small clove garlic, minced
½ teaspoon salt
½ teaspoon thyme leaves
1 egg, beaten
2 tablespoons butter or margarine
6 tablespoons flour
2 cups chicken broth
2 cups dairy sour cream
3 tablespoons paprika

1. Cook cabbage leaves 4 minutes in boiling salted water to cover. Drain and pat dry.
2. Mix chicken, onion, celery, mushrooms, garlic, salt, and thyme; stir in egg.
3. Place ½ cup of the chicken mixture in the center of each cabbage leaf. Fold sides of the cabbage leaf toward center, over filling, and then fold and overlap ends to make a small bundle. Fasten with wooden picks. Place in a 3-quart baking dish.
4. Heat butter in a large skillet. Blend in flour and heat until bubbly. Add chicken broth gradually, stirring until smooth. Blend in sour cream and paprika. Cook over low heat, stirring constantly, until thickened. Pour sauce over cabbage rolls. Cover baking dish.
5. Cook in a 350°F oven 35 minutes.

4 servings

345 *Cauliflower Italiana*

2 packages (10 ounces each) frozen
  cauliflower
2 tablespoons butter or margarine
½ clove garlic, minced
2 teaspoons flour
1 teaspoon salt
1 can (16 ounces) tomatoes
  (undrained)
1 small green pepper, coarsely
  chopped
¼ teaspoon oregano

1. Cook cauliflower following package directions; drain.
2. Meanwhile, heat butter with garlic in a saucepan. Stir in flour and salt and cook until bubbly.
3. Add tomatoes with liquid and bring to boiling, stirring constantly; cook 1 to 2 minutes. Stir in green pepper and oregano.
4. Pour hot sauce over cooked cauliflower.

About 6 servings

346 *Corn Spoon Bread*

1 quart milk
1 cup enriched yellow cornmeal
2 tablespoons finely chopped onion
2 tablespoons chopped parsley
4 eggs
2 tablespoons butter or margarine
2 tablespoons prepared baconlike
  pieces (a soy protein product)

1. Scald milk in top of a double boiler over simmering water.
2. Add cornmeal to scalded milk gradually, stirring constantly. Mix in onion and parsley. Cook over boiling water until thickened, about 10 minutes, stirring frequently and vigorously.
3. Meanwhile, beat eggs in a large bowl until thick and piled softly.
4. Remove double boiler top from water. Stir in butter and

2 teaspoons salt
1 teaspoon sugar
1 teaspoon baking powder
¼ teaspoon seasoned pepper
2 cups corn kernels (fresh, frozen, or canned)

baconlike pieces. Blend salt, sugar, baking powder, and seasoned pepper; stir into cornmeal mixture. Add hot mixture gradually to eggs, beating constantly. Mix in corn. Turn into a buttered 2-quart casserole.
5. Bake at 425°F 40 to 45 minutes, or until top is browned. Serve immediately.

6 to 8 servings

347 *Ratatouille with Spanish Olives*

1 medium eggplant (about 1½ pounds), pared and cut in 3 × ½-inch strips
2 zucchini, cut in ¼-inch slices
2 teaspoons salt
½ cup olive oil
2 onions, thinly sliced
2 green peppers, thinly sliced
2 cloves garlic, minced
3 tomatoes, peeled and cut in strips
1 cup sliced pimento-stuffed olives
¼ cup snipped parsley
¼ teaspoon ground pepper
Parsley, snipped

1. Toss eggplant and zucchini with 1 teaspoon salt and let stand 30 minutes. Drain and then dry on paper toweling.
2. Heat ¼ cup oil in a large skillet and lightly brown eggplant strips and then zucchini slices. Remove with slotted spoon; set aside.
3. Heat remaining oil in the skillet; cook onions and green peppers until tender. Stir in garlic. Put tomato strips on top; cover and cook 5 minutes. Gently stir in eggplant, zucchini, olives, ¼ cup parsley, remaining salt, and the pepper.
4. Simmer, covered, 20 minutes. Uncover and cook 5 minutes; baste with juices from bottom of skillet. Serve hot or cold, garnished with parsley.

6 to 8 servings

348 *Fresh Corn Vinaigrette*

4 ears fresh corn
¼ cup vegetable oil
2 tablespoons cider vinegar
¾ teaspoon lemon juice
1½ tablespoons chopped parsley
1 teaspoon salt
½ teaspoon sugar
¼ teaspoon basil
⅛ teaspoon cayenne pepper
1 large tomato, peeled and chopped
¼ cup chopped green pepper
¼ cup chopped green onion
Greens (optional)

1. Husk corn and remove silks. Fill a large kettle half full of water and bring to boiling. Add corn, cover, and return to boiling. Remove from heat and let stand 5 minutes. Drain and set aside to cool.
2. Mix oil, vinegar, lemon juice, parsley, salt, sugar, basil, and cayenne in a large bowl.
3. Cut corn off cob and add to bowl along with tomato, green pepper, and green onion; mix well. Cover and chill several hours.
4. Drain and serve on greens, if desired.

4 to 6 servings

Note: If desired, substitute 1½ cups (12-ounce can, drained, or 10-ounce package frozen, defrosted) whole kernel corn.

349 *Gingered Turnips*

Oriental seasonings give this often neglected vegetable new flavor appeal.

2 pounds yellow turnips, pared and cubed
1 tablespoon minced onion
1¼ cups Beef Stock
½ teaspoon ground ginger
½ teaspoon sugar
2 teaspoons soy sauce

Combine all ingredients in a saucepan; simmer covered until turnips are tender (about 15 minutes). Drain; mash turnips with potato masher or electric mixer until fluffy, adding cooking liquid as needed for desired consistency.

6 servings

350 *Fresh Peas with Basil*

2 tablespoons butter or margarine
½ cup sliced green onions with tops
1½ cups shelled fresh peas (1½ pounds)
½ teaspoon sugar
½ teaspoon salt
⅛ teaspoon ground black pepper
¼ teaspoon basil
1 tablespoon snipped parsley
½ cup water

1. Heat butter in a skillet. Add green onions and cook 5 minutes, stirring occasionally. Add peas, sugar, salt, pepper, basil, parsley, and water.
2. Cook, covered, over medium heat 10 minutes, or until peas are tender.

About 4 servings

Note: If desired, use 1 package (10 ounces) frozen green peas and decrease water to ¼ cup.

351 *Parsley-Buttered New Potatoes*

18 small new potatoes
Boiling water
1½ teaspoons salt
2 tablespoons butter
1 tablespoon snipped parsley

Scrub potatoes and put into a saucepan. Pour in boiling water to a 1-inch depth. Add salt; cover and cook about 15 minutes, or until tender. Drain and peel. Return potatoes to saucepan and toss with butter and parsley.

About 6 servings

Note: Snipped chives, grated lemon peel, and lemon juice may be used instead of parsley.

352 *Hash Brown Potatoes au Gratin*

1 package (2 pounds) frozen chopped hash brown potatoes, partially defrosted
1½ teaspoons salt
Few grains pepper
¼ cup coarsely chopped green pepper
1 jar (2 ounces) sliced pimentos, drained and chopped
2 cups milk
¾ cup fine dry enriched bread crumbs
⅓ cup soft butter
⅔ cup shredded pasteurized process sharp American cheese

1. Turn potatoes into a buttered shallow 2-quart baking dish, separating into pieces. Sprinkle with salt and pepper. Add green pepper and pimentos; mix lightly. Pour milk over potatoes. Cover with aluminum foil.
2. Cook in a 350°F oven 1¼ hours, or until potatoes are fork-tender. Remove foil; stir potatoes gently. Mix bread crumbs, butter, and cheese. Spoon over top of potatoes. Return to oven and heat 15 minutes, or until cheese is melted.

About 6 servings

353 *Potato Pancakes*

Butter or margarine (enough, melted, for a ¼-inch layer)
2 tablespoons flour
1½ teaspoons salt
¼ teaspoon baking powder
⅛ teaspoon ground black pepper
6 medium potatoes, washed
2 eggs, well beaten

1. Heat butter in a heavy skillet over low heat.
2. Combine flour, salt, baking powder, and pepper and set aside.
3. Pare and finely grate potatoes; set aside.
4. Combine flour mixture with eggs and onion.
5. Drain liquid from grated potatoes; add potatoes to egg mixture and beat thoroughly.
6. When butter is hot, spoon batter into skillet, allowing

1 teaspoon grated onion
Applesauce or maple syrup, warmed

about 2 tablespoonfuls for each pancake and leaving about 1 inch between cakes. Cook over medium heat until golden brown and crisp on one side. Turn carefully and brown on other side. Drain on absorbent paper. Serve with applesauce or maple syrup.

About 20 pancakes

354 *Lacy French-Fried Onion Rings*

1 cup enriched all-purpose flour
1 teaspoon baking powder
¼ teaspoon salt
1 egg, well beaten
1 cup milk
1 tablespoon vegetable oil
4 sweet Spanish onions
Fat for deep frying heated to 375°F
Salt or garlic salt

1. Blend flour, baking powder, and salt.
2. Combine egg, milk, and oil in a bowl and beat until thoroughly blended. Beat in the dry ingredients until batter is smooth. Cover.
3. Cut off root ends of onions; slip off the loose skins. Slice onions ¼ inch thick and separate into rings.
4. Using a long-handled two-tined fork, immerse a few onion rings at a time into the batter, lift out and drain over bowl a few seconds before dropping into heated fat. Turn only once as they brown; do not crowd.
5. When rings are golden brown on both sides, lift out and drain on absorbent paper-lined cookie sheet. Sprinkle with salt and serve hot.

About 6 servings

Lacy Cornmeal Onion Rings: Follow recipe for **355** Lacy French-Fried Onion Rings. Substitute ½ **cup enriched cornmeal** for ⅔ cup flour.

To Freeze French-Fried Onions: Leaving the crisp, tender rings on the absorbent paper-lined cookie sheet on which they were drained, place in freezer and freeze quickly. Then carefully remove rings to moisture-vaporproof containers with layers of absorbent paper between each layer of onions; the rings may overlap some. Cover tightly, label, and freeze.

To Reheat Frozen French-Fried Onions: Removing the desired number of onion rings, arrange them (frozen) in a single layer on a cookie sheet. Heat in a 375°F oven several minutes, or until rings are crisp and hot.

356 *Turnip Custard*

2 pounds turnips
1 egg, well beaten
¼ cup finely crushed soda crackers
⅔ cup (6-ounce can) undiluted evaporated milk
1 teaspoon salt
Few grains black pepper
1 cup (about 4 ounces) shredded sharp Cheddar cheese

1. Wash, pare, and cut turnips into pieces. Cook, uncovered, in boiling water to cover until turnips are tender, 15 to 20 minutes; drain. Mash and, if necessary, again drain turnips (about 2 cups mashed turnips).
2. Blend mashed turnips, egg, cracker crumbs, evaporated milk, salt, and pepper. Turn mixture into a buttered 1¼-quart baking dish. Set dish in a pan and pour in boiling water to a 1-inch depth.
3. Bake at 350°F 15 minutes. Sprinkle cheese over top. Bake 5 minutes, or until a knife inserted halfway between center and edge comes out clean. Remove from water immediately.

About 6 servings

357 *Cracked-Wheat-Stuffed Tomatoes*

½ cup cracked wheat or bulgur
1½ cups hot water
6 firm medium tomatoes, rinsed
⅛ teaspoon *each* sugar, salt, and
    pepper
3 tablespoons crushed dried mint
3 tablespoons warm water
1 small ripe avocado
1½ teaspoons salt
½ teaspoon sugar
2 tablespoons lemon juice
⅓ cup olive oil
¼ cup finely chopped green onion
¼ cup snipped parsley

1. Combine cracked wheat and hot water; set aside 30 minutes. Drain cracked wheat thoroughly and set aside.
2. Peel tomatoes. Cut off and discard a ½-inch slice from the top of each. Seed tomatoes. Scoop out pulp, chop it, and turn into a sieve to drain. Invert tomatoes on absorbent paper to drain 30 minutes. Mix ⅛ teaspoon sugar, ⅛ teaspoon salt, and pepper; sprinkle over pulp and insides of tomatoes.
3. Combine dried mint and warm water; set aside 15 minutes. Squeeze dry.
4. Peel avocado; put pulp into a bowl and mash with a fork. Beat in 1½ teaspoons salt, ½ teaspoon sugar, and lemon juice. Add oil in a thin stream, beating constantly. Mix in drained cracked wheat, tomato pulp, mint, green onion, and parsley. Fill tomatoes. Chill.

6 servings

358 *Spinach Gnocchi*

1½ cups milk
1 tablespoon butter or margarine
¼ teaspoon salt
    Few grains nutmeg
¼ cup farina
½ cup well-drained cooked chopped
    spinach
1 egg, well beaten
1 tablespoon chopped onion, lightly
    browned in 1 teaspoon butter
    or margarine
1½ cups (about 6 ounces) shredded
    Swiss cheese
2 eggs, well beaten
¾ cup milk
1 tablespoon flour
1 teaspoon salt
    Few grains nutmeg

1. Combine milk, butter, salt, and few grains nutmeg in a saucepan. Bring to boiling and add farina gradually, stirring constantly. Cook over low heat until mixture thickens.
2. Stir in spinach, egg, cooked onion, and 1 cup cheese; blend well. Set aside to cool slightly.
3. Drop mixture by tablespoonfuls close together in a well-greased shallow 9-inch baking dish or casserole. Sprinkle remaining cheese over mounds.
4. For topping, combine eggs, milk, flour, salt, and few grains nutmeg, blending well. Pour over spinach mixture in baking dish.
5. Bake at 350°F 35 to 40 minutes, or until golden brown on top. Serve at once.

4 to 6 servings

359 *Apple-Stuffed Acorn Squash*

2 acorn squash
2 tart apples
1½ teaspoons grated fresh lemon peel
1 tablespoon fresh lemon juice
¼ cup butter or margarine, melted
⅓ cup firmly packed brown sugar
Salt
Cinnamon
Apple and lemon slices for garnish (optional)

1. Cut squash into halves lengthwise and scoop out seedy centers. Place cut side down in baking dish and pour in boiling water to a ½-inch depth. Bake at 400°F 20 minutes.
2. Pare, core, and dice apples; mix with lemon peel and juice, 2 tablespoons butter, and brown sugar.
3. Invert squash halves and brush with remaining 2 tablespoons butter; sprinkle with salt and cinnamon.
4. Fill squash halves with apple mixture. Pour boiling water into dish to a ½-inch depth; cover and bake 30 minutes.
5. Before serving, spoon pan juices over squash. If desired, garnish with apple and lemon slices.

4 servings

360 *Spinach-Bacon Soufflé*

2 cups firmly packed, finely chopped fresh spinach (dry the leaves before chopping)
¼ cup finely chopped green onions with tops
½ pound sliced bacon, cooked, drained, and crumbled
3 tablespoons butter or margarine
¼ cup enriched all-purpose flour
½ teaspoon salt
¼ to ½ teaspoon thyme
1 cup milk
3 egg yolks, well beaten
4 egg whites
2 teaspoons shredded Parmesan cheese

1. Toss the spinach, green onions, and bacon together in a bowl; set aside.
2. Heat butter in a saucepan over low heat. Blend in flour, salt, and thyme. Stirring constantly, heat until bubbly. Add milk gradually, continuing to stir. Bring rapidly to boiling and boil 1 to 2 minutes, stirring constantly.
3. Remove from heat and blend spinach-bacon mixture into the sauce. Stir in the beaten egg yolks; set aside to cool.
4. Meanwhile, beat egg whites until rounded peaks are formed (peaks turn over slightly when beater is slowly lifted upright); do not overbeat.
5. Gently spread spinach-bacon mixture over the beaten egg whites. Carefully fold together until ingredients are just blended.
6. Turn mixture into an ungreased 2-quart soufflé dish (straight-sided casserole); sprinkle top with Parmesan cheese.
7. Bake at 350°F 40 minutes, or until a knife comes out clean when inserted halfway between center and edge of soufflé and top is lightly browned. Serve immediately.

6 servings

361 *Spinach-Cheese Bake*

2 packages (10 ounces each) frozen chopped spinach
3 eggs, beaten
¼ cup enriched all-purpose flour
1 teaspoon seasoned salt
¼ teaspoon ground nutmeg
¼ teaspoon ground black pepper
2 cups (16 ounces) creamed cottage cheese
2 cups (8 ounces) shredded Swiss or Cheddar cheese

1. Cook spinach following package directions; drain.
2. Combine eggs, flour, seasoned salt, nutmeg, and pepper in a bowl. Mix in cottage cheese, Swiss cheese, and spinach.
3. Turn into a buttered 1½-quart casserole.
4. Bake at 325°F 50 to 60 minutes.

6 to 8 servings

362 *Vegetable-Rice Medley*

3 tablespoons butter or margarine
¾ cup chopped onion
1½ pounds zucchini, thinly sliced
1 can (16 ounces) whole kernel golden corn, drained
1 can (16 ounces) tomatoes (undrained)
3 cups cooked enriched white rice
1½ teaspoons salt
¼ teaspoon ground black pepper
¼ teaspoon ground coriander
¼ teaspoon oregano leaves

Heat butter in a large saucepan. Add onion and zucchini; cook until tender, stirring occasionally. Add corn, tomatoes with liquid, cooked rice, salt, pepper, coriander, and oregano; mix well. Cover and bring to boiling; reduce heat and simmer 15 minutes.

About 8 servings

363 *Stuffed Baked Sweet Potatoes*

4 medium sweet potatoes, washed
1 small ripe banana, peeled
2 tablespoons butter or margarine
⅓ cup fresh orange juice
1 tablespoon brown sugar
1½ teaspoons salt
¼ cup chopped pecans

1. Bake sweet potatoes at 375°F 45 minutes to 1 hour, or until tender when tested with a fork.
2. Cut a lengthwise slice from each potato. Scoop out sweet potatoes into a bowl; reserve shells. Mash banana with potatoes; add butter, orange juice, brown sugar, and salt and beat thoroughly. Spoon mixture into shells. Sprinkle with pecans. Set on a cookie sheet.
3. Return to oven 12 to 15 minutes, or until heated.

4 servings

364 *Zucchini Boats*

8 medium zucchini, washed and ends removed
1 medium tomato, cut in small pieces
¼ cup chopped salted almonds
1 tablespoon chopped parsley
1 teaspoon finely chopped onion
½ teaspoon seasoned salt
2 teaspoons butter, melted
¼ cup cracker crumbs

1. Cook zucchini in boiling salted water until crisp-tender, 7 to 10 minutes. Drain; cool.
2. Cut zucchini lengthwise into halves; scoop out and discard centers. Chop 2 shells coarsely; set remaining shells aside. Put chopped zucchini and tomato into a bowl. Add almonds, parsley, onion, and seasoned salt; mix well.
3. Spoon filling into zucchini shells. Mix butter and cracker crumbs. Sprinkle over filling. Set on a cookie sheet.
4. Place under broiler 4 inches from heat. Broil 3 minutes, or until crumbs are golden.

6 servings

365 German-Style Green Beans

A savory hot bacon sauce flavored with beer is poured over green beans with palate-pleasing results. Serve with an unsauced main dish.

2 packages (9 ounces each) frozen green beans
4 slices bacon, cut in ½-inch pieces
⅓ cup finely chopped onion
¼ to ½ cup beer
2 tablespoons sugar
¼ teaspoon salt
Dash pepper

1. Cook beans according to package directions.
2. Meanwhile, fry bacon in a skillet until lightly browned. Add onion, beer, sugar, salt, and pepper. Heat to boiling.
3. Drain beans, pour beer mixture over, and toss lightly.

6 to 8 servings

366 Beets Piquant

¼ cup sugar
1 tablespoon cornstarch
1 teaspoon salt
½ teaspoon caraway seed
6 to 8 whole cloves
¼ cup water
1 cup beer
1 can (16 ounces) sliced beets, drained

1. In a medium saucepan, combine sugar, cornstarch, salt, caraway seed, and cloves.
2. Gradually add water and beer while stirring. Cook, stirring constantly, until thickened.
3. Add beets; heat through.

4 servings

367 French-Style Peas

2 cups shelled peas (see Note)
8 small boiling onions, cut in half
1 cup shredded lettuce
1 teaspoon sugar
2 teaspoons snipped parsley
2 teaspoons clarified butter
½ teaspoon salt
¼ teaspoon freshly ground pepper
¾ cup water

Combine all ingredients except water; let stand 1 hour, stirring occasionally. Transfer mixture to a saucepan; add water. Simmer covered until peas and onions are tender (about 15 minutes). Serve hot.

4 servings

Note: Two packages (10 ounces each) frozen peas can be substituted in this recipe; do not mix with other ingredients. Add to saucepan during last 5 minutes of cooking.

368 Brussels Sprouts and Grapes

1½ pounds fresh Brussels sprouts, cut in half
1 can or bottle (12 ounces) beer
2 teaspoons butter, melted
¼ teaspoon salt
⅛ teaspoon freshly ground white pepper
1 cup seedless white grapes
Snipped parsley

1. Simmer Brussels sprouts in beer in a covered saucepan until tender (about 8 minutes); drain.
2. Drizzle butter over sprouts; sprinkle with salt and pepper. Add grapes; heat thoroughly. Sprinkle with parsley.

6 servings

369 *Red Cabbage, Danish Style*

⅓ cup butter or margarine
1 head red cabbage (2 pounds), coarsely shredded
1 can or bottle (12 ounces) beer
⅔ cup red currant jelly
½ teaspoon salt

1. Melt butter in a large, heavy saucepan. Add cabbage; cook about 5 minutes to soften, turning frequently.
2. Stir in beer, jelly, and salt. Cover and simmer about 1½ hours, removing cover during last 30 minutes to evaporate most of liquid; stir occasionally.

10 servings, ½ cup each

370 *French-Fried Onion Rings in Beer Batter*

These light, crisp onion rings have a batter featuring a hint of beer flavor. The batter may also be used for fresh mushrooms.

1¼ cups flour
1 teaspoon baking powder
1 teaspoon salt
2 tablespoons shortening
1 egg, beaten
1 cup beer
1 large sweet Spanish onion
Oil for deep frying

1. Mix flour, baking powder, and salt in a bowl. Cut in shortening until mixture resembles fine crumbs.
2. Add egg and beer; beat until smooth.
3. Cut onion into ¼-inch-thick slices; separate into rings.
4. Using a fork, immerse a few onion rings at a time in the batter. Lift out; allow excess batter to drip off. Drop into hot oil (375°F). Fry until golden brown, turning once. Drain on paper towels. Serve hot.

50 to 60 rings; 6 to 8 servings

371 *Hash Brown Potatoes*

The potatoes absorb beer while boiling, giving the dish an unusual flavor.

6 medium boiling potatoes (2 pounds), pared and cubed
1 can or bottle (12 ounces) beer
⅓ cup chopped onion
⅓ cup chopped green pepper
¼ cup butter or margarine
½ teaspoon salt
Dash pepper

1. In a covered saucepan, boil potatoes in beer until just tender, but not mushy. Remove potatoes with a slotted spoon; chop finely.
2. Add onion and green pepper to saucepan. Add water, if needed, to just cover. Simmer, uncovered, about 5 minutes, or until tender. Drain. Mix with potatoes, salt, and pepper.
3. In a skillet, heat butter until very hot and beginning to brown. Add potato mixture. Cook over medium high heat, turning occasionally, until browned.

6 servings

372 *Beer Pilaff*

Substitute beer for water when cooking rice, and the rice takes on an intriguing flavor.

1 medium onion, chopped
2 tablespoons butter or margarine
1 chicken bouillon cube, or 1 teaspoon chicken stock base
¼ teaspoon salt
Dash pepper
¾ cup uncooked rice (not instant)
1 can or bottle (12 ounces) beer

1. Sauté onion in butter until soft.
2. Add bouillon, salt, and pepper; stir. Add rice. Cook and stir 1 minute.
3. Add beer. (If package directions specify more than 1½ cups liquid for ¾ cup uncooked rice, use water to make up the difference.)
4. Heat to boiling. Cover, reduce heat, and simmer for 15 minutes, or until tender.

2¾ cups; 4 or 5 servings

373 *Vegetable Salad with Yogurt Dressing*

Vivid colors dominate this unusual salad combination.

¾ cup Low-Fat Yogurt
2 tablespoons snipped parsley
½ cup finely chopped dill pickle
½ cup chopped tomato
1 teaspoon salt
1 cup sliced radishes
1 medium zucchini, shredded
2 medium carrots, shredded
1 large beet, shredded

1. Mix yogurt, parsley, pickle, chopped tomato, and salt; refrigerate covered 1 hour.
2. Arrange radish slices around edge of a serving plate. Arrange zucchini, carrots, and beet decoratively in center of plate. Serve yogurt mixture with salad.

4 servings

374 *Layered Casserole*

1 can (14½ ounces) asparagus spears, drained
1 can (17 ounces) green peas
1 can (8½ ounces) water chestnuts, drained and sliced
2 tablespoons chopped pimento
½ cup fine dry bread crumbs
1 can (10¾ ounces) condensed cream of mushroom soup
½ cup (2 ounces) shredded American cheese

1. Arrange asparagus spears in bottom of a 1½-quart shallow baking dish.
2. Drain peas, reserving ¼ cup liquid. Top asparagus spears with peas, water chestnuts, and pimento. Sprinkle with ¼ cup bread crumbs.
3. Combine soup with reserved ¼ cup pea liquid. Evenly spread over bread crumbs. Sprinkle with remaining ¼ cup bread crumbs and cheese.
4. Bake, uncovered, at 350°F 20 minutes, or until heated through.

6 servings

375 *Marinated Artichoke Hearts Supreme*

2 jars (6 ounces each) marinated artichoke hearts
1 garlic clove, minced
½ cup chopped onion
4 eggs, beaten
¼ cup fine dry bread crumbs
2 tablespoons snipped parsley
½ teaspoon salt
½ teaspoon oregano
¼ teaspoon pepper
¼ teaspoon Tabasco
2 cups (8 ounces) shredded Cheddar cheese

1. Cut up artichoke hearts, reserving liquid from 1 jar.
2. Pour liquid into a skillet and sauté garlic and onion.
3. Combine with eggs, bread crumbs, parsley, salt, oregano, pepper, and Tabasco. Stir in cheese and artichoke hearts. Pour into a greased 1½-quart shallow baking dish.
4. Bake, uncovered, at 325°F 30 minutes, or until set.

6 servings

376 *Sweet-and-Sour Green Beans*

8 bacon slices, cut in 1-inch pieces
½ cup sugar
1 tablespoon cornstarch
1 cup vinegar
1 large onion, thinly sliced
2 cans (16 ounces each) cut green beans, drained

1. Fry bacon in a skillet.
2. Combine sugar and cornstarch. Blend in vinegar. Add to bacon and drippings in a skillet, stirring until thickened.
3. Put onion and beans into a 1½-quart casserole. Stir in vinegar mixture.
4. Bake, covered, at 300°F 1 hour, stirring once.

6 servings

377 *Spicy Lima Beans*

6 bacon slices, cut up
½ cup chopped onion
2 tablespoons flour
¼ teaspoon salt
   Dash pepper
1 bay leaf
1 can (16 ounces) tomatoes (undrained)
2 packages (10 ounces each) frozen lima beans, cooked and drained
½ cup fine dry bread crumbs
2 tablespoons butter or margarine, melted

1. Fry bacon and onion in a skillet. Stir in flour, salt, pepper, and bay leaf. Gradually add tomatoes and juice, stirring until thickened.
2. Add lima beans. Put into a 1½-quart casserole.
3. Combine bread crumbs and butter. Sprinkle over beans.
4. Bake, covered, at 350°F 20 minutes. Remove cover and bay leaf. Bake an additional 10 minutes, or until heated through.

6 servings

378 *Broccoli Casserole*

¼ cup chopped onion
¼ cup butter or margarine
2 teaspoons flour
½ cup water
1 jar (8 ounces) pasteurized process cheese spread
2 packages (10 ounces each) frozen chopped broccoli, thawed and squeezed
3 eggs, well beaten
½ cup buttered bread crumbs

1. Sauté onion in butter in a skillet. Stir in flour. Gradually add water, stirring until thickened and smooth.
2. Blend in cheese until melted. Combine with broccoli and eggs. Pour into a greased 1½-quart casserole. Sprinkle with bread crumbs.
3. Bake, uncovered, at 350°F 45 minutes, or until set.

6 servings

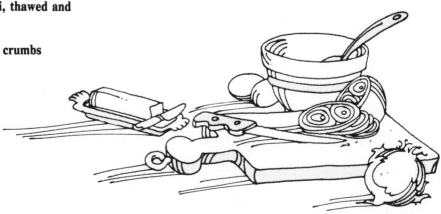

379 *Broccoli Bake*

2 packages (10 ounces each) frozen
   chopped broccoli, cooked and
   drained
1 can (10¾ ounces) condensed cream
   of mushroom soup
½ cup mayonnaise
1 cup (4 ounces) shredded Cheddar
   cheese
1 tablespoon lemon juice
½ cup crumbled cheese crackers

1. Spread broccoli in bottom of 10x6-inch baking dish.
2. Combine soup, mayonnaise, cheese, and lemon juice. Spread over broccoli. Sprinkle with cracker crumbs.
3. Bake, uncovered, at 350°F 30 minutes, or until heated through.

6 servings

380 *Broccoli-Mushroom Casserole*

1 package (10 ounces) frozen chopped
   broccoli, cooked and drained
1 can (4 ounces) mushroom slices,
   drained
2 tablespoons chopped pimento
⅓ cup dairy sour cream
½ cup chopped celery
½ teaspoon salt
   Dash pepper

1. Combine all ingredients. Put into a 1-quart casserole.
2. Bake, covered, at 350°F 25 minutes, or until heated through.

3 servings

381 *Brussels Sprouts in Broth*

2 packages (10 ounces each) frozen
   Brussels sprouts, cooked and
   drained
1 cup water
1 beef bouillon cube
2 tablespoons butter or margarine
½ cup (2 ounces) freshly grated
   Parmesan cheese

1. Put Brussels sprouts into a 1-quart casserole.
2. Heat together water, bouillon cube, and butter. Pour over Brussels sprouts. Sprinkle with cheese.
3. Bake, covered, at 325°F 20 minutes, or until heated through.

6 servings

Note: To improve flavor, cover and refrigerate Brussels sprouts, broth, and butter overnight. Add cheese before baking.

382 Carrot-Apricot Casserole

1 package (11 ounces) dried apricots
1 can (12 ounces) apricot nectar
2 jars (16 ounces each) tiny whole
   Belgian carrots, drained
½ cup firmly packed brown sugar
4 tablespoons butter or margarine
¼ cup slivered almonds

1. Soak apricots in nectar overnight.
2. Put 1 jar carrots into a 2-quart casserole. Top with half the apricots, half the apricot nectar, and ¼ cup brown sugar.
3. Dot with 2 tablespoons butter; repeat layers. Sprinkle with almonds.
4. Bake, covered, at 350°F 30 minutes, or until bubbly.

8 servings

383 Marmalade Carrots

4 cups thinly sliced carrots
⅓ cup orange juice
½ teaspoon salt
¼ teaspoon ginger
⅓ cup orange marmalade
1 tablespoon butter or margarine

1. Combine carrots, orange juice, salt, ginger, and marmalade.
2. Put into a 1½-quart casserole. Dot with butter.
3. Bake, covered, at 350°F 30 minutes, or until carrots are tender. If desired, sprinkle with snipped parsley.

8 servings

384 Brandied Carrots

4 cups thinly sliced carrots
¼ cup butter or margarine
¼ cup water
1 teaspoon lemon juice
½ teaspoon salt
¼ teaspoon pepper
¼ cup brandy
2 tablespoons snipped parsley

1. Put carrots into a large saucepan. Add butter and water. Cover and cook over moderate heat, stirring occasionally, until carrots are just crisp-tender (about 15 minutes).
2. Add lemon juice, salt, pepper, and brandy.
3. Put into a 1½-quart casserole. Cover and refrigerate overnight.
4. Bake, covered, at 350°F 30 minutes, or until heated through. Sprinkle with parsley.

8 servings

385 *Cabbage Casserole*

1 head cabbage, cut in 6 wedges
1½ cups (6 ounces) shredded Cheddar
   cheese
¼ cup butter or margarine
¼ cup flour
½ teaspoon seasoned salt
½ teaspoon sugar
⅛ teaspoon garlic powder
1¾ cups milk

1. Cook cabbage in **boiling salted water** about 10 minutes, or until tender.
2. Layer cabbage and 1 cup cheese in a 2-quart casserole.
3. Melt butter in a saucepan. Stir in flour, seasoned salt, sugar, and garlic powder. Gradually add milk, stirring until thickened and smooth.
4. Pour over cabbage. Sprinkle with remaining ½ cup cheese.
5. Bake, covered, at 350°F 20 minutes, or until heated through. If desired, sprinkle with paprika.

6 servings

386 *Sour Red Cabbage*

1 head red cabbage, shredded
1 onion, finely chopped
2 cooking apples, cored and cut up
¼ cup red wine vinegar
¼ cup water
1 tablespoon firmly packed brown
   sugar
1 teaspoon salt
¼ teaspoon pepper
1 tablespoon butter

1. Combine all ingredients, except butter.
2. Put into a 2-quart casserole. Dot with butter.
3. Bake, covered, at 350°F 1 hour, or until cabbage is tender.

6 servings

387 *Scalloped Corn and Broccoli*

¼ cup chopped onion
2 tablespoons butter or margarine
1 tablespoon flour
1¼ cups milk*
1 cup (4 ounces) shredded Cheddar
   cheese
1 can (12 ounces) whole kernel corn,
   drained
2 packages (10 ounces each) frozen
   broccoli spears, cooked and
   drained

1. Sauté onion in butter in a skillet. Stir in flour. Gradually add milk, stirring until thickened and smooth.
2. Add cheese, stirring until melted. Stir in corn.
3. Arrange broccoli in a 2-quart shallow baking dish.
4. Pour corn sauce over broccoli.
5. Bake, uncovered, at 350°F 30 minutes, or until heated through.

8 servings

* One-fourth cup of the drained corn liquid can be substituted for ¼ cup of the milk.

388 Creole Eggplant

1 eggplant
1¼ teaspoons salt
2 tablespoons butter or margarine
2 tablespoons flour
1 can (28 ounces) tomatoes (undrained)
½ cup chopped onion
½ cup chopped green pepper
2 tablespoons firmly packed brown sugar
¼ teaspoon pepper
¼ cup buttered bread crumbs

1. Pare and cut eggplant into cubes. Sprinkle with 1 teaspoon salt. Let stand 15 minutes.
2. Rinse and drain eggplant. Cook in **boiling water** 10 minutes; drain. Put into a 1½-quart casserole.
3. Melt butter in a saucepan. Stir in flour. Gradually add tomatoes and liquid, stirring until thickened.
4. Add onion, green pepper, brown sugar, pepper, and the remaining ¼ teaspoon salt. Pour over eggplant.
5. Bake, covered, at 350°F 15 minutes. Remove cover; sprinkle with bread crumbs. Bake an additional 5 minutes, or until heated through.

4 to 6 servings

389 Italian Eggplant Casserole

1 large eggplant
¼ cup milk
1 egg, beaten
½ cup fine dry bread crumbs
1 teaspoon salt
¼ cup shortening
1 can (8 ounces) tomato paste
1 can (8 ounces) spaghetti sauce
8 ounces mozzarella cheese, thinly sliced
½ cup (2 ounces) grated Parmesan cheese

1. Pare eggplant and cut into ¼-inch slices.
2. Combine milk and egg. Also combine bread crumbs and salt.
3. Dip eggplant into milk mixture, then bread crumbs. Fry eggplant in shortening in a skillet. Drain on absorbent paper.
4. Combine tomato paste and spaghetti sauce.
5. Alternate layers of half the eggplant, half the sauce, and half the mozzarella cheese in a 2-quart casserole. Repeat layers. Sprinkle with Parmesan cheese.
6. Bake, covered, at 350°F 30 minutes, or until heated through.

8 servings

Paprika Buttered Fish Fillets, page 362

390 *Carrot Soufflé*

3 tablespoons butter or margarine
3 tablespoons flour
1 cup milk
1 teaspoon sugar
½ teaspoon salt
¼ teaspoon pepper
2 cups mashed cooked carrots (about 1 pound fresh)
3 eggs, separated

1. Melt butter in a saucepan. Stir in flour. Gradually add milk, stirring until thickened and smooth.
2. Blend in sugar, salt, pepper, and mashed carrots. Beat in egg yolks.
3. Beat egg whites until stiff but not dry. Fold in carrot mixture. Divide in 2 buttered 1½-quart casseroles.
4. Bake, uncovered, in hot water bath at 325°F 50 minutes, or until set.

8 servings

391 *Vegetable Spoon Bread*

1 cup cornmeal
1½ teaspoons salt
1 cup cold milk
1½ cups milk, scalded
1 tablespoon butter or margarine
1 can (16 ounces) mixed vegetables, drained
5 bacon slices, cooked and crumbled
4 egg yolks
4 egg whites, beaten stiff but not dry

1. Combine cornmeal, salt, and cold milk. Add to scalded milk. Cook until thickened (about 5 minutes), stirring constantly.
2. Remove from heat; add butter, vegetables, and bacon.
3. Beat egg yolks until thick and lemon colored. Stir a small amount of cornmeal mixture into egg yolks; add egg mixture to cornmeal, stirring constantly. Fold in beaten egg white.
4. Pour into a greased 2-quart casserole or soufflé dish.
5. Bake, uncovered, at 350°F 50 to 60 minutes, or until set. Serve immediately.

6 servings

Sweet & Sour Chicken, page 341

392 *Broccoli-Stuffed Onions*

3 medium sweet Spanish onions
2 tablespoons butter or margarine
2 tablespoons flour
¼ teaspoon salt
1 cup milk
1 package (3 ounces) cream cheese, cut in cubes
1 package (10 ounces) frozen chopped broccoli, cooked and drained
½ cup (2 ounces) grated Parmesan cheese
1 teaspoon lemon juice

1. Peel and halve onions. Cook in **boiling salted water** 10 minutes; drain. Remove centers, leaving a ½-inch edge. Chop center portion to equal ½ cup.*
2. Melt butter in a saucepan. Stir in flour and salt. Gradually add milk, stirring until thickened and smooth. Add cream cheese, stirring until smooth.
3. Stir in broccoli, Parmesan cheese, lemon juice, and chopped onion. Spoon into onion halves. Place in a 2-quart shallow baking dish.
4. Bake, uncovered, at 375°F 20 minutes, or until heated through.

6 servings

* Use remaining onion in other casserole mixtures.

393 *Barbecue Potatoes*

8 potatoes
3 tablespoons flour
2¼ cups water
¾ cup barbecue sauce
1 tablespoon vinegar
2 teaspoons salt
2 small onions, thinly sliced
Paprika
1 tablespoon snipped parsley

1. Pare and thinly slice potatoes. Sprinkle with flour.
2. Combine water, barbecue sauce, vinegar, and salt in a large saucepan. Stir in potato and onion. Simmer 5 minutes, stirring frequently.
3. Pour into a 3-quart casserole.
4. Bake, covered, at 350°F 1 hour, or until potatoes are tender. Sprinkle with paprika and parsley.

8 servings

394 *Mushroom Business*

1 pound fresh mushrooms, thickly sliced
¼ cup butter or margarine
7 slices white bread, buttered
½ cup chopped onion
½ cup chopped celery
½ cup chopped green pepper
½ cup mayonnaise
¾ teaspoon salt
¼ teaspoon pepper
2 eggs, slightly beaten
1½ cups milk
1 can (10¾ ounces) condensed cream of mushroom soup
1 tablespoon grated Parmesan cheese

1. Sauté mushrooms in butter in a skillet; set aside.
2. Cut 3 slices bread into 1-inch cubes. Put into a 2½-quart casserole.
3. Combine mushrooms, onion, celery, green pepper, mayonnaise, salt, and pepper. Spoon on top of bread cubes.
4. Cut 3 slices bread into 1-inch cubes and put onto mushroom mixture.
5. Combine eggs and milk. Pour over mushroom mixture. Cover and refrigerate at least 1 hour.
6. Remove from refrigerator; uncover and spoon soup overall.
7. Cut remaining slice bread into 1-inch cubes; arrange over soup. Sprinkle with Parmesan cheese.
8. Bake, uncovered, at 300°F 60 to 70 minutes, or until mixture is set.

8 servings

395 *Mashed Potato Casserole*

2 pounds potatoes
⅓ to ½ cup milk
¼ cup butter or margarine
¼ cup chopped green pepper
1 package (3 ounces) cream cheese, cut in cubes
½ cup dairy sour cream
1 teaspoon salt
1 teaspoon onion salt
Dash pepper

1. Cook potatoes in **boiling water; drain.** Mash with milk and butter.
2. Beat in remaining ingredients. Put into a 1½-quart casserole.
3. Bake, covered, at 350°F 40 minutes, or until heated through. Garnish with **parsley** and **paprika.**

6 servings

396 *Potato-Mushroom Casserole*

3 cups sliced potatoes (about 4 medium)
1 cup sliced fresh mushrooms
1 onion, thinly sliced
3 beef bouillon cubes
1½ cups boiling water
¼ teaspoon salt
¼ teaspoon thyme
Dash pepper

1. Put potatoes, mushrooms, and onion into a 1½-quart casserole.
2. Dissolve bouillon cubes in boiling water. Add salt, thyme, and pepper. Pour over vegetables.
3. Bake, covered, at 350°F 30 minutes. Remove cover and bake an additional 15 minutes, or until vegetables are tender.

6 servings

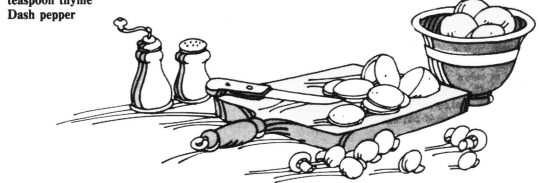

397 *Potato Stuffing*

2 cups chopped pared potatoes
¼ cup butter or margarine
1 medium apple, chopped
¾ cup chopped onion
1 garlic clove, minced
2 tablespoons snipped parsley
1 cup unflavored croutons
1½ teaspoons salt
1 egg, beaten
½ cup milk

1. Sauté potatoes in butter in a skillet 10 minutes, or until lightly browned.
2. Add remaining ingredients. Put into a 1½-quart casserole.
3. Bake, covered, at 325°F 30 minutes, or until heated through.

6 servings

398 Deluxe Scalloped Potatoes

1 package (5.5 ounces) scalloped
  potatoes
2 tablespoons butter or margarine
2½ cups boiling water
⅔ cup milk
⅓ cup crumbled blue cheese

1. Empty potato slices into a 1½-quart casserole. Sprinkle with sauce mix.
2. Stir in butter, water, milk, and blue cheese.
3. Bake, uncovered, at 400°F 30 to 35 minutes, or until potatoes are tender. Let stand a few minutes before serving.

4 servings

399 Apple-Honey Sweet Potatoes

4 sweet potatoes
4 cooking apples
½ cup honey
¼ teaspoon nutmeg

1. Bake sweet potatoes at 350°F 45 minutes, or until tender.
2. Core apples and cut into thin slices. (To avoid darkening, brush with lemon juice.)
3. Peel baked potatoes and cut into ½-inch-thick slices.
4. Alternate layers of potatoes and apples in a greased 2½-quart casserole. Drizzle with honey and sprinkle with nutmeg.
5. Bake, covered, at 350°F 20 minutes, or until heated through.

6 servings

400 Pecan Sweet Potatoes

¼ cup butter or margarine
2 tablespoons cornstarch
¾ cup firmly packed brown sugar
½ teaspoon salt
2 cups orange juice
2 cans (23 ounces each) sweet
  potatoes, drained
¼ cup chopped pecans

1. Melt butter in a saucepan. Blend cornstarch, brown sugar, and salt; mix with butter. Gradually add orange juice, stirring until thickened and clear.
2. Put sweet potatoes into a 1½-quart casserole. Pour sauce over sweet potatoes. Sprinkle with pecans.
3. Bake, covered, at 350°F 45 minutes, or until heated through.

8 servings

401 *Spinach Bake*

2 packages (10 ounces each) frozen chopped spinach, thawed and drained
2 cups milk
6 eggs
½ teaspoon salt
1 tablespoon instant minced onion
¾ cup (3 ounces) shredded Swiss cheese

1. Blend spinach, milk, eggs, and salt in a blender.
2. Pour into an 8-inch square baking dish. Sprinkle with onion and cheese.
3. Bake, uncovered, at 325°F 45 minutes, or until set. Let stand a few minutes. Cut into squares to serve.

6 servings

402 *Spinach-Artichoke Casserole*

1 jar (6 ounces) marinated artichoke hearts, drained
2 packages (10 ounces each) frozen chopped spinach, cooked and squeezed
1 package (8 ounces) cream cheese, softened
2 tablespoons butter or margarine, softened
¼ cup milk
½ teaspoon freshly ground pepper
¼ cup (1 ounce) grated Parmesan cheese

1. Put artichoke hearts into a 1½-quart casserole.
2. Spread spinach over artichoke hearts.
3. Beat together cream cheese and butter. Gradually add milk, beating until smooth. Spread over spinach.
4. Sprinkle pepper and Parmesan cheese over top.
5. Bake, covered, at 350°F 30 minutes. Remove cover. Garnish with **pimento strips** and **hard-cooked egg slices.** Bake an additional 10 minutes, or until heated through.

6 servings

403 *Spinach and Rice*

1 package (10 ounces) frozen chopped spinach, cooked and drained
1 can (10¾ ounces) condensed cream of mushroom soup
1½ cups boiling water
1⅓ cups packaged precooked rice
⅛ teaspoon garlic powder
1 teaspoon lemon juice
2 hard-cooked eggs, sliced
¾ cup (3 ounces) shredded Cheddar cheese
1 can (3 ounces) French-fried onions

1. Combine spinach, soup, boiling water, rice, garlic powder, and lemon juice. Put into a 1½-quart shallow baking dish.
2. Bake, covered, at 400°F 25 minutes, or until rice is tender. Remove cover and stir. Arrange eggs over top. Sprinkle with cheese. Place onions around edge. Bake an additional 5 minutes, or until cheese is melted.

4 servings

404 *Spinach Pudding*

¼ cup chopped onion
¼ cup chopped green pepper
2 tablespoons butter or margarine
1 tablespoon flour
1 teaspoon salt
1 cup milk
2 packages (10 ounces each) frozen chopped spinach, cooked and drained
2 eggs, well beaten

1. Sauté onion and green pepper in butter in a skillet. Stir in flour and salt. Gradually add milk, stirring until thickened and smooth. Remove from heat.
2. Stir in spinach and eggs. Pour into a greased 1-quart casserole. Set casserole in pan of hot water 1 inch deep.
3. Bake, uncovered, at 350°F 30 minutes, or until set. If desired, garnish with pimento strips.

6 servings

405 *Layered Tomato Casserole*

1 cup sliced celery
4 tablespoons butter or margarine
¾ teaspoon basil
½ teaspoon salt
¼ teaspoon pepper
3 tomatoes, sliced
1 large onion, sliced
1 garlic clove, minced
⅓ cup fine dry bread crumbs

1. Put celery into a 1½-quart casserole.
2. Dot with 1 tablespoon butter. Sprinkle with a little basil, a little salt, and a dash of pepper. Repeat with a layer of tomatoes and a layer of onion.
3. Sauté garlic in remaining 1 tablespoon butter. Stir in bread crumbs. Sprinkle over onion.
4. Bake, covered, at 350°F 30 minutes, or until vegetables are tender.

6 servings

406 *Baked Tomato Pudding*

1 can (20 ounces) tomatoes (undrained)
⅔ cup firmly packed brown sugar
1 teaspoon salt
½ cup water
4 slices white bread, cut in ½-inch cubes (about 3 cups)
½ cup butter or margarine, melted

1. Force tomatoes through a sieve into a saucepan; add brown sugar, salt, and water. Bring to a boil; boil 5 minutes.
2. Put bread crumbs into a 1½-quart casserole. Pour melted butter over bread cubes. Add tomato mixture and stir.
3. Bake, uncovered, at 350°F 45 minutes.

6 servings

407 Sue's Best Zucchini

4 small zucchini, thinly sliced
¾ cup shredded carrot
½ cup chopped onion
6 tablespoons butter or margarine, melted
2½ cups herb stuffing cubes
1 can (10¾ ounces) condensed cream of mushroom soup
½ cup dairy sour cream

1. Combine all ingredients. Put into a 1½-quart casserole.
2. Bake, covered, at 350°F 30 to 40 minutes, or until zucchini is tender, stirring once.

6 servings

408 Sauerkraut Casserole

1 tablespoon butter or margarine
2 large onions, chopped
6½ cups drained sauerkraut, snipped
2 medium apples, quartered, cored, and diced
1 small carrot, pared and shredded
2 medium potatoes, shredded (about 1½ cups)
½ cup dry white wine
1 to 2 tablespoons brown sugar
2 teaspoons caraway seed
½ teaspoon seasoned pepper
Brown sugar
Apple, thinly sliced

1. Heat butter in a skillet. Add onion and cook, stirring occasionally, until crisp-tender, 3 to 5 minutes.
2. Meanwhile, combine kraut, diced apple, carrot, and potato in a large bowl. Toss until mixed.
3. Add onion, wine, 1 to 2 tablespoons brown sugar, caraway seed, and seasoned pepper. Toss again. Turn into a 2-quart casserole; sprinkle generously with brown sugar.
4. Overlap thinly sliced apple on top; sprinkle again with brown sugar.
5. Heat in a 350°F oven until thoroughly heated and apples are tender.

10 to 12 servings

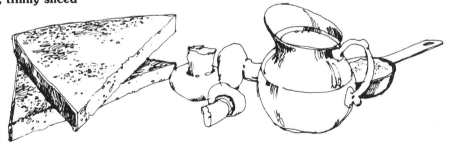

409 Beets in Red Wine Sauce

2 tablespoons butter
1 shallot, minced
2 tablespoons flour
1 jar or can (16 ounces) beets, drained and ⅓ cup liquid reserved
⅓ cup beef bouillon
⅓ cup red wine
Ground cloves (optional)

1. Melt butter in a saucepan; stir in minced shallot. Add flour, stirring constantly for 1 minute.
2. Blend reserved beef liquid, bouillon, and red wine into flour mixture; bring to boiling, stirring until sauce is smooth and thick. Sprinkle lightly with cloves, if desired.
3. Add beets and heat thoroughly.

4 to 6 servings

410 *Red Cabbage and Wine*

1 head (about 2 pounds) red
  cabbage
1 cup red wine
⅓ cup firmly packed brown sugar
1 teaspoon salt
  Few grains cayenne pepper
4 medium apples
¼ cup cider vinegar
¼ cup butter

1. Remove and discard wilted outer leaves of cabbage. Rinse, cut into quarters (discarding core), and coarsely shred (about 2 quarts, shredded). Put cabbage into a saucepan with wine, brown sugar, salt, and pepper.
2. Rinse, quarter, core, and pare apples. Add the apples to the saucepan.
3. Cover and simmer over low heat 20 to 30 minutes, or until cabbage is tender. Add vinegar and butter. Toss together lightly until butter is melted.

6 servings

411 *Celery Coronado*

3 celery hearts
1 tablespoon green pepper,
  chopped
¼ cup butter or margarine
1 cup chicken bouillon or broth
½ cup dry white wine, such as
  sauterne
1 small jar pimentos
  Sliced almonds, sautéed

1. Wash celery and split lengthwise. Sauté celery and green pepper in butter, turning celery gently.
2. Add bouillon and wine. Cover and cook over low heat until celery is tender-crisp.
3. Remove celery to heat-resistant platter and keep warm in oven.
4. Reduce the sauce until it has a glazed appearance. Pour it over the celery. Garnish with strips of pimento and sautéed almonds.

4 to 6 servings

412 *Mushrooms in Wine Sauce on Toast*

1 cup water
½ cup white wine
3 tablespoons butter
1 pound fresh mushrooms,
  cleaned
1 tablespoon flour
  Juice of ½ lemon
1 egg yolk
¼ cup light cream
4 slices toast, sliced diagonally

1. Combine water, wine, and 1 tablespoon of the butter; add to the mushrooms in a saucepan. Bring to boiling; cover and let simmer 10 minutes. Drain, reserving broth.
2. Heat 2 tablespoons butter and blend in flour. Gradually add reserved broth, stirring constantly. Bring to boiling; stir and cook 1 to 2 minutes.
3. Thinly slice the mushrooms; mix into sauce with lemon juice. Cook 5 minutes.
4. Beat the egg yolk with cream. Gradually add mushroom mixture and mix well. Serve mushrooms on toast points.

4 servings

413 *Celery and Green Pepper au Gratin*

4 cups diagonally sliced celery
2 green peppers, thinly sliced
¼ cup dry sherry
3 tablespoons butter or
  margarine, melted
1 cup soft bread crumbs
½ cup crumbled blue cheese

1. Cook celery and green pepper, covered, in a small amount of boiling salted water until crisp-tender (about 5 minutes); drain. Turn vegetables into a shallow 1½-quart baking dish and drizzle with 3 tablespoons sherry.
2. Mix remaining sherry with butter and toss with bread crumbs and blue cheese. Spoon over vegetables.
3. Set under broiler with top 3 to 4 inches from heat. Broil until top is lightly browned.

6 to 8 servings

414 *Sweet and Sour Red Cabbage*

1 head (2 pounds) red cabbage
4 tablespoons brown sugar
1 teaspoon salt
½ cup beef bouillon
¼ cup cider vinegar
4 slices bacon, diced
4 tablespoons butter
2 medium cooking (sour) apples,
   pared and sliced
1 cup red wine

1. Discard tough, outer leaves of cabbage and shred, as for cole slaw.
2. Combine brown sugar, salt, bouillon, and vinegar as a marinade. Let cabbage stand in marinade 1 hour or longer. (This cabbage is limp when served so can be marinated as long as you wish.)
3. Cook bacon until crisp; drain bacon pieces, and pour off all but 2 tablespoons of bacon fat.
4. Melt butter in bacon fat. Add cabbage, marinade and all. Arrange apples on top of cabbage. Cover and cook slowly 1 hour.
5. Add wine, cover, and simmer 30 minutes.

6 servings

415 *Macaroni Vegetable Medley au Vin*

2 cups (8 ounces) elbow
   macaroni
1 package (10 ounces) frozen
   mixed vegetables
2 tablespoons butter or
   margarine
3 ounces fresh mushrooms,
   chopped
½ cup chopped onion
1 can (about 10 ounces)
   condensed cream of celery
   soup
1 soup can milk
2 teaspoons Worcestershire
   sauce
1 teaspoon salt
¼ teaspoon white pepper
1 teaspoon dry mustard
½ cup dry sherry or dry white
   wine
¼ cup chopped pimento
1 cup cooked peas
½ pound Swiss cheese, shredded
   Chopped parsley
   Pimento strips

1. Cook macaroni and frozen vegetables following directions on package. Drain and set aside.
2. Heat butter in a skillet; add mushrooms and onion. Cook, stirring occasionally, until onion is soft; set aside.
3. In a large bowl mix soup, milk, Worcestershire sauce, salt, white pepper, dry mustard, and wine. Add chopped pimento, peas, cheese, mushroom mixture, mixed vegetables, and macaroni; mix well. Turn into a greased 2½-quart casserole.
4. Bake at 300°F until thoroughly heated, about 30 minutes. Garnish with chopped parsley and pimento strips.

About 8 servings

Meat

416 *Italian-Style Meat Stew*

¼ cup olive oil
1 pound lean beef for stew (1½-inch cubes)
1 pound lean lamb for stew (1½-inch cubes)
1 can (28 ounces) tomatoes (undrained)
1½ cups boiling water
1½ cups chopped onion
1 cup diced celery
2 teaspoons salt
½ teaspoon ground black pepper
4 large potatoes, pared and quartered (about 3 cups)
5 large carrots, pared and cut in strips (about 2 cups)
1 teaspoon basil, crushed
¼ teaspoon garlic powder
½ cup cold water
¼ cup enriched all-purpose flour

1. Heat oil in a large saucepot or Dutch oven; add meat and brown on all sides.
2. Add undrained tomatoes, boiling water, onion, celery, salt, and pepper to saucepot. Cover and simmer 1 to 1½ hours, or until meat is almost tender.
3. Add potatoes, carrots, basil, and garlic powder to saucepot; mix well. Simmer 45 minutes, or until meat and vegetables are tender when pierced with a fork.
4. Blend cold water and flour; add gradually to meat-and-vegetable mixture, stirring constantly. Bring to boiling and continue to stir and boil 1 to 2 minutes, or until sauce is thickened. (Leftover sauce may be served the following day on mashed potatoes.)

8 to 10 servings

417 *Oxtail Stew*

½ cup enriched all-purpose flour
1 teaspoon salt
¼ teaspoon ground black pepper
3 oxtails (about 1 pound each), disjointed
3 tablespoons butter or margarine
1½ cups chopped onion
1 can (28 ounces) tomatoes, drained (reserve liquid)
1½ cups hot water
4 medium potatoes, pared
6 medium carrots, pared
2 pounds fresh peas, shelled
1 tablespoon paprika
1 teaspoon salt
¼ teaspoon ground black pepper
¼ cup cold water
2 tablespoons flour

1. Mix ½ cup flour, 1 teaspoon salt, and ¼ teaspoon pepper in a plastic bag; coat oxtail pieces evenly by shaking two or three at a time.
2. Heat butter in a 3-quart top-of-range casserole. Add onion and cook until soft. Remove onion with a slotted spoon and set aside.
3. Put meat into casserole and brown on all sides. Return onion to casserole. Pour in the reserved tomato liquid (set tomatoes aside) and hot water. Cover tightly and simmer 2½ to 3 hours, or until meat is almost tender when pierced with a fork.
4. When meat has cooked about 2 hours, cut potatoes and carrots into small balls, using a melon-ball cutter. Cut the tomatoes into pieces.
5. When meat is almost tender, mix in potatoes, carrots, peas, paprika, 1 teaspoon salt, and ¼ teaspoon pepper. Cover and simmer 20 minutes. Stir in tomatoes and cook 10 minutes, or until meat and vegetables are tender. Put meat and vegetables into a warm dish.
6. Blend cold water and 2 tablespoons flour; add half gradually to cooking liquid, stirring constantly. Bring to boiling; gradually add only what is needed of remaining flour mixture for desired gravy consistency. Bring to boiling after each addition. Cook 3 to 5 minutes after final addition. Return meat and vegetables to casserole and heat thoroughly.

6 to 8 servings

418 *Sauerbraten Moderne*

1 cup wine vinegar
1 cup water
1 medium onion, thinly sliced
2 tablespoons sugar
1 teaspoon salt
5 peppercorns
3 whole cloves
1 bay leaf
2 pounds beef round steak (¾ inch thick), boneless, cut in cubes
1 lemon, thinly sliced
2 tablespoons butter or margarine
1 can (10¾ ounces) beef gravy
1 can (3 ounces) broiled sliced mushrooms (undrained)
6 gingersnaps, crumbled (about ⅔ cup)
Cooked noodles

1. Combine vinegar, water, onion, sugar, salt, peppercorns, cloves, and bay leaf in a saucepan. Heat just to boiling.
2. Meanwhile, put meat into a large shallow dish and arrange lemon slices over it. Pour hot vinegar mixture into dish. Cover and allow to marinate about 2 hours.
3. Remove and discard peppercorns, cloves, bay leaf, and lemon slices; reserve onion. Drain meat thoroughly, reserving marinade.
4. Heat butter in a skillet over medium heat. Add meat and brown pieces on all sides. Stir 1 cup of the reserved liquid with the onion into skillet. Cover, bring to boiling, reduce heat, and simmer about 45 minutes.
5. Blend beef gravy and mushrooms with liquid into mixture in skillet. Bring to boiling and simmer, loosely covered, about 20 minutes longer, or until meat is tender.
6. Add the crumbled gingersnaps to mixture in skillet and cook, stirring constantly, until gravy is thickened. Serve over noodles.

6 to 8 servings

419 *Short Ribs, Western Style*

4 medium onions, peeled and
    quartered
2 teaspoons salt
¼ teaspoon ground black pepper
½ teaspoon rubbed sage
1 quart water
1 cup dried lima beans
3 tablespoons flour
1 teaspoon dry mustard
2 to 3 tablespoons fat
2 pounds beef rib short ribs, cut in
    serving-size pieces

1. Combine onions, salt, pepper, sage, and water in a large heavy saucepot or Dutch oven. Cover, bring to boiling, reduce heat, and simmer 5 minutes. Bring to boiling again; add lima beans gradually and cook, uncovered, 2 minutes. Remove from heat, cover, and set aside to soak 1 hour.
2. Meanwhile, mix flour and dry mustard and coat short ribs evenly.
3. Heat fat in a large heavy skillet and brown short ribs on all sides over medium heat. Add meat to soaked lima beans. Bring to boiling and simmer, covered, 1½ hours, or until beans and meat are tender.

About 6 servings

420 *Kidney Bean Rice Olympian*

2 tablespoons olive oil
1½ pounds beef round steak,
    boneless, cut in 1-inch cubes
2 teaspoons salt
¼ teaspoon ground black pepper
2 large cloves garlic, crushed in a
    garlic press
2 cups beef broth
1 cup sliced celery
1 can (16 ounces) tomatoes, cut in
    pieces (undrained)
2 cans (16 ounces each) kidney
    beans (undrained)
1 large green pepper, diced
3 cups hot cooked rice
1 large head lettuce, finely shredded
3 medium onions, peeled and
    coarsely chopped

1. Heat olive oil in a large heavy skillet. Add meat and brown on all sides. Add salt, pepper, and garlic; pour in beef broth. Bring to boiling, reduce heat, and simmer, covered, about 1 hour.
2. Stir celery and tomatoes and beans with liquid into beef in skillet; bring to boiling and simmer, covered, 30 minutes. Add green pepper and continue cooking 30 minutes.
3. To serve, spoon rice onto each serving plate, cover generously with shredded lettuce, and spoon a generous portion of the bean mixture over lettuce. Top each serving with about 3 tablespoons chopped onion.

About 8 servings

421 *Lamb Crown Roast with Mint Stuffing*

8 slices enriched white bread,
    toasted and cubed
1 unpared red apple, cored and
    diced
1½ tablespoons coarsely chopped
    mint or 1½ teaspoons dried
    mint flakes
¾ teaspoon poultry seasoning

1. Combine toasted bread cubes, apple, mint, poultry seasoning, and salt in a large bowl.
2. Heat butter in a saucepan. Mix in celery and onion and cook about 5 minutes. Pour over bread mixture along with water; toss lightly.
3. Place lamb on a rack, rib ends up, in a shallow roasting pan. Fill center with stuffing.
4. Roast in a 325°F oven about 2½ hours, or until a meat

½ teaspoon salt
6 tablespoons butter
½ cup chopped celery
¼ cup chopped onion
½ cup water
1 lamb rib crown roast (5 to 6 pounds)

thermometer registers 175° to 180°F (depending on desired degree of doneness).

5. Place roast on a heated serving platter. Prepare gravy, if desired. Accompany with Parsley-Buttered New Potatoes (page 68) and Butter-Sauced Asparagus (page 65).

About 8 servings

422 *Lamb Kabobs*

1½ pounds lamb (leg, loin, or shoulder), boneless, cut in 1½-inch cubes
½ cup vegetable oil
1 tablespoon lemon juice
2 teaspoons sugar
½ teaspoon salt
½ teaspoon paprika
¼ teaspoon dry mustard
⅛ teaspoon ground black pepper
¼ teaspoon Worcestershire sauce
1 clove garlic, cut in halves
6 small whole cooked potatoes
6 small whole cooked onions
Butter or margarine, melted
6 plum tomatoes

1. Put lamb cubes into a shallow dish. Combine oil, lemon juice, sugar, salt, paprika, dry mustard, pepper, Worcestershire sauce, and garlic. Pour over meat. Cover and marinate at least 1 hour in refrigerator, turning pieces occasionally. Drain.

2. Alternately thread lamb cubes, potatoes, and onions on 6 skewers. Brush pieces with melted butter.

3. Broil 3 to 4 inches from heat about 15 minutes, or until lamb is desired degree of doneness; turn frequently and brush with melted butter. Shortly before kabobs are done, impale tomatoes on ends of skewers.

6 servings

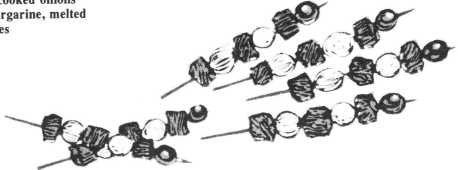

423 *Oven Lamb Stew*

2 pounds lean lamb shoulder, boneless, cut in 2-inch cubes
1¾ teaspoons salt
¼ teaspoon thyme, crushed
1 bay leaf
4 whole allspice
2 tablespoons chopped parsley
1 clove garlic, minced
¼ small head cabbage, shredded
2 leeks, thinly sliced
2 medium onions, sliced
1 cup sliced raw potatoes
4 cups water
8 small onions
4 carrots, cut in 2-inch pieces
2 white turnips, quartered

1. Put lamb into a Dutch oven. Season with salt, thyme, bay leaf, allspice, parsley, and garlic. Add cabbage, leeks, sliced onions, and potatoes. Pour in water. Cover tightly and bring rapidly to boiling.

2. Cook in a 350°F oven about 1½ hours, or until meat is tender.

3. About 30 minutes before cooking time is ended, cook whole onions, carrots, and turnips separately in boiling salted water until tender. Drain.

4. Turn contents of Dutch oven into a food mill set over a large bowl. Return meat to the Dutch oven and add the cooked onions, carrots, and turnips. Discard bay leaf and allspice; force the vegetables through food mill into the bowl containing cooking liquid (or purée vegetables in an electric blender). Heat with meat and vegetables.

6 to 8 servings

424 *Company Beef and Peaches*

1 can (8 ounces) tomato sauce with
    onions
1 can (8 ounces) sliced peaches,
    drained; reserve syrup
¾ cup beef broth
2 tablespoons brown sugar
2 tablespoons lemon juice
1 tablespoon prepared mustard
1 teaspoon Worcestershire sauce
1 clove garlic, minced
1 beef round bottom round roast or
    eye round roast, boneless (2 to 3
    pounds)
    Vegetable oil
    Salt and seasoned pepper
2 tablespoons cold water
2 teaspoons cornstarch
    Watercress or parsley

1. Turn the tomato sauce with onions into a bowl. Mix in the peach syrup (set peaches aside), beef broth, brown sugar, lemon juice, prepared mustard, Worcestershire sauce, and garlic. Set aside.
2. Cut meat across the grain into 6 to 8 slices, about ¾ inch thick.
3. Heat oil in a large skillet. Add the meat slices and brown on both sides. Sprinkle with salt and seasoned pepper. Pour the sauce mixture over the meat. Bring to boiling, reduce heat, and simmer, covered, about 1½ hours, or until meat is fork-tender; turn meat slices occasionally.
4. Overlap meat slices to one side of a heated serving platter.
5. Blend water and cornstarch; stir into sauce in skillet. Bring to boiling; cook about 1 minute. Mix in sliced peaches and heat thoroughly; spoon to the side of meat on the platter. Cover meat with sauce. Garnish with watercress.

6 to 8 servings

425 *Red-Topper Meat Loaf*

Meat loaf:
2 tablespoons butter or margarine
¾ cup finely chopped onion
¼ cup chopped green pepper
1½ pounds lean ground beef
½ pound bulk pork sausage
1 cup uncooked oats, quick or old
    fashioned
2 eggs, beaten
¾ cup tomato juice
¼ cup prepared horseradish
2 teaspoons salt
1 teaspoon dry mustard
½ teaspoon monosodium glutamate

Topping:
1 to 3 tablespoons brown sugar
1 teaspoon dry mustard
¼ cup ketchup

1. For meat loaf, heat butter in a skillet. Mix in onion and green pepper; cook about 5 minutes, or until onion is soft.
2. Meanwhile, lightly mix beef, sausage, and oats in a large bowl. Combine eggs, tomato juice, horseradish, salt, dry mustard, and monosodium glutamate; add to meat mixture and mix lightly. Turn into a 9×5×3-inch loaf pan and press lightly.
3. For topping, mix brown sugar with dry mustard and blend in ketchup. Spread over meat loaf.
4. Bake at 375°F about 1 hour. Remove from oven and allow meat to stand several minutes before slicing.

About 8 servings

426 *Liver-Apple Bake*

1 pound sliced beef liver (about ¼
    inch thick)
2 cups chopped apple
½ cup chopped onion
2 teaspoons seasoned salt
⅛ teaspoon ground black pepper
4 slices bacon, cut in thirds
    Parsley sprigs

1. Remove tubes and outer membrane from liver, if necessary. Put liver slices into a greased shallow baking dish.
2. Combine apple, onion, seasoned salt, and pepper; toss to mix. Spoon over liver. Arrange bacon pieces over top. Cover dish.
3. Cook in a 325°F oven 1 hour. Remove cover and continue cooking about 15 minutes.
4. Garnish with parsley.

4 servings

427 *Roast Leg of Lamb*

1 teaspoon salt
½ teaspoon monosodium glutamate
½ teaspoon ground black pepper
1 teaspoon seasoned salt
½ teaspoon ground marjoram
¼ teaspoon dry mustard
⅛ teaspoon ground cardamom
1 lamb leg, whole (about 6 pounds)
2 cloves garlic, cut in slivers
½ teaspoon ground thyme
  Orange peel, cut in slivers
  Fresh mint sprigs (optional)

1. Mix salt, monosodium glutamate, pepper, seasoned salt, marjoram, dry mustard, and cardamom; rub over lamb. Cut about 16 deep slits in roast. Toss garlic and thyme together. Insert garlic in each slit along with a sliver of orange peel.
2. Place lamb, fat side up, on a rack in a shallow roasting pan. Insert meat thermometer in center of thickest portion of meat.
3. Roast, uncovered, in a 325°F oven 2½ to 3 hours. Meat is medium done when thermometer registers 175°F and is well done at 180°F.
4. Remove meat thermometer. Place roast on a warm serving platter. Put a paper frill around end of leg bone and garnish platter with mint, if desired.

About 10 servings

428 *Pork Loin Roast*

1 pork loin roast (4 to 6 pounds)
  Salt and pepper
  Spiced crab apples

1. Have the meat retailer saw across the rib bones of roast at base of the backbone, separating the ribs from the backbone. Place roast, fat side up, on a rack in an open roasting pan. Season with salt and pepper. Insert meat thermometer in roast so the bulb is centered in the thickest part and not resting on bone or in fat.
2. Roast in a 350°F oven about 2½ to 3 hours, or until thermometer registers 170°F; allow 30 to 40 minutes per pound.
3. For easy carving, remove backbone, place roast on platter, and allow roast to set for 15 to 20 minutes. Garnish platter with spiced crab apples, heated if desired. Accompany with Hash Brown Potatoes au Gratin ●

8 to 10 servings

429 *Veal Glacé*

1 cup dry white wine
1½ teaspoons tarragon leaves
1½ pounds veal cutlets (about ¼ inch thick)
3 tablespoons butter
½ teaspoon salt
⅛ teaspoon ground black pepper
½ cup condensed consommé (undiluted)
½ cup dry vermouth

1. Stir tarragon into white wine. Cover; allow to stand several hours, stirring occasionally.
2. Cut meat into pieces about 3×2 inches. Heat butter in skillet until lightly browned. Add meat and brown lightly. Season with salt and pepper. Reduce heat and pour in tarragon wine mixture with the consommé and vermouth. Simmer uncovered, about 10 minutes, or until veal is tender.
3. Remove veal to a heated dish and cover. Increase heat under skillet and cook sauce until it is reduced to a thin glaze (about 10 minutes), stirring occasionally.
4. Pour glaze over meat, turning meat to coat evenly. Serve hot.

About 6 servings

Note: If desired, accompany with buttered fluffy rice tossed with chopped parsley and toasted slivered almonds.

430 *Curried Veal and Vegetables*

1 pound veal for stew (1-inch cubes)
2 cups water
1 teaspoon salt
3 medium carrots, pared and cut in quarters
½ pound green beans
2 large stalks celery, cut in ½-inch slices
3 tablespoons butter or margarine
2 tablespoons flour
½ teaspoon curry powder
¼ teaspoon salt
Cooked rice
Fresh parsley, snipped

1. Put veal into a large saucepan with water and 1 teaspoon salt. Cover, bring to boiling, reduce heat, and simmer 1 hour. Add carrots, green beans, and celery. Cover, bring to boiling, and simmer 1 hour, or until meat is tender.
2. Remove meat and vegetables from broth with a slotted spoon; set aside. Reserve broth.
3. Heat butter in a saucepan. Blend in flour, curry powder, and ¼ teaspoon salt. Heat until bubbly. Add reserved broth gradually, stirring until smooth. Bring to boiling, stirring constantly, and cook 1 to 2 minutes. Mix in meat and vegetables. Heat thoroughly.
4. Serve over rice. Sprinkle with parsley.

About 6 servings

431 *Saucy Ham Loaf*

Meat loaf:
1½ pounds ground cooked ham
½ pound ground veal
½ pound ground pork
2 eggs, fork beaten
½ teaspoon salt
⅛ teaspoon ground black pepper
½ teaspoon ground nutmeg
½ teaspoon dry mustard
¼ teaspoon ground thyme
¼ cup finely chopped onion
½ cup finely chopped green pepper
2 tablespoons finely chopped parsley
¾ cup soft enriched bread crumbs
¾ cup apple juice

Sauce:
⅔ cup packed light brown sugar
2 teaspoons cornstarch
1 teaspoon dry mustard
1 teaspoon ground allspice
⅔ cup apricot nectar
3 tablespoons lemon juice
2 teaspoons vinegar

1. Combine ham, veal, and pork with eggs, salt, pepper, nutmeg, dry mustard, and thyme in a large bowl. Add onion, green pepper, and parsley and toss to blend. Add bread crumbs and apple juice; mix thoroughly but lightly. Turn into a 9×5×3-inch loaf pan and flatten top.
2. Bake at 350°F 1 hour.
3. Meanwhile, prepare sauce for topping. Blend brown sugar, cornstarch, dry mustard, and allspice in a small saucepan. Add apricot nectar, lemon juice, and vinegar. Bring rapidly to boiling and cook about 2 minutes, stirring constantly. Reduce heat and simmer 10 minutes to allow flavors to blend.
4. Remove meat loaf from oven; pour off and reserve juices. Unmold loaf in a shallow baking pan. Spoon some of the reserved juices and then the sauce over loaf. Return to oven 30 minutes.
5. Place loaf on a warm platter and garnish as desired.

8 to 10 servings

432 *Canadian-Style Bacon and Peaches*

Roast Canadian-Style Bacon:
- 2 pounds smoked pork loin Canadian-style bacon (in one piece)
- 10 whole cloves

Orange-Spiced Peaches:
- ½ cup firmly packed brown sugar
- ⅓ cup red wine vinegar
- 1 tablespoon grated orange peel
- 2 tablespoons orange juice
- 1 teaspoon whole cloves
- ½ teaspoon whole allspice
- 1 can (29 ounces) peach halves, drained; reserve 1½ cups syrup
- Mustard Sauce

1. Remove casing from the meat and place, fat side up, on a rack in a shallow roasting pan. Stud with cloves. Insert a meat thermometer into bacon so bulb is centered. Roast, uncovered, at 325°F about 2 hours, or until thermometer registers 160°F.
2. For Orange-Spiced Peaches, stir brown sugar, wine vinegar, orange peel, orange juice, cloves, allspice, and peach syrup together in a saucepan. Bring to boiling; reduce heat and simmer 5 minutes. Mix in peaches and heat 5 minutes.
3. Remove from heat and allow peaches to cool in syrup. Refrigerate until ready to serve.
4. Shortly before meat is roasted, prepare Mustard Sauce.
5. Remove meat from oven and place on a heated serving platter. Remove thermometer. Arrange peaches on platter. Accompany with Mustard Sauce in a bowl.

About 8 servings

Mustard Sauce: Mix **1 cup firmly packed brown sugar, 2 tablespoons prepared mustard, 1 tablespoon butter or margarine, 3 tablespoons cider vinegar** in a saucepan. Stir over low heat until sugar is dissolved; heat thoroughly, stirring occasionally.

⅔ cup sauce

433 *Savory Sweetbreads*

- 1½ pounds sweetbreads
- Cold water
- ¼ cup lemon juice
- 1 teaspoon salt
- 1½ cups beef broth
- 2 stalks celery with leaves, cut in 1-inch pieces
- 2 sprigs parsley
- ¼ teaspoon savory
- ¼ teaspoon thyme
- ⅛ teaspoon ground allspice
- ⅛ teaspoon ground nutmeg
- ⅓ cup butter or margarine
- 2 tablespoons flour
- 2 teaspoons dry mustard
- 1 teaspoon monosodium glutamate
- ⅛ teaspoon ground black pepper
- 1 tablespoon vinegar
- ¼ cup coarsely snipped parsley
- Melba toast (optional)

1. Rinse sweetbreads with cold water as soon as possible after purchase. Put sweetbreads into a saucepan. Cover with cold water and add lemon juice and salt. Cover saucepan, bring to boiling, reduce heat, and simmer 20 minutes. Drain sweetbreads; cover with cold water. Drain again. (Cool and refrigerate if sweetbreads are not to be used immediately.) Remove tubes and membrane; reserve. Separate sweetbreads into smaller pieces and slice; set aside.
2. Pour broth into a saucepan. Add the tubes and membrane, celery, parsley, savory, thyme, allspice, and nutmeg. Bring to boiling and simmer, covered, 30 minutes. Strain broth, reserving 1 cup.
3. Heat butter in a skillet. Blend in flour, dry mustard, monosodium glutamate, and pepper. Heat until bubbly. Add the reserved broth and vinegar while stirring until smooth. Bring to boiling, stirring constantly, and cook until thickened. Add the sweetbreads and parsley. Heat thoroughly.
4. Serve over Melba toast, if desired.

About 6 servings

434 *Flemish Beef Stew* (Carbonnade à la Flamande)

This world-famous dish of beef, beer, and onions is from Belgium. "Carbonnade" originally meant meat grilled over hot coals or embers, but in this dish it now means slow stewing. It makes a savory, guest-pleasing party dish for a buffet dinner. Spoon it over noodles and complete the menu with a tossed salad, French bread, cake, and steins of beer to drink.

4 **pounds beef chuck or round, boneless, cut in 1-inch cubes**
¼ **cup oil**
2 **tablespoons parsley flakes**
2 **teaspoons each thyme, sugar, and salt**
½ **teaspoon pepper**
2 **garlic cloves, minced**
2 **bay leaves**
2 **cans or bottles (12 ounces each) beer**
8 **medium onions, sliced**
¼ **cup cornstarch**

1. Brown meat in oil; place in a very large casserole or two medium ones, about 2½ quarts each. Add seasonings; stir to coat meat.
2. Add beer plus a little water, if needed, to almost cover meat. Cover casseroles.
3. Bake at 300°F 1½ hours.
4. Parboil onion half covered with water, stirring frequently, until soft. Stir into meat. Cover and continue baking 1 to 1½ hours, or until meat is tender.
5. Make a paste of cornstarch and a little water. Stir into casseroles. Return to oven about 10 minutes, stirring once or twice. Serve over **noodles.**

12 to 14 servings

435 *Munich Beef*

This German-style oven beef stew has a sweet-sour gravy.

1 **can or bottle (12 ounces) beer**
1 **medium onion, chopped**
½ **teaspoon salt**
⅛ **teaspoon pepper**
1½ **pounds beef chuck, boneless, cut in 1-inch cubes**
4 **medium carrots (¾ pound)**
3 **tablespoons flour**
2 **tablespoons currant or grape jelly**
1 **tablespoon grated orange or lemon peel**
1 **tablespoon lemon juice**
4 **cups cooked noodles**

1. In a 2- to 2½-quart casserole, combine beer, onion, salt, and pepper. Add beef. Cover; marinate in refrigerator 10 to 24 hours, stirring occasionally.
2. Place casserole in oven (do not brown beef).
3. Bake at 300°F 1½ hours. Add carrots. Continue baking 1 hour longer, or until meat and carrots are tender.
4. Mix flour, jelly, peel, and lemon juice to a paste. Stir into stew. Bake 15 minutes more, stirring once or twice, until thickened and bubbly. Serve over noodles.

6 servings

436 *Savory Beef Stew*

Beer adds a subtle flavor to the gravy, although it is not a typical beer taste. The alcohol boils off early in the cooking, so the dish may be served to children.

1½ **pounds beef stew meat, boneless, cut in 1½-inch cubes**
¼ **cup flour**
1 **teaspoon salt**
¼ **teaspoon basil**
¼ **teaspoon savory or marjoram**
⅛ **teaspoon pepper**
3 **tablespoons vegetable oil**
2 **onions, sliced**
1 **can or bottle (12 ounces) beer**
½ **cup water**
1 **bay leaf**
5 **medium potatoes (1⅔ pounds)**
1 **pound carrots (8 to 10); or ½ pound each parsnips and carrots**

1. Dredge meat in mixture of flour, salt, basil, savory, and pepper. Reserve excess flour. Brown meat in oil. Add onion, beer, water, and bay leaf. Cover and simmer 1½ hours.
2. Pare potatoes; cut into large cubes. Slice carrots and/or parsnips. Add vegetables to stew. If necessary, add a little more water.
3. Cover and simmer 1 hour more, or until meat and vegetables are tender. Make smooth paste of reserved flour mixture and a little water. Stir into stew during last 10 minutes of cooking.

6 servings

437 *Sausage-Stuffed Rouladen with Tomato-Beer Kraut*

1 **beef round steak, cut ½ inch thick (about 2 pounds)**
  Flour
6 **smoked link sausages**
2 **tablespoons oil**
2 **medium onions, sliced**
1 **can (16 ounces) sauerkraut, rinsed and drained**
1 **can (16 ounces) tomatoes (undrained)**
1 **can or bottle (12 ounces) beer**
2 **teaspoons caraway seed**
1 **teaspoon salt**
¼ **teaspoon pepper**
3 **tablespoons flour**

1. Cut beef into 6 serving pieces approximately rectangular in shape. Dredge in flour. Pound on a floured board until as thin as possible. Roll each piece around a sausage. Fasten with wooden picks.
2. In a large skillet, brown meat in oil; set aside. Sauté onion in same skillet until golden.
3. Add sauerkraut, undrained tomatoes, beer, caraway seed, salt, and pepper. Stir. Add beef rolls. Cover and simmer 1½ to 2 hours, or until tender.
4. Transfer meat and vegetables to a serving platter, using slotted spoon. Make paste of flour and a little water; stir into cooking liquid. Cook, stirring constantly, until thickened. Pass gravy in sauceboat.

6 servings

438 *Scandinavian Sailors' Beef Casserole*

This dish is frequently served in Scandinavian homes during the winter. It is a time-honored favorite among sailors.

1½ to 2 pounds beef round steak, boneless, cut ½ inch thick
Flour
3 medium onions, sliced
¼ cup margarine, oil, or butter
6 medium potatoes, pared and thickly sliced
1 teaspoon salt
¼ teaspoon pepper
1 can or bottle (12 ounces) beer
¼ cup minced parsley (optional)

1. Cut meat into 6 serving pieces. Dredge in flour. Pound to ¼-inch thickness.
2. Sauté onion in 2 tablespoons margarine in a large skillet; set aside.
3. In remaining margarine, brown meat on both sides in same skillet.
4. In a large casserole, layer meat, potatoes, and onion, sprinkling layers with salt and pepper.
5. Pour beer into skillet; stir up brown bits. Add to casserole.
6. Cover and bake at 350°F 1½ hours, or until meat is tender. Sprinkle with parsley. Serve with **pickled beets.**

6 servings

439 *Bachelor's Steak*

A perfect main dish for an intimate dinner for two. Complete the menu with a green vegetable or salad, plus your choice of baked potatoes, white and wild rice, or french-fried potatoes (frozen for ease of preparation). Dessert could be ice cream topped with a liqueur.

2 small single-serving steaks (rib, rib eye, strip, T-bone)
1 garlic clove, halved
1 can (2 to 2½ ounces) sliced mushrooms
¼ to ⅓ cup beer
1 tablespoon flour
¼ teaspoon salt
Dash pepper

1. Rub meat with cut surface of garlic. Broil 2 to 3 inches from heat until as done as desired.
2. Meanwhile, drain mushroom liquid into measuring cup. Add enough beer to measure ⅔ cup total liquid.
3. Pour 2 tablespoons steak drippings into a saucepan; stir in flour, salt, and pepper until smooth. Stir in beer mixture. Cook, stirring constantly, until thickened and smooth. Add drained mushrooms; heat through.
4. Pour beer-mushroom sauce over steak and **potatoes.**

2 servings

440 *English Meat Patties*

Similar to Salisbury steaks, this dish is flavored with beer.

1 pound ground beef
½ cup fine dry bread crumbs
½ cup beer
1 small onion, finely minced
½ teaspoon salt
Dash pepper and garlic powder
Oil

Gravy:
2 tablespoons drippings
2 tablespoons flour
½ cup beer
½ cup water
1 teaspoon Worcestershire sauce
¼ teaspoon salt
Dash pepper

1. Combine beef, crumbs, beer, onion, salt, and pepper. Shape into 4 patties.
2. Pan-fry in a very small amount of oil in a skillet, pouring off drippings as they accumulate. Turn once, carefully, and cook until as done as desired. Place patties on a platter; keep warm.
3. For gravy, pour off drippings from skillet; return 2 tablespoons. Stir in flour. Add beer; stir until smooth. Add water and seasonings. Cook, stirring constantly, until thickened; stir up brown bits. After gravy boils, reduce heat and simmer 2 to 3 minutes to mellow beer flavor.

4 servings

Brewerburgers: Follow recipe for English Meat Patties; omit gravy. If desired, broil or grill over coals. 441

442 *Mushroom-Beer Steaks*

1 beef round steak, cut ½ inch thick (2 pounds)
Flour for dredging
¼ cup shortening or cooking oil
2 large onions, sliced
2 garlic cloves, minced
1 can or bottle (12 ounces) beer
1 cup beef broth (homemade, canned, or from bouillon cubes)
¼ cup ketchup
½ teaspoon salt
¼ teaspoon pepper
1 bay leaf
1 can (4½ ounces) mushroom stems and pieces
¼ cup flour

1. Cut meat into 6 serving pieces. Pound with meat mallet.
2. Dredge meat in flour. Brown in shortening in a large skillet; set meat aside.
3. Add onion and garlic to skillet, adding more fat if needed. Sauté until golden. Remove.
4. To skillet add beer, broth, ketchup, salt, pepper, and bay leaf. Stir up brown bits.
5. Layer meat and onions in skillet. Cover and simmer 1 to 1½ hours, or until meat is tender. Drain mushrooms, reserving liquid. Add mushrooms during last 5 minutes.
6. Place meat, onions, and mushrooms on serving platter; cover with foil to keep warm. Measure liquid. If needed, add water to measure about 2 cups.
7. Mix ¼ cup flour, mushroom liquid, and just enough water to make a smooth paste. Stir into cooking liquid. Cook, stirring constantly, until thickened. Serve gravy over meat and a **noodle** or **potato** accompaniment.

6 servings

443 *Marinated Venison in Cream Gravy*

This marinade may be used for various kinds of game: rabbit, duck, and other birds. Cut proportions, if necessary.

1 venison roast, preferably from leg (4 to 5 pounds)
1 cup chopped onion
⅓ cup oil
2 cans or bottles (12 ounces each) beer
2 tablespoons lemon juice
2 teaspoons salt
1 teaspoon thyme
8 peppercorns
2 garlic cloves, minced
1 bay leaf
½ cup cream or half-and-half (about)
Flour

1. Place venison in a large glass bowl.
2. Sauté onion in oil. Stir in beer and seasonings. Pour over venison. Marinate in refrigerator 24 to 36 hours, turning occasionally.
3. Place venison and marinade in a Dutch oven. Cover.
4. Bake at 325°F 2½ hours, or until tender, basting several times. (Venison may be cooked a shorter time to rare, only if meat is from a young animal.)
5. Transfer venison to a platter. Strain cooking liquid; skim off most of fat. Measure liquid. Make a paste of cream and 2 tablespoons flour for each 1 cup cooking liquid. Combine the paste in a saucepan with liquid and cook, stirring constantly, until thickened. Season to taste. Serve in a sauceboat along with venison.

2 or 3 servings per pound

444 Old-World Short Ribs

Select meaty beef short ribs for this hearty and savory entrée. Serve with noodles, pouring gravy over both. Complete the meal with tossed salad, beverage, and dessert.

3 to 4 pounds beef short ribs
2 tablespoons oil
1 medium onion, chopped
1 can (8 ounces) tomato sauce
1 can or bottle (12 ounces) beer
1 teaspoon caraway seed
½ teaspoon salt
⅛ teaspoon pepper
1 bay leaf
¼ cup flour
2 to 3 cups cooked noodles

1. Brown ribs slowly in oil in a Dutch oven or deep skillet. Remove as they are browned.
2. Add onion and sauté until golden. Add tomato sauce, 1¼ cups beer, and seasonings. Return ribs.
3. Cover and simmer 1½ hours, or until tender.
4. Place ribs on platter; keep warm. Skim fat from cooking liquid (there should be about 2 cups liquid). Stir in paste made from flour and remaining ¼ cup beer. Cook, stirring constantly, until thickened. Serve gravy over ribs and noodles.

4 servings

445 Caraway Meat Loaf

With this meat loaf is a beer-flavored chili sauce to be poured over the slices.

1 pound ground beef
1 cup soft bread crumbs (from 2 slices white or rye bread)
1 small onion, minced
⅔ cup beer
1 egg
½ teaspoon caraway seed
½ teaspoon salt
¼ teaspoon pepper
⅓ cup chili sauce

1. Combine beef, crumbs, onion, ⅓ cup beer, egg, caraway seed, salt, and pepper.
2. Shape into a loaf. Place in a roasting pan. (Or pack into a 7 x 3½ x 2-inch loaf pan.)
3. Bake at 350°F 45 minutes.
4. Simmer chili sauce and remaining ⅓ cup beer about 5 minutes; serve over slices of meat loaf.

4 servings

446 Breaded Pork Chops with Beer Gravy

4 pork chops, cut ½ to ¾ inch thick
1 egg
1 tablespoon water
½ cup fine cracker crumbs (from about 12 saltines)
½ teaspoon salt
¼ teaspoon paprika
2 tablespoons oil
¾ cup beer
2 tablespoons flour
¾ cup beef bouillon
1 tablespoon ketchup

1. Dip chops in a mixture of egg and water, coating both sides. Mix crumbs, salt, and paprika. Dip egg-coated chops in this mixture, coating both sides well.
2. Brown chops slowly in oil, cooking about 15 minutes. Reduce heat; add ¼ cup beer. Cover and simmer 20 to 30 minutes, or until done.
3. Make a paste of flour and a little remaining beer. Place chops on platter. Stir flour paste, rest of beer, bouillon, and ketchup into cooking liquid. Cook, stirring constantly, until thickened. Season to taste, if desired. (Makes enough gravy to pour over meat and potatoes.)

4 servings

447 *Jiffy Beer Chili (Pronto Chili con Cerveza)*

A thick and savory chili that can be prepared in almost no time at all for cold days

½ pound ground beef
½ cup chopped onion (frozen, or 1 medium fresh)
1 can (6 ounces) tomato paste
1 can or bottle (12 ounces) beer
1 can (16 ounces) kidney beans (undrained)
1 to 1½ teaspoons chili powder
1 teaspoon sugar
1 teaspoon garlic salt
½ teaspoon oregano

1. Lightly brown ground beef and onion in a heavy medium saucepan; cook until onion is soft.
2. Add tomato paste and beer; stir up brown bits.
3. Add remaining ingredients. Cook slowly uncovered 10 to 15 minutes, or until onion is tender. Add a little water, if needed.

5 cups; 4 servings

448 *Applesauce-Topped Beef and Sausage Loaf*

Meat Loaf:
1 pound ground beef
½ pound pork sausage
½ cup dry bread or cracker crumbs
½ cup beer
1 small onion, minced
1 egg, slightly beaten
½ teaspoon salt
¼ teaspoon each sage, thyme, and garlic powder
⅛ teaspoon pepper

Topping and Sauce:
1⅓ cups applesauce
¼ cup beer

1. For meat loaf, mix ingredients. Shape into an elongated loaf. Place in a shallow roasting pan.
2. Bake at 350°F 50 minutes.
3. Spoon fat from pan. Spread ⅓ cup applesauce over meat loaf. Bake 10 minutes longer.
4. For sauce, heat 1 cup applesauce and beer to simmering; serve over meat loaf slices.

6 servings

449 *Bavarian Casserole*

A good use for leftover roast pork.

2 celery stalks, chopped
1 medium onion, chopped
3 tablespoons butter or margarine
½ teaspoon salt
¼ teaspoon sage
¼ teaspoon sugar
⅛ teaspoon pepper
1 cup beer
4 cups pumpernickel bread cubes (5 slices)
2 cups cubed cooked pork (10 ounces)

1. Sauté celery and onion in butter until soft; stir in seasonings. Add beer.
2. Place bread and pork in a 1½-quart casserole. Add beer-vegetable mixture. Stir lightly.
3. Cover and bake at 375°F 30 to 35 minutes.

4 servings

450 *Savory Spareribs*

4 pounds pork spareribs
1 can or bottle (12 ounces) beer
½ cup honey
2 tablespoons lemon juice
2 teaspoons salt
1 teaspoon dry mustard
¼ teaspoon pepper

1. Cut spareribs into 2-rib sections.
2. Combine remaining ingredients in a shallow glass or ceramic baking dish. Add ribs. Marinate in refrigerator at least 24 hours, turning and basting occasionally.
3. Arrange ribs in a single layer in a large baking pan; reserve marinade.
4. Bake at 350°F 1½ hours, turning once and basting frequently with marinade.

4 to 6 servings

451 *Lagered Ham and Noodle Casserole*

Beer delicately flavors the cheese sauce in this delicious family-style casserole.

1 medium green pepper, chopped
1 medium onion, chopped
¼ cup butter or margarine
3 tablespoons flour
½ teaspoon dry mustard
½ teaspoon salt
  Dash pepper
⅓ cup instant nonfat dry milk
1 can or bottle (12 ounces) beer
1 cup shredded Cheddar cheese (4 ounces)
8 ounces uncooked medium noodles, cooked and drained
2 cups diced cooked ham (⅔ pound)

1. For sauce, slowly sauté green peeper and onion in butter until soft and almost tender. Stir in flour and seasonings.
2. Mix dry milk and ⅓ cup beer.
3. Gradually add remaining beer to flour mixture. Cook, stirring constantly, until thickened and bubbly. Add cheese; stir until melted. Remove from heat; add beer-milk mixture.
4. Combine sauce, cooked noodles, and ham. Turn into a 2½-quart casserole.
5. Bake at 350°F 20 minutes, or until heated through and bubbly.

6 servings

452 *Orange-Ginger Lamb Chops*

4 lamb leg sirloin or shoulder chops
1 tablespoon oil
¾ teaspoon salt
¼ teaspoon ginger
  Dash pepper
1 orange, peeled
1 small to medium onion
1 can or bottle (12 ounces) beer
2 tablespoons sugar
1 tablespoon cornstarch

1. Brown chops in oil in a skillet; pour off fat. Mix salt, ginger, and pepper. Sprinkle over chops.
2. Cut off a thin slice from each end of orange. Cut remainder of orange into 4 slices. Remove seeds. Repeat with onion; do not separate into rings.
3. Top each chop with an orange slice, then an onion slice. Add 1¼ cups beer. Cover and simmer 30 minutes, or until meat is tender.
4. Transfer chops topped with orange and onion to a platter.
5. Mix sugar, cornstarch, and remaining ¼ cup beer. Add to liquid in skillet. Cook, stirring constantly, until thickened. Add dash of salt, if desired. Strain into a sauceboat. Accompany chops with rice, pouring sauce over both.

4 servings

453 *Fruited Pork Roast, Scandinavian Style*

Prunes and apple are stuffed inside a boneless pork roast to create an unusual entrée that's nice for a party or a special family meal. The slices are especially attractive. The sweetened sauce retains just a hint of beer flavor.

1 pork rolled loin roast, boneless,
    (3 to 3½ pounds)
8 to 10 pitted dried prunes
1 can or bottle (12 ounces) beer
½ teaspoon ginger
1 medium apple, pared and
    chopped
1 teaspoon lemon juice
½ teaspoon salt
   Dash pepper
¼ cup flour

1. Make pocket down center of roast by piercing with a long, sharp tool such as a steel knife sharpener; leave strings on roast. (Alternate method: Remove strings. Using strong knife, cut pocket in pork by making a deep slit down length of loin, going to within ½ inch of the two ends and within 1 inch of other side.)
2. Meanwhile, combine prunes, beer, and ginger in a saucepan; heat to boiling. Remove from heat; let stand 30 minutes.
3. Mix apple with lemon juice to prevent darkening. Drain prunes, reserving liquid; pat dry with paper towels. Mix prunes and apple.
4. Pack fruit into pocket in pork, using handle of wooden spoon to pack tightly. (With alternate method of cutting pocket, tie with string at 1-inch intervals. Secure with skewers or sew with kitchen thread.)
5. Place meat on rack in a roasting pan.
6. Roast at 350°F 2 to 2½ hours, allowing 40 to 45 minutes per pound. During last 45 minutes of roasting, spoon fat from pan; baste occasionally with liquid drained from prunes.
7. Transfer meat to a platter. Skim fat from cooking liquid; measure liquid. Add a little water to roasting pan to help loosen brown bits; add to cooking liquid. Add salt, pepper, and enough additional water to measure 2 cups total. Make a paste of flour and a little more water. Combine with cooking liquid. Cook, stirring constantly, until thickened. Pass in a sauceboat for pouring over meat slices.

8 servings

454 *Piquant Lamb Kabobs*

Grill these colorful kabobs outdoors or broil inside. It's a year-round dish. If you wish, substitute tender beef cubes for the lamb.

1½ pounds boneless lamb (leg or
    sirloin), cut in 1-inch cubes
18 fresh medium mushrooms
    (about ½ pound)
¾ cup beer
1 can (6 ounces) pineapple juice
    (¾ cup)
2 tablespoons oil
2 teaspoons soy sauce
1 garlic clove, quartered
18 cherry tomatoes (about 1 pint)
18 green pepper squares (1 large
    pepper)
4 to 5 cups cooked rice

1. Place lamb cubes and whole mushrooms in a ceramic casserole.
2. Combine beer, pineapple juice, oil, soy sauce, and garlic. Pour over lamb and mushrooms. Add a little more beer, if needed.
3. Cover and refrigerate at least 6 hours, or overnight.
4. On each of 6 long skewers, alternate lamb cubes with mushrooms, cherry tomatoes, and green pepper squares. Use 3 each of the vegetables for each skewer.
5. Broil 3 inches from heat to desired doneness (about 10 to 15 minutes), turning once or twice. Watch that vegetables do not overcook.
6. Heat marinade to pass as sauce. Serve kabobs on or with rice.

6 servings

455 Sausage in Beer

1 can or bottle (12 ounces) beer
3 medium onions, thinly sliced
2 medium carrots, thinly sliced
1 teaspoon Worcestershire sauce
½ teaspoon salt
8 bratwurst, knockwurst, Polish sausage, or large frankfurters
8 frankfurter buns

1. Put beer, onion, carrot, Worcestershire sauce, and salt in a saucepan. Heat to boiling. Cover, reduce heat, and simmer 15 minutes.
2. Add sausage. Cover and simmer 15 minutes more, stirring occasionally.
3. Place sausages in buns. Using a slotted spoon, lift vegetables from liquid and place on sausages.

8 servings

456 Luxemburg Stew

2 pounds boneless veal shoulder or stew meat, cut in 1-inch cubes
⅓ cup flour
6 tablespoons butter or margarine
1 large onion, sliced
2 cans (16 ounces each) tomatoes, broken up
1 can or bottle (12 ounces) beer
6 whole cloves
1 teaspoon salt
½ teaspoon thyme
¼ teaspoon crushed rosemary
¼ teaspoon paprika
8 gingersnaps
2 tablespoons lemon juice

1. Dredge veal in flour. Brown in ¼ cup butter in a saucepot. Remove meat.
2. Add remaining 2 tablespoons butter and onion to saucepot. Sauté until golden.
3. Add veal, tomatoes with liquid, beer, and seasonings. Cover and simmer 1 hour.
4. Moisten gingersnaps with a little water; crush. Stir into meat. Simmer 5 minutes more. Add lemon juice; mix well.
5. Serve over **rice** or **noodles** or with **potatoes.**

8 servings

Note: Poultry or lean pork could be substituted for veal.

457 German Veal Chops

4 veal loin or rib chops
Butter or margarine
2 medium onions, sliced
1 cup dark beer
1 bay leaf
½ teaspoon salt
Dash pepper
2 tablespoons flour

1. Brown veal in butter in a skillet; set meat aside. Sauté onion in same skillet until golden.
2. Add beer, bay leaf, salt, and pepper. Cover and simmer 15 minutes.
3. Transfer veal and onion to a platter. Make a paste of flour and a little water; stir into cooking liquid in skillet. Cook, stirring constantly, until thickened and smooth. Pour over veal and onion.

4 servings

Note: If you do not have dark beer, add ½ **teaspoon molasses** to light beer.

458 Taco Casserole

1 pound ground beef
1 package (1.25 ounces) taco
    seasoning mix
1 cup water
1 can (15 ounces) refried beans with
    sausage
2 cups shredded lettuce
¼ cup chopped onion
1 tablespoon chopped green chilies
1 cup (4 ounces) shredded Cheddar
    cheese
    Nacho-flavored tortilla chips
    Chopped tomato
    Sliced ripe olives
    Dairy sour cream
    Taco sauce

1. Brown ground beef in a skillet; drain off excess fat. Add taco mix and water. Simmer, uncovered, until mixture is thickened (about 15 minutes).
2. Lightly grease bottom of an 11x7-inch baking dish. Spread refried beans evenly on the bottom. Sprinkle with shredded lettuce, onion, and chilies; top with ground beef mixture. (If desired, cover and refrigerate until ready to finish.)
3. Bake, uncovered, at 400°F 15 minutes. Sprinkle with shredded cheese and bake an additional 5 minutes, or until cheese is melted and mixture is heated through.
4. Remove from oven and garnish with tortilla chips.
5. Serve with chopped tomato, sliced olives, sour cream, and taco sauce in separate serving dishes.

6 servings

459 Savannah Beef and Noodles

1 pound ground beef
1 cup chopped onion
1 can (28 ounces) tomatoes
    (undrained)
2 teaspoons salt
2 teaspoons chili powder
1 teaspoon Worcestershire sauce
3 cups cooked noodles
1 can (5¾ ounces) pitted ripe olives,
    sliced
2 cups (8 ounces) shredded Cheddar
    cheese

1. Brown ground beef and onion in a skillet; drain off excess fat. Add tomatoes, salt, chili powder, and Worcestershire sauce; simmer 30 minutes.
2. Alternate layers of half the noodles, half the meat mixture, and half the ripe olives in a 2½-quart casserole; repeat layers. Top with shredded cheese.
3. Bake, covered, at 350°F 30 minutes, or until heated through.

6 to 8 servings

460 Easy Beefy Casserole

1 **pound ground beef**
2 **cans (16 ounces each) tomatoes (undrained)**
1 **can (16 ounces) whole kernel corn, drained**
¼ **cup sliced stuffed olives**
½ **cup chopped green pepper**
1 **teaspoon oregano**
1½ **tablespoons instant minced onion**
1 **teaspoon salt**
½ **teaspoon pepper**
2 **cups (about 4 ounces) uncooked noodles**
¼ **cup (1 ounce) grated Parmesan cheese**

1. Brown ground beef in a skillet; drain off excess fat. Add remaining ingredients, except cheese. Put into a 2-quart casserole.
2. Bake, covered, at 350°F 25 minutes. Remove cover. Sprinkle with grated cheese and bake an additional 5 minutes, or until heated through.

6 servings

461 Baked Steak Patties

1 **pound ground beef**
½ **pound pork sausage meat**
2 **cups cooked white rice**
1 **egg**
6 **bacon slices**
1 **package (1⅜ ounces) dry onion soup mix**
3 **cups water**
2 **tablespoons flour**

1. Combine ground beef, sausage, rice, and egg. Shape to form 6 patties. Wrap each with a bacon slice; secure with wooden pick. Place in an 11x7-inch baking dish.
2. Bake, uncovered, at 350°F 30 minutes; drain off excess fat.
3. Meanwhile, combine soup mix and 2½ cups water in a saucepan. Cook, covered, 10 minutes.
4. Mix the remaining ½ cup water and flour until smooth. Gradually add to soup mixture, stirring until thickened.
5. Pour over steak patties and bake an additional 20 minutes. Remove picks before serving.

6 servings

Note: The gravy may be served with the steak patties or covered and refrigerated. Reheat and serve with mashed potatoes at the next evening's meal.

462 Party Beef Casserole

2 pounds ground beef
¾ cup chopped onion
1 garlic clove, minced
½ cup chopped green pepper
½ cup chopped celery
1 teaspoon salt
½ teaspoon pepper
1 can (15 ounces) tomato sauce
1 can (8 ounces) mushroom stems and
    pieces, drained
1 can (6 ounces) tomato paste
½ cup sherry
2 tablespoons Worcestershire sauce
1 package (7 ounces) shell macaroni,
    cooked and drained
1 cup (4 ounces) shredded Cheddar
    cheese

1. Brown ground beef, onion, garlic, green pepper, and celery in a skillet; drain off excess fat. Combine with remaining ingredients, except shredded cheese. Put into a 3-quart casserole.
2. Bake, covered, at 350°F 45 minutes. Sprinkle with shredded cheese and bake an additional 5 minutes, or until heated through.

8 to 10 servings

463 Spanish Take-Along Casserole

1½ pounds ground beef
½ cup chopped onion
¼ cup chopped green pepper
¼ cup chopped celery
1 can (8 ounces) pizza sauce
2 cups (about 4 ounces) medium
    noodles, cooked and drained
1 teaspoon salt
1 carton (16 ounces) cream-style
    cottage cheese

1. Brown ground beef, onion, green pepper, and celery in a skillet; drain off excess fat. Combine with remaining ingredients.
2. Put into a 2-quart casserole. (If desired, cover and refrigerate until ready to finish.)
3. Bake, covered, at 350°F 30 minutes, or until heated through. Garnish with **green pepper rings.**

6 to 8 servings

464 *Super Macaroni and Beef Bake*

1 package (6 ounces) elbow macaroni
1 package (8 ounces) cream cheese
1 carton (16 ounces) cream-style
    cottage cheese
¼ cup dairy sour cream
1½ pounds ground beef
3 cans (8 ounces each) tomato sauce
½ cup (2 ounces) grated Parmesan
    cheese

1. Cook macaroni in **boiling salted water** until just tender; rinse with cold water. Place half the macaroni in bottom of a greased 13x9-inch baking dish.
2. With mixer beat together cream cheese, cottage cheese, and sour cream; pour over macaroni. Sprinkle remaining macaroni over cheese mixture.
3. Brown ground beef in a skillet; drain off excess fat. Stir in tomato sauce. Evenly spread meat mixture over macaroni. Sprinkle with grated cheese.
4. Bake, uncovered, at 350°F 50 to 60 minutes, or until heated through.

8 servings

Note: This casserole is best when prepared a day in advance. Cover and refrigerate. Remove from refrigerator 1 hour before baking.

465 *Italian Spaghetti Bake*

1 pound ground beef
½ cup chopped onion
1 can (16 ounces) tomatoes, drained
1 can (6 ounces) tomato paste
1 garlic clove, minced
1½ teaspoons salt
½ teaspoon oregano
½ teaspoon basil
¼ teaspoon whole marjoram
1 package (7 ounces) spaghetti
2 cups milk
3 eggs
    Dash of pepper
1 cup (4 ounces) grated Parmesan
    cheese
1 cup (4 ounces) shredded mozzarella
    cheese

1. Brown ground beef and onion in a skillet; drain off excess fat. Stir in tomatoes, tomato paste, garlic, 1 teaspoon salt, oregano, basil, and marjoram.
2. Cook spaghetti in **boiling salted water** until just tender. Spread in bottom of a 13x9-inch baking dish.
3. Combine milk, eggs, pepper, and remaining ½ teaspoon salt. Pour over spaghetti. Sprinkle with Parmesan cheese. Spoon meat mixture over Parmesan cheese. Top with mozzarella cheese.
4. Bake, uncovered, at 350°F 40 to 45 minutes, or until heated through. Let stand 10 minutes. Cut into squares to serve.

8 servings

466 *Lasagne Bolognese*

3 tablespoons butter or margarine
3 tablespoons flour
1 cup milk
1 cup whipping cream
¼ teaspoon salt
Dash of pepper
½ pound lasagne noodles
Meat Sauce Bolognese
1 cup (4 ounces) grated Parmesan
cheese

1. Melt butter in a saucepan; blend in flour. Gradually add milk and cream, stirring until thickened and smooth. Add salt and pepper.
2. Cook lasagne noodles in **boiling salted water** according to package directions. Drain, rinse, and spread on a damp towel.
3. Spread a thin layer of Meat Sauce Bolognese in a 13x9-inch baking dish. Top with a layer of half the lasagne noodles, half the Meat Sauce Bolognese, half the white sauce, and half the cheese; repeat layers.
4. Bake, uncovered, at 375°F 35 to 40 minutes, or until mixture is bubbly and top is golden brown. Let stand 10 minutes. Cut into squares to serve.

8 servings

467 *Meat Sauce Bolognese*

6 bacon slices, diced
1 medium onion, chopped
½ cup chopped celery
½ cup chopped carrot
6 tablespoons butter or margarine
¼ pound chicken livers, diced
1 pound ground beef round
1 teaspoon salt
½ teaspoon oregano
¼ teaspoon nutmeg
1 bay leaf
2 tablespoons vinegar
1 can (8 ounces) tomato sauce
1 cup beef bouillon
1 cup sliced fresh mushrooms
½ cup dry white wine

1. Sauté bacon in a skillet; drain off all but 2 tablespoons fat. Add onion, celery, and carrot; cook until tender.
2. Add 2 tablespoons butter and the chicken livers. Brown lightly; add ground beef round. Cook 10 to 15 minutes, or until well browned.
3. Stir in salt, oregano, nutmeg, bay leaf, vinegar, tomato sauce, and bouillon. Cover and simmer ½ hour.
4. Sauté mushrooms in remaining 4 tablespoons butter. Add to meat sauce along with wine. Remove bay leaf. Simmer ½ hour longer.

1 quart

468 *Beef and Pea Casserole*

1 pound ground beef
1 medium onion, chopped
1 can (10¾ ounces) condensed
tomato soup
⅓ cup water
2 cups cooked noodles
1 can (8 ounces) peas, drained*
1 can (4 ounces) sliced mushrooms,
drained*

1. Brown ground beef and onion in a skillet; drain off excess fat. Combine with remaining ingredients. Put into a 2-quart casserole.
2. Bake, covered, at 350°F 30 minutes, or until heated through. To serve, sprinkle with **Parmesan cheese** and garnish with **pimento strips**.

6 servings

* The liquid from the peas or mushrooms may be substituted for the 1/3 cup water.

469 *Cheese, Beef, 'n' Macaroni Bake*

2 pounds ground beef
½ medium onion, chopped
1 garlic clove, minced
1 jar (15½ ounces) spaghetti sauce
1 can (16 ounces) stewed tomatoes
1 can (3 ounces) mushroom stems and
pieces, drained
2 cups uncooked large macaroni
shells
2 cups dairy sour cream
1 package (6 ounces) provolone
cheese slices
1 cup (4 ounces) shredded mozzarella
cheese

1. Brown ground beef in a skillet; drain off excess fat. Add onion, garlic, spaghetti sauce, tomatoes, and mushrooms. Mix well and simmer 20 minutes.
2. Meanwhile, prepare macaroni shells according to package directions.
3. Put the macaroni shells into a 3-quart casserole. Cover with half the meat sauce. Spread meat with half the sour cream. Top with provolone cheese.
4. Repeat macaroni, meat, and sour-cream layers. Top with mozzarella cheese.
5. Bake, covered, at 350°F 35 to 40 minutes. Remove cover. Bake an additional 10 minutes, or until cheese is lightly browned.

8 to 10 servings

470 *Mock Chop Suey Casserole*

1 pound ground beef
¾ cup chopped onion
2 cups chopped celery
1 can (10¾ ounces) condensed
cream of chicken soup
1 can (10¾ ounces) condensed
cream of mushroom soup
½ cup uncooked white rice
2 cups boiling water
1 tablespoon soy sauce
1 can (5 ounces) chow mein noodles

1. Brown ground beef in a skillet; drain off excess fat. Combine with remaining ingredients, except chow mein noodles. Put into a 13x9-inch baking dish.
2. Bake, covered, at 350°F 45 minutes, or until rice is tender. Uncover; sprinkle with chow mein noodles. Bake an additional 10 minutes, or until noodles are heated through.

6 servings

Gefilte Fish, page 335

471 *Beef and Rice Bake*

1 pound ground beef
1 package (1⅜ ounces) dry onion
    soup mix
¾ cup uncooked white rice
1½ cups boiling water
1 can (16 ounces) tomatoes
    (undrained)
1 cup (4 ounces) shredded Cheddar
    cheese

1. Brown ground beef in a skillet; drain off excess fat. Combine with soup mix, rice, boiling water, and tomatoes. Put into a 2-quart casserole.
2. Bake, covered, at 350°F 45 minutes, or until rice is tender. Uncover; sprinkle with cheese. Bake an additional 5 minutes, or until cheese is melted.

6 servings

472 *Easy Meatball Stroganoff*

1 tablespoon instant minced onion
½ cup milk
1½ pounds ground beef
⅔ cup quick or old-fashioned oats,
    uncooked
1 teaspoon salt
¼ teaspoon pepper
¼ teaspoon dill weed
⅛ teaspoon garlic powder
1 egg, beaten
1 can (10¾ ounces) condensed golden
    mushroom soup
½ cup dairy sour cream

1. Combine onion and milk. Mix ground beef, oats, salt, pepper, dill weed, garlic powder, egg, and onion-milk mixture.
2. Shape to form 24 meatballs. Place in a shallow 10-inch casserole. Spoon soup over meatballs.
3. Bake, covered, at 350°F 35 minutes, or until meatballs are cooked through, stirring occasionally.
4. Uncover; blend in sour cream. Serve over **hot, cooked rice.**

6 servings

473 *Sloppy Joe for a Crowd*

2¼ pounds ground beef
2½ cups chopped onion
1 cup chopped green pepper
1 bottle (14 ounces) ketchup
¼ cup firmly packed brown sugar
¼ cup lemon juice
¼ cup vinegar
¼ cup water
2 teaspoons salt
1 teaspoon pepper
1 teaspoon Worcestershire sauce
½ teaspoon prepared mustard

1. Brown ground beef, onion, and green pepper in a skillet; drain off excess fat. Combine with remaining ingredients. Put into a large oven-proof Dutch oven.
2. Bake, covered, at 325°F 1½ hours. To serve, spoon over **toasted hamburger buns.**

16 servings

Beef Stroganoff Turnovers, page 320

474 Beef-Sour Cream Casserole

4 cups cooked noodles
1 cup (8 ounces) cream-style cottage cheese
1 package (8 ounces) cream cheese
¼ cup dairy sour cream
⅓ cup instant minced onion
2 tablespoons butter or margarine, melted
1½ pounds ground beef
3 cans (8 ounces each) tomato sauce
½ teaspoon salt
1 teaspoon oregano
⅓ cup chopped green pepper
1 can (2 ounces) sliced mushrooms, drained

1. Put half the noodles into a 2-quart casserole.
2. Combine cottage cheese, cream cheese, sour cream, and onion. Spread over noodles. Cover with remaining noodles. Drizzle with butter.
3. Brown ground beef in a skillet; drain off excess fat. Add remaining ingredients. Pour over noodles. Cover and chill overnight.
4. Remove from refrigerator 1 hour before baking.
5. Bake, covered, at 375°F 45 minutes, or until heated through. To serve, sprinkle with **grated Parmesan cheese.**

8 servings

475 Biscuit-Topped Burger

1¼ pounds ground beef
3 tablespoons instant minced onion
½ cup chopped celery
1 can (8 ounces) tomato sauce
2 tablespoons sweet pickle relish
½ teaspoon chili powder
½ teaspoon horseradish
¼ teaspoon salt
1 can (10 ounces) refrigerator biscuits
1 cup (4 ounces) shredded Cheddar cheese
1 tablespoon snipped parsley
½ teaspoon celery seed

1. Brown ground beef, onion, and celery in a skillet; drain off excess fat. Add tomato sauce, pickle relish, chili powder, horseradish, and salt. Simmer 2 minutes, or until heated through.
2. Spoon into an 11x7-inch baking dish.
3. Separate biscuits; then split each biscuit into 2 layers. Place half the biscuit halves over the meat mixture.
4. Combine cheese, parsley, and celery seed. Sprinkle over biscuit layer. Top with remaining biscuit halves.
5. Bake, uncovered, at 375°F 20 to 25 minutes, or until golden brown.

5 servings

476 *Texas Chili*

2 pounds ground beef
2 medium onions, chopped
1 garlic clove, minced
3 tablespoons flour
2 tablespoons chili powder
2 teaspoons salt
½ teaspoon cumin
3 cups hot water
1 can (15½ ounces) kidney beans, drained

1. Brown ground beef, onion, and garlic in a skillet; drain off excess fat.
2. Combine flour, chili powder, salt, and cumin. Gradually stir in hot water. Combine with meat mixture. Pour into a 2½-quart casserole.
3. Bake, covered, at 350°F 1¼ hours. Remove cover. Add beans and bake an additional 15 minutes.

8 servings

477 *Hominy-Beef Bake*

2 pounds ground beef
3 medium onions, chopped
1 can (16 ounces) tomatoes (undrained)
1 can (16 ounces) whole white hominy, drained
1 can (16 ounces) whole kernel corn, drained
1 can (16 ounces) cream-style corn
1 cup sliced pitted ripe olives
2 cans (8 ounces each) tomato sauce
1 package (1.25 ounces) chili mix
1 package (6 ounces) corn tortillas, cut up

1. Brown ground beef and onion in a skillet; drain off excess fat.
2. Combine with remaining ingredients. Put into a 4-quart casserole.
3. Bake, covered, at 300°F 2 hours.

12 servings

478 *Individual Burger Casseroles*

1 pound ground beef
¼ cup finely chopped onion
1 teaspoon salt
¼ teaspoon oregano
2 tablespoons ketchup
1 cup plus 2 tablespoons milk
2 tablespoons butter or margarine
2 tablespoons flour
1 cup cooked mixed vegetables
2 slices American cheese, cut in 4 strips each

1. Combine ground beef, onion, ½ teaspoon salt, oregano, ketchup, and 2 tablespoons milk.
2. Divide into 4 equal portions. Evenly line bottom and sides of 4 individual casseroles with meat mixture.
3. Bake, uncovered, at 350°F 20 minutes, or until meat mixture is done. Pour off excess fat.
4. Meanwhile, melt butter in a saucepan. Stir in flour. Gradually add remaining 1 cup milk, stirring until thickened and smooth.
5. Add vegetables and remaining ½ teaspoon salt. Spoon into meat shells. Top each with crisscross of cheese strips.
6. Bake about 5 minutes or until cheese melts.

4 servings

479 *African Bobotie*

3 slices day-old bread
1½ cups milk
2 medium onions, chopped
1 garlic clove, minced
½ cup slivered almonds
½ cup raisins
1 tablespoon sugar
1 teaspoon salt
1 teaspoon curry powder
⅛ teaspoon pepper
1 tablespoon vinegar
1 teaspoon lemon juice
1½ pounds ground beef
2 eggs

1. Soak bread in milk. Squeeze milk from bread, reserving milk. Combine all ingredients, except milk and 1 egg.
2. Press mixture into an 11x7-inch baking dish.
3. Add enough milk to reserved milk to make ¾ cup. Beat together milk and remaining egg. Pour over meat mixture.
4. Bake, uncovered, at 350°F 1 hour, or until golden brown and firm to the touch.

6 servings

480 *Mediterranean Beef Casserole*

1 can (20 ounces) pineapple chunks
1 cup uncooked white rice
1 teaspoon salt
1 pound ground beef
1 egg, lightly beaten
1 cup fine soft bread crumbs
1 tablespoon instant minced onion
1 teaspoon salt
⅓ cup milk
1 tablespoon vegetable oil
1 can (16 ounces) stewed tomatoes
½ teaspoon dill weed
2 tablespoons snipped parsley

1. Drain pineapple, reserving liquid. Add enough **water** to liquid to make 2½ cups.
2. Combine liquid, rice, and 1 teaspoon of the salt in a saucepan. Bring to a boil. Cover and simmer 25 minutes, or until rice is fluffy.
3. Combine ground beef, egg, bread crumbs, onion, 1 teaspoon salt, and milk. Shape to form 1-inch balls.
4. Brown meatballs in oil in skillet; drain off excess fat.
5. Add pineapple chunks, tomatoes, dill weed, and parsley. Put into a greased 2-quart casserole.
6. Bake, covered, at 375°F 25 minutes, or until meat is done. Serve over pineapple-rice.

6 servings

481 One 'n' One Casserole

1 pound ground beef
1 cup uncooked white rice
1 package (1⅜ ounces) dry onion soup mix
1 can (10¾ ounces) condensed cream of mushroom soup
2½ cups boiling water
½ cup sliced green onion tops

1. Brown ground beef in a skillet; drain off excess fat. Put into a greased 2-quart casserole. Sprinkle with rice and onion soup mix.
2. Combine mushroom soup and boiling water. Pour over rice.
3. Bake, covered, at 350°F 1 hour, or until rice is tender. Remove cover. Sprinkle with onion tops.

4 servings

482 Meatball Supper Pie

1 pound ground beef
½ cup quick or old-fashioned oats, uncooked
¼ cup chopped onion
1 teaspoon salt
¼ teaspoon pepper
¼ teaspoon thyme
1¼ cups milk
1 egg, beaten
1 tablespoon butter or margarine
1 tablespoon flour
Dash ground red pepper
½ cup (2 ounces) grated Parmesan cheese
1 baked 9-inch pie shell
½ cup (2 ounces) shredded American cheese
1 tomato, cut in wedges

1. Combine ground beef, oats, onion, salt, pepper, thyme, ¼ cup milk, and egg. Shape to form 4 dozen small meatballs.
2. Brown meatballs in a skillet; drain off excess fat.
3. Melt butter in a saucepan. Stir in flour and red pepper. Gradually add remaining 1 cup milk, stirring until thickened and smooth. Stir in Parmesan cheese.
4. Place meatballs in pie shell. Pour cheese sauce over meatballs.
5. Bake, uncovered, at 375°F 20 minutes. Sprinkle with American cheese and top with tomato wedges. Bake an additional 5 minutes. Cut into wedges to serve.

6 servings

483 *Layered Hamburger Bake*

1 pound ground beef
1 medium onion, chopped
4 medium potatoes, pared and sliced
¼ teaspoon pepper
1 can (10½ ounces) condensed
   vegetable soup
1 can (10¾ ounces) condensed cream
   of mushroom soup
½ cup water

1. Brown ground beef and onion in a skillet; drain off excess fat.
2. Put half of the potatoes into a greased 2-quart casserole. Top with half the meat mixture; repeat. Sprinkle with pepper.
3. Combine vegetable soup, mushroom soup, and water. Pour over meat.
4. Bake, covered, at 350°F 1 hour, or until potatoes are tender.

4 servings

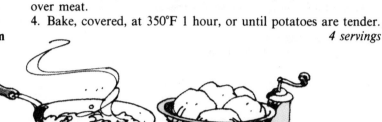

484 *Tamale Pie*

1 cup cornmeal
1¾ teaspoons salt
1 cup cold water
2 cups boiling water
1 pound ground beef
⅓ cup chopped onion
2 tablespoons flour
½ cup chopped pitted ripe olives
1 can (16 ounces) tomatoes (undrained)
2 teaspoons chili powder
½ cup cubed sharp Cheddar cheese

1. Combine cornmeal, 1 teaspoon salt, and cold water. Slowly pour into boiling water in a saucepan, stirring constantly. Cook until thickened, stirring frequently. Cover; continue cooking over low heat about 5 minutes. Stir occasionally.
2. Brown ground beef and onion in a skillet; drain off excess fat. Add flour, olives, tomatoes, chili powder, and remaining ¾ teaspoon salt.
3. Spread mush evenly in bottom of a greased 12x8-inch baking dish. Pour meat mixture over mush. Arrange cheese cubes over meat mixture.
4. Bake, uncovered, at 350°F 20 minutes, or until casserole is bubbly.

6 servings

485 *Szededine Goulash*

2 pounds beef stew meat, cut in
   1-inch pieces
¼ cup vegetable oil
2 cups sliced onion
1 garlic clove, minced
1 teaspoon salt
1 can (10 ounces) tomato purée,
1 cup water
1 cup dairy sour cream
2 teaspoons paprika
2 teaspoons caraway seed
1 can (16 ounces) sauerkraut, rinsed
   and drained
2 tablespoons snipped parsley

1. Brown beef in oil in a skillet. Add onion and garlic. Sauté about 5 minutes; drain off excess fat.
2. Add salt, tomato purée, and water. Put into a 2½-quart casserole.
3. Bake, covered, at 325°F 2 hours, or until meat is tender, stirring occasionally. Remove cover. Stir in sour cream, paprika, caraway seed, and sauerkraut. Bake an additional 15 minutes, or until heated through. Sprinkle with parsley.

8 servings

486 Oven Beef Bake

2 pounds beef stew meat, cut in
    1-inch cubes
1 can (10¾ ounces) condensed cream
    of mushroom soup
1 can (10½ ounces) condensed onion
    soup
¼ cup dry vermouth

1. Put meat into a 2-quart casserole.
2. Combine mushroom soup, onion soup, and vermouth. Pour over meat.
3. Bake, covered, at 325°F 3 hours, or until meat is tender. Serve with **hot, cooked noodles.**

8 servings

487 Beef Bourguignon

¼ cup flour
1 teaspoon salt
½ teaspoon freshly ground black
    pepper
2 pounds beef stew meat, cut in
    2-inch cubes
¼ cup butter or margarine
1 medium onion, chopped
2 medium carrots, chopped
1 garlic clove, minced
2 cups dry red wine
1 can (6 ounces) mushroom crowns,
    drained, reserving liquid
1 bay leaf
3 tablespoons snipped parsley
½ teaspoon thyme
1 can (16 ounces) onions, drained

1. Combine flour, salt, and pepper; coat beef cubes.
2. Brown beef in butter in a skillet. Put into a 2-quart casserole.
3. Add onion, carrots, and garlic to skillet. Cook until tender but not brown. Add wine, liquid from mushrooms, bay leaf, parsley, and thyme. Pour over meat.
4. Bake, covered, at 350°F 2½ hours. Remove cover. Add onions and mushroom crowns. Bake an additional 30 minutes, or until meat is tender.

8 servings

488 Swiss Steak Mozzarella

2 pounds beef round steak, ½ inch
    thick
3 tablespoons flour
½ cup butter or margarine
1 can (16 ounces) tomatoes, cut up
1¼ teaspoons salt
¼ teaspoon basil
½ cup chopped green pepper
1½ cups (6 ounces) mozzarella cheese

1. Cut meat into serving-size pieces; coat with flour.
2. Melt butter in a skillet. Brown meat slowly on both sides. Put into a 12x8-inch baking dish.
3. Combine tomatoes, salt, basil, and green pepper. Pour over meat.
4. Bake, covered, at 350°F 1 hour, or until meat is tender. Remove cover. Sprinkle with cheese and bake an additional 5 minutes, or until cheese is melted.

8 servings

489 *Stew with Cornbread Topping*

1½ pounds beef stew meat, cut in
     ¾-inch cubes
  2 tablespoons butter or margarine
  2 medium onions, sliced
  1 garlic clove, minced
2¼ cups water
  1 can (8 ounces) tomato sauce
  ¼ bay leaf
  2 teaspoons salt
  ¼ teaspoon pepper
  4 carrots, cut in 1-inch pieces
  4 celery stalks, cut in 1-inch pieces
  ½ cup all-purpose flour
  2 teaspoons baking powder
  1 tablespoon sugar
  1 teaspoon salt
  1 cup cornmeal
  1 egg, beaten
  1 cup milk
  2 tablespoons vegetable oil
  1 tablespoon snipped parsley

1. Brown meat in butter in a skillet. Add onion and garlic, cooking until lightly brown. Stir in water, tomato sauce, bay leaf, 2 teaspoons salt, and the pepper. Put into a 2½-quart casserole.
2. Bake, covered, at 350°F 45 minutes. Remove bay leaf. Add carrots and celery. Bake, covered, an additional 25 minutes, or until meat and vegetables are tender.
3. Sift together flour, baking powder, sugar, and 1 teaspoon salt into a bowl. Mix in cornmeal. Add egg, milk, and oil. (Mix only until dry ingredients are moistened.)
4. Remove stew from oven. Pour topping over hot stew. Sprinkle with parsley.
5. Bake, uncovered, at 400°F 20 minutes, or until cornbread is golden brown.

6 servings

490 *Slow Oven Beef Stew*

  2 pounds beef stew meat, cut in
     1½-inch cubes
  2 medium onions, each cut in eighths
  3 celery stalks, cut in 1-inch
     diagonally sliced pieces
  4 medium carrots, pared and cut in
     half crosswise and lengthwise
  3 cups tomato juice
  ⅓ cup quick-cooking tapioca
  1 tablespoon sugar
  2 teaspoons salt
  ¼ teaspoon pepper
  1 bay leaf
  2 medium potatoes, pared and cut in
     ¼-inch-thick slices

1. Put all ingredients, except potatoes, into a 3-quart casserole.
2. Bake, covered, at 300°F 2½ hours. Remove bay leaf and stir in potatoes. Bake, covered, an additional 1 hour, or until meat and vegetables are tender.

8 servings

491 *Cornbread Tamale Pie*

1 pound ground beef
½ cup chopped onion
⅓ cup chopped celery
1 can (16 ounces) tomatoes
    (undrained)
1 can (12 ounces) whole kernel corn,
    drained
1 can (8 ounces) tomato sauce
1 tablespoon chili powder
1 teaspoon salt
¼ teaspoon pepper
¼ cup all-purpose flour
1½ teaspoons baking powder
½ teaspoon salt
¾ cup cornmeal
1 egg, beaten
½ cup milk
2 tablespoons vegetable oil

1. Brown ground beef, onion, and celery in a skillet; drain off excess fat. Add tomatoes, corn, tomato sauce, chili powder, 1 teaspoon salt, and the pepper; simmer 10 minutes.
2. Sift together flour, baking powder, and ½ teaspoon salt into a bowl. Mix in cornmeal. Stir in egg, milk, and oil. (Mix only until dry ingredients are moistened.)
3. Spoon hot meat mixture into a 2-quart casserole. Top with cornbread topping.
4. Bake, uncovered, at 425°F 15 minutes, or until topping is golden brown.

6 servings

492 *Beef 'n' Peppers*

1 garlic clove, minced
1½ pounds lean beef, cut in 1-inch
    cubes
2 tablespoons shortening
1 cup sliced fresh mushrooms
2 cans (10½ ounces each) brown
    gravy with onions
1 green pepper, cut in strips

1. Sauté garlic and beef in hot shortening in a skillet. Put into a 1½-quart casserole.
2. Combine mushrooms and gravy in skillet with drippings. Pour over meat.
3. Bake, covered, at 350°F 2 hours, or until meat is tender. Remove cover. Add pepper strips. Bake an additional 15 minutes, or until pepper is tender but still crisp. Serve over **hot, cooked rice** or **noodles.**

6 servings

493 *Yankee Steak*

2 pounds beef round steak, ½ inch
    thick
½ cup flour
2 teaspoons salt
½ teaspoon pepper
3 tablespoons vegetable oil
2 medium onions, thinly sliced
1 can (15 ounces) tomato sauce
⅛ teaspoon garlic powder

1. Cut meat into serving-size pieces. Combine flour, salt, and pepper; pound into steak.
2. Heat oil in a skillet. Brown meat slowly on both sides. Place in a 13x9-inch baking dish. Top with onion slices.
3. Combine tomato sauce and garlic powder. Pour over meat.
4. Bake, covered, at 350°F 1 hour, or until meat is tender.

8 servings

494 *Creamy Baked Steak*

1 **pound beef round tip steak**
4 **tablespoons flour**
½ **teaspoon salt**
2 **tablespoons vegetable oil**
1 **small onion, sliced**
1 **garlic clove, minced**
1 **can (10½ ounces) condensed beef broth**
1 **cup dairy sour cream**
2 **tablespoons sherry**
1 **can (3 ounces) sliced mushrooms, drained**

1. Cut steak into serving-size pieces. Sprinkle with 1 tablespoon flour and the salt.
2. Brown meat in oil in a skillet. Add onion and garlic.
3. Combine beef broth with remaining 3 tablespoons flour. Stir into skillet. Cook, stirring constantly, until mixture thickens. Put meat and sauce into a 12x8-inch baking dish.
4. Bake, covered, at 350°F 30 minutes, or until steak is tender. Remove cover. Combine sour cream, sherry, and mushrooms. Stir into meat mixture in baking dish. Bake an additional 5 minutes, or until heated through.

3 or 4 servings

495 *Island-Style Short Ribs*

4 **pounds lean beef short ribs**
½ **cup soy sauce**
⅓ **cup sugar**
2 **tablespoons vinegar**
1 **tablespoon vegetable oil**
1 **teaspoon ginger**
½ **teaspoon lemon pepper seasoning**
¼ **teaspoon garlic salt**
1 **large onion, finely chopped**
¼ **cup butter or margarine**
2 **cups water**

1. Cut meat from bones; reserve the bones. Trim off as much fat as possible. Cut meat into cubes. Put meat into a bowl.
2. Combine soy sauce, sugar, vinegar, oil, ginger, lemon pepper seasoning, and garlic salt. Pour over meat. Cover and refrigerate several hours or overnight.
3. Sauté onion in butter in a skillet. Remove onion; set aside.
4. Cook meat in skillet about 10 minutes. Add onion, marinade, and water. Put into a 2-quart casserole. Top with bones.
5. Bake, covered, at 325°F 1½ hours. Remove bones and bake, uncovered, an additional 30 minutes, or until meat is tender. To serve, spoon broth over **hot, cooked rice.**

8 servings

496 *Veal Parmigiano*

1 pound veal steak or cutlet, thinly
    sliced
1 teaspoon salt
⅛ teaspoon pepper
1 egg
2 cups plus 2 teaspoons water
⅓ cup grated Parmesan cheese
⅓ cup fine dry bread crumbs
¼ cup shortening
1 medium onion, finely chopped
1 can (6 ounces) tomato paste
1 teaspoon salt
½ teaspoon basil
6 slices mozzarella cheese

1. Cut veal into 8 pieces; sprinkle with 1 teaspoon salt and the pepper.
2. Lightly beat together egg and 2 teaspoons water.
3. Combine Parmesan cheese and bread crumbs.
4. Dip veal in egg wash, then Parmesan mixture. Refrigerate at least ½ hour.
5. Brown veal on both sides in shortening in a skillet. Remove to a 1½-quart shallow baking dish.
6. Sauté onion in skillet. Stir in tomato paste, 1 teaspoon salt, and basil. Simmer 5 minutes. Pour three fourths of the sauce over veal. Top with mozzarella cheese. Pour remaining sauce over cheese.
7. Bake, uncovered, at 350°F 20 to 25 minutes, or until mixture is bubbly.

4 servings

497 *Northwoods Pork Chops*

1 package (2¾ ounces) instant wild
    rice
¼ cup chopped celery
¼ cup chopped green pepper
¼ cup chopped onion
6 tablespoons butter or margarine
4 pork chops, ¾ inch thick
¼ cup flour
2 cups milk
½ teaspoon salt
⅛ teaspoon pepper
½ cup (2 ounces) shredded American
    cheese

1. Prepare wild rice according to package directions.
2. Sauté celery, green pepper, and onion in 4 tablespoons butter in a skillet. Combine with wild rice. Put into a 1½-quart shallow baking dish.
3. Brown pork chops on both sides in skillet. Place on top of wild rice mixture.
4. Melt remaining 2 tablespoons butter in skillet. Blend in flour. Gradually add milk, stirring until thickened and smooth. Add salt and pepper. Pour over pork chops.
5. Bake, covered, at 350°F 1 hour, or until chops are done. Sprinkle with cheese.

4 servings

498 Golden Pork Chop Bake

6 pork chops, 1 inch thick
2 tablespoons shortening
½ cup sliced celery
1 garlic clove, minced
2 cans (10¾ ounces each) condensed golden mushroom soup
1⅓ cups water
1⅓ cups packaged precooked rice
½ cup chopped tomato

1. Brown pork chops on both sides in shortening in a skillet. Remove chops from skillet; drain off excess fat.
2. Sauté celery and garlic in skillet. Combine with remaining ingredients. Spoon into a 2-quart shallow baking dish.
3. Arrange chops on top of rice mixture.
4. Bake, covered, at 350°F 1 hour, or until chops are tender.

6 servings

499 Baked Stuffed Pork Chops

4 rib pork chops, 1 inch thick
1 tablespoon finely chopped onion
¼ cup diced celery
2 tablespoons butter or margarine
1 cup soft bread crumbs
½ teaspoon salt
⅛ teaspoon poultry seasoning
2 tablespoons shortening
1 can (10¾ ounces) condensed cream of mushroom soup
⅓ cup water

1. Trim excess fat from pork chops. Slit each chop from bone side almost to fat, making a pocket.
2. Sauté onion and celery in butter in a skillet. Combine with bread crumbs, salt, and poultry seasoning. Stuff into pockets in chops.
3. Brown chops in shortening in skillet. Place in a 10x8-inch baking dish.
4. Add soup and water to drippings in skillet. Stir to dissolve brown particles. Pour over chops.
5. Bake, covered, at 350°F 1 hour, or until chops are tender.

4 servings

500 He-Man Casserole

½ cup chopped green onion
½ cup chopped green pepper
½ cup chopped celery
6 tablespoons butter or margarine
6 tablespoons flour
Dash pepper
1 cup chicken broth
1½ cups milk
4 cups cubed cooked ham
1 package (10 ounces) frozen peas, thawed
4 cups hot, cooked mashed potatoes (stiff)
1 egg, beaten
1 cup (4 ounces) shredded Cheddar cheese

1. Sauté onion, green pepper, and celery in butter in a saucepan. Stir in flour and pepper. Gradually add broth and milk, stirring until thickened and smooth.
2. Mix with ham and peas. Put into a 3-quart casserole.
3. Combine potatoes, egg, and cheese. Spoon around edge of casserole mixture.
4. Bake, uncovered, at 375°F 45 minutes, or until mixture is bubbly.

8 servings

501 Calico Ham Bake

1 pound cooked ham
1 package (10 ounces) sharp Cheddar cheese
1 medium green pepper, chopped
4 eggs, beaten
2 cups milk

1. Grind ham and cheese together. Combine with green pepper, eggs, and milk. Put into a greased 8-inch square baking dish.
2. Bake, uncovered, at 325°F 1 hour, or until browned. Cut into squares to serve.

6 servings

502 Wild Rice-Ham Rolls

1½ cups uncooked wild rice
½ cup sliced green onion
¼ cup snipped parsley
¼ pound fresh mushrooms, sliced
¼ cup butter or margarine
¼ cup flour
½ teaspoon salt
¼ teaspoon pepper
¼ teaspoon nutmeg
½ cup dry white wine
2 cups milk
8 slices cooked ham, about ¼ inch thick

1. Prepare wild rice according to package directions. Add ¼ cup green onion and the parsley.
2. Sauté remaining ¼ cup green onion and mushrooms in butter in a skillet. Stir in flour, salt, pepper, and nutmeg. Gradually add wine, then milk, stirring until thickened and smooth.
3. Combine 1 cup sauce with 2 cups wild rice. Divide evenly on top of each ham slice. Spoon remaining rice on bottom of a lightly greased 12x9-inch shallow baking dish.
4. Roll up ham rolls to enclose filling. Place seam side down on rice in casserole. Spoon remaining sauce over ham rolls.
5. Bake, uncovered, at 350°F 20 minutes, or until heated through.

8 servings

503 Ham and Cheese Casserole Bread

⅔ cup chopped onion
3 tablespoons vegetable oil
2 cups all-purpose biscuit mix
1 cup chopped cooked ham
2 eggs
⅔ cup milk
1 teaspoon prepared mustard
1½ cups (6 ounces) shredded Cheddar cheese
2 tablespoons sesame seed
2 tablespoons snipped parsley
3 tablespoons butter or margarine, melted

1. Sauté onion in 1 tablespoon oil in a skillet.
2. Combine biscuit mix and ham.
3. Blend the remaining 2 tablespoons oil, eggs, milk, mustard, onion, and ¾ cup cheese. Stir into ham mixture. Spoon into a greased 1½-quart round casserole. Sprinkle with remaining ¾ cup cheese, sesame seed, parsley, and butter.
4. Bake, uncovered, at 350°F minutes, or until done. Cut into wedges to serve.

6 servings

504 *Calico Supper Pie*

  1 can (10 biscuits) refrigerator
    biscuits
  2 cups diced cooked ham
  1 large tomato, sliced
  ¼ cup chopped green onion
  1 cup (4 ounces) shredded Cheddar
    cheese
  2 eggs, separated
  ½ cup milk
  2 tablespoons flour
  ¼ cup (1 ounce) grated Parmesan
    cheese
  1 tablespoon snipped parsley

1. Separate dough into biscuits. Place in a 9-inch deep pie pan; press over bottom and up sides to form crust. Sprinkle with ham. Top with tomato, green onion, and Cheddar cheese.
2. Beat egg yolks. Stir in milk and flour. Pour over cheese.
3. Beat egg whites until soft peaks form. Fold in Parmesan cheese and parsley. Spread over pie. Cover edge of crust with foil.
4. Bake at 350°F 25 minutes. Remove foil. Bake an additional 10 minutes, or until crust is golden brown. Let stand a few minutes before serving.

6 servings

505 *Ham Wrap-Arounds*

  8 slices cooked ham, about ¼ inch
    thick
  2 packages (10 ounces each) frozen
    broccoli spears, cooked and
    drained
  3 cups cubed French bread, toasted*
  1½ cups dry white wine
  3 cups (12 ounces) shredded Swiss
    cheese
  3 tablespoons flour
  2 teaspoons prepared mustard
  ⅛ teaspoon garlic powder

1. Wrap ham slices around broccoli spears. Place in a 12x8-inch shallow baking dish. Sprinkle with bread cubes.
2. Heat wine in a saucepan. Mix cheese and flour. Gradually add to wine while stirring until smooth. Stir in mustard and garlic powder. Pour sauce over all in dish.
3. Bake, uncovered, at 350°F 30 minutes, or until heated through.

8 servings

* To toast cubed French bread, place on a baking sheet and put into a 350°F oven about 10 minutes.

506 *Saucy Stuffed Peppers*

6 medium green peppers
1½ pounds pork sausage meat
1 cup quick or old-fashioned oats, uncooked
⅔ cup tomato juice
1 can (10¾ ounces) condensed tomato soup
¼ cup milk
1 teaspoon Worcestershire sauce
⅛ teaspoon oregano

1. Cut ¼-inch slice from the top of each green pepper; remove seeds. Cook green peppers in **boiling water** about 5 minutes; drain.
2. Brown sausage in a skillet until lightly browned; drain off excess fat. Combine meat, oats, and tomato juice.
3. Fill green peppers with meat mixture. Stand upright in a 1½-quart shallow baking dish; add a small amount of **water.**
4. Bake, uncovered, at 350°F 45 to 50 minutes, or until done.
5. Serve with sauce made by heating together the soup, milk, Worcestershire sauce, and oregano.

6 servings

507 *Ham and Asparagus Casserole*

3 tablespoons butter or margarine
3 tablespoons flour
½ teaspoon dry mustard
1½ cups milk
1½ cups (6 ounces) shredded Cheddar cheese
2 cups cubed cooked ham
1 package (10 ounces) frozen cut-up asparagus, cooked and drained
⅛ teaspoon onion powder
Dash Tabasco
½ cup toasted slivered almonds

1. Melt butter in a saucepan. Stir in flour and mustard. Gradually add milk, stirring until thickened and smooth. Add cheese, stirring until smooth.
2. Combine with ham, asparagus, onion powder, and Tabasco. Put into a 1½-quart casserole. Sprinkle with almonds.
3. Bake, uncovered, at 350°F 20 minutes, or until heated through.

4 servings

508 *Sausage-Green Bean Casserole*

3 cups hot, cooked mashed potatoes
1 pound pork sausage links, cooked and drained
1 cup (4 ounces) shredded American cheese
1 package (9 ounces) frozen cut green beans, cooked and drained
1 can (8 ounces) small whole onions, drained
1 tablespoon chopped pimento

1. Layer half of the mashed potatoes, half of the sausage, and half of the cheese in a 1½-quart casserole.
2. Combine green beans, onions, and pimento. Spoon over cheese. Top with remaining potatoes, sausage, and cheese.
3. Bake, covered, at 350°F 30 minutes, or until heated through.

6 servings

509 *Super Sausage Supper*

1 cup chopped onion
1 garlic clove, minced
3 carrots, pared and thinly sliced
2 tablespoons shortening
1 jar (32 ounces) sauerkraut, drained
2 cups apple cider
½ cup dry white wine
¼ teaspoon pepper
3 parsley sprigs
1 bay leaf
1 package (12 ounces) pork sausage links, cooked and drained
1 package (5 ounces) tiny smoked sausage links
2 links (8 ounces each) Polish sausage, cooked and drained
2 cans (16 ounces each) small white potatoes, drained
1 apple, cored and cut in chunks

1. Sauté onion, garlic, and carrot in shortening in a skillet. Add sauerkraut, apple cider, wine, pepper, parsley, and bay leaf. Bring to a boil; reduce heat and simmer 15 minutes.
2. Stir in remaining ingredients. Remove bay leaf. Put into a 3-quart casserole.
3. Bake, covered, at 350°F 1 hour.

8 servings

510 *Hearty Sausage Supper*

1 jar (16 ounces) applesauce
1 can (14 ounces) sauerkraut, drained
⅓ cup dry white wine
2 tablespoons firmly packed brown sugar
1 can (16 ounces) small white potatoes, drained
1 can (16 ounces) small whole onions, drained
1 ring (12 ounces) Polish sausage, slashed several times
1 tablespoon snipped parsley

1. Mix applesauce, sauerkraut, wine, and brown sugar. Put into a 2½-quart casserole.
2. Arrange potatoes and onions around edge of casserole. Place sausage in center.
3. Bake, covered, at 350°F 45 to 50 minutes, or until heated through. Sprinkle with parsley.

4 servings

511 *Smoked Sausage Dinner*

1 medium onion, chopped
½ cup chopped green pepper
2 tablespoons butter or margarine
1 pound smoked sausage, cut in ½-inch pieces
1 can (16 ounces) tomatoes, cut up
1 cup uncooked noodles

1. Sauté onion and green pepper in butter in a skillet. Add sausage and brown lightly; drain off excess fat.
2. Stir in remaining ingredients. Put into a 1½-quart casserole.
3. Bake, covered, at 375°F 45 minutes, or until noodles are tender, stirring once.

4 servings

512 *Lamb Curry*

1½ pounds boneless lamb shoulder, cut in ¾-inch cubes
2 tablespoons shortening
1 teaspoon salt
1 teaspoon paprika
¼ teaspoon pepper
1 large onion, sliced
1 cup sliced celery
2¼ cups water
1 teaspoon curry powder
¼ cup flour
1 cup uncooked white rice

1. Brown lamb in shortening in a large saucepan. Sprinkle with salt, paprika, and pepper. Add onion, celery, and 2 cups water. Cover and simmer 1 hour, or until tender.
2. Combine curry powder, flour, and remaining ¼ cup water. Gradually add to saucepan, stirring until thickened and smooth.
3. Meanwhile, prepare rice according to package directions. Press rice in bottom and up sides of a 2-quart casserole. Pour lamb mixture into rice shell.
4. Bake, covered, at 350°F 20 minutes, or until casserole is bubbly. Serve with **chopped peanuts, shredded coconut,** and **chutney.**

6 servings

513 *Smothered Lamb Chops*

6 lamb rib chops
2 tablespoons butter or margarine
4 medium red potatoes, pared and thinly sliced
2 large onions, sliced
1½ cups beef bouillon
2 tablespoons snipped parsley
¼ cup buttered bread crumbs

1. Brown lamb chops on both sides in butter in a skillet. Place in a 2-quart shallow baking dish.
2. Arrange potatoes over chops and onions over potatoes. Season lightly with **salt.** Pour bouillon over all.
3. Bake, covered, at 375°F 1 hour, or until chops and vegetables are tender. Combine parsley and bread crumbs. Remove cover from casserole. Sprinkle with the parsley-bread crumbs. Bake, uncovered, at 450°F 10 minutes, or until crumbs are lightly browned.

6 servings

514 *Franks and Scalloped Potatoes*

    6 medium potatoes, pared and thinly
        sliced
    3 tablespoons finely chopped chives
    3 tablespoons flour
    1 teaspoon salt
    ¼ teaspoon pepper
    3 tablespoons butter or margarine
    2½ cups milk, heated
    6 frankfurters, cut in pieces

1. Place one third of the potatoes in a greased 2½-quart casserole. Sprinkle with one third of the chives, one third of the flour, one third of the salt, and one third of the pepper. Dot with 1 tablespoon butter. Repeat twice. Pour milk over all.

2. Bake, covered, at 350°F 30 minutes. Remove cover. Stir in frankfurters. Bake, uncovered, an additional 50 minutes, or until potatoes are tender.

6 servings

515 *Hot Dogs in Cornbread*

    1 package (8½ ounces) corn muffin
        mix
    1 egg
    ⅓ cup milk
    1 tablespoon instant minced onion
    4 frankfurters, split in half lengthwise
    1 teaspoon oregano
    1 cup (4 ounces) shredded Cheddar
        cheese

1. Prepare corn muffin mix, using egg and milk, according to package directions. Stir onion into batter. Spread into a greased 1½-quart shallow baking dish.

2. Arrange frankfurters over batter. Sprinkle with oregano.

3. Bake, uncovered, at 400°F 15 minutes, or until golden brown. Sprinkle with cheese. Bake an additional 3 minutes, or until cheese is melted. Serve with **prepared mustard.**

4 servings

516 *Macaroni and Cheese with Franks*

    1 package (8 ounces) elbow macaroni,
        cooked and drained
    2 cups (8 ounces) shredded Cheddar
        cheese
    1 can (13 ounces) evaporated milk
    1 small onion, finely chopped
    ⅛ teaspoon pepper
    1 package (16 ounces) frankfurters,
        cut in 1-inch pieces

1. Combine all ingredients. Put into a 2½-quart casserole.

2. Bake, covered, at 350°F 30 minutes, or until heated through, stirring occasionally.

6 servings

517 *Dried Beef 'n' Noodles*

    1 cup diced celery
    1 cup chopped onion
    ½ cup chopped green pepper
    ¼ cup shortening
    2 tablespoons flour
    2 cups milk
    1 tablespoon Worcestershire sauce
        Dash Tabasco
    ½ cup (2 ounces) shredded American
        cheese
    1 package (3 ounces) dried smoked
        beef, cut in pieces
    2 cups cooked wide noodles
    2 hard-cooked eggs, sliced

1. Sauté celery, onion, and green pepper in shortening in a skillet.
2. Stir in flour. Gradually add milk, stirring until thickened and smooth. Add Worcestershire sauce, Tabasco, and cheese, stirring until smooth. Stir in beef and noodles.
3. Put into a 1½-quart casserole. Top with hard-cooked egg slices.
4. Bake, covered, at 350°F 30 minutes, or until heated through.

4 servings

518 *Corned Beef Casserole*

    ½ cup chopped onion
    ¼ cup chopped green pepper
    2 tablespoons shortening
    1 can (12 ounces) corned beef, cut up
    ¾ cup water
    1½ cups ketchup
    1 package (10 ounces) frozen peas,
        thawed
    1½ cups (about 6 ounces) shell
        macaroni, cooked and drained

1. Sauté onion and green pepper in shortening in a skillet. Stir in remaining ingredients. Put into a 2-quart casserole.
2. Bake, covered, at 350°F 30 minutes, or until heated through.

6 servings

519 *Hearty Sandwich Squares*

    2 cups pancake mix
    1 can (11 ounces) condensed Cheddar
        cheese soup
    1 teaspoon prepared mustard
    1¼ cups milk
    8 slices (1 ounce each) luncheon meat
    4 slices (1 ounce each) American
        cheese
    ¼ cup chopped onion
    ¼ cup chopped green pepper

1. Combine pancake mix, ¼ cup soup, mustard, and 1 cup milk.
2. Spread half the batter in a greased 8-inch square baking dish. Top with meat, cheese, onion, and green pepper. Spoon remaining batter over all.
3. Bake, uncovered, at 400°F 25 to 30 minutes, or until done. Cut into squares to serve. Heat together remaining soup and ¼ cup milk. Spoon over squares. Sprinkle with **snipped parsley.**

4 servings

520 *Frankfurter Supper Bake*

1 pound frankfurters
½ cup vegetable oil
1 large garlic clove, minced
8 slices bread, well toasted and cut in
    ½-inch cubes
1 cup diagonally sliced celery
2 tablespoons minced parsley
1 egg
¼ teaspoon salt
⅛ teaspoon pepper
2 cans (8 ounces each) tomato sauce
    with onions

1. Make diagonal slits at 1-inch intervals almost to bottom of each frankfurter. Set aside.
2. Mix oil and garlic and pour about half of mixture into a large skillet; heat thoroughly. Add about half of toast cubes and toss until all sides are coated and browned. Turn into a large bowl. Repeat heating oil; brown remaining toast cubes, and put into bowl along with celery and parsley.
3. Beat egg, salt, and pepper slightly. Add 1 can of tomato sauce; mix well. Pour over the crouton mixture; toss lightly.
4. Turn half of the mixture into a greased 1½-quart casserole. Put half of the franks onto the mixture. Brush franks with 1 teaspoon tomato sauce from remaining can. Repeat layers and brushing.
5. Bake, uncovered, at 350°F 45 minutes.
6. Heat remaining tomato sauce in a small saucepan and pour evenly over casserole mixture. Garnish with **parsley.**

6 servings

521 *Pear-Topped Special*

1 can (12 ounces) luncheon meat,
    shredded
2 medium onions, chopped
⅔ cup diced celery
⅓ cup slivered green pepper
4 medium potatoes, cooked, peeled,
    and cut in cubes
1 cup beef broth
½ teaspoon salt
    Few grains pepper
1 can (29 ounces) pear halves, drained
    Softened butter or margarine
¼ cup firmly packed brown sugar

1. Combine luncheon meat, onion, celery, green pepper, potato cubes, broth, salt, and pepper; toss lightly to mix. Turn into a buttered shallow 1½-quart baking dish.
2. Bake, uncovered, at 400°F 30 minutes. Arrange pear halves, cut side down, over top. Brush pears lightly with softened butter and sprinkle with brown sugar. Bake an additional 15 minutes.

About 6 servings

522 *Parmesan Macaroni Casserole*

1 package (8 ounces) cream cheese
½ teaspoon garlic salt
1 cup milk
½ cup (2 ounces) grated Parmesan
    cheese
1 can (12 ounces) luncheon meat,
    chopped
½ cup sliced celery
¼ cup chopped green pepper
1 cup (4 ounces) elbow macaroni,
    cooked and drained

1. Soften cream cheese over low heat in a saucepan. Add garlic salt. Gradually add milk, stirring until smooth.
2. Stir in remaining ingredients. Put into a greased 1½-quart casserole.
3. Bake, covered, at 350°F 25 minutes, or until heated through and lightly browned.

6 servings

523 Pot Roast of Beef with Wine

3- to 4-pound beef pot roast, bone-
    less (rump, chuck, or round)
2 cups red wine
2 medium onions, chopped
3 medium carrots, washed, pared,
    and sliced
1 clove garlic
1 bay leaf
¼ teaspoon pepper
4 sprigs parsley
¼ cup all-purpose flour
2 teaspoons salt
¼ teaspoon pepper
3 tablespoons butter
2 cups red wine
1 cup cold water
¼ cup all-purpose flour

1. Put the meat into a deep bowl. Add wine, onions, carrots, garlic, bay leaf, pepper, and parsley. Cover and put into re-frigerator to marinate 12 hours, or overnight; turn meat occa-sionally. Drain the meat, reserving marinade, and pat meat dry with absorbent paper.
2. Coat meat evenly with a mixture of flour, salt, and pepper.
3. Heat butter in a large saucepot; brown the meat slowly on all sides in the butter. Drain off the fat. Add the marinade and wine. Cover and bring to boiling. Reduce heat and simmer slowly 2½ to 3 hours, or until meat is tender.
4. Remove meat to a warm platter.
5. Strain the cooking liquid. Return the strained liquid to sauce-pot.
6. Pour water into a screw-top jar and add flour; cover jar tightly and shake until mixture is well blended.
7. Stirring constantly, slowly pour one half of the blended mixture into liquid in saucepot. Bring to boiling. Gradually add only what is needed of the remaining blended mixture for consistency desired. Bring gravy to boiling after each addition. Cook 3 to 5 minutes longer.
8. Serve meat with gravy.

8 to 10 servings

524 Beef Burgundy

This is a family-size recipe. Increase it for a party, as pictured on the cover.

2 slices bacon
2 pounds beef round tip steak, cut
    in 2-inch cubes
2 tablespoons flour
1 teaspoon seasoned salt
1 package beef stew seasoning
    mix
1 cup burgundy
1 cup water
1 tablespoon tomato paste
12 small boiling onions
4 ounces fresh mushrooms, sliced
    and lightly browned in 1
    tablespoon butter or
    margarine
16 cherry tomatoes, stems
    removed

1. Fry bacon in a Dutch oven; remove bacon. Coat meat cubes with a blend of flour and seasoned salt. Add to fat in Dutch oven and brown thoroughly. Add beef stew seasoning mix, burgundy, water, and tomato paste. Cover and simmer gently 45 minutes.
2. Peel onions and pierce each end with a fork so they will retain their shape when cooked. Add onions to beef mixture and simmer 40 minutes, or until meat and onions are tender. Add mushrooms and cherry tomatoes; simmer 3 minutes. Pour into a serving dish.

6 to 8 servings

Note: If cherry tomatoes are not available, use canned whole peeled tomatoes.

525 Easy Corned Beef Bake

½ package (6 ounces) noodles, cooked
    and drained
1 can (12 ounces) corned beef, cut up
1 cup (4 ounces) shredded American
    cheese
¾ cup milk
¼ cup chopped onion
½ cup fine dry bread crumbs
2 tablespoons butter or margarine

1. Combine noodles, corned beef, cheese, milk, and onion. Put into a greased 1½-quart casserole.
2. Top with bread crumbs. Dot with butter.
3. Bake, covered, at 325°F 45 minutes, or until casserole is bub-bly.

4 servings

526 Corned Beef

6-pound beef brisket corned, boneless
2 teaspoons whole cloves
½ cup firmly packed light brown sugar
¼ cup sherry

1. Put the meat into a saucepot and add enough water to cover meat. Cover saucepot tightly and bring water just to boiling over high heat. Reduce heat and simmer about 4 hours, or until meat is almost tender when pierced with a fork.
2. Remove from heat and cool in liquid; refrigerate overnight.
3. Remove meat from liquid and set on rack in roasting pan. Stud with cloves. Put brown sugar over top and press firmly.
4. Roast at 325°F 1½ hours. After roasting 30 minutes, drizzle with sherry.
5. To serve, carve meat into slices.

About 12 servings

527 Roast Beef Filet with Burgundy Sauce

1 beef loin tenderloin roast, center cut (about 4 pounds)
Salt and pepper
½ cup dry red wine, such as burgundy
Sautéed mushroom caps
Parsley-buttered potatoes
Spiced crab apples
Burgundy Sauce:
½ cup warm water
¼ cup flour
1 cup beef broth
½ cup burgundy

1. Have meatman trim all but a thin layer of fat from meat and roll meat like a rib roast (but without adding fat).
2. Rub meat with salt and pepper and place in shallow roasting pan. Insert meat thermometer into center of thickest portion of roast.
3. Roast in a very hot oven, 450°F, about 45 to 60 minutes until thermometer registers 140°F (rare), basting twice with the wine after meat has cooked for 20 minutes.
4. Remove roast to heated serving platter. Garnish with sautéed mushroom caps, parsley-buttered potatoes, and spiced crab apples. Serve with Burgundy Sauce.
5. For sauce, pour off clear fat from drippings, saving ¼ cup.
6. Pour warm water into roasting pan; stir and scrape up all brown bits; strain.
7. Heat the reserved fat in a skillet; stir in flour. Slowly stir in strained liquid, beef broth, and burgundy. Cook and stir until sauce boils and thickens. Add a few drops of gravy coloring, if desired.

6 to 8 servings

528 *Boulettes of Beef Stroganoff*

1 pound ground beef round steak
1 egg, lightly beaten
⅓ cup fine fresh bread crumbs
¼ cup milk
¼ teaspoon grated nutmeg
¼ teaspoon each salt and freshly
    ground pepper
3 tablespoons paprika
¼ cup butter
¼ pound mushrooms, thinly sliced
⅓ cup finely chopped onion
¼ cup dry sherry
2 tablespoons brown sauce or
    canned beef gravy
¼ cup heavy cream
1 cup dairy sour cream
¼ cup finely chopped parsley

1. Put the meat into a mixing bowl and add the egg.
2. Soak the crumbs in milk and add this to the meat. Add the nutmeg, salt, and pepper; mix well with the hands. Shape the mixture into balls about 1½-inches in diameter. There should be about 35 to 40 meatballs.
3. Sprinkle a pan with the paprika and roll the meatballs in it.
4. Heat the butter in a heavy skillet and cook the meatballs, turning gently, until they are nicely browned, about 5 minutes. Sprinkle the mushrooms and onion between and around the meatballs and shake the skillet to distribute the ingredients evenly. Cook about 1 minute and partially cover. Simmer about 5 minutes and add the wine and brown sauce.
5. Stir in the heavy cream. Partially cover and cook over low heat about 15 minutes. Stir in the sour cream and bring just to boiling without cooking. Sprinkle with parsley and serve piping hot with **buttered fine noodles** as an accompaniment.

4 to 6 servings

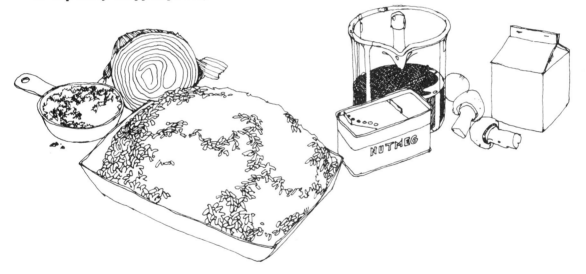

529 *Beef Stroganoff*

1½ pounds well-trimmed beef loin
    top sirloin steak, boneless
2 cups sliced mushrooms
3 tablespoons butter
1 shallot, chopped
¼ bay leaf
¾ cup dry sherry
2 tablespoons cornstarch
1 can (about 10 ounces)
    condensed beef broth
½ teaspoon salt
    Pepper to taste
1 cup dairy sour cream
1 tablespoon finely chopped
    parsley

1. Broil steak until rare. Cool thoroughly, then cut into strips.
2. Saute mushrooms in butter. Add shallot, bay leaf, and sherry; boil 5 minutes, until wine is reduced in volume to about half. Remove bay leaf.
3. Stir cornstarch into a little of the broth. Turn remaining broth over mushrooms, add cornstarch mixture, and cook-stir until sauce boils thoroughly and thickens. Add salt and pepper.
4. Just before serving, reheat sauce, then stir in sour cream and parsley and heat until simmering. Add steak strips and heat, but do not boil. Serve as soon as steak is thoroughly heated.

6 servings

530 Tenderloin Supreme in Mushroom Sauce

1 whole beef loin tenderloin roast
    (4 to 6 pounds)
Mushroom Sauce:
⅓ cup butter
¾ cup sliced mushrooms
¾ cup finely chopped onion
1½ tablespoons flour
¾ teaspoon salt
⅛ teaspoon pepper
⅛ teaspoon thyme
1½ cups beef broth
¾ cup red wine, such as burgundy
1½ teaspoons wine vinegar
1½ tablespoons tomato paste
1½ teaspoons chopped parsley

1. Place tenderloin on rack in roasting pan. Insert roast meat thermometer in center of meat so that tip is slightly more than halfway through meat.
2. Roast, uncovered, at 425°F 45 to 60 minutes. The roast will be rare when meat thermometer registers 140°F.
3. For Mushroom Sauce, heat butter in a skillet. Add mushrooms and cook over medium heat until lightly browned and tender, stirring occasionally. Remove mushrooms with a slotted spoon, allowing butter to drain back into skillet; set aside.
4. Add onion and cook 3 minutes; blend in flour, salt, pepper, and thyme. Heat until mixture bubbles. Remove from heat.
5. Gradually add, stirring constantly, beef broth, wine, and wine vinegar. Cook rapidly until sauce thickens. Blend in the mushrooms, tomato paste, and parsley. Cook about 3 minutes.
6. Serve slices of beef tenderloin with sauce spooned over individual servings.

16 to 24 servings

531 Roast Leg of Lamb with Spicy Wine Sauce

1 cup dry red wine
¼ cup salad oil
1 onion, coarsely chopped
2 cloves garlic, minced
½ teaspoon Tabasco
2 teaspoons salt
1 lamb leg whole (6 to 8 pounds)
    Parsley

1. Combine wine, oil, onion, garlic, Tabasco, and salt; pour over lamb. Cover and refrigerate 6 hours or overnight, turning occasionally.
2. Place lamb on rack in shallow roasting pan. Roast at 325°F about 25 minutes per pound, or until meat thermometer registers 160° to 170°F (medium); baste occasionally with marinade.
3. Garnish with parsley.

12 to 16 servings

532 Company Affair Lamb Chops

3 tablespoons butter
3 tablespoons flour
1 cup rich beef stock
¼ cup diced smoked pork loin,
    Canadian style bacon, or lean
    ham
1 tablespoon butter
¼ cup sherry
2 tablespoons minced green pepper
6 slices eggplant, cut ½ inch
    thick; unpeeled
    Olive oil
6 lamb loin chops
6 broiled mushroom caps

1. Melt butter in saucepan; add flour and cook until lightly browned. Gradually add beef stock and cook sauce until smooth and thick.
2. Combine bacon and butter in skillet and fry at least 2 minutes. Add sherry and green pepper and add to sauce.
3. Brush eggplant with olive oil and broil until lightly browned.
4. Broil lamb chops so that they are pink and juicy inside and crisply browned on outside.
5. Pour hot sauce over eggplant slices and place one lamb chop on each slice of eggplant. Garnish with a mushroom cap.

6 servings

533 *Lamb Chops Burgundy*

8 lamb loin or rib chops, cut 1½ to
   2 inches thick
½ cup burgundy
¼ cup olive oil
⅔ cup chopped red onion
½ clove garlic, minced
¼ teaspoon salt
3 peppercorns, crushed
½ teaspoon cumin seed, crushed

1. Put lamb chops into a shallow dish.
2. Combine burgundy, olive oil, red onion, garlic, salt, peppercorns, and cumin in a screw-top jar and shake to blend.
3. Pour marinade over meat. Cover and set in refrigerator to marinate about 2 hours, turning chops occasionally.
4. Remove chops from marinade and place on broiler rack. Set under broiler with tops of chops 3 to 5 inches from heat. Broil 18 to 22 minutes, or until meat is done as desired; turn once and brush occasionally with remaining marinade. To test, slit meat near bone and note color of meat.

8 servings

534 *Party Lamb Chops*

6 lamb loin chops, about 2 pounds
½ teaspoon salt
⅛ teaspoon pepper
2 tablespoons butter
2 tablespoons prepared mustard
1 can (16 ounces) quartered
   hearts of celery
1 cup tomato juice
½ cup dry white wine, such as
   sauterne
¼ cup finely chopped parsley

1. Sprinkle chops with salt and pepper.
2. Brown chops on both sides in butter in skillet. Spread mustard on chops.
3. Add celery and liquid from can, tomato juice, and wine. Cover and simmer 1 hour over low heat until chops are tender. Place chops on platter and keep warm.
4. Pour pan juices into blender and whirl until smooth, or beat with a rotary beater in small bowl. Pour back into skillet and reheat until bubbly and thick. Spoon over chops. Sprinkle chops with parsley.

6 servings

535 *Lamb Chops with Dill Sauce*

3 tablespoons butter
½ cup chopped onion
4 lamb shoulder arm chops, cut ½
   inch thick
2 tablespoons water
1 tablespoon vinegar
1 teaspoon salt
¼ teaspoon pepper
1 bay leaf
2 tablespoons butter or margarine
2 tablespoons flour
¼ teaspoon salt
   Few grains pepper
½ cup beef broth
1 tablespoon chopped fresh dill
½ cup dry white wine, such as
   chablis or sauterne
2 tablespoons vinegar

1. For chops, melt butter in a large heavy skillet with a tight-fitting cover. Add onion to fat and cook slowly, stirring occasionally, about 5 minutes. Remove onion from skillet with slotted spoon to small dish and set aside.
2. Cut through fat about every inch on outside edges of lamb chops. Be careful not to cut through to lean meat. Place chops in skillet; slowly brown both sides.
3. Meanwhile, combine water, vinegar, salt, pepper, and bay leaf; slowly add this mixture to the browned lamb. Return onion to skillet. Cover skillet and simmer 25 to 30 minutes, or until lamb is tender when pierced with a fork. If needed, add small amounts of water as lamb cooks.
4. For sauce, melt butter in small skillet over low heat. Blend flour, salt, and pepper into butter until smooth. Heat mixture until bubbly and lightly browned. Remove skillet from heat. Gradually add a mixture of the broth and fresh dill, stirring constantly.
5. Bring rapidly to boiling, stirring constantly; cook 1 to 2 minutes longer. Remove sauce from heat and gradually add wine and vinegar, stirring constantly. Serve the sauce over lamb chops.

4 servings

536 *Stuffed Veal Steak*

    4 veal loin top loin chops, 1 inch
        thick (about 1½ pounds)
    1 cup dry white wine, such as chablis
    ½ cup sliced mushrooms
    1 green pepper, cut in ½-inch pieces
    ½ cup butter or margarine
    ½ cup all-purpose flour
    1 egg, fork beaten
    ½ cup fine dry bread crumbs
    ½ cup grated Parmesan cheese
    4 slices proscuitto (Italian ham)
    4 slices (4 ounces) Cheddar cheese

1. Make a cut in the side of each veal chop, cutting almost all the way through. Lay each open and pound flat. Marinate meat for 1 hour in wine.
2. While meat marinates, sauté mushrooms and green pepper in butter for about 10 minutes or until tender. Remove from skillet with slotted spoon, leaving butter in skillet. Set vegetables aside.
3. Dry veal on paper towel. Bread on one side only, dipping first in flour, then in beaten egg, and last in bread crumbs mixed with Parmesan cheese.
4. Lay a slice of proscuitto on one half of unbreaded side of veal. Fold other side over. Panfry for 6 minutes on one side in butter in skillet, adding more butter if needed. Turn veal, and remove skillet from heat.
5. Insert a slice of cheese and ¼ of the mushroom-pepper mixture into the fold of each steak.
6. Return to heat and cook 6 minutes, or until meat is tender.

4 servings

537 *Veal Cutlet in Wine with Olives*

    1½ pounds veal cutlets, cut about ¼
        inch thick
    ¼ cup all-purpose flour
    1 teaspoon salt
    ½ teaspoon monosodium
        glutamate
    ¼ teaspoon pepper
    2 to 3 tablespoons butter or
        margarine
    ⅓ cup marsala
    ⅓ cup sliced green olives

1. Place meat on flat working surface and pound with meat hammer to increase tenderness. Turn meat and repeat process. Cut into 6 serving-size pieces. Coat with a mixture of flour, salt, monosodium glutamate, and pepper.
2. Heat butter in skillet over low heat. Brown meat over medium heat. Add marsala and green olives. Cover skillet and cook over low heat about 1 hour, or until meat is tender when pierced with a fork.

About 6 servings

538 *Veal in Wine-Mushroom Sauce*

1½ pounds thin veal cutlets
1 clove garlic, peeled and cut
1 tablespoon flour
¼ cup butter or margarine
½ pound mushrooms, thinly sliced
½ teaspoon salt
  Dash white pepper
½ cup white wine, such as vermouth
1 teaspoon lemon juice (optional)
  Snipped parsley

1. Pound meat to ¼-inch thickness. Rub both sides with garlic. Cut veal into 2-inch pieces and sprinkle with flour.
2. Sauté veal, a few pieces at a time, in hot butter in a large skillet, until golden brown on both sides.
3. Return all pieces to skillet. Top with mushrooms and sprinkle with salt and pepper.
4. Add wine and cook, covered, over low heat for 20 minutes, or until fork tender, adding 1 tablespoon or so of water if necessary.
5. To serve, sprinkle with lemon juice, if desired, and parsley.

4 to 6 servings

539 *Neapolitan Pork Chops*

2 tablespoons olive oil
1 clove garlic, minced
6 pork loin rib chops, cut about ¾ to 1 inch thick
1 teaspoon salt
½ teaspoon monosodium glutamate
¼ teaspoon pepper
1 pound mushrooms
2 green peppers
½ cup canned tomatoes, sieved
3 tablespoons dry white wine

1. Heat oil in large heavy skillet, add minced garlic and cook until lightly browned.
2. Season pork chops with a mixture of the salt, monosodium glutamate, and pepper. Place in skillet and slowly brown chops on both sides.
3. While chops brown, clean and slice mushrooms and chop green peppers; set aside.
4. When chops are browned, add the mushrooms and peppers. Stir in tomatoes and wine, cover skillet and cook over low heat 1 to 1½ hours, depending on thickness of chops. Add small amounts of water as needed. Test the chops for tenderness by piercing with a fork.

6 servings

540 *Apple-Covered Ham in Claret*

2 smoked ham center slices, fully cooked, about ¾ inch thick (about ½ pound each) or 1 large center cut 1½ inches thick
½ teaspoon dry mustard
3 to 4 medium Golden Delicious apples, cored and cut in rings
4 orange slices
¾ cup dry red wine, such as claret
½ cup packed brown sugar
  Parsley sprigs

1. Place ham slices in large shallow baking dish. Sprinkle each slice with ¼ teaspoon mustard.
2. Cut unpared apple rings in half and place around outer edge of ham, slightly overlapping slices.
3. Place two orange slices in center of each ham slice.
4. Pour wine over top of ham and fruit. Then sprinkle entire dish with brown sugar.
5. Cover; cook in a 350°F oven 45 minutes. Serve on platter or from baking dish, and garnish with parsley.

6 to 8 servings

Poultry

541 *Spiced Fruited Chicken*

12 pieces frying chicken (breasts, legs, and thighs)
1½ teaspoons salt
¼ teaspoon each pepper, cinnamon, and cloves
2 garlic cloves, minced
¼ cup oil
½ cup chopped onion
1 can (13¼ ounces) crushed pineapple
1⅓ cups orange juice (about)
½ cup raisins
½ cup dry sherry

1. Rub chicken with mixture of salt, pepper, cinnamon, cloves, and garlic. Brown in oil in a heavy skillet.
2. Place browned chicken pieces in an attractive range-to-table Dutch oven.
3. Lightly brown onion in oil remaining in skillet.
4. Drain pineapple, reserving liquid. Add enough orange juice to liquid to measure 2 cups.
5. Add onion, pineapple, raisins, and orange juice mixture to chicken. Cover and simmer about 45 minutes, or until chicken is tender.
6. Remove chicken. Add sherry; cook uncovered 15 minutes longer to cook down liquid. Return chicken; heat through.

12 servings

542 *Chicken and Dumplings*

¼ cup butter or margarine
2 broiler-fryer chickens, cut in
    serving-size pieces
½ cup chopped onion
¼ cup chopped celery
2 tablespoons chopped celery leaves
1 clove garlic, minced
¼ cup enriched all-purpose flour
4 cups chicken broth
1 teaspoon sugar
2 teaspoons salt
¼ teaspoon ground black pepper
1 teaspoon basil leaves
2 bay leaves
¼ cup chopped parsley
    Basil Dumplings
2 packages (10 ounces each) frozen
    green peas

1. Heat butter in a large skillet. Add chicken pieces and brown on all sides. Remove chicken from skillet.
2. Add onion, celery, celery leaves, and garlic to fat in skillet. Cook until vegetables are tender. Sprinkle with flour and mix well. Add chicken broth, sugar, salt, pepper, basil, bay leaves, and parsley; bring to boiling, stirring constantly. Return chicken to skillet and spoon sauce over it; cover.
3. Cook in a 350°F oven 40 minutes.
4. Shortly before cooking time is completed, prepare Basil Dumplings.
5. Remove skillet from oven and turn control to 425°F. Stir peas into skillet mixture and bring to boiling. Drop dumpling dough onto stew.
6. Return to oven and cook, uncovered, 10 minutes; cover and cook 10 minutes, or until chicken is tender and dumplings are done.

About 8 servings

Basil Dumplings: Combine **2 cups all-purpose biscuit mix** and **1 teaspoon basil leaves** in a bowl. Add **⅔ cup milk** and stir with a fork until a dough is formed. Proceed as directed in recipe.   543

544 *Chicken Fricassee with Vegetables*

1 broiler-fryer chicken (about 3
    pounds), cut in serving-size
    pieces
1½ teaspoons salt
1 bay leaf
    Water
2 cups sliced carrots
2 onions, quartered
2 crookneck squashes, cut in halves
    lengthwise
2 pattypan squashes, cut in halves
    Green beans (about 6 ounces),
    tips cut off
1 can (3½ ounces) pitted ripe olives,
    drained
1 tablespoon cornstarch
2 tablespoons water

1. Place chicken pieces along with salt and bay leaf in a Dutch oven or saucepot. Add enough water to just cover chicken. Bring to boiling; simmer, covered, 25 minutes until chicken is almost tender.
2. Add carrots and onions to cooking liquid; cook, covered, 10 minutes. Add squashes and green beans to cooking liquid; cook, covered, 10 minutes, or until chicken and vegetables are tender. Remove chicken and vegetables to a warm serving dish and add olives; keep hot.
3. Blend cornstarch and 2 tablespoons water; stir into boiling cooking liquid. Boil 2 to 3 minutes. Pour gravy over chicken.

About 4 servings

545 Chicken Polynesian Style

2 cups chicken broth
1 package (10 ounces) frozen mixed vegetables
½ cup diagonally sliced celery
1½ tablespoons cornstarch
1 teaspoon monosodium glutamate
½ teaspoon sugar
½ teaspoon seasoned salt
⅛ teaspoon ground black pepper
½ teaspoon Worcestershire sauce
1 small clove garlic, minced or crushed in a garlic press
1 tablespoon instant minced onion
1 can (6 ounces) ripe olives, drained and cut in wedges
Cooked chicken, cut in 1-inch pieces (about 2 cups)
Chow mein noodles
Salted peanuts
Soy sauce

1. Heat ½ cup chicken broth in a saucepan. Add frozen vegetables and celery; cook, covered, until crisp-tender. Remove vegetables and set aside; reserve any cooking liquid in saucepan.
2. Mix cornstarch, monosodium glutamate, sugar, seasoned salt, and pepper; blend with ¼ cup of the chicken broth. Add remaining broth, Worcestershire sauce, garlic, and onion to the saucepan. Add cornstarch mixture; bring to boiling, stirring constantly. Cook and stir 2 to 3 minutes.
3. Mix in olives, chicken, and reserved vegetables; heat thoroughly, stirring occasionally.
4. Serve over chow mein noodles and top generously with peanuts. Accompany with a cruet of soy sauce.

About 6 servings

546 Country Captain

1 broiler-fryer chicken (3 to 3½ pounds), cut in serving-size pieces
¼ cup enriched all-purpose flour
½ teaspoon salt
Pinch ground white pepper
3 to 4 tablespoons lard
2 onions, finely chopped
2 medium green peppers, chopped
1 clove garlic, crushed in a garlic press or minced
1½ teaspoons salt
½ teaspoon ground white pepper
1½ teaspoons curry powder
½ teaspoon ground thyme
½ teaspoon snipped parsley
5 cups undrained canned tomatoes
2 cups hot cooked rice
¼ cup dried currants
¾ cup roasted blanched almonds
Parsley sprigs

1. Remove skin from chicken. Mix flour, ½ teaspoon salt, and pinch white pepper. Coat chicken pieces.
2. Melt lard in a large heavy skillet; add chicken and brown on all sides. Remove pieces from skillet and keep hot.
3. Cook onions, peppers, and garlic in the same skillet, stirring occasionally until onion is lightly browned. Blend 1½ teaspoons salt, ½ teaspoon white pepper, curry powder, and thyme. Mix into skillet along with parsley and tomatoes.
4. Arrange chicken in a shallow roasting pan and pour tomato mixture over it. (If it does not cover chicken, add a small amount of water to the skillet in which mixture was cooked and pour liquid over chicken.) Place a cover on pan or cover tightly with aluminum foil.
5. Cook in a 350°F oven about 45 minutes, or until chicken is tender.
6. Arrange chicken in center of a large heated platter and pile the hot rice around it. Stir currants into sauce remaining in the pan and pour over the rice. Scatter almonds over top. Garnish with parsley.

About 6 servings

547 *Chicken with Fruit*

 1 tablespoon flour
 1 teaspoon seasoned salt
 ¾ teaspoon paprika
 3 pounds broiler-fryer chicken
   pieces (legs, thighs, and breasts)
1½ tablespoons vegetable oil
1½ tablespoons butter or margarine
 1 glove garlic, crushed in a garlic
   press or minced
 ⅓ cup chicken broth
 2 tablespoons cider vinegar
 1 tablespoon brown sugar
 ¼ teaspoon rosemary
 1 can (11 ounces) mandarin
   oranges, drained; reserve syrup
 1 jar (4 ounces) maraschino
   cherries, drained; reserve syrup
 1 tablespoon water
 1 tablespoon cornstarch
 ½ cup dark seedless raisins
   Cooked rice

1. Mix flour, seasoned salt, and paprika. Coat chicken pieces.
2. Heat oil, butter, and garlic in a large heavy skillet. Add chicken pieces and brown well on all sides.
3. Mix broth, vinegar, brown sugar, rosemary, and reserved syrups. Pour into skillet; cover and cook slowly 25 minutes, or until chicken is tender.
4. Remove chicken pieces to a serving dish and keep warm; skim any excess fat from liquid in skillet. Blend water with cornstarch and stir into liquid in skillet. Add raisins, bring to boiling, stirring constantly, and cook about 5 minutes, or until mixture is thickened and smooth. Mix in orange sections and cherries; heat thoroughly.
5. Pour sauce over chicken and serve with hot fluffy rice.

About 6 servings

548 *Chicken Livers and Mushrooms*

 2 pounds chicken livers, thawed if
   frozen
 ½ cup enriched all-purpose flour
 1 teaspoon salt
 ¼ teaspoon ground white pepper
 ⅓ cup butter or margarine
 1 cup orange sections, cut in halves
 1 can (6 ounces) broiled mushrooms
   Fresh parsley, snipped

1. Rinse chicken livers and drain on absorbent paper. Mix flour, salt, and pepper; coat chicken livers evenly.
2. Heat butter in a large skillet, add chicken livers, and cook 10 minutes, or until livers are lightly browned and tender. Mix in orange sections; heat.
3. Meanwhile, heat mushrooms in their broth in a small skillet.
4. Arrange cooked chicken livers and heated orange sections on a hot platter. Top with mushrooms and sprinkle with parsley. Serve immediately.

About 6 servings

549 *Chicken Mexicana*

 3 tablespoons vegetable oil
 2 broiler-fryer chickens (2½ to 3
   pounds each), cut in serving-size
   pieces
 2 cans (8 ounces each) tomato sauce
 1 can (13¾ ounces) chicken broth
 2 tablespoons (½ envelope) dry onion
   soup mix
 ¾ cup chopped onion
 1 clove garlic, minced
 6 tablespoons crunchy peanut butter
 ½ cup cream
 ½ teaspoon chili powder
 ¼ cup dry sherry
   Cooked rice

1. Heat oil in a large skillet. Add chicken and brown on all sides.
2. Meanwhile, combine tomato sauce, 1 cup chicken broth, soup mix, onion, and garlic in a saucepan. Heat thoroughly, stirring constantly.
3. Pour sauce over chicken in skillet. Simmer, covered, 20 minutes.
4. Put peanut butter into a bowl and blend in cream and remaining chicken broth; stir into skillet along with chili powder and sherry. Heat thoroughly. Serve with hot fluffy rice.

About 6 servings

550 Stuffed Roast Capon

½ cup butter or margarine
1½ teaspoons salt
¼ teaspoon ground black pepper
¼ teaspoon thyme
¼ teaspoon marjoram
¼ teaspoon rosemary
1½ quarts soft enriched bread cubes
½ cup milk
¼ cup chopped celery leaves
¼ cup chopped onion
1 capon (6 to 7 pounds)
Salt
Fat, melted

1. For stuffing, melt butter and mix in salt, pepper, thyme, marjoram, and rosemary.
2. Put bread cubes into a large bowl and pour in seasoned butter; lightly toss. Mix in milk, celery leaves, and onion.
3. Rub body and neck cavities of capon with salt. Fill cavities lightly with stuffing; truss bird, using skewers and cord.
4. Place, breast side up, on rack in a shallow roasting pan. Brush skin with melted fat and cover with a fat-moistened cheesecloth.
5. Roast in a 325°F oven 2½ hours, or until a meat thermometer inserted in center of inside thigh muscle registers 180° to 185°F. For easier carving, allow capon to stand about 20 minutes after removing from oven. Serve on a heated platter.

6 to 8 servings

551 Turkey 'n' Dressing Bake

3 tablespoons butter or margarine
½ cup diced celery
¼ cup minced onion
3¼ cups chicken broth (dissolve 4 chicken bouillon cubes in 3¼ cups boiling water)
5 cups coarse whole wheat bread crumbs; reserve ½ cup crumbs for topping
¼ cup snipped parsley
½ teaspoon salt
¼ teaspoon ground black pepper
1 egg, slightly beaten
2 tablespoons flour
2 eggs, beaten
⅛ teaspoon ground black pepper
¼ teaspoon crushed leaf sage
¼ teaspoon celery salt
Thin slices of cooked turkey roast (see Note)
1 tablespoon butter or margarine, melted
Parsley, snipped

1. Heat 3 tablespoons butter in a large skillet. Mix in celery and onion and cook about 5 minutes. Combine vegetables with 1¾ cups chicken broth, 4½ cups bread crumbs, ¼ cup parsley, salt, ¼ teaspoon pepper, and 1 egg. Mix lightly with a fork. Spoon the mixture over bottom of a shallow 2-quart baking dish; set aside.
2. Mix flour and ¼ cup cool broth in a saucepan until smooth; heat until bubbly. Add remaining broth gradually, stirring constantly. Cook and stir over medium heat until sauce comes to boiling; cook 2 minutes. Remove from heat and gradually add to eggs while beating. Blend in remaining pepper, sage, and celery salt.
3. Arrange the desired amount of turkey over dressing in baking dish. Pour the sauce over all.
4. Toss reserved bread crumbs with melted butter; spoon over top.
5. Bake at 350°F 30 to 40 minutes, or until egg mixture is set. Garnish generously with parsley.

6 servings

Note: Prepare frozen boneless turkey roast, following package directions.

552 *Roast Turkey with Herbed Stuffing*

Cooked Giblets and Broth
4 quarts ½-inch enriched bread
    cubes
1 cup snipped parsley
2 to 2½ teaspoons salt
2 teaspoons thyme
2 teaspoons rosemary, crushed
2 teaspoons marjoram
1 teaspoon ground sage
1 cup butter or margarine
1 cup coarsely chopped onion
1 cup coarsely chopped celery with
    leaves
1 turkey (14 to 15 pounds)
    Fat
3 tablespoons flour
¼ teaspoon salt
⅛ teaspoon ground black pepper

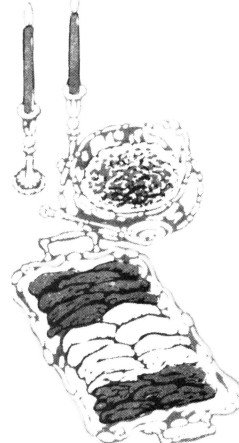

1. Prepare Cooked Giblets and Broth. Measure 1 cup chopped cooked giblets; set the broth aside.
2. Combine bread cubes, reserved giblets, and parsley in a large bowl. Blend salt, thyme, rosemary, marjoram, and sage; add to bread mixture and toss to mix.
3. Heat butter in a skillet. Mix in onion and celery; cook about 5 minutes, stirring occasionally. Toss with the bread mixture.
4. Add 1 to 2 cups broth (depending upon how moist a stuffing is desired), mixing lightly until ingredients are thoroughly blended.
5. Rinse turkey with cold water; pat dry, inside and out, with absorbent paper. Lightly fill body and neck cavities with the stuffing. Fasten neck skin to back with a skewer. Bring wing tips onto back of bird. Push drumsticks under band of skin at tail, if present, or tie to tail with cord.
6. Place turkey, breast side up, on rack in a shallow roasting pan. Brush skin with fat. Insert meat thermometer in the thickest part of the inner thigh muscle, being sure that tip does not touch bone.
7. Roast in a 325°F oven about 5 hours, or until thermometer registers 180° to 185°F. If desired, baste or brush bird occasionally with pan drippings. Place turkey on a heated platter; for easier carving, allow turkey to stand about 30 minutes.
8. Meanwhile, leaving brown residue in roasting pan, pour remaining drippings and fat into a bowl. Allow fat to rise to surface; skim off fat and measure 3 tablespoons into roasting pan. Blend flour, salt, and pepper with fat. Cook and stir until bubbly. Continue to stir while slowly adding 2 cups reserved liquid (broth and drippings). Cook, stirring constantly, until gravy thickens; scrape pan to blend in brown residue. Cook 1 to 2 minutes. If desired, mix in finely chopped cooked giblets the last few minutes of cooking.

About 25 servings

Cooked Giblets and Broth: Put **turkey neck** and **giblets** (except liver) into a saucepan with **1 large onion,** sliced, **parsley, celery with leaves, 1 medium bay leaf, 2 teaspoons salt,** and **1 quart water.** Cover, bring to boiling, reduce heat, and simmer until giblets are tender (about 2 hours); add the liver the last 15 minutes of cooking. Strain through a colander or sieve; reserve broth for stuffing. Chop giblets; set aside for stuffing and gravy.

553 *Turkey-Oyster Casserole*

1 tablespoon butter
2 teaspoons grated onion
4 ounces mushrooms, sliced
    lengthwise
¼ cup butter
¼ cup enriched all-purpose flour
1 teaspoon salt
¼ teaspoon ground pepper
    Few grains cayenne pepper
2 cups milk
1 egg yolk, slightly beaten
2 tablespoons chopped parsley
¼ teaspoon thyme
2 drops Tabasco
1 pint oysters (with liquor)
2 cups diced cooked turkey
    Buttered soft enriched bread
    crumbs

1. Heat 1 tablespoon butter with onion in a skillet; add mushrooms and cook over medium heat until lightly browned, stirring occasionally. Set aside.
2. Heat ¼ cup butter in a saucepan over low heat. Stir in flour, salt, pepper, and cayenne; cook until bubbly. Add milk gradually, stirring until well blended. Bring rapidly to boiling and boil 1 to 2 minutes, stirring constantly.
3. Blend a small amount of the hot sauce into egg yolk and return to remaining sauce, stirring until mixed. Stir in parsley, thyme, and Tabasco.
4. Heat oysters just to boiling; drain. Add oysters, turkey, and the mushrooms to sauce; toss lightly until thoroughly mixed.
5. Turn mixture into a buttered shallow 1½-quart baking dish. Sprinkle with crumbs.
6. Heat in a 400°F oven about 10 minutes, or until mixture is bubbly around edges and crumbs are golden brown.

About 6 servings

554 *Roast Goose with Rice-and-Pickle Stuffing*

3 cups cooked rice; or 1 package (6 ounces) seasoned white and wild rice mix, cooked following package directions
1 package (7 ounces) herb-seasoned stuffing croutons
2 medium navel oranges, pared and sectioned
2 onions, chopped
1 cup cranberries, rinsed, sorted, and chopped
1 cup sweet mixed pickles, drained and chopped
¼ cup sweet pickle liquid
½ to ¾ cup butter or margarine, melted
2 tablespoons brown sugar
1 goose (8 to 10 pounds)
1 tablespoon salt
¼ teaspoon ground black pepper
2 tablespoons light corn syrup
1½ cups orange juice
½ cup orange marmalade

1. Combine rice, stuffing croutons, orange sections, onions, cranberries, pickles and liquid, butter, and brown sugar in a large bowl; toss lightly until blended.
2. Rinse goose and remove any large layers of fat from the body cavity. Pat dry with absorbent paper. Rub body and neck cavities with salt and pepper.
3. Lightly spoon stuffing into the neck and body cavities. Overlap neck cavity with the skin and skewer to back of goose. Close body cavity with skewers and lace with cord. Loop cord around legs; tighten slightly and tie to a skewer inserted in the back above tail. Rub skin of goose with a little salt, if desired.
4. Put remaining stuffing into a greased casserole and cover; or cook in heavy-duty aluminum foil. Set in oven with goose during final hour of roasting.
5. Place goose, breast side down, on a rack in a large shallow roasting pan.
6. Roast in a 325°F oven 2 hours, removing fat from pan several times during this period.
7. Turn goose, breast side up. Blend corn syrup and 1 cup orange juice. Brush generously over goose. Roast about 1½ hours, or until goose tests done. To test for doneness, move leg gently by grasping end of bone; when done, drumstick-thigh joint moves easily or twists out. Brush frequently during final roasting period with the orange-syrup blend.
8. Transfer goose to a heated serving platter. Spoon 2 tablespoons drippings, the remaining ½ cup orange juice, and marmalade into a small saucepan. Heat thoroughly, stirring to blend. Pour into a serving dish or gravy boat to accompany goose.

6 to 8 servings

555 *Rock Cornish Hens with Fruited Stuffing*

1½ cups herb-seasoned stuffing
    croutons
½ cup drained canned apricot
    halves, cut in pieces
½ cup quartered seedless green
    grapes
⅓ cup chopped pecans
¼ cup butter or margarine, melted
2 tablespoons apricot nectar
1 tablespoon chopped parsley
¼ teaspoon salt
4 Rock Cornish hens (1 to 1½
    pounds each), thawed if
    purchased frozen
  Salt and pepper
⅓ cup apricot nectar
2 teaspoons soy sauce

1. Combine stuffing croutons, apricots, grapes, pecans, 2 tablespoons butter, 2 tablespoons apricot nectar, parsley, and ¼ teaspoon salt in a bowl; mix lightly.
2. Sprinkle cavities of hens with salt and pepper. Fill each hen with about ½ cup stuffing; fasten with skewers and lace with cord.
3. Blend ⅓ cup apricot nectar, soy sauce, and remaining butter. Place hens, breast side up, on a rack in a shallow roasting pan; brush generously with sauce.
4. Roast in a 350°F oven about 1½ hours, or until hens are tender and well browned; baste occasionally with sauce during roasting.

4 servings

556 *Chicken with Poached Garlic*

The garlic, poached without peeling, imparts a delicate flavor to the chicken.

1 broiler-fryer chicken (2½ to 3
    pounds)
1 garlic clove, peeled and cut in
    half
  Juice of 1 lime
  Salt
  Freshly ground white pepper
16 garlic cloves (unpeeled)
½ cup Chicken Stock
¼ cup dry vermouth
  Chicken Stock
2 teaspoons arrowroot
  Cold water
¼ cup Mock Crème Fraîche
1 tablespoon snipped parsley
  Salt
  Freshly ground white pepper

1. Rinse chicken; pat dry. Place in a roasting pan. Rub entire surface of chicken with cut garlic clove. Squeeze lime juice over chicken. Sprinkle cavity and outside of chicken lightly with salt and pepper. Place remaining garlic cloves around chicken; pour in ½ cup stock and ¼ cup dry vermouth.
2. Roast in a 325°F oven about 2½ hours, or until done; meat on drumstick will be very tender. Add stock if necessary to keep garlic covered. Remove chicken to platter. Cover loosely with aluminum foil. Let stand 20 minutes before carving.
3. Spoon fat from roasting pan. Add enough stock to pan to make 1 cup of liquid. Mix arrowroot with a little cold water; stir into stock. Simmer, stirring constantly, until thickened (about 3 minutes). Stir in Mock Crème Fraîche and parsley. Season to taste with salt and pepper. Pass sauce with chicken.

4 servings

Note: To eat garlic cloves, gently press with fingers; the soft cooked interior will slip out. The flavor of the poached garlic is very delicate.

557 *Mock Crème Fraîche*

1½ cups Neufchatel cheese
6 tablespoons Low-Fat Yogurt

1. Mix cheese and yogurt in a blender or food processor until smooth and fluffy. Place in small jars; cover tightly.
2. Set jars in a warm place (100° to 125°F) for 2 hours; see Note. Cool and refrigerate. Stir before using.

About 2 cups

Note: Use an oven thermometer in making Mock Crème Fraîche, as temperature is very important. A gas oven with a pilot light will be about 125°F. Turn electric oven to as warm a setting as necessary to maintain temperature. Mock Crème Fraîche can be refrigerated up to 3 weeks.

558 Roast Chicken with Orange-Beer Sauce

1 roasting chicken (4 to 5 pounds)
Stuffing (optional)
Salt and pepper
1 can or bottle (12 ounces) beer
½ cup orange juice
2 tablespoons lemon juice
2 tablespoons tomato paste or ketchup
2 teaspoons sugar
¼ cup flour
Fresh parsley and orange slices

1. Stuff chicken, if desired; truss. Rub with salt and pepper. Place in a roasting pan.
2. Combine 1 cup beer, orange juice, lemon juice, tomato paste, and sugar. Pour a little over chicken.
3. Roast, uncovered, at 375°F 2 to 2½ hours, or until done, basting occasionally with remaining beer mixture.
4. Transfer chicken to platter; keep warm. Skim fat from drippings; measure remaining liquid. If needed, add water to make 1½ cups. Make paste with flour and remaining ½ cup beer. Combine with liquid. Cook, stirring constantly, until thickened. Season with salt and pepper to taste.
5. Garnish chicken with parsley and orange slices. Pass sauce to pour over slices after carving.

6 servings

Ham-Bread Stuffing for Chicken: Combine **3 cups fresh bread cubes, ¼ pound ground ham, 1 small onion, minced, 2 tablespoons melted butter, ½ teaspoon salt, ¼ teaspoon sage, a dash pepper,** and just enough **beer** to moisten.

559 Brewers' Chicken

You don't taste the beer in this creamy, smooth sauce, but it imparts a subtly savory flavor.

1 broiler-fryer chicken (2 to 2½ pounds), cut up
12 small white onions; or 3 medium onions, sliced
3 tablespoons cooking oil
¾ cup beer
1 tablespoon ketchup
½ teaspoon each thyme or rosemary, paprika, and salt
1 bay leaf
½ cup milk or half-and-half
3 tablespoons flour

1. In a large skillet, brown chicken and onions in oil, removing pieces as they brown. Pour off excess fat.
2. Add beer, ketchup, and seasonings to skillet. Stir up brown bits.
3. Return chicken and onions to skillet. Cover and simmer 30 to 35 minutes, or until tender.
4. With a slotted spoon, transfer chicken and onions to serving platter; keep warm. Boil down cooking liquid to about 1½ cups.
5. Stir milk into flour until smooth. Add to liquid in skillet. Cook, stirring constantly, until thickened and smooth. Strain, if desired.

4 servings

560 *Broiled Marinated Chicken*

Cook this chicken indoors in the broiler or outdoors over hot coals.

1 broiler-fryer chicken (2 to 2½ pounds), cut up
1 can or bottle (12 ounces) beer
2 tablespoons lemon juice
2 tablespoons oil
2 tablespoons honey
1 garlic clove, slivered
½ teaspoon crushed rosemary
½ teaspoon salt
⅛ teaspoon pepper

1. Place chicken in a shallow dish just large enough to hold pieces. Combine remaining ingredients; pour over chicken. Marinate in refrigerator at least 6 hours or overnight.
2. Grill or broil 6 to 8 inches from heat, basting often with marinade and turning, 30 to 40 minutes, or until tender.

4 servings

561 *African-Style Chicken*

1 broiler-fryer chicken (2 to 2½ pounds), cut up
2 tablespoons peanut or other cooking oil
1 medium onion, chopped
1 garlic clove, minced
¾ cup beer
⅓ cup ground peanuts
1 tablespoon lemon juice
1 tablespoon honey
½ teaspoon salt
¼ to ½ teaspoon dried ground chili pepper or chili powder
¼ teaspoon ginger
3 tablespoons cream or milk
2 to 3 tablespoons flour
¼ cup flaked coconut

1. Brown chicken in oil in a heavy skillet; set aside.
2. Sauté onion and garlic in same skillet until golden. Add beer, peanuts, lemon juice, honey, and seasonings; mix.
3. Return chicken to skillet. Cover and simmer 35 to 40 minutes, or until tender.
4. Place chicken on a platter; keep warm. Measure cooking liquid. Make a paste of cream and flour, using 2 tablespoons flour per 1 cup cooking liquid. Add coconut. Cook, stirring constantly, until thickened. Pour part of sauce over chicken. Pass remainder to pour over **rice** or **potatoes.**

4 servings

562 *Chicken and Rice in Beer*

Chicken, rice, and flavorings bake together in this meal-in-one casserole. Beer is used in place of water to cook the rice. Complete the dinner with a green salad and fruit or a custard dessert.

1 broiler-fryer chicken (2 to 2½ pounds), cut up
2 tablespoons oil
2 medium onions, chopped
1 garlic clove, minced
¾ cup uncooked rice (not instant)
½ green pepper, chopped
½ cup chopped fresh or canned tomatoes
1½ teaspoons salt
¼ teaspoon pepper
1 can or bottle (12 ounces) beer
2 bay leaves

1. Brown chicken in oil in a large skillet; set chicken aside.
2. In same skillet, sauté onion and garlic until golden.
3. Stir in rice, green pepper, tomatoes, 1 teaspoon salt, and pepper. Put mixture into a large, shallow baking dish.
4. Sprinkle chicken with ½ teaspoon salt; place on top of rice mixture.
5. Add beer to skillet; stir up brown bits. Pour over chicken and vegetables. Add bay leaves.
6. Cover tightly with foil or lid.
7. Bake at 375°F 40 to 60 minutes, or until chicken and rice are tender.

4 servings

563 Crunchy Fried Chicken

Chicken is dipped in a beer batter, then fried. The resulting coating is tender, crisp, and so delicious!

1 cup all-purpose flour
½ teaspoon salt
¼ teaspoon pepper
2 eggs
½ cup beer
1 broiler-fryer chicken (2 to 2½
    pounds), cut up
    Cooking oil

1. Mix flour, salt, and pepper. Beat eggs with beer; add to flour mixture. Stir until smooth.
2. Dip chicken in batter, coating pieces well. Chill 1 hour.
3. Fry chicken in hot oil ½ to 1 inch deep 15 minutes on one side. Turn; fry on other side 5 to 10 minutes, or until browned and done. Drain on absorbent paper.

4 servings

564 Chicken Easy Oriental Style

¼ cup flour
1 teaspoon salt
¼ teaspoon pepper
4 chicken breasts, split in halves
¼ cup shortening
1 can (10¾ ounces) condensed cream
    of chicken soup
¼ cup dry white wine
¼ cup milk
1 can (4 ounces) water chestnuts,
    drained and sliced
¼ teaspoon ground ginger

1. Combine flour, salt, and pepper; coat chicken with mixture.
2. Brown chicken in shortening in skillet. Place in a 13x9-inch baking dish.
3. Combine soup, wine, milk, chestnuts, and ginger. Pour over chicken.
4. Bake, covered, at 350°F 1 hour, or until chicken is tender. If desired, sprinkle with snipped parsley.

4 servings

565 Chicken and Tomato Casserole

1 broiler-fryer chicken (about 3
    pounds), cut up
3 tablespoons shortening
½ cup chopped onion
¼ cup chopped green pepper
1 can (28 ounces) tomatoes
    (undrained)
1 can (8 ounces) tomato sauce
1 can (6 ounces) tomato paste
1 teaspoon salt
1 teaspoon oregano

1. Brown chicken in shortening in a skillet. Place in a 2-quart casserole.
2. Sauté onion and green pepper in fat in skillet. Stir in remaining ingredients and pour over chicken.
3. Bake, covered, at 350°F 1 hour, or until chicken is tender. Serve with **hot, cooked spaghetti.**

4 servings

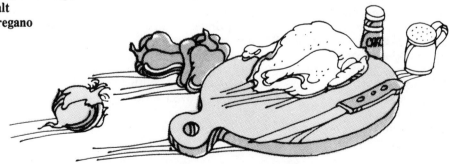

566 *Chicken Novaes*

2 jars (6 ounces each) tamales
1 can (4 ounces) sliced mushrooms, drained
2 cans (8 ounces each) tomato sauce
12 slices cooked chicken
2 cups cooked white rice
1 cup chopped green onion
2 cans (10¾ ounces each) condensed cream of chicken soup
1 cup (4 ounces) shredded Cheddar cheese
½ cup buttered bread crumbs

1. Remove paper from tamales. Cut in half crosswise and arrange in bottom of a 3-quart casserole.
2. Over the tamales, layer mushrooms, 1 can tomato sauce, chicken, rice, and onion. Top with the remaining can of tomato sauce. Spoon chicken soup over all, inserting a knife so soup will seep through.
3. Combine cheese and bread crumbs. Sprinkle over top of casserole mixture.
4. Bake, covered, at 350°F 30 minutes, or until bubbly.

12 servings

567 *Swiss Chicken Bake*

6 chicken breasts, split in halves, boned, and skin removed
1½ cups (6 ounces) shredded Swiss cheese
1 can (10¾ ounces) condensed cream of chicken soup
½ cup sherry
3 cups packaged herb stuffing mix
1 tablespoon butter or margarine

1. Place chicken breasts in a 13x9-inch baking dish. Sprinkle with cheese.
2. Combine soup and sherry; pour over Swiss cheese. Evenly spoon dressing over all. Dot with butter.
3. Bake, covered, at 350°F 1 hour, or until chicken is tender.

6 servings

568 *Thyme-Chicken Casserole*

4 chicken breasts, split in halves
1 teaspoon salt
¼ teaspoon pepper
¼ cup butter or margarine
1 can (10¾ ounces) condensed cream of mushroom soup
¼ cup dry white wine
1 can (4 ounces) sliced mushrooms, drained
¼ cup chopped green pepper
¼ teaspoon thyme
1 tablespoon instant minced onion

1. Season chicken with salt and pepper. Brown in butter in a skillet. Arrange, skin side up, in a 13x9-inch baking dish.
2. Blend soup into drippings. Slowly stir in wine. Add remaining ingredients; heat thoroughly. Pour over chicken.
3. Bake, covered, at 350°F 50 minutes. Remove cover and bake an additional 10 minutes, or until chicken is tender.

4 servings

569 *Italian Baked Chicken*

¼ cup butter or margarine, melted
1 tablespoon lemon juice
1 broiler-fryer chicken (about 3 pounds), cut up
1 package (1½ ounces) spaghetti sauce mix
⅔ cup fine dry bread crumbs
½ to 1 cup half-and-half
1 cup (4 ounces) shredded mozzarella cheese

1. Combine butter and lemon juice. Dip chicken pieces in butter mixture.
2. Combine spaghetti sauce mix and bread crumbs; coat chicken pieces with mixture.
3. Place chicken pieces, skin side up, in a 1½-quart shallow baking dish. Pour half-and-half around and between chicken pieces.
4. Bake, covered, at 350°F 1 hour, or until chicken is tender. Top with cheese and bake 2 minutes, or until cheese is melted.

4 servings

570 *Crispy Chicken with Curried Fruit*

1 cup corn flake crumbs
½ teaspoon salt
Dash pepper
1 broiler-fryer chicken (about 3 pounds), cut up
½ cup evaporated milk
Curried Fruit

1. Combine crumbs, salt, and pepper. Dip chicken pieces in milk. Roll in crumb mixture. Place chicken pieces in a 1½-quart shallow baking dish.
2. Bake, uncovered, at 350°F with Curried Fruit 1 hour, or until chicken is tender.

4 servings

571 *Curried Fruit*

1 can (16 ounces) peach halves, drained*
1 can (8½ ounces) pineapple chunks, drained*
4 maraschino cherries
¼ cup butter or margarine, melted
½ cup firmly packed brown sugar
1 tablespoon curry powder

1. Put fruits into a 1½-quart casserole. Combine butter, brown sugar, and curry powder. Spoon over fruits.
2. Bake, covered, at 350°F 1 hour. Serve with **hot, cooked rice.**

4 servings

* The drained liquids can be refrigerated and used in gelatin salads.

572 *Chicken and Rice*

2 cups cooked white rice
½ cup milk
2 tablespoons chopped pimento
1 can (10¾ ounces) condensed cream of celery soup
1 can (10¾ ounces) condensed cream of mushroom soup
1 broiler-fryer chicken (about 3 pounds), cut up
1 package (1⅜ ounces) dry onion soup mix

1. Combine rice, milk, pimento, celery soup, and mushroom soup. Pour into a greased 13x9-inch baking dish.
2. Dip chicken pieces in **milk,** then roll in onion soup mix. Arrange chicken pieces over rice mixture.
3. Bake, covered, at 350°F 1 hour, or until chicken is tender.

4 servings

573 *Chicken and Rice Valencia*

1 broiler-fryer chicken (about 3 pounds), cut up
¼ cup olive oil
1 medium onion, finely chopped
1 medium green pepper, slivered
1 can (10 ounces) tomatoes (undrained)
1 bay leaf
¾ cup water
Dash ground saffron (optional)
1 cup drained stuffed olives
1 package (6 ounces) Spanish rice mix
½ cup chopped celery

1. Brown chicken pieces in olive oil in a skillet.
2. Add remaining ingredients, except rice and celery. Place in a 2-quart casserole.
3. Bake, covered, at 350°F 1 hour, or until chicken is tender.
4. Meanwhile, prepare rice according to package directions. Stir celery into rice. Spread on hot serving platter.
5. Remove bay leaf from chicken. Spoon chicken and sauce over rice.

4 servings

574 *Chicken Surprise*

½ cup chopped onion
1 tablespoon butter or margarine
1 tablespoon cornstarch
¾ cup orange juice
2 tablespoons prepared mustard
½ cup sherry
2 cups chopped cooked chicken
½ cup raisins
½ cup sliced celery

1. Sauté onion in butter in a skillet. Stir in cornstarch. Gradually add orange juice, then mustard and sherry, stirring until thickened and smooth.
2. Place chicken, raisins, and celery in a 1-quart casserole. Pour sauce over all; mix.
3. Bake, covered, at 325°F 30 minutes, or until heated through. Serve in **chow mein noodle** or **patty shells** and garnish with **orange twists.**

4 servings

575 *Chicken Breasts with Sour Cream*

8 chicken breasts, split in halves, boned, and skin removed
16 bacon slices
3 packages (3 ounces each) smoked sliced beef
1 can (10¾ ounces) condensed cream of mushroom soup
2 cups dairy sour cream

1. Roll each chicken breast in 1 bacon slice. (Another half bacon slice may be needed if the breast is a large one, so that all of it will be surrounded by the bacon.)
2. Shred beef and place in a 13x9-inch baking dish. Top with chicken breasts.
3. Combine soup and sour cream. Spoon over chicken breasts.
4. Bake, uncovered, at 275°F 3 hours, or until chicken is tender. Cover lightly with foil if it begins to get too brown.

8 servings

576 *Chicken Pie*

1¼ cups water
1 cup milk
1 package (⅞ ounce) chicken gravy mix
1 package (10 ounces) frozen peas, thawed
2 tablespoons chopped pimento
2 cups cubed cooked chicken
1 tablespoon finely chopped onion
1 teaspoon snipped parsley
2 cups all-purpose biscuit mix

1. Combine ¾ cup water, milk, and gravy mix in a saucepan; bring to a boil.
2. Stir in peas, pimento, and chicken; heat thoroughly.
3. Stir onion, parsley, and remaining ½ cup water into biscuit mix, stirring until thoroughly moistened.
4. Pour hot chicken mixture into an 11x7-inch shallow baking dish. Roll or pat out dough to fit top of baking dish. Set on chicken mixture.
5. Bake, uncovered, at 450°F 10 to 12 minutes, or until topping is golden brown.

6 servings

577 *Chicken Mac*

1 package (7¼ ounces) macaroni and cheese dinner
1 tablespoon instant minced onion
2 tablespoons chopped celery
2 tablespoons chopped green pepper
1 garlic clove, minced
2 tablespoons butter or margarine
1 can (8¾ ounces) whole kernel corn, drained
1 can (10¾ ounces) condensed cream of chicken soup
1½ cups chopped cooked chicken or turkey
2 tablespoons snipped parsley
⅓ cup buttered bread crumbs

1. Prepare dinner according to package directions, except use ½ cup milk.
2. Sauté onion, celery, green pepper, and garlic in butter in a skillet. Combine with corn, soup, chicken, and prepared dinner. Put into a greased 1½-quart casserole.
3. Combine parsley and bread crumbs. Sprinkle over top of casserole mixture.
4. Bake, covered, at 350°F 25 minutes, or until heated through.

4 servings

578 *Chicken Artichoke Casserole*

⅓ cup butter or margarine
¼ cup flour
1¾ cups milk
　　Dash ground red pepper
1 garlic clove, minced
¼ cup (1 ounce) shredded Cheddar
　　cheese
1½ ounces Gruyère cheese, cut up
2 cups chopped cooked chicken
1 can (4 ounces) button mushrooms,
　　drained
1 can (14 ounces) artichoke hearts,
　　drained

1. Melt butter in a saucepan. Stir in flour. Gradually add milk, stirring until thickened and smooth.
2. Add red pepper, garlic, and cheese, stirring until smooth. Blend in chicken, mushrooms, and artichoke hearts. Pour into a 2-quart casserole.
3. Bake, covered, at 350°F 30 minutes, or until heated through. Sprinkle with **paprika.**

6 servings

579 *Chicken-Green Noodle Casserole*

½ cup chopped onion
½ cup slivered almonds
1 cup sliced fresh mushrooms
¼ cup butter or margarine
3 cups cooked spinach (green) noodles
1 cup milk
2 cans (10¾ ounces each) condensed
　　cream of chicken soup
3 cups chopped cooked chicken
¼ teaspoon pepper
⅓ cup buttered bread crumbs

1. Sauté onion, almonds, and mushrooms in butter in a skillet. Combine with remaining ingredients, except bread crumbs. Put into a 2½-quart casserole.
2. Bake, covered, at 350°F 30 minutes. Remove cover. Sprinkle with bread crumbs and bake an additional 15 minutes, or until heated through.

8 servings

580 Chicken-Chip Bake

2 cups chopped cooked chicken
2 cups sliced celery
1 can (8 ounces) pineapple chunks, drained
¾ cup mayonnaise
⅓ cup toasted slivered almonds
2 tablespoons lemon juice
2 teaspoons finely chopped onion
½ teaspoon salt
½ cup (2 ounces) shredded American cheese
1 cup crushed potato chips

1. Combine chicken, celery, pineapple, mayonnaise, almonds, lemon juice, onion, and salt. Put into a 1½-quart casserole. Sprinkle with cheese and potato chips.
2. Bake, uncovered, at 350°F 30 minutes, or until heated through.

4 to 6 servings

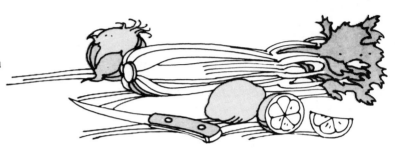

581 Chicken Bake

8 slices white bread, crusts removed
4 cups chopped cooked chicken or turkey
1 jar (4½ ounces) mushroom stems and pieces, drained
1 can (4 ounces) water chestnuts, drained and sliced
8 slices (1 ounce each) Cheddar cheese
¼ cup mayonnaise
4 eggs, well beaten
2 cups milk
1 teaspoon salt
2 cans (10¾ ounces each) condensed cream of mushroom soup
1 tablespoon chopped pimento
½ cup buttered bread crumbs

1. Place bread in a 13x9-inch baking dish. Top with chicken, mushrooms, water chestnuts, cheese, and mayonnaise.
2. Combine eggs, milk, and salt. Pour over all in casserole.
3. Mix soup and pimento; spread over top. Cover and refrigerate overnight.
4. Bake, covered, at 325°F 1 hour. Remove cover; sprinkle with bread crumbs and bake an additional 15 minutes, or until set. Let stand a few minutes before serving.

8 servings

582 Hens in Wine

1 tablespoon rosemary
1 cup dry white wine
⅓ cup flour
1 teaspoon salt
½ teaspoon pepper
1 teaspoon snipped parsley
4 Rock Cornish hens, quartered
½ cup butter or margarine
1 pound small fresh mushrooms

1. Soak rosemary in wine 1 hour.
2. Combine flour, salt, pepper, and parsley. Coat hen quarters with flour mixture.
3. Brown hen quarters in butter in a skillet. Place in a 12x8-inch baking dish. Add wine mixture.
4. Bake, uncovered, at 350°F 30 minutes.
5. Meanwhile, sauté mushrooms in butter in skillet. Add to baking dish. Bake an additional 15 minutes, or until hen quarters are tender.

4 servings

583 *Chicken à la King*

½ cup sliced fresh mushrooms
¼ cup butter or margarine
¼ cup flour
2 cups milk
1 teaspoon salt
1½ cups cooked noodles
2 cups chopped cooked chicken or turkey
¾ cup (3 ounces) shredded Cheddar cheese
1 cup cooked peas
1 tablespoon instant minced onion
2 teaspoons Worcestershire sauce
1 tablespoon ketchup
   Dash Tabasco

1. Sauté mushrooms in butter in a skillet. Stir in flour. Gradually add milk, stirring until thickened and smooth. Stir in remaining ingredients. Put into a 2-quart casserole.
2. Bake, covered, at 350°F 30 minutes, or until heated through.

4 servings

584 *Chicken and Wild Rice*

¾ cup uncooked wild rice
4 cups chopped cooked chicken
1 cup sherry
1 cup chicken broth
1 small onion, chopped
1 can (8 ounces) mushroom slices, drained
¼ cup butter or margarine, melted
1 can (10¾ ounces) condensed cream of mushroom soup
1 can (10¾ ounces) condensed cream of chicken soup
2 packages (10 ounces each) frozen broccoli or asparagus spears, cooked and drained
1 cup (4 ounces) shredded Cheddar cheese

1. Cook wild rice according to package directions.
2. Combine rice with remaining ingredients, except broccoli and cheese.
3. Spread half the rice mixture in a 13x9-inch baking dish. Top with broccoli. Evenly spread remaining rice mixture over all.
4. Bake, uncovered, at 350°F 45 minutes, or until heated through. Sprinkle with cheese and bake an additional 5 minutes, or until cheese is melted.

8 servings

585 Turkey Pot Pie

2 cups chopped cooked turkey
2 cans (10¾ ounces each) condensed
    cream of celery soup
½ cup milk
½ teaspoon Worcestershire sauce
    Dash pepper
6 cooked small onions
1 cup cooked cubed potato
1 cup cooked sliced carrot
⅓ cup shortening
1 cup self-rising flour
4 tablespoons cold water

1. Combine turkey, soup, milk, Worcestershire sauce, pepper, onions, potato, and carrot. Put into a 2-quart casserole.
2. Cut shortening into flour. Add water, a tablespoon at a time, mixing lightly until dough can be formed into a ball. (If necessary, add a little more water to make dough hold together.) Let rest 5 minutes.
3. Roll dough out on a lightly floured board or canvas to fit top of casserole. Cut slits to allow steam to escape. Adjust over filling; flute edges.
4. Bake, uncovered, at 425°F 20 minutes, or until pastry is golden brown.

6 servings

586 Gefüllter Gänsebraten
(Roast Goose with Prune-Apple Stuffing)

2 cups pitted cooked prunes
1 goose (10 to 12 pounds, ready-to-
    cook weight)
    Salt
6 medium (about 2 pounds)
    apples

1. Set out a shallow roasting pan with rack. Have prunes ready, reserving about 8 to 10 prunes for garnish.
2. If goose is frozen, thaw according to directions on package. Clean and remove any layers of fat from body cavity and opening of goose. Cut off neck at body, leaving on neck skin. Rinse and pat dry with absorbent paper. (Reserve giblets for use in gravy or other food preparation.) Rub body and neck cavities of goose with salt. Wash, core, pare and quarter apples.
3. Lightly fill body and neck cavities with the apples and prunes. To close body cavity, sew or skewer and lace with cord. Fasten neck skin to back with skewer. Loop cord around legs and tighten slightly. Place breast side down on rack in roasting pan.
4. Roast uncovered at 325°F 3 hours. Remove fat from pan as it accumulates during this period. Turn goose breast side up. Roast 1 to 2 hours longer, or until goose tests done. To test for doneness, move leg gently by grasping end of bone; drumstick-thigh joint should move easily. (Protect fingers with paper napkin.) Allow about 25 minutes per pound to estimate total roasting time.
5. To serve, remove skewers and cord. Place goose on heated platter. Remove some of the apples from goose and arrange on the platter. Garnish with the reserved prunes. For an attractive garnish, place cooked prunes on top of cooked apple rings, if desired.

8 servings

587 *Brunswick Stew*

1 chicken (about 4 pounds),
   disjointed
¼ cup cooking oil
1 cup coarsely chopped onion
¼ pound salt pork, chopped
4 tomatoes, peeled and quartered
2 cups boiling water
1 cup sherry
1 bay leaf
1 teaspoon Worcestershire sauce
1½ cups fresh lima or butter beans
½ cups sliced fresh okra
1½ cups fresh bread crumbs
2 tablespoons butter
   Salt to taste

1. Sauté chicken in cooking oil until golden; remove chicken. Brown onion and salt pork in the same fat.
2. Put chicken, salt pork, onion, tomatoes, boiling water, sherry, bay leaf, and Worcestershire sauce into Dutch oven or saucepot. Cover and simmer 2 hours, or until chicken is tender.
3. After 1 hour, remove bay leaf; add beans and cook about 15 minutes. Add sliced okra; continue cooking about 15 minutes.
4. Sauté fresh bread crumbs in butter; stir into stew. Add salt to taste before serving.

8 servings

588 *Chicken Breasts with Noodles*

8 whole chicken breasts, flattened
   Salt and pepper to taste
   Dash of crushed marjoram
   Butter to cover skillet
3 pounds fresh mushrooms
½ pound butter
12 ounces noodles
2 tablespoons butter
2 cups Medium White Sauce
   (see recipe)
1 cup cold milk
1 cup chicken broth
   Hollandaise Sauce (see recipe)
½ cup dry white wine
   Parmesan cheese, grated

1. Season chicken breasts with salt, pepper, and marjoram. Sauté in butter until breasts are fully cooked.
2. While chicken is cooking, wash mushrooms and cut into small pieces, then sauté in ½ pound butter.
3. Cook noodles until done; drain and work 2 tablespoons of butter gently into the noodles.
4. Make white sauce; add to it the cold milk and chicken broth. Cook mixture until thickened. Reserve while making hollandaise sauce.
5. Carefully blend hollandaise with white sauce mixture; stir in wine.
6. Butter a small roasting pan; place noodles in the bottom, add the mushrooms, and place chicken breasts on top of the mushrooms. Pour the sauce over all. Heat thoroughly in a 325°F oven about 45 minutes.
7. Remove from oven, sprinkle with grated Parmesan cheese and place under broiler to brown.

8 servings

Medium White Sauce: Melt **¼ cup butter or margarine** in a saucepan. Blend in **¼ cup flour, 1 teaspoon salt,** and **¼ teaspoon pepper.** Cook and stir until bubbly. Gradually add **2 cups milk,** stirring until smooth. Bring to boiling; cook and stir 1 to 2 minutes longer.   589

About 2 cups sauce

Hollandaise Sauce: Beat **4 egg yolks** in the top of a double boiler, then beat in **½ cup cream.** Cook and stir over **hot water** until slightly thickened. Blend in **2 tablespoons lemon juice.** Cut in **4 tablespoons cold butter,** a tablespoon at a time. Sauce will thicken.   590

About 1 cup sauce

591 *Chicken Curry with Rice*

⅔ cup butter or margarine
6 tablespoons chopped onion
6 tablespoons chopped celery
6 tablespoons chopped green apple
24 peppercorns
2 bay leaves
⅔ cup all-purpose flour
5 teaspoons curry powder
1 teaspoon monosodium glutamate
½ teaspoon sugar
¼ teaspoon nutmeg
5 cups milk
4 teaspoons lemon juice
1 teaspoon Worcestershire sauce
½ cup cream
¼ cup sherry
½ teaspoon Worcestershire sauce
6 cups cubed cooked chicken
Hot cooked rice

1. Heat butter in a heavy 3-quart saucepan over low heat. Add onion, celery, apple, peppercorns, and bay leaves, and cook over medium heat until lightly browned, occasionally moving and turning with a spoon.
2. Blend in flour, curry powder, monosodium glutamate, sugar, and nutmeg; heat until mixture bubbles.
3. Remove from heat and add milk gradually, stirring constantly.
4. Return to heat and bring rapidly to boiling. Stirring constantly, cook until mixture thickens; cook 1 to 2 minutes longer.
5. Remove from heat; add lemon juice and 1 teaspoon Worcestershire sauce. Strain mixture through a fine sieve, pressing vegetables against sieve to extract all sauce. Set sauce aside.
6. Reheat the curry sauce and blend in cream, sherry, and ½ teaspoon Worcestershire sauce; add chicken and cook over medium heat 2 to 3 minutes, or until mixture is thoroughly heated. Serve with rice.

8 servings

592 *Chicken à la Winegrower*

2 slices bacon, diced
2 cloves garlic, halved
1 tablespoon butter or margarine
4 chicken legs (thighs and drumsticks)
1 cup chopped onion
½ cup dry white wine
2 tablespoons chopped parsley
2 tablespoons chopped chives
1½ teaspoons salt
¼ teaspoon pepper
1 bay leaf
1 can (4 ounces) sliced mushrooms with liquid
1 cup chicken broth
2 tablespoons flour
Hot cooked rice
½ cup dairy sour cream, warmed
Chopped parsley for garnish

1. Sauté bacon and garlic in butter until bacon is partially cooked. Discard garlic.
2. Add chicken and brown on all sides.
3. Stir in onion and sauté until transparent. Add ¼ cup wine and cook a few minutes, stirring to loosen browned particles.
4. Add parsley, chives, seasonings, mushrooms, and broth. Cover and cook over low heat for 30 minutes, or until chicken is tender. Remove chicken and keep warm. Discard bay leaf.
5. Blend flour with remaining wine. Stir into sauce and cook until thickened.
6. Serve chicken on beds of fluffy rice. Top with sauce and dollops of sour cream. Garnish with parsley.

4 servings

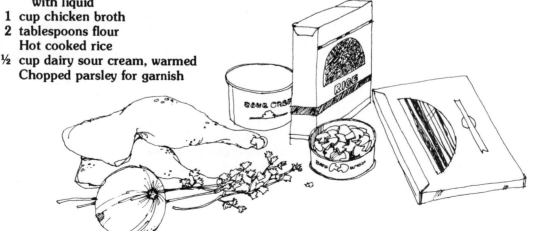

593 Skillet Chicken and Vegetables

1 can (about 10 ounces)
    condensed chicken broth
1 cup dry white wine, such as
    chablis
1 tablespoon instant minced onion
½ teaspoon salt
1 bay leaf
¼ teaspoon rosemary, crushed
6 half breasts of chicken
6 small carrots
6 small zucchini
2 tablespoons cornstarch
2 tablespoons cold water
3 tablespoons chopped pimento
2 tablespoons chopped parsley

1. Combine broth, wine, onion, salt, bay leaf, and rosemary in a large skillet. Heat to boiling.
2. Place chicken breasts in the boiling liquid; cover and simmer 20 minutes.
3. While chicken is cooking, pare carrots and cut in half lengthwise. Cut zucchini in half lengthwise. Add carrots and zucchini to the chicken; cover, and cook 15 minutes longer, or until chicken is tender and vegetables are crisp-tender.
4. Remove chicken and vegetables with a slotted spoon; keep warm.
5. Mix cornstarch with water and stir into liquid remaining in skillet. Cook, stirring until sauce boils thoroughly. Add pimento and parsley, and pour over chicken and vegetables. Serve immediately.

6 servings

594 Chicken Marengo

1 broiler-fryer chicken (2 to 3
    pounds)
⅓ cup all-purpose flour
1 teaspoon salt
¼ teaspoon pepper
¼ cup olive oil
1 clove garlic, crushed
3 tablespoons chopped onion
4 tomatoes, quartered
1 cup white wine
    Herb Bouquet
1 cup (about 4 ounces) sliced
    mushrooms
2 tablespoons butter
½ cup sliced olives
½ cup chicken bouillon
2 tablespoons all-purpose flour

1. Disjoint chicken and cut into serving-size pieces. Rinse and pat dry with absorbent paper.
2. Coat chicken evenly with a mixture of flour, salt, and pepper.
3. Heat oil in a large skillet and brown chicken.
4. Add garlic, onion, tomatoes, wine, and Herb Bouquet to chicken; cover and simmer over low heat about ½ hour, or until thickest pieces of chicken are tender when pierced with a fork.
5. Sauté mushrooms in butter and add to chicken with olives.
6. Put bouillon and flour into screw-top jar; cover and shake well.
7. Remove chicken from skillet and discard Herb Bouquet. Gradually add bouillon-flour liquid to mixture in skillet, stirring constantly. Boil 3 to 5 minutes until mixture thickens.
8. Return chicken to sauce; cover and simmer 10 minutes. Arrange chicken on a hot platter. Cover with the sauce.

4 or 5 servings

Herb Bouquet: Tie neatly together **3 or 4 sprigs of parsley, 1 sprig thyme,** and **½ bay leaf.**

595 Chicken a Seville

3 tablespoons butter or margarine
½ pound fresh mushrooms, cleaned
    and halved lengthwise
3 to 4 tablespoons olive or other
    cooking oil
3 pounds chicken pieces
1 cup uncooked rice
1 large clove garlic, minced
2 cups chicken broth or bouillon

1. Heat butter in a large skillet and stir in mushrooms. Cook until lightly browned, stirring occasionally. Remove from skillet and set aside. Pour oil into skillet and heat.
2. Coat chicken pieces with a blend of **flour, salt,** and **pepper.** Fry in hot oil until browned on all sides. Remove chicken and keep warm.
3. Mix rice and garlic with oil in skillet, then stir in 1 cup of the chicken broth. Turn contents of skillet into a shallow baking dish. Put onions, browned chicken, mushrooms, and olives into dish.

12 **very small white onions**
1 **cup small pimento-stuffed olives**
1 **cup dry white wine**
¾ **teaspoon oregano**
½ **cup toasted blanched almonds, sliced**

Pour remaining broth and the wine over all. Sprinkle oregano over chicken.

4. Cook, covered, in a 375°F oven about 45 minutes, or until rice is tender. Remove from oven and top with the nuts.

About 6 servings

596 Breast of Chicken Savannah

4 **large chicken breasts, split**
2½ **ounces (about ¼ cup) peanut butter**
8 **thin slices cooked ham**
¼ **cup sherry**
Parmesan Sauce:
¼ **cup flour**
2 **cups milk**
½ **teaspoon salt**
6 **tablespoons freshly grated Parmesan cheese**
2 **tablespoons firm butter**

1. Lift skin on chicken breasts slightly, and spread a film of peanut butter on meat under skin; replace skin.
2. Place 1 slice of cooked ham over skin side of each breast.
3. Put sherry into a large casserole or braising pan. Add chicken pieces, ham side up; cover and cook in a 350°F oven 1 hour, or until pieces are tender.
4. Remove breasts from pan and keep warm while preparing Parmesan sauce; reserve ¼ cup pan drippings.
5. For sauce, put the pan drippings into a medium saucepan. Add flour; stir and heat until bubbly. Add milk gradually, stirring well; bring to boiling and cook 1 to 2 minutes.
6. Add salt and Parmesan cheese, stirring until cheese melts. Stir in butter, 1 tablespoon at a time.
7. Pour sauce over chicken and serve.

8 servings

597 Canard à l'Orange
(Roast Duckling with Orange Sauce)

2 **ducklings (4 to 5 pounds each)**
2 **teaspoons salt**
½ **teaspoon pepper**
1 **clove garlic, peeled and cut crosswise into halves**
½ **cup dry white wine**
½ **cup orange marmalade**
Sauce:
2 **tablespoons butter or margarine**
1 **can (13¾ ounces) condensed chicken broth**
½ **cup orange marmalade**
¼ **cup dry white wine**
¼ **cup orange juice**
2 **teaspoons cornstarch**
2 **teaspoons lemon juice**
2 **tablespoons slivered orange peel**

1. If frozen, let ducklings thaw according to package directions. Remove giblets, necks, and livers from ducklings. Reserve livers for sauce; if desired, reserve giblets and necks for soup stock. Remove and discard excess fat. Wash, drain, and pat dry with paper toweling. Rub cavities with salt, pepper, and garlic. Fasten neck skin of each to back with a skewer. Tuck tail ends into cavities. Tie legs together and tuck wing tips under ducklings. Prick skin generously to release fat. Place ducklings, breast side up, on a rack in a large shallow roasting pan.
2. Roast at 350°F 2 to 2½ hours or until legs can be moved easily, basting several times during roasting and removing accumulated drippings about every 30 minutes. Remove ducklings from oven and spread surface with mixture of wine and marmalade. Return to oven and continue roasting for 10 minutes.
3. For sauce, melt butter in a skillet. Add duckling livers and sauté until lightly browned. Remove and chop livers. Add chicken broth, marmalade, wine, orange juice, and cornstarch blended with lemon juice. Cook, stirring constantly over low heat for 10 minutes or until sauce bubbles and thickens. Stir in chopped livers and orange peel.
4. Transfer ducklings to a heated platter. Remove skewers and twine. Garnish, if desired, with watercress and orange slices. Reheat sauce if necessary and serve with duckling.

8 servings

598 Chicken, Cacciatore Style

¼ cup vegetable oil
1 broiler-fryer chicken (about 2½ pounds), cut in serving-size pieces
2 medium onions, sliced
2 cloves garlic, crushed in a garlic press or minced
3 tomatoes, sliced
2 medium green peppers, sliced
1 small bay leaf
1 teaspoon salt
¼ teaspoon ground black pepper
½ teaspoon celery seed
1 teaspoon crushed oregano or basil
1 can (8 ounces) tomato sauce
¼ cup dry white wine
8 ounces spaghetti, cooked

1. Heat oil in a large heavy skillet. Add chicken and brown on all sides. Remove chicken from skillet.
2. Add onion and garlic to oil remaining in skillet and cook until onion is tender but not brown; stir occasionally to cook evenly.
3. Return chicken to skillet and add the tomato, green pepper, and bay leaf.
4. Mix salt, pepper, celery seed, and oregano with tomato sauce; pour over all.
5. Cover and cook over low heat 45 minutes. Blend in wine and cook, uncovered, 20 minutes. Discard bay leaf.
6. Put cooked spaghetti onto a warm serving platter and top with the chicken pieces and sauce.

About 6 servings

599 Herb-Chicken with Mushrooms

2 tablespoons butter or margarine
1 broiler-fryer chicken (3 pounds), cut in quarters
¾ cup cider vinegar
¼ cup water
1 cup (about 3 ounces) sliced mushrooms
1 tablespoon finely chopped parsley
1 tablespoon finely chopped chives
1 teaspoon crushed tarragon
½ teaspoon thyme
½ teaspoon salt
¼ teaspoon black pepper
2 tablespoons flour
1½ cups chicken broth
½ cup sherry

1. Heat butter in a large skillet. Place chicken pieces, skin side down, in skillet and brown on all sides.
2. Meanwhile, pour a mixture of vinegar and water over the mushrooms. Let stand 10 minutes; drain.
3. When chicken is evenly browned, transfer pieces to a shallow baking dish. Sprinkle the seasonings over the chicken. Spoon drained mushrooms over the top; sprinkle evenly with flour. Pour broth and wine over all.
4. Bake at 325°F about 1 hour, or until tender.

About 4 servings

600 Roast Goose with Sauerkraut Stuffing

1 goose (ready-to-cook 10 to
  12 pounds)
1 tablespoon butter or margarine
2 large onions, chopped
6½ cups drained sauerkraut, snipped
2 medium apples, quartered,
  cored, and diced
1 small carrot, pared and shredded
2 medium potatoes, shredded
  (about 1½ cups)
½ cup dry white wine
1 to 2 tablespoons brown sugar
2 teaspoons caraway seed
½ teaspoon seasoned pepper
  Salt

1. Singe and clean goose removing any large layers of fat from the body and neck cavities. Rinse thoroughly, drain, and pat dry with absorbent paper; set aside.
2. Heat butter in a skillet; add onion and cook until crisp-tender, 3 to 5 minutes.
3. Meanwhile, combine kraut, apple, carrot, and potato in a large bowl; toss until mixed. Add the onion, wine, and a blend of brown sugar, caraway seed, and seasoned pepper; toss again.
4. Rub cavities of goose with salt; lightly spoon stuffing into the body and neck cavities. Truss goose; set, breast side up, on a rack in a shallow roasting pan.
5. Roast, uncovered, in a 325°F oven about 3½ hours, or until goose tests done. Remove stuffing to a serving dish and accompany with slices of the roast goose.

About 8 servings

601 Glazed Duckling Gourmet

2 ducklings (about 4 pounds
  each), quartered (do not use
  wings, necks, and backs) and
  skinned
1½ teaspoons salt
¼ teaspoon ground nutmeg
3 to 4 tablespoons butter
1 clove garlic, minced
1½ teaspoons rosemary, crushed
1½ teaspoons thyme
1½ cups burgundy
2 teaspoons red wine vinegar
⅓ cup currant jelly
2 teaspoons cornstarch
2 tablespoons cold water
1½ cups halved seedless green
  grapes
  Watercress

1. Remove excess fat from duckling pieces; rinse duckling and pat dry with absorbent paper. Rub pieces with salt and nutmeg.
2. Heat butter and garlic in a large skillet over medium heat; add the duckling pieces and brown well on all sides.
3. Add rosemary, thyme, burgundy, vinegar, and jelly to skillet. Bring to boiling; cover and simmer over low heat until duckling is tender (about 45 minutes). Remove duckling to a heated platter and keep it warm.
4. Combine cornstarch and water; blend into liquid in skillet; bring to boiling and cook 1 to 2 minutes, stirring constantly. Add grapes and toss them lightly until thoroughly heated.
5. Pour the hot sauce over duckling; garnish platter with watercress.

6 to 8 servings

602 Roast Duckling with Olives

1 duckling (about 4 pounds)
⅓ cup olive oil or other cooking oil
2 medium carrots, coarsely chopped
1 large onion, coarsely chopped
½ teaspoon salt
⅛ teaspoon seasoned pepper
¼ teaspoon rosemary
⅛ teaspoon savory
2 small stalks celery, chopped
3 sprigs parsley, chopped
1 small bay leaf
⅓ cup cognac
2 tablespoons tomato paste
2 cups hot chicken broth or bouillon
⅓ cup dry white wine
16 whole pitted green olives

1. Rinse, pat dry, and cut duckling into quarters. Remove any excess fat from pieces.
2. Heat oil in skillet; add duckling pieces and cook over medium heat until well browned on all sides. Remove pieces from skillet and keep warm.
3. Add carrots, onion, salt, seasoned pepper, rosemary, savory, celery, parsley, and bay leaf to skillet; continue cooking until carrots and onions are lightly browned. Drain off excess fat in skillet.
4. Return duck to skillet and pour cognac over it. Ignite and when flame ceases add a blend of tomato paste, chicken broth, and white wine. Cover skillet and cook in a 350°F oven about 1½ hours, or until duckling is tender.
5. Remove to heated serving platter and keep warm. Strain remaining mixture in skillet into a saucepan and add green olives. Heat until sauce is very hot and pour over duckling.

4 servings

603 Roast Rock Cornish Hen with Wild Rice and Mushrooms

1½ cups water
½ teaspoon salt
½ cup wild rice
2 tablespoons butter or margarine
½ pound mushrooms, sliced lengthwise through caps and stems
1 tablespoon finely chopped onion
3 tablespoons melted butter or margarine
2 tablespoons madeira
4 Rock Cornish hens, about 1 pound each
2 teaspoons salt
¼ cup unsalted butter, melted
Watercress (optional)

1. Bring the water and salt to boiling in a deep saucepan.
2. Wash rice in a sieve. Add rice gradually to water so that boiling will not stop. Boil rapidly, covered, 30 to 40 minutes, or until a kernel of rice is entirely tender when pressed between fingers. Drain rice in a colander or sieve.
3. While rice is cooking, heat 2 tablespoons butter or margarine in a skillet. Add the mushrooms and onion; cook, stirring occasionally, until mushrooms are lightly browned. Combine mushrooms, wild rice, melted butter, and madeira; toss gently until mushrooms and butter are evenly distributed throughout rice.
4. Rinse and pat hens dry with absorbent paper. Rub cavities of the hens with the salt. Lightly fill body cavities with the wild rice stuffing. To close body cavities, sew or skewer and lace with cord. Fasten neck skin to backs and wings to bodies with skewers.
5. Place hens, breast-side up, on rack in roasting pan. Brush each hen with melted unsalted butter (about 1 tablespoon).
6. Roast, uncovered, in a 350°F oven; frequently baste hens during roasting period with drippings from roasting pan. Roast 1 to 1½ hours, or until hens test done. To test, move leg gently by grasping end bone; drumstick-thigh joint moves easily when hens are done. Remove skewers, if used.
7. Transfer hens to a heated serving platter and garnish with sprigs of watercress if desired.

4 to 8 servings

Seafood

604 *Salmon Bake*

1 can (16 ounces) salmon, drained and flaked
1½ cups herb-seasoned stuffing croutons
2 tablespoons finely snipped parsley
2 tablespoons finely chopped onion
3 eggs, well beaten
1 can (10½ ounces) condensed cream of celery soup
½ cup milk
⅛ teaspoon ground black pepper
Lemon, thinly sliced and cut in quarter-slices
Parsley, snipped
Sour cream sauce (prepared from a mix)

1. Toss salmon, stuffing croutons, parsley, and onion together in a bowl. Blend eggs, condensed soup, milk, and pepper; add to salmon mixture and mix thoroughly. Turn into a greased 1½-quart casserole.
2. Bake at 350°F about 50 minutes. Garnish center with overlapping quarter-slices of lemon and parsley.
3. Serve with hot sour cream sauce.

About 6 servings

605 *Baked Fish with Shrimp Stuffing*

1 dressed whitefish, bass, or lake
    trout (2 to 3 pounds)
Salt
1 cup chopped cooked shrimp
1 cup chopped fresh mushrooms
1 cup soft enriched bread crumbs
½ cup chopped celery
¼ cup chopped onion
2 tablespoons chopped parsley
¾ teaspoon salt
    Few grains black pepper
½ teaspoon thyme
¼ cup butter or margarine, melted
2 to 3 tablespoons apple cider
2 tablespoons butter or margarine,
    melted
Parsley sprigs

1. Rinse fish under running cold water; drain well and pat dry with absorbent paper. Sprinkle fish cavity generously with salt.
2. Combine in a bowl the shrimp, mushrooms, bread crumbs, celery, onion, parsley, salt, pepper, and thyme. Pour ¼ cup melted butter gradually over bread mixture, tossing lightly until mixed.
3. Pile stuffing lightly into fish. Fasten with skewers and lace with cord. Place fish in a greased large shallow baking pan. Mix cider and 2 tablespoons melted butter; brush over fish.
4. Bake at 375°F, brushing occasionally with cider mixture, 25 to 30 minutes, or until fish flakes easily when pierced with a fork. If additional browning is desired, place fish under broiler 3 to 5 minutes. Transfer to a heated platter and remove skewers and cord. Garnish platter with parsley.

4 to 6 servings

606 *California Style Red Snapper Steaks*

6 fresh or thawed frozen red snapper
    steaks (about 2 pounds)
Salt and pepper
¼ cup butter or margarine, melted
1 tablespoon grated orange peel
¼ cup orange juice
1 teaspoon lemon juice
    Dash nutmeg
Fresh orange sections

1. Arrange red snapper steaks in a single layer in a well-greased baking pan; season with salt and pepper.
2. Combine butter, orange peel and juice, lemon juice, and nutmeg; pour over fish.
3. Bake at 350°F 20 to 25 minutes, or until fish flakes easily when tested with a fork.
4. To serve, put steaks onto a warm platter; spoon sauce in pan over them. Garnish with orange sections.

6 servings

607 *Sole with Tangerine Sauce*

1 pound sole fillets
5 tablespoons butter or margarine
2 teaspoons finely shredded tangerine
    peel
½ cup tangerine juice
1 teaspoon lemon juice
1 tablespoon finely chopped parsley
1 tablespoon finely chopped green
    onion
1 bay leaf
1 tangerine, peeled, sectioned, and
    seeds removed
3 tablespoons flour
½ teaspoon salt
⅛ teaspoon ground black pepper
3 tablespoons butter or margarine
    Parsley

1. Thaw fish if frozen.
2. Combine 5 tablespoons butter, tangerine peel and juice, lemon juice, 1 tablespoon parsley, green onion, and bay leaf in a saucepan. Bring to boiling and simmer over low heat until slightly thickened, stirring occasionally. Remove from heat; remove bay leaf and mix in tangerine sections. Keep sauce hot.
3. Mix flour, salt, and pepper; coat fish fillets. Heat 3 tablespoons butter in a skillet. Add fillets and fry until both sides are browned and fish flakes easily when tested with a fork.
4. Arrange fish on a hot platter and pour the hot sauce over it. Garnish with parsley.

About 4 servings

608 Two-Layer Salmon-Rice Loaf

Salmon layer:
1 can (16 ounces) salmon
2 cups coarse soft enriched bread crumbs
2 tablespoons finely chopped onion
½ cup undiluted evaporated milk
1 egg, slightly beaten
2 tablespoons butter or margarine, melted
1 tablespoon lemon juice
1 teaspoon salt

Rice layer:
3 cups cooked enriched rice
¼ cup finely chopped parsley
2 eggs, slightly beaten
⅔ cup undiluted evaporated milk
2 tablespoons butter or margarine, melted
¼ teaspoon salt

Sauce:
1 large onion, quartered and thinly sliced
¾ cup water
1 can (10¾ ounces) condensed tomato soup

1. For salmon layer, drain salmon and remove skin. Flake salmon and put into a bowl. Add bread crumbs, onion, evaporated milk, egg, butter, lemon juice, and salt; mix lightly. Turn into a buttered 9×5×3-inch loaf pan; press lightly to form a layer.
2. For rice layer, combine rice with parsley, eggs, evaporated milk, butter, and salt. Spoon over salmon layer; press lightly.
3. Set filled loaf pan in a shallow pan. Pour hot water into pan to a depth of 1 inch.
4. Bake at 375°F about 45 minutes. Remove from water immediately.
5. Meanwhile, for sauce, put onion and water into a saucepan. Bring to boiling, reduce heat, and simmer, covered, 10 minutes. Remove onion, if desired. Add condensed soup to saucepan, stir until blended, and bring to boiling.
6. Cut loaf into slices and top servings with tomato sauce.

About 8 servings

609 Broiled Salmon

6 salmon steaks, cut ½ inch thick
1 cup sauterne
½ cup vegetable oil
2 tablespoons wine vinegar
2 teaspoons soy sauce
2 tablespoons chopped green onion
Seasoned salt
Green onion, chopped (optional)
Pimento strips (optional)

1. Put salmon steaks into a large shallow dish. Mix sauterne, oil, wine vinegar, soy sauce, and green onion; pour over salmon. Marinate in refrigerator several hours or overnight, turning occasionally.
2. To broil, remove steaks from marinade and place on broiler rack. Set under broiler with top 6 inches from heat. Broil about 5 minutes on each side, brushing generously with marinade several times. About 2 minutes before removing from broiler, sprinkle each steak lightly with seasoned salt and, if desired, top with green onion and pimento. Serve at once.

6 servings

610 Broiled Trout

Trout (8- to 10-ounce fish for each serving)
French dressing
Instant minced onion
Salt

1. Remove head and fins from trout, if desired. Rinse trout quickly under running cold water; dry thoroughly. Brush inside of fish with French dressing and sprinkle generously with instant minced onion and salt. Brush outside generously with French dressing.

Lemon slices
Tomato wedges
Mint sprigs or watercress

2. Arrange trout in a greased shallow baking pan or on a broiler rack. Place under broiler with top of fish about 3 inches from heat. Broil 5 to 8 minutes on each side, or until fish flakes easily; brush with dressing during broiling.
3. Remove trout to heated serving platter and garnish with lemon, tomato, and mint.

611 *Trout Amandine with Pineapple*

6 **whole trout**
Lemon juice
Enriched all-purpose flour
6 **tablespoons butter or margarine**
Salt and pepper
2 **tablespoons butter or margarine**
½ **cup slivered blanched almonds**
6 **well-drained canned pineapple slices**
Paprika
Lemon wedges

1. Rinse trout quickly under running cold water; dry thoroughly. Brush trout inside and out with lemon juice. Coat with flour.
2. Heat 6 tablespoons butter in a large skillet. Add trout and brown on both sides. Season with salt and pepper.
3. Meanwhile, heat 2 tablespoons butter in another skillet over low heat. Add almonds and stir occasionally until golden.
4. Sprinkle pineapple slices with paprika. Place pineapple in skillet with almonds and brown lightly on both sides. Arrange trout on a warm serving platter and top with pineapple slices and almonds. Garnish platter with lemon wedges.

6 servings

612 *Planked Halibut Dinner*

4 **halibut steaks, fresh or thawed frozen (about 2 pounds)**
¼ **cup butter, melted**
2 **tablespoons olive oil**
1 **tablespoon wine vinegar**
2 **teaspoons lemon juice**
1 **clove garlic, minced**
¼ **teaspoon dry mustard**
¼ **teaspoon marjoram**
½ **teaspoon salt**
⅛ **teaspoon ground black pepper**
2 **large zucchini**
1 **package (10 ounces) frozen green peas**
1 **can (8¼ ounces) tiny whole carrots**
Au Gratin Potato Puffs
Butter
Fresh parsley
Lemon wedges

1. Place halibut steaks in an oiled baking pan.
2. Combine butter, olive oil, vinegar, lemon juice, garlic, dry mustard, marjoram, salt, and pepper. Drizzle over halibut.
3. Bake at 450°F 10 to 12 minutes, or until halibut is almost done.
4. Meanwhile, halve zucchini lengthwise and scoop out center portion. Cook in boiling salted water until just tender.
5. Cook peas following directions on package. Heat carrots.
6. Prepare Au Gratin Potato Puffs.
7. Arrange halibut on wooden plank or heated ovenware platter and border with zucchini halves filled with peas, carrots, and potato puffs. Dot peas and carrots with butter.
8. Place platter under broiler to brown potato puffs. Sprinkle carrots with chopped parsley.
9. Garnish with sprigs of parsley and lemon wedges arranged on a skewer.

4 servings

Au Gratin Potato Puffs: Pare 1½ pounds potatoes; cook and mash potatoes in a saucepan. Add **2 tablespoons butter** and ⅓ **cup milk**; whip until fluffy. Add **2 slightly beaten egg yolks**, ½ **cup shredded sharp Cheddar cheese**, 1 **teaspoon salt**, and **few grains pepper**; continue whipping. Using a pastry bag with a large star tip, form mounds about 2 inches in diameter on plank. Proceed as directed in recipe. 613

614 *Tuna Fiesta*

1 can (6½ or 7 ounces) tuna, drained
   and separated in large pieces
1 can (16 ounces) stewed tomatoes,
   drained
1 can (15¼ ounces) spaghetti in
   tomato sauce with cheese
1 tablespoon ketchup
1 teaspoon seasoned salt
½ cup (about 2 ounces) shredded
   sharp Cheddar cheese
   Few grains paprika
   Fresh parsley

1. Turn tuna, stewed tomatoes, and spaghetti into a saucepan. Add ketchup, seasoned salt, cheese, and paprika; mix well. Set over medium heat, stirring occasionally, until thoroughly heated (about 8 minutes).
2. Turn into a warm serving dish; garnish with parsley. Serve at once.

About 6 servings

Note: If desired, reserve cheese and paprika for topping. Mix remaining ingredients and turn into a greased 1-quart casserole. Top with the cheese and paprika. Set in a 350°F oven 20 minutes, or until thoroughly heated. Garnish with parsley.

615 *Patio Crab Casserole*

¼ cup butter or margarine
2 cups chopped onion
1 pound frozen or 2 cans (7½
   ounces each) Alaska king crab,
   drained and sliced
½ cup snipped parsley
2 tablespoons capers
2 tablespoons snipped chives
2 pimentos, diced
1½ cups corn muffin mix
⅛ teaspoon salt
1 egg, fork beaten
½ cup milk
1 cup cream-style golden corn
6 drops Tabasco
2 cups dairy sour cream
1½ cups shredded extra sharp
   Cheddar cheese

1. Heat butter in a skillet. Add onion and cook until tender. Stir in crab, parsley, capers, chives, and pimentos; heat.
2. Meanwhile, stir corn muffin mix, salt, egg, milk, corn, and Tabasco until just moistened (batter should be lumpy). Turn into a greased shallow 3-quart dish and spread evenly to edges.
3. Spoon crab mixture and then sour cream over batter. Sprinkle cheese over all.
4. Bake at 400°F 25 to 30 minutes.
5. To serve, cut into squares.

About 12 servings

616 *Savory Oysters*

⅓ cup butter or margarine
1 can (4 ounces) sliced mushrooms,
   drained
⅓ cup chopped green pepper
½ clove garlic
2 cups coarse toasted enriched bread
   crumbs
1 quart oysters, drained (reserve
   liquor)
¼ cup cream
1 teaspoon Worcestershire sauce
1 teaspoon salt
1 teaspoon paprika
⅛ teaspoon ground mace
   Few grains cayenne pepper

1. Heat butter in a large skillet. Add mushrooms, green pepper, and garlic; cook about 5 minutes. Remove skillet from heat; discard garlic. Stir in toasted bread crumbs. Set aside.
2. Mix ¼ cup reserved oyster liquor, cream, and Worcestershire sauce.
3. Blend salt, paprika, mace, and cayenne.
4. Use about a third of crumb mixture to form a layer in bottom of a greased 2-quart casserole. Arrange about half of oysters and half of seasonings over crumbs. Repeat crumb layer, then oyster and seasoning layers. Pour the liquid mixture over all. Top with remaining crumbs.
5. Bake at 375°F 20 to 30 minutes, or until thoroughly heated and crumbs are golden brown.

6 to 8 servings

617 *Scallops Gourmet*

2 pounds scallops
1 cup boiling water
1 teaspoon salt
3 to 4 tablespoons lemon juice
1 medium onion, sliced
2 sprigs parsley
1 bay leaf
¼ cup butter or margarine
½ pound mushrooms, sliced
    lengthwise
3 tomatoes, peeled and diced
2 tablespoons butter or margarine
2 tablespoons flour
¼ teaspoon garlic powder
8 patty shells, heated
    Carrot curls

1. Rinse scallops under running cold water. Put scallops into a saucepan and pour boiling water over them. Stir in salt, lemon juice, onion, parsley, and bay leaf. Cook, covered, over low heat 5 minutes; drain and reserve 1 cup of the stock. If scallops are large, cut into smaller pieces. Set aside.
2. Heat ¼ cup butter in a skillet. Add mushrooms and cook until delicately browned and tender, stirring occasionally. Remove from skillet with slotted spoon; set aside. Add diced tomatoes to skillet and cook 5 minutes. Set aside.
3. Heat 2 tablespoons butter in a saucepan. Blend in flour; heat until bubbly. Add reserved stock gradually, stirring constantly. Continue to stir and bring rapidly to boiling; cook 1 to 2 minutes.
4. Add scallops, mushrooms, tomatoes, and garlic powder to sauce; heat thoroughly.
5. To serve, spoon scallop mixture into patty shells. Garnish with carrot curls.

About 8 servings

618 *Seafood Kabobs*

1 lobster tail (8 ounces), cut in 6
    pieces
6 scallops
6 shrimp, peeled and deveined
12 large mushroom caps
½ cup olive oil
3 tablespoons soy sauce
1 tablespoon Worcestershire sauce
2 tablespoons white wine vinegar
½ teaspoon grated lemon peel
2 tablespoons lemon juice
½ teaspoon ground pepper
2 teaspoons snipped parsley
18 (4-inch) pieces sliced bacon
12 (1-inch) squares green pepper
6 cherry tomatoes

1. Put lobster pieces, scallops, shrimp, and mushroom caps into a shallow dish.
2. Combine olive oil, soy sauce, Worcestershire sauce, vinegar, lemon peel. lemon juice, pepper, and parsley in a screwtop jar and shake vigorously. Pour the marinade over the seafood and mushroom caps and set aside for at least 2 hours.
3. Drain off marinade and reserve.
4. Wrap each piece of seafood in bacon. Thread pieces on skewers (about 10 inches each) as follows: green pepper, lobster, mushroom, scallop, mushroom, shrimp, and green pepper. Arrange on a broiler rack and brush with marinade.
5. Place under broiler 3 inches from heat. Broil 10 to 12 minutes, turning and brushing frequently with marinade. Add a cherry tomato to each skewer during the last few minutes of broiling.

6 servings

619 Deviled Crab

Mustard Sauce:
- 2 tablespoons dry mustard
- 2 tablespoons water
- 2 tablespoons olive oil
- 1 tablespoon ketchup
- ¼ teaspoon salt
- ¼ teaspoon Worcestershire sauce

Crab meat mixture:
- 6 tablespoons butter
- 4 teaspoons finely chopped green pepper
- 2 teaspoons finely chopped onion
- 6 tablespoons flour
- 1 teaspoon salt
- ½ teaspoon dry mustard
- 1½ cups milk
- 1 teaspoon Worcestershire sauce
- 2 egg yolks, slightly beaten
- 1 pound lump crab meat, drained
- 2 teaspoons chopped pimento
- 2 tablespoons dry sherry
- 1 cup fine dry enriched bread crumbs
- Paprika
- Butter, melted

1. For Mustard Sauce, blend dry mustard, water, olive oil, ketchup, salt, and Worcestershire sauce in a small bowl; set aside.
2. For crab meat mixture, heat butter in a large heavy saucepan. Add green pepper and onion; cook until onion is golden in color.
3. Blend flour, salt, and dry mustard; stir in. Heat until bubbly. Add milk gradually, stirring until smooth. Stir in Worcestershire sauce. Bring rapidly to boiling; cook 1 to 2 minutes.
4. Remove mixture from heat and stir a small amount of hot mixture into the egg yolks; return to saucepan and cook 3 to 5 minutes, stirring constantly.
5. Stir in crab meat and pimento; heat thoroughly. Remove from heat and blend in sherry and the Mustard Sauce.
6. Spoon into 6 shell-shaped ramekins, allowing about ½ cup mixture for each. Sprinkle top with bread crumbs and paprika; drizzle with melted butter.
7. Set in a 450°F oven about 6 minutes, or until tops are lightly browned and mixture is thoroughly heated. Serve hot.

6 servings

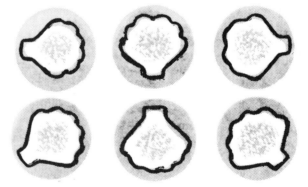

620 Baked Flounder Superb

- 2 pounds flounder fillets
- ½ cup fine Melba toast crumbs
- ¼ cup butter or margarine, melted
- ⅔ cup minced green onion
- 2 tablespoons snipped parsley
- ½ teaspoon poultry seasoning
- ½ pound fresh or thawed frozen sea scallops, chopped
- 1 can (4 ounces) mushroom stems and pieces, drained
- 2 tablespoons butter or margarine
- 2 tablespoons flour
- ¼ teaspoon salt
- Few grains black pepper
- 1 cup milk
- Shredded Parmesan cheese

1. Thaw fish if frozen; cut fish into 12 pieces.
2. Toss crumbs and melted butter together in a bowl. Add green onion, parsley, poultry seasoning, scallops, and mushrooms; mix well.
3. Place a piece of flounder in the bottom of each of 6 ramekins. Spoon stuffing mixture over flounder and top with remaining flounder pieces.
4. Heat butter in a saucepan. Stir in flour, salt, and pepper and cook until bubbly. Add milk gradually, stirring until smooth. Bring rapidly to boiling; boil 1 to 2 minutes, stirring constantly.
5. Spoon sauce over flounder. Sprinkle with Parmesan cheese.
6. Bake at 350°F 20 to 25 minutes. If desired, set ramekins under broiler with tops about 3 inches from heat until lightly browned; watch carefully to avoid overbrowning.

6 servings

621 *Shrimp Exotica*

1½ pounds deveined cooked shrimp
1 can (20 ounces) sliced pineapple, drained; reserve syrup
2 cups water
3 chicken bouillon cubes
1 cup long-grain enriched white rice
¼ cup vegetable oil
1½ cups cubed cooked ham
¼ cup chopped onion
1 clove garlic, crushed in a garlic press or minced
2 tablespoons chopped preserved or crystallized ginger
2 teaspoons soy sauce
2 teaspoons curry powder
½ teaspoon salt
1 medium green pepper, cut in strips

1. Reserve 5 or 6 whole shrimp for garnish. Cut remaining shrimp into pieces. Set aside. Cut 4 pineapple slices into pieces and set aside.
2. Bring water to boiling in a deep saucepan. Add the bouillon cubes, and when dissolved, add the rice gradually, so boiling continues. Cover pan tightly, reduce heat, and simmer 15 to 20 minutes, until a kernel is soft when pressed between fingers.
3. Heat oil in a large skillet. Add ham, onion, and garlic; heat thoroughly, turning with a spoon.
4. Blend ⅔ cup of the reserved pineapple syrup with ginger, soy sauce, curry powder, and salt; add to skillet along with green pepper and heat thoroughly. Add rice and shrimp and remaining pineapple pieces; toss until mixed. Heat thoroughly. Serve on a warm serving platter. Garnish with the pineapple slices and whole shrimp.

About 6 servings

622 *Shrimp Creole*

Cooked shrimp:
1 pound fresh shrimp with shells
2 cups water
2 tablespoons lemon juice
2 teaspoons salt

Sauce:
¼ cup fat
¾ cup finely chopped onion
¾ cup minced green pepper
1 can (16 ounces) tomatoes, sieved
1 teaspoon Worcestershire sauce
1 bay leaf
1½ teaspoons salt
¼ teaspoon ground black pepper
½ teaspoon sugar
½ teaspoon oregano
Cooked rice

1. For cooked shrimp, rinse shrimp under running cold water.
2. Combine water, lemon juice, and salt in a saucepan and bring to boiling. Drop shrimp into boiling water, reduce heat, and simmer, covered, until pink and tender (about 5 minutes).
3. Drain shrimp immediately and cover with cold water to chill; drain again. Remove tiny legs and peel shells from shrimp. Cut a slit to just below surface along back (curved surface) of shrimp to expose the black vein. With knife point, remove vein. Rinse shrimp quickly in cold water.
4. Reserve about ten whole shrimp for garnish and cut remainder into pieces. Refrigerate until ready to use.
5. For sauce, heat fat in a large heavy skillet. Mix in onion and green pepper and cook until vegetables are tender. Stir in sieved tomatoes, Worcestershire sauce, bay leaf, salt, pepper, sugar, and oregano. Bring mixture to boiling and simmer, uncovered, stirring occasionally. Cook about 15 minutes, or until thickened. Stir in shrimp pieces and heat thoroughly.
6. Serve shrimp mixture on hot fluffy rice and garnish with the whole shrimp.

About 4 servings

623 *Mock Lobster, Flemish Style*

The main ingredient in this dish is monk fish, which has a taste and texture somewhat similar to lobster. Served in scallop shells or ramekins, it makes a delectable fish course during a multiple-course dinner

1 **pound monk fish fillets**
1 **can or bottle (12 ounces) beer**
½ **cup water**
1 **small onion, quartered**
1 **small celery stalk with top, cut in chunks**
½ **teaspoon salt**
¼ **teaspoon thyme**
2 **tablespoons butter or margarine**
2 **tablespoons flour**
¼ **cup cream**
1 **egg yolk**
½ **cup shredded cheese (Edam, Gruyère, Cheddar)**

1. Cut fish fillets in half lengthwise; then cut each section into ¾-inch slices.
2. In a large saucepan, place beer, water, onion, celery, salt, and thyme. Heat to boiling. Add fish. Cover and simmer 4 minutes, or until fish flakes.
3. Remove fish with a slotted spoon. Drain well on paper towels. Boil stock 10 minutes to reduce; strain.
4. In another saucepan, melt butter. Stir in flour. Add ¾ cup strained stock and the cream. Cook, stirring constantly, until thickened.
5. Add a little hot mixture to egg yolk; return to pan. Cook slowly, stirring, 1 to 2 minutes. Remove from heat; adjust seasonings.
6. Gently combine fish and sauce. Spoon into scallop shells or individual ramekins. Sprinkle with cheese. Broil 2 minutes, or just until tops are lightly browned.

6 appetizer servings

624 *Saucy Fish Fillets*

This delicately flavored entrée consists of fish poached in beer and a hollandaise-style sauce with egg yolks, cream, butter, and part of the cooking liquid.

1 **pound fish fillets**
1 **can or bottle (12 ounces) beer**
1 **small onion, quartered**
1 **celery stalk, cut in chunks**
2 **tablespoons minced fresh parsley or 1 tablespoon dried parsley flakes**
1 **teaspoon salt**
  Dash white pepper
2 **egg yolks**
2 **tablespoons cream**
2 **tablespoons butter or margarine**

1. Thaw fish, if frozen.
2. Put beer, onion, celery, parsley, salt, and pepper in a skillet. Heat to boiling. Add fish. Cover and simmer about 8 to 10 minutes, or just until fish flakes with a fork.
3. Drain fish and put onto a deep platter. Place in a 300°F oven to keep warm. Boil cooking liquid about 5 minutes to reduce; strain.
4. In top of a double boiler, beat egg yolks with cream. Gradually stir in ½ cup hot strained cooking liquid. Cook over boiling water, stirring constantly, until thickened. Cut butter into small pieces; stir into sauce, one piece at a time. Pour sauce over fish. (Recipe makes about ¾ cup sauce.)

3 or 4 servings

625 Tuna and Swiss Cheese Pie

3 eggs
½ teaspoon salt
½ teaspoon dry mustard
Dash pepper
1 cup whipping cream or half-and-half
¾ cup ale or beer
1 unbaked 9-inch pastry shell, chilled
2 cans (6½ or 7 ounces each) tuna, drained and flaked
6 ounces Swiss cheese, shredded
1 tablespoon flour

1. Beat eggs, salt, dry mustard, and pepper until foamy. Beat in cream and ale.
2. Cover bottom of pastry shell with a layer of tuna. Sprinkle half of cheese over tuna. Repeat layering. Sprinkle flour over cheese. Pour egg mixture over all.
3. Bake at 425°F 15 minutes. Turn oven control to 300°F and bake 25 minutes, or until a knife inserted halfway between center and edge of filling comes out clean.

6 entrée servings;
10 to 12 appetizer servings

626 Tuna-Macaroni Bake

1 package (7¼ ounces) macaroni and cheese dinner
6 cups boiling water, salted
2 tablespoons butter or margarine
1 can or bottle (12 ounces) beer
¼ teaspoon salt
1 can (6½ or 7 ounces) tuna, drained and flaked
¼ cup chopped green pepper
1 canned pimento, chopped
⅓ cup instant nonfat dry milk
2 eggs, slightly beaten

1. Cook macaroni in boiling salted water in a large saucepan, stirring occasionally, until tender (about 7 to 10 minutes). Drain; return macaroni to pan.
2. Add butter, ½ cup beer, contents of cheese sauce packet from dinner, and salt. Stir until butter is melted. Add tuna, green pepper, and pimento. (Two pimentos or ½ cup chopped green pepper may be used instead of some of each, if desired.)
3. Turn into a lightly buttered rectangular 1½-quart baking dish. Combine remaining beer, dry milk, and eggs; pour over macaroni mixture.
4. Bake at 325°F 1½ hours, or until lightly browned on edges and set.

4 servings

627 German Beer Fish (Bier Fisch)

This recipe is an old tradition in Germany. The sauce combines sweet, sour, and spicy flavors. In Germany, fresh carp would be used, but since good fresh carp is hard to find in this country, other fish may be substituted. It should not be too delicate in flavor.

1 whole carp, buffalo fish, or pike (2 to 3 pounds with head); or 1 to 1½ pounds boneless fillets
2 tablespoons butter or margarine
1 medium onion, chopped
1 celery stalk, chopped
½ teaspoon salt
6 peppercorns
3 whole cloves
4 slices lemon
1 bay leaf
1 can or bottle (12 ounces) beer
6 gingersnaps, crushed
1 tablespoon sugar
Fresh parsley for garnish

1. Remove head from fish; discard or use to make fish stock for other recipes. Lay fish out as flat as possible, breaking bones along back.
2. Melt butter in a skillet. Add onion, celery, salt, peppercorns, and cloves; mix. Top with lemon slices and bay leaf. Place fish on top.
3. Add beer. Cover and simmer 15 to 20 minutes, or just until fish flakes with a fork. Transfer fish to a platter; cover with foil to keep warm.
4. Strain cooking liquid, pressing some of vegetables through.
5. Put gingersnaps and sugar in skillet; stir in 1½ cups strained liquid. Cook, stirring constantly, until thickened.
6. Garnish fish with fresh parsley. Pass sauce for pouring over fish and **boiled potato** accompaniment.

4 to 6 servings

628 *Tunaroni Casserole*

¼ cup chopped onion
2 tablespoons snipped parsley
2 tablespoons butter or margarine
2 tablespoons flour
½ teaspoon salt
⅛ teaspoon pepper
2 cups milk
2 cups cooked elbow macaroni
1 can (28 ounces) tomatoes, drained and cut up
2 cans (6½ or 7 ounces each) tuna, drained and flaked
¼ cup buttered bread crumbs

1. Sauté onion and parsley in butter in a skillet. Stir in flour, salt, and pepper. Gradually add milk, stirring until thickened and smooth.
2. Stir in macaroni, tomatoes, and tuna. Put into a 2-quart casserole. Sprinkle with bread crumbs.
3. Bake, covered, at 375°F 30 minutes, or until mixture is bubbly.

6 servings

629 *Seviche*

In this specialty of Mexico, the lemon juice actually "cooks" the fish.

1¼ pounds whitefish fillets, skinned and cut in 2x¼-inch strips
1 cup fresh lemon juice
2 green chilies, seeded and minced
1 teaspoon snipped fresh or ½ teaspoon dried oregano leaves
1 tablespoon snipped fresh or 1½ teaspoons dried coriander leaves
1 tablespoon olive oil
1 teaspoon salt
¼ teaspoon freshly ground pepper
2 large tomatoes, peeled, seeded, and chopped
1 medium green pepper, finely chopped
1 small yellow onion, finely chopped
¼ cup fresh lime juice
Radish slices
Ripe olives

1. Place fish in a shallow glass bowl; pour lemon juice over it. Refrigerate covered 6 hours, stirring occasionally. Drain; discard lemon juice.
2. Mix remaining ingredients except radish slices and olives with fish in a medium bowl. Refrigerate 30 minutes.
3. Serve on chilled plates; garnish with radish slices and olives. Or spoon into **fluted lemon shells.**

8 servings (½ cup each)

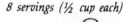

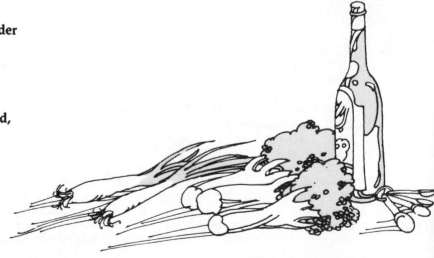

Walnut Torte, page 376

630 Tuna-Idaho Casserole

¼ cup finely chopped onion
½ cup chopped celery
3 tablespoons butter or margarine
3 tablespoons flour
1¾ cups milk
1 tablespoon lemon juice
1 teaspoon grated lemon peel
½ teaspoon salt
¼ teaspoon dill weed
   Dash pepper
1 package (10 ounces) frozen peas,
   cooked and drained
1 can (12 ounces) tuna, drained and
   flaked
2 cups frozen Idaho potato puffs

1. Sauté onion and celery in butter in a saucepan. Stir in flour. Gradually add milk, stirring until thickened and smooth.
2. Add remaining ingredients, except potatoes. Spoon into a 1½-quart casserole. Top with potato puffs.
3. Bake, uncovered, at 450°F 20 minutes, or until puffs are golden brown and mixture is heated through.

4 servings

631 Confetti Casserole

1 can (10¾ ounces) condensed cream
   of mushroom soup
1 can (16 ounces) peas (undrained)
2 tablespoons chopped pimento
¼ cup chopped celery
¼ cup chopped green pepper
1 tablespoon Worcestershire sauce
2 cans (6½ or 7 ounces each) tuna,
   drained and flaked
1 cup (4 ounces) shredded American
   cheese
1 can (3 ounces) French-fried onions

1. Combine soup, peas with ½ cup liquid, pimento, celery, green pepper, and Worcestershire sauce. Mix in tuna and cheese.
2. Put half the mixture into a 2-quart casserole. Sprinkle with half the onions; repeat.
3. Bake, uncovered, at 375°F 30 minutes, or until mixture is bubbly.

6 servings

632 Tuna-Rice Pie

2 cups cooked white rice
2 tablespoons butter or margarine,
   melted
3 eggs, beaten
⅓ cup chopped pitted ripe olives
¾ cup milk
1 can (6½ or 7 ounces) tuna, drained
   and flaked
3 green onions, sliced
   Dash ground red pepper
1 cup (4 ounces) shredded Swiss
   cheese

1. Combine rice, butter, 1 egg, and ripe olives. Spread evenly onto sides and bottom of a greased 9-inch pie plate.
2. Combine remaining 2 eggs, milk, tuna, onion, and red pepper. Pour into rice-lined pie plate. Sprinkle with cheese.
3. Bake, uncovered, at 350°F 15 minutes. Turn oven control to 300°F and bake an additional 10 minutes, or until set.

4 servings

Cherries Jubilee, page 331

633 *Tuna Dinner*

2 cups cooked green beans
1 can (10¾ ounces) condensed cream
    of chicken soup
1 cup mayonnaise
2 cans (7 ounces each) tuna packed in
    water (undrained)
½ cup corn flakes
1 tablespoon butter or margarine

1. Combine beans, soup, mayonnaise, and tuna. Put into a 1½-quart casserole. Top with corn flakes. Dot with butter.
2. Bake, uncovered, at 350°F 30 minutes, or until heated through.

6 servings

634 *Salmon with Rice*

1⅓ cups cooked white rice
1 can (15½ ounces) salmon, drained
    and flaked
1 large tomato, chopped
¼ cup chopped onion
1 tablespoon snipped parsley
½ cup whipping cream, whipped
½ teaspoon salt
    Dash ground red pepper
1 tablespoon lemon juice
½ cup (2 ounces) freshly grated
    Parmesan cheese

1. Combine all ingredients, except cheese. Put into a 1½-quart casserole. Sprinkle with cheese.
2. Bake, covered, at 350°F 20 minutes, or until bubbly.

4 servings

635 *Individual Salmon-Green Bean Casseroles*

1 package (9 ounces) frozen Italian
    green beans, cooked and drained
1 package (9 ounces) frozen artichoke
    hearts, cooked and drained
1 can (15½ ounces) salmon, drained
    and flaked
½ cup canned Hollandaise sauce
½ cup dairy sour cream
½ teaspoon grated lemon peel
¼ teaspoon crushed tarragon
⅛ teaspoon pepper
⅓ cup toasted slivered almonds

1. Combine beans, artichoke hearts, and salmon. Spoon into 6 individual casseroles.
2. Combine Hollandaise sauce, sour cream, lemon peel, tarragon, and pepper. Spoon evenly over salmon mixture. Sprinkle with almonds.
3. Bake, uncovered, at 350°F 20 minutes, or until heated through.

6 servings

636 *Baked Salmon Squares*

1 can (15½ ounces) salmon, drained
   and flaked
½ cup fine dry bread crumbs
1 can (10¾ ounces) condensed cream
   of celery soup
¼ cup dairy sour cream
2 eggs, beaten

1. Combine all ingredients. Put into a greased 8-inch square baking dish.
2. Bake, uncovered, at 325°F 1 hour, or until set. Cut into squares and serve with **creamed spinach.**

6 servings

637 *Shrimp and Rice Supreme*

1 medium onion, thinly sliced
⅓ cup chopped green pepper
½ cup sliced fresh mushrooms
¼ cup butter or margarine
¼ cup flour
½ teaspoon salt
   Dash ground red pepper
2 cups milk
1 tablespoon Worcestershire sauce
2 cups cooked white rice
1 pound cooked and cleaned shrimp

1. Sauté onion, green pepper, and mushrooms in butter in a skillet. Stir in flour, salt, and red pepper. Gradually add milk, stirring until thickened and smooth.
2. Combine sauce with remaining ingredients. Put into a 2-quart casserole.
3. Bake, covered, at 350°F 30 minutes, or until bubbly.

6 servings

638 *Shrimp Florentine*

1 package (10 ounces) frozen spinach,
   cooked and squeezed
1 pound cooked and cleaned shrimp
1 can (10¾ ounces) condensed cream
   of chicken soup
¼ cup sherry
1 tablespoon snipped parsley
   Dash pepper
½ cup (2 ounces) shredded Cheddar
   cheese
¼ cup buttered bread crumbs

1. Put spinach into a 1½-quart casserole.
2. Blend shrimp, soup, sherry, parsley, and pepper. Spoon over spinach.
3. Combine cheese and crumbs. Sprinkle over all.
4. Bake, covered, at 350°F 30 minutes, or until heated through.

4 servings

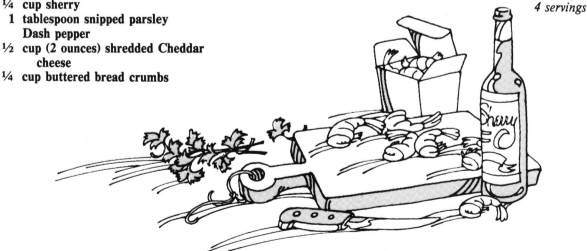

639 *Shrimp Lasagne*

½ cup chopped onion
1 garlic clove, minced
2 tablespoons butter or margarine
2 cans (8 ounces each) tomato sauce
1 can (6 ounces) tomato paste
½ cup water
1 tablespoon basil
2 teaspoons oregano
¼ teaspoon pepper
½ pound lasagne noodles
12 ounces cooked and cleaned shrimp
⅓ cup sliced pitted ripe olives
2 cups (8 ounces) shredded mozzarella cheese
1 carton (16 ounces) cream-style cottage cheese
½ cup (2 ounces) grated Parmesan cheese

1. Sauté onion and garlic in butter in a saucepan. Add tomato sauce, tomato paste, water, and seasonings. Simmer 25 minutes.
2. Meanwhile, cook noodles according to package directions.
3. Add shrimp and olives to sauce.
4. Layer half the noodles, half the mozzarella cheese, half the cottage cheese, and half the sauce in a 13x9-inch baking dish. Repeat layers. Sprinkle with Parmesan cheese.
5. Bake, covered, at 350°F 20 minutes. Remove cover and bake an additional 15 minutes, or until heated through. Let stand a few minutes before serving.

8 servings

640 *Seafood Creole*

1 medium onion, chopped
1 garlic clove, minced
½ cup chopped green pepper
½ cup sliced celery
3 tablespoons butter or margarine
1½ tablespoons flour
1 can (28 ounces) tomatoes (undrained)
1 bay leaf
1 teaspoon salt
1 teaspoon sugar
½ teaspoon allspice
1 tablespoon Worcestershire sauce
¼ teaspoon Tabasco
1 can (6½ or 7 ounces) tuna, drained and flaked
1 pound cooked and cleaned shrimp
1 can (7½ ounces) Alaska King crab, drained and flaked
2 tablespoons snipped parsley

1. Sauté onion, garlic, green pepper, and celery in butter in a skillet. Stir in flour. Add tomatoes, stirring until slightly thickened.
2. Combine with remaining ingredients, except parsley. Put into a 2-quart casserole.
3. Bake, covered, at 350°F 30 minutes, or until bubbly. Remove bay leaf. Sprinkle with parsley and serve over **hot, cooked rice.**

8 servings

641 *Pimento-Crab Meat Strata Supreme*

1 can (7½ ounces) Alaska King crab, drained and flaked
½ cup chopped celery
¼ cup chopped onion
¾ cup mayonnaise
Dash ground red pepper
12 slices white bread, crusts removed
Butter or margarine, softened
3 jars (4 ounces each) whole pimentos, each pimento cut in 2 or 3 large pieces
4 cups (1 pound) shredded Swiss cheese
5 eggs
3 cups milk
1 teaspoon salt
⅛ teaspoon pepper
¼ teaspoon dry mustard

1. Mix crab, celery, and onion. Blend in mayonnaise and red pepper. Set aside.
2. Spread both sides of the bread slices with butter. Place half the bread slices in a layer in a 3-quart shallow baking dish.
3. Arrange half the pimento pieces, half the crab mixture, and one third the cheese over the bread. Repeat layering, using remainder of the crab mixture, pimento, and second third of the cheese. Cover with reserved bread slices and sprinkle with the remaining cheese.
4. Beat together remaining ingredients until frothy and blended. Pour over all. Let stand 1 hour.
5. Bake, uncovered, at 325°F 1 hour, or until puffed and brown. If desired, garnish with pimento strips, green pepper strips, and sprigs of parsley.

6 to 8 servings

642 *Smoked Oyster and Corn Casserole*

1 egg, beaten
½ cup evaporated milk
1 can (16 ounces) whole kernel corn, drained
1 tablespoon instant minced onion
1 teaspoon soy sauce
1 can (3½ ounces) smoked oysters, drained
¼ cup coarsely crushed soda crackers

1. Combine egg, evaporated milk, corn, onion, and soy sauce. Put into a 1-quart casserole.
2. Scatter oysters over top. Sprinkle with cracker crumbs.
3. Bake, uncovered, at 325°F 30 minutes, or until mixture is bubbly. Stir before serving.

4 servings

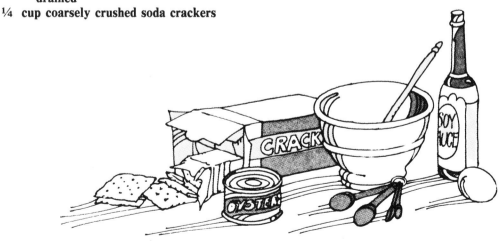

643 *Savory Rice and Lobster*

1 large lobster tail (about 10 ounces)
   Paprika
3 tablespoons butter or margarine
2 teaspoons lemon juice
¼ teaspoon salt
¼ teaspoon garlic powder
¼ teaspoon onion powder
¼ teaspoon oregano
   Dash pepper
2 tablespoons dry white wine
1 package (6 ounces) long-grain and
   wild rice, cooked according to
   package directions

1. Cook lobster in **boiling salted water** 5 minutes.
2. Rinse lobster tail with cold water. Remove meat from shell and cut up. Sprinkle lobster pieces with paprika.
3. Brown lobster lightly in butter in a skillet. Sprinkle with lemon juice. Combine with remaining ingredients. Put into a 1-quart casserole.
4. Bake, covered, at 325°F 25 minutes, or until heated through. If desired, sprinkle with snipped parsley.

4 servings

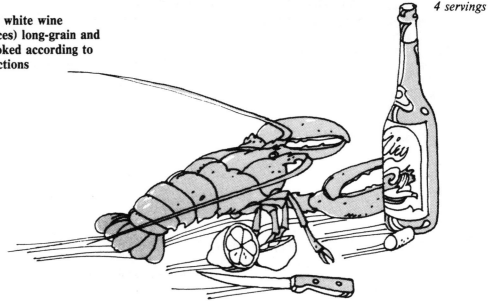

644 *Scallops au Gratin*

2 tablespoons butter or margarine
2 tablespoons flour
1 cup milk
1 package (12 ounces) frozen scallops,
   thawed and drained
1 can (4 ounces) mushroom slices,
   drained
¼ cup chopped green onion
1 teaspoon grated lemon peel
½ teaspoon salt
⅛ teaspoon garlic powder
½ cup (4 ounces) shredded Cheddar
   cheese
¼ cup fine dry bread crumbs
4 English muffins, split and toasted
8 tomato slices

1. Melt butter in a skillet. Stir in flour. Gradually add milk, stirring until thickened and smooth.
2. Stir in scallops, mushrooms, green onion, lemon peel, salt, and garlic powder. Put into a 1-quart casserole.
3. Mix cheese and bread crumbs. Sprinkle over all.
4. Bake, covered, at 325°F 25 minutes, or until mixture is bubbly. To serve, top each English muffin half with a tomato slice. Spoon scallop mixture over tomato.

4 servings

645 *Fish and Vegetable Casserole*

1½ pounds frozen fish steaks, thawed and cut in chunks
1 can (16 ounces) cut green beans, drained
1 can (16 ounces) sliced carrots, drained
¼ cup butter or margarine
¼ cup flour
1 teaspoon salt
½ teaspoon pepper
⅔ cup milk
1½ cups chicken broth
1 can (10¾ ounces) condensed tomato soup
½ teaspoon rosemary
3 cups hot, cooked mashed potatoes

1. Put fish, green beans, and carrots into a 2½-quart casserole.
2. Melt butter in a saucepan. Stir in flour, salt, and pepper. Gradually add milk and broth, stirring until thickened and smooth.
3. Stir in soup and rosemary. Pour over fish and vegetables.
4. Bake, covered, at 350°F 15 minutes. Remove cover and spoon potatoes around edge of casserole. Bake an additional 15 minutes, or until fish is flaky and mixture is heated through.

6 servings

646 *Seafood Continental*

6 sole fillets
¼ cup chopped celery
¼ cup chopped green pepper
⅛ teaspoon leaf tarragon
2 tablespoons butter or margarine
1⅓ cups water
1½ cups packaged precooked rice
½ pound cooked and cleaned shrimp, cut up
1 can (10¾ ounces) condensed cream of celery soup
⅓ cup dry white wine

1. Line the sides of 6 well-greased 6-ounce individual casseroles or custard cups with sole fillets.
2. Sauté celery, green pepper, and tarragon in butter in a saucepan. Add water; bring to a boil. Stir in rice. Cover and cook 5 minutes.
3. Stir in half the shrimp and ¼ cup soup. Spoon into fish-lined cups.
4. Bake, uncovered, at 350°F 30 minutes. Unmold onto a serving platter. Serve with sauce made by heating together remaining soup, wine, and remaining shrimp. If desired, garnish with celery leaves.

6 servings

647 Curried Prawns

1 pound large prawns, peeled
    and deveined
2 tablespoons butter
1 tablespoon chopped scallions
1 tablespoon flour
1 teaspoon curry powder
¼ cup sauterne
2 cups cream
    Hot rice

1. Sauté prawns in heated butter in skillet 2 to 3 minutes; add scallions and sauté 3 to 4 minutes longer. Sprinkle with a mixture of flour and curry powder. Cook and stir about 3 minutes.
2. Stir in the wine and cream and simmer mixture 10 minutes, stirring occasionally. Transfer prawns to a chafing dish using a slotted spoon.
3. Continue cooking the sauce over low heat to desired consistency. Add seasoning, if desired, and pour over the prawns. Serve with hot rice.

2 servings

648 Oysters in Mushroom Purée

1 pound mushrooms, coarsely
    chopped
1 quart oysters, liquor reserved
¼ cup dry sherry
½ cup soft bread crumbs
2 garlic cloves, minced
1 teaspoon salt
¼ teaspoon freshly ground
    pepper
    Beef Stock
    Watercress

1. Simmer mushrooms and 1 cup of the oysters in the sherry in a covered saucepan 8 to 10 minutes. Drain; press all moisture out of mushrooms.
2. Purée mushrooms and cooked oysters in a food processor or blender; pour into a shallow 1½-quart casserole. Stir in the bread crumbs, garlic, salt, and pepper. Stir in reserved oyster liquor. Stir in stock, if necessary, to make purée of a thick sauce consistency. Arrange remaining oysters in purée.
3. Bake covered at 350°F 20 minutes.
4. Serve in shallow bowls or ramekins. Garnish with watercress.

6 to 8 servings

649 Fresh Vegetables and Shrimp en Brochette

1¾ pounds fresh shrimp (23 to 25
    uncooked shrimp), washed,
    peeled, and deveined
1 pound fresh mushrooms (about
    12 mushrooms) with stem
    ends removed
2 medium tomatoes, quartered
2 medium green peppers, seeded
    and cut in 1½-inch cubes
2 medium onions, peeled and
    quartered
¾ cup oil
½ cup dry white wine or sherry
¼ cup chopped parsley
1 teaspoon salt
¼ teaspoon pepper

1. Combine shrimp and vegetables in a bowl.
2. Prepare marinade by combining oil, wine, parsley, salt, and pepper. Pour over shrimp and vegetables. Allow to marinate for 3 hours.
3. String shrimp on skewers alternately with vegetables. Broil about 3 inches from heat until shrimp are browned and flake easily; about 4 minutes on one side, 3 minutes on the other.

4 to 6 servings

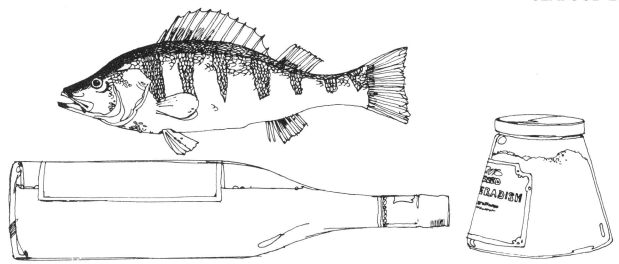

650 *Poached Fish with Horseradish Sauce*

1½ **pounds fish fillets, such as perch or bass**
Boiling water (enough to just cover fish)
½ **cup dry white wine**
1 **small onion, chopped**
2 **tablespoons chopped parsley**
1 **teaspoon salt**
⅛ **teaspoon pepper**
Horseradish Sauce:
1 **cup dairy sour cream**
2 **to 3 tablespoons prepared horseradish**
2 **tablespoons grated lemon peel**

1. For poached fish, tie fish loosely in cheesecloth to prevent breaking and place in a skillet. Add boiling water, wine, onion, parsley, salt, and pepper. Cover skillet and simmer about 10 minutes, or until fish flakes (can be separated with a fork into thin, layer-like pieces). Meanwhile, prepare sauce.
2. For sauce, blend well sour cream, horseradish, and lemon peel. Pour sauce into serving dish; set aside.
3. Drain fish; remove cheesecloth. Place fish on warm platter. Serve with sauce.

4 servings

651 *Shrimp à la King*

2 **cups white wine**
2 **shallots, minced, or ¼ cup minced onion**
1 **cup oyster liquor, fish stock, or chicken broth**
1½ **pounds fresh shrimp, peeled and deveined**
2 **tablespoons flour**
2 **tablespoons butter**
Juice of ¼ lemon (about 2 teaspoons)
½ **cup light cream**
2 **egg yolks, well beaten**
Toast points
Parsley

1. Combine wine, shallots, and oyster liquor in a saucepan; bring to boiling and add shrimp. Simmer 15 minutes. Drain and reserve ¾ cup stock.
2. Meanwhile, stir flour into melted butter in a saucepan, making a roux. Blend in reserved stock; cook and stir until mixture thickens. Add shrimp and cook over low heat. Stir in lemon juice.
3. Add cream to beaten yolks. Mix well and add hot shrimp mixture, stirring constantly. Serve on toast points and garnish with parsley.

4 to 6 servings

652 Fish Stew with Red Wine

2 pounds fish
2 cups red wine
1 carrot, sliced
1 onion, minced
2 cloves garlic, cut in halves
1 teaspoon salt
¼ teaspoon pepper
   Herb Bouquet
3 tablespoons brandy
3 tablespoons melted butter
2 tablespoons all-purpose flour

1. Set out a deep heavy skillet with a tight-fitting cover.
2. Clean, wash, dry, and cut fish into thick slices. Put fish into skillet and add wine, carrot, onion, garlic, salt, pepper, and Herb Bouquet; bring to boiling.
3. Heat brandy in a small saucepan. Ignite brandy and immediately pour over the fish. When the flame has burned out, cover the pan. Cook fish slowly 15 to 20 minutes, or until the fish flakes when pierced with a fork. Remove fish to a warm serving dish. Keep hot. Strain and reserve cooking liquid.
4. Blend thoroughly in same skillet butter and flour. Cook over low heat until mixture bubbles. Remove from heat; gradually stir in cooking liquid. Cook rapidly; stir constantly until sauce thickens. Boil 1 to 2 minutes longer. Pour sauce over the fish.
5. Serve with **garlic croutons.** Garnish with **tiny cooked onions, sautéed mushrooms,** or **cooked shrimp.**

4 servings

Herb Bouquet: Tie together neatly **3 or 4 sprigs of parsley, 1 sprig thyme,** and **½ bay leaf.** If dry herbs are used, enclose in fine cheesecloth bag.

653 Mussels Cooked in Wine Sauce

2 quarts mussels
2 cups dry white wine such as chablis
1 cup finely chopped shallots
½ cup finely chopped parsley
⅓ cup unsalted butter
   Freshly ground white pepper
   Juice of ½ lemon
   Salt
Hollandaise Sauce:
2 egg yolks
2 tablespoons cream

1. Scrub mussels under running water and trim off the beards.
2. Pour wine over mussels in a saucepot; add shallots, parsley, butter, and white pepper to taste. Cover tightly and cook over high heat about 2 minutes; stir the mixture and cook, covered, 2 minutes longer, or until mussel shells open.
3. Remove the mussels from saucepot; remove and discard top shells, placing the filled bottom shells in a serving dish. Keep warm.
4. Cook the pan juice over high heat to reduce the amount by one half. Remove from heat. Add lemon juice, salt, and white pepper to taste.
5. For hollandaise sauce, in the top of a double boiler, beat egg

¼ teaspoon salt
Few grains cayenne pepper
2 tablespoons lemon juice or
tarragon vinegar
½ cup butter

yolks, cream, salt, and cayenne pepper until thick with a whisk beater. Set over hot (not boiling) water. (Bottom of double-boiler top should not touch water.)

6. Add the lemon juice gradually, while beating constantly. Cook, beating constantly with the whisk beater, until sauce is the consistency of thick cream. Remove double boiler from heat, leaving top in place.

7. Beating constantly, add the butter, ½ teaspoon at a time. Beat with whisk beater until butter is melted and thoroughly blended in. Mix with wine sauce.

8. Pour the sauce over the mussels and serve immediately.

4 servings

654 *Scallops Baked in Shells*

2 cups dry white wine
Herb Bouquet
2 pounds (1 quart) scallops
½ teaspoon salt
½ pound mushrooms
6 shallots or ¼ cup minced onions
1 tablespoon minced parsley
3 tablespoons butter
2 tablespoons water
1 teaspoon lemon juice
¼ cup melted butter
¼ cup all-purpose flour
2 egg yolks, slightly beaten
¼ cup heavy cream
⅓ cup buttered dry bread crumbs

1. Butter 6 baking shells or ramekins.
2. Heat wine in a saucepan with Herb Bouquet.
3. Wash scallops in cold water and drain.
4. Add scallops and salt to wine, cover and simmer about 10 minutes, or until tender. Remove Herb Bouquet, drain scallops, and reserve the liquid. Cut scallops into fine pieces and set aside.
5. Clean and chop mushrooms.
6. Add mushrooms, shallots, parsley, butter, water, and lemon juice to a saucepan; cover and simmer 5 to 10 minutes. Strain liquid into seasoned wine. Add vegetable mixture to scallops. Set aside.
7. Make a roux by blending butter and flour in a saucepan. Cook over low heat until mixture bubbles. Remove from heat and gradually stir in wine and vegetable liquid. Return to heat and bring rapidly to boiling, stirring constantly; cook 1 to 2 minutes longer.
8. Remove sauce from heat and add egg yolks and cream gradually, stirring vigorously. Then stir in the scallop mixture.
9. Fill shells or ramekins, piling high in center. Sprinkle with about ⅓ cup of buttered bread crumbs.
10. To brown, set shells on a baking sheet and place in oven at 450°F 8 to 10 minutes, or place under broiler 3 to 4 minutes from heat to top of the creamed mixture. Serve when browned.

6 servings

Herb Bouquet: Tie neatly together **3 or 4 sprigs of parsley, 1 sprig thyme,** and **½ bay leaf.** If dry herbs are used, enclose in fine cheesecloth bag.

655 Lobster Newburg/Crab Meat Newburg

2 cups cooked lobster meat
¼ cup butter
2 cups cream
¾ teaspoon salt
⅛ teaspoon pepper
⅛ teaspoon nutmeg
4 egg yolks, slightly beaten
2 tablespoons sherry
Toast points or cooked rice

1. Cut lobster meat into 1-inch pieces and set aside.
2. Melt butter in the top of a double boiler. Blend in cream, salt, pepper, and nutmeg; bring just to boiling. Stir in lobster and cook over low heat until lobster is thoroughly heated.
3. Vigorously stir about 3 tablespoons of hot mixture into egg yolks. Immediately blend into hot mixture. Place over simmering water and cook 3 to 5 minutes, or just until mixture thickens. Stir slowly to keep mixture cooking evenly. (Do not overcook as sauce will curdle.)
4. Remove immediately from heat and blend in sherry. Serve on toast points or cooked rice.

About 6 servings

Crab Meat Newburg: Follow recipe for Lobster Newburg substituting **2 cups cooked crab meat** for the lobster. Remove and discard bony tissue from meat.

656

657 Sole Véronique in Parchment

Baked in parchment paper, the fish retains its natural moisture and flavor.

2 pounds sole fillets
¾ teaspoon salt
3 tablespoons snipped parsley
2 teaspoons minced lemon peel
1½ cups seedless white grapes
⅔ cup dry white wine
Lemon wedges

1. Lay each fillet on a piece of parchment paper or aluminum foil, 12x12 inches. Sprinkle fillets with salt, parsley, and lemon peel. Divide grapes over fish; sprinkle with wine. Bring edges of parchment up, crimp edges and seal; place on a jelly-roll pan.
2. Bake at 350°F 20 minutes.
3. Place parchment packets on individual plates; let each person open packet. Serve with lemon wedges.

4 servings

Desserts

658 *Pie-Pan Apple Dessert*

1 egg
¾ cup firmly packed brown sugar
½ cup enriched all-purpose flour
1 teaspoon baking powder
¼ teaspoon salt
¼ to ½ teaspoon ground nutmeg
1½ cups chopped pared apple
½ cup chopped pecans
   Lemon Sauce, whipped cream, or
     ice cream

1. Beat egg until light and fluffy. Beat in brown sugar. Mix flour, baking powder, salt, and nutmeg; add to egg mixture and blend.
2. Stir in apple and pecans. Spread in well-greased 8- or 9-inch pie pan or plate.
3. Bake at 350°F about 30 minutes, or until top is golden brown.
4. Serve warm with Lemon Sauce or desired topping.

About 6 servings

Lemon Sauce: Mix ⅓ cup sugar, 2 teaspoons corn- **659** starch, and a **few grains salt** in a saucepan. Add **1 cup boiling water** gradually, stirring constantly. Continue to stir and bring to boiling; simmer 5 minutes. Remove from heat. Blend in **2 tablespoons butter**, ¾ **teaspoon grated lemon peel**, and 1½ **tablespoons lemon juice.** Serve warm.

660 *Peaches 'n' Corn Bread, Shortcake Style*

1 cup sifted enriched all-purpose
    flour
½ teaspoon baking soda
¼ teaspoon salt
1 cup enriched yellow cornmeal
¾ cup firmly packed light brown
    sugar
1 egg, beaten
½ cup buttermilk
⅓ cup dairy sour cream
    Peach Butter Elégante
    Sweetened fresh peach slices

1. Blend flour, baking soda, salt, cornmeal, and brown sugar in a bowl; set aside.
2. Beat egg, buttermilk, and sour cream until well blended; add to dry ingredients and stir until just smooth (do not overmix).
3. Turn into a greased 11×7×1½-inch pan and spread batter evenly.
4. Bake at 425°F about 20 minutes.
5. While still warm, cut corn bread into serving-size pieces, remove from pan, and split into two layers. Spread Peach Butter Elégante generously between layers. Top with peach slices.

9 or 12 servings

661 *Peach Butter Elégante:* Thaw **1 package (10 or 12 ounces) frozen sliced peaches.** Drain peaches and cut into pieces; set aside. Put **1 cup firm unsalted butter** or **1 cup margarine** into a small mixing bowl. Beat with electric mixer on high speed just until butter is whipped. Add **½ cup confectioners' sugar** gradually, beating thoroughly. Add the peaches, about 1 tablespoon at a time, beating thoroughly after each addition. (Do not allow butter to become too soft.) Chill until ready to use.

About 2 cups peach butter

662 *Spicy Peach Cobbler*

1 can (29 ounces) sliced peaches,
    drained; reserve 1 cup syrup
½ cup firmly packed brown sugar
2 tablespoons cornstarch
⅛ teaspoon salt
⅛ teaspoon ground cinnamon
⅛ teaspoon ground cloves
2 tablespoons cider vinegar
1 tablespoon butter or margarine
1 cup all-purpose biscuit mix
½ cup finely shredded sharp Cheddar
    cheese
2 tablespoons butter or margarine,
    melted
¼ cup milk

1. Put drained peaches into a shallow 1-quart baking dish. Set aside.
2. Mix brown sugar, cornstarch, salt, cinnamon, and cloves in a saucepan. Blend in reserved peach syrup and vinegar; add 1 tablespoon butter. Bring mixture to boiling, stirring frequently; cook until thickened, about 10 minutes. Pour over peaches and set in a 400°F oven.
3. Combine biscuit mix and cheese. Stir in melted butter and milk to form a soft dough. Remove dish from oven and drop dough by heaping tablespoonfuls on top of hot peaches.
4. Return to oven and bake 20 minutes, or until crust is golden brown. Serve warm.

6 servings

663 *Cantaloupe Sherbet*

2 cups ripe cantaloupe pieces
1 egg white
½ cup sugar
2 tablespoons fresh lime juice

1. Put melon pieces, egg white, sugar, and lime juice into an electric blender container. Cover and blend until smooth.
2. Turn into a shallow baking dish. Set in freezer; stir occasionally during freezing.
3. To serve, spoon into chilled dessert dishes.

About 1½ pints sherbet

Pineapple Sherbet: Follow recipe for Cantaloupe Sherbet; substitute **2 cups fresh pineapple pieces** for cantaloupe. **664**

Watermelon Sherbet: Follow recipe for Cantaloupe Sherbet; substitute **2 cups watermelon pieces** for cantaloupe and, if desired, decrease sugar to ¼ cup. **665**

666 *Banana-Pineapple Ice Cream*

2 cups mashed ripe bananas (about 5 medium)
1 cup sugar
1 teaspoon grated orange peel
1 teaspoon grated lemon peel
3 tablespoons lemon juice
2 tablespoons lime juice
1½ cups unsweetened pineapple juice
⅓ cup orange juice
2 cans (14½ ounces each) evaporated milk

1. Crushed ice and rock salt will be needed. Wash and scald cover, container, and dasher of a 3- or 4-quart ice cream freezer. Chill thoroughly.
2. Combine bananas, sugar, orange peel, lemon peel, lemon juice, and lime juice; blend thoroughly. Set aside about 10 minutes.
3. Stir fruit juices into banana mixture. Add evaporated milk gradually, stirring until well blended.
4. Fill chilled freezer container no more than two-thirds full with ice cream mixture. Cover tightly. Set into freezer tub. (For electric freezer, follow the directions.)
5. Fill tub with alternate layers of crushed ice and rock salt, using 8 parts ice to 1 part salt. Turn handle slowly 5 minutes. Then turn rapidly until handle becomes difficult to turn (about 15 minutes), adding ice and salt as necessary.
6. Wipe cover and remove dasher. Pack down ice cream and cover with waxed paper or plastic wrap. Replace lid. (Plug dasher opening unless freezer has a solid cover.) Repack freezer container in ice, using 4 parts ice to 1 part salt. Cover with heavy paper or cloth. Let ripen 2 hours.

About 2 quarts ice cream

667 *Quick Applesauce Whip*

1 can (16 ounces) applesauce
½ teaspoon grated lemon peel
2 teaspoons lemon juice
½ teaspoon ground cinnamon
3 egg whites
⅛ teaspoon salt
6 tablespoons sugar
Ground nutmeg

1. Combine applesauce, lemon peel, juice, and cinnamon.
2. Beat egg whites and salt until frothy. Add sugar gradually, beat well. Continue beating until rounded peaks are formed. Fold beaten egg whites into applesauce mixture.
3. Spoon immediately into dessert dishes. Sprinkle nutmeg over each serving.

About 6 servings

668 *Bananas with Royal Pineapple Sauce*

3 tablespoons dark brown sugar
2 teaspoons cornstarch
1 can (8¼ ounces) crushed pineapple
   (undrained)
1 tablespoon butter
⅛ teaspoon almond extract
¼ teaspoon grated lemon peel
1 tablespoon lemon juice
¼ cup butter
4 firm bananas, peeled
2 tablespoons flaked coconut

1. Mix sugar and cornstarch in a saucepan. Add pineapple with syrup, 1 tablespoon butter, and almond extract; mix well. Bring to boiling, stirring constantly until thickened.
2. Remove from heat and stir in lemon peel and juice. Set the sauce aside.
3. Heat ¼ cup butter in a heavy skillet. Add bananas; turn them by rolling to cook evenly and brown lightly. (Do not overcook or fruit will lose its shape.)
4. Allowing one-half banana per person, serve at once topped with the warm pineapple sauce. Sprinkle with coconut.

8 servings

669 *Purple Plum Crunch*

5 cups pitted, quartered fresh purple
   plums
¼ cup firmly packed brown sugar
3 tablespoons flour
½ teaspoon ground cinnamon
1 cup enriched all-purpose flour
1 cup sugar
1 teaspoon baking powder
¼ teaspoon salt
¼ teaspoon ground mace
1 egg, well beaten
½ cup butter or margarine, melted
   and cooled

1. Put plums into a shallow 2-quart baking dish or casserole.
2. Mix brown sugar, 3 tablespoons flour, and cinnamon; sprinkle over plums and mix gently with a fork.
3. Blend 1 cup flour, sugar, baking powder, salt, and mace thoroughly. Add to beaten egg and stir with a fork until mixture is crumbly. Sprinkle evenly over plums in baking dish. Pour melted butter evenly over the topping.
4. Bake at 375°F 40 to 45 minutes, or until topping is lightly browned. Serve warm.

6 to 8 servings

Note: Other fresh fruits may be substituted for the plums.

670 *Chocolate Peanut Butter Pudding*

1 small package chocolate pudding
   and pie filling (not instant)
1 can (14½ ounces) evaporated milk
⅔ cup water
⅓ cup peanut butter
   Slightly sweetened whipped cream
   (optional)
   Chopped salted peanuts (optional)

1. Empty pudding mix into a saucepan, then stir in evaporated milk and water.
2. Cook and stir over moderate heat until thickened, about 5 minutes. Remove from heat and stir in peanut butter. Cover and chill.
3. To serve, spoon into dessert dishes. If desired, top with whipped cream and peanuts.

4 to 6 servings

671 *Steamed Pumpkin Pudding*

Pudding:
- 1¼ cups fine dry bread crumbs
- ½ cup enriched all-purpose flour
- 1 cup firmly packed brown sugar
- 1 teaspoon baking powder
- ½ teaspoon baking soda
- ½ teaspoon salt
- ½ teaspoon ground cinnamon
- ½ teaspoon ground cloves
- ½ cup salad oil
- ½ cup undiluted evaporated milk
- 2 eggs
- 1½ cups canned pumpkin

Lemon Nut Sauce:
- ½ cup butter or margarine
- 2 cups confectioners' sugar
- ¼ teaspoon salt
- ¼ teaspoon ground ginger
- ¼ cup lemon juice
- ½ cup chopped walnuts

1. Blend bread crumbs, flour, brown sugar, baking powder, baking soda, salt, cinnamon, and cloves in a large bowl.
2. Beat oil, evaporated milk, eggs, and pumpkin. Add to dry ingredients; mix until well blended.
3. Turn into a well-greased 2-quart mold. Cover tightly with a greased cover, or tie greased aluminum foil tightly over mold. Place mold on trivet or rack in a steamer or deep kettle with a tight-fitting cover.
4. Pour in boiling water to no more than one half the height of the mold. Cover steamer, bring water to boiling, and keep boiling at all times. If necessary, add more boiling water during cooking period.
5. Steam the pudding 2½ to 3 hours, or until a wooden pick inserted in center comes out clean.
6. For Lemon Nut Sauce, beat butter in a bowl. Blend confectioners' sugar, salt, and ginger; add gradually to butter, beating well. Add lemon juice gradually, continuing to beat until blended. Mix in walnuts.
7. Remove pudding from steamer and unmold onto a serving plate. Serve pudding with Lemon Nut Sauce.

About 12 servings

Note: If pudding is to be stored and served later, unmold onto a rack and cool thoroughly. Wrap in aluminum foil or return to mold and store in a cool place. Before serving, resteam pudding about 3 hours, or until thoroughly heated.

672 *Individual Fruit Puddings*

Pudding:
- 2 medium oranges
- 1½ cups sifted enriched all-purpose flour
- 1 teaspoon baking soda
- ¼ teaspoon salt
- ¼ teaspoon ground cinnamon
- ¼ teaspoon ground cloves
- ¼ teaspoon ground nutmeg
- ¼ cup shortening
- 1 cup firmly packed brown sugar
- 1 egg, well beaten
- 1 cup dark seedless raisins
- ½ cup pitted dates, cut in pieces
- ½ cup walnuts, coarsely chopped

Orange Sauce:
- ¾ cup sugar
- 2 tablespoons cornstarch
- ⅛ teaspoon salt
- ¾ cup orange juice
- ½ cup water
- 1 teaspoon grated orange peel
- 1 tablespoon butter or margarine

1. For pudding, grease eight 5-ounce custard cups. Set aside.
2. Peel oranges; slice into cartwheels, and cut into pieces; reserve juice as it collects.
3. Blend flour, baking soda, salt, cinnamon, cloves, and nutmeg. Set aside.
4. Beat shortening; add brown sugar gradually, beating until fluffy. Add egg and beat thoroughly.
5. Mix in the orange pieces, reserved juice, raisins, dates, and walnuts. Blend in the dry ingredients.
6. Fill custard cups about two-thirds full with mixture; cover tightly with aluminum foil. Set in a pan and fill pan with water to a 1-inch depth. Cover pan with aluminum foil.
7. Cook in a 325°F oven 2 hours.
8. For Orange Sauce, mix sugar, cornstarch, and salt in a saucepan. Add orange juice and water gradually, stirring constantly. Bring to boiling, stirring constantly until thickened; cook over low heat 6 to 8 minutes, stirring occasionally.
9. Remove from heat. Blend in orange peel and butter. Keep warm.
10. Unmold puddings while hot onto dessert plates and spoon sauce over each.

8 servings

673 *Blueberry-Orange Parfaits*

2 tablespoons cornstarch
1 cup sugar
½ teaspoon salt
2 cups orange juice
2 eggs, beaten
½ teaspoon grated lemon peel
2 tablespoons sugar
2 cups fresh blueberries
Whipped cream (optional)

1. Mix cornstarch, 1 cup sugar, and salt in a heavy saucepan. Add a small amount of the orange juice and blend until smooth. Stir in remaining orange juice.
2. Bring mixture to boiling, stirring constantly, and cook 3 to 5 minutes.
3. Stir about 3 tablespoons of the hot mixture into beaten eggs; immediately blend with mixture in saucepan.
4. Cook and stir about 3 minutes. Remove from water and cool. Stir in lemon peel. Chill.
5. Meanwhile, sprinkle 2 tablespoons sugar over blueberries and allow to stand at least 30 minutes. Spoon alternating layers of custard and blueberries in parfait glasses, beginning with a layer of custard and ending with blueberries. Top with whipped cream, if desired.

6 servings

674 *Ginger-Yam Mousse*

1½ cups mashed cooked yams (about 3 medium yams)
1 cup sugar
2 teaspoons ground ginger
1 teaspoon ground nutmeg
½ teaspoon ground cinnamon
Few grains salt
3 egg yolks, fork beaten
2 cups milk
½ teaspoon grated lemon peel
½ teaspoon lemon juice
½ cup half-and-half
3 egg whites
¼ cup sugar
Whipped dessert topping
Toasted slivered almonds

1. Put mashed yams into a heavy saucepan. Blend 1 cup sugar, spices, and salt. Mix with yams, then mix in egg yolks and milk. Cook over medium heat, stirring constantly, until mixture is thick. Remove from heat when mixture just comes to boiling.
2. Cool, stirring occasionally. Blend in lemon peel, juice, and half-and-half.
3. Beat egg whites until frothy; add ¼ cup sugar gradually, continuing to beat until stiff peaks are formed. Fold into completely cooled yam mixture.
4. Turn into a 6½-cup ring mold, spreading evenly. Freeze until firm, about 3½ hours.
5. Allow mousse to soften slightly at room temperature before unmolding. Unmold onto a chilled plate. Spoon whipped dessert topping into center and sprinkle with almonds.

6 to 8 servings

675 *Citrus Bundt Cake*

¾ cup butter
2 teaspoons grated lemon peel
2 teaspoons grated orange peel
1¾ cups sugar
3 eggs
3⅓ cups sifted enriched all-purpose flour
1 tablespoon baking powder
½ teaspoon salt
1 cup milk
2 tablespoons lemon juice
2 tablespoons orange juice
⅓ cup sugar
Fruit sauce (optional)

1. Cream butter, grated peels, and 1¾ cups sugar until light and fluffy. Add eggs, one at a time, beating thoroughly after each addition.
2. Blend flour, baking powder, and salt. Mix into creamed mixture alternately with milk. Turn into a generously buttered 10-inch Bundt pan or angel food cake pan.
3. Bake at 325°F 60 to 75 minutes, or until a cake tester comes out clean. Remove from pan immediately and place on wire rack set over a shallow pan.
4. Combine fruit juices and ⅓ cup sugar in a small saucepan. Bring to boiling and boil 3 minutes. Drizzle over warm cake; cool completely before serving.
5. Slice and serve with a fruit sauce, if desired.

One 10-inch Bundt cake

676 *Chocolate Pound Cake Loaf*

3 cups sifted enriched all-purpose flour
2 teaspoons baking powder
¼ teaspoon salt
½ cup cocoa, sifted
1 cup butter or margarine
½ cup lard
1 tablespoon vanilla extract
½ teaspoon almond extract
3 cups sugar
1 cup eggs (5 or 6)
1¼ cups milk

1. Lightly grease (bottom only) two 9×5×3-inch loaf pans. Line bottoms with waxed paper; grease paper. Set aside.
2. Combine flour, baking powder, salt, and cocoa and blend thoroughly. Set aside.
3. Cream butter and lard with extracts in a large bowl. Add sugar gradually, creaming thoroughly after each addition. Add eggs, one at a time, beating until fluffy after each addition.
4. Beating only until blended after each addition, alternately add dry ingredients in fourths and milk in thirds to creamed mixture.
5. Turn equal amounts of batter into prepared loaf pans. Spread batter evenly. (Top of baked cakes may have a slight crack down center.) Place pans on center of oven rack so that top of batter will be at center of oven.
6. Bake at 325°F about 65 minutes, or until cake tester inserted in center comes out clean.
7. Cool cakes in pans 15 minutes on wire racks. Loosen sides with a spatula and turn onto rack. Peel off paper, turn right side up, and cool completely.

Two loaf cakes

Dutch Cocoa Loaf Cake: Follow directions for 677 Chocolate Pound Cake Loaf except substitute ⅔ cup **Dutch process cocoa** for the ½ cup cocoa and increase butter or margarine to 1½ cups; omit lard.

678 *Cranberry Upside-Down Cake*

Topping:
¼ cup butter or margarine
⅔ cup sugar
1 tablespoon grated orange peel
½ teaspoon vanilla extract
2 cups fresh cranberries, washed and coarsely chopped
⅓ cup sugar

Cake:
1½ cups sifted enriched cake flour
2 teaspoons baking powder
½ teaspoon salt
½ cup butter or margarine
1 teaspoon vanilla extract
½ cup sugar
1 egg
½ cup milk

1. For topping, heat butter in a saucepan. Add ⅔ cup sugar, orange peel, and vanilla extract; blend thoroughly. Spread mixture evenly in an 8×8×2-inch pan.
2. Combine cranberries and ⅓ cup sugar. Spread over mixture in pan; set aside.
3. For cake, blend flour, baking powder, and salt; set aside.
4. Cream butter with vanilla extract. Add sugar gradually, creaming until fluffy after each addition. Add egg and beat thoroughly.
5. Beating only until smooth after each addition, alternately add dry ingredients in thirds and milk in halves to creamed mixture. Turn batter over cranberry mixture and spread evenly.
6. Bake at 350°F about 50 minutes.
7. Remove from oven and let stand 1 to 2 minutes in pan on wire rack. To remove from pan, run spatula gently around sides. Cover with a serving plate and invert; allow pan to remain over cake 1 or 2 minutes. Lift pan off. Serve cake warm or cool.

One 8-inch square cake

679 *Date Spice Cake*

2¼ cups sifted enriched all-purpose flour
2 teaspoons baking powder
¼ teaspoon baking soda
½ teaspoon salt
2 teaspoons ground nutmeg
2 teaspoons ground ginger
⅔ cup shortening
1 teaspoon grated orange peel
1 teaspoon grated lemon peel
1 cup sugar
2 eggs
1 cup buttermilk
1 cup chopped dates

1. Grease a 9×9×2-inch pan. Line with waxed paper cut to fit bottom; grease paper. Set aside.
2. Blend flour, baking powder, baking soda, salt, nutmeg, and ginger.
3. Beat shortening with orange and lemon peels. Add sugar gradually, creaming until fluffy after each addition.
4. Add eggs, one at a time, beating thoroughly after each addition.
5. Beating only until smooth after each addition, alternately add dry ingredients in fourths and buttermilk in thirds to creamed mixture. Mix in dates. Turn batter into prepared pan.
6. Bake at 350°F about 45 minutes.
7. Remove from oven. Cool 5 to 10 minutes in pan on wire rack. Remove cake from pan and peel off paper; cool cake on rack.

One 9-inch square cake

680 *Carrot Cupcakes*

1½ cups sifted enriched all-purpose flour
1 teaspoon baking powder
1 teaspoon baking soda
1 teaspoon ground cinnamon
½ teaspoon salt
1 cup sugar
¾ cup vegetable oil
2 eggs
1 cup grated raw carrots
½ cup chopped nuts

1. Blend flour, baking powder, baking soda, cinnamon, and salt. Set aside.
2. Combine sugar and oil in a bowl and beat thoroughly. Add eggs, one at a time, beating thoroughly after each addition. Mix in carrots. Add dry ingredients gradually, beating until blended. Mix in nuts.
3. Spoon into paper-baking-cup-lined muffin-pan wells.
4. Bake at 350°F 15 to 20 minutes.

About 16 cupcakes

681 *Triple-Treat Walnut Bars*

½ cup butter or margarine
1 package (3 ounces) cream cheese
½ cup firmly packed dark brown sugar
1 cup whole wheat flour
⅓ cup toasted wheat germ
1 package (6 ounces) semisweet chocolate pieces
2 eggs
½ cup honey
⅓ cup whole wheat flour
⅓ cup instant nonfat dry milk
¼ teaspoon salt
¼ teaspoon ground cinnamon
¼ teaspoon ground mace
1½ cups chopped walnuts

1. Cream butter, cheese, and sugar in a bowl until light. Add 1 cup whole wheat flour and wheat germ and mix until smooth. Turn into a greased 13×9×2-inch pan; spread evenly.
2. Bake at 375°F 15 to 18 minutes, until edges are very lightly browned and top is firm.
3. Remove from oven and sprinkle with chocolate. Let stand about 5 minutes, or until chocolate softens, then spread it evenly over baked layer.
4. Combine eggs and honey; beat just until well blended. Add ⅓ cup whole wheat flour, dry milk, salt, cinnamon, mace, and walnuts; mix well. Spoon over the chocolate.
5. Return to oven and bake 18 to 20 minutes, or until top is set. Cool in pan, then cut into bars or diamonds.

About 3 dozen cookies

682 *Swiss Chocolate Squares*

Cake:
- 1 cup water
- ½ cup soft margarine
- 1½ ounces (1½ squares) unsweetened chocolate
- 2 cups enriched all-purpose flour
- 2 cups sugar
- 2 eggs
- ½ cup dairy sour cream
- 1 teaspoon baking soda
- ¼ teaspoon salt

Milk Chocolate Frosting:
- ½ cup soft margarine
- 6 tablespoons milk
- 1½ ounces (1½ squares) unsweetened chocolate
- 4½ cups confectioners' sugar
- 1 teaspoon vanilla extract
- ½ cup chopped nuts

1. For cake, combine water, margarine, and chocolate in a saucepan. Set over medium heat and bring to boiling, stirring occasionally. Remove from heat.
2. Blend flour and sugar; stir into the cooked chocolate mixture. Beat in eggs and sour cream. Blend baking soda and salt; beat in. Turn into a greased 15×10×1-inch jelly-roll pan and spread evenly.
3. Bake at 375°F 20 to 25 minutes. Cool on a wire rack.
4. For Milk Chocolate Frosting, combine margarine, milk, and chocolate in a saucepan. Set over medium heat and bring to boiling; boil 1 minute, stirring constantly. Remove from heat.
5. Stir in confectioners' sugar, adding gradually, and beat until smooth. Stir in vanilla extract.
6. Turn frosting onto warm cake and spread evenly. Sprinkle with nuts. Cool completely before cutting into squares.

1½ to 3 dozen cake squares

683 *Choco-Raisin Candy*

- ¾ cup dark seedless raisins
- ½ cup canned chocolate frosting
- Finely chopped nuts, flaked coconut, cocoa, or equal parts confectioners' sugar and cocoa

Mix raisins and chocolate frosting. Chill thoroughly. Working quickly, form mixture into 1-inch balls and coat as desired. Refrigerate before serving.

1½ dozen candy balls

684 *Peanut Butter Fudge*

- 1 cup undiluted evaporated milk
- 2 cups sugar
- ¼ cup butter or margarine
- 1 cup miniature marshmallows
- 1 jar (12 ounces) crunchy peanut butter
- 1 teaspoon vanilla extract

1. Combine evaporated milk, sugar, and butter in a heavy 10-inch skillet. Set over medium heat, bring to boiling, and boil 4 minutes, stirring constantly.
2. Remove from heat and stir in marshmallows, peanut butter, and vanilla extract until evenly blended.
3. Turn into a buttered 8-inch square pan and spread to corners. Chill before cutting into squares.

About 2 pounds fudge

Note: This fudge may be prepared in an electric skillet. Set temperature at 280°F, bring mixture to boiling, and boil about 5 minutes.

685 *Spicy Walnut Diamonds*

2½ cups sifted all-purpose flour
2 tablespoons cocoa
1½ teaspoons baking powder
1 teaspoon salt
½ teaspoon ground nutmeg
¼ teaspoon ground cloves
2 cups firmly packed brown sugar
3 eggs
½ cup honey
½ cup butter or margarine, melted
1½ cups chopped walnuts (1 cup medium and ½ cup fine)
½ cup confectioners' sugar
2 to 3 teaspoons milk

1. Blend flour, cocoa, baking powder, salt, nutmeg, and cloves.
2. Combine brown sugar and eggs in a large bowl; beat until well blended and light. Add honey, butter, and flour mixture and mix until smooth.
3. Stir in the 1 cup medium walnuts, and spread evenly in a greased 15×10×1-inch jelly-roll pan. Sprinkle the ½ cup fine walnuts over top.
4. Bake at 375°F about 20 minutes, or just until top springs back when touched lightly in center. Cool in pan.
5. Mix confectioners' sugar and enough milk to make a smooth, thin glaze. Spread over cooled layer. Cut into diamonds or bars.

About 4 dozen cookies

686 *Tropichocolate Wafers*

1½ cups sifted enriched all-purpose flour
½ teaspoon baking soda
½ teaspoon salt
½ cup cocoa
½ cup butter or margarine
½ teaspoon vanilla extract
1 cup firmly packed brown sugar
1 egg
¾ cup flaked coconut

1. Blend flour, baking soda, salt, and cocoa. Set aside.
2. Cream butter with vanilla extract. Add brown sugar gradually, creaming until fluffy. Add egg and beat thoroughly.
3. Mixing until well blended after each addition, add dry ingredients in thirds to creamed mixture. Stir in coconut.
4. Chill dough in refrigerator until easy to handle, then shape into 2 rolls about 1½ inches in diameter. Wrap each roll in waxed paper, aluminum foil, or plastic wrap. Chill several hours or overnight.
5. Remove rolls of dough from refrigerator as needed. Cut dough into ⅛-inch slices. Place slices about 1½ inches apart on lightly greased cookie sheets.
6. Bake at 400°F 5 to 8 minutes. Cool cookies on wire racks.

About 5 dozen cookies

687 *Butterscotchies*

½ cup undiluted evaporated milk
¾ cup sugar
¼ teaspoon salt
2 tablespoons butter or margarine
1 package (6 ounces) butterscotch-flavored pieces
1 teaspoon vanilla extract
1 cup flaked coconut
½ cup coarsely chopped walnuts
2 to 2½ cups crisp enriched ready-to-eat cereal

1. Put evaporated milk, sugar, salt, and butter into a heavy 2-quart saucepan. Bring to a full boil, stirring constantly, and boil 2 minutes.
2. Remove from heat. Add butterscotch pieces and vanilla extract; stir until smooth. Add coconut, walnuts, and cereal; toss lightly until well coated.
3. Drop by rounded teaspoonfuls onto a cookie sheet lined with waxed paper or aluminum foil. Allow to stand until set.

About 1½ pounds candy

688 *Peanut Blonde Brownies*

½ cup chunk-style peanut butter
¼ cup butter or margarine
1 teaspoon vanilla extract
1 cup firmly packed light brown
  sugar
2 eggs
½ cup enriched all-purpose flour
1 cup chopped salted peanuts
  Confectioners' sugar

1. Cream peanut butter, butter, and vanilla extract in a bowl. Add brown sugar gradually, beating well after each addition.
2. Add eggs, one at a time, beating thoroughly after each addition until creamy.
3. Add flour in halves, beating until blended after each addition. Stir in peanuts. Turn mixture into a greased 8×8×2-inch pan and spread evenly.
4. Bake at 350°F 30 to 35 minutes.
5. Remove from oven and cool in pan 5 minutes. Cut into 2-inch squares. Remove from pan and cool on a wire rack. Sift confectioners' sugar over tops.

16 brownies

689 *Pineapple Volcano Chiffon Pie*

2 envelopes unflavored gelatin
½ cup sugar
¼ teaspoon salt
3 egg yolks, fork beaten
½ cup water
1 can (20 ounces) crushed pineapple
  (undrained)
¼ teaspoon grated lemon peel
1 tablespoon lemon juice
3 egg whites
  Frozen dessert topping, thawed, or
  whipped dessert topping
1 baked 9-inch graham cracker crust
1 can (8¼ ounces) crushed pineapple,
  drained

1. Mix gelatin, ¼ cup sugar, and salt in the top of a double boiler.
2. Beat egg yolks and water together. Stir into gelatin mixture along with undrained pineapple.
3. Set over boiling water. Thoroughly beat mixture and continue cooking 5 minutes to cook egg yolks and dissolve gelatin, stirring constantly.
4. Remove from water; mix in lemon peel and juice. Chill, stirring occasionally until mixture mounds slightly when dropped from a spoon.
5. Beat egg whites until frothy. Gradually add remaining ¼ cup sugar, beating until stiff peaks are formed. Fold into gelatin mixture.
6. Turn filling into crust; chill.
7. Garnish pie with generous mounds of the dessert topping. Spoon on remaining crushed pineapple to resemble "volcanoes."

One 9-inch pie

690 *Cherry-Rhubarb Pie*

1 can (16 ounces) pitted tart red
  cherries (water packed),
  drained
1 pound fresh rhubarb, sliced about
  ⅛ inch thick
1¼ cups sugar
¼ cup quick-cooking tapioca
⅛ teaspoon baking soda
½ teaspoon almond extract
  Few drops red food coloring
  Pastry for a 2-crust 9-inch pie

1. Mix cherries, rhubarb, sugar, tapioca, baking soda, almond extract, and red food coloring; let stand 20 minutes.
2. Prepare pastry. Roll out enough pastry to line a 9-inch pie pan or plate; line pie pan. Roll out remaining pastry for top crust and slit pastry with knife in several places to allow steam to escape during baking.
3. Pour filling into pastry-lined pan; cover with top crust and flute edge.
4. Bake at 450°F 10 minutes. Turn oven control to 350°F and bake 40 to 45 minutes. Remove from oven and set on a wire rack. Serve warm or cooled.

One 9-inch pie

691 *Lemon-Beer Sponge Pie*

This pie bakes with a puddinglike layer on the bottom, a cakelike layer on the top. The beer flavor is subtle.

1 unbaked 9-inch pie shell
4 eggs, separated
¾ cup sugar
¼ cup flour
3 tablespoons butter or
   margarine, softened
2 teaspoons grated lemon peel
1 can or bottle (12 ounces) beer
2 tablespoons lemon juice

1. Bake pie shell at 450°F 10 minutes.
2. Beat egg whites until foamy. Gradually add half of sugar, continuing beating until stiff peaks form.
3. In a separate bowl, beat remaining sugar, flour, butter, peel and egg yolks. Mix in beer and lemon juice.
4. Fold beaten egg whites into yolk mixture. Turn into partially baked pie shell.
5. Bake at 350°F about 50 minutes, or until set. Cool to room temperature before slicing.

One 9-inch pie

692 *Peanuts-and-Beer Pie*

Peanuts and beer are frequent partners—for snacking, at the ball park, at parties. So what a natural idea it would be to combine peanuts and beer in a sweet dessert pie. It's a memorable combination. This is a chiffon-type pie made fluffy with beaten egg whites and firmed with gelatin. It goes into a prebaked shell.

Pastry for 9-inch pie shell
1 can or bottle (12 ounces) beer
1 envelope unflavored gelatin
½ cup packed brown sugar
3 eggs, separated
1 teaspoon vanilla extract
6 ounces salted peanuts (1¼
   cups), chopped
¼ cup granulated sugar

1. Roll out pastry and fit into pie plate. Do not cut off excess pastry, but fold under and make high fluted sides. Prick bottom and sides thoroughly with fork.
2. Bake at 450°F 15 minutes, until light golden brown. Cool.
3. Pour beer into top of a double boiler; sprinkle with gelatin. Add brown sugar and slightly beaten egg yolks.
4. Cook over boiling water, stirring constantly, until slightly thickened and gelatin is dissolved (8 to 10 minutes). Add vanilla extract.
5. Chill until partially thickened. Stir in peanuts.
6. Beat egg whites until foamy. Gradually add granulated sugar, continuing beating until stiff peaks form. Fold in peanut-gelatin mixture. Turn into baked shell. Chill.

One 9-inch pie

693 *Cheese-Stuffed Strawberries*

A traditional French dessert, served in an elegant manner. If berries are small, slice them and serve the cheese mixture as a sauce.

½ cup low-fat ricotta cheese
1 teaspoon grated lemon peel
1 teaspoon fresh lemon juice
1 teaspoon honey or sugar
48 large strawberries
   Mint sprigs (optional)

1. Mix cheese, lemon peel, lemon juice, and honey in a food processor or blender until fluffy; refrigerate until chilled (about 1 hour).
2. Gently scoop centers from strawberries with melon-baller or fruit knife. Fill with cheese mixture.
3. Arrange filled strawberries on small individual plates. Garnish with mint.

4 servings

694 *Brewmaster's Poppyseed Cake*

A scrumptious, moist, and tender cake that everyone will rave about. It needs no frosting.

Cake:
- 1 package (2-layer size) regular yellow cake mix
- 1 small package instant vanilla pudding and pie filling
- 4 eggs
- 1 cup beer
- ½ cup oil
- ¼ cup poppyseed

Glaze:
- ½ cup sugar
- ½ cup beer
- ¼ cup butter

1. Place cake mix, dry pudding, eggs, beer, oil, and poppyseed in an electric mixer bowl. Blend on low speed. Then beat on medium speed for 2 minutes.
2. Turn into a well-greased and floured 10-inch Bundt or tube pan.
3. Bake at 350°F 50 to 55 minutes, or until done.
4. Cool in pan 15 minutes. Turn out on rack.
5. To prepare glaze, boil ingredients for 5 minutes. Prick warm cake with skewer in many places. Brush warm glaze generously over top and sides. Cool. (If desired, sift confectioners' sugar over top; cake needs no frosting.)

1 large cake; 16 servings

695 *Velvety Chocolate Cake*

This excellent chocolate cake has an extremely moist and tender crumb.

- 2¾ cups sifted cake flour
- 2 teaspoons baking powder
- 1 teaspoon baking soda
- ¼ teaspoon salt
- ¾ cup butter or margarine
- 1 cup packed brown sugar
- ⅔ cup granulated sugar
- 3 eggs
- 3 ounces (3 squares) unsweetened chocolate, melted and cooled
- 1 can or bottle (12 ounces) beer

1. Sift dry ingredients together.
2. Cream butter and sugars until very light and fluffy.
3. Add eggs, one at a time, beating thoroughly at medium speed of electric mixer. Beat in chocolate.
4. Add sifted dry ingredients alternately with beer, beating at low speed until blended after each addition.
5. Turn into 2 greased and waxed-paper-lined 9-inch round layer cake pans.
6. Bake at 350°F 35 minutes, or until done. Cool in pans 10 minutes; turn out on wire racks. When cool, frost with favorite icing.

One 2-layer 9-inch cake

696 *Nutmeg Cake*

A moist, flavorful cake with a very tender crumb. Fill it with Lemon-Beer Filling or Orange-Beer Filling. Frost with any white frosting.

- 3 cups sifted cake flour
- 1 tablespoon baking powder
- 2 teaspoons nutmeg
- ½ teaspoon salt
- ¾ cup butter or margarine
- 2 teaspoons vanilla extract
- 1 cup granulated sugar
- ¾ cup packed brown sugar
- 2 whole eggs
- 2 egg whites
- 1 can or bottle (12 ounces) beer
- ● Lemon-Beer Filling
  White frosting, any type

1. Sift dry ingredients together.
2. Cream butter with vanilla extract and sugars until light and fluffy. Add eggs and whites, one at a time, beating well after each addition (medium speed of mixer).
3. Alternately add sifted dry ingredients in thirds and beer in halves to creamed mixture, beating on low speed just until smooth after each addition.
4. Turn into 2 greased and waxed-paper-lined 9-inch round layer cake pans.
5. Bake at 350°F 30 to 35 minutes, or until cake tests done. Cool in pans about 10 minutes. Turn out onto wire racks. Cool completely before filling and frosting.

One 2-layer 9-inch cake

Note: If not making a filling requiring egg yolks, use 3 whole eggs in batter.

697 *Raisin-Nut Spice Cake*

Serve this moist, dark, and delectable cake any time of year with whipped cream, ice cream, or Beer Dessert Sauce on top. It is delicious served warm with hard sauce during the holiday season.

3 cups sifted cake flour
2 teaspoons baking powder
1 teaspoon baking soda
½ teaspoon cinnamon
½ teaspoon nutmeg
¼ teaspoon ginger
¼ teaspoon salt
1 can or bottle (12 ounces) beer
1 cup raisins (5 ounces)
¾ cup butter or margarine
1 cup sugar
½ cup molasses
2 eggs
¾ cup chopped nuts (3 ounces)
Glaze

1. Sift dry ingredients together. Set aside.
2. Heat beer and raisins to simmering; let stand about 15 minutes to plump.
3. Cream butter and sugar until light and fluffy; add molasses.
4. Add eggs, one at a time, beating well after each addition.
5. Add dry ingredients alternately in thirds with beer drained from raisins, beating just until well blended. Stir in raisins and nuts.
6. Turn into a well-greased and floured 10-inch Bundt pan or angel food cake pan (nonstick pan preferred).
7. Bake at 350°F 1 hour, or until done.
8. Let stand in pan about 10 minutes; invert onto cake rack. Cool. Cover with foil or store in airtight container. Cake slices better if made a day in advance.
9. Prepare a glaze by thinning **1 cup sifted confectioners' sugar** with **beer** or **milk.** Drizzle over cake shortly before serving.

1 large cake; 16 servings

698 *Old English Cheesecake*

Raisins, almonds, lemon peel, and beer delectably perk up the flavor of this rich dessert.

Crust:
1¼ cups all-purpose flour
¼ cup sugar
⅓ cup butter or margarine
4 tablespoons cold beer

Filling:
½ cup golden raisins (2½ ounces), chopped
⅓ cup almonds (2 ounces), finely chopped
1 tablespoon grated lemon peel
1 pound cottage cheese
½ cup flour
4 eggs
1 cup sugar
¾ cup beer
⅛ teaspoon nutmeg

1. For crust, mix flour and sugar; cut in butter until crumbly. Add beer 1 tablespoon at a time, stirring with a fork. Shape dough into a ball. Chill.
2. Roll out on floured surface to a 13- to 14-inch circle. Fold in quarters. Gently unfold in a 9-inch springform pan. Even edge of crust so it extends about 2 inches up sides of pan (1½ inches up sides if using a 10-inch pan). Prick all over with fork.
3. Bake at 425°F 10 minutes. Prick again and press to sides. Bake 10 minutes more, or until slightly golden.
4. For filling, mix chopped raisins, almonds, and peel.
5. Process cottage cheese, flour, and eggs until smooth, using food processor or electric blender. (Do in several batches in blender.)
6. Add sugar, beer, and nutmeg; blend until smooth. Stir in raisin mixture. Pour into cooled shell.
7. Bake at 300°F 1¼ to 1½ hours, or until set. Cool to room temperature for serving. Dust with **confectioners' sugar** and top with **whole unblanched almonds.**

8 to 10 servings

699 *Easy Walnut Cake*

When filled with Orange-Beer Filling or Lemon-Beer Filling, this cake doesn't even need an icing—but add one of your choice, if you wish. Otherwise, sift confectioners' sugar over the top.

1 package (2-layer size) yellow
   cake mix
Beer
Water
2 eggs
⅔ cup finely chopped walnuts
Orange-Beer Filling or
   Lemon-Beer Filling

1. Mix cake batter according to package directions. Use the exact amount of liquid called for, but substitute beer for all or part of the water. (If making Orange-Beer Filling, set aside ½ cup beer from a can for filling and use 1 cup in cake. For Lemon-Beer Filling, set aside ¾ cup beer for filling and use ¾ cup in cake. If not making beer-flavored filling, substitute beer for all of the water in cake.)
2. Blend in walnuts.
3. Turn batter into 2 greased and waxed-paper-lined 9-inch round layer cake pans.
4. Bake at 350°F 30 minutes, or until a wooden pick inserted in center comes out clean. Cool in pans 10 minutes; turn out onto wire racks. Cool completely before filling and frosting.

One 2-layer 9-inch cake

700 *Orange-Beer Filling*

⅓ cup sugar
1½ tablespoons cornstarch
⅛ teaspoon salt
½ cup beer
⅓ cup orange juice
1 egg yolk
2 teaspoons grated orange peel
2 teaspoons butter or margarine

1. In top of a double boiler, combine sugar, cornstarch, and salt. Stir in beer and orange juice. Cook over direct heat, stirring constantly, until thickened and clear.
2. Add a little hot mixture to egg yolk; return to double-boiler top. Cook over hot water, stirring constantly, 4 to 5 minutes.
3. Stir in peel and butter. Cool before spreading on cake.

About 1 cup; enough to fill two 8- or 9-inch layers

701 *Lemon-Beer Filling*

A tart filling to spread between two layers of an 8- or 9-inch cake.

½ cup sugar
2 tablespoons cornstarch
⅛ teaspoon salt
¾ cup beer
2 teaspoons grated lemon peel
2 tablespoons lemon juice
2 egg yolks

1. In top of a double boiler, combine sugar, cornstarch, and salt. Stir in beer. Cook over direct heat, stirring constantly, until thickened and clear.
2. Stir in lemon peel and juice.
3. Add a little hot mixture to egg yolks; return to double boiler top. Cook over hot water, stirring constantly, for 4 to 5 minutes. Cool before spreading on cake.

About 1 cup

702 *White Beer Icing*

3 tablespoons butter
3 cups sifted confectioners' sugar
3 to 4 tablespoons beer

1. Cream butter.
2. Add confectioners' sugar alternately with beer, until frosting is fluffy and of spreading consistency.

1⅔ cups; for tops and sides of 2 round 8- or 9-inch layers

703 *Cocoa-Beer Icing*

A light chocolate icing with a very mild beer flavor.

¼ **pound butter or margarine,**
softened
3½ **cups sifted confectioners' sugar**
⅓ **cup cocoa**
⅛ **teaspoon salt**
⅓ **cup beer (about)**

1. Cream butter with part of confectioners' sugar.
2. Add cocoa, salt, and a little beer. Beat until smooth.
3. Add remaining sugar alternately with enough beer to make icing of spreading consistency, beating until fluffy.

2 cups; for tops and sides of two 9-inch layers

704 *Spicy Fruit Gelatin "with a Head"*

Serve this fruited gelatin dessert in pilsner glasses, if you have them, and top with whipped cream or whipped topping to simulate the foam on beer.

1 **can or bottle (12 ounces) beer**
2 **tablespoons packed brown**
sugar
1 **stick cinnamon**
4 **whole cloves**
1 **package (3 ounces)**
orange-flavored gelatin
1 **can (8¼ ounces) crushed**
pineapple
Water

1. Place beer, brown sugar, cinnamon, and cloves in a saucepan. Heat to boiling. Add gelatin; stir until dissolved.
2. Let stand at room temperature until lukewarm to mellow flavors. Remove spices.
3. Drain pineapple thoroughly, reserving liquid. Add water to liquid to measure ½ cup. Stir into gelatin mixture. Chill until partially thickened.
4. Fold in pineapple. Spoon into pilsner or parfait glasses. Chill until firm.
5. To serve, top with a "head" of whipped cream or prepared whipped topping.

4 or 5 servings

705 *Zesty Beer Ice*

You've heard of champagne sherbet, so why not a beer ice? Those who try it are in for a delicious surprise. It's especially nice on hot days or following a heavy meal. Lemon gives a zest to the taste.

1 **envelope unflavored gelatin**
2 **cans or bottles (12 ounces each)**
beer
1 **cup sugar**
2 **teaspoons grated lemon peel**
½ **cup lemon juice**

1. Sprinkle gelatin over 1 can beer in a saucepan. Let stand 5 minutes to soften.
2. Add sugar. Cook over low heat just until dissolved.
3. Add remaining 1 can beer, lemon peel, and juice. Turn into a shallow pan.
4. Freeze until firm, stirring several times. Pack into a 1-quart covered container.

1 quart

706 *Baked Stuffed Apples*

6 **medium cooking apples (about**
2 pounds)
½ **cup raisins**
½ **cup packed brown sugar**
1 **teaspoon cinnamon**
1 **cup beer**

1. Core apples. Remove 1-inch strip of peel around top.
2. Mix raisins, brown sugar, and cinnamon. Fill apple centers.
3. Place apples in a baking dish. Pour beer over.
4. Bake at 350°F 40 to 45 minutes, or until tender, basting occasionally.
5. Cool to room temperature, basting while cooling. Serve with its own sauce. If desired, add cream or Beer Dessert Sauce (page 76).

6 servings

707 *Beer Bread Pudding*

1½ cups milk
1 can or bottle (12 ounces) beer
3 eggs
½ cup packed brown sugar
½ teaspoon vanilla extract
¼ teaspoon cinnamon
¼ teaspoon nutmeg
¼ teaspoon salt
4 cups dry bread cubes (6 slices)

1. Scald milk and beer.
2. Beat eggs with brown sugar, vanilla extract, cinnamon, nutmeg, and salt. Add scalded milk and beer gradually while stirring. Add bread.
3. Turn into a greased 1½- or 2-quart casserole. Set in a pan of boiling water.
4. Bake at 325°F 50 minutes, or until a knife inserted in center comes out clean. Serve hot or cold.

6 servings

708 *Raisin-Beer Pudding*

Try putting beer in a simple pudding. You'll discover a surprisingly delicious and unusual flavor treat.

2 eggs
1½ cups milk
½ cup sugar
¼ cup quick-cooking tapioca
¼ teaspoon nutmeg
⅛ teaspoon salt
1 can or bottle (12 ounces) beer
½ cup raisins

1. In a heavy 2-quart saucepan, beat eggs. Add milk, sugar, tapioca, nutmeg, and salt. Let stand 5 minutes.
2. Cook, stirring constantly, to simmering. Add beer gradually while stirring; add raisins. Cook and stir just to boiling.
3. Pour into dessert dishes.

About 1 quart; 6 to 8 servings

709 *Spicy Butterscotch Pudding*

This pudding may also be put in 4 to 6 baked tart shells or an 8-inch baked pie shell.

1 package (4-serving size) butterscotch pudding and pie filling (not instant)
⅔ cup instant nonfat dry milk
1 teaspoon pumpkin pie spice
1 cup beer
1 cup water
Whipped cream or thawed frozen whipped dessert topping

1. In a heavy saucepan, combine pudding mix, dry milk, and spice. Stir in beer and water.
2. Cook over medium heat, stirring constantly, until mixture boils.
3. Pour into 4 pudding dishes. Cover surfaces with plastic wrap. Chill until set. Serve topped with whipped cream or dessert topping.

4 servings

710 Chocolate-Beer Pudding Cake

A fun dessert to make and bake. A hot chocolate-beer syrup is poured over cake batter in the pan. After baking, a puddinglike layer forms in the bottom. The cake is then inverted.

Batter:
- 1½ cups all-purpose flour
- ¾ cup sugar
- 1 tablespoon unsweetened cocoa
- 1½ teaspoons baking powder
- ½ teaspoon baking soda
- ¼ teaspoon salt
- ¾ cup beer
- ⅓ cup oil
- 1 egg, slightly beaten

Syrup:
- 1 tablespoon unsweetened cocoa
- ¾ cup beer
- ⅓ cup packed brown sugar
- ⅓ cup granulated sugar

1. For batter, mix dry ingredients; make a well in center. Add beer, oil, and egg. Beat just until smooth.
2. For syrup, make a paste of cocoa and a little beer. Add remaining beer and sugars. Heat to boiling.
3. Pour batter into a greased 8-inch square baking pan. Drizzle syrup over top.
4. Bake at 350°F 40 minutes.
5. Cool about 5 minutes. Loosen sides of cake from pan; invert onto platter. Even out pudding layer with knife. Serve warm or cool.

6 to 8 servings

711 Currant-Apple Fritters

Serve as a hot dessert sprinkled with confectioners' sugar. Or top with syrup and serve for breakfast.

- 1 cup all-purpose flour
- 1½ teaspoons baking powder
- ¼ teaspoon cinnamon
- ¼ teaspoon salt
- ½ cup beer
- ½ cup currants
- ½ cup chopped pared apple
- 2 eggs, slightly beaten
- 1 teaspoon oil
- Fat for deep frying
- Confectioners' sugar

1. Combine flour, baking powder, cinnamon, and salt. Add beer, currants, apple, eggs, and oil. Stir to blend well.
2. Drop by rounded teaspoonfuls into hot deep fat heated to 365°F. Fry until browned. Drain on paper towels.
3. Keep hot in oven until serving time. While still hot, roll in confectioners' sugar.

About 30 fritters; 6 to 8 servings

712 Peach Cobbler

- 1 can (29 ounces) sliced peaches
- 2 teaspoons lemon juice
- ¼ teaspoon cinnamon
- 1½ tablespoons cornstarch
- ¾ cup beer
- 1 cup all-purpose flour
- 1½ teaspoons baking powder
- ¼ teaspoon salt
- 3 tablespoons shortening

1. Drain peaches, reserving syrup.
2. Lightly toss together peaches, lemon juice, and cinnamon. Arrange in a buttered shallow 1½-quart baking dish, 10 x 6 inches, or 8 inches square.
3. In a small saucepan, blend cornstarch, ¼ cup reserved syrup, and ¾ cup beer. Cook, stirring constantly, until thickened and clear. Pour over peaches.
4. Bake at 400°F 10 to 15 minutes, or until bubbly.
5. Meanwhile, mix flour, baking powder, and salt. Add ½ cup more reserved syrup (or use ½ cup beer plus 1 tablespoon sugar). Stir just until dough forms a ball.
6. Drop by large spoonfuls onto peaches. Continue baking 25 minutes.

8 servings

713 *Lemon Crunch Dessert*

Lemon mixture:
- ¾ cup sugar
- 2 tablespoons flour
- ⅛ teaspoon salt
- 1 cup water
- 2 eggs, well beaten
- 1 teaspoon grated lemon peel
- ⅓ cup lemon juice

Crunch mixture:
- ½ cup butter or margarine
- 1 cup firmly packed brown sugar
- 1 cup all-purpose flour
- ½ teaspoon salt
- 1 cup whole wheat flakes, crushed
- ½ cup finely chopped walnuts
- ½ cup shredded coconut

1. For lemon mixture, mix sugar, flour, and salt in a heavy saucepan. Gradually add water, stirring until smooth. Bring mixture to boiling and cook 2 minutes.
2. Stir about 3 tablespoons of the hot mixture vigorously into beaten eggs. Immediately blend into mixture in saucepan. Cook and stir about 3 minutes.
3. Remove from heat and stir in lemon peel and lemon juice. Set aside to cool.
4. For crunch mixture, beat butter until softened; add brown sugar gradually, beating until fluffy. Add flour and salt; mix well. Add wheat flakes, walnuts, and coconut; mix thoroughly.
5. Line bottom of an 8-inch square baking dish with one third of the crunch mixture. Cover with the lemon mixture, spreading to form an even layer. Top with remaining crunch mixture.
6. Bake, uncovered, at 350°F 40 minutes, or until lightly browned. Serve warm or cold.

8 servings

714 *Hot Spicy Fruit Pot*

- 1 can (16 ounces) pear halves
- 1 can (16 ounces) peach halves
- 1 can (16 ounces) purple plums, halved and pitted
- 1 cup firmly packed brown sugar
- 1 cinnamon stick
- ¼ teaspoon nutmeg
- ¼ teaspoon allspice
- ⅛ teaspoon ginger
- ¼ cup lemon juice
- 2 teaspoons grated orange peel
- 2 tablespoons butter or margarine

1. Drain fruits, reserving 1 cup liquid. Put fruit into a buttered 2-quart casserole.
2. Combine reserved liquid with remaining ingredients, except butter. Pour over fruit. Dot with butter.
3. Bake, covered, at 350°F 30 minutes, or until bubbly. Serve hot or cold. If desired, spoon over ice cream or cake.

8 servings

715 *Buttery Baked Apples*

8 medium baking apples, cored
1 cup sugar
6 tablespoons butter or margarine
1 tablespoon cornstarch
1 tablespoon cold water
½ teaspoon vanilla extract
½ cup milk

1. Put apples into a 1½-quart baking dish. Sprinkle with sugar. Dot with butter.
2. Bake, uncovered, at 450°F 20 minutes, or until fork-tender, basting occasionally.
3. Remove baking dish from oven and apples from baking dish.
4. Combine cornstarch, water, and vanilla extract; add to milk. Stir into liquid in baking dish. Return apples to baking dish.
5. Bake an additional 8 to 10 minutes, or until sauce is thickened. To serve, spoon sauce over each apple.

8 servings

716 *Cherry-Pineapple Cobbler*

1 can (21 ounces) cherry pie filling
1 can (13¼ ounces) pineapple tidbits, drained
¼ teaspoon allspice
3 tablespoons honey
1 egg, slightly beaten
½ cup dairy sour cream
1½ cups unflavored croutons

1. Combine cherry pie filling, pineapple tidbits, allspice, and 1 tablespoon honey. Put into a 1½-quart baking dish.
2. Blend egg, sour cream, and remaining 2 tablespoons honey. Stir in croutons. Spoon over cherry-pineapple mixture.
3. Bake, uncovered, at 375°F 30 minutes, or until heated through. If desired, top with ice cream.

8 servings

717 *Indian Pudding*

3 cups milk
½ cup cornmeal
1 tablespoon butter or margarine
½ cup light molasses
½ teaspoon salt
½ teaspoon ginger
1 cup cold milk

1. Scald 2½ cups milk in top of double boiler over boiling water.
2. Combine cornmeal and the remaining ½ cup milk. Add to scalded milk, stirring constantly. Cook about 25 minutes, stirring frequently.
3. Stir in butter, molasses, salt, and ginger.
4. Pour into a greased 1½-quart baking dish. Pour the 1 cup cold milk over pudding.
5. Set in a baking pan. Pour boiling water around dish to within 1 inch of top.
6. Bake, covered, at 300°F about 2 hours. Remove cover and bake an additional 1 hour. Serve warm or cold with **cream** or **ice cream.**

6 servings

Glazed Apple Tart in Wheat Germ Crust, page 262

718 *Bread Pudding*

1 cup raisins
½ cup sherry
8 slices white bread
Butter
4 eggs
½ cup sugar
Dash salt
1 quart half-and-half
1½ teaspoons vanilla extract

1. Soak raisins in sherry 2 hours, stirring occasionally.
2. Trim crusts from bread and spread with butter. Place bread, buttered side down, in a 2½-quart casserole or soufflé dish.
3. Drain raisins and sprinkle over bread.
4. Beat remaining ingredients together. Pour over bread and let stand 30 minutes. Sprinkle with **cinnamon.**
5. Bake, covered, at 350°F 30 minutes. Remove cover and bake an additional 30 minutes, or until set.

8 servings

719 *Peach Meringue Pudding*

2 cans (21 ounces each) peach pie filling
¼ cup butter or margarine, melted
½ teaspoon cinnamon
⅛ teaspoon nutmeg
⅛ teaspoon allspice
½ cup slivered almonds
3 egg whites
½ cup sugar

1. Combine peach pie filling, butter, cinnamon, nutmeg, allspice, and almonds. Put into a 1½-quart casserole.
2. Bake, uncovered, at 350°F 30 minutes, or until bubbly. Remove from oven.
3. Beat egg whites until stiff, but not dry. Gradually beat in sugar until glossy. Evenly spread over hot peaches. Sprinkle with **cinnamon.**
4. Bake an additional 12 to 15 minutes, or until lightly browned.

6 servings

720 *Apple Cream*

6 cups sliced apples (about 2 pounds)
½ cup sugar
1 teaspoon cinnamon
1 teaspoon nutmeg
¼ cup butter or margarine
⅔ cup sugar
1 egg
½ cup flour
½ teaspoon baking powder
½ teaspoon salt
1 cup whipping cream

1. Toss the apple slices with a mixture of the ½ cup sugar, cinnamon, and nutmeg. Spread evenly in bottom of a buttered 9-inch square baking dish.
2. Cream together butter and ⅔ cup sugar. Add egg and continue beating until mixture is light and fluffy.
3. Blend flour, baking powder, and salt; beat into creamed mixture until just blended. Spread evenly over apples.
4. Bake, uncovered, at 350°F 30 minutes. Pour cream over surface and bake an additional 10 minutes, or until topping is golden brown. Serve warm with cream, if desired.

8 servings

Raspberry Mousse, page 350

721 *Favorite Apple Pudding*

6 or 7 medium firm, tart cooking apples, quartered, cored, pared, and cut in ⅛-inch slices
¾ cup firmly packed brown sugar
3 tablespoons flour
½ teaspoon salt
1 teaspoon cinnamon
¼ teaspoon nutmeg
3 tablespoons butter or margarine
1 teaspoon grated orange peel
¾ cup (3 ounces) shredded Cheddar cheese
5 slices white bread, toasted, buttered on both sides and cut in halves
¼ cup orange juice
½ cup buttered soft bread cubes

1. Arrange one third of the apple slices on bottom of a greased 2-quart casserole.
2. Thoroughly blend brown sugar, flour, salt, cinnamon, and nutmeg. Using a pastry blender or 2 knives, cut in butter and grated orange peel until mixture is in coarse crumbs. Mix in cheese.
3. Sprinkle one third of the sugar-cheese mixture over apples and cover with one half of the toast. Repeat layers. Cover the top with remaining apples and sugar-cheese mixture.
4. Pour orange juice over surface and top with the buttered bread cubes.
5. Bake, covered, at 425°F 30 minutes. Remove cover and bake an additional 10 minutes.

6 to 8 servings

722 *Baked Apricot Pudding*

1 tablespoon confectioners' sugar
1¼ cups (about 6 ounces) dried apricots
1 cup water
1½ tablespoons butter or margarine
1½ tablespoons flour
¾ cup milk
4 egg yolks
½ teaspoon vanilla extract
4 egg whites
6 tablespoons granulated sugar
Whipped cream

1. Lightly butter bottom of a 1½-quart casserole and sift confectioners' sugar over it.
2. Put apricots and water into a saucepan. Cover; simmer 20 to 30 minutes, or until apricots are plump and tender. Force apricots through a coarse sieve or food mill (makes about ¾ cup purée).
3. Heat butter in saucepan. Stir in flour. Gradually add milk, stirring until thickened and smooth. Remove from heat.
4. Beat egg yolks and vanilla extract together until mixture is thick and lemon colored. Spoon sauce gradually into beaten egg yolks while beating vigorously. Blend in apricot purée.
5. Using clean beater, beat egg whites until frothy. Add sugar gradually, beating constantly. Continue beating until rounded peaks are formed. Spread apricot mixture gently over beaten egg whites and fold until thoroughly blended. Turn mixture into prepared casserole. Set casserole in a pan of very hot water.
6. Bake, uncovered, at 350°F 50 minutes, or until a knife inserted halfway between center and edge comes out clean. Cool slightly before serving. Top with whipped cream.

6 servings

723 *Chocolate Custard*

1 package (6 ounces) semisweet
    chocolate pieces
3 tablespoons half-and-half
3 cups milk
3 eggs
1 teaspoon vanilla extract
⅓ cup sugar
¼ teaspoon salt

1. Melt 2/3 cup chocolate pieces with half-and-half in top of a double boiler over hot (not boiling) water. Stir until smooth; spoon about 1 tablespoon into each of 8 custard cups or 10 soufflé dishes. Spread evenly. Put cups into a shallow pan; set aside.
2. Scald milk. Melt remaining 1/3 cup chocolate pieces and, adding gradually, stir in scalded milk until blended.
3. Beat together eggs, vanilla extract, sugar, and salt. Gradually add milk mixture, stirring constantly. Pour into chocolate-lined cups.
4. Set pan with filled cups on oven rack and pour boiling water into pan to a depth of 1 inch.
5. Bake, uncovered, at 325°F 25 minutes, or until a knife inserted halfway between center and edge comes out clean.
6. Set cups on wire rack to cool slightly. Refrigerate and serve when thoroughly cooled. Unmold and, if desired, garnish with whipped cream rosettes.

8 to 10 servings

724 *Brazilian Pudim Moka with Chocolate Sauce*

3 cups milk
1 cup half-and-half
5 tablespoons instant coffee
2 teaspoons grated orange peel
4 eggs
1 egg yolk
½ cup sugar
½ teaspoon salt
1 teaspoon vanilla extract
    Nutmeg
    Chocolate sauce
    Chopped Brazil nuts

1. Combine milk and half-and-half in top of a double boiler and heat over simmering water until scalded.
2. Add instant coffee and orange peel, stirring until coffee is dissolved. Remove from simmering water and set aside to cool (about 10 minutes).
3. Beat together eggs and egg yolk slightly. Blend in sugar and salt.
4. Gradually add coffee mixture, stirring constantly. Mix in vanilla extract. Strain through a fine sieve into eight 6-ounce custard cups. Sprinkle with nutmeg. Set cups in pan of hot water.
5. Bake, uncovered, at 325°F 25 to 30 minutes, or until a knife inserted in center of custard comes out clean.
6. Cool and chill. To serve, invert onto serving plates. Pour chocolate sauce over top and sprinkle with Brazil nuts.

8 servings

725 *Rosy Rhubarb Swirls*

1½ cups sugar
1¼ cups water
⅓ cup red cinnamon candies
2 or 3 drops red food coloring
2¼ cups all-purpose flour
4 teaspoons baking powder
½ teaspoon salt
⅔ cup milk
⅓ cup half-and-half
3 cups finely diced fresh rhubarb (if
    tender do not peel)

1. Put sugar, water, and cinnamon candies into a saucepan. Stirring occasionally, cook over medium heat until candies are melted and mixture forms a thin syrup (about 10 minutes). Stir in food coloring.
2. Meanwhile, sift together into a bowl the flour, baking powder, and salt. Add a mixture of milk and half-and-half and stir with a fork only until dry ingredients are moistened. Turn onto a floured surface and knead lightly about 10 times with fingertips.
3. Roll dough into a 13x11x¼-inch rectangle. Spoon rhubarb evenly over dough. Beginning with longer side, roll dough and seal edges. Cut crosswise into 12 slices.
4. Pour syrup into a shallow baking dish and arrange rolls, cut side up, in syrup. Sprinkle with additional sugar (¼ to ⅓ cup) and top each roll with a small piece of **butter**.
5. Bake, uncovered, at 400°F 25 to 30 minutes. Serve warm with **half-and-half**.

12 servings

726 Vanilla Soufflé

1 tablespoon confectioners' sugar
¼ cup butter or margarine
3 tablespoons flour
1 cup milk
4 egg yolks
½ cup sugar
1 tablespoon vanilla extract
4 egg whites

1. Butter bottom of a 1½-quart soufflé dish (straight-sided casserole) and sift confectioners' sugar over it.
2. Heat butter in a saucepan. Stir in flour. Gradually add milk, stirring until thickened and smooth. Remove from heat.
3. Beat egg yolks, sugar, and vanilla extract together until mixture is very thick. Spoon sauce gradually into egg-yolk mixture while beating vigorously. Cool to lukewarm.
4. Using clean beater, beat egg whites until rounded peaks are formed. Spread egg-yolk mixture gently over egg whites and fold until thoroughly blended. Turn mixture into prepared soufflé dish. Set dish in a pan of very hot water.
5. Bake, uncovered, at 400°F 15 minutes. Turn oven control to 375°F and bake 30 to 40 minutes, or until a knife inserted halfway between center and edge comes out clean. Serve immediately.
6. Accompany with **puréed thawed frozen strawberries or raspberries.**

About 6 servings

727 Wine Fruit Compote

1 can (16 ounces) pear halves
1 can (16 ounces) cling peach halves
1 can (13½ ounces) pineapple chunks
½ lemon, thinly sliced and quartered
2 cups fruit juices and water
5 whole cloves
1 stick cinnamon
1 package (3 ounces) strawberry-flavored gelatin
2 teaspoons lemon juice
1 cup cherry kijafa wine

1. Drain fruit and reserve juice. Arrange fruit in a shallow 1½-quart dish. Scatter lemon slices over top.
2. Combine juices from fruit and water, cloves, and cinnamon in a saucepan. Heat to boiling. Simmer for 5 minutes. Strain.
3. Dissolve gelatin in the hot liquid. Add lemon juice and cherry wine. Pour over fruit. Chill 1 to 1½ hours, or until gelatin is only partly set. Baste fruit occasionally with gelatin mixture while chilling.

6 to 8 servings

728 Elegant Creamed Peaches

1 envelope plain gelatin
½ cup sweet red wine, such as port or muscatel
1 pint whipping cream
3 tablespoons powdered sugar
Dash salt
1 can (29 ounces) cling peach halves
½ cup glacé fruit
2 tablespoons roasted diced almonds
1 tablespoon honey
1 tablespoon sweet red wine

1. Combine gelatin and ½ cup wine in saucepan; place over low heat and stir until gelatin is dissolved.
2. Cool until mixture begins to thicken.
3. Whip cream with powdered sugar and salt.
4. Fold gelatin mixture into whipped cream. Spoon into 6 to 8 dessert dishes or 9-inch round pan.
5. Drain peaches; place cup-sides up in cream mixture.
6. Combine glacé fruit, almonds, honey, and 1 tablespoon wine. Spoon into peach cups. Chill.

6 to 8 servings

729 *Stuffed Peaches*

½ cup almond macaroon crumbs
6 large firm peaches
½ cup blanched almonds, chopped
2 tablespoons sugar
1 tablespoon chopped candied orange peel
⅓ cup sherry or Marsala
2 tablespoons sugar

1. Using an electric blender, grind enough almond macaroons to make ½ cup crumbs. Set crumbs aside.
2. Rinse, peel, and cut peaches into halves. Remove pit and a small portion of the pulp around cavity.
3. Combine and mix macaroon crumbs, chopped almonds, 2 tablespoons sugar, and orange peel.
4. Lightly fill peach halves with mixture. Put two halves together and fasten with wooden picks. Place in baking dish.
5. Pour sherry over peaches and sprinkle remaining sugar over peaches.
6. Bake at 350°F 15 minutes and serve either hot or cold.

6 servings

730 *Port Wine Molds*

1 envelope unflavored gelatin
1¼ cups sparkling water
½ cup ruby port
⅓ cup sugar

1. Soften gelatin in ½ cup of the sparkling water. Dissolve over hot water.
2. Combine remaining sparkling water, wine, and sugar; stir until sugar is dissolved. Mix in the gelatin.
3. Pour into 6 individual molds and chill until firm.
4. Unmold gelatin onto a chilled serving plate. Serve as a meat accompaniment.

6 servings

731 *Sherry Elegance*

3 envelopes unflavored gelatin
1½ cups sugar
3 cups water
1 cup plus 2 tablespoons sherry
¾ cup strained orange juice
⅓ cup strained lemon juice
9 drops red food coloring

1. Combine the gelatin and sugar in a large saucepan; mix well. Add water and stir over low heat until gelatin and sugar are dissolved.
2. Remove from heat and blend in remaining ingredients. Pour mixture into a 1½-quart fancy mold or a pretty china bowl. Chill until firm.
3. To serve, unmold gelatin onto chilled platter or serve in china bowl without unmolding. Serve with whipped cream or whipped dessert topping, if desired.

6 to 8 servings

732 *Glazed Apple Tart in Wheat Germ Crust*

Wheat Germ Crust (see recipe)
8 medium apples
1 cup red port
1 cup water
⅓ cup honey
2 tablespoons lemon juice
⅛ teaspoon salt
3 drops red food coloring
1 package (8 ounces) cream cheese
1 tablespoon half-and-half
1 tablespoon honey
1½ tablespoons cornstarch

1. Prepare crust and set aside to cool.
2. Pare, core, and cut apples into eighths to make 2 quarts.
3. Combine port, water, ⅓ cup honey, lemon juice, salt, and food coloring in large skillet with a cover. Add half the apples in single layer, cover, and cook slowly about 5 minutes, until apples are barely tender. Remove apples with slotted spoon and arrange in a single layer in a shallow pan. Cook remaining apples in same manner. Chill apples, saving cooking liquid for glaze.
4. Beat cream cheese with half-and-half and 1 tablespoon honey. Spread in even layer over bottom of cooled crust, saving about ¼ cup for decoration on top of tart, if desired.
5. Arrange apples over cheese.
6. Boil syrup from cooking apples down to 1 cup.
7. Mix cornstarch with 1½ tablespoons cold water. Stir into syrup, and cook, stirring, until mixture clears and thickens. Set pan in cold water, and cool quickly to room temperature. Spoon carefully over apples.
8. Chill until glaze is set before cutting.

One 10-inch tart

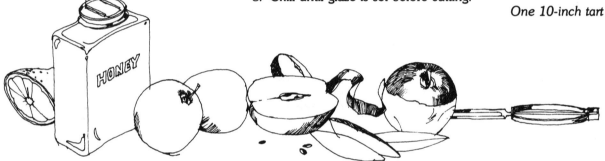

733 *Wheat Germ Crust*

1½ cups sifted all-purpose flour
3 tablespoons wheat germ
3 tablespoons packed brown sugar
¾ teaspoon salt
⅛ teaspoon cinnamon
6 tablespoons shortening
2 tablespoons butter
2 tablespoons milk (about)

1. Combine flour, wheat germ, brown sugar, salt, and cinnamon in mixing bowl.
2. Cut in shortening and butter as for pie crust.
3. Sprinkle with just enough milk to make dough stick together.
4. Press dough against bottom and up sides of 10-inch springform pan to make shell 1¾ inches deep. Prick bottom. Set on baking sheet.
5. Bake at 375°F on lowest shelf of oven for about 20 minutes, or until golden.

734 *Crêpes Superbe with Wine Sauce*

⅔ cup all-purpose flour
3 tablespoons sugar
¼ teaspoon salt
⅛ teaspoon baking soda
2 eggs

1. Combine the flour, sugar, salt, and baking soda in a mixing bowl; mix well.
2. Using an electric or hand rotary beater, beat the eggs; add milk, melted butter, orange peel and juice, and rum.
3. Combine egg mixture with dry ingredients and continue beat-

¾ cup milk
¼ cup butter or margarine,
   melted and cooled
1½ teaspoons grated orange peel
3 tablespoons orange juice
1 tablespoon rum
Wine Sauce:
1½ tablespoons butter or
   margarine
1½ teaspoons sugar
¾ cup apricot jam
1 cup port wine
3 tablespoons brandy
3 tablespoons Cointreau or rum

ing until smooth. (Batter should be consistency of heavy cream. Add more orange juice, if necessary.)

4. Heat and lightly butter the bottom of a 6- or 8-inch skillet. Pour in about 2 tablespoons of the batter and tilt skillet to spread batter evenly. Cook over medium heat until small bubbles form in the batter. Turn over and brown crêpe very lightly on second side. Repeat process using all the batter.

5. Keep crêpes warm by placing them in a pan over simmering water.

6. For wine sauce, heat butter in a chafing dish blazer over direct heat. Stir in sugar, jam, port wine, brandy, and Cointreau. Heat until mixture comes to boiling. Reduce heat and ignite the sauce.

7. To serve, roll crêpes jelly-roll fashion on serving plates; allow 2 or 3 per serving. Ladle hot wine sauce over them.

6 to 8 servings

735 *Chocolate Cream Cups*

1 package (3 ounces) chocolate
   or butterscotch pudding
1½ cups milk
¼ cups sherry
1 teaspoon instant coffee powder
⅛ teaspoon salt
½ cup whipping cream, whipped
Spiced Cream Topping:
½ cup whipping cream, whipped
1 tablespoon sugar
½ teaspoon instant coffee powder
⅛ teaspoon cinnamon

1. Prepare pudding mix according to package directions using milk and sherry for the liquid.

2. Add instant coffee and salt. Cover and chill.

3. Fold in whipped cream and spoon into 6 or 8 individual serving dishes. Serve with a bowl of Spiced Cream Topping.

4. For Spiced Cream Topping, whip cream; fold in sugar, instant coffee powder, and cinnamon.

6 to 8 servings

736 *Trifle*

Day-old pound cake (enough
   to line bottom of casserole)
½ cup brandy or rum
1 envelope unflavored gelatin
¼ cup cold water
5 egg yolks, slightly beaten
½ cup sugar
1½ cups milk, scalded
3 egg whites
¼ cup whipping cream, whipped

1. Cut the pound cake into 1-inch pieces. Arrange over bottom of a 2-quart shallow casserole. Pour brandy over cake pieces.

2. Soften gelatin in the cold water. Combine egg yolks with ¼ cup of the sugar in top of a double boiler. Add the scalded milk gradually, blending well. Cook over simmering water, stirring constantly until mixture coats a metal spoon. Immediately remove from heat and stir in gelatin until dissolved. Cool and chill until mixture becomes slightly thicker.

3. Beat the egg whites until frothy; gradually add the remaining ¼ cup sugar, beating constantly until stiff peaks are formed.

4. Spread egg whites and whipped cream over gelatin mixture and gently fold together. Turn into the casserole. Chill until firm.

5. When ready to serve, garnish with **candied cherries, slivered almonds,** and pieces of **angelica.** If desired, garnish with a border of sweetened whipped cream forced through a pastry bag and star decorating tube.

About 12 servings

737 *Walnut Cake*

2 cups (about 10 ounces) dark seedless raisins
⅔ cup sherry
4 cups sifted all-purpose flour
2 teaspoons baking powder
¼ teaspoon salt
1 teaspoon nutmeg
4 cups (about 1 pound) walnuts
1¼ cups butter or margarine
2 teaspoons grated orange peel
2 cups sugar
6 eggs, well beaten
⅔ cup orange juice
½ cup molasses

1. Lightly grease a 10-inch tube pan. Line bottom with waxed paper cut to fit pan. Lightly grease paper.
2. Put raisins into a bowl. Pour sherry over raisins. Set aside.
3. Sift together flour, baking powder, salt, and nutmeg and set aside.
4. Chop walnuts and set aside.
5. Cream butter and orange peel until softened. Add sugar gradually, creaming until fluffy after each addition.
6. Add eggs gradually, beating thoroughly after each addition. Set aside.
7. Drain raisins, reserving liquid. Mix liquid with orange juice and molasses.
8. Alternately add dry ingredients in fourths and liquid in thirds to creamed mixture, beating only until smooth after each addition. Finally, blend in the raisins and walnuts. Turn batter into pan, spreading evenly to edges.
9. Bake at 275°F 2½ hours, or until cake tests done. Cool completely on cooling rack and remove from pan.

One 10-inch tube cake

738 *Sherried Holiday Pudding*

1 package (14 ounces) gingerbread mix
¾ cup orange juice
¼ cup sherry
½ cup chopped walnuts
½ teaspoon grated orange peel
Golden Sherry Sauce (see recipe)
Hard Sauce Snowballs (see recipe)

1. Prepare gingerbread according to package directions using orange juice and sherry for liquid. Add walnuts and orange peel.
2. Turn batter into a well-greased 6-cup mold (batter should fill mold ½ to ⅔ full).
3. Bake at 350°F for 50 to 55 minutes, until pudding tests done. Serve warm with Golden Sherry Sauce and Hard Sauce Snowballs.

8 servings

Golden Sherry Sauce: Combine **½ cup each granulated and brown sugar (packed), ¼ cup whipping cream,** and **⅛ teaspoon salt** in saucepan. Heat slowly to boiling, stirring occasionally. Add **¼ cup sherry** and **1 teaspoon grated lemon peel.** Heat slightly to blend flavors. 739

About 1⅓ cups sauce

Hard Sauce Snowballs: Beat together **⅔ cup soft butter or margarine, 2 cups confectioners' sugar,** and **1 tablespoon sherry,** adding a little more sherry if more liquid is needed. Shape into small balls and roll in **flaked coconut.** 740

About 1½ cups or 16 balls

741 *New Orleans Holiday Pudding*

3 cups boiling water
1¼ cups prunes
1 cup dried apricots
1 cup sugar
1 teaspoon ground cinnamon
1 teaspoon ground nutmeg

1. Pour boiling water over prunes and apricots in a saucepan. Return to boiling, cover, and simmer about 45 minutes, or until fruit is tender. Drain and reserve 1 cup liquid. Set liquid aside until cold. Remove and discard prune pits.
2. Force prunes and apricots through a food mill or sieve into a large bowl. Stir in a mixture of the sugar, cinnamon, nutmeg,

1 teaspoon ground allspice
1 cup orange juice
3 tablespoons ruby port
3 envelopes unflavored gelatin
1½ cups golden raisins, plumped
2¼ cups candied cherries
⅓ cup diced candied citron
⅓ cup diced candied lemon peel
1½ cups walnuts, coarsely
    chopped
3 envelopes (2 ounces each)
    dessert topping mix, or 3
    cups whipping cream,
    whipped

and allspice, mixing until sugar is dissolved. Blend in orange juice and wine; mix thoroughly.

3. Soften gelatin in the 1 cup reserved liquid in a small saucepan. Stir over low heat until gelatin is dissolved. Stir into fruit-spice mixture. Chill until mixture is slightly thickened, stirring occasionally.

4. Blend raisins, cherries, citron, lemon peel, and walnuts into gelatin mixture.

5. Prepare the dessert topping according to package directions or whip the cream. Gently fold into fruit mixture, blending thoroughly. Turn into 10-inch tube pan. Chill until firm.

6. Unmold onto chilled serving plate.

20 to 24 servings

742 *Sherry Baba Ring*

1 package active dry yeast
¼ cup warm water
¼ cup hot milk
½ cup soft butter
3 tablespoons sugar
1 teaspoon salt
4 eggs
2 cups all-purpose flour
  Sherry Syrup
  Whipped cream
  Glacé fruits

1. Soften yeast in water.
2. Combine hot milk, soft butter, sugar, and salt.
3. Beat eggs. Beat in yeast mixture, then butter mixture. Beat in flour thoroughly to make a smooth, thick batter.
4. Turn into a well-buttered 2-quart mold with tube center. Let rise in a warm place until almost doubled in bulk, 1 to 1½ hours.
5. Bake at 375°F for 30 minutes, or until cake tests done. Make sherry syrup while baba is baking.
6. Remove baked baba from oven and allow to cool in pan 10 minutes. Turn baba onto a serving plate. Prick sides and top with tines of a fork. Slowly baste with sherry syrup. Let stand until syrup is almost absorbed.
7. Fill center of ring with slightly sweetened whipped cream and garnish with glacé fruits.

About 8 servings

Sherry Syrup: Simmer 1½ cups sugar with ⅔ cup water and 1 tablespoon grated orange peel 10 minutes. Mix in ½ cup California Cream Sherry and ¼ cup apricot-pineapple jam. Simmer 5 minutes; cool.

743 *Biscuit Tortoni*

⅓ cup confectioners' sugar
1 tablespoon sherry
½ cup plus 2 tablespoons fine dry
    macaroon crumbs
1 cup whipping cream, whipped
1 egg white

1. Fold sugar, sherry, and ½ cup macaroon crumbs into whipped cream until well blended.
2. Beat egg white until stiff, not dry, peaks are formed. Fold into whipped cream mixture.
3. Divide mixture equally into ten 2-inch heavy paper baking cups and sprinkle with the remaining crumbs. Freeze until firm.

10 servings

744 *Sherry Almond Chiffon Pie*

1 unbaked 9-inch pastry shell
¼ cup blanched almonds, toasted
    (see Note)
⅓ cup sugar
1 envelope unflavored gelatin
½ teaspoon salt
3 egg yolks, slightly beaten
1¾ cups milk
½ cup chilled heavy cream
3 egg whites
¼ cup sugar
3 tablespoons sherry
½ teaspoon almond extract
1 ounce (1 square) unsweetened
    chocolate

1. Chill a bowl and a rotary beater in refrigerator.
2. Bake pastry shell and set aside to cool.
3. Coarsely chop toasted almonds and set aside.
4. Mix ⅓ cup sugar, gelatin, and salt thoroughly in the top of a double boiler.
5. Beat egg yolks with milk until blended; add the milk mixture gradually to gelatin mixture in double boiler top, stirring constantly until blended.
6. Set over boiling water and cook, stirring constantly, until gelatin is completely dissolved, about 5 minutes.
7. Remove the gelatin mixture from heat. Cool; chill in refrigerator or over ice and water until the mixture mounds when dropped from a spoon. (If mixture is placed over ice and water, stir frequently; if placed in refrigerator, stir occasionally.)
8. Beat cream until medium consistency (piles softly) using chilled bowl and beater. Set whipped cream in refrigerator while preparing the meringue.
9. Using a clean beater, beat egg whites until frothy; add ¼ cup sugar gradually, beating well after each addition. Beat until stiff peaks are formed.
10. Fold the meringue and whipped cream into custard mixture with sherry and almond extract. Fold in the chopped toasted almonds. Turn into cooled pie shell.
11. Chill in refrigerator 2 to 3 hours, or until firm. When ready to serve, top with chocolate curls made by pulling chocolate across a shredder.

One 9-inch pie

Note: To toast almonds, place nuts in a shallow baking dish or pie pan and, if desired, brush lightly with butter, margarine, or cooking oil. Heat in a 350°F oven until delicately browned; move and turn occasionally. Or put nuts into a heavy skillet in which butter (about 1 tablespoon per cup of nuts) has been heated. Heat until nuts are lightly browned, moving and turning constantly.

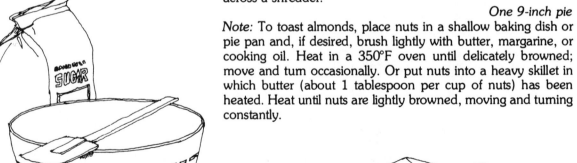

Fondue

745 Cheese Fondue with Apples

1 can (11 ounces) condensed Cheddar cheese soup
2 packages (8 ounces each) cream cheese, softened and cut into pieces
1 cup dairy sour cream
½ teaspoon salt
½ teaspoon dry mustard
⅛ teaspoon garlic powder
½ teaspoon Worcestershire sauce
2 drops Tabasco
¼ cup sherry
4 or 5 apples
Lemon juice for dipping apple slices

1. In a fondue pot or chafing dish, combine soup with cream cheese, blending well.
2. Add remaining ingredients, except apples; mix well. Cook over low heat, stirring occasionally, until cheese melts and mixture is smooth.
3. Meanwhile, slice apples and dip in lemon juice.
4. Keep fondue warm while dipping apple slices.

About 4½ cups fondue

746 Cheesy Tuna-Onion Fondue

2 cans (6½ or 7 ounces each) tuna
1 pound pasteurized process American cheese, shredded (about 4 cups)
1 cup milk
3 tablespoons chopped parsley
1 tablespoon instant minced onion
Unsalted crackers
Corn chips
Potato chips

1. Drain tuna and flake, if desired.
2. Put shredded cheese into a saucepan and set over medium heat. Pour milk over the cheese. Stir until cheese is completely melted.
3. Mix in tuna, parsley, and onion. Heat thoroughly, stirring constantly.
4. Turn into a fondue saucepan and keep warm while serving with bowls of crackers, corn chips, and potato chips for dippers.

6 servings

747 Tomato Bagna Cauda

1 can (8 ounces) tomato sauce
¼ cup cooking oil
1 tablespoon anchovy paste
1 clove garlic, crushed in a garlic
   press
⅛ teaspoon pepper
¼ teaspoon tarragon leaves
   Fresh mushrooms, broccoli and
      cauliflower flowerets, celery
      sticks, carrot sticks,
      zucchini strips

1. In a fondue pot or chafing dish, stir together all ingredients except fresh vegetables. Stir over low heat until smooth and thoroughly heated.
2. Keep hot and serve fresh vegetables as dunkers.

About 1¼ cups sauce

748 Swiss Cheese Fondue

1 tablespoon cornstarch
2 tablespoons kirsch
1 clove garlic, halved
2 cups Neuchâtel or other dry
   white wine
1 pound natural Swiss cheese,
   shredded (about 4 cups)
   Freshly ground black pepper to
      taste
   Ground nutmeg to taste
1 loaf French bread, cut into
   1-inch cubes

1. Mix cornstarch and kirsch in a small bowl; set aside.
2. Rub the inside of a nonmetal fondue pot with cut surface of garlic. Pour in wine; place over medium heat until wine is about to simmer (do not boil).
3. Add cheese in small amounts to the hot wine, stirring constantly until cheese is melted. Heat cheese-wine mixture until bubbly.
4. Blend in cornstarch mixture and continue stirring while cooking 5 minutes, or until fondue begins to bubble; add seasoning.
5. Dip bread cubes in fondue. Keep the fondue gently bubbling throughout serving time.

About 6 servings

749 Brussels Sprouts with Dunking Sauce

2¼ cups chicken broth (dissolve
   2 chicken bouillon cubes in
   2¼ cups boiling water)
1 pound fresh Brussels sprouts
   (or two 10-ounce packages
   frozen Brussels sprouts)
2 tablespoons butter or margarine
1 tablespoon flour
1 teaspoon salt
½ teaspoon caraway seed
¼ teaspoon cayenne pepper
1 cup milk
1½ cups dairy sour cream

1. Heat broth in a saucepan until boiling. Add Brussels sprouts and boil, uncovered, 5 minutes. Cover and boil 5 to 10 minutes, or until just tender. (Cook frozen Brussels sprouts in the chicken broth following package directions.)
2. Meanwhile, heat butter in a fondue saucepan; stir in a mixture of flour, salt, caraway seed, and cayenne pepper. Heat until mixture bubbles. Add milk, cooking and stirring until mixture comes to boiling. Boil 1 to 2 minutes, stirring constantly.
3. Reduce heat and stir in sour cream. Heat thoroughly (do not boil). Keep sauce hot during serving.
4. Drain cooked Brussels sprouts and turn into a serving dish. Spear each sprout and dunk into the sauce.

About 8 servings

750 *Cheese Rabbit Fondue*

1 small clove garlic
2 cups beer
1 pound sharp Cheddar cheese, shredded (about 4 cups)
3 tablespoons flour
1 teaspoon Worcestershire sauce
½ teaspoon dry mustard
2 tablespoons chopped chives or green onion top (optional)
1 loaf sourdough French bread, cut into 1-inch cubes

1. Rub inside of a nonmetal fondue pot with garlic; discard garlic. Heat beer in the pot until almost boiling.
2. Dredge cheese in flour and add about ½ cup at a time, stirring until cheese is melted and blended before adding more.
3. When mixture is smooth and thickened, stir in Worcestershire sauce and dry mustard.
4. Sprinkle chives on top and serve with bread cubes. Keep fondue warm while serving.

4 to 6 servings

751 *Cheesy Potato Fondue*

3 cups sliced pared potatoes
3 cups water
1 tablespoon butter
1 tablespoon flour
1½ cups milk
¾ cup coarsely grated Parmesan or Romano cheese
2 egg yolks, fork beaten
¾ teaspoon salt
⅛ teaspoon cayenne pepper
Cooked ham, cut into cubes
Cherry tomatoes, halved
Zucchini slices

1. Cook potatoes in a small amount of water until soft (about 15 minutes). Drain, reserving the water; sieve or rice potatoes.
2. Melt butter in a large fondue saucepan. Add flour and cook 1 or 2 minutes without browning.
3. Stir in potatoes with reserved water and milk. Blend until smooth and simmer 10 minutes, stirring occasionally.
4. Stir in cheese and beat in egg yolks. Continue beating until mixture is smooth, hot, and thick. Stir in salt and cayenne.
5. Serve warm with ham, tomatoes, and zucchini for dippers.

4 to 6 servings

752 *Buttermilk Fondue*

1 pound Swiss cheese, shredded (about 4 cups)
3 tablespoons cornstarch
½ teaspoon salt
⅛ teaspoon white pepper
¼ teaspoon dry mustard
2 cups buttermilk
1 clove garlic, split in half
1 loaf dark rye bread, cut into 1-inch cubes

1. Toss cheese with a mixture of cornstarch, salt, pepper, and dry mustard. Set aside.
2. In a fondue saucepan, heat buttermilk with garlic over low heat. When hot, remove garlic and add cheese; stir constantly until cheese is melted.
3. Keep fondue warm over low heat while dipping bread cubes.

4 to 6 servings

753 *Beef à la Fondue*

2 teaspoons butter
1 tablespoon flour
½ cup dry white wine
8 ounces Swiss cheese, shredded
    (about 2 cups)
1½ pounds beef top sirloin steak,
    cut into bite-size pieces
Oil for deep frying
Sauces for dipping

1. Melt butter in top of a double boiler over boiling water. Remove from heat; add flour and part of wine, mixing to a smooth paste.
2. Add remaining wine; heat over water until thickened. Add cheese; heat until melted. Keep warm.
3. At serving time, fill a metal fondue pot half full with oil. Heat oil to 375°F. Cook a cube of beef in the hot oil and dip it into the cheese sauce, and then into other sauces and side dishes. **Horseradish sauce** (sour cream and horseradish), **tartar sauce, mustard sauce, chopped chives** and **chutney** are suitable sauces and accompaniments. These should be in small individual dishes clustered around each place setting.

4 servings

754 *Fondue Bourguignonne*

Sauces for dipping (three or
    or more)
Cooking oil
1½ to 2 pounds beef tenderloin
    or sirloin, cut into 1-inch pieces

1. Prepare sauces and set aside until serving time.
2. Fill a metal fondue pot half full with oil. Heat oil to 375ºF. Spear pieces of meat with dipping forks and plunge into hot oil, cooking until done as desired.
3. Dip cooked meat in desired sauce and transfer to plate. Place another piece of meat in hot oil to cook while eating cooked meat.

4 servings

755 *Velvet Lemon Sauce*

2 eggs
½ teaspoon salt
2 tablespoons lemon juice
½ cup butter, softened
Few grains white pepper
½ slice onion
½ cup hot water

1. Put eggs, salt, lemon juice, butter, pepper, and onion into an electric blender container. Blend until smooth. Add hot water, a little at a time, while blending.
2. Turn into top of double boiler. Cook over simmering water, stirring constantly until thickened (about 10 minutes).

About 1½ cups sauce

756 *Rémoulade Sauce*

1 cup mayonnaise
1½ teaspoons prepared mustard
¼ teaspoon anchovy paste
2 tablespoons finely chopped dill
    pickles
1 tablespoon chopped capers
1½ teaspoons minced parsley
½ teaspoon finely crushed chervil
½ teaspoon crushed tarragon

Blend all ingredients in a small bowl. Cover; chill thoroughly.

About 1 cup sauce

757 *Paprika Sauce*

2 tablespoons butter or margarine
2 tablespoons flour
½ teaspoon salt
⅛ teaspoon pepper
1 cup milk
1 teaspoon minced onion
Few grains nutmeg
2 to 3 teaspoons paprika

1. Heat butter in a saucepan. Blend in flour, salt, and pepper; heat and stir until bubbly.
2. Gradually add milk, stirring until smooth. Bring to boiling; cook and stir 1 to 2 minutes longer.
3. Blend in onion, nutmeg, and paprika.

About 1 cup sauce

Jiffy Sauces for Fondue Bourguignonne

Onion-Chili: Combine ½ envelope (about 1½ ounces) dry onion soup mix and ¾ cup boiling water in a saucepan. Cover partially and cook 10 minutes. Adding gradually, mix in 1½ tablespoons flour mixed with ¼ cup water. Bring to boiling, stirring constantly; cook until thickened. Remove from heat; mix in 2 tablespoons chili sauce. 758

Onion-Horseradish: Blend ½ envelope (about 1½ ounces) dry onion soup mix, 1 tablespoon milk, 2 teaspoons prepared horseradish, and desired amount of snipped parsley into 1 cup dairy sour cream. 759

Horseradish: Blend 3 tablespoons prepared horseradish, 1 teaspoon grated onion, and ½ teaspoon lemon juice with 1 cup mayonnaise. 760

Curry: Blend 1 tablespoon curry powder, 1 teaspoon grated onion, and ½ teaspoon lemon juice with 1 cup mayonnaise. 761

Mustard: Blend 1 tablespoon half-and-half with 1 cup mayonnaise and stir in prepared mustard to taste. 762

Caper: Mix 1 tablespoon chopped capers and 1 cup bottled tartar sauce; blend in 1 tablespoon half-and-half. 763

Béarnaise: Blend 1 tablespoon parsley flakes, ½ teaspoon grated onion, ¼ teaspoon crushed tarragon, and 1 teaspoon tarragon vinegar into hollandaise sauce prepared from a mix according to package directions. 764

Barbecue: Blend prepared horseradish to taste with a bottled barbecue sauce. 765

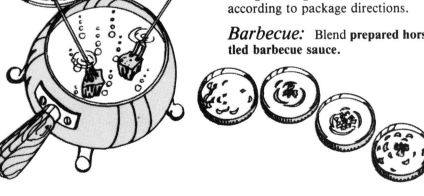

766 *Chicken Fondue*

Cooking oil
1 teaspoon salt
2 pounds chicken breasts, skinned, boned, and cut into ¾-inch cubes
Sauces for dipping

1. Pour cooking oil into a metal fondue pot, not more than half full. Heat on range to 425°F. Add salt.
2. Transfer to fondue heating element. Spear chicken cube with a fondue fork and cook in hot oil 2 to 3 minutes.
3. Dip in desired sauce.

4 servings

Note: To maintain a high enough cooking temperature, it may be necessary to return pot to kitchen range and heat oil.

767 *Easy Tomato Sauce*

1 medium clove garlic, crushed in a garlic press
1 teaspoon oregano
½ teaspoon thyme
1 can (8 ounces) tomato sauce
3 tablespoons grated Parmesan cheese
Salt and pepper to taste

Combine all ingredients in a saucepan and simmer, uncovered, 5 minutes.

768 *Béarnaise Sauce*

4 egg yolks
1 cup butter
1 tablespoon lemon juice
1 tablespoon tarragon vinegar
¼ teaspoon salt
1 teaspoon chopped parsley
1 teaspoon onion juice
Dash cayenne pepper

1. Blend egg yolks with a third of the butter in a fondue saucepan. Place over low heat. Add remaining butter as sauce thickens, stirring constantly.
2. Remove from heat and add remaining ingredients.

1 cup sauce

769 *Jiffy Curry Sauce*

⅔ cup condensed cream of celery soup
1½ teaspoons instant minced onion
½ teaspoon curry powder
6 tablespoons milk
1 egg, slightly beaten
1½ teaspoons butter or margarine

1. Combine soup, onion, and curry powder in a fondue saucepan; stir until well blended. Stir in milk. Heat thoroughly over low heat, stirring occasionally.
2. Stir about ¼ cup of the hot sauce into the beaten egg; immediately return mixture to fondue saucepan.
3. Cook over low heat 3 to 5 minutes, stirring occasionally to keep mixture cooking evenly. Blend in the butter.

About 1 cup sauce

770 Sloppy Joe Fondue

1 tablespoon butter or margarine
1 pound ground beef
1 envelope (about 1½ ounces)
    Sloppy Joe seasoning mix
1 can (6 ounces) tomato paste
    Water
⅓ cup chopped celery
¼ cup chopped green pepper

1. Heat butter in a large skillet. Add meat and brown, breaking into small pieces with a spoon. Stir in seasoning mix, tomato paste, and water called for in package directions. Mix in celery and green pepper. Bring to boiling, stirring occasionally.
2. Reduce heat, cover, and simmer 10 minutes, stirring occasionally.
3. Turn into a fondue saucepan and keep warm.
4. To serve, spoon over halves of **toasted buttered buns** or **English muffins.**

4 servings

771 Oriental Chicken Fondue

3 cups chicken broth or bouillon
2 pounds chicken breasts, skinned, boned, and cut into paper-thin strips
    Sauces for dipping

1. Heat chicken broth to boiling. Adjust heat so broth will continue to boil gently throughout dipping.
2. Spear chicken strip with a fondue fork and cook in boiling broth 2 to 3 minutes, or until chicken turns white and is tender.
3. Transfer cooked piece of chicken to plate and start cooking another before dipping in desired sauce.

4 servings

772 Teriyaki Sauce

½ cup pineapple juice
¼ cup brown sugar
2 tablespoons soy sauce
1 tablespoon cooking oil
¾ teaspoon ground ginger
¼ teaspoon salt
1 clove garlic, minced

Combine all ingredients in a saucepan. Heat to blend flavors.
About ⅔ cup sauce

773 Tangy Plum Sauce

1 can or jar (17 ounces) purple plums, drained (reserve syrup)
½ cup frozen orange juice concentrate, thawed
½ teaspoon Worcestershire sauce

Pit plums, and force through a sieve or food mill into a bowl. Blend in reserved syrup, orange juice, and Worcestershire sauce. Heat just to blend flavors.
About 1½ cups sauce

774 Mustard Sauce

1 cup undiluted evaporated milk
2 tablespoons dry mustard
¼ cup sugar
3 egg yolks, well beaten
⅓ cup cider vinegar

1. Scald evaporated milk in top of a double boiler over boiling water. Blend a small amount of hot evaporated milk with dry mustard until smooth; return to remaining evaporated milk along with sugar and stir until sugar is dissolved. Add a small amount of the hot mixture to the beaten egg yolks, blending well, and return to double-boiler top.
2. Cook over boiling water about 3 minutes, stirring constantly.
3. Remove from heat. Mix in vinegar. Serve hot.
About 1¼ cups sauce

775 *Colby-Crab Fondue*

⅓ cup butter
¾ cup dry white wine
1 pound colby cheese, shredded (about 4 cups)
2 tablespoons flour
1 can (6½ ounces) crab meat
⅛ teaspoon garlic powder
1 teaspoon salt
⅛ teaspoon Tabasco
1 teaspoon prepared mustard
1 teaspoon bottled steak sauce
1½ teaspoons Worcestershire sauce

1. Melt butter in a nonmetal fondue pot. Stir in wine and heat until bubbles appear around the edges.
2. Toss cheese with flour and stir into the hot mixture, a handful at a time. Heat and stir until completely melted.
3. Rinse, drain, and flake crab meat. Stir into cheese mixture with remaining ingredients. Heat thoroughly, stirring occasionally.
4. To serve, dip cubes of **French bread** in the warm fondue.

4 servings

776 *Deep-Fried Zucchini*

1¼ cups all-purpose flour
1 teaspoon salt
¼ teaspoon pepper
2 eggs, well beaten
¾ cup milk
1 teaspoon Worcestershire sauce
1 tablespoon butter or margarine, melted
   Oil for deep frying
6 medium (about 2 pounds) zucchini, cut in halves crosswise and into ¾-inch sticks lengthwise

1. Blend flour, salt, and pepper in a bowl. Add a mixture of eggs, milk, Worcestershire sauce, and butter; beat just until smooth.
2. Heat oil in a fondue pot to 365°F.
3. Dip zucchini sticks into batter, using a fork to coat evenly. Allow any excess coating to drip off.
4. Fry 2 to 3 minutes, or until golden brown. Lift from oil and drain a few seconds before removing to absorbent paper.
5. Sprinkle with **salt.**

6 servings

777 *Orange Chocolate Fondue*

2 packages (3¼ ounces each) chocolate pudding and pie filling
3 cups orange juice
1 cup milk
2 tablespoons butter or margarine
   Marshmallows
   Pound cake cubes
   Ladyfingers, cut in thirds
   Maraschino cherries with stems
   Walnut halves

1. In a large saucepan, mix together pudding, orange juice, and milk. Cook over low heat, stirring constantly, until mixture thickens and comes to boiling. Remove from heat.
2. Stir in butter until melted. Pour mixture into a fondue pot. Serve with marshmallows, cake cubes, ladyfingers, cherries, and walnuts.

8 servings

778 *Banana Split Fondue*

2 king-size chocolate crunch
    candy bars (about 6½
    ounces each)
1 cup milk
    Ripe bananas, cut into bite-
    size pieces
    Large marshmallows
    Maraschino cherries with
    stems

1. Break candy bars into pieces over fondue saucepan. Pour milk over candy-bar pieces.
2. Place saucepan over low heat just long enough to warm mixture. Stir occasionally until chocolate melts. If mixture becomes too thick for dipping, stir in 1 to 2 tablespoons milk.
3. Spear banana pieces and marshmallows; dip in melted chocolate. Cherries may be held by the stems for dipping.

4 to 6 servings

779 *Chocolate Fondue*

4 ounces (4 squares) unsweetened
    chocolate
1 cup sugar
½ cup whipping cream
5 tablespoons butter or margarine
2 tablespoons orange liqueur
½ teaspoon vanilla extract
    Assorted dippers (marshmallows,
    strawberries with hulls, apple
    slices, banana chunks,
    mandarin orange segments,
    cake cubes)

1. Cut up chocolate and melt in fondue pot over low heat. Stir in sugar, whipping cream, and butter.
2. Cook over low heat until thickened (about 5 minutes), stirring constantly. Stir in orange liqueur and vanilla extract.
3. Place over very low heat to keep warm while dipping.

4 servings

780 *Eggnog Fondue*

2 eggs, beaten
2 tablespoons sugar or honey
⅛ teaspoon salt
1½ cups milk
½ teaspoon vanilla extract
3 tablespoons arrowroot
3 tablespoons dark rum
    Nutmeg
    Fruitcake, cut into ¾-inch
    pieces

1. Beat together eggs, sugar, and salt. Stir in milk and vanilla extract.
2. Pour eggnog into a nonmetal fondue pot. Mix arrowroot with 1 tablespoon rum and stir into the eggnog.
3. Cook over medium heat until mixture thickens, stirring occasionally. Stir in remaining rum.
4. Keep fondue warm while dipping fruitcake pieces.

6 to 8 servings

781 *Teriyaki*

1 teaspoon ground ginger
⅓ cup soy sauce
¼ cup honey
1 clove garlic, minced
1 teaspoon grated onion
1 pound beef sirloin tip, cut into
  2x½x¼-inch strips
2 to 3 tablespoons cooking oil
1 tablespoon cornstarch
½ cup water
⅛ teaspoon red food coloring

1. Blend ginger, soy sauce, honey, garlic, and onion in a bowl. Add meat; marinate about 1 hour.
2. Remove meat, reserving marinade, and brown quickly on all sides in the hot oil in a large wok. Remove meat from wok.
3. Stir a blend of cornstarch, water, and food coloring into the reserved marinade and pour into wok. Bring rapidly to boiling and cook 2 to 3 minutes, stirring constantly.
4. Add meat to thickened marinade to glaze; remove and drain on wire rack.
5. Insert a frilled wooden pick into each meat strip and serve with the thickened marinade.

About 24 appetizers

WOK

782 Fried Shrimp with Dunking Sauce

2 pounds uncooked shrimp
Salt
2 eggs, slightly beaten
1 can (3 ounces) chow mein
noodles, finely crushed
Oil for deep frying
Dunking Sauce or Zesty Sauce

1. Wash shrimp; remove shells (not tails) and black veins. Drain shrimp and sprinkle with salt.
2. Dip each shrimp into beaten egg and then into finely crushed chow mein noodles, coating well.
3. Pour oil into a wok, filling not more than a third full yet at least 1 inch deep. Heat to 375 °F.
4. Drop shrimp, about 6 at a time, into hot oil. Fry, turning as necessary, until golden, and drain on absorbent paper.
5. Serve hot with desired sauce.

About 60 appetizers

Dunking Sauce: Add enough water to **2 tablespoons dry mustard** to make a smooth paste. Blend in ½ **cup soy sauce.**

Zesty Sauce: Blend **1 tablespoon ground ginger,** ¼ **clove garlic** (crushed in a garlic press), ¼ **cup water, 2 tablespoons sugar,** and ½ **cup soy sauce.**

783 Fried Oriental Shrimp Balls

2 pounds fresh uncooked shrimp
1 can (5 ounces) water chestnuts,
drained and coarsely chopped
1 egg, slightly beaten
1 tablespoon cornstarch
¼ teaspoon sherry extract
½ teaspoon salt
Oil for deep frying

Sauce:

1 tablespoon cornstarch
¼ teaspoon sugar
1 tablespoon soy sauce
¾ cup chicken bouillon

1. Wash, shell, devein, and finely chop shrimp. Combine with water chestnuts, egg, cornstarch, sherry extract, and salt. Form into balls about 1 inch in diameter.
2. Pour oil into a wok, filling it not more than a third full, but at least 1 inch deep. Heat oil to 375ºF. Fry shrimp balls about 6 at a time until golden brown. Drain on paper towels and keep shrimp balls warm in a low oven, if necessary.
3. Combine ingredients for sauce in a small fondue pot. Cook over low heat until thickened, stirring constantly.
4. Keep the sauce warm and serve with hot shrimp balls.

About 4 dozen appetizers

784 *Peanut Cocktail Fritters*

½ cup boiling water
¼ cup peanut oil
¼ teaspoon salt
½ cup flour
2 eggs
1 cup finely chopped dry roasted
  peanuts
Peanut oil for deep frying
Salt

1. In a saucepan, combine water, ¼ cup peanut oil, and ¼ teaspoon salt. Bring to a full boil. Add flour all at once, and stir vigorously over low heat until mixture forms a ball and leaves sides of pan. Remove from heat.
2. Add eggs, one at a time, beating thoroughly after each is added. Stir in chopped peanuts, blending well. Form into 1-inch balls.
3. Heat oil to 365°F in a wok. Fry fritters, about 10 at a time, until golden brown (3 to 4 minutes).
4. Drain on paper towels, sprinkle with salt, and serve while hot.

5 dozen fritters

785 *Beef Sub Gum Soup*

½ pound beef round, cut into
  small cubes
1 tablespoon cooking oil
1 can (20 ounces) Chinese
  vegetables, drained
2 cans (10½ ounces each) condensed beef broth or bouillon
2 cups water
¼ cup uncooked rice
2 tablespoons soy sauce
¼ teaspoon monosodium glutamate
⅛ teaspoon pepper
1 egg, beaten

1. In a large wok, brown beef in hot oil. Chop vegetables and add to the browned meat with remaining ingredients, except egg.
2. Bring soup to boiling, stirring to blend. Cover and simmer 40 minutes.
3. Remove soup from heat and slowly stir in the egg. Let stand until egg is set.

About 6 servings

786 *Chinese Chicken-Mushroom Soup*

1 pound chicken breasts
½ teaspoon salt
1 tablespoon cooking oil
10 medium-size mushrooms, sliced
4 chicken bouillon cubes
4 cups hot water
1 tablespoon cornstarch
3 tablespoons cold water
1 tablespoon soy sauce
2 tablespoons lemon juice

1. Bone chicken breasts, remove skin, and cut into ¼-inch-wide strips, 1½ to 2 inches long. Sprinkle with salt and let stand 30 minutes.
2. Heat oil in a wok and sauté mushrooms a few minutes until golden. Remove from wok. Dissolve bouillon cubes in hot water and set aside.
3. Mix cornstarch with cold water. Stir in soy sauce. Combine with chicken bouillon in the wok. Bring to boiling, add chicken pieces, and simmer, covered, 5 minutes.
4. Add mushrooms and lemon juice to soup, adding more salt, if necessary. Heat gently without boiling.
5. Serve with a thin **lemon slice** in each bowl.

5 servings

787 *Carrot Nibblers*

1	pound carrots
2 to 3	tablespoons cooking oil
2	large cloves garlic, minced
1	tablespoon chopped onion
¼	cup vinegar
1½	teaspoons salt
⅛	teaspoon pepper
½	teaspoon dry mustard
1	tablespoon whole pickling spices
1	onion, thinly sliced

1. Wash and pare carrots. Cut into 3x¼-inch strips, and set aside.
2. Heat oil in a large wok. Stir in garlic and onion and cook over low heat about 5 minutes. Stir in vinegar, salt, pepper, dry mustard, spices (tied in cheesecloth), and carrots.
3. Cook, covered, over low heat about 10 minutes, or until carrots are crisp-tender. Remove spice bag and turn carrots into a shallow dish. Top with sliced onion, cover, and refrigerate overnight.

8 servings

788 *Cheese Balls*

4	ounces Cheddar cheese, shredded (about 1 cup)
1	teaspoon flour
¼	teaspoon salt
	Dash pepper
1	egg white
	Oil for deep frying

1. Mix cheese, flour, salt, and pepper.
2. Beat egg white to stiff, not dry, peaks. Fold beaten egg white into cheese mixture. Form into small balls, using a rounded tablespoon of the mixture for each.
3. Heat the oil to 365° F in a wok. Fry the cheese balls, a few at a time, until brown. Serve while warm.

12 cheese balls

789 *Ham Nibbles*

2	cups ground cooked ham
1	can (12 ounces) vacuum-packed whole kernel corn, drained
2	cups cheese-cracker crumbs
¼	cup mayonnaise
2	eggs, well beaten
	Oil for deep frying

1. Combine the ham, corn, 1 cup of the crumbs, mayonnaise, and eggs.
2. Shape mixture into ¾- to 1-inch balls. Roll in remaining crumbs. Set aside about 30 minutes.
3. Fill a large wok with oil not more than a third full, and heat to 375°F. Fry balls uncrowded in hot fat 2 minutes, or until browned. Remove to drain on absorbent paper.
4. Serve on a heated platter accompanied with picks.

About 7 dozen appetizers

790 *Chinese Cabbage Soup*

1 chicken breast (¾ pound),
    cooked
7 cups chicken broth
6 cups sliced Chinese cabbage
    (celery cabbage)
1 teaspoon soy sauce
1¼ teaspoons salt
¼ teaspoon pepper

1. Cut chicken into strips about ⅛ inch wide and 1½ to 2 inches long. Combine with chicken broth in a large wok and heat only until hot. Add Chinese cabbage and cook 3 to 4 minutes (only until cabbage is crisp-tender; do not overcook).
2. Stir in soy sauce, salt, and pepper. Serve hot.

6 servings

Note: If desired, romaine may be substituted for the cabbage. Reduce cooking time to 1 minute

791 *Oriental Soup*

2 tablespoons cooking oil
2 cups diagonally sliced celery
½ cup chopped onion
1 can (16 ounces) bean sprouts,
    drained
1 can (5 ounces) water chestnuts,
    drained and chopped
2 quarts rich beef broth (made
    with bouillon cubes, if desired)
Salt and pepper to taste

1. In a large wok, heat oil and stir in celery and onion. Cook until crisp-tender, stirring frequently.
2. Stir in remaining ingredients and heat thoroughly.
3. Serve with crisp chow mein noodles sprinkled over individual bowls, if desired.

6 servings

792 *Spanish Chicken Soup with Sausage*

1 pound bulk pork sausage
1 teaspoon sage
1 teaspoon ground thyme
¼ teaspoon salt
½ cup finely chopped almonds
1 onion, cut into 8 wedges
1 large clove garlic, minced
1 can (10½ ounces) condensed
    chicken broth
1 can (10½ ounces) condensed
    cream of chicken soup
1 cup dry white wine
¼ cup dry sherry
¾ cup diced green pepper
1 bay leaf
⅛ teaspoon Tabasco
½ cup slivered almonds, toasted
    (see Note)
1 ounce (1 square) semisweet
    chocolate, shaved

1. Mix sausage with sage, ½ teaspoon thyme, salt, and the chopped almonds. Shape into balls about 1½ inches in diameter.
2. In a large wok, cook the meatballs over medium heat until evenly browned and thoroughly cooked. Remove meatballs from wok.
3. Stir in onion and garlic; sauté 5 minutes. Add chicken broth, condensed soup, wines, green pepper, bay leaf, Tabasco, and remaining thyme. Salt to taste.
4. Cover and simmer about 5 minutes, stirring occasionally. Uncover and simmer 10 minutes. Ladle into soup bowls and garnish with slivered almonds and shaved chocolate.

4 servings

Note: To toast almonds, spread in a shallow pan. Heat in a 350°F oven or on top of range, stirring occasionally, until almonds are lightly browned.

793 *Bacon 'n' Egg Croquettes*

3 tablespoons butter or margarine
2 tablespoons chopped onion
3 tablespoons flour
½ teaspoon salt
⅛ teaspoon pepper
¾ teaspoon dry mustard
¾ cup milk
6 hard-cooked eggs, coarsely chopped
8 slices bacon, cooked and finely crumbled
1 egg, fork beaten
2 tablespoons water
⅓ cup fine dry bread or cracker crumbs
Oil for deep frying

1. Melt butter in a saucepan; stir in onion and cook about 2 minutes, or until tender. Stir in a mixture of flour, salt, pepper, and dry mustard. Heat until bubbly. Add milk gradually, stirring constantly. Cook and stir until mixture forms a ball.
2. Remove from heat and stir in chopped eggs and crumbled bacon. Refrigerate about 1 hour, or until chilled.
3. Shape into 8 croquettes (balls or cones). Mix egg with water. Roll croquettes in crumbs, dip into egg, and roll again in crumbs.
4. Fill a large wok no more than half full with oil. Slowly heat to 385°F. Fry croquettes without crowding in the hot oil 2 minutes, or until golden. Remove croquettes with a slotted spoon; drain over fat and place on paper towel to drain.

4 servings

Herbed Egg Croquettes: Follow recipe for Bacon 'n' Egg Croquettes. Decrease mustard to ¼ teaspoon and bacon to 4 slices. Add ½ **teaspoon summer savory**, crushed, with mustard and **4 teaspoons snipped parsley** with chopped egg.

794 *Eggs Pisto Style*

1 large clove garlic
1 cup thinly sliced onion
1 cup slivered green pepper
½ cup olive oil
1 cup thin raw potato strips
1 tablespoon chopped parsley
⅓ cup (2 ounces) diced cooked ham
2 cups small cubes yellow summer squash
2 cups finely cut peeled ripe tomatoes
2 teaspoons salt
1 teaspoon sugar
⅛ teaspoon pepper
6 eggs, beaten

1. Add garlic, onion, and green pepper to heated olive oil in a large wok; cook until softened, then remove garlic.
2. Add remaining ingredients except eggs to wok; cook over medium heat, stirring frequently, about 10 minutes, or until squash is just tender.
3. Pour beaten eggs into vegetables, and cook over low heat. With a spatula, lift mixture from bottom and sides as it thickens, allowing uncooked portion to flow to bottom. Cook until eggs are thick and creamy.

6 servings

795 *Cottage Cheese Croquettes*

3 tablespoons butter or margarine
¼ cup flour
1 teaspoon salt
Dash pepper
½ teaspoon dill weed
1 cup milk
1 teaspoon instant minced onion
1 cup elbow macaroni, cooked and drained
1 pound (2 cups) creamed cottage cheese
1½ cups corn-flake crumbs (more if needed)
3 eggs, slightly beaten
Oil for deep frying

1. In a 3-quart saucepan, melt butter. Blend in flour, salt, pepper, and dill weed.
2. Combine milk with onion. Add gradually to flour mixture, stirring constantly. Stir while cooking until thickened. Reduce heat and cook 2 minutes longer.
3. Stir in macaroni and cheese; mix well. Chill 1 to 2 hours, or until firm enough to handle.
4. Shape into 12 croquettes, coating with crumbs as soon as shaped. Dip in egg and again in crumbs.
5. Fill wok not more than half full with oil. Slowly heat oil to 375°F. Fry 3 croquettes at a time in hot oil until golden brown. Remove to a baking sheet lined with paper towels to drain. When all croquettes are drained, remove paper towels.
6. Bake croquettes at 350°F 10 to 15 minutes. Serve hot.

6 servings

Note: If desired, fine dry bread crumbs can be substituted for the corn-flake crumbs.

796 *Chinese Beef and Pea Pods*

1½ pounds flank steak, thinly
    sliced diagonally across grain
to 2 tablespoons cooking oil
1 bunch green onions, chopped
    (tops included)
1 or 2 packages (7 ounces each)
    frozen Chinese pea pods,
    partially thawed to separate
1 can (10½ ounces) condensed
    beef consommé
3 tablespoons soy sauce
¼ teaspoon ground ginger
2 tablespoons cornstarch
2 tablespoons cold water
1 can (16 ounces) bean sprouts,
    drained and rinsed

1. Stir-fry meat, a third at a time, in hot oil in a large wok until browned. Remove from wok and keep warm.
2. Put green onions and pea pods into wok. Stir in a mixture of condensed consommé, soy sauce, and ginger. Bring to boiling and cook, covered, about 2 minutes.
3. Blend cornstarch with water and stir into boiling liquid in wok. Stirring constantly, boil 2 to 3 minutes. Mix in the meat and bean sprouts; heat thoroughly.
4. Serve over **hot fluffy rice.**

6 servings

797 *Chinatown Chop Suey*

1¼ pounds pork, boneless
1 pound beef, boneless
¾ pound veal, boneless
3 tablespoons cooking oil
1 cup water
3 cups diagonally sliced celery
2 cups coarsely chopped onion
3 tablespoons cornstarch
¼ cup water
¼ cup soy sauce
¼ cup bead molasses
1 can (16 ounces) bean sprouts,
    drained and rinsed
2 cans (5 ounces each) water
    chestnuts, drained and sliced

1. Cut meat into 2x½x¼-inch strips. Heat oil in a large wok. Stir-fry ½ pound of meat at a time, browning pieces on all sides. Remove the meat from the wok as it is browned. When all the meat is browned, return it to the wok. Cover and cook over low heat 30 minutes.
2. Mix in 1 cup water, celery, and onions. Bring to boiling and simmer, covered, 20 minutes.
3. Blend cornstarch, the ¼ cup water, soy sauce, and molasses. Stir into meat mixture. Bring to boiling and cook 2 minutes, stirring constantly. Mix in bean sprouts and water chestnuts; heat.
4. Serve on **hot fluffy rice.**

8 servings

798 *Spicy Beef Strips*

1½ pounds beef round steak (¼
    inch thick)
2 tablespoons cooking oil
1 clove garlic
2 beef bouillon cubes
1 cup boiling water
1 tablespoon instant minced onion
½ teaspoon salt
    Few grains cayenne pepper
¼ teaspoon chili powder
¼ teaspoon ground cinnamon
¼ teaspoon ground celery seed
2 tablespoons prepared mustard

1. Cut round steak into 2x½-inch strips; set aside.
2. Heat cooking oil in a large wok. Add garlic and stir-fry until browned. Remove the garlic.
3. Add the round steak strips, half at a time, and stir-fry until browned.
4. Dissolve bouillon cubes in boiling water. Add to wok with all the ingredients; stir to mix. Cover and simmer 25 to 30 minutes, or until meat is fork-tender.
5. Serve over **hot fluffy rice.**

6 servings

799 *Nectarine Sukiyaki*

1 tablespoon cooking oil
2 pounds beef sirloin steak, boneless, cut 1½ inches thick, sliced ¹⁄₁₆ inch thick, and cut into about 2½-inch pieces
2 large onions, cut in thin wedges
8 green onions (including tops), cut into 2-inch pieces
5 ounces fresh mushrooms, sliced lengthwise
1 can (5 ounces) bamboo shoots, drained and sliced
2 cups unpared sliced fresh nectarines
½ cup soy sauce
½ cup canned condensed beef broth
2 tablespoons sugar

1. Heat oil in a large wok. Add meat, 1 pound at a time, and stir-fry over high heat until browned. Remove meat and set aside.
2. Arrange vegetables and nectarines in mounds in wok; top with the beef. Pour a mixture of soy sauce, condensed beef broth, and sugar over all. Simmer 3 to 5 minutes, or until onions are just tender.
3. Serve immediately over **hot fluffy rice**.

6 to 8 servings

800 *Sukiyaki*

½ cup Japanese soy sauce (shoyu)
½ cup sake or sherry
⅓ cup sugar
3 tablespoons cooking oil
1½ pounds beef tenderloin, sliced ¹⁄₁₆ inch thick and cut into pieces about 2½x1½ inches
12 scallions (including tops), cut into 2-inch lengths
½ head Chinese cabbage (cut lengthwise), cut into 1-inch pieces
½ pound spinach leaves, cut into 1-inch strips
2 cups drained shirataki (or cold cooked very thin long egg noodles)
12 large mushrooms, sliced lengthwise
12 cubes tofu (soybean curd)
1 can (8½ ounces) whole bamboo shoots, drained and cut in large pieces

1. Mix soy sauce, sake, and sugar to make the sauce; set aside.
2. Heat oil in a wok and add enough sauce to form a ¼-inch layer in bottom of wok.
3. Add half the beef and stir-fry just until pink color disappears; remove and stir-fry remaining meat, adding more of the sauce if necessary. Remove meat and set aside.
4. Arrange all other ingredients in individual mounds in skillet. Top with beef.
5. Cook until vegetables are just tender. Do not stir. Serve immediately with bowls of **hot cooked rice**.

4 servings

801 *Beef Chow Mein*

2 to 4 tablespoons cooking oil
1 pound beef tenderloin or sirloin
    steak, cut into 3x½x⅛-inch
    strips
½ pound fresh mushrooms, sliced
    lengthwise
2 cups sliced celery
2 green onions, sliced ½ inch thick
1 small green pepper, cut into
    narrow strips
1½ cups boiling water
1 teaspoon salt
½ teaspoon monosodium glutamate
⅛ teaspoon pepper
2 tablespoons cold water
2 tablespoons cornstarch
2 teaspoons soy sauce
1 teaspoon sugar
1 can (16 ounces) Chinese
    vegetables, drained
2 tablespoons coarsely chopped
    pimento

1. Heat 2 tablespoons oil in a large wok. Add beef and stir-fry until browned evenly. Remove meat; set aside.
2. Heat more oil, if necessary, in wok. Stir in mushrooms, celery, green onions, and green pepper; stir-fry 1 minute. Reduce heat and blend in boiling water, salt, monosodium glutamate, and pepper. Bring to boiling; cover and simmer 2 minutes. Remove vegetables; keep warm.
3. Bring liquid in wok to boiling and stir in a blend of cold water, cornstarch, soy sauce, and sugar. Cook and stir 2 to 3 minutes. Reduce heat; mix in the browned beef, vegetables, Chinese vegetables, and pimento. Heat thoroughly.
4. Serve piping hot with **chow mein noodles.**

4 to 6 servings

802 *Veal Scaloppine with Mushrooms*

1 tablespoon flour
¾ teaspoon salt
    Pinch pepper
1 pound veal cutlets
2 tablespoons cooking oil
4 ounces fresh mushrooms,
    quartered lengthwise
½ cup sherry
2 tablespoons finely chopped
    parsley

1. Combine flour, salt, and pepper; sprinkle over veal slices. Pound slices until thin, flat, and round, working flour mixture into both sides. Cut into ¼-inch-wide strips.
2. Heat oil in a large wok. Add veal strips and stir-fry over high heat until golden.
3. Sprinkle mushrooms on top and pour sherry over all. Simmer, uncovered, about 15 minutes, or until tender.
4. Toss with parsley and serve.

4 servings

803 *Beef Polynesian*

2 tablespoons cooking oil
1 pound lean ground beef
1 can (4 ounces) mushrooms, drained
½ cup golden raisins
1 package (10 ounces) frozen green peas
½ cup beef broth
1 teaspoon curry powder
1 tablespoon soy sauce
1 orange, sliced
½ cup salted cashews
Fried Rice

1. Heat oil in a large wok. Add ground beef and separate into small pieces; cook until lightly browned.
2. Add mushrooms, raisins, peas, broth, curry powder, and soy sauce. Break block of peas apart, if necessary, and gently toss mixture to blend.
3. Arrange orange slices over top. Cover loosely and cook over low heat 15 minutes.
4. Mix in cashews and serve with Fried Rice.

About 4 servings

Fried Rice: Cook **½ cup chopped onion** in **2 tablespoons butter** until golden. Mix in **2 cups cooked rice** and **2 tablespoons soy sauce.** Cook over low heat, stirring occasionally, 5 minutes. Stir in **1 slightly beaten egg** and cook until set. 804

805 *Deep-Fried Beef Pies*

Pastry:
1 cup all-purpose flour
½ teaspoon salt
⅓ cup shortening
2 or 3 tablespoons cold water

Filling:
¾ pound lean ground beef
2 tablespoons shortening
1½ teaspoons olive oil
1 teaspoon salt
¼ teaspoon black pepper
⅛ teaspoon cayenne pepper
1 ripe tomato, peeled and cut in pieces
⅓ cup finely chopped green pepper
¼ cup finely chopped carrot
¼ cup finely chopped celery
¼ cup finely chopped onion
¼ cup finely chopped green onion
1 tablespoon chopped hot red pepper
1 tablespoon snipped parsley
1 tablespoon snipped seedless raisins
1 tablespoon chopped pitted green olives
1 tablespoon capers
¼ cup water
Oil for deep frying

1. To make pastry, sift flour and salt together into a bowl. Cut in shortening with pastry blender or two knives until pieces are the size of small peas.
2. Sprinkle water over mixture, a teaspoonful at a time, mixing lightly with a fork after each addition. Add only enough water to hold pastry together. Shape into a ball and wrap in waxed paper; chill.
3. To make filling, cook ground beef in hot shortening and olive oil in a large skillet, separating meat with a spoon. Remove from heat and drain off fat. Mix in remaining ingredients except the oil for deep frying. Cover and simmer 30 minutes.
4. Working with half the chilled pastry at a time, roll out ⅛ inch thick on a lightly floured surface. Using a lightly floured 4-inch cutter, cut into rounds. Place 1 tablespoon filling on each round. Moisten edges with cold water, fold pastry over, press edges together, and tightly seal.
5. Slowly heat the oil for deep frying in a wok to 375°F.
6. Fry one layer at a time in the heated oil until lightly browned on both sides (about 3 minutes.) Drain on absorbent paper.

About 16 pies

806 *Stir-Fry Beef and Broccoli*

2 pounds broccoli
2 pounds beef round or chuck, boneless
¼ cup olive oil
2 cloves garlic, minced
3 cups hot chicken broth
4 teaspoons cornstarch
¼ cup cold water
3 tablespoons soy sauce
1 teaspoon salt
2 cans (16 ounces each) bean sprouts, drained and rinsed

1. Cut broccoli into pieces about 2½ inches long and ¼ inch thick; set aside. Slice beef very thin and cut diagonally into 4x½-inch strips; set aside.
2. Heat 1 tablespoon olive oil with garlic in a large wok. Add half the beef and stir-fry until evenly browned. Remove cooked meat from the wok and stir-fry remaining beef, adding more olive oil, if necessary.
3. Pour 1 tablespoon olive oil in the wok. Add half the broccoli and stir-fry over high heat ½ minute. Remove cooked broccoli from the wok and stir-fry remaining broccoli ½ minute, adding more oil, if necessary.
4. Place all the broccoli in the wok; cover and cook 3 minutes. Remove broccoli and keep warm.
5. Blend into broth a mixture of cornstarch, cold water, soy sauce, and salt. Bring to boiling, stirring constantly, and cook until mixture thickens.
6. Add bean sprouts, broccoli, and beef; toss to mix. Heat thoroughly and serve over **hot fluffy rice.**

8 servings

807 *Chicken with Almonds*

2 tablespoons cooking oil
⅓ cup chopped onion
1 cup chopped celery
1 can (4 ounces) mushrooms, liquid included
2 cups diced cooked chicken
1 can (5 ounces) water chestnuts, drained and sliced
2 tablespoons cornstarch
¼ teaspoon ground ginger
3 tablespoons soy sauce
¾ cup chicken bouillon
½ cup toasted almonds

1. Heat oil in a large wok. Add onion and celery; cook until soft. Stir in mushrooms and chicken and heat gently, stirring occasionally. Mix in water chestnuts and push mixture up on sides of wok.
2. Combine cornstarch, ginger, soy sauce, and bouillon. Stir into liquid in middle of wok. Cook until sauce thickens, stirring constantly.
3. When sauce thickens, combine with chicken mixture and almonds. Serve immediately over **hot fluffy rice.**

6 servings

Note: If desired, cashew nuts may be used instead of almonds.

808 *Batter-Fried Chicken*

1 broiler-fryer, cut into serving
    pieces
1½ cups sifted flour
½ teaspoon salt
    Dash pepper
1½ teaspoons baking powder
1 egg, beaten
1½ cups milk
    Oil for deep frying

1. Steam chicken in a large wok until
tender. Dry and refrigerate until time to fry.
2. Just before frying the chicken, combine the dry ingredients.
Blend the egg with milk and combine the liquid with the dry ingredients.
3. Slowly heat oil in a wok to 375 °F. Sprinkle chicken pieces
with salt and pepper. Dip chicken in batter, allow excess to
drain off, and fry a few pieces at a time until brown. Drain and
serve either hot or cold.

2 to 4 servings

809 *Good Fortune Chicken with Pineapple Piquant*

1 egg, fork beaten
⅓ cup water
1 tablespoon milk
¼ cup flour
1 tablespoon cornstarch
1 tablespoon cornmeal
⅛ teaspoon baking powder
12 small chicken legs
    Oil for deep frying heated to
    365 °F
1 tablespoon cooking oil
½ cup green pepper chunks
½ cup onion chunks
1 can (about 15 ounces) pineapple
    chunks (reserve syrup)
½ cup cider vinegar
½ cup packed brown sugar
2 tablespoons soy sauce
¼ cup water
1 tablespoon cornstarch

1. Beat egg, water, and milk with a mixture of flour, cornstarch, cornmeal, and baking powder in a bowl until smooth.
Dip each chicken leg into the batter and drain over bowl a few
seconds.
2. Fry pieces in hot oil 15 minutes, or until chicken is crisp-
brown and tender. Remove with a slotted spoon and drain over
fat; place on absorbent paper.
3. Meanwhile, heat 1 tablespoon cooking oil in a large wok,
and cook green pepper and onion until crisp-tender, stirring occasionally. Push vegetables up on sides of wok.
4. Pour in reserved pineapple syrup; add vinegar, brown
sugar, soy sauce, and a mixture of water and cornstarch. Stir
until blended. Mix in pineapple. Bring rapidly to boiling, stirring constantly; cook 3 minutes.
5. Pour sauce over chicken legs and serve. If desired, add 1
tablespoon sesame seed to sauce, or sprinkle over chicken when
served.

4 to 6 servings

810 *Chicken Tokay*

6 **chicken breasts (about 4 pounds),**
skinned, boned, and split
1½ **teaspoons salt**
¼ **teaspoon pepper**
1 **teaspoon crushed rosemary**
3 **tablespoons butter or margarine**
¼ **cup chopped onion**
2 **chicken bouillon cubes**
1 **cup boiling water**
1 **tablespoon lemon juice**
4 **teaspoons cornstarch**
2 **tablespoons cold water**
1½ **cups seeded and halved Tokay**
grapes (about 1 pound)

1. Rub chicken breasts with a mixture of the salt, pepper, and rosemary. Brown chicken slowly and evenly in hot butter in a large wok, pushing chicken up on sides of wok as it is browned.
2. Stir the onion into center of wok and cook until lightly browned, stirring occasionally. Stir chicken into onion.
3. Dissolve bouillon cubes in the boiling water and combine with lemon juice. Pour over chicken and onion. Cover and simmer until chicken is tender when pierced with a fork (about 20 minutes). Remove chicken from wok; keep hot.
4. Blend cornstarch with cold water. Stir into liquid in wok, blending thoroughly. Bring rapidly to boiling and boil 3 minutes, stirring constantly. Add grapes and chicken to wok and spoon sauce over all. Heat to serving temperature and serve immediately sprinkled with snipped **parsley.**

About 6 servings

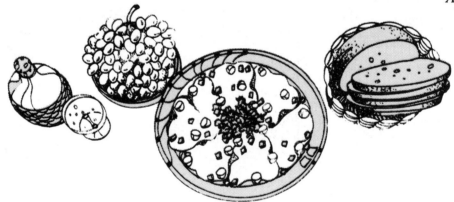

811 *Chicken Croquettes*

5 to 6 **tablespoons butter or**
margarine
5 to 6 **tablespoons flour**
¼ **teaspoon salt**
Few grains pepper
1½ **cups milk**
2 **cups finely chopped or ground**
cooked chicken
1 **tablespoon finely chopped**
parsley
1 **tablespoon lemon juice**
½ **teaspoon onion juice**
½ **teaspoon salt**
¼ **teaspoon celery salt**
1 **cup fine dry bread crumbs**
1 **egg, slightly beaten**
1 **tablespoon milk**
Oil for deep frying

1. Heat butter in saucepan over low heat. Blend in flour, salt, and pepper. Heat until mixture is bubbly. Remove from heat and gradually stir in milk.
2. Cook rapidly, stirring constantly, until sauce thickens. Cook 1 to 2 minutes longer.
3. Mix together lightly the chicken, parsley, lemon juice, onion juice, salt, and celery salt. Combine with the sauce. Refrigerate until chilled.
4. Shape chilled mixture into balls, cones, or cylinders. Roll in bread crumbs, then dip in a mixture of the egg and milk. Roll again in bread crumbs, shaking off loose crumbs.
5. Slowly heat oil in a wok to 375°F. Deep-fry the croquettes, a few at a time, turning frequently to brown evenly. Drain on absorbent paper and serve immediately.

6 servings

Chinatown Chop Suey, page 282

812 *Oriental Pineapple Chicken*

12 chicken wings
½ teaspoon monosodium glutamate
¼ teaspoon ground ginger
2 tablespoons cooking oil
1 clove garlic, minced
Chicken broth (about 1½ cups)
1 can (8½ ounces) pineapple slices (reserve syrup)
½ cup soy sauce
2 tablespoons cider vinegar
2 tablespoons cornstarch
1 cup diagonally sliced celery
4 green onions, diagonally sliced
1 can (5 ounces) water chestnuts, drained and halved
1 can (16 ounces) bean sprouts, drained and rinsed
¼ cup toasted blanched almonds

1. Remove and discard tips from chicken wings; cut wings in half at joint. Toss with a mixture of monosodium glutamate and ginger.
2. Heat oil in a large wok and stir in garlic. Brown the chicken pieces.
3. Add enough chicken broth to the pineapple syrup to make 1⅔ cups liquid; gradually pour into the wok. Cover and simmer 15 minutes, or until wings are tender.
4. Push chicken up on sides of wok. Stir in a mixture of soy sauce, vinegar, and cornstarch. Add celery and green onion. Bring to boiling and cook 3 minutes, stirring constantly. Mix in water chestnuts, bean sprouts, almonds, and 2 pineapple slices, cut in large pieces. Move chicken through mixture. Heat thoroughly.
5. Turn into a heated serving dish. Garnish with remaining pineapple slices.

4 servings

813 *Pineapple Trout*

4 trout (about 6 ounces each)
1 lemon, cut in half
2 tablespoons flour
¼ teaspoon salt
Pinch pepper
2 to 3 tablespoons cooking oil
3 tablespoons finely sliced green onions (including tops)
5 tablespoons sugar
1½ tablespoons cornstarch
½ teaspoon ground ginger
1 can (13½ ounces) pineapple chunks, drained (reserve syrup)
¼ cup wine vinegar
1 tablespoon soy sauce
½ teaspoon bead molasses

1. Remove fins and heads from trout; rinse fish under running cold water and pat dry with absorbent paper. Rub inside of fish with lemon. Coat fish with a mixture of the flour, salt, and pepper.
2. Fry the trout in hot oil in a wok over medium heat until golden brown on one side. Turn and cook until browned on other side and fish flakes easily; sprinkle green onion over fish the last 2 or 3 minutes of cooking.
3. Transfer to a serving platter and keep warm. If desired, remove bones from fish.
4. Pour out any oil remaining in wok. Combine sugar, cornstarch, and ginger in wok. Stir in the reserved pineapple syrup plus enough water to make 1⅓ cups, the vinegar, soy sauce, and molasses. Bring rapidly to boiling; boil 2 to 3 minutes, stirring constantly. Stir in the pineapple chunks. Spoon over the fish and serve immediately.

4 servings

Eggnog Fondue, page 275

814 *Steamed Fish Slices*

1 **pound frozen sole or turbot fillets, thawed**
3 **green onions including tops, sliced**
½ **teaspoon minced ginger root**
8 **medium mushrooms, thinly sliced**
1 **tablespoon cider vinegar**
1 **tablespoon soy sauce**
1 **tablespoon cooking oil**
¼ **teaspoon sugar**
   Generous dash pepper

1. Place fish fillets on a plate, skin side down, so that they fit in a large wok. Scatter onion, ginger root, and mushrooms over fish.
2. Combine remaining ingredients and pour over fish and vegetables.
3. Steam fish 10 minutes, or until fish flakes easily (see steaming instructions, page 7), and serve immediately.

2 or 3 servings

815 *Sweet and Sour Fish*

1 **bass or other firm white fish (about 1½ pounds), cleaned and dressed with tail left on**
½ **cup flour**
2 **medium carrots, pared and cut diagonally into ⅛-inch slices**
   Oil for deep-frying
2 **green onions (including tops), sliced diagonally into ¼-inch pieces**
¼ **teaspoon ground ginger**
2 **medium green peppers, cleaned and cut in thin strips**
4 **large mushrooms, thinly sliced**
½ **teaspoon salt**
5 **tablespoons sugar**
5 **tablespoons cider vinegar**
2 **tablespoons Japanese soy sauce**
1 **tablespoon dry sherry**
2 **tablespoons cornstarch**
1 **cup cold water**

1. Rinse fish in cold water and pat dry on inside and outside. With a sharp knife or cleaver, cut off head and discard. Lay the fish on its side and split in half along the backbone, removing backbone but not the tail.
2. Make three or four diagonal cuts on each side of the fish on the inside, not the skin side. Coat the fish with flour on inside and outside. Shake off excess.
3. Place carrot slices in boiling salted water. Bring to rapid boil and cook 2 to 3 minutes. Remove and set aside to drain.
4. Heat oil in a large wok to 375°F. Lower the fish into hot oil by holding it by its tail, keeping fish open and almost flat. Deep-fry 5 to 8 minutes, or until it is golden. Lift the fish out of the oil and drain on absorbent paper toweling. Keep fish warm while making sauce.
5. Remove all but 2 tablespoons oil from wok. Stir in green onion tossed with ginger, stir-frying a minute or two. Add carrots, green pepper, and mushrooms; stir-fry 2 to 3 minutes.
6. Add salt, sugar, vinegar, soy sauce, and sherry. Combine cornstarch with water and stir into mixture in wok. Cook, stirring, until sauce is thickened and vegetables are glazed.
7. Place fish on a warm platter, pour sauce over fish, and serve.

3 or 4 servings

816 *Fried Clams*

1 **quart fresh clams, shucked**
2 **eggs, beaten**
2 **tablespoons milk**
2 **teaspoons salt**
   Few grains pepper
3 **cups dry bread crumbs**
   Oil for deep frying

1. Drain clams and set aside.
2. Combine egg, milk, salt, and pepper. Dip clams in egg mixture and roll in bread crumbs.
3. Heat oil to 350°F in a wok. Fry a few clams at a time in the hot oil 1 to 2 minutes, or until brown. Drain on absorbent paper.
4. Serve hot with **tartar sauce.**

About 6 servings

817 *Rock Lobster, Cantonese Style*

6 South African rock lobster tails
   (3 to 5 ounces each), thawed
   Lime butter*
2 cups shredded cabbage
1½ cups diagonally sliced celery
1 cup thawed frozen or fresh
   peas
6 green onions, cut into ½-inch
   pieces
4 carrots, cut into thin diagonal
   slices
3 to 4 tablespoons cooking oil
1 cup vegetable broth
¼ cup soy sauce
1 teaspoon monosodium glutamate
1 teaspoon sugar

1. Using scissors, cut away the thin underside membrane of lobster tails. Remove meat and cut into ½- to ¾-inch pieces.
2. Cook lobster pieces slowly in hot lime butter in a large wok 5 minutes, or until lobster is opaque and tender. Set aside and keep warm.
3. Cook vegetables 5 minutes in hot oil in a wok over medium heat, stirring frequently. Stir in vegetable broth, soy sauce, monosodium glutamate, and sugar. Simmer, uncovered, 10 minutes.
4. Toss lobster with vegetables; serve with **hot fluffy rice.**

6 to 8 servings

*Blend desired amount of lime juice with melted butter.

818 *Shrimp Jambalaya*

2 to 3 tablespoons cooking oil
½ cup chopped onion
½ cup chopped green onion
½ cup chopped green pepper
½ cup chopped celery
¼ pound diced cooked ham
2 cloves garlic, minced
2 cups chicken broth
3 large tomatoes, coarsely
   chopped
¼ cup chopped parsley
½ teaspoon salt
⅛ teaspoon pepper
¼ teaspoon thyme
⅛ teaspoon cayenne pepper
1 bay leaf
1 cup uncooked rice
3 cans (4½ ounces each) shrimp,
   rinsed under running cold
   water
¼ cup coarsely chopped green
   pepper

1. Heat oil in a large wok over low heat. Stir in onion, green onion, green pepper, celery, ham, and garlic. Cook over medium heat about 5 minutes, or until onion is tender, stirring occasionally.
2. Stir in chicken broth, tomatoes, parsley, salt, pepper, thyme, cayenne pepper, and bay leaf; cover and bring to boiling.
3. Add rice gradually, stirring with a fork. Simmer, covered, 20 minutes, or until rice is tender.
4. Mix in shrimp and remaining green pepper. Simmer, uncovered, about 5 minutes longer.

6 to 8 servings

819 *Noodle Supper*

½ pound lean ground beef
1 teaspoon salt
¼ cup chopped parsley
1 package (1½ ounces) dry
   onion soup mix
1 quart hot water
1 cup sliced carrots
4 ounces medium noodles

1. Place ground beef in a large wok. Sprinkle with salt and brown lightly, stirring frequently.
2. Stir in parsley, soup mix, water, and carrots. Bring to boiling. Reduce heat and simmer 10 to 15 minutes, stirring occasionally.
3. Stir in noodles and cover. Cook about 10 minutes, or until noodles are tender.

4 servings

820 Stir-Fried Shrimp and Vegetables

¾ pound fresh bean sprouts
2 tablespoons cornstarch
2 teaspoons sugar
1½ cups water
2 tablespoons Japanese soy sauce
3 tablespoons white wine vinegar
½ teaspoon pepper
2 tablespoons sesame oil
1 teaspoon salt
1 cup diagonally sliced celery
6 green onions, sliced diagonally into 1-inch pieces
1 cup thinly sliced fresh mushrooms
1 tablespoon sesame oil
2 cloves garlic, minced
1 teaspoon minced fresh ginger root
¾ pound cleaned and cooked shrimp
1 package (6 ounces) frozen snow peas, thawed and well drained

1. Blanch bean sprouts by turning half of them into a sieve or basket and setting in a saucepan of boiling water. Boil 1 minute. Remove from water and spread out on absorbent paper to drain. Repeat with remaining bean sprouts.
2. Blend cornstarch, sugar, water, soy sauce, vinegar, and pepper; set aside.
3. Heat 2 tablespoons sesame oil in a large wok. Stir in salt, celery, green onion, and mushrooms. Stir-fry vegetables about 1 minute. Add bean sprouts and stir-fry 1 minute more. Remove vegetables from wok.
4. Heat 1 tablespoon sesame oil. Add garlic and ginger root; stir-fry briefly. Add shrimp and snow peas; stir-fry 1 minute longer. Return other vegetables to wok and mix together. Stir-fry briefly to heat.
5. Push vegetables and shrimp up sides of wok. Stir cornstarch mixture into liquid in center of wok. Cook until thickened and combine with shrimp and vegetables. Serve immediately.

4 servings

821 Noodle Omelet

1½ cups (4 ounces) noodles
3 tablespoons butter
2 tablespoons chopped onion
3 eggs
2 tablespoons milk or water
½ teaspoon salt
⅛ teaspoon pepper

1. Cook noodles according to package directions. Drain well.
2. Melt butter in a large wok over low heat. Add onion and cook until soft but not browned. Stir in noodles.
3. Meanwhile, beat eggs, milk, salt, and pepper with a fork; beat just enough to mix well. Pour over noodle mixture.
4. Cook rapidly, lifting mixture with fork, at the same time tilting wok to let uncooked egg mixture flow to bottom.
5. When mixture is set, reduce heat and cook 1 or 2 minutes longer to brown the bottom. Loosen edges and slide a spatula underneath to be sure omelet is free. Fold in half and slide out of wok onto a warm platter.

4 servings

822 Deep-Fried Noodles

6 ounces fine noodles
Oil for deep frying

1. Cook noodles in boiling salted water according to package directions. Rinse with cold water, drain, separate, and place on absorbent paper to dry.
2. Heat oil in a wok to 375°F. Place about ½ cup noodles in the hot oil. Fry until golden brown, turning once.
3. Drain on absorbent paper and sprinkle with salt, if desired. If not to be used immediately, noodles may be reheated in a 400°F oven.

4 to 6 servings

823 *Curried Rice*

1 tablespoon cooking oil
1 cup minced onion
1 cup chopped green pepper
½ cup currants
2 cups uncooked rice
1 teaspoon salt
½ teaspoon pepper
½ teaspoon curry powder
1 quart chicken broth

1. Heat oil in a large wok. Stir in onion, green pepper, and currants. Stir-fry until tender (about 10 minutes).
2. Stir in rice and seasonings; brown slightly.
3. Pour broth over rice and mix well. Bring to boiling, cover, and simmer 20 to 25 minutes, or until rice is tender.

8 servings

824 *Bacon-and-Egg Fried Rice*

10 slices bacon
½ cup chopped onion
1 cup diagonally sliced celery
1 cup sliced mushrooms
3 cups cooked rice
2 tablespoons Japanese soy sauce
1 egg, slightly beaten

1. Cook bacon, 5 slices at a time, in a large wok until crisp. Remove bacon and pour out all but 3 tablespoons bacon drippings.
2. Stir-fry onion and celery in the hot fat until almost tender. Stir in mushrooms, rice, and soy sauce. Cook 5 minutes over low heat, stirring occasionally.
3. Stir in egg and cook only until egg is set. Turn into a serving dish. Crumble bacon over top and serve immediately.

6 servings

825 *Fried Rice*

2 tablespoons butter
¾ cup uncooked rice
2 tablespoons very finely chopped fresh mushrooms
½ teaspoon grated onion
3 chicken bouillon cubes
2½ cups boiling water
1 tablespoon finely chopped carrot
1 tablespoon finely chopped green pepper

1. Melt butter in a wok over low heat. Add rice, mushrooms, and onion. Cook until golden brown.
2. Dissolve bouillon cubes in boiling water and stir into rice mixture. Cover and cook over low heat 30 minutes, or until rice is tender.
3. Add carrot and green pepper; toss lightly.

About 8 servings

826 *French-Style Green Beans with Water Chestnuts*

1 can (5 ounces) water chestnuts, drained, sliced, and slivered
3 tablespoons chopped onion
¼ cup butter or margarine
½ teaspoon salt
Few grains pepper
2 tablespoons lemon juice
1 teaspoon soy sauce
1 pound fresh green beans, frenched, cooked, and drained

1. Brown slivered water chestnuts and onion in hot butter in a large wok. Stir in a mixture of salt, pepper, lemon juice, and soy sauce. Heat thoroughly.
2. Add green beans and toss with sauce. Turn into a heated serving dish.

About 6 servings

827 *Old-fashioned Green Beans*

¾ pound fresh green beans
8 slices bacon, diced
2 medium potatoes, pared and cut into ½-inch pieces
1 small onion, sliced
¼ cup water
½ teaspoon salt

1. Cut green beans into 1-inch pieces. Cook in boiling salted water until tender; drain.
2. Fry bacon in a wok until crisp. Stir in green beans, potatoes, onion, water, and salt.
3. Cook, covered, over medium heat about 15 minutes, or until potatoes are tender.

About 4 servings

828 *Fried Green Pepper Strips*

2 large green peppers
½ cup fine dry bread crumbs
⅓ cup grated Parmesan cheese
1½ teaspoons salt
⅛ teaspoon pepper
1 egg, fork beaten
2 tablespoons water
Oil for frying

1. Clean green peppers and cut into ⅛-inch rings. Cut each ring into halves or thirds.
2. Coat with a mixture of bread crumbs, cheese, salt, and pepper. Dip into a mixture of egg and water. Coat again with crumb mixture. Chill 1 hour.
3. Heat a 1-inch layer of oil to 375°F in a large wok. Cover surface with chilled green pepper strips. Fry about 30 seconds, or until golden brown. Remove strips with fork or slotted spoon. Drain on absorbent paper.

4 servings

829 *Mushrooms in Sour Cream*

1½ pounds fresh mushrooms
½ cup butter
½ large clove garlic, chopped
1 small onion, sliced
¼ teaspoon paprika
2 tablespoons white wine
½ cup dairy sour cream

1. Wash mushrooms and pat dry. Slice lengthwise through caps and stems.
2. Heat butter in a large wok. Add garlic and onion; cook until onion is soft.
3. Add mushrooms and paprika; stir-fry mushrooms about 5 minutes, or until mushrooms are lightly browned.
4. Add wine to wok, reduce heat, and cook mushrooms several minutes, stirring occasionally.
5. Just before serving, blend in sour cream and heat about 1 minute. Serve immediately on **hot fluffy rice.**

4 to 6 servings

830 *Stir-Fried Peas*

1 package (10 ounces) frozen
    peas, thawed
1 tablespoon vegetable oil
½ teaspoon salt
⅛ teaspoon pepper
1 medium onion, peeled, cut in
    half lengthwise, and sliced
   ¼ inch thick

1. Drain peas on paper toweling to remove as much moisture as possible.
2. Heat oil in a large wok. Stir in salt and pepper. Add drained peas; stir-fry to coat with oil and heat through. Simmer, covered, over medium heat 2 minutes.
3. Stir in onion and continue cooking 2 minutes.
4. Serve immediately.

4 servings

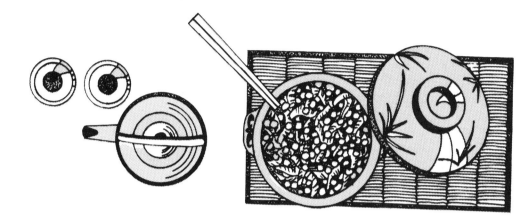

831 *Summer Squash with Bacon*

2 pounds (about 4 small)
    summer squash (yellow
    straight-neck), washed
3 slices bacon, diced
¼ cup finely chopped onion
1 teaspoon salt
   Few grains pepper

1. Trim ends from squash and cut squash into thin diagonal slices; set aside.
2. Cook bacon in a wok until crisp and brown. Remove bacon from wok and all but 3 tablespoons of the bacon drippings.
3. Stir in squash, onion, salt, and pepper. Cover and cook over medium heat 12 minutes, or until squash is tender. Stir in bacon and serve.

About 6 servings

832 *Creole Fried Tomatoes*

1 small clove garlic, minced
1 tablespoon finely chopped
    parsley
½ teaspoon salt
   Dash pepper
¼ cup finely chopped onion
1 tablespoon olive oil
2 large tomatoes, cut into
   ½- inch-thick slices
2 tablespoons cornmeal
2 teaspoons olive oil

1. Combine garlic, parsley, salt, pepper, and onion. Mix in 1 tablespoon olive oil.
2. Spread both sides of each tomato slice with mixture. Sprinkle slices with cornmeal.
3. Heat 2 teaspoons olive oil in a large wok. Fry tomato slices until lightly browned, pushing slices up sides as they are cooked. (Additional oil may be added, if necessary.)

4 servings

833 *Mallow Sweet Potato Balls*

3 cups warm mashed sweet
    potatoes
Salt and pepper to taste
3 tablespoons melted butter
8 large marshmallows
1 egg
1 tablespoon cold water
1 cup almonds, blanched and.
    chopped
Oil for deep frying

1. Season potatoes and add butter. Mold potato mixture around marshmallows, forming 8 balls with a marshmallow in center of each.
2. Beat egg and mix with cold water. Dip sweet potato balls in egg and then in almonds.
3. Slowly heat oil in a wok to 365°F. When oil is hot, fry sweet potato balls until brown, turning occasionally.

8 servings

834 *Zucchini Parmesan*

2 tablespoons cooking oil
1 small clove garlic, minced
4 medium zucchini, thinly sliced
⅓ cup coarsely chopped onion
1 tablespoon chopped parsley
1 teaspoon salt
⅛ teaspoon pepper
¼ teaspoon oregano
¼ teaspoon rosemary
2 cups chopped peeled tomatoes
¼ cup grated Parmesan cheese

1. Heat oil in a large wok. Add garlic and stir-fry about 1 minute. Stir in zucchini, onion, and parsley. Sprinkle with a mixture of salt, pepper, oregano, and rosemary. Stir together and cover.
2. Heat about 5 minutes over medium heat. Stir in tomatoes and cook, uncovered, 1 to 2 minutes, or until tomatoes are thoroughly heated.
3. Turn mixture into a serving dish and sprinkle with cheese.

4 or 5 servings

835 *Fried Cream*

⅓ cup sugar
¼ cup cornstarch
¼ teaspoon salt
4 egg yolks
¼ cup milk
2 cups whipping cream, scalded
½ teaspoon vanilla extract
Fine dry bread crumbs
2 eggs, slightly beaten
Oil for deep frying

1. Mix sugar, cornstarch, and salt in a heavy saucepan.
2. Mix egg yolks with milk; blend with dry ingredients. Add scalded cream, stirring until smooth.
3. Cook and stir mixture until thickened and smooth.
4. Remove from heat and stir in vanilla extract. Turn into a lightly greased 8-inch square dish or pan. Chill thoroughly.
5. Cut cream into squares. Coat with bread crumbs, then with slightly beaten eggs, and again with bread crumbs.
6. Pour oil into wok, filling wok not more than a third full. Heat to 365°F. Fry cream squares in hot oil until browned (about 2 minutes).

25 pieces

Chafing Dish

836 *Hot Cheese Dunk*

3 tablespoons butter or
    margarine
1 tablespoon flour
¼ teaspoon white pepper
¼ teaspoon Tabasco
½ cup instant nonfat dry milk
    solids
1 can (10½ ounces) chicken
    bouillon
½ medium onion
1 cup freshly grated Parmesan
    cheese
4 ounces Swiss cheese, shredded
    (about 1 cup)

1. In cooking pan of a chafing dish, melt butter. Blend in flour, pepper, and Tabasco.
2. Dissolve nonfat dry milk in bouillon. Gradually stir into flour mixture and add onion. Cook over medium heat, stirring constantly, until sauce thickens.
3. Remove onion and stir in cheeses until melted. Place over hot water to keep mixture warm.
4. Serve hot as a dunking sauce for cooked shrimp, ham cubes, rye toast, apple slices, or fresh uncooked vegetables.

About 2 cups dunk

Note: Dunk thickens upon standing and may be thinned with small amounts of chicken bouillon.

837 *Shrimp Mexican Style*

1 can (4 ounces) peeled green
    chilies
½ cup minced onion
3 medium cloves garlic, minced
¼ cup olive oil
2 tablespoons flour
1 cup half-and-half
8 ounces Monterey Jack cheese,
    shredded (about 2 cups)
4 ounces sharp Cheddar cheese,
    shredded (about 1 cup)
¼ cup dry white wine
½ teaspoon paprika
1 pound cooked shrimp, shelled,
    deveined, and cut in bite-size
    pieces

1. Rinse seeds from chilies; dice and set aside.
2. In cooking pan of chafing dish, sauté onion and garlic in oil over medium heat until soft but not browned. Add flour, stirring constantly. Stir over medium heat 3 minutes.
3. Gradually add half-and-half, stirring until very smooth. Add both cheeses gradually, stirring after each addition until the mixture is smooth.
4. Stir in wine, paprika, diced chilies, and shrimp. Heat thoroughly and place over simmering water to keep warm.
5. Serve warm with **corn chips**, pieces of **crisp fried tortillas,** or **crackers**.

4 to 6 servings

838 *Chili con Queso Dip*

1 cup chopped onion
2 cans (4 ounces each) green
    chilies, chopped and drained
2 large cloves garlic, mashed
2 tablespoons cooking oil
1 pound process sharp Cheddar
    cheese, cut into chunks
1 teaspoon Worcestershire sauce
¼ teaspoon paprika
¼ teaspoon salt
½ cup tomato juice

1. Sauté onion, green chilies, and garlic in oil in cooking pan of chafing dish over medium heat until onion is tender.
2. Reduce heat to low, and add remaining ingredients, except tomato juice. Cook, stirring constantly, until cheese is melted.
3. Add tomato juice gradually until dip is the desired consistency. Place over hot water to keep warm.
4. Serve with **corn chips**.

3¼ cups dip

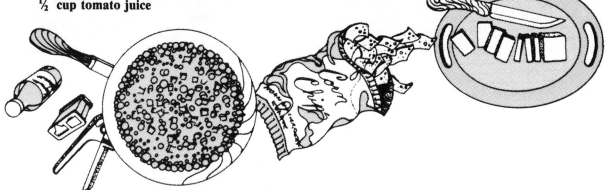

839 *Hot Cheese Dunking Sauce*

½ cup shredded Cheddar cheese
¾ cup milk
3 tablespoons condensed cream of
    mushroom soup
⅛ teaspoon pepper
1½ teaspoons Worcestershire sauce
2 tablespoons prepared horseradish
    French bread, cut into 1-inch
    cubes

1. In cooking pan of chafing dish or in fondue pot, combine cheese and milk. Place over low heat, add soup, and stir constantly until cheese is melted,
2. Stir in pepper, Worcestershire sauce, and horseradish.
3. Keep hot in chafing dish and serve with French bread cubes.

1½ cups sauce

840 *Hot Crab Meat Dip*

2 tablespoons butter or
    margarine
3 tablespoons flour
½ teaspoon salt
1 cup milk
¼ cup shredded Cheddar
    cheese
½ cup mayonnaise
2 tablespoons tomato paste
¼ teaspoon Worcestershire
    sauce
1 cup flaked crab meat

1. Melt butter in cooking pan of chafing dish. Stir in flour and salt. Add milk, stirring until mixture thickens. Blend in cheese.
2. Combine mayonnaise, tomato paste, and Worcestershire sauce. Stir in some of the hot mixture. Pour back into cooking pan. Stir in crab meat.
3. Keep warm while serving with **crackers, toast rounds, potato chips,** or **corn chips.**

About 1½ cups dip

841 *Beef Stroganoff*

1 pound beef tenderloin, sirloin,
   or rib, boneless, cut into
   2x½x¼-inch strips
¼ cup flour
½ teaspoon salt
   Pinch black pepper
3 tablespoons butter or margarine
¼ cup finely chopped onion
1 cup beef broth
1½ tablespoons butter or margarine
¼ pound fresh mushrooms, sliced
   lengthwise
½ cup dairy sour cream
1½ tablespoons tomato paste
½ teaspoon Worcestershire sauce

1. Coat meat strips evenly with a mixture of flour, salt, and pepper.
2. Heat 3 tablespoons butter in a large heavy skillet. Add meat strips and onion. Brown on all sides over medium heat, turning occasionally. Add broth; cover and simmer about 20 minutes.
3. Heat 1½ tablespoons butter in cooking pan of a chafing dish over medium heat. Add mushrooms and cook until lightly browned and tender. Add meat and liquid to mushrooms.
4. Blending well after each addition, add a mixture of sour cream, tomato paste, and Worcestershire sauce in small amounts. Place over simmering water and continue cooking, stirring constantly, until thoroughly heated (do not boil).

About 4 servings

842 *Hamburger Stroganoff*

1½ pounds lean ground beef
2 large onions, sliced
2 cans (10½ ounces each) condensed cream of chicken soup
1 pint dairy sour cream
1 teaspoon salt
   Dash black pepper

1. Sauté ground beef and onions in a small amount of fat in cooking pan of a chafing dish until meat is well browned.
2. Stir in condensed soup, sour cream, salt, and pepper.
3. Cook, covered, over direct heat of chafing dish until thoroughly heated.

About 6 servings

843 *Embassy Veal Glacé*

1½ teaspoons dry tarragon leaves
1 cup dry white wine
1½ pounds veal round steak (about
   ¼ inch thick)
3 tablespoons butter or margarine
½ teaspoon salt
⅛ teaspoon pepper
½ cup condensed beef consommé
½ cup dry vermouth

1. Stir tarragon into white wine; cover and set aside ʳᵃl hours, stirring occasionally.
2. Cut meat into pieces about 3x2 inches. Heat butter in cooking pan of chafing dish until lightly browned. Add meat and lightly brown on both sides; season with salt and pepper.
3. Reduce heat and pour in tarragon-wine mixture with the consommé and vermouth. Simmer, uncovered, about 10 minutes, or until veal is tender.
4. Remove veal to a platter and cover.
5. Increase heat under pan and cook sauce until it is reduced to a thin glaze, stirring occasionally. Return veal to pan and spoon sauce over meat, turning meat once.
6. Cover and place over direct heat of chafing dish until warm.

About 6 servings

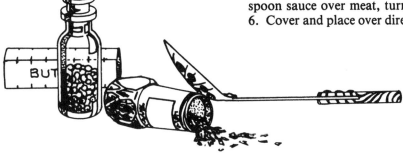

844 *Orange Pork Chops*

1 cup orange juice
3 tablespoons instant minced
onion
2 teaspoons grated orange peel
1 tablespoon brown sugar
½ teaspoon marjoram, crushed
¼ teaspoon thyme, crushed
4 pork chops, cut about 1 inch
thick
½ teaspoon salt
⅛ teaspoon pepper
Cooking oil
Oranges, pared and sectioned

1. Combine orange juice, onion, orange peel, brown sugar, marjoram, and thyme; set aside.
2. Season pork chops with salt and pepper. Brown chops well on both sides in a small amount of oil in a heavy skillet.
3. Place chops in cooking pan of a chafing dish. Add orange juice mixture. Cook, covered, over low heat about 45 minutes, or until chops are very tender. If desired, thicken the sauce slightly with a cornstarch-water mixture.
4. Add orange sections and heat 5 to 10 minutes over direct heat of chafing dish.

4 servings

845 *Peach 'n' Pork Chop Barbecue*

6 pork chops, cut 1 inch thick
1 tablespoon fat
¼ cup lightly packed brown sugar
1 teaspoon ground cinnamon
½ teaspoon ground cloves
1 can (8 ounces) tomato sauce
6 canned cling peach halves,
drained (reserve ¼ cup syrup)
¼ cup cider vinegar
1 teaspoon salt
¼ teaspoon pepper

1. Brown chops on both sides in hot fat in a large heavy skillet.
2. Meanwhile, blend a mixture of brown sugar, cinnamon, and cloves with tomato sauce, reserved peach syrup, and vinegar.
3. Place pork chops in cooking pan of chafing dish. Sprinkle with salt and pepper. Place a peach half on each chop. Pour sauce over all.
4. Cover skillet and simmer about 30 minutes, or until pork is tender; baste occasionally with the sauce.

6 servings

846 *Dutch Sausage with Gravy*

1 pound bulk pork sausage
1 to 2 tablespoons water
1 small onion, minced
1 tablespoon flour
1 cup beef broth

1. Shape sausage into 4 to 6 flat cakes. Put sausage cakes into a skillet. Add water; cover tightly and cook slowly about 5 minutes. Remove cover and cook slowly until well browned on both sides.
2. Remove cakes to cooking pan of a chafing dish and keep warm.
3. Drain off all but 3 tablespoons fat from skillet. Brown onion in the fat. Stir in flour and cook 1 minute. Stir in broth; simmer 5 minutes.
4. Pour gravy over sausage cakes and heat thoroughly.

4 to 6 servings

847 *Sausage, Hominy, and Tomato Scramble*

1 pound bulk pork sausage
½ cup fine dry bread crumbs
⅔ cup undiluted evaporated milk
½ teaspoon rubbed sage
¼ cup flour
2 cans (16 ounces each) tomatoes
1 can (20 ounces) hominy, drained
1 teaspoon salt
¼ teaspoon rubbed sage

1. Combine sausage, bread crumbs, evaporated milk, and ½ teaspoon sage. Mix well and shape into 16 balls. Roll balls in flour to coat, reserving remaining flour.
2. In cooking pan of a chafing dish, brown meatballs over low heat, turning frequently.
3. Remove all but 3 tablespoons of the fat from the pan. Stir in reserved flour, tomatoes, hominy, salt, and sage; blend well.
4. Cook, covered, over low heat about 15 minutes, or until sauce is thickened. Keep warm over chafing dish burner until ready to serve.

6 to 8 servings

848 *Ham à la Cranberry*

2 cups sugar
¼ teaspoon salt
2 cups water
1 pound (about 4 cups) cranberries, washed and sorted
2 teaspoons grated lemon peel
6 cups cubed cooked smoked ham or luncheon meat
½ cup seedless raisins (optional)

1. Combine sugar, salt, and water in a saucepan and heat to boiling. Boil, uncovered, 5 minutes. Add cranberries and continue to boil, uncovered, without stirring, about 5 minutes, or until skins pop.
2. Turn cranberry sauce into cooking pan of a chafing dish. Blend in lemon peel, ham, and raisins, if desired. Cook over direct heat until mixture starts to bubble; stir occasionally.
3. Place over simmering water to keep mixture hot. Serve over **toast triangles, patty shells,** or **hot biscuits.**

8 to 10 servings

849 *Lamb and Rice*

3 tablespoons butter or margarine
½ cup chopped onion
½ cup diced green pepper
1 can (10½ ounces) tomato purée
1 teaspoon bottled brown bouquet sauce
¼ cup ketchup
1 can (8¼ ounces) diced carrots
2 cups ground cooked lamb
1 teaspoon salt
1 cup packaged precooked rice
1 cup chicken bouillon

1. In cooking pan of a chafing dish, melt butter. Stir in onion and green pepper; cook over medium heat until vegetables are lightly browned.
2. Stir in remaining ingredients and cover. Cook over low heat 10 minutes, or until thoroughly heated and rice is tender.
3. Place over simmering water to keep warm.

4 to 6 servings

850 *Cherried Chicken*

2 large chicken breasts, skinned
    and boned
3 to 4 tablespoons flour
½ teaspoon salt
¼ teaspoon paprika
⅛ teaspoon curry powder
2 to 3 tablespoons butter
½ cup dry white wine
1 can (8¼ ounces) pitted dark
    sweet cherries, drained
¼ cup pineapple chunks

1. Dredge chicken in a mixture of flour, salt, paprika, and curry powder. Heat butter in cooking pan of a chafing dish. Cook chicken slowly in the butter until golden brown on all sides.
2. Add wine and cover pan tightly. Simmer 30 minutes, or until chicken is tender.
3. Add cherries and pineapple. Heat over simmering water until heated through.

2 servings

851 *Mexican Chicken*

2 tablespoons cooking oil
1 cup slivered almonds
1 cup chopped onion
1 medium clove garlic, minced
⅛ teaspoon cinnamon
⅛ teaspoon cloves
¼ teaspoon pepper
1 ounce (1 square) unsweetened
    chocolate, coarsely chopped
2 cans (7 ounces each) green
    chili sauce
1 can (15 ounces) tomato sauce
2 cups bite-size pieces cooked
    chicken or turkey

1. In cooking pan of a chafing dish, heat the oil, Sauté almonds, onion, and garlic 10 minutes over medium heat, stirring often.
2. Stir in remaining ingredients except chicken. Heat, stirring, until chocolate melts. Purée mixture in a blender or force through a food mill.
3. Return mixture to cooking pan and stir in chicken. Simmer 5 minutes.
4. Serve over **hot fluffy rice**. Garnish with **avocado** or **orange slices, dairy sour cream,** or **slivered almonds.**

4 servings

852 *Chicken Livers Superb*

2 pounds chicken livers
¼ cup flour
1 cup finely chopped onion
½ cup butter
5 ounces fresh mushrooms,
    cleaned, sliced lengthwise
    through stems and caps, and
    lightly browned in butter
2 tablespoons Worcestershire sauce
2 tablespoons chili sauce
1 teaspoon salt
¼ teaspoon pepper
½ teaspoon rosemary
½ teaspoon thyme
2 cups dairy sour cream

1. Rinse and drain chicken livers. Pat free of excess moisture with absorbent paper. Coat lightly with flour. Set aside.
2. Lightly brown onion in heated butter in a large skillet, stirring occasionally. Remove half the onion-butter mixture and set aside for second frying of livers. Add half the chicken livers and cook, occasionally moving and turning with a spoon, about 5 minutes, or until lightly browned. Turn into the cooking pan of a chafing dish. Fry remaining livers, using all the onion-butter mixture; turn into the cooking pan. Set aside.
3. After browning mushrooms, blend a mixture of Worcestershire sauce, chili sauce, salt, pepper, rosemary, and thyme with the mushrooms. Heat thoroughly.
4. Adding sour cream in small amounts at a time and stirring constantly, quickly blend with mushroom mixture. Heat thoroughly (do not boil). Mix gently with livers to coat.
5. Set cooking pan over simmering water. Before serving, garnish with wreaths of **sieved hard-cooked egg white, watercress, and sieved hard-cooked egg yolk.** Serve with buttered toasted **English muffins.**

About 8 servings

Note: If desired, blend in ¼ cup dry sauterne or sherry with the sour cream.

853 *Chicken Curry with Rice*

⅓ cup butter or margarine
3 tablespoons chopped onion
3 tablespoons chopped celery
3 tablespoons chopped green apple
12 peppercorns
1 bay leaf
⅓ cup sifted flour
2½ teaspoons curry powder
½ teaspoon monosodium glutamate
¼ teaspoon sugar
Pinch nutmeg
2½ cups milk
2 teaspoons lemon juice
½ teaspoon Worcestershire sauce
3 cups cubed cooked chicken
¼ cup cream
2 tablespoons sherry
¼ teaspoon Worcestershire sauce

1. Heat butter in a heavy saucepan over low heat. Add onion, celery, apple, peppercorns, and bay leaf. Cook over medium heat until lightly browned, stirring occasionally.
2. Blend in a mixture of flour, curry powder, monosodium glutamate, sugar, and nutmeg. Heat until mixture bubbles. Remove from heat and gradually add milk, stirring constantly.
3. Return pan to heat and bring sauce rapidly to boiling. Stirring constantly, cook until sauce thickens; cook 1 to 2 minutes longer. Remove from heat and stir in lemon juice and Worcestershire sauce. Strain sauce through a fine sieve, pressing vegetables against sieve to extract all the sauce.
4. Transfer the sauce to cooking pan of a chafing dish and place over simmering water. Blend cream, sherry, and Worcestershire sauce into the warm sauce. Add cubed chicken and cook, covered, until mixture is thoroughly heated.
5. Serve with **hot fluffy rice,** and curry condiments such as **preserved kumquats, chutney, shredded coconut,** and **finely chopped roasted peanuts.**

4 servings

854 *Chinese Chicken Crepes*

16 crepes
2 tablespoons butter or margarine
½ cup thinly sliced green onion
1 cup cooked rice
¼ cup chopped parsley
1 can (8 ounces) water chestnuts, drained and sliced
2 cups bite-size pieces cooked chicken
1 teaspoon lemon juice
Chinese Sauce

1. Prepare crepes and set aside.
2. Melt butter in a large skillet. Add green onion and rice. Cook 5 minutes over low heat, stirring occasionally.
3. Stir in parsley, water chestnuts, chicken, and lemon juice. Remove from heat and stir in 1 cup Chinese Sauce.
4. Spoon a heaping ¼ cup of chicken filling onto one end of each crepe on the unbrowned side. Roll up crepes and set aside.
5. Heat about half the remaining Chinese Sauce in the cooking pan of a chafing dish. Add half the filled crepes and heat over simmering water. As crepes are heated, serve them, and place other crepes in the sauce to heat.

8 servings

855 *Basic Crepes*

1 cup all-purpose flour
⅛ teaspoon salt
3 eggs
1½ cups milk
2 tablespoons melted butter or oil

1. Sift flour and salt. Add eggs, one at a time, beating thoroughly. Gradually add milk, mixing until blended. Add melted butter or oil and beat until smooth. (Or mix in an electric blender until smooth.)
2. Let batter stand for 1 hour before cooking crepes.
3. Heat a 7-inch skillet or crepe pan over moderately high heat. Grease lightly. Pour 3 tablespoons batter into pan and tilt pan with a swirling motion to cover bottom evenly. When brown on first side, turn over and cook other side.
4. Continue making crepes with remaining batter, greasing pan as necessary. Stack crepes on a plate or sheet of waxed paper until ready to fill.

16 crepes

856 *Chinese Sauce*

¼ cup cornstarch
4 cups chicken broth
¼ cup soy sauce
¾ cup sherry
1 teaspoon sugar

1. In a saucepan, mix cornstarch with chicken broth. Stir in remaining ingredients.
2. Cook over medium heat, stirring occasionally, until mixture thickens and comes to boiling. Remove from heat.

857 *Chicken and Ham en Crème*

¼ cup butter or margarine
¼ cup flour
½ teaspoon salt
⅛ teaspoon white pepper
½ teaspoon dry mustard
1 cup chicken broth
1½ cups cream
2 egg yolks, slightly beaten
1 cup cooked ham pieces
1½ cups cooked chicken or turkey
      pieces
¾ teaspoon grated lemon peel

1. Heat butter in a large saucepan over low heat. Blend in a mixture of the flour, salt, pepper, and dry mustard. Heat until bubbly.
2. Gradually add chicken broth and cream, stirring constantly. Bring to boiling, stir and cook 1 to 2 minutes.
3. Vigorously stir about 3 tablespoons of the hot mixture into the egg yolks. Immediately blend into mixture in saucepan, stirring constantly. Cook and stir 2 to 3 minutes. Mix in ham, chicken, and lemon peel.
4. Turn mixture into cooking pan of a chafing dish. Place over simmering water and heat thoroughly (do not boil).

About 6 servings

Chicken and Ham Almond: Follow recipe for 858 Chicken and Ham en Crème. Omit lemon peel. Add ¾ **cup salted almonds.**

Creamed Chicken and Ham with Olives: 859 Follow recipe for Chicken and Ham en Creme. Add ¾ **cup coarsely chopped ripe olives** with chicken and ham.

860 *Chicken à la King with Ham Rolls*

⅓ cup butter or margarine
⅓ cup flour
1 cup chicken broth
1 cup milk
½ teaspoon salt
⅛ teaspoon pepper
1 teaspoon grated onion
1½ cups large-diced cooked chicken
¼ cup diced green pepper
1 pimento, diced
1 can (4 ounces) sliced mushrooms
      (liquid included)
2 tablespoons dry sherry (optional)
6 slices boiled ham
12 cooked asparagus tips

1. Melt butter in a saucepan; add flour and stir over medium heat until bubbly. Stir in broth and milk. Cook, stirring constantly, until thickened and smooth.
2. Stir in next seven ingredients and heat thoroughly. Stir in wine, if desired.
3. Roll two asparagus tips in each ham slice. Place in cooking pan of a chafing dish. Spoon chicken à la king over ham rolls and cover pan.
4. Place over simmering water until thoroughly heated.

About 6 servings

861 *Turkey Royal*

¼ cup butter or margarine
1 tablespoon minced onion
6 tablespoons flour
1 teaspoon salt
Few grains cayenne pepper
Few grains nutmeg
2 cans (4 ounces each) button mushrooms
Milk
3 egg yolks, slightly beaten
2 cups dairy sour cream
1 tablespoon minced parsley
1 tablespoon minced chives
¼ cup pimento strips
½ cup cooked peas
2 cups cooked turkey pieces

1. Heat butter in cooking pan of a chafing dish. Add onion and cook over low heat, stirring occasionally, until onion is transparent.
2. Blend in flour, salt, cayenne, and nutmeg. Heat until bubbly. Drain mushrooms and add enough milk to mushroom liquid to make 1 cup liquid.
3. Remove cooking pan from heat and gradually add liquid, stirring constantly. Return to heat and cook over low heat until mixture thickens, stirring constantly. Cook 1 to 2 minutes longer; remove from heat.
4. Vigorously stir about 3 tablespoons of the hot mixture into the egg yolks. Immediately blend into mixture in cooking pan. Cook over simmering water 5 to 10 minutes, or until thoroughly heated. Stir slowly to keep mixture cooking evenly. Remove from heat.
5. Using a French whip, wire whisk, or fork, vigorously stir sour cream, a little at a time, into hot mixture. Mix in parsley, chives, pimento strips, peas, mushrooms, and turkey.
6. Cook over simmering water, stirring constantly, 3 to 5 minutes, or until thoroughly heated.

6 servings

Chicken Royal: Follow recipe for Turkey Royal, substituting **cooked chicken** for the turkey. **862**

863 *Salmon Rabbit*

4 ounces sharp Cheddar cheese, shredded (about 1 cup)
1 cup tomato purée
½ teaspoon salt
1 teaspoon prepared mustard
1 tablespoon Worcestershire sauce
2 eggs, slightly beaten
1 cup evaporated milk
1 can (16 ounces) salmon, drained

1. In cooking pan of a chafing dish, melt cheese over simmering water. Gradually blend in tomato purée, salt, mustard, and Worcestershire sauce, stirring constantly.
2. Combine eggs with milk and slowly stir into cheese mixture. Add salmon, separated into large chunks, and heat thoroughly. Serve on **hot buttered toast.**

6 servings

864 *Tuna Supreme*

⅔ cup chopped onion
1 green pepper, cut into slivers
2 tablespoons cooking oil
1 can (10¾ ounces) condensed tomato soup
2 teaspoons soy sauce
2 to 3 tablespoons brown sugar
1 teaspoon grated lemon peel
3 tablespoons lemon juice
2 cans (6½ or 7 ounces each) tuna, drained

1. Cook onion and green pepper until almost tender in hot oil in cooking pan of a large chafing dish; stir occasionally.
2. Mix in condensed tomato soup, soy sauce, brown sugar, and lemon peel and juice. Bring to boiling; simmer 5 minutes.
3. Mix in tuna, separating it into small pieces. Cover and heat thoroughly over simmering water.
4. Serve with **hot fluffy rice.** Garnish with **toasted sesame seed** and **chow mein noodles.**

About 6 servings

865 *Crab Ravigote*

¼ cup butter
¼ cup flour
1 teaspoon salt
  Few grains cayenne pepper
2 cups milk
⅔ cup chopped cooked green
    pepper
⅔ cup coarsely chopped pimento
2 tablespoons capers
2 teaspoons tarragon vinegar
2 cups lump crab meat
⅔ cup Hollandaise Sauce

1. Heat butter in cooking pan of a chafing dish; blend in flour, salt, and cayenne pepper; heat until bubbly. Gradually add milk, stirring constantly. Cook and stir until boiling; cook 1 minute.
2. Stir in remaining ingredients and heat thoroughly over simmering water.
3. Serve on **rusks**.

4 servings

Hollandaise Sauce: In the top of a double boiler, beat **2 egg yolks, 2 tablespoons cream, ¼ teaspoon salt,** and a **few grains cayenne pepper** until thick with a whisk beater. Set over hot (not boiling) water. Add **2 tablespoons lemon juice or tarragon vinegar** gradually, while beating constantly. Cook, beating constantly with the whisk beater, until sauce is consistency of thick cream. Remove double boiler from heat, leaving top in place. Beating constantly, add **½ cup butter,** ½ teaspoon at a time, until the butter is melted and thoroughly blended in.

About 1 cup

866 *Lobster Newburg*

¼ cup butter or margarine
2 cups cream
¾ teaspoon salt
⅛ teaspoon pepper
⅛ teaspoon nutmeg
2 cups cooked lobster meat
    (1-inch pieces)
4 egg yolks, slightly beaten
2 tablespoons sherry

1. Melt butter in cooking pan of a chafing dish. Blend in cream, salt, pepper, and nutmeg. Bring just to boiling. Stir in lobster and cook over low heat until lobster is thoroughly heated.
2. Vigorously stir about 3 tablespoons of the hot mixture into the egg yolks. Immediately blend into hot mixture. Place over simmering water and cook 3 to 5 minutes, or just until mixture thickens. Stir slowly to keep mixture cooking evenly. (Do not overcook as sauce will curdle.) Remove immediately from heat.
3. Blend in sherry and serve on **toast points** or over **hot fluffy rice.**

About 6 servings

Crab Meat Newburg: Follow recipe for Lobster Newburg. Substitute **2 cups cooked crab meat** for the lobster. Remove and discard bony tissue from meat.

867 *Creamed Crab Meat and Mushrooms*

1 can (6½ ounces) crab meat
    (about 1⅓ cups, drained)
½ pound mushrooms
    Milk
5 tablespoons butter or margarine
1 tablespoon minced onion
1 tablespoon chopped chives
1 tablespoon chopped parsley
6 tablespoons flour
1 teaspoon salt
    Few grains cayenne pepper
    Few grains nutmeg
3 egg yolks, slightly beaten
2 cups dairy sour cream
¼ cup sherry
6 Croustades

1. Remove and discard bony tissue from crab and set aside to drain.
2. Remove stems from mushroom caps. Slice both stems and caps. Set caps aside. Place stems in a small saucepan and pour in just enough cold water to barely cover the sliced stems.
3. Slowly bring to boiling, reduce heat and simmer 15 minutes. Remove from heat and drain stems, reserving liquid. Add enough milk to liquid to make 1 cup; set aside.
4. Melt butter in cooking pan of a chafing dish. Add sliced mushroom caps, drained mushroom stems, onion, chives, and parsley. Cook over medium heat until mushrooms are lightly browned and tender; stir occasionally. Remove vegetables with a slotted spoon and set aside.
5. Blend flour, salt, cayenne pepper, and nutmeg into butter in cooking pan. Heat until mixture bubbles; remove from heat.
6. Add mushroom liquid mixture gradually while stirring constantly. Return to heat and cook, stirring constantly, until mixture thickens. Cook 1 to 2 minutes longer and remove from heat.
7. Vigorously stir about 3 tablespoons of the hot mixture into the egg yolks. Immediately return to cooking pan and place over simmering water. Cook 3 to 5 minutes, stirring slowly to keep mixture cooking evenly.
8. Add the crab meat and vegetable mixture. Stirring occasionally, cook 10 to 12 minutes, or until thoroughly heated. Remove from heat.
9. Stirring vigorously with a French whip, wire whisk, or fork, add sour cream to sauce in small amounts. Stir in sherry.
10. Serve over Croustades immediately.

6 servings

868 *Croustades*

1 loaf dry bread, unsliced
    Melted butter or margarine

1. Cut bread loaf into 1¼ to 2-inch thick slices. Remove crusts and cut bread into desired shapes (see Note).
2. Brush outside and inside surfaces of shells with melted butter and place on a baking sheet.
3. Bake at 325°F 12 to 20 minutes, or until lightly browned and crisp. If shells are not to be used immediately, reheat in oven for a few minutes before filling.

6 croustades

Note: Bread slices may be cut into triangles, squares, or diamonds; or cut into rounds or fancy shapes with a large biscuit or cookie cutter. (If cutter is not deep enough, mark with it and finish cutting with the point of a sharp knife.) Following outline of shaped piece, carefully cut out center ¼ to ½ inch from edge, and down to within ¼ to ½ inch of bottom, leaving a neatly cut shell.

869 *Creamed Oysters and Turkey*

6 tablespoons butter or margarine
6 tablespoons flour
¾ teaspoon salt
¼ teaspoon pepper
3 cups milk or cream
1 can (2¼ ounces) deviled ham
3 cups cooked turkey pieces
½ pint oysters (shell particles removed)
8 toast cups

1. Heat butter in cooking pan of a chafing dish over direct heat. Blend in flour, salt, and pepper. Heat until mixture bubbles, stirring constantly.
2. Gradually add milk, stirring constantly; cook 1 to 2 minutes longer. Mix in the deviled ham, turkey, and oysters. Heat thoroughly, stirring occasionally. Keep hot over simmering water, if necessary.
3. Fill toast cups with creamed mixture. Serve immediately.

8 servings

Toast cups: To make 8 toast cups, cut crusts from **8 thin bread slices.** Lightly brush both sides with **melted butter or margarine** and press each slice into a muffin pan well, corners pointing up. Toast in a 325°F oven 12 to 20 minutes, or until crisp and lightly browned.

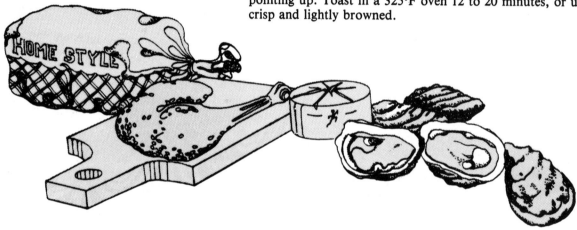

870 *Oysters à la Newburg*

1 pint oysters
1 teaspoon water
½ teaspoon dry mustard
¼ cup butter or margarine
2 tablespoons flour
1 teaspoon salt
⅛ teaspoon nutmeg
⅛ teaspoon pepper
2 cups half-and-half
¼ teaspoon Worcestershire sauce
4 egg yolks, slightly beaten
2 tablespoons sherry

1. Heat oysters in their own liquor just until edges curl. Drain; set aside and keep warm. Blend water with dry mustard and set aside.
2. Heat butter in top of a double boiler over direct heat. Blend in flour, salt, nutmeg, and pepper. Heat until mixture is bubbly. Remove from heat.
3. Gradually add half-and-half and Worcestershire sauce, stirring constantly. Blend mustard mixture into sauce. Bring rapidly to boiling over direct heat, stirring constantly. Cook 1 to 2 minutes longer.
4. Vigorously stir about 3 tablespoons of the hot mixture into the egg yolks. Immediately blend into mixture in top of double boiler and place over simmering water. Cook 3 to 5 minutes, stirring slowly to keep mixture cooking evenly. Remove from heat.
5. Blend in sherry; add oysters and turn into cooking pan of a chafing dish. Keep warm over simmering water and serve on crisp toast.

6 servings

871 *Oysters Royale*

6 tablespoons butter
½ clove garlic, minced
½ cup diced celery
½ cup diced green pepper
6 or 7 tablespoons flour
½ teaspoon salt
¼ teaspoon white pepper
    Few grains cayenne pepper
2 cups half-and-half
1½ pints oysters, drained
    (reserve ⅓ cup liquor)*
1 teaspoon prepared mustard
2 ounces Gruyère cheese, cut into
    pieces
¼ cup dry sherry

1. Heat butter in a saucepan. Add garlic, celery, and green pepper; cook about 5 minutes, or until vegetables are crisp-tender. Remove vegetables with a slotted spoon and set aside.
2. Blend a mixture of flour, salt, and peppers, into butter in saucepan; heat until mixture bubbles. Remove from heat; add half-and-half and reserved oyster liquor gradually, stirring constantly. Continue stirring, bring to boiling, and boil 1 to 2 minutes. Remove from heat.
3. Blend in mustard and cheese, stirring until cheese is melted. Mix in wine, vegetables, and oysters. Bring just to boiling and remove from heat. (Edges of oysters should just begin to curl.) Turn into cooking pan of a chafing dish and set over simmering water.
4. Accompany with a basket of **toasted buttered 3½-inch bread rounds** sprinkled lightly with **ground nutmeg.**

10 to 12 servings

*The amount of liquor in a pint of oysters varies; using slightly less than ⅓ cup will not affect the recipe.

872 *Neapolitan Shrimp*

3 tablespoons olive or other
    cooking oil
2 cloves garlic, minced
2 pounds cleaned and shelled
    shrimp (thawed if frozen)
8 anchovies, cut into pieces
2 cans (16 ounces each) tomatoes,
    forced through a food mill
8 pimento-stuffed olives, sliced
8 pitted ripe olives, sliced
2 teaspoons capers
1 teaspoon dried basil
⅛ teaspoon Tabasco
¼ teaspoon sugar

1. In cooking pan of a chafing dish, heat oil. Add garlic and cook over low heat until tender but not browned.
2. Stir in shrimp. Cook until shrimp turns pink and flesh is firm (about 5 minutes). Remove shrimp from pan and set aside.
3. Add anchovies to liquid in cooking pan; cook 1 minute. Add tomatoes and simmer over low heat 10 minutes. Add olives, capers, basil, Tabasco, and sugar. Cook, uncovered, 15 minutes.
4. Add shrimp to sauce and heat 10 minutes. Keep warm over simmering water. Serve over **hot fluffy rice.**

6 servings

873 *Shrimp Meunière*

1½ pounds uncooked shrimp, shelled
½ cup butter
1 tablespoon lime juice
¼ teaspoon salt
⅛ teaspoon freshly ground
    black pepper
1 teaspoon minced fresh
    parsley

1. Wash shelled shrimp and pat dry. Melt butter in cooking pan of a chafing dish. Stir in the shrimp and cook, turning often, until lightly browned (about 10 minutes).
2. Using a slotted spoon, remove shrimp to a warm platter. Add lime juice, salt, and pepper to butter in pan. Heat thoroughly, return the shrimp to the cooking pan, and coat with the butter sauce.
3. Sprinkle parsley over top and serve shrimp with **hot fluffy rice.**

4 to 6 servings

874 *Shrimp Aphrodite*

1 can (12 ounces) apricot
    nectar
1¼ cups water
2 tablespoons cider vinegar
2 tablespoons sugar
½ teaspoon ground ginger
½ teaspoon dry mustard
½ teaspoon dried tarragon
¼ teaspoon salt
5 cups julienned cooked ham
1½ cups thinly sliced celery
2 cups cooked shrimp, halved
    lengthwise
1 jar (4 ounces) pimentos,
    cut into strips
3 tablespoons butter
¾ cup thinly sliced white
    onion
1½ tablespoons cornstarch
3 tablespoons lime juice

1. Combine apricot nectar, water, vinegar, sugar, ginger, dry mustard, tarragon, and salt. Cover and chill at least 4 hours.
2. Combine ham, celery, shrimp, and pimento. Cover and chill.
3. When ready to serve, melt butter in cooking pan of a chafing dish. Sauté the onion until soft but not brown. Stir in the chilled apricot mixture; cover and simmer 10 minutes.
4. Stir in the chilled ham, celery, shrimp, and pimento. Cover and simmer 10 minutes. Blend cornstarch with lime juice. Stir carefully into mixture until sauce bubbles. Cook 1 to 2 minutes, stirring constantly. Serve over **hot fluffy rice.**

6 to 8 servings

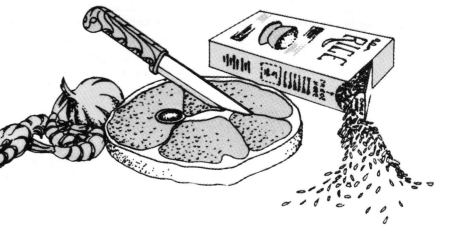

875 *Noodles with Cream and Eggs*

8 ounces medium noodles
½ cup butter
¾ cup freshly grated Parmesan
    cheese
    Freshly ground black pepper
2 egg yolks, slightly beaten
½ cup whipping cream, warmed

1. Cook noodles in boiling salted water as directed on package; drain.
2. Melt butter in cooking pan of a chafing dish. Place cooking pan over simmering water, add noodles to pan, and toss gently with butter. Sprinkle on cheese and a generous amount of pepper while tossing.
3. When cheese is well mixed and noodles are coated, stir egg yolks into the noodles.
4. Toss the noodles again and add whipping cream. Toss again and serve immediately in hot soup bowls.

4 to 6 servings

876 *Shupp Noodles*

6 ounces uncooked noodles
½ cup butter
3 eggs
½ teaspoon salt
    Pinch pepper

1. Cook noodles in boiling salted water about 10 minutes. Rinse and drain well.
2. Melt butter in cooking pan of a chafing dish. Add the cooked noodles and cook over low heat until lightly browned, stirring occasionally.
3. Beat eggs with salt and pepper, and stir into the noodles. Cook over simmering water until eggs are set.

4 to 6 servings

877 *Shrimp Creole*

¼ cup butter or margarine
½ cup chopped onion
½ cup chopped celery
⅓ cup chopped green pepper
3 tablespoons flour
1 can (16 ounces) tomatoes, sieved
1 bay leaf
1 large sprig parsley
1½ teaspoons salt
1 teaspoon sugar
¾ teaspoon Worcestershire sauce
¼ teaspoon freshly ground
    black pepper
2 or 3 drops Tabasco
¾ pound cooked shrimp

1. Heat butter in cooking pan of a chafing dish. Add onion, celery, and green pepper. Cook over medium heat, stirring occasionally, until onion is transparent and other vegetables are tender.
2. Blend in flour and heat until mixture is bubbly. Gradually stir in remaining ingredients except shrimp.
3. Simmer sauce, covered, 30 minutes. Remove bay leaf and parsley. Stir in shrimp and cook over simmering water until thoroughly heated. Serve over **hot fluffy rice.**

4 or 5 servings

878 *Shrimp in Sour Cream Sauce*

¼ cup butter or margarine
2 tablespoons olive oil
1 cup chopped scallions or
    green onions
1 pound fresh mushrooms,
    sliced
¼ cup finely chopped parsley
¼ cup Madeira
1½ pounds fresh shrimp, peeled,
    deveined, rinsed, and drained
½ to 1 teaspoon salt
⅛ teaspoon black pepper
1 cup dairy sour cream

1. Heat butter and olive oil in cooking pan of a chafing dish over direct heat. Add scallions and cook 2 minutes. Add mushrooms and cook 5 minutes. Mix in parsley and wine. Add shrimp and cook until they turn pink. Season with salt and pepper.
2. Remove from heat. Blend in sour cream and heat (*do not boil*). Sprinkle with an additional 2 teaspoons wine, if desired. Place cooking pan over hot water. Serve on **toast rounds.**

About 6 servings

879 *Spaghetti-Cheese Pie*

8 ounces spaghetti, cooked
    and drained
½ cup chopped celery
¼ cup chopped onion
1 tablespoon poppy seed
½ teaspoon salt
¼ teaspoon pepper
½ cup evaporated milk
3 tablespoons butter or margarine
8 ounces sharp Cheddar cheese,
    shredded (about 2 cups)

1. Combine spaghetti, celery, onion, poppy seed, salt, pepper, and evaporated milk in a large bowl.
2. Heat butter in cooking pan of a chafing dish. Spoon half the spaghetti mixture into the pan, spreading evenly. Sprinkle with 1½ cups cheese. Top with remaining spaghetti mixture and cheese.
3. Cover and cook over simmering water 15 to 25 minutes, running a spatula under mixture occasionally to prevent sticking.
4. Cut into six wedges and serve.

6 servings

880 *Chili Don Pedro*

8 ounces medium noodles,
    cooked and drained
1 tablespoon butter or margarine
3 cans (about 16 ounces each)
    chili with beans
8 ounces creamed cottage cheese
1 package (8 ounces) cream
    cheese, cut into ¾-inch cubes
½ cup dairy sour cream

1. Toss cooked noodles with butter; keep warm.
2. Mix chili, cheeses, and sour cream in cooking pan of a large chafing dish. Cover and simmer until the mixture is thoroughly heated, stirring occasionally. If necessary, blend in additional sour cream until of desired consistency.
3. To serve, combine noodles with the chili mixture and sprinkle **snipped parsley** over top.

8 servings

881 *Garlic-Buttered Noodles*

½ cup butter
1 clove garlic, minced
1 teaspoon salt
¼ teaspoon pepper
8 ounces medium noodles,
    cooked and drained
1 cup bread crumbs, browned
    in butter

1. Place butter, garlic, salt, and pepper in cooking pan of a chafing dish. Heat just until butter is lightly browned.
2. Place cooking pan over simmering water. Add noodles and crumbs. Toss lightly until noodles are well coated and crumbs are evenly distributed.

About 8 servings

882 *Glossy Carrots*

24 small whole carrots, pared
    and cooked
¼ cup butter or margarine
¼ cup thawed frozen orange
    juice concentrate
2 teaspoons honey
½ teaspoon ground ginger
½ teaspoon salt

1. While carrots are cooking, melt butter in cooking pan of a chafing dish. Blend in orange juice concentrate, honey, and a mixture of ginger and salt.
2. Add carrots and heat over chafing dish burner, turning carrots until well glazed.

About 4 servings

883 *Corn with Mushrooms*

2 tablespoons butter or margarine
¼ cup thinly sliced green onion
⅔ cup coarsely chopped
    mushrooms
1 can (12 ounces) whole kernel
    corn, drained
½ cup cream
½ teaspoon salt
⅛ teaspoon pepper
2 tablespoons snipped parsley

1. Melt butter in cooking pan of a chafing dish. Add onion and mushrooms and sauté 5 minutes.
2. Add corn and stir mixture gently over medium heat until thoroughly heated.
3. Add cream, salt, pepper, and parsley. Place over simmering water to keep warm until ready to serve.

4 to 6 servings

884 *Green Beans with Tomato*

1 pound fresh green beans, cut
    diagonally into 1-inch pieces
¼ cup butter or margarine
¼ cup finely chopped onion
1 small clove garlic, crushed in
    a garlic press
1 tablespoon lemon juice
2 medium-size ripe tomatoes, cut
    into pieces
1 tablespoon brown sugar
1 teaspoon salt
⅛ teaspoon black pepper
½ teaspoon oregano

1. Cook green beans in boiling salted water until tender; drain.
2. While beans are cooking, heat butter in cooking pan of a chafing dish. Add onion and garlic and cook over medium heat 3 minutes. Add remaining ingredients and heat thoroughly, stirring occasionally.
3. Add green beans to tomato mixture; mix gently. Place over simmering water to keep warm.

6 to 8 servings

885 *Mushrooms Supreme*

2 pounds mushrooms
3 tablespoons lemon juice
¼ teaspoon salt
⅛ teaspoon white pepper
½ cup butter or margarine
2 tablespoons grated onion
¼ teaspoon Worcestershire
    sauce
¼ teaspoon salt
¼ teaspoon white pepper
    Few grains cayenne pepper
¼ cup shredded sharp Cheddar
    cheese

1. Remove stems from mushrooms. (Use stems for other food preparation.) Put mushroom caps into a shallow dish and drizzle with a mixture of lemon juice, ¼ teaspoon salt, and ⅛ teaspoon white pepper. Cover and marinate in refrigerator about 1 hour, turning gently several times.
2. Remove mushrooms from marinade and drain thoroughly on absorbent paper. Heat half the butter in cooking pan of a chafing dish over direct heat. Add about half the mushroom caps and half the grated onion.
3. Cook 10 to 15 minutes, or until caps are lightly browned and tender, turning with a spoon occasionally. Remove mushroom caps to a bowl and cook remaining mushrooms.
4. Place all mushroom caps in cooking pan and add Worcestershire sauce, salt, white pepper, and cayenne pepper. Toss gently to mix.
5. Sprinkle cheese over mushrooms and set pan over simmering water to keep hot while serving. Serve mushrooms on **toast triangles** and garnish with **parsley sprigs.**

6 to 8 servings

886 *Caramel Sweet Potatoes*

⅓ cup butter
½ cup walnut pieces
1 cup firmly packed brown sugar
½ teaspoon salt
½ cup orange juice
6 medium (about 2 pounds) sweet potatoes, cooked
⅓ cup brandy

1. Melt butter in cooking pan of a chafing dish. Stir in walnut pieces. Cook over moderate heat until lightly toasted.
2. Remove walnuts from pan. Add brown sugar, salt, and orange juice to butter remaining in cooking pan; stir to blend. Bring to boiling and boil 3 to 4 minutes, stirring occasionally.
3. Peel the sweet potatoes and cut in halves lengthwise. Add to the syrup with walnut pieces.
4. Place cooking pan over chafing dish burner. Heat the potatoes gently, basting with the syrup. Warm the brandy, pour over potatoes, and ignite. Serve when flames die out.

6 servings

887 *Glazed Fruit in Chafing Dish*

2 tart red apples, cored
2 tablespoons lemon juice
2 tablespoons butter
3 tablespoons brown sugar
1 large banana
½ cup pineapple chunks, fresh or unsweetened canned
1 cup pineapple juice
1 tablespoon cornstarch
Vanilla ice cream

1. Cut apples into wedges. Dip in lemon juice and place in medium-size bowl.
2. Melt butter in cooking pan of a chafing dish over medium heat. Toss apple slices with half the brown sugar and stir into melted butter. Cover and cook over medium heat 7 to 8 minutes, stirring occasionally.
3. When apple slices are almost tender, slice banana into chunks and add with pineapple to apple mixture. Sprinkle remaining brown sugar over fruit, cover, and cook several minutes until bananas are glazed.
4. Remove fruit from cooking pan. Stir in pineapple juice mixed with cornstarch. Simmer a few minutes, stirring occasionally, until sauce thickens.
5. Return fruit to sauce, warm, and serve over ice cream.

4 servings

888 *Fruit Topaz*

3 apples, pared, cored, and sliced
3 pears, pared, cored, and sliced
1 cup firmly packed light brown sugar
1 tablespoon nutmeg
1 cup golden raisins
½ cup slivered almonds
¼ cup butter or margarine
¼ cup lemon-lime carbonated beverage

1. Place apple and pear slices in cooking pan of a chafing dish. Combine sugar and nutmeg and sprinkle over fruit.
2. Sprinkle raisins and almonds over fruit. Dot top of mixture with butter. Pour carbonated beverage over all.
3. Cook over medium heat until fruit is tender (15 to 20 minutes).
4. Keep warm over simmering water while serving.

6 servings

889 *Brandied Bananas*

4 large green-tipped bananas,
    sliced diagonally into 1-inch
    pieces
3 tablespoons lime juice
¼ cup butter or margarine
½ cup sugar
½ cup apricot brandy
1 cup dairy sour cream or yogurt
    Brown sugar

1. Sprinkle bananas with lime juice. Heat butter in cooking pan of a chafing dish over medium flame of chafing dish burner.
2. Add bananas and heat quickly. Stir in sugar and all but 2 tablespoons apricot brandy. Heat remaining brandy in a ladle or a large serving spoon. Ignite the warm brandy and pour over the bananas. Shake the pan gently or stir until flame dies down.
3. Serve the bananas topped with dairy sour cream and a sprinkling of brown sugar.

4 servings

890 *Peach Flambée Ambrosia*

1 tablespoon butter
¼ cup slivered almonds
2 tablespoons light brown sugar
2 tablespoons orange juice
1 package (16 ounces) frozen
    sliced peaches, thawed
    Vanilla ice cream
¼ cup shredded coconut
¼ cup Grand Marnier

1. Heat butter in cooking pan of a chafing dish over low heat. Add almonds and brown lightly. Stir in brown sugar and orange juice. Add peaches and heat.
2. Place scoops of vanilla ice cream in dessert dishes and sprinkle with coconut.
3. Warm liqueur in a ladle. Ignite and pour over the peaches. Shake the pan gently or stir until flames die out. Spoon over ice cream.

4 to 6 servings

891 *Strawberry-Pear Flambée*

2 packages (10 ounces each) frozen
    strawberries
1 cup sugar
6 tablespoons butter
½ cup orange juice
1½ teaspoons grated lemon peel
1 can (29 ounces) large pear halves,
    drained
⅓ cup cognac

1. Drain strawberries; reserve juice. Put berries through a sieve to purée. Add desired amount of reserved juice to sweeten and thin purée; set aside.
2. In cooking pan of a chafing dish, caramelize sugar with butter over medium heat. Stir in orange juice, lemon peel, and purée. Simmer sauce 1 to 2 minutes, stirring gently.
3. Place pears in sauce and roll in sauce until they are thoroughly heated and have a blush.
4. In a separate pan, heat cognac just until warm. Ignite the cognac and pour over the pears. Spoon the sauce over pears until the flames die out.
5. Serve the pears in dessert dishes with the sauce.

4 servings

892 *Crepes Suzette*

Crepes:

    1 cup all-purpose flour
    1 teaspoon sugar
    1 pinch salt
    1 egg, well beaten
    1 cup milk
    2 tablespoons butter

Sauce:

    ½ cup sugar
       Peelings (white portion removed) and juices of 1 orange and ½ lemon
    ¼ cup butter
    1 ounce Grand Marnier
    1 ounce cognac
    1 ounce Cointreau

1. To prepare crepes, mix all ingredients except butter in a bowl; beat until smooth (batter should be the consistency of thin cream).
2. Put a small amount of butter in an 8-inch skillet; heat until the butter bubbles. Pour in enough batter to form a 6-inch circle, quickly rotating the pan to spread the batter thinly and evenly. Cook over medium heat about ½ minute; turn crepe and cook other side.
3. With the aid of a fork and a spoon, carefully fold the crepe in fourths. Transfer to a heated plate and keep warm. Repeat process until all the batter is used.
4. To prepare sauce, heat ¼ cup of the sugar in cooking pan of a chafing dish over low heat, stirring until sugar is caramelized. Add the citrus peelings and the butter; stir until butter is melted.
5. Add the citrus juices; cook and stir several minutes. Remove the peelings from the sauce.
6. To serve, transfer folded crepes to the sauce. Sprinkle the remaining sugar over crepes. Add the liqueurs to sauce and ignite.
7. Serve 3 crepes per person on hot dessert plates.

4 servings

893 *Emperor's Dessert (Kaiserschmarren)*

    2 tablespoons butter
    1 cup all-purpose flour
    ¼ cup sugar
    ¼ teaspoon salt
    3 eggs, beaten
    1 cup milk
    ¾ cup butter
    ¾ cup sugar
    ½ teaspoon ground cinnamon
    ½ cup golden raisins, plumped
    ½ cup flaked or sliced almonds, toasted

1. Melt 2 tablespoons butter in a heavy 6-inch skillet and set aside.
2. Combine flour, ¼ cup sugar, and salt in a bowl. Add a mixture of eggs, milk, and melted butter. Beat until smooth.
3. Heat skillet to moderately hot. Pour in just enough batter to cover bottom. Immediately tilt skillet to spread batter thinly and evenly.
4. Cook each crepe over medium heat until light brown on bottom and firm to touch on top. Turn and brown other side. As each crepe is cooked, transfer to a hot platter.
5. Using two forks, gently tear the crepes into 1-inch irregular-shaped pieces; set aside and keep warm.
6. Melt ¾ cup butter in cooking pan of a chafing dish; stir in ¾ cup sugar. Mix in cinnamon, raisins, and almonds, stirring occasionally until heated.
7. Add crepe pieces and toss lightly to coat.

8 to 10 servings

Crepes

894 Dinner Crepes

1 cup all-purpose flour
⅛ teaspoon salt
3 eggs
1½ cups milk
2 tablespoons melted butter or oil

1. Sift flour and salt. Add eggs, one at a time, beating thoroughly. Gradually add milk, mixing until blended. Add melted butter or oil and beat until smooth. (Or mix in an electric blender until smooth.)
2. Let batter stand for 1 hour before cooking crepes.

About 18 crepes

895 Dessert Crepes

1 cup all-purpose flour
¼ cup sugar
Pinch salt
3 eggs
1½ cups milk
2 tablespoons melted butter or oil
2 tablespoons brandy

1. Sift flour, sugar, and salt. Add eggs, one at a time, beating thoroughly. Gradually add milk, melted butter or oil, and brandy, beating until smooth. (Or mix in an electric blender until smooth.)
2. Let batter stand 1 hour before cooking crepes.

About 18 crepes

Cocoa Crepes: Follow recipe for Dessert Crepes; then mix **2 tablespoons cocoa** with flour, sugar, and salt, and substitute **2 tablespoons rum** for brandy.

896

897 Wheat Crepes

1 cup whole wheat flour
1 tablespoon sprouted wheat or
    wheat germ
3 eggs
Pinch salt
½ cup whipping cream
¾ cup water
2 tablespoons butter or margarine, melted

Make batter the same way as basic crepes

About 16 crepes

898 Corn Crepes

⅔ cup all-purpose flour
6 tablespoons cornmeal
3 eggs
Pinch salt
1 cup milk or cream
2 tablespoons oil

Make batter the same way as basic crepes

About 10 crepes

899 *Wafer Crepes*

2½ cups crepe batter (see Note)
Cooking oil

1. Heat a skillet or griddle over medium heat, and brush with oil.
2. Pour ½ tablespoon batter in skillet, but do not swirl the pan. Pour 3 or 4 more crepes, turn when brown, and brown on other side. Place crepes on ungreased baking sheet.
3. Bake at 350°F about 15 minutes, turning over halfway through baking. Remove from baking sheet and serve with dips, spreads, or cheese.

About 8 dozen wafers

Note: Any of the crepe batters may be used to make Wafer Crepes. If desired, batter may be thinned with a little liquid for thinner, crisper wafers.

900 *Pinwheel Party Platter*
(with Turkey, Ham, and Asparagus)

½ pound mushrooms, cleaned and chopped
5 tablespoons butter or margarine
5 tablespoons flour
½ cup water
½ cup whipping cream
¼ teaspoon salt
2 dashes pepper
¼ teaspoon dry mustard
Dash cayenne pepper
¼ pound Swiss cheese, shredded
15 dinner crepes
10 asparagus spears, cooked and salted
5 (1-ounce) slices boiled ham
5 (1-ounce) slices cooked turkey breast, lightly salted

1. Lightly sauté mushrooms in 1 tablespoon butter about 3 minutes. Set aside.
2. Melt remaining butter over low heat. Add flour and stir until smooth. Slowly stir in water and cream. Add mushrooms. Over medium heat, stir and bring to boiling. Blend in dry seasonings and Swiss cheese. Cook and stir until cheese melts.
3. Spread mixture over crepes. Pinwheels are made by placing a ham or turkey slice, tightly rolled around one asparagus spear, at the bottom edge of each crepe. Roll up, forming a tight roll. Put into a baking dish.
4. Bake at 375°F 10 minutes. Cool 30 minutes.
5. Slice each roll into 6 pinwheels. Serve with picks. Arrange in a colorful pattern on a platter.

90 hors d'oeuvres

901 *Dilled Beef Rolls*

⅓ cup dairy sour cream
2 tablespoons grated cucumber
⅛ teaspoon dill weed
Dash Worcestershire sauce
1 can (4½ ounces) roast beef spread
4 dinner crepes

1. Combine sour cream, cucumber, dill weed, and Worcestershire sauce. Let stand 30 minutes.
2. Spread roast beef mixture on the crepes. Top with a thin layer of sour cream mixture. Roll up jelly-roll fashion. Place on a cookie sheet.
3. Bake at 375°F 15 minutes.
4. Cut each roll into thirds and serve warm as a snack or hors d'oeuvres.

1 dozen hors d'oeuvres

902 Anchovy Bits

4 dinner crepes
½ cup shredded mozzarella
　cheese
8 to 16 anchovy fillets packed in
　oil, drained
¼ teaspoon garlic powder
½ teaspoon oregano

1. On each crepe sprinkle mozzarella cheese, top with 2 to 4 (depending on taste) anchovy fillets, and sprinkle with garlic powder and oregano.
2. Roll up jelly-roll fashion. Place on a cookie sheet.
3. Bake at 375°F 10 minutes.
4. Rolls can be served individually as appetizers, or each roll can be cut into bite-size pieces and served as hors d'oeuvres.

4 large appetizers or 2 dozen hors d'oeuvres

903 Cheddar-Nut Log

8 ounces sharp Cheddar cheese
　spread
¼ cup chopped nuts
1 tablespoon chopped parsley
3 dinner crepes
　Paprika

1. Blend cheese, nuts, and parsley well. Refrigerate 30 minutes.
2. Form mixture into 3 logs. Place a log on one end of each crepe and roll. Sprinkle log with paprika. Freeze 1 hour.
3. Slice while frozen. Spear with picks and serve at room temperature.

3 nut logs

904 Sardine Pinwheels

1 can (1½ ounces) sardines in oil
1 scallion, minced
½ teaspoon dry mustard
1 to 2 tablespoons dairy sour cream
　Salt and pepper
6 dinner crepes

1. Drain and mash sardines; stir in scallion, mustard, and just enough sour cream to make it spreadable. Season to taste with salt and pepper.
2. Spread on crepes and roll up jelly-roll fashion. Slice into bite-size pieces (about 6 per crepe).

About 3 dozen hors d'oeuvres

905 Red Reuben

1 can (4½ ounces) corned beef
　spread
4 dinner crepes
½ cup drained canned sweet 'n' sour
　red cabbage
½ cup shredded Swiss cheese

1. Smooth ¼ can of corned beef spread on each crepe: spread 2 tablespoons of red cabbage over corned beef. Sprinkle with 2 tablespoons cheese.
2. Roll up jelly-roll fashion.
3. Bake at 375°F 10 minutes.
4. Serve one or two as a snack or slice into bite-size pieces for hors d'oeuvres. If desired, spear with picks and dip into Dijon Sauce ●

4 rolls or 2 dozen hors d'oeuvres

906 *Beef Stroganoff Turnovers*

2 tablespoons butter or
    margarine
½ medium onion, minced
½ pound mushrooms, cleaned and
    sliced
1 pound skirt steak, cut in
    thin strips (sirloin,
    round, or flank can be
    substituted)
1 medium clove garlic, crushed in a
    garlic press
⅛ teaspoon cumin
⅛ teaspoon dill weed
⅛ teaspoon marjoram
1 teaspoon Worcestershire sauce
2 tablespoons ketchup
⅓ cup red wine
1 beef bouillon cube
    Salt and pepper
8 ounces dairy sour cream
6 dinner crepes

1. Melt butter. Sauté onion and mushrooms. Add meat strips, garlic, cumin, dill weed, marjoram, Worcestershire sauce, and ketchup. Sauté until meat is browned. Stir in wine and bouillon cube. Simmer until meat is tender. Season with salt and pepper to taste. Stir in sour cream. Cook over low heat 5 minutes.
2. Using a slotted spoon, assemble by turnover method. Place on baking sheet.
3. Bake at 350°F 10 minutes. Serve topped with any remaining sauce.

6 turnovers

907 *Steak and Kidney Pie*

½ pound lamb kidneys
⅓ cup butter or margarine
1 cup chopped onion
½ pound diced beef (top sirloin,
    round, or flank)
1 cup dry red wine
¼ teaspoon marjoram
1 small clove garlic, crushed in
    a garlic press
1 tablespoon flour
¾ cup beef broth (1 beef
    bouillon cube dissolved in ¾ cup
    boiling water)
    Salt and pepper
6 dinner crepes

1. Peel, core, and dice kidneys.
2. Melt butter. Sauté kidneys over low heat until browned. Add onion and beef. Continue cooking until onion is browned and meat is tender. Stir in wine, marjoram, and garlic. Simmer, covered, 15 minutes.
3. Stir in flour. Gradually add broth, stirring constantly. Cook until sauce thickens. Add salt and pepper to taste.
4. Assemble, using tube method. Arrange, seam side down, on a baking sheet.
5. Bake at 375°F 10 minutes. Crepe will be crisp but filling will be moist and tasty. Serve immediately.

6 filled crepes

Note: One crepe, accompanied by soup, salad, vegetable, and dessert, is a filling dinner.

908 *Cannelloni*

½ pound Italian sausage, cooked and finely chopped
1 cup cooked chopped beef
1 package (10 ounces) frozen chopped spinach, thawed and well drained
¼ cup plus 2 tablespoons grated Parmesan cheese
⅛ teaspoon ground thyme
⅛ teaspoon pepper
Salt
8 dinner crepes
● ½ cup Basic White Sauce

Nutmeg

1. Combine sausage, beef, spinach, ¼ cup cheese, thyme, pepper, and salt to taste.
2. Divide filling among crepes. Assemble, using tube method. Top with white sauce, remaining Parmesan, and nutmeg.
3. Bake at 350°F 20 minutes.

8 filled crepes

909 *Creamed Chipped Beef Turnovers*

● 1½ cups Basic White Sauce
2 hard-cooked eggs, chopped
5 ounces dried beef, rinsed
½ teaspoon Worcestershire sauce
8 ounces canned peas
8 dinner crepes

1. Make white sauce; stir in eggs, beef, and Worcestershire sauce. Cook 5 minutes. Stir in peas.
2. Assemble, using turnover method. Place on a baking sheet.
3. Bake at 350°F 15 minutes.

8 turnovers

910 *Veal Cordon Bleu*

¼ cup butter or margarine
1 pound thin veal cutlets, pounded and cut in short strips
2 tablespoons white wine
½ cup shredded Swiss cheese
Salt and pepper
8 dinner crepes
¼ pound thinly sliced boiled ham
Paprika

1. Melt butter, add veal strips, and sauté until tender. Add wine; simmer 3 minutes. Remove from heat; stir in ⅓ cup Swiss cheese. Season with salt and pepper.
2. Spread crepes out on a work surface. Divide ham slices among crepes. Spoon veal mixture onto ham. Continue assembling, using square turnover method. Place, seam side down, on a baking sheet and top with remaining cheese. Sprinkle with paprika.
3. Bake at 375°F 15 minutes. Serve piping hot.

8 filled crepes

Note: Substitute chicken for veal, if desired.

911 *Chicken Italiano*

2 whole chicken breasts (about 1 pound)
2 tablespoons oil
½ pound mushrooms, cleaned and chopped
1 can (16 ounces) stewed tomatoes
1 medium clove garlic, crushed in a garlic press
1 teaspoon oregano
½ teaspoon thyme
1 can (8 ounces) tomato sauce
⅓ cup grated Parmesan cheese
Salt and pepper
6 dinner crepes

1. Bone chicken and cut into 1-inch strips.
2. Heat oil, sauté chicken and mushrooms until chicken turns white. Stir in stewed tomatoes, garlic, oregano, thyme, tomato sauce, and 3 tablespoons grated cheese. Add salt and pepper to taste. Simmer, uncovered, 5 minutes.
3. Using a slotted spoon, spoon onto crepes. Assemble, using tube method, place on a baking sheet, and sprinkle tops of crepes with remaining cheese.
4. Bake at 375°F until cheese browns (about 15 minutes) Serve immediately with any remaining sauce.

6 filled crepes

912 *Creamed Chicken*

3 tablespoons butter or margarine
¼ cup flour
1 tablespoon chopped parsley
¼ teaspoon dried tarragon
1½ cups whipping cream
2 cups diced cooked chicken
Salt and pepper
6 dinner crepes
Paprika

1. Melt butter (do not brown); stir in flour. Add parsley, tarragon, and cream. Cook until thick. Add chicken and salt and pepper to taste.
2. Divide among crepes. Fold in half; place on a baking sheet. Sprinkle with paprika.
3. Bake at 375°F 15 minutes.

6 filled crepes

913 *Curried Chicken Salad in Butterfly Crepes*

1 chicken (2½ pounds), cut in pieces
1 bay leaf
1 teaspoon thyme
½ teaspoon salt
Boiling water
¼ cup mayonnaise
¼ teaspoon curry powder
¼ teaspoon poultry seasoning
2 teaspoons curry powder
2 tablespoons chutney
⅔ cup dairy sour cream

1. Place chicken, bay leaf, thyme, and salt in a deep saucepan and cover with boiling water. Cover. Simmer, do not boil, 1 hour, or until tender.
2. While chicken is simmering, combine mayonnaise and ¼ teaspoon curry powder. Cover. Chill.
3. Remove skin and bones from chicken. Finely dice chicken; cool.
4. Mix cool chicken, poultry seasoning, remaining curry powder, and chutney. Add sour cream and mix until all ingredients are moist and mixture holds its shape. Add salt and pepper to taste.
5. Assemble crepes using butterfly method, with chicken salad

Salt and pepper
6 dinner crepes
Chopped peanuts or cashews
Flaked coconut
2 spiced peaches, cut in 8 wedges

for filling and topping. Garnish wings by dotting with curried mayonnaise and sprinkling with chopped nuts and coconut. Form antennae with peach wedges. Serve at room temperature.

4 servings

Note: Salad may be made in advance and stored in refrigerator until ready to assemble.

914 *Mandarin Chicken Turnovers*

1 chicken (2½ pounds)
2 scallions, minced
⅓ cup diced celery
¼ cup butter or margarine
1 can (11 ounces) mandarin oranges, drained; reserve syrup
2 teaspoons soy sauce
Dash cayenne pepper
⅛ teaspoon minced crystallized ginger
2 teaspoons cornstarch
8 dinner crepes

1. Skin, bone, and dice chicken.
2. Sauté chicken, scallions, and celery in butter until chicken is cooked.
3. Make mandarin sauce by adding water to reserved syrup, if necessary, to equal ⅔ cup liquid. Combine this liquid with soy sauce, cayenne, ginger, and cornstarch. Stir until well blended. Cook, stirring constantly, over medium heat until mixture turns clear and thickens. Stir in mandarin oranges.
4. Stir half the sauce into hot sautéed chicken.
5. Assemble, using turnover method.
6. Serve immediately, topped with remaining sauce; or for a crispy crepe, place on a baking sheet and bake at 375°F 10 minutes. Serve immediately with remaining warm sauce.

8 turnovers

915 *Sicilian Chicken*

1 pound boned chicken
1 package (10 ounces) frozen chopped broccoli, thawed
2 tablespoons oil
¼ pound mushrooms, cleaned and sliced
● ⅔ cup Pesto Sauce
8 dinner crepes
● ½ cup Basic White Sauce
Parsley

1. Cut chicken into 1×¼-inch strips. Drain broccoli.
2. Heat oil and sauté chicken, mushrooms, and broccoli until tender. Drain off any liquid; stir in Pesto Sauce.
3. Assemble, using square turnover method. Place on a baking sheet, separating slightly; top with white sauce.
4. Bake at 375°F 10 minutes. Serve garnished with parsley.

8 filled crepes

916 Chicken and Shrimp Egg Roll

3 tablespoons oil
½ pound raw chicken, cut in julienne
   strips*
½ pound shrimp, cleaned and diced
1 can (16 ounces) bean sprouts,
   well drained
⅓ cup coarsely chopped celery
8 scallions, thinly sliced
½ cup shredded cabbage
1 tablespoon soy sauce
1 teaspoon salt
12 dinner crepes
   Oil for frying

1. Heat 3 tablespoons oil in skillet. Sauté chicken, stirring frequently. Add shrimp, bean sprouts, celery, scallions, and cabbage. Cook 4 minutes. Season with soy sauce and salt. Cool 10 minutes.
2. Assemble, using egg-roll method.
3. Fry in ⅛ inch heated oil in a skillet until golden. Serve hot.

12 egg rolls

Note: Egg rolls can be stored in the refrigerator or freezer. To reheat, bake at 375°F 15 minutes.

*If desired, use all chicken or all shrimp, or substitute pork for chicken.

917 Chicken Curry Turnovers

1 chicken (2½ pounds)
2½ tablespoons Curry Powder
3 tablespoons butter or margarine
½ cup chopped onion
¾ cup unsweetened applesauce
● 2 tablespoons Peach Chutney

Salt and pepper
6 dinner crepes

1. Skin, bone, and dice chicken. Toss chicken with Curry Powder.
2. Sauté coated chicken in butter with onion until tender. Stir in applesauce and chutney. Simmer 10 minutes.
3. Assemble, using turnover method.
4. Bake at 375°F 10 minutes.
5. Serve with Condiments for Curry.

6 turnovers

Curry Powder: Put **1 teaspoon cumin seed, 2 teaspoons coriander seed, 2½ tablespoons sesame seed, 2 teaspoons turmeric, ½ teaspoon chili powder, ¼ teaspoon ground ginger, ¼ teaspoon garlic powder,** and **1 teaspoon salt** into an electric blender container. Blend at medium-high speed until well blended and a powder. Store in a tightly covered container. 918

⅓ cup powder

Condiments for Curry: Chutney, chopped peanuts or cashews, chopped green pepper, flaked coconut, diced bananas, chopped raisins, quartered kumquats, sliced scallions, shredded cucumber, crushed or chunk pineapple, yogurt, diced apple, diced banana, or crumbled bacon.

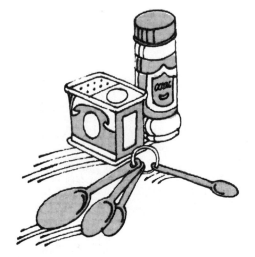

919 Chicken Liver and Green Grape Turnovers

1 pound chicken livers
¼ cup butter or margarine
2 tablespoons minced onion
¼ teaspoon salt
⅛ teaspoon ginger
⅛ teaspoon pepper
1 teaspoon Worcestershire sauce
1 cup seedless green grapes, cut in half
1 tablespoon sherry
1 chicken bouillon cube
¼ cup water
⅓ cup dairy sour cream
2 tablespoons chopped parsley
8 dinner crepes

1. Sauté chicken livers in butter 3 minutes. Stir in onion and sauté 4 minutes more.
2. Add salt, ginger, pepper, Worcestershire sauce, grapes, sherry, bouillon cube, and water. Simmer 3 minutes. Remove from heat. Stir in sour cream and parsley.
3. Assemble, using turnover method.
4. Bake at 350°F 10 minutes. Serve immediately.

8 turnovers

920 Chicken Polynesian Turnovers

2 chicken breasts, boned (about 1 pound)
¼ cup bottled teriyaki sauce
¼ cup oil
1 large banana, diced
1 can (8 ounces) crushed pineapple, drained; reserve juice
¼ cup chopped green pepper
1 tablespoon honey
1 tablespoon soy sauce
1 tablespoon cornstarch
4 dinner crepes

1. Cut boned chicken breasts into short strips. Marinate in teriyaki sauce for 20 minutes.
2. Heat oil; sauté chicken until tender. Stir in diced banana, crushed pineapple, and green pepper. Simmer 3 to 5 minutes to heat fruit.
3. Assemble, using turnover method. Place on a baking sheet.
4. Bake at 375°F 15 minutes.
5. While crepes are baking, make a sauce with ½ cup reserved pineapple juice, honey, soy sauce, and cornstarch; cook until mixture thickens.
6. Serve hot crepes with sauce on top. Accompany with stir-fried vegetables, if desired.

4 turnovers

921 Ham Foldovers

● 1½ cups Basic White Sauce
1 tablespoon Dijon mustard
1 pound cooked ham, cut in ¼-inch cubes
½ pound American cheese, cut in ¼-inch cubes
1 can (16 ounces) green peas, drained
8 dinner crepes
¼ pound Swiss cheese, coarsely shredded

1. Prepare sauce. Reserve ½ cup of sauce for topping.
2. To the remaining sauce, add mustard, ham, American cheese, and peas. Mix gently.
3. Divide filling among crepes. Fold crepes in half. Put on a baking sheet. Spread reserved sauce over tops of crepes and sprinkle with Swiss cheese.
4. Bake at 350°F 15 minutes. Serve at once.

8 filled crepes

Sausage Foldovers: Follow recipe for Ham Foldovers; substitute **1 pound cooked Italian sausage** for ham. 922

923 Turkey à la King

2 tablespoons butter or margarine
¼ cup chopped onion
¼ pound mushrooms, cleaned and sliced
• 1½ cups Basic White Sauce

½ teaspoon Worcestershire sauce
1½ tablespoons chopped pimento
6 dinner crepes
1 cup diced cooked turkey

1. Melt butter. Sauté onion and mushrooms until tender. Stir in white sauce, Worcestershire sauce, and pimento. Simmer 5 minutes.
2. To assemble, spread crepe with some sauce, divide turkey among crepes, and proceed, using turnover method.
3. Bake at 375°F 10 minutes.
4. Keep remaining sauce warm. Serve crepes topped with remaining sauce.

6 filled crepes

Note: Substitute 1 cup diced cooked chicken, pork, or veal for turkey, if desired.

924 Lobster Newburg

¼ cup butter or margarine
6 tablespoons flour
1½ cups light cream
1 tablespoon cooking liquid from lobster (if possible)
3 tablespoons sherry
¼ teaspoon nutmeg
3 dashes cayenne pepper
  Pinch of paprika
1 egg yolk, slightly beaten
1 egg white
2 cups cubed, cooked lobster
12 dinner crepes

1. Melt butter, stir in flour, and cook 1 minute. Slowly stir in light cream and liquid from lobster. Cook, stirring continuously, until smooth and thick.
2. Blend in sherry, nutmeg, cayenne, and paprika. Slowly add egg yolk, blend well, and cook until smooth and thick (about 3 minutes).
3. Combine half of the sauce with the lobster meat. Reserve the rest.
4. To assemble, place a heaping tablespoon of the lobster mixture on one quarter of the crepe. Brush remaining three quarters of crepe with egg white. Fold into cone-shaped packages. Place in baking dish, one cone overlapping the other, with the open part of the cone upward.
5. Bake at 375°F 10 minutes. Serve 2 for an appetizer or 3 for dinner, topped with warmed remaining sauce.

12 filled crepes

925 **Lobster Duxelles:** Sauté ½ **pound sliced mushrooms** in **1 tablespoon butter or margarine** and add to the sauce. This will increase yield to fill 15 crepes.

926 **Crab Newburg:** Substitute **2 cups cooked, flaked crab** for lobster.

927 **Shrimp Newburg:** Sauté ⅓ **cup minced celery** and ¼ **pound sliced mushrooms** in **2 tablespoons butter or margarine.** Substitute **celery, mushrooms,** and **1½ cups cooked shrimp** for lobster.

928 **Scallop Newburg:** Sauté ¼ **pound sliced mushrooms** and **2 tablespoons snipped parsley** in **1 tablespoon butter.** Substitute **mushrooms, parsley,** and **2 cups scallops** for lobster. This will increase the filling yield slightly, so fill each crepe with 2 level tablespoons scallop mixture.

929 Pesto Crab Squares

1 pound ricotta cheese
2 eggs, slightly beaten
1 teaspoon oregano
1 medium clove garlic, crushed
2 tablespoons grated Parmesan
   cheese
• ⅓ cup Pesto Sauce
6 ounces frozen king crab, drained
   well
12 dinner crepes
• 1 cup Basic White Sauce

Nutmeg

1. Beat ricotta cheese and eggs until smooth. Stir in oregano, garlic, Parmesan cheese, Pesto Sauce, and crab.
2. Assemble, using square turnover method. Arrange in baking dish so crepes are just touching. Top with Basic White Sauce; sprinkle with nutmeg.
3. Bake at 375°F 20 minutes. Cool 5 minutes before serving. Serve 1 for an appetizer; 2 for a dinner.

12 squares

930 Curried Crab Florentine

3 tablespoons butter or margarine
2 cans (7½ ounces each)
   Alaska king crab meat, drained
Salt to taste
1 scallion, chopped
1 can (4 ounces) sliced
   mushrooms, drained
1 teaspoon curry powder
Dash cayenne pepper
Dash Worcestershire sauce
1 tablespoon chutney
• 1 cup Creamy Lemon Sauce

8 dinner crepes
¼ cup flaked coconut

1. Melt butter, add crab, salt (if necessary), scallion, mushrooms, curry powder, cayenne, and Worcestershire sauce.
2. Sauté until scallions are tender and mixture is thoroughly heated. Remove from heat.
3. Stir in chutney and ¼ cup Creamy Lemon Sauce. Divide mixture among crepes and assemble, using tube method.
4. Arrange snugly in a baking dish. Top with remaining sauce and sprinkle on coconut.
5. Broil about 5 inches from source of heat 3 minutes or until lightly browned.

8 filled crepes

931 Crab Cannelloni

1 pound ricotta or cottage cheese
1 egg, slightly beaten
¼ cup grated Parmesan cheese
1 teaspoon oregano
¼ teaspoon ground thyme
1 medium clove garlic, crushed
1 teaspoon butter or margarine
2 tablespoons minced onion
½ cup diced broccoli
6 ounces frozen king crab meat,
   drained and crumbled
10 dinner crepes
• 1 cup Basic White Sauce

Nutmeg

1. Beat ricotta or cottage cheese until smooth.
2. Blend in egg, Parmesan cheese, oregano, thyme, and garlic.
3. Melt butter or margarine; sauté onion and broccoli until tender; drain well.
4. Stir onion, broccoli, and crab into cheese mixture. Assemble, using tube method; fit snugly into a baking dish.
5. Bake at 350°F 20 minutes. Cool for 5 minutes. Serve topped with warm white sauce and sprinkled with nutmeg.

10 filled crepes

932 Crab à la King

¼ cup minced onion
¼ pound mushrooms, cleaned
  and sliced
2 tablespoons butter or
  margarine
●1½ cups Basic White Sauce

1½ teaspoons Worcestershire sauce
1 tablespoon chopped pimento
1 teaspoon lemon juice
6 ounces frozen crab meat,
  flaked
4 dinner crepes

1. Sauté onion and mushrooms in butter until tender; stir into Basic White Sauce.
2. Add Worcestershire sauce, pimento, and lemon juice to white sauce mixture; blend well.
3. Simmer 3 minutes to blend flavors. Stir ½ cup sauce into crab meat.
4. Assemble, using tube method. Place in baking pan; top with remaining sauce.
5. Bake at 375°F 15 minutes. Serve piping hot.

4 filled crepes

933 Coral Shrimp

½ cup finely chopped onion
1 tablespoon butter or margarine
● 2 cups Basic White Sauce

1 to 2 teaspoons tomato paste
¼ cup dry white wine
½ teaspoon salt
¼ teaspoon white pepper
1 pound cooked medium shrimp
  (fresh or frozen)

1. Sauté onion in butter until tender. Mix onion into white sauce. Stir in tomato paste, wine, salt, and pepper. Fold in shrimp.
2. Assemble, using tube method. Spoon extra sauce over crepes. Garnish with **fresh tomato** and **Bibb lettuce**.

12 filled crepes

934 Scallops and Broccoli au Gratin

2 tablespoons butter or margarine
5 ounces frozen chopped broccoli
1 scallion, chopped
1 pound frozen scallops
2 tablespoons white wine
1½ teaspoons lemon juice
2 dashes cayenne pepper
1 sprig parsley, chopped
⅓ cup shredded Swiss cheese
2 tablespoons grated Parmesan
  cheese
  Salt and pepper
8 dinner crepes
● ½ cup Basic White Sauce

Nutmeg

1. Melt butter. Sauté broccoli and scallion in butter until broccoli is cooked.
2. Stir in scallops, wine, lemon juice, cayenne, and parsley. Simmer until scallops are tender.
3. Drain off liquid. Stir in cheeses. Salt and pepper to taste.
4. Assemble, using square turnover method. Place on baking sheet.
5. Bake at 375°F 10 minutes. Spoon 1 tablespoon white sauce over each square, sprinkle with nutmeg, and serve.

8 squares

Note: Crab or shrimp may be substituted for scallops.

935 Asparagus Supreme

3 tablespoons softened butter or
    margarine
3 teaspoons prepared mustard
6 dinner crepes
6 slices (1 ounce each) cooked
    ham
18 cooked asparagus spears
6 slices Swiss cheese, cut
    diagonally in half
6 slices American cheese, cut
    diagonally in half

1. Cream butter with mustard. Spread butter mixture on crepes. Cover with a slice of ham. Place 3 asparagus spears in center of each crepe. Fold in thirds. Put on a baking sheet. Arrange 2 triangles of each cheese alternately over each crepe.
2. Broil until cheese begins to melt. Serve immediately.

6 filled crepes

936 Mushroom Stack

1 pound mushrooms, cleaned and
    finely chopped
2 tablespoons butter
● 1 cup Creamy Brown Sauce

8 dinner crepes
    Parsley for garnish

1. Sauté mushrooms in butter until mushrooms are cooked and pan is almost dry. Stir in sauce.
2. Assemble by stacking 1 crepe, mushroom filling, crepe, mushroom filling, crepe, filling, crepe; form 2 stacks. Put on a baking sheet.
3. Bake at 375°F 10 minutes.
4. Cut into wedges and serve for brunch or as an appetizer. Garnish with parsley.

8 servings

Mushroom-Chicken Stack: Follow recipe for Mushroom Stack. Spread contents of a **4½-ounce can chicken spread** on 2 crepes. Stack crepe, mushroom filling, crepe with chicken, crepe, mushroom, crepe. If desired, mix **1 cup Basic White Sauce** ●   and **1 cup cooked chopped spinach;** spread on each stack before serving.

937

938 Spinach-Bacon Turnovers

4 slices bacon, diced
⅓ cup chopped onion
1 package (10 ounces) frozen
    chopped spinach, thawed
¼ cup mayonnaise
    Salt and pepper
4 dinner crepes
● 1 cup Basic White Sauce

1. Sauté bacon and onion until bacon is cooked.
2. Drain spinach well. Stir-fry spinach with bacon and onion for 3 minutes. Drain mixture well. Stir in mayonnaise and season with salt and pepper to taste.
3. Assemble, using turnover method. Place on a baking sheet.
4. Bake at 375°F 10 minutes. If desired, serve topped with white sauce and sprinkled with bacon bits.

4 turnovers

939 *Tomato Rabbit*

4 slices bacon, diced
2 tablespoons flour
½ cup shredded Cheddar cheese
2 tablespoons sherry
Dash cayenne pepper
2 medium tomatoes
4 dinner crepes

1. Cook bacon until crisp. Remove bacon and drain; reserve bacon drippings.
2. To 2 tablespoons of bacon drippings add flour, ¼ cup cheese, sherry, and cayenne. Stir until well blended. Cook over medium heat until thick; cool.
3. Core tomatoes and dice. Mix tomato and cooked bacon pieces with sauce.
4. Divide sauce among crepes, fold in half, top with remaining cheese, and serve.

4 filled crepes

940 *Zucchini Italiano*

1 pound zucchini, diced
1 large clove garlic, crushed in a garlic press
1 can (16 ounces) tomatoes, drained and diced
½ cup chopped onion
Salt and pepper
¼ cup grated Parmesan cheese
8 dinner crepes

1. Combine diced zucchini, garlic, tomatoes, onion, salt, and pepper in a saucepan. Simmer 25 to 30 minutes over medium heat, or until squash is tender.
2. Place crepes on a baking sheet. Drain zucchini mixture as you spoon it equally onto each crepe. Sprinkle with 2 tablespoons cheese. Fold crepes in half, brush with juice from cooked squash, and sprinkle with remaining 2 tablespoons cheese.
3. Bake at 375°F 15 minutes. Serve immediately while crisp and hot.

8 filled crepes

Note: Serve without baking, if desired.

941 *Zucchini with Pesto Sauce*

1 pound zucchini
Water
3 tablespoons grated onion
½ teaspoon salt
¼ teaspoon pepper
●⅔ cup Pesto Sauce
8 dinner crepes

1. Wash, remove stems, and dice zucchini. Place in a saucepan and cover with water. Stir in onion, salt, and pepper. Simmer 7 to 10 minutes, or until squash is tender. Drain well. Toss with Pesto Sauce. Spoon onto crepes and fold in half. Put into a baking dish.
2. Bake at 375°F 10 minutes. Serve immediately.

8 filled crepes

942 *Crepes Benedict*

12 eggs
Salt and pepper
2 tablespoons butter or margarine
8 thin slices boiled ham, heated
8 dinner crepes
●1 cup hollandaise

1. Beat eggs with salt and pepper to taste.
2. Melt butter. Soft-scramble eggs in butter.
3. To assemble, put 1 slice of ham on each crepe and spoon eggs on top. Fold crepe and ham over eggs and serve topped with warm hollandaise.

8 filled crepes

943 *Creamy Vegetable Squares*

2 tablespoons butter or margarine
2 tablespoons minced scallion
2 tablespoons grated carrot
¼ pound mushrooms, cleaned and sliced
1 package (10 ounces) frozen chopped spinach, thawed and well drained
1 pound cottage cheese
1 egg, slightly beaten
½ teaspoon Italian seasoning
¼ teaspoon ground thyme
¼ cup grated Parmesan cheese
12 dinner crepes

1. Melt butter. Sauté scallion, carrot, mushrooms, and spinach until all are tender. Drain well. Cool.
2. Beat cottage cheese and egg until well blended. Add Italian seasoning, thyme, and 2 tablespoons of grated cheese.
3. Assemble, using square turnover method. Place on a baking sheet, seam side down. Sprinkle with remaining cheese.
4. Bake at 350°F 20 minutes. Cool 5 minutes before serving.

12 filled crepes

944 *Cherries Jubilee*

1 package (16 ounces) frozen pitted tart cherries
⅓ cup sugar
¾ cup Cherry Heering
Dash salt
1 tablespoon cornstarch
1 tablespoon butter or margarine
1 tablespoon grated lemon peel
18 dessert crepes
¼ cup brandy
1 pint vanilla ice cream

1. Thaw cherries, drain, and reserve juice.
2. Combine juice (adding water to make 1 cup), sugar, ¼ cup Cherry Heering, salt, and cornstarch in chafing dish. Cook over medium heat, stirring constantly, until sauce begins to thicken. Stir in cherries, butter, and lemon peel. Simmer 3 minutes.
3. Using hot sauce method, fill chafing dish with crepes.
4. Warm ½ cup Cherry Heering and brandy in saucepan. Pour in chafing dish and ignite. When flames die down, place 3 crepes on a plate, top with vanilla ice cream, and spoon warm sauce and cherries over all.

6 servings

945 *Peach Chutney*

1 cup peach preserves
½ cup golden raisins
¼ cup chopped pecans or walnuts
¼ cup cider vinegar
½ teaspoon orange peel
1 tablespoon chopped crystallized ginger
1 teaspoon instant minced onion

1. In a saucepan, combine all ingredients. Cook 3 to 5 minutes.
2. Cool 1 hour before serving. Store in refrigerator.

1½ cups chutney

946 *Pesto Sauce*

This spicy nut-and-cheese sauce is excellent with vegetables, eggs, fish, or poultry.

1½ to 2 teaspoons dried basil
3 tablespoons chopped walnuts
3 tablespoons grated Parmesan cheese
1 medium clove garlic, crushed in a garlic press
3 sprigs fresh parsley
1 tablespoon olive oil
2 tablespoons vegetable oil
2 tablespoons butter or margarine, melted

1. In an electric blender, combine basil, nuts, cheese, garlic, and parsley. Blend at medium speed until nuts are the size of a split pea.
2. Combine oils and butter. Slowly pour this liquid into blender while it is still on medium speed. Turn off as soon as liquid is added. It's ready to serve.

About ⅓ cup sauce

947 Basic White Sauce

¼ cup butter or margarine
5 tablespoons flour
2 cups milk
¼ teaspoon salt

1. Melt butter over low heat. Stir in flour. Gradually add milk, stirring constantly. Cook and stir until mixture comes to boiling; boil 1 minute.
2. Remove from heat. Mix in salt.

2 cups sauce

Dijon Sauce: Follow recipe for Basic White Sauce; blend in **2 tablespoons Dijon mustard** after adding milk. 948

Curry Sauce: Follow recipe for Basic White Sauce; blend **2 teaspoons curry powder** and **⅛ teaspoon dry mustard** into sauce after adding milk. 949

Parmesan Sauce: Follow recipe for Basic White Sauce; after sauce has thickened, stir in **⅓ cup grated Parmesan cheese.** Remove from heat. 950

951 Standard Hollandaise

¼ pound butter or margarine
3 egg yolks
2 tablespoons lemon juice
Pinch salt
Dash nutmeg
Dash cayenne pepper
2 tablespoons hot water

1. Melt butter (do not brown) and keep hot.
2. Put egg yolks in top of double boiler over hot (not boiling) water. Beat until smooth but not fluffy. Add lemon juice and dry seasonings; drizzle in butter and hot water. Beat with a whisk until sauce begins to thicken. Do not reheat.

1 cup sauce

Béarnaise Sauce: Combine **¼ cup dry white wine, 2 scallions, chopped, ½ teaspoon dried tarragon, pinch fresh ground pepper,** and **¼ cup vinegar.** Simmer over medium heat until reduced to 2 tablespoons. Follow recipe for Standard Hollandaise. Blend in liquid along with butter. 952

Dilled Cucumber Hollandaise: Follow recipe for Standard Hollandaise; add **½ cup chopped cucumber** and **½ teaspoon dried dill weed** to mixture immediately after butter has been added. 953

Hollandaise Verde: Follow recipe for Standard Hollandaise; chop **3 sprigs parsley, 1 whole scallion,** and **1 tablespoon capers.** Combine with **2 teaspoons Worcestershire sauce** and add to mixture immediately after butter has been added. 954

955 Creamy Lemon Sauce

¼ cup whipping cream
3 ounces cream cheese, softened
2 tablespoons lemon juice
2 tablespoons butter or margarine, melted
Dash salt
Dash cayenne pepper

1. Whip cream. Gradually add small pieces of softened cream cheese. Blend in lemon juice, butter, salt, and cayenne.
2. Serve with vegetables and fish.

1 cup sauce

Creamy Brown Sauce: Follow recipe for Creamy Lemon Sauce; substitute a **beef bouillon cube** dissolved in **2 tablespoons hot water** for lemon juice. Taste before adding salt. 956

Food Processor

957 Caraway Cheese Twists

2 ounces sharp Cheddar cheese
    (1 cup shredded)
1 cup flour
¼ teaspoon salt
1 tablespoon shortening
8 tablespoons butter (1 stick), frozen
    and cut in 6 pieces
1 tablespoon caraway seed
3 tablespoons ice water

1. Using **shredding disc,** shred cheese and set aside.
2. Using **steel blade,** add flour, salt, shortening, and butter to bowl and process until butter is cut into flour.
3. Add caraway seed and shredded cheese to bowl. With machine on, add water through feed tube and process until dough forms into a ball.
4. Roll dough ¼ inch thick and cut into strips 4×¾ inches. Twist strips and place on baking sheet.
5. Bake at 425°F about 15 minutes.

About 3 dozen twists

958 Spicy Steak Tartare

1 small green onion, cleaned,
    trimmed, and cut in 1-inch
    pieces
2 tablespoons fresh parsley, cleaned
    and trimmed (1 tablespoon
    chopped)
1 radish, cleaned and trimmed
½ pound beef (sirloin, tenderloin, or
    fillet), cut in 1-inch cubes
1 egg yolk
1 tablespoon lemon juice
1 tablespoon capers
    Drop of Dijon mustard
    Salt
    Freshly ground black pepper to
    taste
3 drops Tabasco

Using **steel blade,** process green onion, parsley, and radish together until finely chopped. Add meat and remaining ingredients and process, using quick on/off motions, to desired consistency. Serve with triangles of **black bread.**

959 *Eggs in Parsley Sauce*

8 hard-cooked eggs
1 small clove garlic
2 cups fresh parsley, cleaned and
  trimmed (1 cup chopped)
1 small boiled potato, chilled
6 tablespoons lemon juice
¼ cup olive oil
½ cup vegetable oil
2 tablespoons capers or 1 small dill
  pickle
2 anchovy fillets
⅛ teaspoon pepper

1. Cut hard-cooked eggs in half lengthwise and place cut side down in a shallow serving dish.
2. Using **steel blade,** mince garlic. Add parsley and process until chopped. Add remaining ingredients and process until creamy and thoroughly blended.
3. Pour over eggs and serve.

8 servings

Note: This herb sauce is excellent served with hot or cold meats, or it makes a very tasty salad dressing.

960 *Chopped Chicken Livers*

1 pound chicken livers
3 medium onions, peeled and
  quartered
3 tablespoons chicken fat
3 hard-cooked eggs
½ teaspoon salt
⅛ teaspoon pepper

1. Wash and trim livers.
2. Using **steel blade,** process onions, with quick on/off motions, until chopped.
3. Sauté onion in chicken fat until golden. Add livers and continue to cook until no longer pink inside (10 to 15 minutes).
4. Using **plastic blade,** add livers and onion, 2 of the hard-cooked eggs, salt, and pepper to bowl and process to desired consistency. (For a smooth patélike consistency, use **steel blade.**) You may need to add additional chicken fat.
5. Chill in refrigerator for at least 2 hours. Serve garnished with **finely chopped hard-cooked egg yolk** and **fresh parsley.**

961 *Guacamole*

1 small clove garlic
2 large ripe avocados, peeled
2 tablespoons lemon juice
1 teaspoon chili powder (optional)
  Salt to taste

1. Using **steel blade,** mince garlic. Add avocado and remaining ingredients and process to desired consistency. (Remember to use quick on/off motions if a coarse, chunky consistency is desired.)
2. Serve as a dip with tortilla chips, on lettuce as a salad, or as a filling for tacos.

About 2 cups dip

Note: If not served immediately, refrigerate in a covered bowl with avocado pits immersed in guacamole. This will help prevent the avocado from darkening on standing.

962 Gefilte Fish

3 pounds fresh fish (whitefish, carp, and/or pike)
2 quarts water
2 teaspoons salt
½ teaspoon pepper
8 carrots, pared
4 medium onions, peeled and cut to fit feed tube
2 eggs
6 tablespoons ice water
4 tablespoons matzoh meal
2 teaspoons salt
½ teaspoon pepper

Horseradish

1. Have fish filleted, reserving head, bones, and skin.
2. In a large pot, place water, 2 teaspoons salt, ½ teaspoon pepper, 7 carrots, head, bones, and skin of fish.
3. Using **slicing disc,** slice 3½ onions (cut remaining ½ onion in half and reserve). Add sliced onion to the pot, bring to a boil, lower heat, and simmer while fish is being prepared.
4. Cut fish into 2-inch pieces. Using **steel blade,** process fish in 1-pound batches to pastelike consistency. Remove to a large bowl and repeat 2 more times with remaining fish. After all fish has been processed, thoroughly mix together by hand to blend fish together.
5. Using **steel blade,** process remaining carrot and ½ onion together until finely chopped. Remove half of this mixture from the bowl.
6. Add half of fish mixture to the bowl. To this add 1 egg, 3 tablespoons ice water, 2 tablespoons matzoh meal, 1 teaspoon salt, and ¼ teaspoon pepper. Process, using quick on/off motions, until thoroughly blended. Remove mixture from bowl and repeat procedure, using remaining ingredients.
7. Remove head, bones, and skin of fish from stock.
8. With wet hands, shape fish into shapes the size of a small baking potato and place in fish stock. Simmer slowly 2 hours.
9. Remove fish balls with a slotted spoon and place on a lettuce-lined platter. Cool and chill. Cool fish stock and save for later use for storing leftover fish.
10. Garnish with pieces of cooked carrots left over from stock and serve with freshly made horseradish.

About 20 balls

963 Horseradish

½ cup horseradish root, cut in 1-inch cubes
Beet juice

Using **steel blade,** process until finely chopped. Add a few drops of beet juice to get desired color. Step back from bowl before removing lid!

964 Eggplant Caviar

1 large eggplant (2 pounds)
1 clove garlic
1 large onion, peeled and quartered
1 small green pepper, trimmed and cut in 1-inch pieces
6 tablespoons olive oil
2 tablespoons tomato paste
2 teaspoons lemon juice
1 teaspoon salt
¼ teaspoon pepper

1. Bake eggplant in a 400°F oven for about 1 hour, or until skin is wrinkled and eggplant is soft. Cool.
2. Using **steel blade,** mince garlic. Add onion and green pepper and process until finely chopped.
3. In a skillet, sauté garlic, onion, and green pepper in 4 tablespoons olive oil until tender, but not browned.
4. When eggplant has cooled sufficiently to handle, remove the skin. Using **steel blade,** process until finely chopped.
5. Add chopped eggplant to skillet with onion mixture. Add 2 tablespoons oil and tomato paste and cook slowly, stirring occasionally, about 20 minutes.
6. Mix in lemon juice, salt, and pepper. Serve well chilled with **black bread.**

Note: The flavor of this dish improves on standing overnight. It keeps up to a week in the refrigerator.

965 *Shrimp Dumplings in Chicken Broth*

1 slice ginger
1 green onion, cut in
   1-inch pieces
½ pound fresh shrimp, shelled and
   deveined
1 egg white
½ teaspoon cornstarch
1 tablespoon sherry
2 teaspoons soy sauce
¼ teaspoon salt
8 cups chicken stock

1. Using **steel blade,** with machine on, drop ginger slice down through the feed tube and process until minced.
2. Add green onion pieces and process until finely chopped.
3. Add shrimp and process until of a pastelike consistency. Add egg white, cornstarch, sherry, soy sauce, and salt and process until thoroughly blended.
4. In a large shallow saucepan, heat chicken stock to boiling and simmer over low heat. Using two teaspoons, drop 1-inch balls of batter into simmering chicken stock. Cover and cook over medium heat until done (about 8 to 10 minutes).
5. Just before serving, garnish soup with **sliced green onion.**

About 30 (1-inch) balls or
8 servings

966 *Block Island Quahog Chowder*

1 cube (2 inches) salt pork, partially
   frozen
1 large onion, peeled and quartered
2 to 3 medium potatoes, pared and
   diced
¼ teaspoon pepper
2 dozen large quahogs (hard-shelled
   clams)

1. Using **slicing disc,** slice salt pork. In a large saucepan, cook salt pork until browned.
2. Using **steel blade,** process onion until finely chopped. Add onion to crisp salt pork and cook until onion is transparent. Remove salt pork and discard.
3. Cook diced potatoes in 1 quart water, with pepper added, until almost tender. Do not drain.
4. Meanwhile, rinse quahogs well and open with a clam knife. (If you are not adept at opening clams in this manner, see Note for an alternate method.) Be sure that all the juice is retained. Strain quahogs, and add reserved juice to saucepan with cooked onions. Using **steel blade,** process clams in two batches until finely chopped. Add to saucepan.
5. Add cooked potatoes and water they were cooked in. Add 2 cups water, more or less, if the flavor is too strong. Simmer 15 to 20 minutes but do not boil. Serve with **chowder crackers.**

8 to 10 servings

Note: An alternate method for opening clams: Rinse clams thoroughly under cold water. Place clams in a saucepan and add 2 cups water. Cook, covered, over medium heat only until shells start to open. Remove clams, reserving clam broth for chowder. Remove clams from shells and proceed as above.

967 *Escarole Soup with Tiny Meatballs*

Soup:
4 pounds beef soup bones
1 can (6 ounces) tomato paste
2½ teaspoons salt
2 quarts water
1 pound escarole, cleaned and
   drained

1. For soup, put all ingredients, except escarole, into a saucepot. Cover and simmer for 1 hour. Remove bones.

2. For meatballs, using **steel blade,** separately process bread to fine crumbs, Parmesan cheese to fine powder, and parsley until chopped; set aside. Next, mince garlic. Add meat in two batches and process until finely chopped and remove to bowl.
3. Using **plastic blade,** add chopped meat, egg, salt, pepper,

Meatballs:

   1 **slice dry bread, cut in quarters (¼ cup crumbs)**
   2 **cubes (1 inch each) Parmesan cheese (¼ cup grated)**
  ¼ **cup fresh parsley, cleaned and trimmed (2 tablespoons chopped)**
   1 **clove garlic**
  ¾ **pound beef, cut in 1-inch cubes**
   1 **egg**
  ½ **teaspoon salt**
  ¼ **teaspoon pepper**

bread crumbs, Parmesan cheese, and chopped parsley to bowl. Process, using quick on/off motions, until thoroughly blended.

4. Shape into ¾-inch balls and add to hot soup. Simmer 10 minutes.

5. Using **steel blade,** process escarole, using quick on/off motions, until coarsely chopped. Add escarole to soup and simmer 30 minutes longer.

8 servings

968 *Greens Soup*

   2 **cubes (1 inch each) Parmesan cheese (¼ cup grated)**
   1 **pound mixed greens (lettuce, spinach, watercress, as well as any others), cleaned and trimmed**
   6 **tablespoons butter**
   3 **tablespoons flour**
   1 **quart chicken stock, heated**
   2 **egg yolks**
   1 **cup milk**

1. Using **steel blade,** separately process Parmesan cheese to a fine powder, and greens (in small batches) until coarsely chopped.

2. Sauté greens in 2 tablespoons butter for a few minutes until wilted.

3. Meanwhile, in another saucepan, melt remaining 4 tablespoons butter, add flour, and cook for 5 minutes. Add heated stock, stirring with a whisk until smooth. Add greens, cover, and simmer for 20 minutes.

4. Strain soup. Purée vegetable mixture with **steel blade** until smooth and return to soup. Heat thoroughly and remove from heat.

5. With **plastic blade** in bowl, process egg yolks and milk together. With machine on, add 1 cup hot soup through feed tube and then add all of egg mixture to soup, stirring thoroughly. Add Parmesan cheese and simmer 5 minutes, being careful not to let soup boil after egg yolks have been added.

6 servings

969 *Cranberry-Beet Borscht*

 1½ **cups whole cranberries**
   5 **cups chicken stock**
   2 **medium onions, peeled and quartered**
  ½ **small head cabbage**
   1 **tablespoon sugar**
   1 **can (8 ounces) whole beets and juice**

1. Wash cranberries. In a large saucepan, combine cranberries and chicken stock and cook about 20 minutes, or until cranberries are soft. Sieve cranberries and return liquid to saucepan. Using **steel blade,** process sieved cranberries until puréed and return to saucepan.

2. Using **steel blade,** process onions until chopped. Add to saucepan.

3. Using **slicing disc,** slice cabbage and add to saucepan. Add sugar and simmer uncovered for about 20 minutes.

4. Just before serving, drain beets, adding juice to pan. Shred beets with **shredding disc** and add also. Simmer until thoroughly heated. Serve with a dollop of **dairy sour cream.**

6 servings

Note: This borscht can also be served chilled.

970 *Cream of Carrot Soup*

6 **large carrots, pared and cut in**
   1-inch pieces
1 **onion, peeled and quartered**
1 **stalk celery, trimmed and cut in**
   1-inch pieces
4 **tablespoons butter**
2 **tablespoons flour**
6 **cups chicken stock**
¼ **cup uncooked rice**
1 **tablespoon sugar**
  Pinch nutmeg
1 **cup whipping cream**

1. Using **steel blade,** process carrots, onion, and celery together until finely chopped.
2. In a large saucepan, sauté chopped vegetables in butter for about 15 minutes. Stir in flour and cook for 2 minutes.
3. Gradually add chicken stock and rice, stirring constantly with a whisk until smooth. Cook slowly for 45 minutes, or until carrots and rice are tender.
4. Strain soup, returning liquid to saucepan. Using **steel blade,** process carrot mixture until puréed and return to saucepan. Add sugar and nutmeg. Bring to a boil, add ½ cup cream, and heat thoroughly.
5. Using a mixer, whip remaining cream. Serve each portion of soup with a dollop of whipped cream.

8 servings

971 *Leek and Potato Soup*

1 **pound potatoes, pared and cut to**
   fit feed tube
1 **pound leeks, cleaned and cut in**
   3½-inch pieces
2 **quarts chicken stock**
½ **cup whipping cream**
  Chopped parsley for garnish

1. Using **slicing disc,** slice potatoes and leeks.
2. Put vegetables and chicken stock into a saucepan, partially cover, and cook for 30 minutes, or until vegetables are tender. Strain vegetables, reserving liquid.
3. Using **steel blade,** process vegetables to a smooth purée.
4. Add vegetable purée to reserved liquid and reheat to a simmer. Off heat and just before serving, stir in cream.
5. Garnish with parsley.

About 12 servings

972 *Chilean Chicken*

3 **pounds chicken, cut in serving**
   pieces
¾ **cup flour**
2 **teaspoons salt**
½ **teaspoon pepper**
2 **tablespoons butter**
2 **tablespoons oil**
1 **clove garlic**
1 **large carrot, pared and cut in**
   1-inch pieces
3 **stalks celery, cleaned and cut in**
   1-inch pieces
1 **medium green pepper, seeded and**
   cut in 1-inch pieces
1 **large onion, peeled and quartered**
1 **teaspoon cumin**
1 **can (28 ounces) whole tomatoes,**
   drained
1 **cup pimento-stuffed olives**
1 **can (8 ounces) corn, drained**

1. In a paper bag, dredge chicken in flour, salt, and pepper.
2. In a large skillet, brown chicken on both sides in butter and oil and remove from pan.
3. Using **steel blade,** separately process garlic until minced; carrot, celery, green pepper, and onion until finely chopped. Add to the skillet in which chicken was browned, sauté for about 5 minutes, and remove from pan.
4. Still using **steel blade,** process drained tomatoes until finely chopped.
5. Place chicken in a large Dutch oven or covered casserole. Add cooked chopped vegetables, sprinkle with cumin, and top with chopped tomatoes. Cover Dutch oven.
6. Bake at 350°F 45 minutes.
7. Using **slicing disc,** slice olives. Add sliced olives and corn and cook 15 minutes longer, or until chicken is tender. Serve with rice

6 servings

973 *Barbecued Spareribs*

3 pounds spareribs, cracked through
    the center
  Salt and pepper
1 small green pepper, trimmed and
    cut in 1-inch pieces
1 small onion, peeled and quartered
1 stalk celery, peeled and cut in
    1-inch pieces
3 tablespoons butter
½ cup cider vinegar
½ cup ketchup
¼ cup brown sugar
1 tablespoon Worcestershire sauce
½ teaspoon dry mustard
½ teaspoon chili powder
2 lemon slices

1. Cut ribs into serving-size pieces, sprinkle with salt and pepper, and place, meaty side up, in a shallow roasting pan. Bake at 350°F 30 minutes, turning once.
2. Using **steel blade,** place green pepper, onion, and celery in bowl and process until coarsely chopped. In a saucepan, heat butter and sauté chopped vegetables until tender, stirring occasionally.
3. Return mixture to bowl with **steel blade.** Add remaining ingredients except lemon slices and process until puréed. Return to saucepan, add lemon slices, and simmer 10 minutes, stirring frequently. Remove from heat and set aside.
4. After ribs have baked for 30 minutes, remove them from oven and pour off excess fat. Spoon one half of the sauce over the ribs. Cover and continue baking, basting frequently, 1 to 1½ hours, or until meat is tender. Uncover the pan for the last 15 minutes.

6 servings

974 *Roast Duckling à l'Orange with Apricot-Rice Stuffing*

Duck:
1 duckling (about 4 pounds)
1 teaspoon salt
1½ cups orange juice
3 tablespoons butter

Apricot-Rice Stuffing:
2 cups cooked rice (1 cup wild and
    1 cup white rice)
¼ cup fresh parsley, cleaned and
    trimmed (2 tablespoons
    chopped)
6 ounces dried apricots
1 small onion, peeled and quartered
1 stalk celery, trimmed and cut in
    1-inch pieces
¼ cup orange juice
3 tablespoons butter, melted
¼ teaspoon salt
⅛ teaspoon pepper
⅛ teaspoon nutmeg
⅛ teaspoon cloves

Orange Sauce:
1 tablespoon flour
2 oranges, sectioned
2 tablespoons orange liqueur
    (optional)
  Salt and pepper to taste

1. Rinse duckling and pat dry with paper towel. Rub cavity with salt.
2. In a saucepan, heat orange juice and butter over low heat until butter is melted. Remove from heat and using a pastry brush, brush cavity with mixture.
3. For stuffing, using **steel blade,** separately process parsley, dried apricots, onion, and celery until finely chopped. Combine all ingredients for stuffing in a large bowl and toss until thoroughly mixed.
4. Lightly fill body and neck cavity with the stuffing. Do not pack. To close body cavity, sew or skewer and lace with a cord. Fasten neck skin to back and wings to body with skewers. Place duckling, breast up, on a rack in a roasting pan. Brush with juice mixture.
5. Roast, uncovered, at 325°F 2½ to 3 hours. Brush frequently with orange juice mixture. Pour off drippings as they accumulate. When duckling is done, drumstick should move easily.
6. Place duckling on a heated platter. Pour off fat from roasting pan, reserving 2 tablespoons, leaving brown residue in the bottom. Put reserved fat into roasting pan and blend in 1 tablespoon flour, stirring constantly over medium heat until mixture bubbles. Remove from heat and continue to stir while slowly adding remaining orange juice mixture and sectioned oranges. Return to heat and cook rapidly, stirring constantly, until gravy thickens. Cook 1 to 2 minutes longer, while stirring; scrape bottom and sides of pan to blend in brown residue. Add orange liqueur and/or more orange juice to reach desired consistency. Adjust seasonings. Remove from heat, pour into gravy boat, and serve hot with duckling.

3 or 4 servings

975 *Stuffed Flank Steak*

6 slices dry bread, cut in quarters (1½ cups crumbs)
4 cubes (1 inch each) Parmesan cheese (½ cup grated)
½ cup fresh parsley, cleaned and trimmed (¼ cup chopped)
1 clove garlic
2½ medium onions, peeled and quartered
2 tablespoons butter
¼ pound mushrooms, cleaned and trimmed
¼ teaspoon tarragon
½ teaspoon salt
¼ teaspoon pepper
1 egg
1 beef flank steak (about 2 pounds)
1 carrot, pared and cut in 1-inch pieces
1 stalk celery, cut in 1-inch pieces
½ cup red wine
1 cup beef stock

1. Using **steel blade,** separately process bread to coarse crumbs, Parmesan cheese to a fine powder, and parsley until chopped; remove from bowl.
2. Still using **steel blade,** mince garlic. Add 2 onions and process until chopped.
3. In a skillet, heat butter and sauté onion and garlic until lightly browned.
4. Using **steel blade,** process mushrooms until chopped and add to skillet along with tarragon, salt, pepper, and parsley; cook a few minutes more.
5. Using **plastic blade,** lightly beat egg. Add bread crumbs and mushroom mixture to bowl and process, with quick on/off motions, until blended.
6. Spread the mixture on the steak. Roll lengthwise in a jelly-roll fashion and tie with string at 1-inch intervals.
7. In a heavy skillet or Dutch oven, brown the meat on all sides and remove from pan.
8. Using **steel blade,** process carrot, celery, and remaining ½ onion together until finely chopped. Add to skillet, along with wine and beef stock. Place stuffed flank steak on top and cover tightly.
9. Bake at 350°F about 2 hours, or until tender.
10. When meat is done, remove from pan, and keep warm. Using **steel blade,** process pan drippings until puréed. Add more water or milk to reach desired consistency.
11. Put steak on a platter and surround with cooked vegetables such as **sliced zucchini, julienne carrots,** and **frenched green beans.**
12. Cut steak into 1-inch slices and serve with gravy on the side.

4 to 6 servings

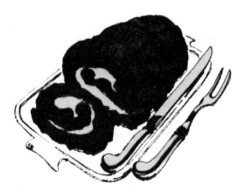

976 *Baked Sole in Champagne*

2 ounces Swiss cheese (1 cup shredded)
¼ cup fresh parsley, cleaned and trimmed (2 tablespoons chopped)
1 small onion, peeled and quartered
¼ pound fresh mushrooms, washed and trimmed
1 cup champagne
2 tablespoons butter
1 bay leaf
¼ cup whipping cream
4 sole fillets
Salt and pepper

1. Using **shredding disc,** shred Swiss cheese and set aside.
2. Using **steel blade,** separately process parsley until chopped, and onion until finely chopped. Set aside.
3. Using **slicing disc,** slice mushrooms.
4. In a saucepan, combine champagne, butter, bay leaf, parsley, onion, and mushrooms. Bring to boiling, reduce heat, and cook slowly until reduced by half. Remove bay leaf and mix in cream. Remove from heat.
5. Sprinkle sole fillets with salt and pepper. Place in a baking dish and pour sauce over them. Sprinkle with shredded cheese.
6. Bake at 350°F 25 minutes, or until fish is tender and top is lightly browned.

4 servings

977 *Shrimp Pancakes with Cheese Sauce*

Pancakes:

8 cubes (1 inch each) Parmesan cheese (1 cup grated)
½ pound fresh shrimp, shelled and cooked
2 eggs
¾ cup flour
1 cup cream
5 tablespoons milk
1 tablespoon butter, melted
¼ teaspoon salt

Cheese Sauce:

3 ounces sharp Cheddar cheese (1½ cups shredded)
3 tablespoons butter
3 tablespoons flour
2½ cups milk, scalded
¼ teaspoon salt
⅛ teaspoon nutmeg

1. For pancakes, using **steel blade,** process Parmesan cheese to a fine powder. Set aside.
2. Using **steel blade,** process cooked shrimp until finely chopped. Set aside.
3. Using **steel blade,** add eggs to bowl and beat lightly. Add remaining ingredients for pancakes and ½ cup grated Parmesan cheese and process until thoroughly blended.
4. In a hot well-buttered 8-inch skillet (crêpe or omelet), drop 3 tablespoons batter. Tilt pan to spread batter evenly into a 6-inch pancake. Fry until lightly browned. Turn and brown other side. Remove to a platter, cool about 1 minute, then roll up and place on a serving dish.
5. Before cooking next pancake, add 1 teaspoon melted butter to the skillet to coat bottom, and pour off excess. Cook next pancake and repeat process until all batter is used up.
6. Sprinkle rolled pancakes generously with remaining Parmesan cheese and keep them hot in a 250°F oven.

7. For sauce, using **shredding disc,** shred cheese and set aside.
8. In a saucepan, melt butter, gradually stir in flour, and cook 2 to 3 minutes. Slowly stir in milk, and continue to cook, stirring with a whisk until sauce is thickened and smooth. Add shredded cheese, salt, and nutmeg and stir until cheese is melted.
9. Serve Cheese Sauce on the side.

15 (6-inch) pancakes;
3 cups Cheese Sauce

978 *Sweet and Sour Chicken*

Sauce:

¾ cup chicken stock
¼ cup brown sugar
¼ cup sugar
½ cup vinegar
¼ cup ketchup
1 tablespoon sherry
1 tablespoon cornstarch
2 tablespoons soy sauce
¼ cup pineapple juice

Chicken:

1 chicken breast, boned, skinned, and partially frozen
1 clove garlic
2 slices fresh ginger, each slice cut in quarters (1 teaspoon minced)
3 tablespoons peanut oil
1 green pepper, cut in 1-inch pieces
1 tomato, cut in 1-inch pieces
½ cup pineapple chunks, drained (reserving liquid)

1. For sauce, combine stock, sugars, vinegar, ketchup, and sherry in a saucepan. Bring to a boil, stirring to dissolve sugar.
2. Blend cornstarch, soy sauce, and pineapple juice. Stir into mixture in saucepan and cook over low heat until thickened.
3. For chicken, using **slicing disc,** slice meat (page 13). Set aside.
4. Using **steel blade,** mince garlic and ginger root by starting machine and adding ingredients through feed tube. Set aside.
5. Heat 2 tablespoons peanut oil in a wok. Add minced garlic and ginger root and stir-fry a few seconds. Add sliced chicken and stir-fry until just tender. Remove from pan and set aside.
6. Heat 1 tablespoon peanut oil in wok and stir-fry green peppers 2 to 3 minutes. Add tomato, pineapple, and chicken and stir-fry only to heat through.
7. Remove to a serving dish and spoon sauce over the top. Serve at once with **rice.**

4 servings

979 *Veal Chops with Onion-Cheese Sauce*

6 large veal chops
Milk
4 cubes (1 inch each) Parmesan
    cheese (½ cup grated)
2 ounces Swiss cheese (1 cup
    shredded)
4 large onions, peeled and quartered
Butter (about ⅔ cup)
Flour
2 tablespoons oil
½ teaspoon salt
¼ teaspoon pepper

1. Cover veal with milk and soak for 1 hour.
2. Using **steel blade,** process Parmesan cheese to a fine powder and set aside.
3. Using **shredding disc,** shred Swiss cheese and set aside.
4. Using **steel blade,** process onions, one at a time with quick on/off motions, until finely chopped. In a large skillet, sauté onion in 4 tablespoons butter for about 5 minutes. Cover and steam onion over low heat until transparent and tender, but not browned.
5. Remove chops from milk, reserving milk in a 2-cup measure. Dry on a paper towel, then dust lightly with flour. In a separate skillet, heat 4 tablespoons butter and the oil and brown chops on both sides.
6. Lower the heat, and cook until chops are tender, turning once. Place cooked veal chops in a flat baking dish and keep warm.
7. Meanwhile, drain cooked onion and add liquid to the reserved milk. Add milk, if necessary, to fill to the 1½-cup line.
8. To the skillet in which veal chops were cooked, add enough butter to' make 3 tablespoons fat. Add ¼ cup flour, stirring constantly, and cook for about 3 minutes. Slowly add milk-onion mixture, stirring with a wire whisk until smooth and thickened. Add salt, pepper, and Parmesan cheese and cook until thoroughly blended and cheese has melted.
9. Top each veal chop with some of the drained steamed onion. Pour sauce over all and sprinkle with shredded Swiss cheese.
10. Heat in a 475°F oven until cheese melts and browns lightly.

6 servings

980 *Lamb Leg on a Bed of Spinach*

Lamb:
1 lamb leg (6 pounds)
4 cloves garlic
2 carrots, pared and cut in 1-inch
    pieces
2 stalks celery, trimmed and cut in
    1-inch pieces
1 large onion, peeled and quartered
2 tablespoons fresh parsley, cleaned
    and trimmed (1 tablespoon
    chopped)
⅛ teaspoon each thyme, oregano,
    savory, and basil
1 cup beef stock

Spinach:
3 pounds spinach, cleaned and
    trimmed

1. For lamb, put lamb in a roasting pan and stud with 2 cloves garlic, cut in slivers. Bake at 400°F 15 minutes to brown.
2. Meanwhile, using **steel blade,** process remaining garlic, carrots, celery, onion, and parsley all together until finely chopped.
3. After meat has browned, remove from pan. Turn oven down to 350°F. Add chopped vegetables, spices, and beef stock to roasting pan. Place lamb on top. Cover tightly and return to oven. Roast 20 to 25 minutes per pound.
4. For spinach, put spinach into a saucepan with just the water that clings to the leaves, sprinkle with salt, and cook until almost tender (8 to 10 minutes). Remove to a colander and immediately rinse with cold water. Take the spinach in handfuls and squeeze out as much water as possible.
5. Using **steel blade** and working with small batches, process the spinach, using quick on/off motions, until chopped.
6. In an enameled pan, heat 2 tablespoons butter and add

1 teaspoon salt
6 tablespoons butter
⅛ teaspoon pepper
Pinch nutmeg

chopped spinach. Cook over high heat 2 to 3 minutes, stirring constantly, until moisture has cooked away.

7. Add remaining butter, pepper, and nutmeg. Cover and cook slowly 10 minutes until butter is absorbed and spinach is tender. Season with more salt and pepper if necessary.

8. To assemble, remove lamb from roasting pan. Let it stand at room temperature for about 15 minutes. Remove fat and strain sauce, reserving liquid. Using **steel blade,** process vegetable mixture until puréed. With machine running, add strained liquid through the feed tube. Return sauce to pan and simmer.

9. Spread spinach on a serving dish and keep warm.

10. Carve lamb into thin slices and overlap them on the bed of spinach. Serve the sauce separately.

8 servings

981 *Puffy Omelets with Crab Meat Sauce*

Crab Meat Sauce:
1 small onion, peeled and quartered
1 apple, pared, cored, and quartered
1 carrot, pared and cut in 1-inch pieces
1 stalk celery, trimmed and cut in 1-inch pieces
6 tablespoons butter
2 cans (7 ounces each) crab meat
3 tablespoons flour
2 cups milk, heated
1 teaspoon grated lemon peel
1 tablespoon lemon juice
⅛ teaspoon dry mustard
½ teaspoon curry powder
½ teaspoon salt
Pinch nutmeg

Omelets:
8 eggs, separated
½ cup milk
1 teaspoon baking powder
½ teaspoon salt
3 tablespoons butter

1. For sauce, using **steel blade,** process onion, apple, carrot, and celery together until finely chopped.

2. In a saucepan, sauté mixture in 3 tablespoons butter for 5 minutes.

3. Drain crab meat, reserving liquid. Go over crab meat carefully, removing any tendons. Measure crab meat liquid and add enough water to make ½ cup liquid. Add to vegetables; cover and simmer 20 minutes, or until tender.

4. Meanwhile, in another saucepan, melt remaining butter, add flour, and cook 2 to 3 minutes. Off heat, add heated milk and stir with a whisk until thickened and smooth. Add vegetable mixture and remaining ingredients, except crab meat. Simmer 10 minutes.

5. Strain sauce and return to saucepan. Add crab meat and heat thoroughly.

6. For omelets, using **plastic blade,** add egg yolks, milk, and baking powder to the bowl. Process until foamy and lemon colored.

7. Using a mixer, beat egg whites with salt until stiff, but not dry, peaks are formed. Gently fold in egg-yolk mixture.

8. Melt butter in a 12-inch skillet. Add egg mixture, cover, and cook over a medium-low heat 12 to 15 minutes, or until firm. Turn upside down on a platter. Top with some of Crab Meat Sauce and cut into wedges. Serve with remaining Crab Meat Sauce on the side.

6 to 8 servings

982 *Mushroom Kugel*

5 matzoh
¼ cup fresh parsley, cleaned and trimmed (2 tablespoons chopped)
2 medium onions, peeled and quartered
¼ pound fresh mushrooms, cleaned and trimmed
2 tablespoons butter
1 egg
1 cup cottage cheese
½ teaspoon salt
¼ teaspoon pepper

1. Soak matzoh in cold water for 2 minutes. Squeeze out as much water as possible and set aside.

2. Using **steel blade,** separately process parsley and onions until chopped. Set aside.

3. Using **slicing disc,** slice mushrooms.

4. In a skillet, sauté chopped onion and sliced mushrooms in butter until onion is soft.

5. Using **plastic blade,** beat egg lightly. Add squeezed-out matzoh, mushroom-onion mixture, and remaining ingredients. Process, using quick on/off motions, until blended.

6. Pour into a buttered 2-quart casserole.

7. Bake at 375°F 40 to 45 minutes.

6 servings

983 *German Apple Pancakes*

3 small apples, pared, cored, and quartered
10 tablespoons butter
3 tablespoons sugar
1 teaspoon cinnamon
4 eggs
⅓ cup milk
¼ cup flour
¼ teaspoon salt
Confectioners' sugar

1. Using **slicing disc,** slice apples. Heat 4 tablespoons butter in a 10-inch skillet. Add apple slices, cover, and cook over medium heat until apples are almost tender, gently turning slices several times during cooking. When almost tender, sprinkle a mixture of 2 tablespoons sugar and the cinnamon evenly over the apples. Continue cooking, uncovered, until apples are just tender. Turn into a bowl and keep warm.
2. Using **plastic blade,** beat eggs thoroughly and blend in milk. Add flour, 1 tablespoon sugar, and salt and process a few seconds until blended and smooth.
3. Heat 3 tablespoons of the butter in the skillet until moderately hot. Pour in enough batter to cover bottom of skillet. Spoon about one half of the apple mixture evenly over batter. Pour in just enough batter to cover apples.
4. Bake pancake over medium heat until golden brown on the bottom. Loosen edges with a spatula and carefully turn and brown the other side.
5. When pancake is baked, remove skillet from heat and brush pancake generously with melted butter. Roll up and transfer to a warm serving platter. Sift confectioners' sugar over the top. Keep pancake hot. Repeat procedure with remaining batter and apples.

2 apple pancakes

984 *Cynthia's Cottage Cheese Pancakes*

6 eggs, separated
2 cups cottage cheese
2 tablespoons sugar
½ teaspoon salt
⅔ cup flour
Pinch cinnamon and nutmeg
⅛ teaspoon cream of tartar

1. Using **plastic blade,** process egg yolks, cottage cheese, sugar, salt, flour, cinnamon, and nutmeg until thoroughly blended.
2. Using a mixer, beat egg whites in a large bowl with cream of tartar until stiff, but not dry, peaks are formed. Gently add egg-yolk mixture to bowl and fold together.
3. Drop batter by large spoonfuls to make 4-inch pancakes on an oiled skillet or griddle. Fry until golden on both sides and puffy.
4. Sprinkle with confectioners' sugar and serve with sour cream, preserves, honey, or applesauce on the side.

About 30 (4-inch) pancakes

985 *Asparagus Supreme*

1 slice dry bread, cut in quarters
    (¼ cup crumbs)
2 ounces sharp Cheddar cheese
    (1 cup shredded)
1 small onion, peeled and quartered
2 tablespoons butter
1 tablespoon flour
¼ teaspoon salt
½ teaspoon paprika
¼ teaspoon dry mustard
½ teaspoon Worcestershire sauce
1 cup evaporated milk
2 pounds fresh asparagus, trimmed,
    cooked, and drained
1 tablespoon butter, melted

1. Using **steel blade,** process bread to fine crumbs. Set aside.
2. Using **shredding disc,** shred cheese and set aside.
3. Using **steel blade,** process onion until finely chopped. In a saucepan, cook onion in butter until tender, but not browned. Blend in flour, salt, paprika, dry mustard, and Worcestershire sauce. Heat until bubbly.
4. Remove from heat. Add evaporated milk gradually, stirring constantly. Return to heat; bring to boiling and cook 1 to 2 minutes.
5. Turn asparagus into a 1-quart shallow baking dish. Pour sauce over asparagus. Sprinkle with shredded cheese. Mix bread crumbs and melted butter together and sprinkle over the top.
6. Set under broiler with top of mixture 3 inches from heat and broil 3 to 5 minutes, or until crumbs are lightly browned and cheese is melted.

6 to 8 servings

986 *Broccoli, Sicilian Style*

1 clove garlic
1 medium onion, peeled and cut to
    fit feed tube
2 tablespoons olive oil
1½ tablespoons flour
¼ teaspoon pepper
1 cup chicken stock
3 ounces sharp Cheddar cheese (1½
    cups shredded)
½ cup ripe olives
4 anchovy fillets
2 pounds fresh broccoli, cooked and
    drained

1. Using **steel blade,** mince garlic.
2. Using **slicing disc,** slice onion.
3. In a saucepan, cook onion and garlic in olive oil until onion is soft. Blend in a mixture of flour and pepper and heat until bubbly.
4. Add chicken stock, stirring constantly. Bring to boiling and cook 1 to 2 minutes, or until sauce thickens.
5. Using **shredding disc,** shred cheese.
6. Using **slicing disc,** slice olives.
7. Using **steel blade,** process anchovy fillets until finely chopped.
8. Add shredded cheese, sliced olives, and chopped anchovy fillets to sauce. Stir over low heat until cheese melts. Pour sauce over hot broccoli and serve immediately.

6 servings

987 *Sour Cream Blintzes*

Blintzes:
- 1 egg
- ¾ cup dairy sour cream
- ¾ cup milk
- ⅛ teaspoon salt
- 1 teaspoon sugar
- 1 cup flour
- 1 tablespoon butter, melted

Filling:
- 1 carton (8 ounces) cottage cheese
- 1 package (8 ounces) cream cheese, cut in quarters
- 1 egg
- 2 tablespoons butter, melted
- 2 tablespoons sugar
- 1 teaspoon vanilla extract
- ¼ cup golden raisins (optional)

Apricot Sauce:
- 1 pound dried apricots
- ¾ cup sugar
  Orange liqueur (optional)

1. For blintzes, using **steel blade,** add egg, sour cream, milk, salt, and sugar to bowl. Process until light and fluffy. Add flour and butter and process until smooth.
2. Drop 2 tablespoons batter into a hot buttered 8-inch omelet or crêpe pan. Tilt pan to spread batter evenly into a 5-inch circle. Cook until light golden brown. Turn and cook other side briefly but do not brown. Repeat process until all batter is used. Remember to butter pan before each blintz is cooked and pour off excess butter.
3. Stack blintzes, browned side up, on a plate and cover with a dome-type cover to prevent them from drying out.

4. For filling, using **steel blade,** place all ingredients, except raisins, in the bowl and process until smooth and creamy. Add raisins, if desired, and process, with quick on/off motions, until blended.
5. Place a heaping tablespoon of cheese filling on each pancake. Tuck in opposite sides and roll up.
6. Arrange rolled pancakes in a buttered baking dish.
7. Set in a 350°F oven 10 to 15 minutes, or until heated through.

8. For Apricot Sauce, cover apricots with water and cook until soft. Drain, reserving juice.
9. Using **steel blade,** process until puréed, adding additional strained juice to reach desired consistency. Add sugar and process until sugar is blended into sauce. Return to saucepan and heat thoroughly. Sauce can be flavored with orange liqueur, if desired.
10. Serve with blintzes and **sour cream.**

988 *Blue Cheese Potato Salad*

- 5 medium potatoes, pared, cooked, and diced
- ½ teaspoon salt
- ¼ teaspoon pepper
- 4 hard-cooked eggs
- 3 stalks celery, trimmed and cut in 1-inch pieces
- 4 green onions, trimmed and cut in 1-inch pieces
- ½ medium green pepper, trimmed and cut in 1-inch pieces
- 1 cup cottage cheese
- ½ teaspoon dry mustard
- ¼ teaspoon salt
- ⅛ teaspoon pepper
- ⅔ cup (6-ounce can) evaporated milk
- ½ cup crumbled blue cheese
- 2 tablespoons cider vinegar
  Lettuce
  Green pepper slices and tomato wedges for garnish

1. Put potatoes into a large bowl and sprinkle with salt and pepper.
2. Using **steel blade,** process hard-cooked eggs, using quick on/off motions, until finely chopped. Add to potatoes.
3. Using **steel blade,** separately process celery, green onion, and green pepper until finely chopped. Add to potatoes and toss lightly.
4. Using **steel blade,** put cottage cheese, dry mustard, salt, pepper, evaporated milk, blue cheese, and vinegar in the bowl. Process until thoroughly blended.
5. Pour dressing over potato mixture in bowl and toss lightly and thoroughly. Chill well before serving to blend the flavors.
2. Spoon chilled potato salad into a bowl lined with lettuce. Garnish with green pepper slices and tomato wedges.

8 servings

989 *Crêpes Farcie*

Crêpes:
- ½ pound fresh spinach, cleaned and trimmed
- 2 egg yolks
- ¼ teaspoon salt
  Dash pepper
- 1 cup flour

Filling:
- 3 cubes (1 inch each) Parmesan cheese (6 tablespoons grated cheese)
- 1 medium onion, peeled and quartered
- 4 tablespoons butter
- 2 ounces mushrooms, cleaned and trimmed
- 1 pound cooked chicken, cut in 1-inch pieces
- 2 tablespoons flour
- 1 cup milk
- 1 tablespoon sherry

Sauce:
- 4 tablespoons butter
- 4 tablespoons flour
- 2 cups milk
- ¾ teaspoon salt
- ¼ teaspoon pepper
  Pinch nutmeg
- 1 tablespoon sherry
  Parmesan cheese

1. For crêpes, cook spinach and drain well. Using **steel blade,** process until finely chopped. Add egg yolks, salt, and pepper and process a few seconds until blended. Add flour and process until dough forms into a ball.

2. On a lightly floured surface, roll out dough ¹⁄₁₆ inch thick. Cut into 4-inch squares.

3. Add squares one at a time to boiling salted water and cook 4 to 5 minutes, or until tender. Remove with a slotted spoon and cool separately.

4. For filling, using **steel blade,** separately process Parmesan cheese to a fine powder and onion until chopped. In a saucepan, sauté chopped onion in butter until transparent.

5. Using **steel blade,** separately process mushrooms and chicken, using quick on/off motions, until finely chopped. You should have about 1½ cups chopped chicken. Add mushrooms and chicken to saucepan and cook about 5 minutes, stirring occasionally. Add flour and cook 1 or 2 minutes. Gradually add milk, stirring constantly until thickened. Mix in sherry and 2 tablespoons grated Parmesan cheese.

6. Spoon filling along center of each pasta square and roll to form a tube.

7. For sauce, in same saucepan in which chicken was cooked, melt butter and blend in flour. Stir until bubbly. Gradually add milk, stirring with a whisk until smooth. Bring to boiling. Cook and stir 1 to 2 minutes. Mix in salt, pepper, nutmeg, and sherry.

8. Spread a thin layer of sauce in a shallow baking dish. Arrange filled rolls on top and pour cream sauce over all. Sprinkle with remainder of grated Parmesan cheese.

9. Set in a 350°F oven until thoroughly heated.

4 servings

990 *Harvest Soufflé*

- 3 ounces sharp Cheddar cheese (1½ cups shredded)
- 4 tablespoons butter
- ¼ cup flour
- ¼ teaspoon salt
- ⅛ teaspoon garlic powder
- ⅓ cup milk
- 1 can (17 ounces) cream-style corn
- ½ teaspoon Worcestershire sauce
- 6 eggs, separated

1. Using **shredding disc,** shred cheese and set aside.

2. In a saucepan, melt butter, add flour, salt, and garlic powder and heat until bubbly. Remove from heat and blend in milk, corn, and Worcestershire sauce. Return to heat and bring mixture to a boil, stirring constantly. Cook 2 minutes and remove from heat.

3. Add shredded cheese and stir until cheese is melted.

4. Using **plastic blade,** add egg yolks to bowl and process until well beaten. Add corn mixture and process until thoroughly blended, stopping to scrape down sides, if necessary.

5. Using a mixer, beat egg whites until stiff, not dry, peaks are formed. Gently spread egg-yolk mixture over egg whites. Carefully fold together until just blended. Gently turn the mixture into an ungreased 2-quart soufflé dish (deep casserole with straight sides).

6. Bake at 350°F 40 to 45 minutes, or until a knife inserted in the center of the soufflé comes out clean. Serve immediately.

6 servings

991 *Bavarian Carrots*

1 pound carrots, pared and cut in
    2½-inch pieces
1 tablespoon sugar
3 slices bacon
1 large onion, peeled and quartered
2 apples, pared, cored, and
    quartered
½ cup chicken stock
½ teaspoon salt
⅛ teaspoon pepper
    Pinch nutmeg

1. Place carrots horizontally in the feed tube and slice with **slicing disc.**
2. In a saucepan, cover carrots with water and add sugar; cook until barely tender. Drain thoroughly.
3. Meanwhile, in a large saucepan, cook bacon until crisp, reserving drippings. Drain well on paper towel. Using **steel blade,** process until coarsely chopped.
4. Still using **steel blade,** process onion until chopped. Sauté in bacon drippings until golden.
5. Slice apples with **slicing disc.** Add sliced apples and chopped bacon to onions and cook together for 5 minutes. Add cooked carrots and toss gently. Add chicken stock, salt, pepper, and nutmeg and simmer for 5 minutes.

6 servings

992 *Greek-Style Carrots and Green Beans*

1 pound carrots, pared and cut in
    2½-inch pieces
1 clove garlic
1 medium onion, peeled and
    quartered
1 pound fresh green beans, cleaned,
    trimmed, and cut in 2½-inch
    pieces
2 tablespoons butter
2 tablespoons oil
1 can (15 ounces) tomato sauce
¼ teaspoon cinnamon
½ teaspoon salt
¼ teaspoon pepper

1. Place carrots horizontally in the feed tube and slice with **slicing disc.** Set aside.
2. Using **steel blade,** mince garlic. Add onion and process until chopped.
3. In a saucepan, sauté green beans, sliced carrots, onion, and garlic in butter and oil about 15 minutes.
4. Add tomato sauce, cinnamon, salt, and pepper; simmer, partially covered, until vegetables are tender (about 30 minutes).

8 servings

993 *Braised Cucumbers*

¼ cup parsley, cleaned and trimmed
    (2 tablespoons chopped)
2 medium onions, peeled and
    quartered
4 tablespoons butter
6 large cucumbers
2 tablespoons flour
½ cup chicken stock
    Salt and pepper to taste
    Pinch sugar
2 tablespoons lemon juice
1 teaspoon dried dill
½ cup dairy sour cream
    Dash nutmeg

1. Using **steel blade,** separately process parsley and onions until chopped. Set aside.
2. In a saucepan, sauté chopped onion in butter until transparent.
3. Pare cucumbers, cut in half lengthwise, and remove seeds. Cut into 3-inch lengths.
4. Add cucumbers to sautéed onions and cook until lightly browned. Add flour and cook for 2 minutes. Add chicken stock, salt, pepper, sugar, and lemon juice. Sprinkle with chopped parsley and dill and simmer for 10 minutes. Just before serving, add sour cream and nutmeg. Bring to a boil and reduce heat. Simmer for 5 minutes.

8 servings

994 *Green Salad Vinaigrette*

1 hard-cooked egg
1 clove garlic
2 tablespoons fresh parsley, cleaned and trimmed (1 tablespoon chopped)
⅛ teaspoon chervil
⅛ teaspoon tarragon
1 teaspoon Dijon mustard
1 tablespoon wine vinegar
1 tablespoon lemon juice
4 tablespoons vegetable oil
.2 tablespoons olive oil
¼ teaspoon salt
⅛ teaspoon pepper
1 head romaine lettuce

1. Using **plastic blade,** process hard-cooked egg until finely chopped. Set aside.
2. Using **steel blade,** mince garlic. Add parsley and process until chopped. Add remaining ingredients, except chopped hard-cooked egg and romaine, and process until thoroughly blended.
3. Wash and thoroughly dry romaine; tear into pieces into a salad bowl, pour dressing over lettuce, and gently toss together. Sprinkle chopped hard-cooked egg over the top.

8 servings

995 *Spinach Salad with Hot Sweet and Sour Dressing*

½ pound bacon
1 medium onion, peeled and quartered
1 pound fresh spinach

Dressing:
¼ cup water
¼ cup vinegar
½ cup sugar
1½ cups mayonnaise

1. Cook bacon until crisp and set aside. Reserve 1 tablespoon bacon drippings.
2. Using **steel blade,** process onion until chopped and cook in bacon drippings until golden.
3. Wash and trim spinach and drain thoroughly.
4. For dressing, combine water, vinegar, and sugar in a saucepan and boil until sugar dissolves. Add mayonnaise and onion and heat thoroughly, stirring until smooth.
5. Using **steel blade,** process bacon, using quick on/off motions, until coarsely chopped.
6. Pour hot salad dressing over spinach, sprinkle bacon over top, and toss gently.

6 to 8 servings

Note: Any leftover salad dressing can be stored in refrigerator and reheated before serving.

996 *Greek Salad*

Salad Dressing:
- ⅓ cup olive oil
- ¼ cup wine vinegar
- ½ teaspoon salt
- 1 teaspoon oregano

Salad:
- 1 large head romaine, trimmed and torn in pieces
- 1 cucumber, pared and cut in 3½-inch pieces
- 1 small bunch radishes, cleaned and trimmed
- 2 small green peppers, trimmed and cored
- 1 can (8 ounces) whole beets, drained
- 4 tomatoes
- ⅓ pound feta cheese
  Greek olives
  Anchovy fillets (optional)

1. For salad dressing, mix all ingredients and refrigerate.

2. For salad, put romaine pieces in a large salad bowl.
3. Using **slicing disc,** slice cucumber, radishes, green pepper, and beets.
4. Cut tomatoes into quarters.
5. Using **plastic blade,** process feta cheese, using quick on/off motions, until crumbled.
6. Combine prepared salad ingredients with romaine in a bowl, sprinkle with crumbled feta cheese, and top with olives and, if desired, anchovy fillets. Pour salad dressing over salad and serve.

8 servings

997 *Raspberry Mousse*

- 5 packages (10 ounces each) frozen raspberries
- 2 packages unflavored gelatin
- 2 tablespoons lemon juice
- 5 whole eggs
- 4 egg yolks
- ½ cup sugar
- 3 tablespoons raspberry liqueur (optional)
- 2½ cups whipping cream
- 2 tablespoons confectioners' sugar

1. Drain raspberries, reserving juice. Using **steel blade,** process raspberries until pureed. Strain to remove seeds. Discard seeds and set puree adiseset puree aside.
2. In a saucepan, combine lemon juice and 6 tablespoons of reserved raspberry juice. Add gelatin and stir to soften. Stir over low heat until gelatin is dissolved. Let cool.
3. Using **steel blade,** add 5 whole eggs, 4 egg yolks, and sugar to bowl. Process for about 4 to 5 minutes, until very thick. Add raspberry puree and process until combined.
4. With machine on, add cooled gelatin mixture through the feed tube. Process until thoroughly blended. Add raspberry liqueur, if desired.
5. Using a mixer, beat whipping cream until it begins to thicken. Add confectioners' sugar and continue to beat until it holds its shape. Remove one quarter of the whipped cream and save it to decorate the finished mousse.
6. Gently fold whipped cream and raspberry mixture together. Turn into a decorative crystal bowl.
7. Chill mousse until set, at least 2 hours, and decorate with remaining whipped cream put through a pastry bag.

10 to 12 servings

Microwave

998 Seafood Crackers

1 can (8 ounces) crab or shrimp,
    drained, or 1½ pounds cooked
    fresh fish
1 tablespoon sliced green onion
1 cup shredded Swiss cheese
½ cup mayonnaise
1 teaspoon lemon juice
25 crisp crackers

1. In a 1-quart mixing bowl, combine seafood, onion, cheese, mayonnaise, and lemon juice.
2. Spread 1 teaspoon filling on each cracker. Arrange 10 to 12 crackers in a circle on glass plate or waxed paper.
3. Cook 45 seconds to 1 minute, rotating dish one-quarter turn halfway through cooking time. Serve hot.

25 appetizers

999 Sweet-and-Sour Wiener Fondue

1 jar (5 ounces) currant jelly
½ cup prepared mustard
1 pound wieners, cut in bite-size
    pieces

1. In a small glass mixing bowl, combine jelly and mustard. Cook 2 minutes, stirring halfway through cooking time.
2. Add wieners and cook 3 to 4 minutes, stirring halfway through cooking time.
3. Serve warm.

60 to 70 appetizers

1,000 Stuffed Mushrooms

1 bunch green onions, chopped
¼ cup dairy sour cream
½ teaspoon Worcestershire sauce
½ teaspoon oregano
½ cup bulk pork sausage
1 pound fresh mushrooms, washed,
    drained, and stemmed

1. In a 1-quart glass casserole, blend green onions, sour cream, Worcestershire sauce, oregano, and sausage. Cook 2 to 3 minutes, stirring halfway through cooking time.
2. Stuff mushroom caps with filling. Place stem in top of filling and secure in place with wooden pick.
3. Arrange 10 to 12 mushrooms evenly around the edge of a glass pie plate and cook, covered, 6 to 8 minutes.
4. Serve warm.

25 to 30 appetizers

1,001 *Appetizer Kabobs*

8 large precooked smoked sausage
    links
1 can (16 ounces) pineapple chunks,
    drained
1 tablespoon brown sugar
2 tablespoons soy sauce
1 tablespoon vinegar

1. Arrange sausage evenly around edge of roasting rack set in a glass dish or directly on glass plate and cook 2 to 3 minutes, rotating dish one-quarter turn halfway through cooking time. Drain sausage and cut each sausage link into 5 pieces.
2. Make kabobs, using 1 sausage piece and 1 pineapple chunk threaded on a round wooden pick. Arrange evenly in a large shallow dish.
3. In a 1-cup glass measure, blend brown sugar, soy sauce, and vinegar and pour over kabobs. Refrigerate 1 or 2 hours until serving time.
4. Arrange 20 kabobs on a large glass plate and cook 2 to 3 minutes, rotating dish one-quarter turn and spooning sauce over top halfway through cooking time.
5. Cook additional kabobs as needed. Serve warm.

40 appetizers

Snackin' Nuts

¼ cup sugar
½ teaspoon cinnamon
1 tablespoon brown sugar
2 tablespoons butter
2 cups pecan halves

1. Combine sugar, cinnamon, and brown sugar; set aside.
2. In a 2-quart glass casserole, heat butter 30 seconds. Add nuts and cook 4 to 5 minutes, stirring every minute.
3. Add sugar mixture to nuts and stir to coat nuts evenly. Spread out on wooden board to cool.
4. Serve warm or cold.

2 cups nuts

Note: May be stored in freezer.

Mock Bouillabaisse

1 small onion, sliced
1 clove garlic, minced
1 bay leaf
¼ teaspoon thyme
2 tablespoons olive oil
1 can (10¾ ounces) condensed
    tomato soup
¾ soup can water
2 cups cooked seafood
1 teaspoon lemon juice
    Dash Tabasco
3 or 4 slices French bread, toasted

1. In a 3-quart glass casserole, combine onion, garlic, bay leaf, thyme, and olive oil. Cook 3 to 4 minutes, stirring halfway through cooking time, until onion is tender.
2. Stir in soup, water, seafood, lemon juice, and Tabasco.
3. Heat 6 to 8 minutes, stirring every 2 minutes, until boiling.
4. Cover and cook an additional 2 minutes.
5. Rest 5 minutes. Ladle soup over toast in bowls.

3 or 4 servings

Leek Soup, page 36
Peasant Black Bread, page 275

Creamed Onion Soup

4 medium onions, sliced
½ cup butter
¼ cup flour
1 quart milk
2 cups chicken broth or 2 chicken bouillon cubes dissolved in 2 cups boiling water
1 to 1½ teaspoons salt
1 egg yolk
1 tablespoon minced parsley
½ cup croutons

1. In a 3-quart glass casserole, sauté onions in butter 4 to 5 minutes, stirring every minute. Stir in flour and cook until sauce bubbles, about 1 minute.
2. Add milk slowly, stirring gently. Cook until slightly thickened, about 6 to 8 minutes, stirring every 2 minutes.
3. Add broth and cook 5 minutes, stirring twice.
4. Stir in salt to taste. Blend some of the hot soup with egg yolk and return to remaining soup. Cook 1 minute, stirring every 15 seconds.
5. Serve topped with minced parsley and croutons.

8 servings

Spaghetti Meat Sauce

1 pound ground beef
1 clove garlic, minced
1 small onion, chopped
1 can (15 ounces) tomato sauce
1 teaspoon oregano
½ teaspoon basil
½ teaspoon salt
¼ teaspoon pepper
½ cup tomato juice or ketchup

1. In a 2-quart glass casserole, brown ground beef 2 to 3 minutes, stirring to crumble.
2. Stir in garlic and onion. Cook, covered, 5 minutes, stirring halfway through cooking time.
3. Add tomato sauce, oregano, basil, salt, pepper, and tomato juice.
4. Cook, covered, 15 to 20 minutes, stirring several times. Rest, covered, 5 minutes.
5. Serve over **cooked spaghetti,** and sprinkle with **grated Parmesan cheese.**

4 servings

Gravy

¼ cup flour
¼ cup drippings
2 cups broth, water, or milk
1 teaspoon salt
¼ teaspoon pepper

1. In a 4-cup glass measure, blend flour into drippings to make a smooth paste. Gradually stir in liquid until smooth.
2. Cook 1 to 3 minutes, stirring every minute, until smooth and thickened. Add salt and pepper; stir to blend.
3. Cook 30 seconds to 1 minute.

2 cups

Pumpkin Bread

1½ cups sugar
⅓ cup salad oil
2 eggs
1 cup canned pumpkin
1½ cups all-purpose flour
¾ teaspoon salt
½ teaspoon cinnamon
½ teaspoon nutmeg
½ teaspoon cloves
½ teaspoon allspice
1 teaspoon baking soda
¼ teaspoon baking powder
½ cup coarsely chopped walnuts

1. In a large mixing bowl, blend sugar, oil, eggs, and pumpkin. When ingredients are well mixed, stir in flour, salt, cinnamon, nutmeg, cloves, allspice, baking soda, and baking powder, blending well. Stir in walnuts. Pour batter into an 8×4-inch glass dish.
2. Cook 12 to 14 minutes, rotating dish one-quarter turn every 4 minutes. Knife inserted in the center should come out clean when bread is done.
3. Rest 5 minutes and remove from pan. Serve either warm or cold with **butter** or **cream cheese.**

1 loaf bread

Strawberry Pear Flambee, page 315

Blueberry Streusel

1½ cups all-purpose flour
¾ cup uncooked oats
1 cup firmly packed brown sugar
½ teaspoon baking soda
½ teaspoon salt
½ cup butter
1 can (21 ounces) blueberry pie
   filling

1. In a large mixing bowl, blend flour, oats, brown sugar, baking soda, and salt. Cut butter into dry mixture until crumbly. Spread one half of mixture into an 8-inch glass baking dish, and press firmly in bottom.
2. Spread pie filling evenly over crumb mixture. Top pie filling with remaining crumb mixture.
3. Cook 12 to 15 minutes, rotating dish one-quarter turn halfway through cooking time.
4. Serve warm or cold.

8 or 9 servings

Note: Any fruit pie filling may be used.

Raisin Bran Muffins

½ cup sugar
⅓ cup shortening
1 egg
1 cup all-purpose flour
2 teaspoons baking powder
½ teaspoon baking soda
½ teaspoon salt
2 cups raisin bran flakes
1 cup buttermilk

1. In a medium mixing bowl, cream sugar and shortening. Add egg and beat until light and fluffy.
2. Add flour, baking powder, baking soda, and salt; stir to blend. Fold in raisin bran flakes and buttermilk. Stir just to moisten.
3. Line custard cups, paper drinking cups, or cupcaker with paper cups. Fill each cup no more than half full. Arrange 6 cups in a circle and cook 3 to 3½ minutes, rearranging cups halfway through cooking time.
4. Serve warm with **butter** and **jelly.**

12 to 14 muffins

Quick Cheese Bread

2½ cups all-purpose biscuit mix
1 cup shredded sharp Cheddar
　　cheese
1 tablespoon poppy seed
1 egg
1 cup milk

1. In a medium mixing bowl, blend biscuit mix, cheese, poppy seed, egg, and milk. Stir just to moisten. Pour into a buttered 8-inch square glass baking dish.
2. Cook 5 to 7 minutes, rotating dish one-quarter turn halfway through cooking time. Allow to stand 5 minutes. Center will be soft but will set with standing.

9 to 12 servings

Note: A glass may be placed in the center of dish before pouring in batter to help the bread cook. A 9-inch round glass baking dish may also be used.

The bread may be browned under a conventional broiler for 1 to 2 minutes, but only if a glass ceramic baking dish is used, or the bread is transferred to a metal pan.

Quick Cheese Muffins: Follow recipe for Quick Cheese Bread. Line custard cups, paper drinking cups, or cupcaker with paper baking cups. Fill each cup half full with batter. Arrange 6 cups in a circle in microwave oven. Bake for 2 to 2½ minutes, rearranging cups halfway through cooking time.

About 1½ dozen muffins

Assorted Hot Rolls

The microwave oven is a real aid in serving piping hot rolls at every meal. Heating times may vary, depending on whether the roll has a filling, icing, or nut coating. Always undercook rolls rather than overcook them. Any complaints about dry, tough rolls are always an indication of overcooking.

Rolls (plain or sweet)

1. Place rolls in a napkin, terry towel, or napkin in a wooden bread basket.
2. Heat as follows: 1 roll, 10 to 15 seconds; 2 rolls, 20 to 30 seconds; 4 rolls, 40 to 60 seconds; and 6 rolls, 1 to 1¼ minutes. Always start with the shortest time, and heat longer if necessary.
3. Serve immediately while warm.

Peanut Butter Coffee Cake

2 cups all-purpose biscuit mix
2 tablespoons sugar
¼ cup peanut butter, chunky or
　　smooth
⅔ cup milk
1 egg
½ cup jelly or jam (optional)

1. Combine biscuit mix and sugar; cut in peanut butter with a fork. Stir in milk and egg; blend evenly. Pour into a buttered 9-inch glass dish. Swirl jelly through batter, if desired.
2. Cook 8 to 10 minutes, rotating dish one-quarter turn halfway through cooking time.
3. Rest 5 minutes before serving.

4 to 6 servings

Coffee Cake Ring

½ cup butter
¾ cup brown sugar
1 egg
1 cup whole wheat pancake mix
1 teaspoon vanilla extract
¼ cup water
1 cup quick-cooking oats
½ cup butterscotch-flavored pieces
½ cup chopped walnuts

1. In a mixing bowl, blend butter, brown sugar, egg, and pancake mix.
2. Add vanilla extract, water, oats, butterscotch-flavored pieces, and walnuts. Stir until evenly blended.
3. Place small glass, open end up, in center of 8-inch glass dish. Pour batter into dish around glass.
4. Cook 4 to 6 minutes, rotating dish one-quarter turn halfway through cooking time. Rest 5 minutes.
5. Serve warm.

6 to 8 servings

Muffin Bread

5 cups all-purpose flour
2 packages active dry yeast
1 tablespoon sugar
2 teaspoons salt
2½ cups milk
½ teaspoon baking soda
1 tablespoon warm water
¼ cup cornmeal

1. In a large bowl, blend 3 cups flour, yeast, sugar, and salt.
2. In a 4-cup glass measure, heat milk 2 to 3 minutes until warm.
3. Stir milk into flour mixture and blend well. Stir in remaining flour. Cover; let rise in a warm place until doubled, about 1 hour.
4. Blend baking soda and water, then stir into batter, blending well. Divide batter in half; place in two 8×4-inch loaf dishes. Cover; let rise until doubled, about 1 hour.
5. Sprinkle 2 tablespoons cornmeal on top of each loaf.
6. Cook loaves individually 5 to 6 minutes, rotating dish one-quarter turn every 2 minutes.
7. Rest 5 minutes and remove from dish.
8. Slice and toast before serving.

2 loaves bread

Sour Cream Coffee Cake

½ cup butter
1 cup sugar
3 eggs
1 teaspoon vanilla extract
1 cup dairy sour cream
2 cups all-purpose flour
1 teaspoon baking powder
1 teaspoon baking soda
¾ cup firmly packed brown sugar
¼ cup butter
¼ cup all-purpose flour
¼ teaspoon salt
¼ teaspoon cinnamon
1 cup chopped walnuts

1. In a mixing bowl, cream butter and sugar. Add eggs and stir to blend. Stir in vanilla extract and sour cream. Add flour, baking powder, and baking soda. Stir until well mixed.
2. Line bottom of two 8-inch round glass baking dishes with waxed paper. Pour one quarter of the batter into each cake pan.
3. In a small mixing bowl, combine brown sugar, butter, flour, salt, and cinnamon; stir until crumbly. Mix in nuts.
4. Sprinkle one quarter of the nut mixture on each cake layer. Divide remaining batter between each dish, and pour over nut mixture. Cover with remaining nut mixture.
5. Cook 1 dish at a time, covered with waxed paper, 4 to 5 minutes, rotating dish one-quarter turn halfway through cooking time.
6. Rest 5 minutes before serving.

12 to 16 servings

Note: Cooked coffee cake may be frozen.

Chinese Tomato Beef

2 pounds beef steak (sirloin, round, flank, or chuck)
2 tablespoons sugar
½ cup soy sauce
1 clove garlic, minced
¼ teaspoon ginger
3 tablespoons salad oil
2 large green peppers, cut in strips
3 green onions, cut in 1-inch pieces
2 large tomatoes, peeled and cut in wedges
2 tablespoons cornstarch
¼ cup water

1. Slice steak diagonally across the grain in ⅛-inch-thick slices. Meat will slice easier if placed in the freezer 30 minutes.
2. In a 2-cup glass measure, combine sugar, soy sauce, garlic, and ginger. Pour over meat in a 9-inch baking dish. Marinate at least 30 minutes, turning meat occasionally.
3. Preheat browning dish 6 minutes. Remove meat from marinade; reserve marinade. Add oil and meat to dish. Fry meat 5 to 6 minutes in microwave oven, stirring halfway through cooking time. Drain cooking juices into marinade.
4. Stir green pepper and onion into meat. Cook 3 to 4 minutes, stirring halfway through cooking time. Top with tomato wedges.
5. In a 1-cup glass measure, combine cornstarch and water, and blend with marinade. Cook 1 to 2 minutes, stirring halfway through cooking time, until thickened. Pour over meat and vegetables and heat 1 to 2 minutes.
6. Rest 5 minutes and serve over **hot fluffy rice.**

8 servings

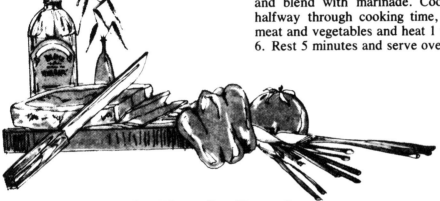

Marinated Flank Steak

⅓ cup soy sauce
2 tablespoons vinegar
¼ cup minced onion
¼ teaspoon garlic powder
1½ teaspoons ground ginger
2 tablespoons sugar
2 pounds beef flank steak

1. In a 2-quart glass baking dish, blend soy sauce, vinegar, onion, garlic powder, ginger, and sugar. Dip meat in mixture and marinate 4 hours, turning occasionally.
2. Cut steak into serving pieces. Pound to tenderize.
3. Return to 2-quart dish with sauce and cook, covered, 12 to 14 minutes, rotating dish one-quarter turn halfway through cooking time.
4. Serve with **hot rice.**

6 or 7 servings

Many-Way Meatballs

1 pound ground beef
¼ cup dry bread crumbs
¼ cup minced onion
1 egg
¼ teaspoon salt
1 can (10½ ounces) condensed Cheddar cheese, cream of celery, or cream of mushroom soup
½ cup water
2 tablespoons parsley flakes

1. In a mixing bowl, combine beef, bread crumbs, onion, egg, and salt. Shape into 16 meatballs, and place in a 2-quart baking dish.
2. Cook, covered, 5 to 6 minutes, stirring halfway through cooking time. Pour off drippings.
3. Stir in soup, water, and parsley. Cover and cook 6 to 8 minutes, stirring halfway through cooking time.
4. Rest 5 minutes before serving.

3 or 4 servings

Marvelous Eggs

3 tablespoons butter
1 tablespoon minced green onion
6 eggs, slightly beaten
⅓ cup milk
½ teaspoon salt
¼ teaspoon lemon juice
1 package (3 ounces) cream cheese,
    cut in ½-inch cubes

1. In a 2-quart glass casserole, heat butter 30 seconds. Add onion and cook 2 minutes, stirring once. Stir in eggs, milk, salt, and lemon juice.
2. Cook, covered, 4 to 5 minutes, stirring every 2 minutes. When almost set, lightly fold in cream cheese.
3. Cook 1 minute longer, rest 5 minutes, and serve.

4 servings

Mushroom Eggs on Toast

1 pound fresh mushrooms, cleaned
    and sliced
¼ cup butter
4 slices hot buttered toast
2 tablespoons butter
2 tablespoons flour
1 cup milk
½ cup grated Parmesan cheese
¼ teaspoon dry mustard
4 poached eggs
    Paprika (optional)

1. In a 1-quart glass casserole, cook mushrooms in ¼ cup butter 3 to 4 minutes, stirring halfway through cooking time. Cover each slice toast with one-fourth of the mushrooms.
2. In a 2-cup glass measure, heat 2 tablespoons butter 30 seconds. Stir in flour to blend. Stir in milk and cook 2 to 3 minutes, stirring every minute, until sauce becomes thick. Add cheese and dry mustard; stir to blend.
3. Place an egg on top of mushrooms on each toast slice and cover with sauce. Sprinkle with paprika, if desired.

3 or 4 servings

Confetti Eggs

2 tablespoons butter
½ cup diced ham
2 green onions, including tops,
    chopped
4 eggs
    Dash Tabasco
½ teaspoon salt
¼ teaspoon pepper

1. In a 2-quart glass casserole, cook butter, ham, and green onions 3 to 4 minutes, stirring every minute.
2. Add eggs, Tabasco, salt, and pepper; stir to blend.
3. Cook, covered, 3 to 4 minutes, stirring halfway through cooking time.
4. Rest, covered, 5 minutes.

3 or 4 servings

Tangy Pork Chops

4 to 6 pork chops
    Prepared mustard
1 can (10½ ounces) condensed cream
    of celery soup

1. Spread both sides of each pork chop with mustard and place in a 10-inch glass baking dish.
2. Cook pork chops 6 to 8 minutes, rotating dish one-quarter turn halfway through cooking time.
3. Remove drippings from pan. Pour soup over pork chops. Cook, covered, 5 to 6 minutes, rotating dish one-quarter turn halfway through cooking time.
4. Rest, covered, 5 minutes before serving.

4 to 6 servings

Breakfast Kabobs

8 ounces link pork sausage
6 ounces Canadian bacon, or 12
    ounces canned luncheon meat
1 can (8 ounces) pineapple chunks,
    drained
16 maraschino cherries
    Maple syrup
8 bamboo skewers

1. Cut each sausage link in 3 or 4 pieces. Cut bacon in small cubes.
2. Thread meat and fruit alternately on skewers. Arrange in a 2-quart glass baking dish and brush with maple syrup.
3. Cook, covered, 4 to 6 minutes, rotating one-quarter turn and basting with syrup halfway through cooking time.

4 to 6 servings

Sausage Ring

1 pound bulk pork sausage
2 eggs
2 tablespoons minced onion
½ cup bread crumbs
2 tablespoons parsley flakes

1. In a 1-quart glass casserole, blend sausage, eggs, onion, bread crumbs, and parsley flakes. Mold into a ring and place a small glass, open end up, in the center of the ring.
2. Cook 5 to 6 minutes, rotating dish one-quarter turn halfway through cooking time.
3. Rest 5 minutes, remove glass from center, and invert ring on plate to serve. Center may be filled with **cooked rice** or **noodles.** If using for breakfast, center may be filled with **scrambled eggs.**

4 or 5 servings

Note: Leftover Sausage Ring makes good sandwiches when reheated.

Fresh Ham

5- to 6-pound cook-before-eating ham

1. Place ham on roasting rack in a 2-quart glass baking dish. Shield protruding corners or shank end with foil. Do not allow foil to touch walls inside microwave oven.
2. Cook 40 to 50 minutes, allowing 8 to 9 minutes per pound. Turn ham over and rotate dish one-quarter turn halfway through cooking time.
3. Rest 10 to 15 minutes before carving or serving.

10 to 12 servings

Cooked Ham: Follow recipe for Fresh Ham, but allow 6 to 7 minutes per pound cooking time, or 30 to 40 minutes for a 5- to 6-pound ham.

Fresh Pork Roast: Follow recipe for Fresh Ham, allowing 8 to 9 minutes per pound cooking time.

Creamed Chicken Casserole

4 chicken breasts, halved
1 can (10½ ounces) condensed cream of chicken soup
2 tablespoons brandy
½ cup dairy sour cream
2 green onions, chopped
Dash pepper
¼ cup cashews
Parsley, chopped
Paprika

1. Wash chicken and pat dry. Arrange in a 2-quart baking dish. Cook 10 to 12 minutes, rotating one-quarter turn halfway through cooking time.
2. In a mixing bowl blend soup, brandy, sour cream, onion, pepper, and cashews. Pour over chicken.
3. Cook, covered, 12 to 15 minutes, rotating one-quarter turn halfway through cooking time.
4. Garnish with parsley or paprika, if desired.

4 servings

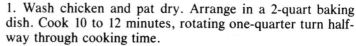

Chicken Hawaiian

1½ cups sliced celery
1 green pepper, cut in strips
3 tablespoons butter
3 cups cubed cooked chicken
1 can (21 ounces) pineapple pie filling
¼ cup soy sauce
2 teaspoons instant chicken bouillon
Chow mein noodles
Parsley (optional)

1. In a 2-quart glass casserole, blend celery, green pepper, and butter. Cook 3 to 4 minutes, stirring halfway through cooking time.
2. Add chicken, pie filling, soy sauce, and bouillon; mix well.
3. Cook, covered, 10 to 12 minutes, stirring halfway through cooking time.
4. Serve over chow mein noodles and garnish with parsley, if desired.

5 or 6 servings

Dinner Chicken Wings

2 to 3 pounds chicken wings
1 teaspoon ginger
1 teaspoon dry mustard
1 tablespoon brown sugar
⅓ cup soy sauce
3 tablespoons salad oil
3 cloves garlic, quartered
2 tablespoons sesame seed

1. Clip wing tips from each wing. Divide each wing at the joint, in two pieces. Place wing pieces in a 2-quart glass baking dish.
2. In a mixing bowl, blend ginger, mustard, brown sugar, soy sauce, oil, and garlic. Pour over chicken pieces and marinate overnight.
3. Remove the garlic pieces from the marinade. Cook the chicken in marinade 12 to 14 minutes, rotating dish one-quarter turn halfway through cooking time.
4. Rest, covered with waxed paper, 10 minutes. Pour off marinade. Sprinkle chicken with sesame seed and heat 1 minute.

5 or 6 servings

Note: Dinner Chicken Wings may be served with rice for a main dish or used as an appetizer.

Roast Turkey

8- to 15-pound turkey
2 tablespoons butter
1 tablespoon bottled brown bouquet
  sauce

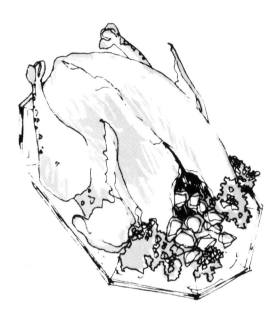

1. Clean and prepare turkey for cooking as directed on turkey wrapper. Place turkey, breast down on roasting rack in a glass baking dish; cover with waxed paper.
2. Estimate the total cooking time. For an 8- to 12-pound turkey allow 7 to 8 minutes per pound, and for a 12- to 15-pound turkey allow 6 to 7 minutes per pound. Cook the turkey for a fourth of the estimated cooking time
3. Melt the butter in a custard cup and mix with the bottled brown bouquet sauce. Brush the turkey with the mixture. Cover the bottom half of wings and legs with small pieces of aluminum foil. Secure legs and wings close to body with string. Cover with waxed paper. Do not allow foil to touch inside walls of microwave oven.
4. Place turkey on its side and cook a fourth of estimated roasting time. Turn turkey on its other side and cook for another fourth of estimated roasting time. Cut strings to allow legs and wings to stand free, remove foil, place turkey breast up, and cook until turkey reaches internal temperature of 175°F. Each time turkey is turned rotate dish one-quarter turn and baste with drippings. Remove drippings as they accumulate, or additional cooking time will be needed.
5. When cooking time is up, rest the turkey 15 to 20 minutes; temperature should reach 190°F. Return to oven for additional cooking if needed.
6. Garnish with green grapes and serve.

About 2 servings per pound

Note: If desired, turkey cavity may be filled with Apple Dressing. Follow Roast Turkey recipe, but add 6 minutes per pound to the cooking time.

Apple Dressing

1½ cups finely chopped celery
⅔ cup finely chopped onion
1 cup butter
1 teaspoon salt
1 teaspoon sage or thyme
½ to ¾ cup water
12 cups dry bread cubes
3 cups pared and chopped apple

1. In a 3-quart glass casserole, sauté celery and onion in butter 2 to 3 minutes, stirring after every minute.
2. Mix together salt, sage, and water. Pour over bread cubes, tossing lightly to mix.
3. Add bread cubes to vegetable mixture. Stir in apple, blending evenly.
4. Stuff turkey just before roasting, or cook dressing in a 3-quart casserole dish 10 to 12 minutes, rotating dish one-quarter turn halfway through cooking time.
5. Rest 5 minutes before serving.

10 to 12 servings

Note: This dressing is also good with pork chops. Extra dressing may be frozen and reheated later.

Microwave Fried Chicken

1 broiler-fryer (2½ to 3 pounds)
1 cup corn flake crumbs
¼ cup butter
   Paprika

1. Wash chicken and coat with crumbs. In a 1-cup glass measure, heat butter 45 seconds.
2. On roasting rack in a 2-quart glass baking dish, arrange chicken with meatier pieces around edges of dish, and smaller pieces, such as wings, in the center. Pour a small amount of butter over each piece. Sprinkle with paprika.
3. Cook 10 to 12 minutes. Turn chicken pieces over and coat each piece with remaining butter and paprika. Cook 10 to 12 minutes.
4. Rest 5 minutes before serving.

4 to 6 servings

Note: The chicken may be covered during cooking, which will steam the chicken, producing a soft, not crisp, skin. If the chicken is in a glass ceramic baking dish or is transferred to a metal pan, additional browning can be achieved by placing cooked chicken under a conventional broiler 1 to 2 minutes.

Paprika Buttered Fish Fillets

1 package (1 pound) frozen fish fillets
   (perch, haddock, cod, or halibut),
   thawed
   Flour
   Salt and pepper
2 tablespoons butter
   Paprika

1. Dip fillets in flour seasoned with salt and pepper; coating well. Set aside.
2. Melt butter in an 11x7-inch baking dish. Dip fillets in butter and arrange in baking dish. Sprinkle with paprika.
3. Cook, uncovered, 2 to 4 minutes. Do not turn fish over, but do rotate dish one-quarter turn halfway through cooking time.
4. Serve garnished with **cooked asparagus spears** and **carrots**.

About 4 servings

Stuffed Flounder

¼ cup chopped green onion
¼ cup butter
1 can (4 ounces) chopped mushrooms
1 can (6½ ounces) crab meat,
   drained
½ cup cracker crumbs
2 tablespoons parsley flakes
½ teaspoon salt
¼ teaspoon pepper
2 pounds flounder fillets, cut in
   serving pieces
2 tablespoons butter
2 tablespoons flour
¼ teaspoon salt
   Milk
⅓ cup sherry
1 cup shredded Cheddar cheese
½ teaspoon paprika
1 teaspoon parsley flakes

1. In a 2-quart glass casserole, combine green onion and butter and cook 2 to 3 minutes, stirring after every minute.
2. Drain mushrooms and reserve liquid. Combine mushrooms, crab meat, cracker crumbs, 2 tablespoons parsley flakes, salt, and pepper with cooked onion. Spread mixture over fish fillets. Roll up each piece of fish and secure with a wooden pick. Place seam side down in a 10-inch glass baking dish.
3. In a 4-cup glass measure, heat butter 30 seconds. Stir in flour and salt.
4. Add enough milk to reserved mushroom liquid to make 1 cup. Gradually stir milk and sherry into flour mixture. Cook sauce 2 to 3 minutes, stirring every minute, until thickened. Pour sauce over flounder.
5. Cook flounder 6 to 8 minutes, rotating dish one-quarter turn halfway through cooking time.
6. Sprinkle cheese, paprika, and 1 teaspoon parsley flakes over fish. Cook 3 to 5 minutes, or until fish flakes easily with fork.

6 to 8 servings

Fish with Caper Stuffing

1 dressed trout, pike, haddock, perch, or flounder (about 1½ pounds)
1 teaspoon salt
1 cup coarse dry bread crumbs
¼ cup capers
2 tablespoons finely chopped green onion
2 tablespoons finely chopped parsley
1 egg, slightly beaten
2 to 4 tablespoons half-and-half
Lemon wedges

1. Rinse fish under cold water; drain well and pat dry with paper towels. Sprinkle cavity with salt and set aside.
2. Combine bread crumbs, capers, green onion, and parsley. Blend egg with 2 tablespoons half-and-half and pour over bread crumb mixture. Mix until moistened, adding additional half-and-half if necessary.
3. Lightly pile stuffing into fish. Fasten with wooden picks or secure with string. Place in an 11×7-inch baking dish. Cover with waxed paper.
4. Cook fish 8 to 10 minutes, or until fish flakes when tested with a fork; rotate dish one-quarter turn halfway through the cooking time. Allow to stand 2 minutes after cooking before serving. Garnish with lemon wedges.

4 servings

Red Snapper à l'Orange

1 pound red snapper, cut in serving pieces
2 tablespoons orange juice
1 teaspoon grated orange peel
1 tablespoon butter
½ teaspoon lemon juice
½ teaspoon salt
¼ teaspoon pepper
Parsley sprigs

1. In a 2-quart glass baking dish, arrange fish evenly around edge.
2. In a 1-cup glass measure, blend orange juice, orange peel, butter, lemon juice, salt, and pepper. Heat 30 seconds and pour over fish.
3. Cook fish, covered, 5 to 6 minutes, rotating dish one-quarter turn halfway through cooking time.
4. Rest, covered, 5 minutes before serving. Garnish with parsley.

4 servings

Sole Sauté Amandine

3 tablespoons flour
¾ teaspoon salt
¼ teaspoon pepper
1 pound sole or other white fish
  fillets
1 tablespoon oil
¼ cup butter
¼ cup sliced almonds
1 tablespoon fresh lemon juice
1 tablespoon chopped parsley

1. Combine flour, salt, and pepper in a shallow dish. Dip fillets into mixture, coating on all sides.
2. In a 10-inch glass dish, heat oil and 1 tablespoon butter 1 minute. Place fillets in dish and cover.
3. Sauté 4 to 5 minutes, turning fillets over and rotating dish one-quarter turn halfway through cooking time. Rest, covered, 5 minutes.
4. In a 1-cup glass measure, combine 3 tablespoons butter, almonds, and lemon juice. Cook and stir 1 to 2 minutes, until brown.
5. Pour sauce over fillets, sprinkle with parsley, and serve immediately.

3 or 4 servings

Salmonburgers

1 can (16 ounces) salmon
½ cup chopped onion
¼ cup salad oil
⅓ cup dry bread crumbs
2 eggs, beaten
1 teaspoon dry mustard
½ teaspoon salt
½ cup dry bread crumbs

1. Drain salmon, reserving ⅓ cup liquid; set aside.
2. In a 2-cup glass measure, cook onion in oil 2 to 2½ minutes. In a large mixing bowl, combine onion, ⅓ cup dry bread crumbs, reserved salmon liquid, eggs, mustard, salt, and salmon; mix well. Shape into 6 patties.
3. Roll patties in ½ cup bread crumbs. Place on roasting rack in a 2-quart baking dish. Cook patties 5 to 6 minutes, rotating dish one-quarter turn halfway through cooking time. Rest 5 minutes before serving.

3 or 4 servings

Salmon Ring: Follow recipe for Salmonburgers. Form mixture into a ring in a 1½-quart glass baking dish. Place a glass, open end up, in center of ring. Cook 5 to 6 minutes, rotating dish one-quarter turn halfway through cooking time. Rest 5 minutes before serving.

Shrimp Creole

3 tablespoons butter
½ cup chopped onion
½ cup thin strips green pepper
½ cup diced celery
1 clove garlic, minced
1 can (16 ounces) tomatoes, drained
1 can (8 ounces) tomato sauce
1 tablespoon Worcestershire sauce
1 teaspoon salt
1 teaspoon sugar
½ teaspoon chili powder
  Dash Tabasco
1 tablespoon cornstarch
1 pound cooked shrimp, peeled and
  deveined

1. In a 3-quart glass casserole, blend butter, onion, green pepper, celery, and garlic. Cook 3 to 4 minutes, stirring halfway through cooking time.
2. Stir in tomatoes, tomato sauce, Worcestershire sauce, salt, sugar, chili powder, and Tabasco. Cook 8 minutes, stirring every 3 minutes.
3. In a 1-cup glass measure, blend cornstarch with 2 tablespoons liquid from tomato mixture, and blend into casserole.
4. Cook 3 to 4 minutes, stirring halfway through cooking time. Fold in shrimp and heat 2 to 3 minutes.
5. Rest 10 minutes before serving.

5 or 6 servings

Lasagna

4 cups water
8 ounces lasagna noodles
1 tablespoon salad oil
1½ pounds ground beef
1 clove garlic, crushed in a garlic
  press
1 cup small curd cottage cheese
4 ounces mozzarella cheese,
  shredded
½ teaspoon salt
½ cup mayonnaise
1 jar (16 ounces) spaghetti sauce
  without meat
½ teaspoon oregano
  Grated Parmesan cheese

1. In a large pan on range, bring the water to boiling. Add noodles and salad oil. Cook 5 to 6 minutes until tender; drain.
2. In a medium glass mixing bowl, break apart ground beef. Add garlic and cook 6 to 7 minutes, stirring every 2 minutes. Drain off drippings.
3. Add cottage cheese, mozzarella cheese, salt, and mayonnaise to meat mixture; stir to blend.
4. In a 9-inch glass baking dish, place a layer of noodles on the bottom and cover with a layer of meat mixture. Continue layering with remaining noodles and meat. Pour spaghetti sauce over top and sprinkle with oregano and desired amount of Parmesan cheese.
5. Cook, covered, 6 to 8 minutes, rotating dish one-quarter turn halfway through cooking time.
6. Rest, covered, 10 minutes before serving.

4 to 6 servings

Macaroni-Franks Dinner

8 ounces macaroni
1 pound frankfurters, cut in 1-inch
  pieces
1 cup mayonnaise
2 ounces Cheddar cheese, cut in thin
  strips
½ cup sliced green onion
2 tablespoons prepared mustard
½ teaspoon salt
¼ teaspoon pepper

1. Cook macaroni as directed on package. Drain well.
2. In a 1½-quart casserole, combine frankfurters, mayonnaise, cheese, green onion, mustard, salt, and pepper; stir to blend. Stir in cooked macaroni.
3. Cook, covered, 6 to 8 minutes, rotating dish one-quarter turn halfway through cooking time.
4. Rest 5 minutes before serving.

6 to 8 servings

Tortilla Casserole

1½ pounds ground beef
1 medium onion, chopped
1 clove garlic, minced
1 tablespoon chili powder
1 can (15 ounces) tomato sauce
⅔ cup water
8 corn tortillas
2½ cups shredded Cheddar cheese

1. In a 2-quart glass casserole, crumble ground beef and combine with onion and garlic. Cook 5 to 6 minutes, stirring halfway through cooking time.
2. Stir in chili powder, tomato sauce, and water. Cook 3 to 4 minutes, stirring halfway through cooking time.
3. In a 2-quart glass casserole, alternate layers of tortillas, meat sauce, and cheese, reserving ½ cup cheese for the top.
4. Cook, covered, 6 to 8 minutes, rotating dish one-quarter turn halfway through cooking time.

6 to 8 servings

Chili

1 pound ground beef
1 medium onion, diced
2 teaspoons flour
2 cans (16 ounces each) tomatoes
    (undrained)
2 cans (16 ounces each) kidney beans
1 tablespoon salt
1 to 2 tablespoons chili powder
¼ teaspoon thyme
1 cup water or ketchup

1. In a 3-quart glass casserole, sauté ground beef and onion 6 minutes, stirring every 2 minutes.
2. Mix flour with tomatoes and add to meat mixture. Blend in kidney beans, salt, chili powder, thyme, and water.
3. Cook, covered, 10 to 12 minutes, stirring halfway through cooking time.
4. Rest 5 minutes before serving.

4 to 6 servings

Conventional oven: Bake at 350°F 1 hour.

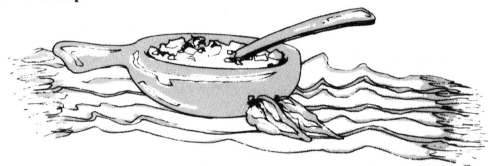

Quick Beef Pie

1½ pounds ground beef
1 medium onion, finely chopped
½ teaspoon salt
1 can (10½ ounces) condensed
    tomato soup
1 can (16 ounces) cut green beans,
    drained
¼ teaspoon pepper
1½ cups seasoned mashed potatoes
½ cup shredded Cheddar cheese

1. In a 10-inch glass dish, crumble beef. Add onion and salt; cook 6 to 7 minutes, stirring halfway through cooking time, until browned. Drain off excess drippings.
2. Add soup, green beans, and pepper to meat mixture. Cook 3 to 4 minutes, stirring halfway through cooking time.
3. Press meat mixture into dish. Drop potatoes in mounds around edge of hot mixture, and sprinkle with cheese.
4. Cook 3 to 4 minutes, rotating dish one-quarter turn halfway through cooking time.
5. Rest 5 minutes before serving.

5 or 6 servings

Conventional oven: Bake at 350°F 25 to 30 minutes.

Note: If desired, the pie may be browned under a conventional broiler, but only if it is in a glass ceramic dish.

Macaroni in Cheese Sauce

3 cups macaroni
¼ cup butter
¼ cup flour
½ teaspoon salt
2 cups milk
½ teaspoon dry mustard
1½ cups shredded Cheddar cheese

1. Cook macaroni as directed on package.
2. In a 1½-quart glass casserole, heat butter 30 seconds. Stir in flour and salt. Add milk slowly, stirring continuously.
3. Cook 4 to 5 minutes until mixture thickens. Add mustard and cheese; stir to blend. Cook 1 minute.
4. Mix in cooked macaroni and heat 2 to 3 minutes.

5 or 6 servings

Texas Hash

1 pound ground beef
2 large onions, sliced
2 medium green peppers, chopped
½ cup chopped celery
2 cans (16 ounces each) tomatoes
¾ cup rice
½ teaspoon salt
Pepper to taste

1. In a 3-quart glass baking dish, cook crumbled ground beef 5 minutes, stirring halfway through cooking time. Spoon off drippings.
2. Add onion, green pepper, celery, tomatoes, rice, salt, and pepper; stir to blend.
3. Cook, covered, 20 minutes, rotating dish one-quarter turn halfway through cooking time.
4. Rest, covered, 10 minutes before serving.

4 to 6 servings

Artichokes

Fresh artichokes

1. Slice off about 1 inch from top of artichoke. Cut off stem about 1 inch from base so artichoke will sit upright. Remove tough outside leaves. With scissors, clip tips of remaining leaves. Wash well.
2. Arrange artichokes upright in a glass baking dish. Cover and cook as follows: for 1 artichoke, 6 to 8 minutes; for 2, 12 to 15 minutes; for 4, 20 to 25 minutes.
3. Rest, covered, 10 minutes before serving. Serve with **lemon butter, hollandaise sauce, melted butter,** or **mayonnaise.**

Note: Artichokes may be chilled after resting and served cold.

Asparagus Amandine

2 packages (10 ounces each) frozen asparagus
¼ cup finely chopped almonds
¼ cup butter
1 teaspoon wine vinegar

1. Pierce asparagus packages with fork. Cook 6 to 8 minutes, rotating one-quarter turn halfway through cooking time.
2. In a 3-cup glass measure, combine almonds and butter. Cook 1 to 2 minutes, stirring halfway through cooking time. Stir in vinegar.
3. Drain asparagus well and arrange in a 10-inch glass baking

dish. Pour sauce over asparagus and cook, covered, 1 to 2 minutes.
4. Rest, covered, 5 minutes before serving.

4 to 6 servings

Note: If desired, serve cold on lettuce leaves as a salad.

Tangy Pork and Beans

2 cans (16 ounces each) pork and beans, drained
½ cup minced onion
1 cup dry white wine
½ cup firmly packed dark brown sugar
½ cup honey
1 teaspoon finely crushed bay leaf
1 teaspoon pepper
¼ teaspoon Tabasco

1. In a 2-quart glass casserole, combine pork and beans, onion, wine, brown sugar, honey, bay leaf, pepper, and Tabasco.
2. Cook, covered, 10 to 12 minutes, stirring halfway through cooking time.
3. Rest, covered, 5 minutes before serving.

6 to 8 servings

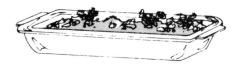

Creamed Green Beans

1 jar (8 ounces) pasteurized process cheese spread
1 can (10½ ounces) condensed cream of mushroom soup
Tabasco
1 tablespoon soy sauce
1 medium onion, chopped
3 tablespoons butter
5 fresh mushrooms, cleaned and chopped
1 can (8 ounces) water chestnuts, drained and sliced
2 cans (16 ounces each) French-style green beans, drained
Slivered almonds

1. In a 4-cup glass measure, blend cheese spread, soup, Tabasco, and soy sauce. Cook 3 to 5 minutes, stirring halfway through cooking time.
2. In a 1½-quart glass casserole, cook onion and butter 3 to 4 minutes, stirring halfway through cooking time until onions are transparent. Stir in mushrooms and water chestnuts and cook 1 minute.
3. Add green beans and soup mixture to mushroom mixture; stir to blend. Garnish with almonds.
4. Cook 5 minutes, rotating dish one-quarter turn halfway through cooking time.
5. Rest 5 minutes before serving.

6 to 8 servings

Sweet-and-Sour Beets

2 tablespoons brown sugar
1 tablespoon cornstarch
¼ teaspoon salt
1 can (8 ounces) pineapple tidbits (undrained)
1 tablespoon butter
1 tablespoon lemon juice
1 can (16 ounces) sliced beets, drained

1. In a 1-quart glass casserole, combine brown sugar, cornstarch, and salt. Stir in pineapple with its juice.
2. Cook 3 to 4 minutes, stirring after every minute, until mixture thickens.
3. Add butter, lemon juice, and beets. Cook, covered, 4 to 5 minutes, stirring halfway through cooking time.
4. Rest, covered, 5 minutes.

4 or 5 servings

Easy Broccoli Casserole

2 packages (10 ounces each) frozen broccoli spears
1 can (10½ ounces) condensed cream of mushroom soup
1 cup crushed potato chips or French-fried onion rings
½ cup grated Cheddar cheese

1. Pierce broccoli packages with fork. Cook broccoli 7 to 9 minutes, rotating dish one-quarter turn halfway through cooking time. Rest 5 minutes.
2. Place drained broccoli in a 2-quart glass casserole. Gently stir in soup. Sprinkle potato chips and cheese on top.
3. Cook, covered, 2 to 3 minutes. Remove cover and cook an additional 2 minutes. Serve immediately.

5 or 6 servings

Brussels Sprouts with Buttered Chestnuts

2 packages (10 ounces each) frozen Brussels sprouts
1 tablespoon finely chopped onion
⅔ cup sliced cooked chestnuts (see Note)
½ teaspoon salt

1. Pierce Brussels sprouts packages with fork. Cook 6 to 8 minutes, rotating one-quarter turn halfway through cooking.
2. In a 1-quart glass casserole, heat butter 30 seconds. Stir in onion, chestnuts, and salt, Cook 3 to 4 minutes, stirring halfway through cooking time.
3. Drain Brussels sprouts and combine with chestnut mixture. Cook, covered, 3 to 4 minutes.
4. Rest, covered, 5 minutes before serving.

6 to 8 servings

Note: To cook chestnuts, slash each chestnut crosswise through skin on flat end of shell. In a glass pie plate, arrange 20 to 24 chestnuts in an even layer. Cook 3 to 4 minutes, stirring every minute, until nuts are soft when squeezed. Rest 5 minutes. Peel off shells and use as directed.

Sweet-and-Sour Cabbage

1 small onion, chopped
3 tablespoons butter
1 cup meat stock or water
1 small head cabbage, shredded
1 small tart apple, cored and diced
3 tablespoons vinegar
1 tablespoon brown sugar
¼ teaspoon allspice
½ teaspoon salt

1. In a 2-quart glass casserole, sauté onion in butter 2 minutes, stirring after 1 minute. Stir in stock, cabbage, and apple.
2. Cover casserole and cook 6 to 8 minutes, stirring halfway through cooking time.
3. Add vinegar, brown sugar, allspice, and salt to cabbage; mix well. Cook 3 to 4 minutes.
4. Rest, covered, 5 minutes before serving.

4 to 6 servings

Orange-Glazed Carrots

6 to 8 medium carrots, pared and
    diagonally sliced
2 tablespoons butter
¼ cup brown sugar
2 tablespoons orange juice
1 teaspoon grated orange peel
1 teaspoon lemon juice
¼ teaspoon salt

1. In a 1½-quart glass casserole, combine carrots, butter, brown sugar, orange juice, orange peel, lemon juice, and salt.
2. Cover carrots and cook 10 to 12 minutes, stirring halfway through cooking time.
3. Rest, covered, 10 minutes before serving.

6 to 8 servings

Cauliflower au Gratin

½ cup butter
1 medium head cauliflower, cut in
    flowerets
¼ teaspoon garlic salt
¼ teaspoon salt
¼ teaspoon pepper
2 large tomatoes, cut in wedges
¼ cup seasoned bread crumbs
¼ cup grated Parmesan cheese
½ cup shredded Swiss cheese

1. In a 1½-quart glass casserole, heat butter 30 seconds. Add cauliflower, garlic salt, salt, and pepper, and stir to coat cauliflower with butter.
2. Cover cauliflower and cook 5 to 6 minutes, rotating dish one-quarter turn halfway through cooking time.
3. Arrange tomatoes on top of cauliflower and cook 2 minutes.
4. Add bread crumbs, Parmesan cheese, and Swiss cheese. Cook 1 to 2 minutes until cheese begins to melt.
5. Rest, covered, 5 minutes before serving.

3 or 4 servings

Sautéed Celery and Tomatoes

2 tablespoons butter
6 cups diagonally cut celery (½-inch
    slices)
½ pound cherry tomatoes, stems
    removed
½ teaspoon basil
½ teaspoon salt
¼ teaspoon pepper

1. In a 2-quart glass casserole, heat butter 30 seconds. Stir in celery. Cover and cook 10 to 12 minutes, stirring halfway through cooking time.
2. Stir tomatoes, basil, salt, and pepper into celery. Cook, covered, 3 to 4 minutes.
3. Rest, covered, 5 minutes before serving.

4 to 6 servings

Creamed Corn Casserole

2 tablespoons butter
1 egg
⅓ cup soda cracker crumbs
1 can (17 ounces) cream-style corn
½ teaspoon salt
¼ teaspoon pepper

1. In a 1-quart glass casserole, heat butter 30 seconds. Add egg, cracker crumbs, corn, salt, and pepper; blend evenly.
2. Cook 4 to 6 minutes, stirring halfway through cooking time.
3. Rest 5 minutes before serving.

4 or 5 servings

Eggplant Casserole

1 eggplant (about 1½ pounds)
Salt
Flour
½ cup salad oil for skillet
2 cans (8 ounces each) tomato sauce
1 cup thinly sliced mozzarella cheese
½ cup grated Parmesan cheese

1. Peel eggplant and cut in ½-inch-thick slices. Sprinkle both sides with salt, and set aside 20 to 30 minutes.
2. Dip eggplant slices in flour. Brown eggplant in hot microwave browning dish or in hot salad oil in hot skillet on a conventional range. Drain slices on paper towel.
3. Pour 1 can tomato sauce in a 10-inch glass baking dish. Lay eggplant slices in sauce, and cover with other can of sauce. Place mozzarella cheese over the sauce and sprinkle Parmesan cheese on top.
4. Cover with waxed paper or lid. Cook 12 to 14 minutes, rotating dish one-quarter turn halfway through cooking time.
5. Rest, covered, 5 minutes.

4 to 6 servings

Sautéed Mushrooms

2 tablespoons butter
¼ teaspoon tarragon
½ pound fresh mushrooms, cleaned and sliced
3 tablespoons chopped green onion
Salt
Pepper

1. In a 1-quart glass casserole, heat butter and tarragon 30 seconds, until butter is melted. Stir in mushrooms, cover, and cook 2 minutes.
2. Add green onion and stir to blend. Cook 3 to 4 minutes, stirring halfway through cooking time. Season with salt and pepper.
3. Rest, covered, 5 minutes before serving.

4 servings

Mustard Greens and Bacon

4 slices bacon, diced
¼ cup finely chopped onion
¾ pound mustard greens
Salt and pepper

1. In a 3-quart glass casserole, cook bacon 2 to 3 minutes, stirring halfway through cooking time.
2. Stir in onion and cover. Cook 3 to 4 minutes, stirring halfway through cooking time, until bacon is crisp. Pour off all drippings, except 1½ tablespoons.
3. Rinse and coarsely chop the mustard greens. Stir the greens into onion mixture, coating them with the drippings.
4. Cover the casserole and cook 2 to 3 minutes. Season with salt and pepper to taste.
5. Rest, covered, 5 minutes before serving.

3 or 4 servings

Note: Fresh spinach may be substituted for mustard greens.

Cooked Onions

1½ pounds small white onions
2 tablespoons butter
1 teaspoon minced sage leaves
½ teaspoon salt

1. In a 1½-quart glass casserole, combine onions, butter, sage, and salt.
2. Cook, covered, 8 to 10 minutes, stirring twice during cooking time.
3. Rest, covered, 5 minutes before serving.

4 servings

Snow Peas with Water Chestnuts

1 tablespoon salad oil or bacon
   drippings
1 can (5 ounces) water chestnuts,
   drained and sliced
½ pound fresh (or 1 10-ounce
   package frozen) snow peas
1 cup water
1 chicken bouillon cube
1 tablespoon cornstarch
2 tablespoons cold water

1. In a 1½-quart glass casserole, heat oil 15 seconds. Add water chestnuts and snow peas.
2. In a 1-cup glass measure, heat water 2 minutes. Dissolve bouillon cube and add to vegetable mixture.
3. Cook vegetables, covered, 4 to 6 minutes, stirring once halfway through cooking time.
4. Combine cornstarch and cold water; mix well. Push vegetables to one side of casserole and stir cornstarch mixture into broth.
5. Stir vegetables into sauce. Cook 2 to 4 minutes, stirring every minute, until sauce is slightly thickened. Salt to taste.

4 servings

Herbed Peas

2 packages (10 ounces each) frozen
   peas
¼ cup butter
½ cup minced onion
¼ cup minced celery
½ cup minced parsley
¼ teaspoon crushed rosemary
¼ teaspoon basil
¾ teaspoon salt

1. Pierce pea packages with fork and cook 6 to 8 minutes, rotating one-quarter turn halfway through cooking time.
2. In a 1½-quart glass casserole, heat butter 30 seconds. Stir in onion and celery. Cook 3 to 4 minutes, stirring halfway through cooking time. Add parsley, rosemary, basil, salt, and drained peas; stir to blend.
3. Cook, covered, 3 to 4 minutes, rotating dish one-quarter turn halfway through cooking time.
4. Rest, covered, 5 minutes.

6 to 8 servings

Cheesy Potato Casserole

1 package (12 ounces) frozen
   shredded hash brown potatoes
1 cup shredded Cheddar cheese
1 tablespoon flour
¼ cup chopped onion
1 teaspoon salt
¼ teaspoon pepper
1 tablespoon dried chives

1. Pierce hash brown potato package. Cook the potatoes 3 to 4 minutes, rotating one-quarter turn halfway through cooking time.
2. In a 2-quart glass casserole, blend hash brown potatoes, cheese, flour, onion, salt, pepper, and chives.
3. Cook, covered, 6 to 8 minutes, rotating dish one-quarter turn halfway through cooking time.
4. Rest, covered, 5 minutes.

4 servings

Hard Sauce

2 tablespoons butter
1 cup sifted confectioners' sugar
1 to 2 tablespoons rum or brandy
Dash salt

1. In a 2-cup glass measure, combine butter, confectioners' sugar, rum, and salt.
2. Cook 1 minute, stirring after 30 seconds. Serve hot or cold.

1½ cups

Cake-Mix Layer Cake

1 package (about 18½ ounces) cake mix

1. Prepare cake mix as directed on package, reducing the liquid by one-quarter the amount called for in mixing instructions.
2. Line bottoms of two 8-inch glass baking dishes with paper towel. Pour batter into baking dishes, filling no more than half full. Save extra batter and make cupcakes. Rest batter 10 minutes, if desired.
3. Cook, one layer at a time, 5 to 6 minutes, rotating dish one-quarter turn halfway through cooking time. When wooden pick stuck in center comes out slightly moist, cake is done.
4. Rest each layer 5 minutes before removing from dish. Cool completely before frosting.

Two 8-inch cake layers

Note: Square baking dishes hold more batter than round and will require 2 to 3 minutes more cooking time per pan.

Cake-Mix Sheet Cake: Follow recipe for Cake-Mix Layer Cake. Pour batter into an 11×7-inch glass baking dish, filling no more than half full. Cook 9 to 11 minutes, rotating one-quarter turn twice during cooking time. If cake begins to overcook in corners, shield with small pieces of foil. Cool 5 minutes before removing from dish; or cake may be left in dish. Frost when completely cool.

Apricot Almond Upside-Down Cake

⅓ cup butter
½ cup firmly packed brown sugar
1 can (16 ounces) apricot halves
½ cup blanched almonds, slivered
2 eggs
⅔ cup sugar
1 teaspoon almond extract
1 cup all-purpose flour
½ teaspoon baking powder
¼ teaspoon salt

1. In a 9-inch glass dish, heat butter 30 to 45 seconds. Blend with brown sugar and spread evenly over bottom of pan. Drain apricots and reserve juice. Arrange almonds and apricot halves over sugar mixture.
2. In a medium mixing bowl, beat eggs until thick. Using an electric mixer, beat about 5 minutes on high speed. Gradually add sugar. Add 6 tablespoons liquid from apricots and almond extract; beat well.
3. Add flour, baking powder, and salt to egg mixture; beat until well blended. Pour over fruit.
4. Cook 5 to 6 minutes, rotating dish one-quarter turn halfway through cooking time.
5. Rest 5 minutes, invert onto serving dish, and serve.

6 to 8 servings

Cupcakes

Prepared cake batter

1. Line glass custard cups, drinking cups, or cupcaker with paper baking cups. Pour 3 tablespoons batter into each cup.
2. Arrange cups in a circle on a glass plate, if not using cupcaker. Cook as follows, rotating plate or cupcaker one-quarter turn halfway through cooking time: 1 cupcake, 10 to 20 seconds; 2 cupcakes, 30 to 45 seconds; 3 cupcakes, 45 to 60 seconds; 4 cupcakes, 1 to 1¼ minutes; and 6 cupcakes, 1½ to 2 minutes.

Date Cake

Cake:
2 cups boiling water
½ cup chopped dates
2 teaspoons baking soda
1 cup butter
2 cups sugar
2 eggs
3 cups all-purpose flour
2 teaspoons vanilla extract
1 teaspoon salt

Topping:
3 tablespoons butter
1 cup brown sugar
¼ cup milk or cream
1 cup coarsely chopped walnuts

1. In a 4-cup glass measure, heat water about 5 to 6 minutes, to boiling. Stir in dates and sprinkle baking soda over water. Cool until just warm.
2. Cream butter with sugar and eggs. Add flour, vanilla extract, and salt to creamed mixture. Blend with date mixture and pour into a buttered 2-quart glass ceramic baking dish.
3. Cook 9 to 11 minutes, rotating dish one-quarter turn every 3 minutes.
4. Rest 5 minutes before removing from dish.
5. To make topping, heat butter 30 seconds in a 2-cup glass measure. Add brown sugar, milk, and nuts. Blend ingredients evenly and spread on top of cake.
6. Place cake under conventional broiler 1 to 2 minutes, until mixture starts to bubble. Remove and serve warm.

20 to 24 servings

Conventional oven: Bake at 350°F 45 minutes.

Apple Cake

Cake:
1½ cups all-purpose flour
¾ teaspoon baking soda
¾ teaspoon nutmeg
½ teaspoon salt
¼ cup salad oil
¾ cup sugar
1 egg, beaten
3 tablespoons buttermilk
1½ cups diced pared apples

Topping:
3 tablespoons butter, softened
⅓ cup firmly packed brown sugar
2 tablespoons milk or cream
¼ teaspoon vanilla extract
½ cup shredded coconut

1. Sift together flour, soda, nutmeg, and salt; set aside. Cream oil with sugar; beat until light and fluffy. Blend in egg.
2. Add buttermilk and flour mixture alternately to creamed mixture. Beat 2 minutes until smooth. Fold in apples.
3. Pour batter into a buttered 8-inch square glass ceramic baking dish. Cook 5 to 7 minutes, rotating dish one-quarter turn halfway through cooking time. Rest 5 minutes before removing from pan.
4. To make topping, heat butter 30 seconds in a 2-cup glass measure. Add brown sugar, milk, vanilla extract, and coconut. Stir to blend ingredients.
5. Spread evenly over top of cake and place under conventional broiler 1 to 2 minutes, until mixture starts to bubble. Remove and serve warm.

9 to 12 servings

Conventional oven: Bake at 350°F 45 minutes.

Poppy Seed Ring Cake

1 package (18½ ounces) prepared
    yellow cake mix
1 package (3¾ ounces) lemon instant
    pudding and pie filling
4 eggs
½ cup cooking oil
1 cup water
⅓ cup poppy seed
    Butter
    Sugar

1. In a large mixing bowl, combine cake mix, pudding and pie filling, eggs, oil, water, and poppy seed. Beat mixture at low speed of electric mixer until ingredients are moistened, then beat on high speed 3 to 4 minutes. If beating by hand, stir until ingredients are moistened; then beat about 150 strokes per minutes for 3 to 4 minutes.
2. Butter the bottom and sides of a 3-quart glass casserole. Sprinkle sugar over the butter. Place a drinking glass open end up in the center of the dish. Remove 1 cup of batter from the bowl and save to make cupcakes. Pour remaining batter in dish around the glass.
3. Cook 10 to 12 minutes, rotating dish one-quarter turn two times, more if needed, during cooking time. A wooden pick inserted in the cake that comes out slightly moist indicates cake is done.
4. Rest cake 5 minutes until it begins to pull away from sides of dish Remove glass from center of cake and invert cake onto serving plate. Sprinkle sifted confectioners' sugar over top, if desired.

10 to 12 servings

Note: The cake may be made in a 10-cup glass tube mold, if available.

Pineapple Upside-Down Cake

2 tablespoons butter
1 can (8 ounces) crushed pineapple
½ cup firmly packed brown sugar
6 maraschino cherries
1 package (9 ounces) yellow cake mix

1. Heat butter 30 seconds in an 8-inch round glass baking dish.
2. Drain pineapple, reserving juice.
3. Blend together butter, brown sugar, and drained pineapple; spread evenly in bottom of pan. Arrange maraschino cherries in bottom of pan.
4. Prepare cake mix as directed on package, substituting the reserved pineapple juice for water. Pour batter evenly over pineapple mixture.
5. Cook 5 to 7 minutes, rotating dish one-quarter turn halfway through cooking time. Rest 5 minutes until cake pulls away from sides of pan.
6. Invert onto serving dish.

6 to 8 servings

Note: If desired, pineapple slices may be used. Blend the melted butter and the brown sugar in baking dish and arrange slices on top. Other fruits, such as apricots or peaches, may be used, also.

Walnut Torte

4 eggs
1 cup sugar
1 cup graham cracker crumbs
½ cup chopped walnuts
1 cup apricot jam
Whipped cream

1. Beat eggs well. Combine sugar, graham cracker crumbs, and walnuts. Add to beaten eggs, mixing well. Pour into a buttered 9-inch glass cake dish with small glass, open end up, in center of dish.
2. Cook 5 to 6 minutes, rotating dish one-quarter turn halfway through cooking time.
3. Rest 5 minutes. Invert cake on plate. Spread jam over top, and serve warm or cold with whipped cream.

One 9-inch cake

Lemon Meringue Pie

1½ cups sugar
¼ teaspoon salt
1½ cups boiling water
2 tablespoons butter
6 tablespoons cornstarch
⅓ cup lemon juice
1 tablespoon grated lemon peel
3 egg yolks, slightly beaten
1 baked 9-inch pastry pie shell
3 egg whites
6 tablespoons sugar
½ teaspoon lemon juice

1. In a 4-cup glass measure, combine 1½ cups sugar, salt, water, and butter. Cook 3 to 4 minutes, stirring halfway through cooking time until sugar is dissolved.
2. Blend cornstarch with 3 tablespoons water and stir into hot sugar mixture. Cook 2 to 3 minutes, stirring after every minute.
3. Stir in ⅓ cup lemon juice and lemon peel. Gradually add egg yolks, taking care to avoid overcooking them. Cook mixture 3 to 4 minutes, stirring after every minute. Cool and pour into pie shell.
4. Using an electric mixer, beat egg whites until stiff. Continue beating while adding 6 tablespoons sugar, 1 tablespoon at a time, until rounded peaks are formed. Beat in ½ teaspoon lemon juice.
5. Spread meringue evenly over cooked filling, sealing to edges of pie shell.
6. Bake in a conventional oven at 450°F 5 to 6 minutes, or until lightly browned.

6 or 7 servings

Pumpkin Pie

1 egg, beaten
1 can (14 ounces) sweetened condensed milk
1 can (16 ounces) cooked pumpkin
½ teaspoon salt
1 teaspoon cinnamon
¼ teaspoon nutmeg

1. Combine all ingredients except pie shell. Mix until well blended.
2. Pour filling into pie shell. Cook 4 to 5 minutes until the edges begin to set. Stir the cooked edges to the center.
3. Cook 5 to 6 minutes, until the center is almost set. Rest 10 minutes. Check to see if pie is done by inserting a knife in the center. The knife should come out clean if the pie is done.

½ teaspoon allspice
¼ cup firmly packed dark brown sugar
1 tablespoon flour
¼ cup hot water
1 baked 9-inch pastry pie shell

4. Cool pie before serving. Top with **whipped cream** or **vanilla ice cream** and serve.

One 9-inch pie

Conventional oven: Pour filling into unbaked pastry pie shell and bake at 375°F 50 to 55 minutes.

Brownie Pie

2 ounces (2 squares) unsweetened chocolate
2 tablespoons butter
3 eggs, beaten
½ cup sugar
¾ cup dark corn syrup
¾ cup pecan halves
1 baked 9-inch pastry pie shell

1. In a 2-cup glass measure, heat chocolate and butter 1 to 2 minutes, until melted.
2. In a large mixing bowl, combine eggs, sugar, and corn syrup; blend evenly. Slowly blend in chocolate mixture. Stir in pecan halves and pour into pie shell in glass pie plate.
3. Cook 4 to 5 minutes and rotate dish one-quarter turn.
4. Continue cooking 3 to 4 minutes until center is just beginning to set.
5. Rest pie 10 minutes. Serve slightly warm or cold with **ice cream** or **whipped cream.**

One 9-inch pie

Conventional oven: Bake at 375°F 40 to 50 minutes.

Strawberry Tarts

1 package (10 ounces) frozen strawberries
1 tablespoon cornstarch
Dash cinnamon
Dash cloves
½ teaspoon lemon juice
6 cooked pastry tart shells
Whipped cream (optional)

1. In a 1-quart glass casserole, cook strawberries 1 to 1½ minutes. Separate berries with a fork. Add cornstarch, cinnamon, and cloves; stir to blend evenly.
2. Cook strawberries 5 to 6 minutes, stirring after every minute, until mixture is thickened and clear. Stir in lemon juice.
3. Cool slightly and spoon into tart shells. Refrigerate until ready to serve. Top with whipped cream.

6 tarts

Fresh Strawberry Pie: Follow recipe for Strawberry Tarts. Use 4 cups fresh strawberries, cook as directed above, and pour into a **9-inch baked pastry pie shell.**

Gingerbread

½ cup shortening
⅔ cup sugar
2 eggs
⅔ cup molasses
2 cups all-purpose flour
¾ teaspoon salt
¾ teaspoon ginger
¾ teaspoon cinnamon
¼ teaspoon baking soda
¾ cup boiling water

1. In a medium mixing bowl, cream shortening with sugar. Stir in eggs, one at a time. Gradually add molasses.
2. Combine flour, salt, ginger, cinnamon, and baking soda. Blend into creamed mixture. Add boiling water and mix until smooth.
3. Cut paper towel to line bottom of 9-inch glass baking dish. Pour batter into dish, filling no more than half full.
4. Cook 5 to 6 minutes, rotating dish one-quarter turn halfway through cooking time.
5. Rest 5 minutes before removing from pan. Serve with Lemon Sauce •   or Hard Sauce •

10 to 12 servings

Note: If desired, cupcakes may be made from mixture. Use cupcaker or custard cups lined with paper baking cups. Allow 15 seconds per cupcake.

Basic Pastry Pie Shell

4 cups all-purpose flour
1 tablespoon sugar
1 teaspoon baking powder
2 teaspoons salt
1¾ cups shortening
1 egg, beaten
⅓ cup cold water
1 tablespoon cider vinegar

1. In a large mixing bowl, combine flour, sugar, baking powder, and salt.
2. Cut in shortening with a pastry blender or two knives, until particles are the size of small peas. In a 1-cup measure, combine egg, cold water, and vinegar. Stir into flour mixture until well moistened. Chill 15 minutes.
3. Divide pastry into 5 portions and form each into a ball (see Note). Flatten one ball on a lightly floured pastry cloth, and roll to about ⅛ inch thick. Ease pastry into a 9-inch glass pie plate, and flute edges.
4. Make a waxed paper starburst pattern (follow step-by-step instructions). Center waxed paper on shell and place an 8-inch glass pie plate on top.
5. Cook pastry 3 minutes. Remove 8-inch glass pie plate and waxed paper. Rotate dish one-quarter turn and cook 2½ to 3 minutes.
6. Cool on rack.

Five 9-inch pie shells

Note: If not to be used immediately, wrap balls individually in waxed paper and freeze. When needed, remove from freezer, thaw, roll, and bake as directed.

Pastry Tart Shells: Follow recipe for Basic Pastry Pie Shell. Roll one ball on floured pastry cloth, as directed. Using an inverted 10-ounce custard cup, cut out six pastry rounds. Invert six 6-ounce glass custard cups. Cover each first with a paper towel and then a pastry round. Flute each tart edge in four evenly spaced places. Place in oven in a circle and cook 4 to 5 minutes, rearranging cups one-quarter turn halfway through cooking time. Rest 3 to 4 minutes. Place upright and carefully lift out custard cup and paper towel. Cool thoroughly before filling.

6 tart shells

Index